COMPETITION AND FINANCE

Also by Kevin Dowd

CURRENT ISSUES IN FINANCIAL AND MONETARY
ECONOMICS (*edited with M. K. Lewis*)

LAISSEZ-FAIRE BANKING

PRIVATE MONEY: The Path to Monetary Stability

THE EXPERIENCE OF FREE BANKING (*editor*)

THE STATE AND THE MONETARY SYSTEM

Competition and Finance

A Reinterpretation of Financial and Monetary Economics

Kevin Dowd
Yorkshire Bank Professor of Financial Economics
Sheffield Hallam University

St. Martin's Press
New York

COMPETITION AND FINANCE
Copyright © 1996 by Kevin Dowd

St. Martin's Press, Scholarly and Reference Division,
175 Fifth Avenue, New York, N.Y. 10010

First published in the United States of America in 1996

Printed in Great Britain

ISBN 0–312–16218–9

Library of Congress Cataloging-in-Publication Data
Dowd, Kevin.
Competition and finance : a reinterpretation of financial and
monetary economics / Kevin Dowd.
p.   cm.
Includes bibliographical references and index.
ISBN 0–312–16218–9
1. Free banking.   2. Free enterprise.   3. Monetary policy.
I. Title.
HG1685.D68   1996
332.1—dc20   96–13141
                                                       CIP

Contents

Preface

This book sets out a new interpretation of financial and monetary economics. Some such effort is long overdue. The two basic subjects, financial and monetary economics, have long since gone off in their own directions, and it seems increasingly the case that experts in one area have relatively little feel for the other. Furthermore, while financial economics is in generally good shape, monetary economics is most definitely not. Monetary economics lacks a coherent structure, and there is no consensus among monetary economists about how the subject should be structured. As a result, we can't collectively agree on how we should even *think* about monetary economics, let alone agree about the answers to many important monetary economic questions.

This book tries to resolve some of these difficulties by offering a (fairly) unified conceptual framework that integrates financial and monetary economics, and offers tentative answers to many of the questions they raise. This framework has two essential features. The first is an emphasis on market 'frictions', for want of a better term. A great deal of work has been done on these 'frictions' in recent years – most particularly, in the fields of agency and information economics – and there is no doubt in my view that this new microeconomics holds the key to explaining the main features of real-world institutions. Most particularly, it provides us with a sensible economic theory of security design and corporate capital structure, and this theory, in turn, can be used to provide an intellectually coherent and empirically acceptable economic theory of banking.

The second feature of this framework is unrestrained competition, or *laissez-faire*. The reader can think of this conceptual world as being an anarchy or a world with a government that keeps strictly out of the financial and monetary arenas. This approach has many attractions. One attraction is that it enables us to endogenise the monetary standard: the monetary standard emerges here as an equilibrium feature of the system, determined from within it, and is *not* something that the system takes as given (e.g., as in most free banking literature). Another attraction is that it helps us to think more clearly about the rationale, or lack of it, for government intervention, but I also hope that the basic framework would still be useful to other scholars even if they disagree with some of the answers I offer. After all, advocates of government intervention ought to know what the *laissez-faire* outcome would look like, even if they feel that the government can improve upon it: they *must* know, because they cannot possibly provide any economic justification for government intervention if they do not know what the government is supposed to improve upon. That said, I also believe that this framework does naturally lead to pro-*laissez-faire* answers, and I make no secret of the fact that I hope it will help win over many of my professional colleagues to the free-banking side. At the very least, however, I hope to have provided a restatement of the free-banking position that does justice to recent theoretical developments and addresses some of the concerns about free banking that have been raised by other economists.

KEVIN DOWD

Acknowledgements

I started working on this book in the summer of 1989. It started as an attempt to put some rigour into an earlier book I had written – *The State and the Monetary System* (Philip Allan/St Martin's Press, 1989) – but I had no idea at the time what I had let myself in for. (Realistic planning of research projects has never been a strong point of mine.) What I had naively imagined would take a few months instead dragged on for years and years, and, as the project evolved, it occurred to me that it would be a good idea to try to get bits of it published elsewhere. Consequently, versions of some parts of this book have already appeared as articles in various academic journals, and I would like to express my sincere thanks to the many editors, referees and others whose comments have done much to improve these articles, and therefore improve this book. To be precise: part of the material used in Chapter 2 appeared as 'Optimal Financial Contracts', *Oxford Economic Papers*, 44 (October 1992, pp. 672–693); parts of Chapter 8 appeared as 'Is Banking a Natural Monopoly?', *Kyklos*, 45(3) (1992, pp. 379–392), and also as 'Competitive Banking, Bankers' Clubs, and Bank Regulation', in the *Journal of Money, Credit, and Banking*, 26(2) (May 1994, pp. 289–308); much of Chapter 9 appeared as 'Models of Banking Instability: A Partial Review of the Literature', *Journal of Economic Surveys*, 6(2) (1992, pp. 107–132); some of the material used in Chapter 11 appeared as 'Currency Competition, Network Externalities and Switching Costs: Towards an Alternative View of Optimal Curency Areas', *Economic Journal*, 103 (420) (September 1993, pp. 1180–1189 (under David Greenaway's name as well as my own); much of Chapter 12 appeared as 'The Mechanics of Indirect Convertibility', *Journal of Money, Credit, and Banking*, 27 (1) (February 1995, pp. 67–88), part of Chapter 14 appeared as 'A Proposal to End Inflation', *Economic Journal*, 104 (425) (July 1994, pp. 828–840); part of Chapter 15 is due to appear as 'The Costs of Inflation and Disinflation', forthcoming in the *Cato Journal*; and virtually all of the Appendix to Chapter 15 appeared as 'Deflating the Productivity Norm', *Journal of Macroeconomics*, 17 (4) (Fall 1995). Finally, part of Chapter 13 draws heavily from 'The Analytics of Bimetallism', which is forthcoming in the *Manchester School*. I would therefore to thank the various editors and copyright holders – Blackwells (for the *EJ*, *JES*, and *Manchester School*), the Cato Institute (for the *CJ*), Helbing and Lichtenhahn Verlag AG (for *Kyklos*), Louisiana State University Press (for *JMACRO*), Ohio State University Press (for the *JMCB*), and Oxford University Press (for *OEP*) – for their permission to use this material here. I also wish to thank University of Chicago Press for permission to reproduce Figure 16.1, from F. E. Kydland and E. C. Prescott, 'Rules rather than discretion', *Journal of Political Economy* (1977). I would also like to thank the Yorkshire Bank for its sponsorship of my chair at Sheffield Hallam University which, among other things, has helped to free time for me to finish the book.

Finally, it is a real pleasure to thank many friends, colleagues and family for their contributions, direct and indirect, to this book. I cannot mention everyone here, but particularly thank Mark Billings, Dave Campbell, Dave Chappell, Tony Courakis, Tyler Cowen, Giovanna Davitti, Charles Goodhart, David Goacher, Keith Harrison, Barbara Hollman, Steve Horwitz, Duncan Kitchin, Mervyn Lewis, Tony McGuiness, Paul Mizen, Imad Moosa, Keith Povey, Willy Seal, Bob Sedgwick, George Selgin, John Smithin, Scott Sumner, Chris Tame, Dick Timberlake, Peter Vincent-Jones, John Whittaker, Bill Woolsey, and Basil Zafiriou – and I apologise in advance to those whom I have inadvertently omitted. I also thank long-suffering librarians at the Federal Reserve Bank of St Louis, Sheffield Hallam University, and the University of Nottingham, and I thank Kevin White for some research assistance with Chapter 15. Most of all, I thank my family – my parents, my brothers, Brian and Victor, my wife, Mahjabeen, and my daughters, Raadhiyah and Safiah – for too many things to mention. I would like to dedicate the book to Raadhiyah and Safiah – I hope some day that they will be able to understand it, but have better things to do.

SHEFFIELD   SEPTEMBER 1995

1 Introduction

The principal purpose of this book is to explore financial and monetary *laissez-faire*. In so doing, I also hope to provide some insight into real-world financial and monetary problems, and, in particular, into the issue of the appropriate role of the state. The issue of financial *laissez-faire* – or *free banking* – is of course highly controversial, and there is little doubt that free banking is still a minority view.[1] Nonetheless, I believe that free banking is both feasible and desirable, and that the main criticisms levelled against it are essentially unsound. My main theme, therefore, is that free trade is just as desirable in the financial sector of the economy as it is in any other sector. However, financial free trade in its broadest sense means much more than just, say, the deregulated banking on a *given* monetary standard (e.g., a gold standard) on which much of the free banking literature has hitherto focused. To examine financial *laissez-faire* in the context of a given monetary standard is useful, but limited, and we really need to go further and examine *laissez-faire* in a broader framework in which the monetary standard itself – that is, the set of rules governing the issue of currency, which indirectly determine the price level and other nominal variables – is endogenised. Financial *laissez-faire* in its broadest sense therefore includes the various monetary issues related to the determination and operation of the monetary standard, as well as the financial issues on which free bankers have hitherto tended to focus.

The relevant literature on financial and monetary economics is, to put it mildly, both massive and extremely complex. Our first requirement is therefore to organise the material in a form that enables us to go through it systematically and, I hope, sensibly. It seems to me that it is perhaps most convenient to organise the material in two stages, with the first stage introducing some basic issues and the second stage the more formal organisation into which the later chapters fit. The first stage is therefore a preliminary organisation which takes the form of a conjectural history – a thought-exercise in which we trace the development of a social order from some initial state, given the driving principle that all individuals are motivated by their self-interest.[2] The evolutionary process is essentially very simple. Each individual is always trying to make himself better off in an environment that he takes as given. He himself usually has a negligible effect on the general social order, but the effects of individual actions taken together can add up and change the environment within which they all operate. The individual efforts of many different people can therefore profoundly alter the social order itself. These far-reaching changes are generally unforeseen, and are certainly not 'planned' in the sense in which an idealised central planner would plan them. A standard example is the textbook account of the goldsmiths in which banknotes replace gold as the dominant

1

exchange medium: initially everyone uses full-bodied coins as their medium of exchange, but coins are costly to protect and store, and so goldsmiths start to take deposits of gold coins for safekeeping; they issue receipts to those who make such deposits, and over time merchants adopt these receipts as exchange media; the goldsmiths' receipts then become banknotes, and the goldsmiths become bankers. The story of the goldsmiths thus explains how a paper currency can evolve from the use of full-bodied coins even though no-one involved actually 'planned' or even foresaw it.

Our conjectural history serves three interrelated purposes. The first is that it gives an intuitively appealing framework which provides the foundation on which we can then set out the more complex analytical structure of later chapters. A second purpose of the conjectural history is that it helps to highlight key issues and themes before descending into more detailed and complicated discussions later on. It provides an aerial view, and is also a particularly effective way of explaining (or at least introducing) the roles and functions of the various institutions involved (e.g., in the story of the goldsmiths, it provides a simple but powerful explanation of the emergence of paper currency). The third purpose of the conjectural history is that it illustrates very effectively the book's main theme, namely, the plausibility and attractiveness of financial *laissez-faire*. Seeing the conjectural history unfold gives one a feel for how *laissez-faire* actually works and helps to break the conditioning against it that most of us were given when we first learned our economics. The problem with traditional treatments is that they *presume* that a central bank is necessary and make *laissez-faire appear* as though it is missing something essential. Central banking then seems 'natural', and free banking seems odd. If we look through a conjectural history, on the other hand, *laissez-faire* comes across as very natural, and perhaps even desirable, and it is the departures from *laissez-faire* that appear out of place.

The particular kind of conjectural society on which I shall focus is a society without a state, that is, an *anarchy*. An anarchy differs from currently existing statist social orders in that there is free competition in the provision of law and legal process, and there is free entry in the law-enforcement industry. One can think of law and law enforcement as goods provided on markets just like any other goods, and if one wants a real-world example one can think of the legal system under anarchy – the laws and the courts – as similar to the spontaneous common law systems that existed before kings and legislatures started to tinker with them.[3] Since the anarchy is ruled by law, there is no reason to suppose that it is chaotic or 'disorderly', and one must forget the unfortunate connotations that the term sometimes brings to mind. The anarchy is a pure spontaneous order with no element of order imposed on it from 'outside'.[4] In Hayek's terminology, it is all 'nomos' and no 'taxis'.

There are several reasons for choosing to examine an anarchy. The most basic one is that there is a sense in which the analysis of anarchy *must* logically come prior to the study of other forms of social order. One cannot assess claims for the necessity of some form of government intervention – the establishment of a central bank, say – without analysing the properties of a social order in which this intervention is absent. To illustrate: to claim that central banking is superior to free banking is to imply the existence of a problem inherent in free banking that central banking puts right, but regardless of whether such a claim is valid or not, one cannot justify it without some study of the properties of a free banking system. One must analyse the system without the intervention if one is to be able to assess whether the intervention itself is justified. Dealing with an anarchic social order also has the advantage that it helps to focus on the extent to which the solutions to social problems emerge or fail to emerge spontaneously from 'within' the social order, without relying on the *deus ex machina* of the state to sort them out. Since there is no state under anarchy, there is no 'guardian' to solve the problems that arise within it, and either the individuals involved solve those problems for themselves or else they have to live with them unsolved. If one studies a society with a state, on the other hand, there is often a temptation to underrate the extent to which the parties involved can solve their problems and a corresponding temptation to see the state as the solution to whatever problem one is dealing with. All too often, a writer will identify a problem, think of a way in which the government can ameliorate it, and presume that he has found a 'solution'. Regardless of whether the state intervention happens to be appropriate or not, I would argue that this kind of approach is not a helpful way to address the problem. Assuming the government away provides a mental discipline that helps us avoid the distraction of such spurious 'solutions' and concentrate on the real issue – the extent to which individuals in society can solve their own problems.

A conjectural history is a benchmark to help assess the world we live in, but it is *not* meant to provide an accurate historical description of how the world *actually* evolved. The conjectural history is merely a useful myth, and it is no criticism to say that the world failed to evolve in the way that a conjectural history postulates. Suppose for example that it could be proved beyond doubt that Doge of Venice in the sixteenth century had been shrewd enough to recognise that a bank need not maintain a 100 percent reserve ratio:

What then of our goldsmiths' story? Does the fact that the Doge beat the invisible-hand [i.e., conjectural history] explanation to it rob the invisible-hand explanation of its explanatory import? I suggest that the answer is No, and that the argument for this answer goes beyond the mere 'feeling' that we may have that the account of how something could have arisen without anyone devising it is 'interesting' or 'illuminating' in its own right.

The argument ... is that even if the invisible-hand explanation turns out not to be the correct account of how the thing *emerged*, it may still not be devoid of validity with regard to the question of how (and why) it is *maintained*, ... The availability ... of a cogent invisible-hand story of how the pattern in question could have arisen ... may, I believe, contribute to our understanding of the inherently self-reinforcing nature of this pattern and hence of its being successful and lasting. (Ullman-Margalit, 1978, 275, her emphasis)

The conjectural history therefore helps to explain why certain institutions *persist* – regardless of its strict historical accuracy – which in turn helps to illustrate the *functions* they perform. It also suggests questions that we may wish to pursue further and sheds light on their possible answers – an obvious example being the question of the inherent stability of free banking, a question which seems bizarre if one thinks in terms of the traditional monetary economics that took the existence of the central bank for granted.

The Early Evolution of the Economy

Suppose we now begin with an initial 'primitive' state of society. Individuals live in groups (e.g., clans), have well-defined preferences, and have endowments consisting of various commodities, chattels, and natural abilities. Individuals can combine these endowments with their own time and effort to produce goods (e.g., they can harvest food) and engage in other economic activity (i.e., exchange and consumption) to improve their well-being. To begin with, most economic activity is organised hierarchically, there is little exchange between groups or between individuals within groups, and concepts of private property are primitive.

However, over time people gradually discover that they can make themselves better off by exchange, and the practice of barter spreads. Trade is initially more or less sporadic (e.g., potential trading partners meet each other randomly as in Jones, 1976), but as it spreads a set of social conventions develops spontaneously around it. These relate to good places to find trading partners, the rules of bargaining, and so on. These conventions reduce the costs to individuals of searching for trading partners and carrying out trades with them. The trading process therefore becomes more orderly, and trading fairs and *markets* gradually evolve at which people meet every so often to exchange their goods. At the same time, trade also alters individuals' relationships to their groups. Individual activity is increasingly directed at people outside their group, and the old group hierarchy slowly breaks down. Individuals form new relationships with each other, and principal among these are *firms* – organisations in which some individuals agree to take certain kinds of orders from others, in return for agreed compensation. Firms enable certain types of activities to be co-ordinated more efficiently than would otherwise be the case, and thereby enable individuals to reap specialisation gains that would otherwise be unobtainable (as explained, e.g., by Coase, 1937). As time goes on, an increasing proportion of economic activity is carried on through markets and firms, people become increasingly specialised, and the older groups lose their distinctiveness and merge into a unified economy.

Indirect Exchange and the Emergence of a Dominant Medium of Exchange

Barter nonetheless has the drawback of being costly to carry out. Individuals can only trade if they overcome both coincidence of wants and coincidence of timing problems (see, e.g., Goodhart, 1989, 2). A lot of search – and consequently a lot of (valuable) time – is typically required to carry out a trade, and the outcome of a search is often very uncertain. At some point, individuals then start to resort to indirect exchange – instead of accepting only for the good they want to consume, they accept another good with the intention of exchanging that for the good they are really looking for. If the intermediate good is well-chosen, an individual who resorts to indirect exchange ought to be able to obtain the good he wants with less difficulty than he otherwise would and reduce his overall trading costs (see, e.g., Menger, 1892, 247–249). A good choice of intermediate commodity would be a good that is heavily traded, so that the person who has the commodity one wants will be more likely to accept the commodity one has to offer, but also have a readily recognisable exchange value, be easily portable and non-perishable. Over time, individuals gradually switch to indirect exchange and converge on these kinds of goods to carry out their trades, and this convergence makes these goods even more saleable and therefore further increases their desirability as intermediate goods (Menger, 1892, 250–252). In the end this self-reinforcing process leads to a relatively small number of goods – and perhaps only one – becoming generally accepted as the dominant intermediate good(s). Historically, the preferred intermediary goods have often been precious metals – mainly gold and silver. These were well-suited to be intermediate goods because their quantity and quality were relatively easy to assess, compared to most other goods, and the fact that their value was high relative to their weight meant that storage and transport costs were relatively low (Menger, 1892, 252–255). For the sake of simplicity, we shall assume that the process converges on one single good – gold – as the dominant intermediary commodity.

The Unit of Account

The use of an intermediate commodity considerably simplifies the exchange process. Individuals with goods to sell need look only for individuals with the recognised intermediary good, and trade fairs now become much simpler because of the associated reduction in the number of trading posts. If there are n goods to be traded, there would be $n(n-1)/2$ separate trading posts under pure barter, one for each pair of goods. However, with a dominant intermediary good, the number of trading posts can be cut to $(n-1)$ – one trading post for every commodity to be exchanged for the intermediate good, and an individual with a particular good to sell need only operate (or look for) a single trading post, instead of the $(n-1)$ separate posts that previously dealt with his good under barter. Indirect exchange also means that he need keep account of only $(n-1)$ exchange ratios (or prices) instead of having to keep account of $n(n-1)/2$ exchange ratios as he did before.

Since the intermediary good, gold, is now handed over in most (if not all) trades, it is natural that prices – the exchange rates of goods – be quoted in terms of gold weights. A trader with a good to sell (buy) will post prices in terms of the weight of gold he is willing to accept (pay):

A seller pursues his self-interest by posting prices in terms of the media of exchange he is routinely prepared to accept. This practice economizes on time spent in negotiation over what commodities are acceptable in payment and at what rate of exchange. More importantly, it economizes on the information necessary for the buyer's and the seller's economic calculation. Posting prices in terms of a numeraire commodity not routinely accepted in payment, by contrast, would force buyer and seller to know and agree upon the numeraire price of the payment media due. This numeraire price of the payment medium would naturally be subject to fluctuation, so that updated information would be necessary. A non-exchange-medium numeraire would furthermore be subject to greater bid–ask spreads in barter against other commodities, as by hypothesis it is less saleable, than the medium of exchange. It would therefore serves less well as a tool of economic calculation. (White, 1984b, 704)

The economy has now evolved to the point where gold is not only used as the dominant *medium of exchange*, but where agents also use gold units to express the prices of other goods. Gold therefore provides the *medium of account*, and the *unit of account* – the unit in terms of which prices are expressed – is a specified weight of gold. A good real-world example of this evolutionary process is the POW camp described by Radford:

> Starting with simple direct barter, such as a non- smoker giving a smoker friend his cigarette issue in exchange for a chocolate ration, more complex exchanges soon became an accepted custom ... Within a week or two, as the volume of trade grew, rough scales of exchange values came into existence ... It was realised that a tin of jam was worth 1/2 lb. of margarine plus something else; that a cigarette issue was worth several chocolate issues, and a tin of diced carrots was worth practically nothing ... By the end of a month, when we reached our permanent camp, there was a lively trade in all commodities and their relative values were well-known, and expressed not in terms of one another – one didn't quote bully in terms of sugar – but in terms of cigarettes. The cigarette became the standard of value ... [Everyone,] including non-smokers, was willing to sell for cigarettes, using them to buy at another time and place. Cigarettes became the normal currency. (Radford, 1945, 191)

Cigarettes thus became both medium of exchange and medium (and unit) of account. In our hypothetical economy, gold is both medium of exchange and medium of account, and the unit of account is a particular unit of gold. If we call this unit the dollar, we can then say that prices are expressed in terms of dollars, but the dollar itself is a specific amount of gold.

The Evolution of Coinage

Although gold might be the most convenient intermediate good to use, individuals still have the inconvenience of having to assess the weight and purity of heterogeneous lumps of gold. To avoid having to reassess the value of each amount of gold they are presented with, traders begin to deal in standardised lumps of gold (e.g., gold rings or bars) and put their own marks on them so that they do not need to reassess their value when they next see them. A trader can then look at the marking and shape of any piece of gold he is offered, and if he recognises them he can have some confidence that they are of their claimed weight and dispense with the inconvenience of weighing them again. We therefore arrive at the beginning of *coinage*. There is now a demand for readily authenticated pieces of gold, and *mints* arise to meet this demand by casting gold into coins and charging a fee for the service. Since the demand for each mint's service depends on the reputation of its coins, each mint has an incentive to maintain its reputation by making it as difficult as possible to tamper with its coins without being detected (e.g., by making coins round, so that tampering is more easily detected), and by issuing coins of full-bodied weight (see, e.g., Glasner, 1989a, 7–8). Market forces will also lead mints to issue coins of standardised weight and fineness, so coins will be issued in standard dollar amounts: any mint that issued non-standardised coins would impose additional inconvenience on its customers and have to charge a lower minting fee to compensate them, and would therefore find it difficult to survive against competitors who issued standardised coins.

The Development of Market Makers

At the same time as these other developments, the economy also witnesses the growth of *middlemen* or *market-makers*. (A more detailed and very good discussion of these is to be found in Goodhart, 1989, 6–19) A market-maker is a bridge between the producer of a good and the ultimate consumer. He obtains inventories of goods from the producer, and aims to sell them at a profit to consumers. Market-makers are typically able to make a profit – and perform a socially useful role in the process – because they can bring suppliers and consumers 'together' at less cost and inconvenience than if they traded directly with each other. Market-makers are able to able to make bulk orders, for example, and therefore exploit transaction economies that many consumers are too small to exploit on their own. They can also reduce the costs of bringing suppliers and consumers together by solving important *information problems*. Without an intermediary, consumers and producers would have little knowledge of each other, and the costs of searching each other out would be sufficiently high to discourage many from making the effort. A consumer may be willing to buy a good if he can find it at the local market, but be reluctant to engage in a search for it further afield, while a producer will typically have little comparative advantage in marketing to distant consumers. A market-maker can bridge these information gaps by specialising in the intermediary role, conveying information to consumers about the availability and terms of sale of goods, and conveying information to producers about the potential demand for their produce.

A market-maker will hold inventories of goods and post prices at which he is willing to trade. These prices are both *bid prices* (i.e., the prices at which he is willing to buy) and *ask prices* (i.e., the prices at which he is willing to sell), and his objective is to set and periodically revise these prices and his inventory holdings to maximise his expected profit. The market-maker will let his inventory holdings absorb some shock, at least in the first instance, but will eventually change his prices if his inventories rise or fall too much. The market-maker's inventory behaviour therefore helps to absorb shocks and smooth out their effects on prices. There are several reasons why he acts in this way: (1) Changing prices generally involves some *'resource'* or *menu costs* – advertised prices must be changed, regular customers might need to be informed, and so on – and there is no point bearing these costs for shocks that are very small and transitory. (2) A market-maker who absorbs shocks and smooths prices helps to convey valuable information to potential customers, and in so doing provides them with a form of *liquidity insurance*. Customers can be reasonably confident that they can trade at particular prices, and this kind of information is destroyed if prices are constantly changed. Many customers would have engaged in search processes to find their current market-maker, and the market-maker knows that too many price changes will drive them away again (see, e.g., Goodhart, 1989, 13). (3) Smoothing prices provides customers with insurance against the danger of misrepresentation that arises from the intermediary's information advantage over the customer. Without it, an intermediary might claim that he is charging more because market prices are rising, and his customer could not easily refute that claim at low cost. A market-maker who engages in price smoothing can therefore expect to attract customers who want protection against this kind of misrepresentation. To use one of Goodhart's examples, a hotel manager has no incentive to lie about the occupancy rate if that implies turning a customer away instead of charging him more.

Price Flexibility and Market Structure

These factors typically imply that a market-maker will set his prices in line with longer run, 'permanent' demands and supplies, and it will normally take more than a temporary change in demand to persuade him that underlying 'permanent' factors had altered to make a price change worthwhile. To the extent that markets are 'made' by specialist middlemen – and the majority of markets have middlemen of one form or another – we should then expect prices in those markets to have some degree of 'stickiness'. At one extreme, we have certain markets – such as labour markets and some financial ones – where prices, once fixed, remain fixed for some considerable period of time, whereas at the other extreme we have markets where prices move all the time or are only held fixed for very short periods. It follows, then, that we should not think of markets in terms of a mythical Walrasian 'auctioneer' who costlessly changes prices all the time to equate demand and supply. As Goodhart says:

> While there do remain a relatively few pure auction markets where price changes respond nearly instantaneously to changing market conditions, these

represent the exception and, therefore, for most practical purposes the concept of the auction as the basic market structure can be put aside.

In place of the auction, we should *generally* think of markets being run through specialist market makers who quote publicly announced prices ... Sir John Hicks originated the distinction between flex-price and fix-price markets. This has often been associated with the difference between auction and long-term contract markets. While these concepts have proved useful and illuminating, the bifurcation is too stark and may even serve to deter analysis of the factors determining the speed of price adjustment. Instead, I believe that a more promising approach is to view most markets as being operated via specialist market makers. There is then a possible continuum between those markets in which specialists revise prices very rapidly to incoming news, and those in which the specialists adjust prices more slowly. (Goodhart, 1989, 11, his emphasis)

Most markets are therefore 'made', to a greater or lesser extent, and cases where markets function as if under the guidance of a mythical 'auctioneer' are few and far between.

The Development of Financial Intermediaries

There is one particular kind of market-maker in which we are particularly interested – *financial intermediaries* or market-makers in financial markets. These bring together those with funds to invest and those seeking funds to borrow, and they perform a valuable social function because they enable these parties to trade at lower cost or inconvenience than would be the case if they dealt directly with one another. Intermediaries take three basic forms. The first is a *broker*, an intermediary who literally does nothing more than provide information to 'bring together' those with funds and those who need them so that they can agree on a contract. Brokers will arise where information about sources of funds or investment opportunities is scarce, and where it is difficult for the individuals seeking such information to collect it themselves. Under such circumstances, it may be profitable for brokers to specialise in collecting this information, disseminate it to the individuals who want it, and charge a fee for the service. Apart from providing information about the potential supply of and demand for funds, brokers can also provide credit ratings, independent assessments or audits, and various other specialist information services (e.g., market research).

There are also more sophisticated intermediaries that go beyond the mere provision of information to trade on their own account. These intermediaries take in funds from investors and issue the latter with claims against themselves, and then invest those funds in their own name with the aim of earning a profit from the difference between what they make on their investments and what they pay to the investors whose funds they use. These intermediaries are either *mutual funds*, which issue investors with a *single* type of claim, or *banks*, which issue investors with *two or more* different types of claim.[5] We can think of mutual funds as investment companies that pool their investors' funds and issue them with *shares* proportional to the amounts they invest. The net return from the fund's investments is then divided *pro rata* among the company's shareholders. While a mutual fund issues only shares, a bank issues both *debt* claims (i.e., claims with a given face value, at least outside of bankruptcy) and shares or *equity* (i.e., claims to the intermediary's residual income after debt claimants have been paid off). Banks thus have more sophisticated capital structures than mutual funds, and (as we shall see later) this greater sophistication gives them a competitive edge over mutual funds in many, though not all, of the markets in which intermediaries compete. Banks therefore dominate the financial system, and mutual funds have in comparison a minor role to play.

The Development of Bank-issued Exchange Media

Over time, individuals also come to use exchange media issued by financial intermediaries in place of the gold coinage used earlier. One way to think about this process is suggested by the familiar story of the goldsmiths, and this story of course also gives us one account of how banks might evolve. The use of coins still involves considerable costs, particularly those of storing, protecting and moving coins around. To save on some of these costs, some people would be prepared to pay others with the means to do so to store their gold for them. Goldsmiths and some merchants would already have facilities to keep large amounts of gold, and could therefore keep additional quantities of it at a relatively low marginal cost. These people would find it profitable to accept gold for safekeeping for a fee that many current holders of gold would be willing to pay, and depositors would be issued with receipts that gave them the right to demand their gold back. As the practice of making gold deposits spreads, it increasingly happens that when two parties agree to an exchange, one would go and withdraw his gold, and then hand it over to the other who would promptly deposit it again, often with the same goldsmith. Provided that the party accepting payment was satisfied that the goldsmith would still honour his commitment to pay back the gold, it would be more convenient for him simply to accept the goldsmith's receipt and save everyone the trouble of withdrawing the gold and depositing it again. The receipts of goldsmiths therefore begin to circulate as media of exchange in their own right, and the practice of using such receipts as exchange media will gradually replace the older practice of using gold coins (see also Selgin, 1988a, 19–21). The receipts now become banknotes, and the goldsmiths who issue them become bankers.

The Development of Fractional-reserve and Deposit Banking

At the same time, the goldsmith–bankers also notice that demands for redemption and new deposits of gold largely tend to cancel each other out over most periods, and so *net* withdrawals are generally quite low. They then realise that they could lend out much of the gold deposited with them to earn interest on it, and yet still face little danger of being unable to meet depositors' demands for redemption. They therefore start to lend out the gold (i.e., they reduce their reserve ratios below 100 percent) and then compete for additional gold deposits to lend out. Their competition eliminates the earlier fees charged for accepting deposits, and instead they are soon offering interest payments to attract deposits. As the use of bank liabilities as exchange media spreads, bank borrowers will increasingly accept loans of bank liabilities instead of loans of gold, and so the banks can make loans simply by issuing more of their own debt. The practice of making gold loans then gradually diminishes, and gold loans have effectively disappeared by the time that gold itself has lost its role as medium of exchange. However, even then the banks hold gold because they need it to satisfy public demands for redemption.

To make their deposits even more attractive, banks would also provide depositors with transfer banking facilities, so that they can have deposits transferred to pay their debts (e.g., by writing cheques against them). In so doing, the banks enable depositors to use or draw on their deposits as exchange media, and they would profit from this service by reducing the interest rates they offer on transferable deposits or by charging explicit fees for transfer services. Initially, perhaps, a bank might only allow transfers among its own deposits, but each bank would realise that its deposits would be more attractive if they could be used to make transfers into deposits at other banks, and their mutual interest would soon lead the banks to agree to facilitate deposit transfers among themselves. Each bank would then agree to accept cheques drawn on other banks and subsequently redeem them at the banks on which they were drawn. Initially, each bank might simply collect the cheques of each of its counterparts and redeem them every so often, but it would soon become clear that it would be more convenient and involve less movement of specie if the banks simply returned each other's cheques and arranged to pay only the net difference in specie. The banks would then have entered into bilateral clearing arrangements with each other. Depending on the number of banks involved, it may be even more efficient if they agreed to have representatives meet centrally, in a central clearing-house, and have *multilateral* rather than bilateral clearing. Each bank would then pay (or receive) whatever specie it owed (or was owed by) the other banks as a whole. Instead of a bank taking gold from banks which owe it gold, and paying gold to the banks to whom it owes gold, it will simply settle the net debit or credit to a central fund that does the same with every other bank. Multilateral clearing economises further on the transactions cost of clearing, as well as on the amount of specie that must be moved around between banks for clearing purposes.

The Convertibility of Bank Currency, the 'Law of Reflux' and Note Clearing

While the use of bank liabilities as exchange media gradually spreads, competition still forces the banks to keep their notes and deposits convertible into gold. These liabilities are legally binding promises on the part of the bank that issued them to redeem them (i.e., buy them back) under the conditions called for in the contract, and those conditions will normally call for the bank to do so on demand. The holder of a $1 bill (which is legally only a claim to a dollar, not a dollar itself) will therefore have the right to demand redemption for one dollar (i.e., for gold), and a bank that failed to meet such a demand would expose itself to the penalty for defaulting on a contract.

To see *why* banks would maintain the convertibility of their liabilities, one has to appreciate that convertibility is a guarantee that those liabilities will retain their value in terms of gold. A bank cannot simply discontinue convertibility without notice, since it would be bound to honour the contractual promise on outstanding notes to redeem them when required to. A bank could therefore only abandon convertibility by announcing its intention to retire its convertible notes and replace them with inconvertible ones, and any potential noteholder would interpret such an announcement as an indication that the bank intended to allow the value of its notes to depreciate. If the bank has no such intention, he will think, then why would it want to dispense with the convertibility guarantee? He will therefore refuse to accept the inconvertible notes, and the bank would lose its market share to those competitors who were willing to provide the public with the convertible currency they wanted. To abandon convertibility unilaterally is thus tantamount to surrendering one's market share to rivals. Even if the banks *as a whole* organised a concerted abandonment of convertibility, they would still have no way to prevent *new* banks from undercutting them by offering the public the convertible currency they want. Any concerted abandonment of convertibility would *ipso facto* create profit opportunities for new entrants who were willing to satisfy the public demand for convertible currency, and all the banks that abandon convertibility would lose their market share. Under conditions of free entry, the threat of potential competition therefore prevents even the banks as a whole from being able to abandon the convertibility guarantee. Competition among the banks forces them to maintain convertibility because the public demand it.

The commitment to maintain convertibility then implies that banks can only keep in circulation those issues the public are willing to hold. If a bank issues more notes than the public want to hold, the excess issues will be returned and banks will be legally compelled to redeem them – a 'law of reflux' operates by which unwanted issues are returned to the banks who must redeem them. The circulation of bank liabilities is then limited by the demand to hold them. Banks cannot issue notes *and* keep them in circulation, *without* the public demand to hold them. If a bank wishes to increase its note circulation, it must therefore increase the public demand for its notes – it must fight more aggressively for market share, open more branches, improve its reputation, and advertise more.

One other way in which a bank can increase the demand for its notes is by getting other banks to accept them. A member of the public would more willing to accept the note of a particular bank if he saw that other banks were also willing to, and if he could redeem the note at banks other than the bank that issued it. As with deposit banking, each bank usually has an incentive to enter into mutual acceptance arrangements with other banks, and the most likely result would be clearing arrangements similar to those that would arise when banks accept each other's cheques. The use of bank notes as exchange media therefore leads to the mutual acceptance of each other's notes and the establishment of note clearing arrangements among the banks.

Bank Safety and Soundness

Since a bank will normally find it profitable to operate on a fractional reserve, it will not have the gold on hand to meet redeem all its outstanding liabilities if they were all presented for redemption at once. The bank can therefore only continue to operate if it can persuade a major proportion of its liability-holders *not* to demand redemption, and it can only do that if it maintains their confidence by persuading them that their investments are safe (i.e., that they can get their money back any time they want it), so that over any given period of time most of them will feel no need to redeem.

In order to provide this reassurance, the bank must persuade its customer that its finances are sound – that is, the bank must be seen as having a sufficiently high *net worth* (or *capitalisation*) that it can not only pay off current debts, but could still pay them off even in plausible bad-case scenarios where it suffered major losses on its loan portfolio. If a bank has a sufficiently high capitalisation that it can withstand any plausible losses and still pay off its creditors without too much difficulty, then those creditors can be reasonably confident that their investments are safe. A bank can also supplement its capital by having its shareholders take on some degree of extended liability for bank debts and by issuing *subordinated debt*. Subordinated debt is debt that is automatically converted into equity when the bank's capital falls to some critical value. It provides for an automatic recapitalisation of the bank when the bank's capital has fallen to potentially dangerous levels and shores up the bank's capital strength just when the bank presumably needs it. A bank can also take measures to maintain its soundness by avoiding excessive risks in its lending, employing qualified and reliable staff, and having its books regularly audited and its credit-worthiness regularly rated.

The bank must also maintain its liquidity (i.e., its ability to meet immediate demands for redemption if they should arise). At the very minimum, a bank must maintain a certain amount of gold coins, relative to its outstanding demandable liabilities, so that it could meet demands for redemption as they occur. Given that such reserves are costly to hold, the bank will need to trade off the liquidity benefits of holding them against their holding costs, but experience over time will indicate what an appropriate reserve ratio might be. The bank would also supplement this 'primary' liquid reserve by holding 'secondary' reserves consisting of assets that were less expensive to hold, but which could also be sold quickly at relatively little cost, in case the bank needed to buy more reserves. It could also take out credit lines with other institutions, giving it the right to draw credit if it needed to. Should the bank be faced with unexpected demands for redemption, it would respond in the first instance by drawing down its primary reserve. If the demands continued, it would replenish its gold reserves by drawing down credit lines it had taken out earlier, by taking out new loans, or by selling some of its secondary reserve assets. Provided the bank maintains its soundness, it should have little difficulty obtaining the loans it needs, and it can be reasonably confident of being able to protect its liquidity and meet its redemption demands without defaulting. Indeed, those redeeming a bank's liabilities would have no desire to hold gold as such, but would convert them into other assets instead. Much of the gold would therefore be redeposited in the banking system. Other banks would then be particularly flush with gold and, provided they were satisfied about the soundness of the bank wanting the loan, it would be in their interests to lend it. A sound bank should therefore have no real difficulty obtaining the gold it needs.

The irony is that a bank that protects its soundness and liquidity would be very unlikely to face large demands for redemption *precisely because* liability-holders would have confidence in it. The very fact that it can persuade its creditors that they *could* have their funds back whenever they want them is usually enough to ensure that most of them will not *want* to redeem – in most cases, there is no point demanding redemption if one's investment in the bank appears to be safe. The bottom line is that although a safe and liquid bank always faces the theoretical *possibility* of a run, a run will not *actually* occur unless something happens that shatters public confidence and gives creditors explicit reason to fear for the safety of their funds. However, if a bank *fails* to take appropriate measures to maintain its soundness, a point *will* come when creditors lose confidence and run, and the bank will have difficulty withstanding the run when it occurs. A run thus serves the socially useful purpose of putting a 'bad' bank out of business, and the potential *threat* of a run keeps the other banks healthy by forcing them to keep their houses in order.

Financial Instruments Replace Gold as Redemption Media

While banks want to protect themselves against demands for redemption, they also have an incentive to reduce the cost of the reserves they hold to meet such demands. These costs will fall anyway as the banking system develops, because public demands for redemption will fall as their confidence in banks gradually grows, and the lower demands for redemption imply that the banks can operate on lower reserve ratios. However, at some point the banks will reduce these costs further by offering alternative, lower-cost redemption media instead of gold. One must keep in mind that gold is still relatively costly to store and hold, and bears no explicit return, while financial instruments involve lower holding costs and often yield explicit returns for the holder. It is therefore in a bank's interest to offer to redeem its liabilities using less costly redemption media – and it is in the public's interest to prefer such redemption media to gold. To qualify as a suitable redemption medium, an asset should have a value largely independent of the bank that uses it as a redemption medium (i.e., the bank cannot redeem its own liabilities using more of the same). Obvious examples are the debt or equity of other firms, including the debt or equity of another bank. If a bank uses a financial instrument instead of gold as a redemption medium there may be a possibility that the issuer would default, that the asset would fall in value, and so on, but if members of the public were not satisfied with a particular redemption medium they could always refuse to accept it (e.g., by refusing to accept bank debt that specified that particular redemption medium). If the public accept a particular redemption medium, the very fact that they do so implies that they consider that redemption medium to be at least 'as good as gold' and that they are willing to accept any risks that its use entails.

Banks now redeem their issues, not with a particular *weight* of gold as they did before, but with financial instruments (or other redemption media) of the same *value* as that weight of gold. The earlier directly convertible gold standard in which banks redeemed their liabilities directly with gold has thus given way to an indirectly convertible gold standard in which they redeem their liabilities with something else (see, e.g., Yeager, 1985a; Dowd, 1989). The only remaining 'monetary' purpose of gold is now to provide a definition for the dollar.

The Development of the Monetary Standard

The unit of account, the dollar, is still legally defined as a particular weight of gold and, legally speaking, a banknote with a face value of $1 is still only a claim to a dollar. Nonetheless, by this stage in the economy's evolution gold will have disappeared from circulation, and when he posts a price of one dollar in his shop window the vendor indicates that he is willing to accept a dollar note issued by a reputable bank rather than gold as such. Indeed, since gold has disappeared from circulation he might be quite unfamiliar with gold coins and be willing to accept them, if at all, only at a discount. The dollar note would be more liquid than gold itself, even though it was legally only a claim to some redemption medium of the same value as the gold itself. What this means is that even though the dollar is still legally defined in terms of a particular weight of gold, the term 'dollar' as used in everyday trade by now refers to the units in which exchange media are denominated (i.e., to what might be referred to as the 'banknote dollar') and *not* to units of gold or gold dollars as such. This banknote dollar can be regarded as tied to the gold dollar by virtue of the contract under which notes or deposits are issued, but it is *not* identical to it.

Given this distinction between the banknote dollar and the (gold) dollar itself, we can now say that when they issue their convertible currency, the banks do so according to a rule by which they maintain the price of gold in terms of banknote dollars. The fixed banknote price of gold then ties down the market price of gold by arbitrage forces. If the price of gold on the market rises significantly above the par value maintained by the banks, arbitragers will make a profit by redeeming banknotes (or deposits) for redemption media, selling the redemption media for banknotes and ending up with more notes than they started with. In the process, the outstanding quantity of banknotes will fall, and the falling quantity of notes will put downward pressure on the market (banknote) price of gold. Conversely, if the market price of gold falls too low, arbitragers will demand more notes from the banks and use the notes obtained in this way to buy more redemption media, and end up with more redemption media than they started with. The supply of bank liabilities will rise, and the market (banknote) price of gold will rise back towards par. Any discrepancy of the market price of gold from the 'par' price maintained by the banks sets in motion arbitrage forces that return the market price to par.

The price level under this system is then determined by the forces that determine the relative price of gold (i.e., the exchange rate of gold against goods and services in general). Since the (banknote) price of gold is effectively fixed by the rules of the indirectly convertible gold standard, the price level must move inversely with the relative price of gold. Hence, any factor that causes the relative price of gold to rise will cause the price level to fall, and any factor that causes the relative price of gold to fall will cause the price level to rise. For example, an event such as unexpected discovery of gold ore will lead to a greater gold supply. Given the demand for gold, the gold market will then only equilibrate if the price of gold falls relative to goods and services. Since the nominal price of gold is fixed, the relative price of gold can only fall if the price level itself rises. Hence, the gold discovery leads to a higher price level. Conversely, a factor such as a rise in the demand for gold will lead to a rise in the relative price of gold, and the relative price of gold can only rise if the price level falls.

The price level under the gold standard thus depends on supply and demand in the gold market, but these factors are unlikely to produce the degree of price-level stability that the agents living in our economy would prefer. The price-level instability produced by the gold standard would impose various costs on the public – they would find it harder to distinguish between 'true' price signals and 'irrelevant' price noise, and therefore make 'mistaken' decisions they would otherwise have avoided; they would have less peace of mind about the future; and so forth. A time would therefore come when the banks would decide to reduce price-level instability by changing the gold 'anchor' that ties down the nominal price level. Given that the price level under the gold standard is only as stable as the relative price of gold, the banks could generate a more stable price level by replacing the gold price-level anchor with an alternative anchor based on a commodity or commodities with a more stable relative price. The most likely candidate would be a basket of goods and services rather than any single alternative commodity. The banks would then announce that from a certain future date onwards they would use the term 'dollar' in new contracts to refer, not to a particular amount of gold as previously, but to a particular amount of a specified basket of goods and services (or something equivalent). This new 'basket dollar' would have the same value as the earlier gold dollar on the day it was first introduced, so as to avoid any jumps in the relative price of the 'anchor' (and, hence, the price level) when the new dollar was brought in, and the public would accept the new basket dollar because they themselves would prefer the greater price-level stability it would produce.

The monetary standard has now evolved into an indirectly convertible system based on a commodity-basket anchor chosen for its desirable price-level stability properties. Gold no longer has any 'monetary' purposes whatsoever – as medium of exchange, medium of redemption or unit of account – and the only vestige of gold in the monetary system is the use of the term 'dollar' as the name of the unit of account, but even the dollar itself is now legally defined in terms of a basket of goods and services.

The Mature *Laissez-Faire* Financial System

Stability

The financial system is now fully mature, and we can step back and assess its main features. Consider first its stability. We can talk about the *laissez-faire* system being stable in a number of different senses:

- First of all, the *laissez-faire* system is stable in so far as it is self-sustaining – it leaves no group willing and able to overturn some essential feature of it. The *laissez-faire* system is self-sustaining because everyone already pursues their own welfare subject to their various personal and environmental constraints. No-one therefore has any desire to change anything, given the various constraints under which they operate. In particular, the system does not depend on any 'guardian' who must sacrifice his own welfare and assume an unwanted burden to protect the public good – the safety of the system does not depend on any underpaid night-watchman. And, since there is no night-watchman, we do not have to worry about what he might get up to while everyone else is asleep – there is no problem of 'guarding the guardians'.
- The system is also stable in that it provides financial institutions with appropriate incentives to maintain their financial health and cultivate public confidence. The public want stable banks, and competition ensures that they get them. A bank that is not regarded as sufficiently strong by the public will lose public confidence, and without public confidence it will lose its market. A bank that wishes to remain in business must satisfy its customers and maintain its financial strength. Such a bank will be able to absorb non-catastrophic loan losses relatively easily and still retain public confidence, and, while it will always be subject to the threat of a run, runs will not actually occur unless some event shatters public confidence in it. Far from destabilising banks, as is often supposed, it is the threat of a run that forces banks to maintain their strength in the first place.
- The financial system is also stable in its response to other shocks. Banks accommodate changes in the public's demand for bank liabilities rapidly and automatically, in much the same way that current banking systems accommodate the public demands to change one form of bank deposit into another. However, with the *laissez-faire* system, it makes little difference what kind of bank liabilities are involved. Deposits can be converted into notes as easily as into other forms of deposit, or *vice versa*. Nor do banks have any difficulty meeting demands to redeem their liabilities for 'outside' redemption

media. The banks simply run down their reserves and if necessary obtain more, and accommodating these changes does not generally require major disturbances to interest rates, credit markets or economic activity.

- Finally, and following on from the last section, the *laissez-faire* system is stable in that it delivers nominal price stability (and therefore, other things being equal, interest-rate stability as well). The public demand such stability, and competition forces the banks to choose an anchor that generates it.

Optimality

This system is also optimal by virtually any sensible criterion. All feasible and mutually beneficial trades take place because there are no barriers to prevent them. The banks provide the public with exactly the exchange media they want, and deposit interest rates, bank charges and the like are all competitively determined. The rents from issuing exchange media are therefore competed away to the public. Similarly, competition among the banks ensures that expected rents from the loan side of their business are also competed away. Competition also ensures that banks provide the degree of stability their customers want. If the public want stronger (i.e., better capitalised) banks, competition for market share will lead banks to increase their capitalisation, and the public will get the stronger banks they want. At the same time, since capital is costly, excessively capitalised banks will not be competitive either, so competition produces banks of optimal strength, bearing in mind the public willingness to pay for it. Banks will also optimise their reserve holdings, and select appropriate redemption media, and the costs of maintaining convertibility and maintaining the price-level 'anchor' should be minimal. Unlike modern central banking systems, this free banking system is also entirely automatic. There is no 'policy problem' as conventionally understood – no need to worry about the incentives faced by the monetary or banking authorities, the time consistency of their policies, and so on – because these authorities do not exist to worry about. Everyone pursues his own self-interest, and all interests are harmonised by the market.

The Effects of Government Intervention

The conjectural history outlined above suggests that unfettered private interest would have produced a highly sophisticated, efficient and stable financial system. It would also have produced various institutions that are readily recognisable in the current 'real world' – amongst these the existence of financial intermediaries including brokers, mutual funds, and banks, and the widespread use of bank-issued currency. Yet there are also certain key features of our current financial systems that the conjectural history fails to explain, and prominent amongst these are the replacement of convertible currencies by *inconvertible* (or *fiat*) ones, and the existence of central banks and the apparatus of 'official' (i.e., government-sponsored) financial regulation that often accompanies them. The hypothetical *laissez-faire* system also differs from our contemporary world in that it lacks some of its most prominent problems – in particular the problems of inflation and financial instability – and I would suggest that the absence of these problems under *laissez-faire* is far from accidental.

We therefore need to explain these discrepancies between our hypothetical *laissez-faire* economy and the 'real-world' economy in which we actually live. These discrepancies can be summarised in four basic questions: (1) Why were convertible currencies replaced by fiat ones? (2) Why have we had so much inflation? (3) Why (and how) did central banks and 'official' regulation evolve? (4) And why do we appear to observe more financial instability than our hypothetical economy 'predicts'?

The answers to these questions relate to what is missing from our hypothetical story, and the missing ingredient is of course the state and what it does. While we have assumed so far that the state either does not exist, or, if it does, adopts a strictly *laissez-faire* approach to the financial system, the fact is that it was the historical norm for states to intervene in the financial system, and instances of *laissez-faire* approach are very much exceptional. We therefore need to introduce an interventionist state into our story and see what happens. Since the defining characteristics of the state are its monopolies over law making and law enforcement, we need to consider what happens when we give the individuals who control the state apparatus (i.e., the politicians and civil servants) the unique power that such control gives them. Since control of the state apparatus implies the power to change the law, those who control the state can wield very considerable power and influence over everyone else. They can compel other people to do what they want them to do (e.g., such as make payments to them), and they can change the rules under which everyone operates (e.g., by changing property laws). We must also presume that they will exercise this power to further their own ends, whatever those ends might be.

For what purposes is state power then used? As far as the financial system is concerned, one of the main reasons for state interference is to raise revenue. Raising revenue from the financial system can be politically attractive because it can often be done in heavily disguised ways, and indeed, in some cases those who are paying the tax do not even perceive that they are being taxed (e.g., when the government raises revenue by debasing the currency). Another attraction of taxing the financial system is that the public often fail to distinguish between nominal and effective tax burdens, and are therefore sometimes ready to acquiesce in taxes on financial institutions without realising that much of the burden will be passed back to them. Also, governments often intervene in the financial system to seize surpluses and transfer them to special-interest groups that have the political influence to mount successful lobbies. (A good example is the US Banking Act of 1933 which cartelised the banking industry by preventing 'commercial' and 'investment' banks from encroaching on each other's territory.) Finally, politicians sometimes raise revenue from the financial system because doing so enables them to by-pass the normal constitutional constraints against raising (other) taxes. The most conspicuous example is the use of the inflation tax, but the same end can also be achieved by other means such as selling monopoly privileges and compelling financial institutions to give them subsidised loans.

State intervention in the financial system can also be motivated by special-interest groups bringing pressure to bear on the government to sort out particular 'problems'. While much of this intervention is often some form of rent-seeking (e.g., such as the use of interest rate controls to protect mortgage-holders), much of it also arises, ironically, because of the mess created by previous government interventions. It has often been the case that government intervention in the financial system creates problems – often unforeseen ones – as a side-effect. Pressure is then brought on the government to 'do something', but the most natural solution – to undo the earlier intervention – is ruled out on political grounds. The government therefore intervenes again to correct the side-effects of its own earlier intervention, but the new intervention has side-effects of its own. The pressure therefore grows for the government to intervene again, and so it goes. This process also interacts with periodic government attempts to intervene in the financial system to raise revenue, and the danger is that these two main motives – intervention to raise revenue, and intervention to 'sort things out' – reinforce each other, each intervention producing further problems and calls for even more intervention. A good example of this process at work can be seen in the history of the USA since the outbreak of the Civil War in 1861. The USA had a reasonably good financial system by 1861, but when the Civil War broke out the federal government intervened to impose the National Banking System regulations on it. The principal purpose of this intervention was to raise revenue, but the consequence was to introduce considerable instability in the US financial system (see, e.g., Dowd, 1989, 141–146). Yet rather than repeal the legislation that caused the instability, Congress eventually responded by establishing the Federal Reserve System as the financial system's lender of last resort. Unfortunately, the Federal Reserve cure was worse than the disease, and the Fed's failure to protect the banking system led to the spectacular collapses of the early 1930s. But rather than abolish the Fed and go back at least to the National Banking System, Congress responded to the crisis of the 1930s by increasing the powers of the Federal Reserve and setting up elaborate systems of compulsory federal deposit insurance. The new system encouraged banks to reduce their capitalisation and take excessive risks, and led ultimately to the great deposit insurance disaster of recent years. One intervention led to another, and with each intervention the financial system became progressively less stable – and further intervention apparently even more 'necessary' than it was before.

The Creation of a Fiat Currency

There are two basic aspects to state intervention in the financial system – intervention that affects the currency, and intervention into the financial system *per se*. Of the former interventions, the most important is the creation of a fiat currency.

The process usually begins when the state intervenes to give privileges to one particular bank – the typical privilege being a monopoly over the issue of notes. The usual motive is to raise revenue by selling the privileges concerned. Since notes are a convenient redemption medium, other banks gradually become accustomed to using the notes of the privileged bank as their primary reserve and eventually cease handing out gold when presented with requests to redeem their deposits. The other banks end up making deposits redeemable, not into gold, but into the notes or deposits of the privileged bank, which has by now become a recognisable central bank. For a while, the central bank continues to issue convertible currency, but a point comes where the government tires of the discipline that convertibility imposes, and legislation is passed to order the bank to abandon convertibility. A classic example of this process is provided by the experience of the Bank of England in the 1790s: the obligation to maintain convertibility limited the extent to which the Bank could lend to the government; the government's demands for credits to finance the war against revolutionary France nonetheless continued to rise, and a point came where a comparatively minor shock set off a run that the Bank had not the reserves to meet; accordingly, the government passed an Order in Council to suspend specie payments, and the UK found itself with a fiat currency until convertibility was restored again in 1821.

Once convertibility is abolished, the value of the central bank's liabilities – and, by implication, the price level – depends on the amount of currency the central bank creates: the price level now depends on central bank *policy*. Central bank policy in turn depends on the views and interests of those who make that policy – government politicians and central bankers – and the balance of power between them as implied by the legislative framework under which the central bank operates. We might then expect, among other things, that the politicians would want to use monetary policy to court popularity, especially with elections coming up (see, e.g., Nordhaus, 1975). They would therefore be tempted to engage in lax monetary policies before elections – to reduce unemployment, create an air of prosperity, and reduce interest rates – and put off any 'painful' monetary policy decisions until later. They might also want to use monetary policy for fiscal purposes (i.e., to levy an inflation tax). The printing of additional fiat currency not only gives them more wherewithal to purchase goods and services, but the resulting inflation also reduces the real value of outstanding government debt and, if the fiscal system is imperfectly indexed, generates additional revenue from 'bracket creep' as people are pushed into higher tax brackets. There is therefore a tendency for a central bank issuing a fiat currency not only to produce inflation, but also to produce erratic and unpredictable inflation as well.

Financial Regulation, the Lender of Last Resort, and Liability Insurance

Governments also intervene to regulate the banking system in all sorts of ways. It is very common for banks to face restrictions on the liabilities they are allowed to issue. Legislation normally gives the central bank a monopoly over the note issue –

more often than not, for fiscal reasons – and this monopoly becomes one of the sources of the central bank's influence over the banking system. Commercial banks then have to seek more notes from the central bank, and the central bank always has the power to refuse to issue them. It has also been common historically for banks to face limits on the interest rates they can offer on their deposits or charge on their loans, and to face reserve requirements compelling them to hold more reserves – typically, more central bank liabilities – than they would otherwise choose to do. Reserve requirements increase the demand for central bank liabilities, and therefore increase the *seignorage* revenue the central bank can extract from the financial system. Banks can also face restrictions on the assets they may hold. In the USA, for example, it was traditional for legislation to divide banks into two artificially separate industries, with one (i.e., the 'regular' commercial banks) specialising in regular commercial lending and facing restrictions against real-estate lending, and the other (i.e., the thrifts and savings and loan institutions) specialising in real estate lending and facing restrictions against 'regular' commercial lending. The main function of such separation is usually to cartelise banking and exploit the consumer by ensuring that 'regular' banks and real-estate banks do not intrude on each other's turf. Finally, banks often face various forms of *prudential regulation* (i.e., regulations designed to protect their financial health), of which the most important are capital adequacy requirements (i.e., requirements to maintain minimum capital standards). Yet, as our earlier discussion indicated, the irony is that such regulations are not necessary under genuine *laissez-faire* because unfettered market forces will lead banks to maintain the financial strength that their customers demand. Prudential regulation is only 'necessary', to the extent that it is necessary at all, because *other* government interventions have prevented those customers' demands from being realised and left the banks weaker than they would otherwise be: prudential regulation is a classic case of intervention to correct the side-effects of previous interventions.

As well as restricting the activities permitted to financial institutions, the authorities often intervene to alter the incentives that institutions face. The most important such interventions are the establishment of the central bank as a lender of last resort and the setting up of systems of state-sponsored liability insurance. A lender of last resort provides banks with 'last resort' loans – loans that they cannot obtain anywhere else – while liability insurance protects them by discouraging liability-holders from running on them. Yet, paradoxically, each of these interventions only serves to weaken the banks and make them artificially dependent on state support. As the earlier discussion indicated, if the public want strong banks, competitive forces under *laissez-faire* conditions should ensure that they get them. The introduction of a lender of last resort or deposit insurance into a previously *laissez-faire* system will then undermine a bank's incentives to maintain its strength and cause it to weaken itself. In the absence of a lender of last resort, a bank management knows that it must protect its own liquidity, and will therefore ensure that it is financially strong enough to be able to get loans if it needs them. If a lender of last resort facility becomes available, a bank will become weaker – not to mention dependent on the last resort facility – because it has less reason to be concerned about maintaining its financial health. Deposit insurance has a similar effect. Once creditors are assured that their funds are safe, bank managements no longer have the same incentive to maintain their capital adequacy, forego risks, or generally behave conservatively, and their banks' financial health naturally deteriorates.

Apart from undermining the market forces that would otherwise translate the public demand for strong banks into actual bank strength, these interventions also make banks artificially dependent on state or central bank support. It can then *appear* that financial institutions need support because they are weak, whereas banks are really weak only *because* of the government or central bank support. In addition, this artificial weakness can also make it *appear* that other interventions are required to counteract the 'problem' of bank weakness. Capital adequacy restrictions might appear to be 'needed' to prop up banks' financial health, restrictions on bank lending might appear to be 'needed' to prevent excessively risky lending, and so on. The establishment of a lender of last resort or a system of liability insurance can create an apparent 'need' for regulation, but that 'need' only arises because the intervention distorts the incentives managers face. Remove the distortion, and the 'need' for support or regulation disappears.

OUTLINE OF THE BOOK

Having set the scene with the conjectural history, we can now outline the analytical structure of the material to be covered. This outline also serves the purpose of providing a 'road map' to guide the reader through the later chapters and give some idea of how these chapters fit together.

Financial Contracts, Capital Structure and Corporate Financial Policy

Before we can do anything else, we first need to lay our financial foundations by explaining the basic types of securities that agents use, how these securities produce a firm's financial structure, and how firms manage their financial structures (i.e., what financial policies they adopt). Accordingly, we begin in Chapter 2 by looking at the design of the simplest types of financial contract, those between two agents or two classes of agent. This chapter highlights the main justifications for the basic contract types – debt contracts with provision for costly 'bankruptcy', in which the party issuing the liability agrees to make certain specified payments, failing which he is held to default on the contract and the other party has the recourse of a bankruptcy court; and equity contracts, in which ownership and residual income are shared between both parties. It turns out that debt contracts are often optimal because they reduce the costs of verifying the actions or claims of the insider. If output is high, for example, a debt contract means that the outsider has no reason to care what the insider says or does – and, hence, no reason to spend resources checking up on him – provided he makes his debt payment. The possibility of bankruptcy or default then emerges a natural corollary of debt contracts. The state of bankruptcy is 'bad' if it occurs, in the sense that it implies relatively low welfare, but it is worth their while for the parties involved to write contracts that imply a *risk* that bankruptcy *might* occur for the sake of the benefits that the debt-with-costly-bankruptcy contract would give them if bankruptcy does *not* occur. However, debt contracts are not always optimal, and there are circumstances where debt contracts are dominated by others, the most important being income-sharing or equity contracts.

The chapter then considers a number of related issues. We find that pledges of one sort or another generally help to alleviate contracting problems, but in the presence of limits to what can be pledged they do not eliminate them entirely. If a pledge is limited, as it usually will be, the principal might also respond by curtailing the amount he would be willing to advance to the agent (i.e., he would ration credit). The principal might also insist on the right to re-assess the project periodically (e.g., by offering a short-term loan and requiring the agent to renegotiate it from time to time) or insist on certain conditions (i.e., covenants) being written into the contract. These covenants would place restrictions on the agent's behaviour (e.g., by obliging him to provide information or make periodic payments) and give the principal the right to impose penalties (e.g., the right to foreclose on the project) if these restrictions are violated. We also look at the role of other possible features of contracts such as clauses giving the agent the right to buy his debt back (i.e., call clauses), the extent to which contracts might involve the lender monitoring a loan, and so on. We then take a closer look at bankruptcy issues in these more sophisticated environments and discuss the main features of optimal bankruptcy law, the extent of debtor liability, and so on. We also relax the assumption that both agents are risk- neutral and examine the impact of the agent's risk-aversion on optimal contract forms, and the final section ends with a few observations on observed contract forms (e.g., about why observed contracts forms appear to be relatively 'simple').

Chapter 3 elaborates on the various economies that can be reaped if there are three or more agents who each adopt specialised roles. Instead of there being one class of equity-holder and one class of debt-holder, there might be equity-holders and two classes of debt-holder, one with first claim on the firm's resources in the event of default and the other with a junior claim. Another case is where the manager of a debt-issuing firm is no longer the only owner, and so we have two different types of equity – the *'inside' equity* he holds and the *'outside' equity* held by the other owner(s). There are various reasons why this more sophisticated contract structure might be preferable to the simple debt-and-equity contract structures considered earlier, but perhaps the main one is that it helps to specialise the monitoring function among investors and thereby ensure that monitoring is done, but not excessively duplicated. The basic idea here is that investors adopt a seniority structure among themselves, and this seniority structure gives the most junior investors a strong incentive to monitor; provided the junior investors maintain a large enough stake in the firm, the other investors can then safely monitor less, because they can 'trust' the junior investor(s) to monitor for them. The relative amounts of different securities that a firm issues (i.e., its capital structure) thus basically emerges as a way of handling agency problems, but capital structure is also influenced by need to get around information asymmetries and send credible signals to interested parties (e.g., a firm might use its capital structure to signal that it has good investment opportunities available to it). Our treatment of capital structure opens up the whole subject of corporate financial policy, and we then proceed to go through the main area covered by it – firm dividend policy, corporate governance, and the impact of the takeover market. The chapter ends with a brief overview of the 'new' financial theory of the firm that emerges from recent work and explains how it accounts for some of the main features of observed economic fluctuations.

Financial Intermediation

Having discussed corporate financial policy, we then turn to examine financial intermediation. The essence of financial intermediation is the use of a third party to facilitate the transfer of information or wealth between two others. Financial intermediaries exist because they make the agents with whom they deal better off than they would otherwise be, and we begin our discussion of financial intermediaries by discussing these benefits in general terms in Chapter 4. (1) One important way in which intermediaries can help other agents is by giving individual investors access to economies of scale that would otherwise be closed to them. Individual investors might be too small to be able to invest in profitable but large investment projects, for example, but an intermediary can solicit funds from a group of them and invest those funds on their behalf. (2) Relatedly, individuals might be averse to risk, but each individual might be too small to reap the risk-reduction benefits of holding a diversified portfolio, while an intermediary could give them the benefits of diversification by holding a diversified portfolio and giving them claims against it. (3) An intermediary can also economise on the costs of searching out profitable investment opportunities and monitoring their progress once investments are made. In the absence of an intermediary, such activity might be duplicated or not take place at all, and all would suffer, but an intermediary can ensure that such activity is efficiently carried out because the intermediary itself earns the marginal return from it. (4) An intermediary can also benefit its investors by providing them with liquidity. Investment projects usually take time to mature but in the meantime individual investors often face the possibility that they may be 'caught short' for liquidity in the period before the projects mature. If the proportion of individuals who get caught short can be predicted, an intermediary can offer investors a way to share these liquidity risks and insure themselves against getting caught short. Individuals who are caught short then get higher returns than they would otherwise get, at the *ex post* expense of those who are not, but everyone is better off *ex ante* because they value the liquidity 'insurance' the intermediary provides.

Broker Intermediaries

Chapter 5 is then devoted to the simplest form of financial intermediation, brokerage. A broker is an intermediary who sells information but does not as such purchase financial assets from his clients or issue his own financial assets to them. There are many different kinds of brokers – search specialists who bring investors and savers together, accounting firms that provide specialist advice and auditing services, insurance brokers, credit valuers, forecasters, consultants of one sort or another, and others. All sell information, but do not normally take a direct stake in the quality of the information they sell (e.g., because of superior expertise). However, the viability of brokerage is also limited by two factors. In the first place, clients will only commission a broker if they have some confidence that the information he will provide will be worth its cost. By and large, brokers try to overcome this problem by taking an indirect stake in the reliability of the information sold (e.g., by cultivating a good reputation which he can offer as a hostage for his 'good behaviour'). Potential clients will then appreciate that the need to protect his reputation gives him an incentive to maintain his quality of service. The other problem with brokers is that of preventing resale. If his information is of value to more than one potential customer, a customer to whom he has sold his information might undercut the broker by selling the information himself. The broker must therefore find ways to restrict resale or else assume that he will make only one sale and charge accordingly.

Mutual Funds

Chapter 6 then considers the next form of intermediary, the mutual fund. A mutual fund is an intermediary that holds its own assets and issues liabilities on its own account, but all its liabilities are identical. Mutual funds give small investors the opportunity to benefit from diversification opportunities that would otherwise be unavailable to them. They can also offer investors a large variety of portfolios tailored to their individual risk–return preferences. The size of each fund would be determined by public demand. If a member of the public wished to redeem his shares, the fund would normally sell off the bundle of assets to which his shares are a claim, and the size of the fund would contract accordingly. The price of mutual fund shares will reflect the value of the fund's assets, and if the fund's assets are 'perfectly' marketable, investors will have no problems pricing fund shares – the price of a fund's share would be consistent with the market value of the underlying assets to which the share is a claim. Should the fund's assets alter in value, the price of the fund's shares would change *pari passu* and the net worth of the fund would remain unaltered. Unlike the case with banks, the net worth of a fund is not affected by changes in the value of its assets, and the observation that a fund has suffered losses on its assets does not give fund shareholders any particular reason to lose confidence in the fund and run on it.

Nonetheless, mutual funds are also subject to serious limitations relative to banks. First, there is a large demand among investors for debt-type investments (i.e., investments of predetermined nominal value outside of bankruptcy), and mutual funds are ill-equipped to meet this demand. A fund that tried to offer debt liabilities would have to offer *only* debt liabilities, and any shock to the value of its assets would drive a wedge between the value of its assets and the value of its liabilities that would lead the demand for fund shares to rise or fall without limit. A debt-issuing fund would therefore be highly unstable. Second, many investment assets are imperfectly marketable (e.g., because of verification costs), and mutual funds are generally unable to holding such assets in their portfolios. The only mutual funds that could hold them are closed-end ones (i.e., funds that do not redeem their shares before their assets have matured), but close-end funds cannot by definition issue redeemable assets in the normal sense. A fund that wishes to issue redeemable assets must therefore restrict itself to holding assets of 'perfect' or near-perfect marketability. A bank, by contrast, has no problems holding imperfectly marketable assets *and* issuing liabilities that are redeemable on demand. Finally, the fact that a mutual fund's shares vary in value to reflect the value of the fund's assets puts the fund at a disadvantage relative to a bank in providing exchange media. A fund share could not circulate like a banknote, for example, because it would have no fixed nominal value and a person accepting it would need to check the value of the fund's assets to see what the share was worth.

Banking

Chapters 7–9 examine the third, and in many ways most important form of intermediation, banking. As explained already, a bank is a financial intermediary that holds assets and issues its own liabilities, but it differs from a mutual fund in that it issues *more than one* type of liability. The basics of banking are dealt with in Chapter 7, and we begin by examining bank liability management, paying particular attention to the trade-off between issuing debt and issuing equity. Bank equity capital has a very important role in reassuring bank debt-holders, and issuing more equity generally makes the bank stronger and more reassuring. However, equity is a relatively expensive source of funds, so the bank's optimal debt–equity ratio will involve a trade-off between the greater security of equity and the cheaper financing costs of debt. But whatever precise value it takes, the optimal debt–equity ratio will be low enough to ensure that debtholders continue to have confidence in the bank, and the management will be conscious that losing that confidence could be very costly, and perhaps fatal, to the bank.

We then examine various specific issues in bank liability management, the main ones being the redeemability of bank liabilities, the provision of liquidity to bank debt-holders, and the use of bank debt as media of exchange. After discussing these, we turn to the management of bank assets. Unlike mutual funds, banks have a relatively unrestricted choice of assets, but the basic trade-off they face is between holding low-yielding but relatively marketable assets, on the one hand, and holding high-yielding assets that are imperfectly marketable for one reason or another (e.g., because they need monitoring, or because verification costs need to be paid if they are sold), on the other. A bank will usually want to hold some imperfectly marketable assets for the sake of their higher expected returns, but if this investment strategy is to work the bank must also ensure that it can hold these assets until they mature, which in turn means that they must be able to maintain their debt-holders' confidence. Various other asset management issues also arise that we need to discuss. Foremost amongst these are the issues of credit rationing and collateral policy, bank monitoring activities, loan syndicates, and loan sales. We then examine bank 'off-balance-sheet' activities (i.e., activities that do not appear in conventional bank balance sheets), the principal ones being loan commitments, underwriting activity, acceptances, and bank participation in derivatives markets.

Finally, there is the general question of banking stability and bank runs. We therefore examine what happens when a bank or group of banks lose the confidence of their creditors and the creditors decide to run. There are various issues here. How does a bank respond to a run, and what effect does the run have on it? How does a run on a single bank or group of banks affect the banking system as a whole and, in particular, is there a danger that a run might be 'contagious' and spread to other, presumably healthy, banks? What effects do bank runs and bank distress have on the broader economy? And, what are the costs and consequences of the failure of a bank or group of banks? By and large, our discussion suggests that bank runs are not the problem that traditional accounts have suggested they are. Runs are generally restricted to individual banks or groups of banks that have discernible problems such as bad loans, and there is little evidence of bank run contagion that might turn runs on weak banks into runs on the banking system as a whole. The available evidence on the costs of bank failures also suggests these costs are lower than used to be thought, and indeed, not that much different from the costs imposed by the failures of other comparably-sized firms.

Chapter 8 then discusses the structure of the banking industry. There are two key issues we need to address here. The first is whether the banking industry shows sufficient economies of scale that only one firm can survive in the competitive equilibrium (i.e., is banking a natural monopoly?). We therefore review the arguments for economies of scale in banking to investigate whether these economies are large enough to make banking a natural monopoly. The theoretical arguments suggest several reasons why banking might be subject to economies of scale – there may be economies of scale in reserve holding or in the diversification of risk, and there are also various other arguments that turn out to be spurious – but the empirical evidence suggests that these economies are *not* sufficiently pronounced to make the industry a natural monopoly. Indeed, there is not a *single* recorded case where one bank has emerged as natural monopolist under conditions of free competition.

Given that banking is not a natural monopoly, the second issue is whether banks might usefully form an interbank organisation to which they might delegate certain functions – such as providing emergency loans to banks in difficulty or dealing with bank run contagion – while still retaining some degree of independence. Would individual banks delegate some of their independence to banking clubs that would take decisions on their behalf and perhaps impose their own 'regulations' on them? This is an important issue because some economists have argued that 'central banking' would evolve (or has in fact evolved) spontaneously from free banking, a claim, which, if correct, might make the establishment of free banking effectively pointless. There are indeed certain reasons why they might conceivably establish a club – clubs might reduce the transactions or monitoring costs of inter-bank loans, there might be reserve-holding 'externalities', or they might want to club to counter bank run contagion – but even if they do, the banking clubs that emerge would *still* be very much different from current systems of central banking. To the extent they impose regulations at all, their regulations would be 'voluntary' in the sense that individual banks would always be free to leave the club and ignore them. Furthermore, club officials would be accountable to the clearing banks, and not to some 'external' central bank, and would have to be viable under competitive conditions. These clubs would therefore be quite different from contemporary systems of central banking, so there can be little question of justifying central banking on the grounds that it mimics the 'regulations' that would emerge spontaneously from the membership rules of free banking clubs. Central banking cannot therefore be defended on the grounds that it would have evolved anyway even if governments had not imposed it.

Chapter 9 then takes something of a detour and considers some of the recent theoretical work on banking instability. The main emphasis of this literature is to justify the regulations imposed by current systems of central banking, and in particular to justify the 'need' for a lender of last resort or a system of state-sponsored deposit insurance to protect banks against runs. The key paper is that of Diamond and Dybvig (1983) which sets out a theoretical framework that has since become standard in the literature. Diamond and Dybvig suggest that banks are subject to potentially damaging runs because investment projects take time to mature and investors are uncertain about their future demands for liquidity. The possibility therefore arises that, having made their investments in a financial institution, investors might panic because they feel that other investors will demand redemption before the underlying investments have matured. If other investors demand redemption too early, the intermediary will have to liquidate investments at a loss, and this loss will be borne by those investors who fail to demand redemption sufficiently quickly. Individual investors will therefore rush to demand redemption (i.e., they will run), and Diamond and Dybvig suggest that some form of government intervention is required to protect the banking system to reassure them and prevent the run occurring.

However, this literature *fails* to justify the intervention it purports to. A key problem is that the intermediaries that arise in this framework do not resemble real-world banks – and therefore cannot be used to justify government intervention into real-world banking regulation. In the Diamond–Dybvig world, individuals make investments in a financial intermediary that issues identical claims to all investors. The Diamond–Dybvig intermediary is therefore a mutual fund – and, as we shall see, a peculiar one at that. Runs arise then because the fund tries to fix the value of its liabilities, but has no capital to absorb losses. If some outside investor were to come along in the Diamond–Dybvig world and pledge his own capital to guarantee other investors against loss, the latter would then flock to him and away from the Diamond–Dybvig intermediary. There would no longer be any reason to 'panic', and government intervention would not be necessary. The point is that *this* is exactly what those who invest equity into a bank actually do – they invest their capital to protect other investors against loss, and in so doing remove any reason for them to demand redemption of their investments before the underlying assets have matured. Diamond and Dybvig thus fail to justify government intervention in the banking system.

Media of Exchange and Payments Systems

Chapter 10 examines the economics of exchange media and payments systems. We begin by explaining the development of a commonly or generally accepted medium of exchange. As explained in our conjectural history, media of exchange arise because they economise on the costs of barter, and we eventually end up with one or maybe a small number of them that are commonly or even universally accepted. However, what happens after the development of commonly accepted commodity exchange media is more controversial. Some economists have claimed that the commodity currency would directly give way to *fiat* or *inconvertible* paper currency, but such a development is in fact most implausible. Instead, it is more likely that the commodity currency would give way to *convertible* paper currency and that the currency would remain convertible thereafter. Convertibility persists because the public demand it, and fiat currencies only arose historically because of government intervention to suppress the convertibility guarantee.

The chapter also examine two other issues stemming from the new monetary economics (NME) literature. The first is the 'legal restrictions' theory that effectively implies that currency would disappear under *laissez-faire*; the second is the 'monetary separation' hypothesis that maintains that the medium of exchange and the medium of account would be 'separate' (i.e., be different and move apart from each other) under *laissez-faire*. If either of these is correct, a *laissez-faire* system would look very different in certain respects to presently existing systems. However, I suggest that both claims are theoretically questionable and empirically falsified; *laissez-faire* would therefore lead neither to the disappearance of currency nor to the 'separation' of the medium of exchange and the medium of account. A *laissez-faire* monetary system is not as 'different' from current systems, theoretically speaking, as the NME literature would have us believe.

We then turn to payment system issues. Our main concern is with 'advanced' payment systems – sometimes called accounting systems of exchange – in which payments are made by the transfer of bookkeeping entries without the use of a medium of exchange as such. One important concern with payments systems is systemic risk – the danger that the failure of one of the principal participants to settle would threaten other agents and hence the system as a whole. We therefore need to explain how payment systems can handle systemic risk, and whether the existence of a systemic risk problem represents a 'market failure' that justifies government intervention into the payment system. (The answer, as usual, is 'no'.) We then examine whether accounting systems are likely to displace monetary systems (i.e., systems that use a medium of exchange) entirely – another issue that has been given considerable prominence by the NME literature – but suggest that such an outcome is unlikely. The use of exchange media might diminish over time, but is most unlikely to disappear.

The Monetary Standard

The Unit of Account

Chapters 11–15 focus on issues relating to the *monetary standard*, or the rules and institutions that determine the value of the currency. We begin in Chapter 11 with the *unit of account*. There are three principal issues to be examined here. The first is the nature and uses of a unit of account. The unit of account is the unit of that commodity or asset – the medium of account – in units of which prices are expressed. In the contemporary USA, for example, the medium of account is the US dollar, taken generically, but the unit of account is the (US) dollar-unit. It is not so much the *size* of the units that matters, but the *choice of medium* in which to express them. It would not have made that much difference if the US had adopted the cent-unit instead of the dollar-unit as its unit of account in the 1790s, but it *would* have made a major difference if the USA had adopted the pound sterling as its medium of account instead of the US dollar – American inflation and interest rates would then have been determined by the policy of the Bank of England, and so on.

Our second main concern is with the determinants of the area (or network) – the *unit-of-account area* or *unit-of-account network* – over which a particular unit or medium of account is used. The principal theoretical issue here is the presence of *network externalities* in the use of a particular unit or medium of account – situations in which the value of a unit of account to one user depends on how many others also choose to use it. A good example of this type of externality occurs with the choice of whether or not to install a telephone – the greater the number of other users, generally speaking, the more useful the telephone would be to me, and hence the more inclined I would be to get a telephone myself. These network factors have a critical bearing on the choice of unit of account because they introduce elements of strategic interdependence into agents' decisions. My decision whether to use a particular unit of account might depend on how many others I expect to use that unit, but other agents are just like me and make the same calculations. Multiple equilibria can then arise, depending on what agents expect each other to do. If agents expect each other to use a particular unit of account, they might each individually decide to use it themselves, and so everyone uses it; but if they expect each other not to, then no-one might see any point in adopting it, and so no-one actually adopts it. The outcome depends on agents' strategic expectations, but there is no way to 'tie down' those expectations to ensure that any particular outcome actually occurs.

Having set out a model that explains how a unit of account area is determined in the presence of network externalities, the rest of the chapter develops the implications of this model for competition between different units of account. If an existing currency has a network attached to it, anyone contemplating switching to a new unit of account will appreciate that they will (normally) lose the benefits of that network if they switch. They might then be reluctant to switch, even if the new unit is better than their current one (e.g., because it inflates at a lower rate). Individuals can become 'locked in' to an demonstrably inferior unit of account because they lack the means to co-ordinate a simultaneous switch and no-one wants to switch themselves because they have no confidence that others will switch with them. Nonetheless, it does *not* follow that competition between units of account necessarily 'fails'. Competition only 'fails' if the new unit of account is *incompatible* with the old one's network – if price tags have to be changed, and so on. If a new unit is *compatible* with the old network, on the other hand – if it is another 'brand' of the same currency unit, rather than an unfamiliar new unit – then there is no reason why it cannot access the existing network, and the existence of that network would not constitute an entry barrier against it. Compatibility thus eliminates the network entry barrier and the market 'failure' disappears. Competitive forces then deliver the inflation rate that the public want.

The Mechanics of Convertibility

Chapters 12–14 deal with various mechanical issues. Chapter 12 deals with the mechanics of currency convertibility. When we say a currency is convertible, we normally mean that the issuer promises to maintain its value against something else (e.g., gold, under a gold standard), but also commits itself to buy and sell its currency (usually on demand) for some redemption media whose value is specified by the terms of the contract under which the currency is issued. Underpinning this system is the existence of a good or service, or bundle of goods and services, or financial asset, whose nominal value is pegged by the currency-issuing banks. This is the *anchor commodity* or *anchor asset*. In the gold standard the anchor would be gold, in a silver standard it would be silver, and so forth. We can then think of the prices of other goods and services throughout the economy as being tied down by the combination of the given nominal price of the anchor and the various economic forces that determine the relative values of other goods and services against the anchor.

We are interested in three different types of convertible system. The first and most familiar is a system of *direct convertibility* in which the banks redeem their currency with the same commodity or asset as that which serves as the system's anchor. The medium of redemption and anchor are therefore identical. Directly convertible systems are relatively easy to understand. Should the market price of the anchor deviate from its par price maintained by the banks, individual agents will exploit the opportunity to make arbitrage profits and in so doing set in motion changes in the supply of currency that return the market price of the anchor back to par. However, convertible systems have the drawbacks that a single commodity (or whatever) is unlikely to be the most efficient anchor *and* the most efficient redemption medium, and they also have the potential to destabilise the financial system in the face of shocks to the demand for the redemption-medium/anchor. These drawbacks are avoided by *indirectly convertible systems* in which the roles of redemption medium and anchor are performed by *different* commodities or assets, but the arbitrage mechanism by which equilibrium is restored then becomes more complicated. An appendix to the chapter then examines a third system which is best regarded as a degenerate form of convertibility – the infamous *'real-bills' system* in which bank currency is redeemable against redemption media of a given nominal value, but there is no anchor to tie down any nominal value. Prices and the supply of currency are therefore theoretically indeterminate, and a real-bills system in practice would be subject to very considerable nominal-value instability.

Commodity-based Monetary Systems

Chapters 13–14 consider commodity-based monetary standards – monetary systems where the value of the unit of account is tied by some rule to specific quantities of one or more 'real' commodities. Commodity-based monetary systems are to be distinguished from *fiat* or *inconvertible* monetary systems in which there is no obligation on the issuer to peg the value of its currency. Commodity-based systems were the historical norm until the twentieth century, but convertibility was undermined and then eventually abolished by government intervention, and no major central bank at the present time maintains even the pretence of a commodity-based currency or the desire to re-establish one in the future. Commodity-based systems fall into two general categories – those based on a *single* commodity (e.g., gold or silver), and those systems related to them that involve 'switching' between individual commodities (e.g., bimetallism); and those systems based on *baskets* of commodities (and perhaps services too). Chapter 13 deals with the former, and chapter 14 with the latter.

Chapter 13 begins by setting out a model of the determination of the price level in a gold-standard world where the nominal price of gold is held fixed. It explains how the price level under the gold standard moves inversely with the relative price of gold against goods and services generally, and then shows how various factors might affect that relative price (e.g., a discovery of gold or an improvement in gold-mining technology would reduce it, and hence raise the price level). We then examine the historical record of the gold standard, paying particular attention to its record on price stability, and go on to examine the properties of mono-commodity systems based on other commodities besides gold (e.g., bricks, and non-durable commodities). The second half of the chapter then examines the switching standard, of which the most prominent example is the historical bimetallism that was abolished in the late nineteenth century. The defining characteristic of this type of system is that one or other party to a contract – historically, the debtor – can choose which commodity to use to discharge his debt. The main difference between the switching standard and the monometallic standard – *but* one that only applies to systems in which there is some positive monetary demand for the precious metals – is that bimetallism provides a stabilising mechanism to cushion the effects of most shocks on the price level, relative to the impact that those shocks would have on the price level under a monometallic system. This stabilising mechanism – the so-called *parachute effect* – operates because the two metals are perfect substitutes in their monetary uses, and so the monetary use of one metal will absorb part of the impact of any shock to the other.

After bimetallism, we turn in Chapter 14 to commodity-basket monetary systems. The underlying principle behind these systems is to peg the price of a basket of goods (and, maybe, services) instead of the price of a single good. In its simplest form – that of symmetallism as suggested by Alfred Marshall – a bank would peg the price of a basket of gold and silver, but leave the individual prices of gold and silver free to float. Shocks to the relative prices of each metal will to some extent cancel out, so the relative price of the basket should be more stable than the relative prices of the individual commodities in it. The price level under the basket system should therefore be more stable than the price level under either gold or silver monometallism. If we extend this logic further, a 'broad basket' that includes a large number of goods and services should have a more stable relative price than any 'narrow' basket, and should therefore generate a more stable price level. How, though, do we make such a scheme operationally feasible? One suggestion that gets around the costs of physically handling broad baskets is the 'compensated dollar' scheme of Irving Fisher (1911). This scheme is essentially a proposal to stabilise a target price index, but it turns out that Fisher's proposal is seriously flawed and would not in fact have been feasible. Part of the problem is that it would have been open to speculative attack, but it is also highly doubtful that it would in fact have delivered price-level stability. We go on to examine more recent relatives of the Fisher scheme (e.g, Robert Hall's *ANCAP* proposal) and summarise their generic weaknesses. We now arrive at the point where we can set out a new scheme that should deliver price-level stability without running into the problems that make 'compensated dollar' schemes unworkable. This new scheme involves the creation of a new financial instrument – a 'quasi' price-index futures contract – whose price the banks would peg at periodic intervals. We can then explain how this scheme would work and set out the necessary operational details. The chapter ends with a brief appendix that discusses the 'tabular standard' – essentially a proposal for indexing payments against the price level – as an alternative to stabilising the price level itself.

Price-level Optimality

Having cleared up these issues, we can now turn in Chapter 15 to the fundamental question of *price-level optimality* – the *optimal* path of the price level over time. The absolute level of the price level is of very little interest in itself, but how it *changes* over time can have very profound and complex implications. Most economists agree that a continually rising price level – inflation – damages the economy, and perhaps the social order more generally, but how it does so, and large the costs might be, are still very controversial issues. Economists who agree that inflation are bad are also divided on the most suitable alternative, with a majority arguing for price-level stability – a zero trend for the price level, and a low variance – and some arguing for prices to fall with the real interest rate or the rate of productivity growth. This chapter reviews these issues to determine the factors on which price-level optimality depends and the costs implied by deviations from optimality – principally, the costs of inflation. It then tries to make an assessment of what the optimal price-level path actually is.

We start with a very simple framework and gradually extend it to take account of various complications and in so doing build up a cumulative picture of the effects of a changing price level. Our starting point is a highly simplified model of the effects of perfectly anticipated inflation on economic growth and welfare. This framework enables us to estimate some of the welfare costs that arise from inflation, in particular, the costs of inflation associated with reduced money holdings, and the costs related to the effects of inflation on the capital stock. Having provided some estimates of these costs, we go on to consider the 'optimal quantity of money', estimate the costs of not having an optimal quantity of money, and examine the effects of anticipated inflation on relative prices. We then turn to sporadic inflation, and examine in general terms the various ways in which unpredictable inflation can interfere with the operation of markets and lead them to malfunction. This leads to an investigation of the effects of price-level misperceptions of one form or another, and of the ways in which unanticipated inflation can redistribute income and wealth. After that we leave theoretical issues for a while and look at some of the empirical work on the effects of inflation, as well as the empirical work linking inflation, inflation variability and inflation uncertainty. Particularly important is the evidence linking inflation variables to lower income or lower economic growth which gives us more potentially quantifiable estimates of (some of) the costs of inflation. We then go on to examine some of the 'deeper' effects of inflation that have received relatively little attention in the theoretical literature, paying particular attention to the various social effects of inflation and the extreme disruption and other problems that occur when there is hyperinflation. We end the chapter with some thoughts on price-level optimality, and end up siding with those who argue that the optimal price-level path is a stable price level. An appendix at the end of the chapter looks at 'productivity norm' arguments that the price level should fall with productivity growth, but concludes that these arguments are ultimately unconvincing.

Financial and Monetary Reform

Finally, what happens if we introduce an interventionary state into the picture, and what, if anything, should we do about government intervention? The first question we have already reviewed, and there is no need to go into details again here. Once the government intervenes in the economy, the banking system becomes weaker and inefficient, the currency becomes debauched, and so on. The banking system becomes weak because the government preys on it, or because it sets up a system of deposit insurance or lender of last resort that undermines the banks' own incentives to maintain their financial health; inflation arises because the government severs the link between the currency unit and gold, and then pressures the central bank to reduce interest rates or finance its own fiscal deficits, and so forth. Many problems also arise because special interest groups use the power of the state to acquire privileges at the expense of society as a whole, or because the government or its agents insist on taking on responsibilities that they cannot discharge properly, if only because they lack the necessary knowledge and understanding of how the economy operates.

If *laissez-faire* works, and government intervention fails, then we presumably want 1a package of reforms to roll back the government intervention and establish *laissez-faire*. This programme of reforms outlined in Chapter 16 should have three essential elements. The first is a programme of *financial* reform that based on the following general principles.

(1) The first is the prohibition of government predation on the financial system. The reason for such a prohibition is fairly obvious – government predation has been one of the major causes of historical banking system weakness and, indeed, of inflation as well.

(2) The second would be thorough-going financial liberalisation. The more liberal the legal framework is, the greater the number of mutually beneficial trades that can take place, and the better off people will generally be. Trade in financial services should operate under a liberal (i.e., permissive) general commercial law, and not be subject to any restrictions designed to bring about specific results (e.g., redistributions from one group to another). Financial liberalisation would include: the repeal of discriminatory legal tender laws to allow courts to enforce contracts made in any medium or unit of account the parties involved freely choose; the amendment of existing laws to eliminate, or at least reduce, discrimination between different liability arrangements; and most importantly, the abolition of 'official' regulations on financial institutions, including, among other measures, the abolition of reserve requirements, capital adequacy requirements, and interest rate ceilings.

(3) The third principle in the financial reform package would be the abolition of the artificially distorted incentives created by compulsory deposit insurance and the existence of an 'official' lender of last resort. However, it is important that these latter reforms be carried out carefully, since banks would need time to build up their financial strength in order to be strong enough to survive without government support.

There would also need to be a programme of *monetary* reform. We need a monetary standard that would maximise price-level stability, but also be compatible with free banking. The best option, I believe, would be to re-convert the currency, but choose a 'broad-basket' anchor that would stabilise the value of a chosen price index such as the CPI (or RPI in the UK). The broad basket approach could be implemented using the quasi-futures contract (QFC) scheme suggested in Chapter 14. The scheme could be initially set up by the central bank, which could then be abolished once the scheme was up and running. The central bank would issue the new financial instrument, the QFC, and be legally committed to pegging the price of this instrument at periodic intervals. This new instrument would be similar though not identical to a price index futures contract, and would promise the holder a payment on maturity that was contingent on the 'announced' value of a price index on that date. The expected price level would then be determined by a market equilibrium condition, and arbitrage operations would correct deviations of the expected price level from its equilibrium value. The expected value of the price level should therefore be stable, and there should be relatively little 'slippage' between expected prices and the subsequently realised actual price level. The actual price level should therefore be reasonably stable as well. Once the new monetary system was up and running, the issue of currency could be transferred entirely to commercial financial institutions and the central bank could be abolished. Once the free banking system is up and running, the only remaining task is to protect it against the danger of future government intervention. The third and final task is therefore one of *constitutional* reform – to amend the constitution to protect financial and monetary institutions by making it as difficult as possible for governments to interfere with them in the future.

2 Bilateral Financial Contracts*

Economists have long been interested in how firms and individuals finance their activities, and there is a vast literature dealing with the relative supplies of different types of financial instruments. Two types of financial instrument are particularly important: debt contracts that promise investors a specified return in 'normal', non-default states and first claim to the issuer's assets in default states; and equity contracts that give holders a claim on an issuer's residual income (i.e., its profit) and ultimate control over its assets provided the issuer does not default. Traditionally, the finance literature has tended to focus on the supply of and demand for these financial instruments, but had relatively little to say on why those *particular* contract forms are used in the first place.[1] This latter question – the 'security design' problem, as Harris and Raviv (1991, 2) call it – was neglected, and yet it has become increasingly apparent in recent years that the answers to some of the most basic issues in financial economics actually depend on it. If we do not understand why agents use the contract forms they do, then we can only have, at most, a limited understanding of firm capital structure and financing decisions, and, therefore, of everything that depends on them (e.g., the activities of financial intermediaries). A clear understanding of contract form is thus essential if we are to understand the more sophisticated issues to be considered later. Our first task must therefore be to establish what 'optimal' contracts look like, and how they relate to the contracts we observe in the 'real' world.

It is convenient to distinguish between *bilateral security design* (i.e., the design of contracts involving two agents, or by extension, two classes of agent) and *multilateral security design* (i.e., contract design involving three or more agents, or classes of agent). We need to deal with bilateral design before we deal with multilateral design, so we focus on bilateral design in this chapter and multilateral design in Chapter 3. This chapter therefore focuses on explaining the basic contract types – debt contracts with provision for costly bankruptcy, equity contracts, and certain other types of contract – as well as the different varieties these contract forms can take. One of the most important results that emerges is that debt contracts are often optimal because they minimise the costs associated with asymmetric information or unobserved actions. The possibility of bankruptcy then emerges as a natural by-product of debt-type contracts, and though the bankruptcy state is usually 'bad' if it occurs, the agents involved accept the risk that bankruptcy *might* occur for the sake of the benefits that the debt-with-costly-bankruptcy contract *would* give them if bankruptcy does *not* occur. We can also show how various important features of real-world debt contracts – the use of collateral or inside equity, 'credit rationing', covenant restrictions, and so on – can be explained by

* Part of this chapter appeared as 'Optimal Financial Contracts', *Oxford Economic Papers*, 44 (October 1992), pp. 672–693.

fairly straightforward extensions of the 'basic' economic environment. However, debt contracts are by no means always optimal, and there are readily identifiable circumstances in which alternative contracts – equity contracts, or contracts that are neither debt nor equity – are optimal. For example, while debt contracts are often optimal where the entrepreneur knows more about the project outcome than the outside investor, equity contracts are often optimal where the outside investor *can* observe the project outcome but *not* the amount of risk the entrepreneur takes in his choice of project. The choice of contract form is thus influenced by the features of the economic environment within which the contracting parties find themselves, but it can of course also influenced by their preferences, and, in particular, by their attitudes to risk. Security design can therefore involve an element of risk-trading, as well as an attempt to minimise the agency, information and other costs implied by the economic environment.

Chapter 3 then elaborates on the various economies that can arise if there are three or more agents. If there are two or more 'outside' investors instead of one, these investors can often adopt specialised roles that economise on the costs that would be incurred if they were all to perform the same role (e.g., one agent could monitor the production process or verify output claims on behalf of the others). The various agents consequently adopt interdependent roles, and the financial contracts involved will reflect this interdependence. The investor who accepts the monitoring or verification role might accept the status of junior creditor (i.e., accept a contract under which he only gets paid when other creditors have been paid in full) which would give him an incentive to monitor (or verify) efficiently. The other creditors could then reduce their monitoring efforts, and some costly monitoring could safely be dispensed with. In return for accepting the greater responsibility and risk his status implies, the junior claimant would be rewarded with a higher promised return in non-default states, and it is this higher promised return that would give him the incentive to accept the role of junior claimant/monitor in the first place. But whatever particular form these arrangements take, they all have the common feature that one investor holds a particular asset conditional on the behaviour of one or more *other* investors: our focus of interest in Chapter 3 is consequently the *interdependence* of these asset-holding decisions, and, therefore, the *structure* of the liabilities that a firm will issue when it raises finance from others. In short, Chapter 3 focuses on *capital structure*, while this chapter focuses on 'primary' contract design.

BASIC ANALYTICAL FRAMEWORK

A Benchmark Example

The following example provides a convenient way to begin thinking about these issues. There are two individuals, a principal, P, and an agent, A. The principal P provides funds to A for an investment project, and A undertakes to make some sort of repayment. We assume that A's promise is credible because there exists a legal system that can enforce the promise, and we abstract from any issues relating to the cost of enforcement. Neither agent can influence the investment process which yields a random net outcome θ distributed in a range $[\theta_-, \theta_+]$, where θ_- might be negative (i.e., there may be a loss). Both agents know the distribution of θ *ex ante* and observe its realisation *ex post*. The problem they face is to select a scheme to share out the future profits or losses. At one extreme, if A has sufficient wealth to absorb any possible losses, he could guarantee P a fixed return and himself absorb any profits or losses that arise from the realisation of θ, at the other extreme, if P has sufficient wealth to absorb any possible losses, he could absorb any profits or losses and guarantee A a fixed return; and between these two extremes, they might also agree to share the profits or losses between them according to some formula. If each agent is risk-neutral, then neither of them has any reason to prefer any one of these schemes to any other, and the payout structure would be indeterminate. The payout structure would also be trivial in the sense that these contracts are equally efficient and their differing allocations of *ex post* profits or losses would be of no broader consequence – finance is irrelevant in a sense reminiscent of the famous Modigliani–Miller result that firm financial policy is irrelevant (Modigliani and Miller, 1958). It follows, then, that if we are to derive a determinate payout structure that 'matters', we must relax one or more of the underlying assumptions on which this benchmark example is based. The explanation for a determinate, contract structure therefore lies in the *absence* of one or more of these conditions.

We can now investigate security design by showing how the optimal contract structure becomes determinate and then changes as we relax these assumptions in plausible directions. Before proceeding, it might help the reader to indicate the order in which these assumptions are to be changed. Relaxing the assumptions that the agents involved have unlimited wealth and that verification is costless takes us to the *costly state verification* (CSV) model which yields the important result that the optimal contract is *debt-with-costly-bankruptcy* (or debt contract, for short). Underlying costly state verification is the idea that the agent, A, has more knowledge of the outcome state than the principal, P, and the debt contract arises as a means of dealing with the problems caused by this *hidden knowledge* on A's part. We then consider the possibility that A might be able to influence the outcome state by means of actions that are either unobservable to P or else observable only at a cost (e.g., it might be difficult for P to observe A's effort). A's *hidden actions* thus produce a potential *moral hazard* problem, which may require P to expend resources monitoring A's behaviour, but it turns out that hidden action produces an alternative justification for the basic debt contract. We then consider *adverse selection* where the principal does not observe one or more characteristics of the project itself, and find that the optimal contract form depends on the precise unobserved characteristic. Debt contracts are again (often) optimal where the unobserved characteristic is the 'quality' of the investment project, but in the important case where the unobserved feature is the project's *riskiness*, the optimal contract turns out to be an equity contract that gives the investor P a proportional share in the project's net income. In short, the optimal contract is debt when there is hidden knowledge or hidden action on A's part, but it can be debt or equity when there is adverse project selection.

Having established a basic framework, we then consider various extensions. We begin with those issues raised by the possibility that the agent, A, might be able to alleviate verification or moral hazard problems by making pledges (e.g., with his own assets). A might take an 'inside' stake by investing his own capital in the project, or he might offer some form of collateral. We find that pledges of one sort or another alleviate these problems, but do not eliminate them entirely unless the agent has particularly large amounts of assets to pledge. If what can be pledged is limited, as it will normally be, the principal P might respond by curtailing the amount he would advance to the agent (i.e., he would ration credit). Alternatively, or in addition, he might insist on the right to re-assess the project periodically (e.g., by offering a short-term loan and requiring the agent to renegotiate it from time to time) or he might insist on certain conditions (i.e., covenants) being written into the contract. These covenants would place restrictions on the agent's behaviour (e.g., by obliging him to provide information or make periodic payments) and give the principal the right to impose penalties (e.g., the right to foreclose on the project) if these restrictions were violated. They might also give him the right to monitor the agent's actions as well. We also look at the role of other contract features such as clauses that give the agent the right to buy his debt back (i.e., call clauses) or give the principal the right to convert his debt into equity (i.e., convertibility clauses). We then turn to bankruptcy issues in these more sophisticated environments and discuss the nature and costs of bankruptcy, the main features of optimal bankruptcy law, the appropriate extent of debtor liability, and the various credibility issues to which bankruptcy gives rise. The next section relaxes the assumption that both parties are risk-neutral and examines the impact of risk-aversion on security design, and the final section summarises some of the main points and ends with a few further observations (e.g., on the simplicity) of observed contract forms.

The Impact of Verification Costs

Suppose we begin by dropping the assumption that A always has sufficient wealth to absorb all possible losses. Where this wealth constraint binds, he can no longer credibly offer P a fixed return in all states of nature and P must absorb at least some possible profit or loss himself. If there are also limits on P's wealth, then P cannot guarantee a fixed return either, and there will be states in which A must absorb at least some profit or loss as well. Limitations on wealth thus rule out the two extreme contract forms we mentioned earlier in which one agent alone absorbs all the fluctuation in θ. Now suppose that we also drop the assumption that both individuals observe the output θ at no cost, and assume instead that the borrower–agent observes θ costlessly but a verification cost has to be paid if the lender–principal (or anyone else) is to observe it. We can think of this cost for the moment as the cost of auditing the borrower's books, but a more detailed motivation for these costs will be provided shortly.[2] We then arrive at the CSV models of Townsend (1979), Sappington (1983), Gale and Hellwig (1985), Lacker (1989, 1990) and others which provide a motivation for debt contracts with costly bankruptcy. Assuming for the moment that the decision to verify is deterministic, the optimal contract involves the borrower paying the lender a fixed amount θ^* in all states where there is no verification, but the borrower gives over his whole proceeds to the lender if verification takes place.[3] Verification is paid for by the lender and takes place if the value of θ announced by the borrower falls short of θ^*. Verification does not take place otherwise. Several features of this contract contribute to its optimality:

- It dispenses with the need for costly verification in 'good' states when output is high.
- The requirement that the borrower receives nothing when verification takes place ensures that he minimises the probability of verification taking place, and so minimises expected verification costs.
- While verification depends on what the borrower claims his output was, he still has no incentive to lie (i.e., the contract is incentive-compatible). The borrower will never give a false announcement that θ is less than θ^* because he would incur verification and lose the whole output, and he never has anything to gain from falsely announcing that θ exceeds θ^*.

This CSV framework provides a natural motivation for primitive 'bankruptcy' states which occur when A cannot or will not meet a minimum payment and forfeits what he has left to P. The costs of verification can then be viewed as bankruptcy costs which include not only the costs of auditing the borrower, but also the time costs, lawyers' fees, lost goodwill, and so forth, involved in a legal process. It is important to emphasise that while bankruptcy (or verification, if one prefers) is 'bad' if it occurs – that is, the *occurrence* of bankruptcy might lead one or both agents to regret having made the contract in the first place – the *possibility* of bankruptcy is part of the optimal arrangement. Both agents choose to expose themselves to the risk that bankruptcy might occur for the sake of the benefits they would receive in 'good' states where it does not occur, and they strictly prefer such an arrangement to any other where bankruptcy could not occur. We shall have more to say on bankruptcy states presently.

Hidden Actions and Moral Hazard

We now leave verification issues and consider the effects on contracts of the possibility that output depends on A's *hidden actions* which the principal finds costly to monitor (i.e., there is a *moral hazard* problem).[4] The hidden action usually referred to is A's choice of effort, and the moral hazard problem in this context relates to the tendency of A to reduce his effort on the grounds that some of the results of his effort (in some states, at least) would go to the principal. Let us assume that A's choice of effort can only be monitored at a cost which is sufficiently high to make monitoring unworthwhile. If output is observable at no cost and A's wealth provides no binding constraint, Harris and Raviv (1979) show that moral hazard over A's level of effort leads to an optimal contract in which A makes a fixed payment in all states of nature. The idea is that the optimal contract gives A the appropriate incentive to work by giving him all the marginal returns beyond the fixed repayment amount specified in the contact. A thus 'internalises' the moral hazard problem, and his promised fixed payment is credible because he has sufficient wealth to honour it regardless of how his investment project turns out. If A's wealth imposes a binding constraint on the payments he can credibly offer, a completely non-contingent contract is no longer feasible, but Bester and Hellwig (1989, 162) show that the optimal contract when there is moral hazard relating to the entrepreneur's level of effort is a debt contract in which a pre-agreed fixed payment is made in 'good' states and everything is paid over in 'bad' states where A cannot make that fixed payment. A again gets all the marginal return in 'good' states, and the threat of losing everything in a 'bad' state still gives him the incentive to make the appropriate effort to prevent a 'bad' state occurring.

Adverse Project Selection

A related problem can arise with respect to the type of project undertaken by the entrepreneur. This problem arises where some important feature of the investor's project (or choice of project) is not observed by the investor. One such case is where the investor does not observe the (appropriately defined) 'quality' of the project. In this case, debt contracts are still optimal over a wide of circumstances (Innes, 1993). The reason, of course, is that the entrepreneurs with better quality projects prefer debt contracts to maximise their residual profits, and the entrepreneurs with poorer quality projects need to imitate them to avoid revealing themselves.

However, there can also be adverse selection relating to the riskiness of the investment project, and in this case debt contracts may no longer be optimal. Suppose that the investor makes a debt contract with the entrepreneur but cannot monitor the riskiness of the entrepreneur's choice of project. Imagine, for example, that the entrepreneur has a choice between a safe project and a high-risk one, both of which yield the same total expected return, R^e, and the entrepreneur owes the investor a payment of D in non-default states, and $D < R^e$. The safe project is perfectly safe, so if the entrepreneur adopts it he can repay his debt with probability one. The expected return to the investor is therefore D and the entrepreneur's expected return is $R^e - D$. If the entrepreneur adopts the high-risk project, however, the project yields returns of 0 and $2R^e$ with equal probability. If the project yields the low return, 0, neither party gets any return; but if the project yields the high return, $2R^e$, the investor gets D and the entrepreneur gets $2R^e - D$. The expected returns to the investor and entrepreneur from the high-risk project are therefore $D/2$ and

$(2R^e - D)/2$ (or $R^e - D/2$), and so the entrepreneur is better off choosing the high-risk project, but the investor is better off with the low-risk one. Since the expected return is the same regardless of which project is chosen, the entrepreneur maximises his own expected profit by maximising the expected default losses he passes back to the investor. (This tendency for a borrower to prefer riskier projects (or assets) to less risky ones so he can pass expected losses to the creditor is known as *asset substitution*, and it surfaces in a variety of contexts, as we shall see.)

A more appropriate contract in these circumstances would be equity. With an equity contract, the investor gets a given proportion of the net income from the project, and so the entrepreneur cannot manipulate the investor's expected profit or loss by choosing a more risky project. Provided the output is still verifiable at zero or negligible cost – which rules out the agent misrepresenting output – the entrepreneur then has no incentive (as he would have under the debt contract) to choose an excessively risky project. Since profits are shared, if he chooses a project to maximise his own expected profit, he also maximises the investor's expected profit as well. The investor would then have no reason to object to the project choice even if he somehow got to know what it was. The equity contract thus circumvents the problem posed by adverse project selection and delivers an optimal outcome, or, put another way, adverse project selection makes equity contracts optimal.

Note, however, that this result depends on the output from the project being verifiable at negligible cost. If output is not verifiable at all, the entrepreneur can reduce the payoff to the investor by declaring that output was lower than it actually was, and the investor would never be able to prove he was lying. In fact, the entrepreneur would always declare that output was at its minimum possible level, and knowing that he had this incentive, the investor would presumably prefer to invest elsewhere. On the other hand, if output is verifiable at some positive but not prohibitive cost, we are then back to costly state verification, but what the optimal contract might be in the presence of *both* costly state verification *and* adverse project selection is, to say the least, not an easy matter to resolve. The debt contract that handles the costly state verification issue also encourages the entrepreneur to take excessive risks, but the equity contract that leads the entrepreneur to take the 'right' project risk also encourages him to misrepresent output. The optimal contract under these conditions is not obvious, and is even less so when one adds hidden actions to the picture as well, but to some extent we can view the various extensions to the basic framework – inside equity, collateral, covenant restrictions, and so on – as ways of coping with the difficulties to which these factors give rise.

INSIDE EQUITY AND COLLATERAL

Inside Equity and 'Primary' Collateral

Following on from this last point, the basic debt and equity contract forms might also be supplemented by the entrepreneur taking a stake in the project himself, and the provision of security of some sort is very common in practice (Kanatas, 1992, 381). The entrepreneur might do so either by investing his own capital in the project (i.e., by taking an 'inside' equity stake) or by offering the lender some form of collateral. The simplest case is where the entrepreneur has enough wealth of his own to guarantee the investor against loss in any state of the world (see, e.g., Bester, 1985, 1987; Bernanke and Gertler, 1989, 21). The investor would be guaranteed against loss and would no longer have any interest in the outcome of the project. The fact that the entrepreneur might know more about the project or be able to influence the project outcome (e.g., by choice of effort) would then be irrelevant because the entrepreneur would bear all the gains or losses himself.

However, in most cases the entrepreneur would not be able to offer the investor a fully guaranteed return, and the investor would have to take into account the possibility that he might suffer a loss. In these cases, the entrepreneur will generally maximise the reassurance he provides the investor by committing as much as possible of his own personal wealth to the project: (1) One reason, emphasised in the hidden knowledge literature, is that a bigger stake by the entrepreneur gives the investor more to recover if the entrepreneur defaults (e.g., Gale and Hellwig, 1985, 654). (2) A second reason, emphasised in the hidden action literature, is that a greater own stake by the entrepreneur reduces agency costs – the greater his stake, the greater his incentive to make an effort, and the lower the gap between the effort he makes and the effort the investor wants him to make. (3) A third reason, emphasised in the adverse selection literature, is that a greater inside stake reduces adverse selection problems – the entrepreneurs with better projects want to distinguish themselves from the others, and the entrepreneurs with poorer projects are unwilling to offer such high inside stakes precisely because they know their projects are poor; the investor can therefore judge the quality of the investment project by the willingness of the entrepreneur to stake his own wealth on it (e.g., Bester, 1985, 1987; Chan and Kanatas, 1985; Besanko and Thakor, 1987). Each of these factors provides a reason for the optimal contract to require that the entrepreneur commit *all* his wealth to the project – to maximise the investor's recoverable assets, in the hidden knowledge model; to minimise agency costs, in the hidden actions model; and to maximise the quality of the pool of investment assets, in the adverse selection model – and the investor can always induce the entrepreneur to agree to this arrangement by lowering his cost of finance in return for it. The stake itself could take the form of capital invested directly in the project (i.e., 'inside equity'), but the entrepreneur might use his personal wealth to provide collateral to the investor in the event the project fails (e.g., Berger and Udell, 1990a; Bester 1990).

Empirically, the influence of the borrower's own stake in his project can be broadly captured by his net worth (and, in more general models, by his retained earnings as well, e.g., as in Moore, 1993). We can therefore say that a rise in borrower net worth (and retained earnings) should ease the lender's concerns about default losses and therefore lead him to grant a bigger loan (e.g., Bernanke and Gertler, 1985, 1987, 1989, 1990; Schreft and Villamil, 1990; Calomiris and Hubbard, 1990). A strengthened balance sheet means that a borrower has more resources available to invest directly in a project or to use as collateral to obtain outside funds, and this increased 'inside stake' (and/or increased collateral) reassures the lender and encourages him to lend more. It also helps to explain the well-documented effects of balance-sheet variables on investment.

Leaving aside debt contracts for the moment, the entrepreneur might also take a stake in his own project even if he makes an equity contract with the investor – the entrepreneur can take an inside equity stake even if the investor takes an 'outside' equity one. As we have already seen, the investor might take an equity claim on the project if there is adverse project selection (e.g., if he cannot observe the riskiness of the project selected by the entrepreneur). However, merely taking an outside equity claim on the project is not enough to eliminate all problems of adverse selection, and an important adverse selection problem that still remains is the need to distinguish between good and bad quality projects. One way to resolve this problem is for the entrepreneur to take a stake in the project himself – to post inside equity. The size of his stake then helps the investor to screen projects and tell good from bad. In the basic model, that of Leland and Pyle (1977) and Campbell and Kracaw (1980), the investor's concerns about the quality of the projects he faces would (in the absence of inside equity) lead him to regard all projects as average-value projects and lead him to pay average prices for all (outside) equity shares. Those with good projects would then get lower prices for their shares than would be the case if investors were fully informed. Good entrepreneurs would have an incentive to signal the value of their projects by investing in them themselves, and more they invest, the higher the quality rating that the investors will give them. Inside equity can therefore be important when the (outside) investor takes an equity stake, as well as when he takes a debt one.

'Secondary' Collateral

It will often be the case that the entrepreneur's assets will be worth less to someone else than to him, or can only be sold off at a loss (i.e., they will be illiquid). Such assets provide an imperfect substitute for inside equity, and the optimal contract will call for them to be used as 'secondary' collateral to supplement the entrepreneur's commitment of inside equity and 'primary' (i.e., liquid) collateral. The basic idea is illustrated by Lacker (1990). In this model the entrepreneur has both types of wealth – 'liquid' assets, that an investor values as much as the entrepreneur does, and 'illiquid' assets that the investor values less – and the optimal contract is a debt contract that calls for him to make a fixed nominal payment in non-default states. However, if he defaults, he pays over whatever he can of the liquid good, and, if his 'repayments' still fall short of the specified nominal payment, he then hands over whatever he can of the 'secondary' asset as well. Since the investor attaches a lower value to the secondary good than the entrepreneur does, he obviously prefers that the entrepreneur hand over liquid wealth, but is willing to accept illiquid wealth instead if the entrepreneur has no more liquid wealth to give him. Lacker gives a good example:

> Imagine a loan to a farmer who will repay out of the (private) proceeds from the next harvest. The collateral good corresponds to the chattels of the farmer: durable, portable, personal property ... [But] if chattels are unique and specially suited to an individual, the borrower's chattels might be of only limited direct utility to the lender. So the optimal contract has the farmer repay a fixed amount out of the harvest, with any shortfall made up by the surrender of some of the farmer's chattels. (Lacker, 1990, 3)

The principle that a defaulting entrepreneur hand over his secondary assets to the investor continues to hold even if the secondary assets are of *no* value to the investor. Such assets obviously give the investor no pecuniary compensation in the event of default, but pledging them can *still* be useful because the threat of losing them will influence the entrepreneur's behaviour. (Remember that the entrepreneur still values them even if the investor does not; hence, pledging them gives the entrepreneur more to lose, and the prospect of losing them will influence his behaviour.) The pledged assets are therefore effectively hostages to give credibility to the entrepreneur's promise of 'good behaviour':

> While it may seem strange to consider the possibility of an asset that has no 'market value' serving as collateral, one need only note that collateral can perform its functions *either* by reducing the creditor's costs in the event of default, *or* by making it costly for the debtor to default. Although a tradable asset (or one that yields income or service value to the creditor in the event of default) serves 'double duty' in this regard, an asset that is 'worthless' to the creditor but valuable to the debtor can nevertheless facilitate the formation of a mutually agreeable contract [provided the investor knows that the entrepreneur values them] ... Although the fingers of a concert pianist yield little if any services to the creditor in a fractured condition, the prospect of their fracture will be a strong incentive toward repayment. A less sensational example of the same class of collateral is found in credit ratings: although non-traded and capable of yielding no gain to the creditor in the event of default, the prospect of the capital loss implicit in a bad credit report again serves as an incentive to a debtor to pay his bills. (Benjamin, 1978, 341, his emphasis)

Clearly, the optimal contract will call for the entrepreneur to pledge his most liquid wealth first, his less liquid wealth after that, and his hostages last, in a distinct pecking order. He will begin by pledging as much liquid wealth – inside equity or a pledge of liquid collateral – as he can. If his liquid wealth does not suffice, he will offer whatever secondary collateral he can, beginning with the more liquid assets first. If his secondary collateral still does not suffice, he will then offer his hostages which, though of no pecuniary use to the investor, are still useful in the contract because of their influence on the entrepreneur's behaviour.

CREDIT RATIONING

Even where he can reassure the investor by taking a stake of his own in a project, it will often be the case that the entrepreneur's stake will still be too small to provide the investor with the amount of reassurance he desires. The scarcity or inadequacy of the borrower's guarantees might therefore lead the lender to *ration credit* (i.e., to provide a borrower with few funds than he would want at the given contract terms). But the question arises, why would a lender ever ration credit in preference to letting the loan interest rate rise to clear the market? To answer this question, recall that the lender aims to maximise his expected profit. He will therefore raise his loan interest rate *only* if doing so increases his expected profit, and yet the expected profit from a loan depends, not just on the promised interest, but also on the perceived probability of default. A higher interest rate will certainly increase the promised return, but it can also increase the probability of default and, if the latter effect is large enough, can *decrease* expected profits overall.

One reason is provided by Stephen Williamson (e.g., Williamson, 1986). Suppose we have a costly state verification (CSV) world where all borrowers are identical, but only the borrowing firm costlessly observes the outcome of its investment project and the lender has to pay a cost to verify the output. The optimal contract is a standard debt-with-costly-bankruptcy contract, where bankruptcy is the state where the lender verifies output and takes whatever there is. A rise in the interest rate then increases the lender's payoff in non-default states, but also increases the probability of default, and, hence, the expected bankruptcy cost. The overall effect of a rise in interest on the lender's expected profits depends on the balance between these two effects, and the lender will ration credit if the latter effect is strong enough. *Williamson credit rationing* can thus occur in a CSV framework when a rise in the interest rate would raise the expected cost of bankruptcy (or verification) by more than it would raise the expected return to loans in the non-bankruptcy state.

- Suppose, for example, that entrepreneurs have no (or relatively small) collateral and that each project requires a minimum level of investment to succeed, an assumption that captures an extreme form of economies of scale. Since it then makes no sense for the lender to give a borrower a loan less than a certain amount, the lender gives out loans of that minimum size until he runs out of funds. All loan applicants would be identical, as far as the lender is concerned, yet some would get the full amount of the loan they asked for and others would get nothing.
- Conceivably, however, a different form of credit rationing could occur if entrepreneurs had more collateral and the investment projects did not show such strong economies of scale. If entrepreneurs each had collateral to offer and the investment project showed constant returns to scale, the lender would share out his lending funds among all entrepreneurs, treating each identically. The reason is simple: since production shows constant returns to scale, the way in which the

lender allocates funds makes no difference to the gross expected returns from the investment projects, but the more firms he lends to, the greater the total amount of collateral that is pledged against that the (given) loan total, and, hence, the lower the lender's expected bankruptcy costs. The lender will therefore lend to every entrepreneur, and, if he has to ration credit, he will do so by rationing *loan size* rather than rationing the *number of loans* he makes.

More generally, the presence of economies of scale in the investment technology leads the lender to prefer to make large-size loans, and therefore ration the number of loans he makes, but the pledging of entrepreneurial inside equity and/or collateral to projects encourages the lender to maximise the number of loans he makes, and therefore ration by restricting the size of his loans. But whichever form it takes, this credit rationing is also an equilibrium phenomenon, and borrowers who are denied credit or given smaller loans than they want cannot induce the lender to give them more credit by offering to pay more interest.

Credit rationing might also arise because of the effect of borrower moral hazard on the lender's expected bankruptcy cost. The probability of default could rise because higher interest leads borrowers to take more risks which the bank cannot monitor. This is the moral hazard explanation for a greater probability of default (see, e.g., Keeton, 1979; Stiglitz and Weiss, 1981). Assuming he can, an entrepreneur will choose a level of risk that provides an appropriate balance, to him, between the upside and downside consequences of the risk he takes, but this balance can also depend on the interest rate. If the interest rate then rises, the lender takes a greater slice of whatever return is made, but the rise in interest has a *proportionately greater* effect on the entrepreneur's return if he plays safe. The entrepreneur's previous privately optimal degree of risk is now too low, and he can make himself better off by taking more risk. He therefore does so, but the additional risk increases the probability of default and hence the expected losses that default would impose on the lender. In extreme cases, the rise in interest rates can even lead the lender to stop lending altogether to certain classes of borrower. Again, this credit rationing, when it occurs, is an equilibrium phenomenon, and borrowers who are rationed credit cannot induce the lender to give them more credit by offering to pay more interest.[5]

THE CONTRACT MATURITY STRUCTURE

Short-term versus Long-term Debt

We now turn to intertemporal issues. The simplest such issue is whether to finance an investment project with a loan that comes due for repayment when the investment itself matures, or whether to finance it with a series of consecutive short-term loans. This is the *maturity structure* issue. One argument is that the entrepreneur would prefer long-term debt because of the implicit liquidity insurance it gives him: if he issues short-term debt, he will need to roll it over when it comes due, and the prospect of doing so involves some degree of risk (e.g., over future interest rates or the possibility of credit rationing) and transaction/negotiation cost, both of which can be eliminated by issuing long-term debt instead. However, the lender's willingness to give a long-term loan will depend, in part, on the durability of the underlying collateral. The more durable the firm's assets, the more long-term value they have, and hence the more reassurance they give a lender who commits himself to a long-term loan (Hart and Moore, 1994). A lender would therefore be more willing to provide a long-term loan when the loan is secured against fixed plant or real-estate, than when the loan is secured against working capital or inventories – the maturity structure of the firm's liabilities will to some extent match that of its assets.

Another advantage of issuing short-term debt is that it enables a borrower with private information about his project to signal 'good' information about it, while at the same time forcing a borrower with 'bad' private information to expose himself and risk revealing that information to the lender when the loan comes due for renewal (see, e.g., Boyd and Prescott, 1986; Bolton and Scharfstein, 1990, 98). In these models entrepreneurs have private information about the quality of their projects. The lender is not aware of this information, but interim results will become available in future periods that will (at least partially) reveal that information to him. If a borrower has information that indicates his project is 'good', he would anticipate good interim results which would lead the lender to give him a favourable future loan. He might therefore prefer a short-term loan with the intention of renewing it when the interim information comes out. A firm with 'bad' information about its investment project would feel obliged to imitate the 'good' firm – since it would otherwise stand out and reveal itself – and so it too would take out short-term loans. However, when the interim information came out, the lender would be better able to tell the firms apart and make more informed decisions about extending the loans further.

Apart from dealing with adverse project selection, short-term debt increases the lender's liquidity and can also mitigate conventional agency problems. Making the entrepreneur return to the lender for funding to continue the project restricts his ability to slack off or otherwise benefit at the lender's expense (e.g., by diverting 'excess funds', as in Jensen, 1986 and Hart and Moore, 1993). Short-term debt also forces the entrepreneur to provide useful information to the lender (Chang, 1990). This information enables the latter to keep a better hold on the project and pull the plug if it looks as though it is not going to work out, which in turn enables him to keep down the probability of default and the losses he would suffer if default occurs.

However, long-term debt can also have its advantages. Apart from reducing the borrower's liquidity risk and transactions/renegotiation costs, long-term debt can also reduce 'long-term' agency costs by constraining management from financing unprofitable investments (e.g., managerial golf courses) against future earnings (Hart and Moore, 1993). The optimal debt maturity structure thus represents a trade-off between conflicting factors such as short-term versus long-term agency costs (as in Hart and Moore, 1993, a trade-off that is fairly self-evident, or between the effects of asymmetric information and liquidity risk, as in Diamond, 1991). In this latter model, firms that have very favourable private information about the project outcome will anticipate that interim information will be very good for their future credit rating, and they regard the possibility of bad interim news as very unlikely. They therefore face a very low liquidity risk, and are sufficiently confident about their future credit rating that they prefer short-term loans so they can cash in on the positive interim information they expect to receive. However there are also firms that are less confident about their future credit rating, even if they expect, on balance, that the interim information will be good. Such firms will be more concerned about their liquidity risk and might prefer the security of long-term debt even if it means they cannot cash in on the good news they expect. There is, in short, a trade-off between the signalling and other benefits of short-term debt and the renegotiation costs and liquidity risk it entails, and the presence of renegotiation costs or liquidity risks can mean that even 'good' borrowers might prefer long-term debt because of the additional protection it would give them.

Liquidity Risk from Insufficient Borrower Credibility

Leaving aside renegotiation and interim monitoring costs, much of the reason why the borrower might prefer long-term debt is because of the protection it gives him against liquidity risk. At the same time, the lender might be reluctant to give him that protection because he doubts the borrower's judgement and/or integrity (i.e., the borrower lacks credibility). The borrower faces a number of credibility problems. In the first place, he might have difficulty persuading the lender to make any loan at all, because he (i.e., the borrower) might lack a credible means of conveying his private information about the project to the lender. The borrower can also have a problem transmitting interim news to the lender because the lender would appreciate that the borrower has an incentive to 'paint a rosy picture' regardless of the true position. From the lender's point of view, the best response to these problems is often to keep the borrower on a tight leash and retain as much flexibility as he can to respond to new developments (e.g., to pull the plug on the project if new developments are bad). The lender would therefore keep the borrower liquidity-constrained and force him to keep coming back to him if he needs more finance, but at the same time, his tendency to disbelieve the borrower will sometimes make him reluctant to give the borrower what he asks for. The resulting arrangement consequently suffers from a lack of credibility and useful opportunities can be lost because of the lender's reluctance to grant further finance (see, e.g., Jensen, 1986; Hart and Moore, 1989; or Kahn, 1990). These problems can be particularly acute if agency and asymmetric information problems have already led the borrower to use his own wealth as collateral which he cannot then use to get a new loan, or if they have led the borrower to restrict his own freedom by entering into covenants which he might wish to renegotiate

(Berlin and Mester, 1990). There is also a danger that firms in such liquidity straits can make easy targets for competitors (Bolton and Scharfstein, 1990). One possible solution, suggested by Hart and Moore (1989), is for the lender to provide the borrower with more finance than is required for his initial investment to give him 'excess' funds for contingencies, but this can only be a partial solution at best because it will generally aggravate the underlying agency and other problems which are solved by leaving the firm liquidity-constrained in the first place.

One way to introduce greater flexibility into lending arrangements whilst still meeting the lender's concerns about borrower credibility is for the latter to invest in a reputation which he can use as a hostage for his good behaviour. If it is believed that the borrower will want to get additional loans in the future, he has an incentive to maintain his good standing with the lender to get favourable future loan terms, and his desire to maintain his good standing discourages him from 'abusing' the lender in ways he might otherwise do (see, e.g., Diamond, 1989; Townsend, 1982). The Diamond (1989) model gives a good analysis of these issues. Suppose there are three kinds of agents: those with only good (i.e., safe) projects, those with only bad (i.e., risky) ones, and those who can choose their project type. The agent's choice of project is not observable, and equity contracts are ruled out because the project output is unobservable. The investor makes loans, but appreciates that he faces an asset substitution problem, and the only information observable to him is a borrower's track record (i.e., whether or not he has defaulted on a past loan). Agents can only default if they select the risky project, and once a borrower has defaulted, the lender can presume that he will continue to choose the risky project. In the first period, the lender pools all the borrowers with good track records (i.e., those who have not defaulted) together, and offers them a loan contract. Some of these borrowers will then select risky projects, and some of those who select risky projects will default. These defaulting borrowers are then revealed as 'bad' risks, and treated appropriately in future periods. Since some of the bad risks have been eliminated, a greater proportion of those left are 'good' risks, and the lender offers them a more favourable contract reflecting their better aggregate credit rating. The next period, more borrowers will default and reveal themselves as bad risks. These borrowers are then eliminated from the pool, the average credit rating of those left improves further, and the lender improves their credit terms accordingly. At each stage, more bad risks are eliminated, the perceived quality of the borrowers who remain in the pool improves, and those who are left get a better credit deal relative to the bad credit risks who have been eliminated from it. The value of having a good reputation and remaining in the pool therefore increases at each stage. An established firm with a good reputation will therefore never endanger it by switching from safe to risky projects, but it will sometimes be the case that a young firm with little or no track record will start off taking risks which, if they succeed, will lead to it acquiring a good track record and, in time, a reputation too valuable to endanger by taking further risks. It will then switch to safe projects and to all intents and purposes be indistinguishable from a firm that had been investing in safe projects all along. Reputation (i.e., credit history) thus serves two interdependent purposes: it not only helps the lender distinguish good from bad risks, but a good reputation also gives the borrower a further incentive to avoid default – the threat of losing a valuable reputation that keeps down its cost of credit – and encourages him to act in ways that promote the lender's self-interest.

A borrower's desire to promote his reputation in order to secure future finance can also create scope for a longer-term *relationship* between the borrower and lender. To the extent that reputation is costly to observe (e.g., because it depends on a variety of factors which are themselves difficult to observe or assess), a borrower will have difficulty signalling his reputation to capital markets, and it may make sense for him to form an ongoing relationship with a particular lender which induces the lender to invest the resources to learn the borrower's 'true' credit status. Once the lender has informed himself about the borrower, he can offer him better terms than some other lender could, because any other lender would face adverse selection if he did not investigate the borrower or would have to pay the costs of learning about the borrower, if he did. A lender who has already made that information investment could therefore undercut a new lender, so once the 'set-up' cost has been paid, he would try to induce the borrower to stay with him and maintain their relationship by sharing the gains and offering him terms that were at least as good as he could get elsewhere. The borrower is then to some extent 'locked-in' (i.e., can only go elsewhere at a cost), but this lock-in is an inevitable consequence of the information set-up costs (see, e.g., Sharpe, 1989).

Apart from economising in the 'set-up' costs that must be incurred if the two parties are to deal with each other, a multi-period relationship can also reduce ongoing monitoring costs. Repeated lending allows a lender to produce information and enforce contract compliance in a less costly way than checking out a loan application from scratch each time the borrower applies for a loan. Instead of resorting to 'intensive' monitoring each time a borrower takes out a loan, a lender simply monitors the net outcome over time and uses the threat of withholding future credit if he is not satisfied with the outcome:

> Rather than directly monitor the agent, the principal can observe the claimed outcome of the agent, and then do a statistical test to see if the agent is cheating or shirking. In a one-period principal–agent setting, the agent can claim that he worked hard, but that the productivity variable had a bad draw and so output was low. Several hundred 'bad draws' in a row might make the principal suspicious, and he could then punish the agent. This then should make the basic strategy of the principal clear: compare the sample mean of what the agent has declared with the (known) mean that would occur if the agent were honest and not shirking. If the mean of the reported sequence deviates too far from the true mean, punish the agent (for example, refuse to lend to him ...). Notice that the statistical test employed by the principal must be somewhat delicate. The bound on the permitted deviations from mean must be tight, or the agent will have room to cheat. On the other hand, the bound cannot be too tight

or it will punish honest but unlucky agents who really did have a bad draw in that period. (Haubrich, 1989, 11)

A lender can therefore make loans to a firm whose manager announces its output each period and makes a repayment to the lender that depends on the declared output value. The lender would then monitor the net outcome over time and punish those firms that appear to be 'cheating'. The lender would regard the borrower as cheating if he believed that poor output was due to lack of effort on the entrepreneur's part or if he believed that output was higher than reported, and the lender would punish the firm by depriving it of credit (e.g., by putting its name on a credit 'blacklist' for a while). If punishment and trigger periods are appropriately chosen, cheating firms should be continually without loans, and honest ones would be constrained only occasionally when they had a string of bad luck that made them look as though they were cheating even though they were not. These occasional errors could always be avoided by intensive monitoring each time, but such monitoring would be expensive and *ex ante* a firm might prefer the risk of occasional errors because a lender that monitored only the net outcome could charge lower fees than one which monitored intensively all the time.

Liquidity Risk from Insufficient Lender Credibility

If the borrower faces liquidity risk from his own lack of credibility, he can also face liquidity risk because *he* distrusts the lender. The lender can therefore have a credibility problem as well. A short-term loan might put him at the lender's mercy when the loan came up for renewal, and, since the borrower 'needs' the loan, the borrower might be afraid that the lender would use his superior bargaining power to impose unfavourable terms on him. Of course, the borrower could 'promise' not to abuse his position in this way, but unless that promise takes the form of a hard-and-fast commitment – which would then be equivalent in many ways to a long-term loan – the borrower may not believe him. After all, an unscrupulous lender might promise anything to get the borrower to sign the contract, and then renege on the 'promise' later on and leave the borrower without any real recourse. The problem is that this mistrust may make the borrower reluctant to agree to short-term finance in cases where short-term finance would otherwise have been appropriate, and can therefore hinder both sides from making mutually beneficial deals that could have been struck had the borrower been reassured.

One way to meet this problem is for the lender to build up a reputation and use this reputation to reassure the borrower. A lender who wished to do more business in the future would have an incentive to avoid abusing his current bargaining power over any particular borrower, and the knowledge that he has this incentive gives a borrower some reason to 'trust' him. In effect, the lender's ability to do business in the future depends on his future reputation, and his future reputation depends on how he treats current customers when their loans come to be rolled over. The greater the amount of business the lender hopes to do in the future, the more valuable his reputation would be to him, and the less inclined he would be to abuse current customers. Lender credibility can also be enhanced by him issuing and following decent codes of practice; making investments in ongoing relationships with borrowers, which he would lose if he started alienating customers; and so on.

Good credibility on the part of the lender can also have other benefits. In particular, it can save on the costs of negotiating and drawing up the original contract by encouraging the borrower to accept less explicit reassurance. Instead of insisting on every detail being written explicitly into a contract, the borrower might accept a more implicit contract in which there were certain 'understandings' between the two parties as to what they could expect from each other in the future. A borrower might still expect the lender to treat him sympathetically when his loan comes to be refinanced, but it might be better for both sides to come to an 'understanding' about refinancing the loan than to try to agree upon a complex legally binding contract that enumerates every possible contingency on which the loan would later be refinanced.

These sorts of reputational considerations also help to explain why so much lending is done by professional lenders such as banks. A lender needs to lend repeatedly, and to many different borrowers, if he is to be able to recoup any investment in reputation, and therefore have an incentive to invest in a reputation in the first place. Such investments then help to reassure borrowers, and this reassurance in turn makes short-term finance much more attractive to borrowers than it would otherwise be. We can therefore explain, not just why so much finance is short-term, but also why there is so much reliance on more or less implicit 'understandings' about the terms on which finance would be renewed. These 'understandings' are not legally watertight, but they would make contracts much easier and cheaper to agree. Similar logic also helps to explain the widespread use of longer-term, flexi-rate loans in which the lender commits himself to provide long-term funds but the loan terms are periodically revised during the period of the loan (e.g., as with typical house mortgages).

COVENANTS, CONVERTIBILITY AND OTHER FEATURES OF FINANCIAL CONTRACTS

Covenants in Financial Contracts

Many projects generate useful interim information, and it often makes sense to design the contract to make use of it (e.g., by revealing it). Many contracts therefore include *covenants* that require the entrepreneur–manager to reveal certain information directly to the creditor (e.g., by providing audited financial statements), or else take or abstain from specific actions that indirectly reveal information to him. Two of the simplest are the commitments to make *coupon payments* or *payments into a sinking fund*. A coupon payment is a periodic fixed payment that the issuer of a bond commits himself to make before the bond matures, and a sinking fund is a fund into which the borrower makes certain payments to amortise all of part of a loan before it matures. The obligation to make sinking fund payments is therefore something like an instalment loan (see, e.g., Smith and Warner, 1979, 139). If an investment project yields an interim return before it finally matures, and this return provides information about the eventual project outcome, then it will often be the case that the optimal contract will call for a debt repayment when the project matures, as in the basic one-period model, but will also require an interim payment that can be interpreted as a coupon or sinking fund payment, and default will occur if this payment is not made. Whether or not the borrower makes the contractual payments sends out a valuable signal about the state of the underlying investment project, and the creditor can use this signal to reappraise his commitment to the project. This interim payment therefore allows investors to detect problems before it is too late or costly to correct them so they can cut their losses and cancel the project if it is going badly (see, e.g., Chang, 1990, 70; Bolton and Scharfstein, 1990, 97).

Coupon and sinking fund payments have the further attraction that they help reduce the creditor's exposure in line with the decline in the value of the assets supporting the debt. Should the firm default, the creditor's loss would then be lower than it would otherwise and have been. Coupon and sinking fund payments also help overcome general agency problems. To the extent the creditor has already been repaid, or has had funds set aside in a sinking fund, the borrower has less incentive to play agency games against him, and there is less conflict of interest between them. These payments can also help to siphon off a firm's 'excess' cash flow which the entrepreneur or manager might otherwise be tempted to squander on privately beneficial activities (e.g., playing golf) that contribute little to the firm itself (Jensen, 1986). In each of these cases, as with the other cases to be discussed below, the covenant restriction helps to reassure the potential creditor about the particular problem concerned, and the borrower has an incentive to offer this reassurance to get a better deal than the lender would otherwise give him. A borrower who refused to agree to a covenant might find that he would otherwise have to pay higher interest, post more collateral or otherwise accept a less favourable deal, and if the agency problem was particularly severe might not be able to secure any deal at all.

Covenants might also be tailored to facilitate monitoring by the lender (Berlin and Loeys, 1988). Suppose an investment project generates interim information (e.g., a certain amount of cash flow) about the eventual project outcome, but this information is only a noisy indicator of the project outcome. For example, the project might generate a low interim cash flow, but still succeed in the end; or it might generate a high interim cash flow, but fail. If these indicators are incorporated into covenant restrictions (e.g., by means of an obligation to make certain coupon payments) then the firm might violate its covenant restrictions even though the project would still succeed if allowed to continue. Similarly, the firm might meet its covenant conditions, but still default in the end. Since the indicator is noisy, the lender would not rely only on the monitor when deciding whether to continue financing a project, but might decide instead to use the indicator to tell him when to examine or monitor a project more closely. However, since 'monitoring' is costly and the indicator provides *some* information about the likely outcome, there is no point 'monitoring' the firm more closely when the indicator gives a good reading – if the lender did so, he would have to monitor all the time, in which case it is not clear why he would bother with the interim indicator in the first place. The optimal contract therefore stipulates that the lender will assume that the firm will not default when the interim indicator is good (i.e., when covenant conditions are met), but will have the right to 'monitor' the firm if the indicator is bad (i.e., if the covenant is violated), and to take control and liquidate the firm if the monitoring exercise indicates that the project is likely to fail.

Covenants can also be useful to combat various conflicts of interest that can arise between the entrepreneur or shareholder and his creditor(s). One important such case relates to payments made to the entrepreneur or shareholders. When the investment project ends after one period, there is generally relatively little problem having the entrepreneur or shareholder wait until the project has ended before he gets his reward. However, the longer the project goes on, the more difficult it is for the entrepreneur or shareholder to wait till the project ends to get his return. Some provision might therefore have to be made for the entrepreneur or shareholder to receive interim payments while the project or firm is still ongoing, and such provision is clearly an absolute necessity in cases where the project/firm has no fixed end-date and is meant to go on indefinitely. The contract will then allow for some form of *dividend* payment to the entrepreneur or shareholder(s), presumably in proportion to their capital investment in the project. But once provision for such payments is made, the entrepreneur or the manager acting on behalf of the shareholders can use it to advance his or their interests against those of the creditors, and new agency problems arise that are absent when the entrepreneur or shareholder gets paid only when the project (or firm) ends.

The main concern in this context is the possibility of *excess dividends* – the danger, from the creditor's point of view that the firm might pay 'excessive' dividends (or other payments) to the entrepreneur or shareholder(s) that excessively raise the probability of default and reduce the recoverable assets of the firm, and hence unduly raise the creditors' expected losses from default. The entrepreneur or shareholder will of course generally want *some* dividend payment, and other things being equal, *any* such payment will raise the expected bankruptcy cost to the creditor because it makes it more likely that the firm will default and leave less for creditors to recover, but at the same time it is also important to keep dividend payments down to 'reasonable' levels. The source of the problem is that when a firm has debt outstanding, the entrepreneur–shareholder will normally attach more value to the payments he receives himself than to future returns to the firm. (Why? Because he keeps all returns to himself, but some of the returns to the firm go to pay its creditors.) If there were no constraints against it, the firm's dividend policy might therefore be biased towards it making 'excessive' dividend payments. The more heavily indebted the firm is, and the less of his own wealth the entrepreneur or shareholder has pledged to the project, the more inclined he will be to excessive dividend payments. Indeed, the entrepreneur might even be tempted to make a 'liquidating dividend' – a dividend payment designed to transfer the firm's wealth to himself and leave the creditor(s) holding an empty, perhaps worthless, shell. The temptation to make excess dividends can also distort real investment decisions both *ex post* and *ex ante*. It can cause problems *ex post* because it can lead to 'good' investment projects being liquidated prematurely so the entrepreneur or shareholder can get his hands on the proceeds; and it can cause problems *ex ante* because a prospective creditor could be expected to anticipate the problem and respond to it by charging a higher rate of interest, demanding more collateral or other security to protect himself, or by refusing to lend at all.

It can therefore be useful for covenants to restrict dividends, and covenant dividend constraints usually restrict dividends to be paid out of the proceeds of retained earnings and sales of equity whilst also prohibiting dividend payments from asset sales or the issue of new debt. A typical dividend constraint sets up a reservoir of funds from which dividends may be paid. Retained earnings and the proceeds of equity sales, if any, are then put into the reservoir, and the firm is allowed to pay dividends from the reservoir as it chooses. When it makes dividend payments the reservoir goes down accordingly, but the reservoir must never become negative; when it does not make payments, the reservoir grows over time in accordance with whatever funds flow into it (see, e.g., Smith and Warner, 1979). Since the reservoir cannot become negative and the firm cannot put the proceeds of asset sales or new debt issues into it, the covenant puts an upper limit on dividend payments and also makes it difficult for the firm to run its assets down to make excessive dividends. To the extent dividends are restricted, the firm might also be discouraged from forgoing or liquidating profitable investment opportunities in order to give the funds to its shareholders.

Covenants can also sometimes be used to constrain investment. One reason for such a constraint is to combat asset substitution. Certain types of risky investment might be banned, or only allowed if the firm meets specific capitalisation or other requirements drawn up to protect the creditor. Covenants might also restrict investment to protect the value of the assets the creditor would lay claim to in the event of bankruptcy (i.e., to protect the value of collateral, broadly considered). Such a constraint will generally limit the acquisition of intangible assets (e.g., R&D) that might be of relatively little use to the creditor if the firm went bankrupt, and a typical restriction is that net tangible assets somehow defined should at least be a certain multiple of debt.

Apart from imposing restrictions *against* specified activities, covenants might also require that a firm *undertakes* specific activities as well. A firm might be required to maintain the value of its capital stock and working capital, purchase specific assets (e.g., insurance), and so forth. Such requirements serve a number of purposes: they help to protect the firm (e.g., by making it more difficult for incompetent managers to run it into the ground); they help to protect the value of the assets the creditor would recover in the event of bankruptcy; and, like the coupon and sinking fund payments discussed earlier, they send credible signals to creditors about the firm's financial condition. Since the violation of such a condition constitutes breach of contract, the firm has a strong incentive to ensure that it meets its conditions, and failure to meet them sends a strong signal that the firm is in difficulties. As with other covenant restrictions, those on investment usually involve forgone opportunities and restrictions on investments can be especially costly to enforce since investment decisions are particularly difficult to monitor. For this reason observed covenants tend to place relatively few restrictions on actual investment and rely more on indirect means of controlling it such as restrictions on dividends and financial ratios (Smith and Warner, 1979, 124).

Similar considerations suggest that firms might also enter into covenants obliging them to maintain minimum standards (e.g., with respect to observable financial indicators). Covenants that try to maintain a firm's financial health help to counter the more pronounced conflicts of interest between entrepreneurs (or shareholders) and bondholders that arise as the firm's condition deteriorates. A weakening of the firm's financial condition aggravates managerial moral hazard in at least two important respects:

- The weakening of the firm transfers downside risk from the entrepreneur to the bond-holder, and this transfer encourages the entrepreneur to take more risks at the same time as the bondholder wants the firm to take fewer of them.
- The weakening of the firm aggravates the problem of *Myers under-investment* (Myers, 1977). This problem occurs where the firm forgoes positive-net-value (PNV) investments because too many of the expected benefits would go to the creditor(s) in the form of reductions in their expected bankruptcy costs rather than to the entrepreneur or shareholder as profit.[6] Since expected bankruptcy costs rise as the financial health of the firm deteriorates, the firm is increasingly likely to pass up PNV projects as its financial health worsens.

These factors mean that a reduction in net worth widens the gap between the interests of the entrepreneur and those of the creditor, and as with the various conflicts of interest already discussed, the possibility of this kind of outcome discourages investors from buying bonds in the first place. A firm might therefore reassure its bond-holders by writing covenants that impose penalties on the entrepreneur or manager or allow bond-holders to take over if the firm fails to satisfy certain observable standards of financial health. Such covenants can include the requirements to maintain minimum capital–asset or liquidity ratios, or a minimum credit rating, or the obligations to submit to a particular monitoring regime (e.g., to submit to random audits) or purchase insurance. In some cases, there might also be the obligation to issue short-term debt, on the grounds that the need to maintain the confidence of the creditor on a continuous short-term basis would exert a similar discipline to a more explicit covenant (see, e.g., Hart and Moore, 1990; Calomiris and Kahn, 1991).

Call Provisions

Bonds sometimes contain *call provisions* that gives the issuer the right to buy back his debt prior to its maturity date at some pre-specified price. A contract with a call provision can be considered as a combination of a 'pure' debt contract that requires the borrower to make specified payments at specified times or face bankruptcy, and a *call option* contract that gives the borrower the right to buy back his own debt at a specific price before it matures. Typically, call provisions give the issuer the right to buy the bond back at a price equal to the face value of the bond plus a premium equal to a year's coupon payment if redeemed in the first year in which calls are allowed – usually, calls are prohibited in the first few years after a bond is issued – but decreasing thereafter if redeemed in subsequent years (Narayanan, 1992, 269). If the market price of the 'straight' debt contract rises above the price specified in the call option, the option-bearer (i.e., here the debt-issuer) can then make a profit by buying the debt at the call price. He profits because calling the debt enables him to retire his own debt more cheaply than buying it up at prevailing market prices.

One reason for issuing debt with a call option is to overcome the Myers (1977) under-investment problem, i.e. the problem that the manager of a firm with risky debt outstanding might not undertake socially profitable investments because too much of the gain would go to debt-holders. Without the call option, the firm might not otherwise be able to buy its debt back at a price that would make the investment worthwhile. One or more debt-holders might guess the reason why the firm wanted to buy its debt back and hold out in the hope of a better price, or refuse outright to sell. A call option gives the firm the means to overcome such 'holdout' attempts by debt-holders, by forcing them to sell, and can therefore ensure that the firm has the incentive to make socially useful investments. Alternatively, call options can be help overcome a Myers under-investment problem by enabling firms to circumvent covenant restrictions in their debt contracts that might otherwise prevent the firm investing in positive present-value projects. If the firm is to invest in such projects, it needs to channel the benefits to shareholders, and one way to do so is to finance such projects by issuing additional secured debt. However, covenants often restrict the issue of additional secured debt to protect the interests of existing creditors, but a firm can get always nullify an awkward covenant by calling the debt to which the covenant is attached. Making debt callable thus helps to mitigate under-investment problems in two ways – directly, by enabling the firm to buy back its outstanding debt at prices that do not incorporate the value of the new investment projects; and indirectly, by enabling the bank to nullify covenant restrictions that would otherwise prevent it from financing such projects in other ways such as issuing secured debt.

A call option also offers a firm a way to exploit new investment opportunities that avoids certain drawbacks with the obvious alternative of merely seeking renegotiation of an existing loan. Seeking renegotiation involves potentially higher negotiation and bargaining costs, and renegotiation can be particularly difficult when there are multiple lenders to deal with, and where lenders try to hold out against the firm to get some of the benefits of the new opportunities for themselves. Reliance on renegotiation also involves the risk that the lender might not share the borrower's assessment of the new opportunity and prevent the borrower exploiting it by vetoing any renegotiation. Call provisions enable the firm to avoid these problems by giving it the right to proceed without having to secure the lender's (or lenders') subsequent agreement.

Bond Convertibility

Another option often used in bond contracts is a *convertibility* provision that allows the holder to exchange a bond for a given number of shares at any time until the bond matures. A convertible bond is similar to a combination of a corresponding straight bond (i.e., one without a convertibility provision) and a warrant to purchase common shares at a particular bond-share exchange rate (see, e.g., Brennan and Schwartz, 1992). Since the bond is convertible at the option of the holder, the holder will decide whether or not to exercise the option in his own best interests, and he will decide to convert if the conversion value of the bond (i.e., the value of the shares he would get) exceeds its straight value (i.e., the value of the bond without the option to convert). Since the conversion value varies directly with the share value, the option to convert becomes more valuable as the firm's equity becomes more valuable relative to its debt.

Bond convertibility therefore allows the bond-holder to protect himself against a fall in value of the debt he holds relative to the firm's equity. Anything that causes the straight value of the bond to fall (e.g., something that causes expected bankruptcy costs to rise) or the value of the firm's equity to rise, will cause the conversion value of the bond to rise relative to its straight value. If bonds sufficiently fall or equity sufficiently rises, it then becomes worthwhile for the bondholder to convert and become a shareholder instead. Convertibility thus provides the bondholder with some protection against policies by the firm – such as asset substitution, or investment in negative present-value projects because they significantly increase the firm's risk – that might otherwise enrich the shareholders at the bondholders' expense (see, e.g., Green, 1984). Suppose, for example, that a creditor cannot monitor the firm's choice of project. If he makes a straight loan, he exposes himself to the risk that the firm will choose riskier projects to increase expected profits to the shareholder(s) at his expense (i.e., the firm will engage in asset substitution). However, if the firm pursues such a policy with a convertible loan, it can expect to trigger conversion, and conversion will give the former bondholder the right to ditch the depreciated debt and get some of the shareholders' gains. Convertibility therefore reduces the firm's incentive to engage in such policies, and one can regard the convertibility option as a device by which the firm (partially) precommits itself against exploiting the bondholder(s). By the same token, convertibility also protects a bondholder against adverse selection by giving him the prospect of compensation if the firm's project turns out to be riskier than the bondholder anticipated (Brennan and Schwartz, 1982). Indeed, in some cases it might even be possible to design the warrant so that it encourages the firm to reveal its risk and eliminate adverse selection altogether (e.g., Nyborg, 1991).

It is also frequently the case that firms issue bonds that are *both* callable *and* convertible. In these contracts, the firm issues debt which it has the right to call at a specified price before maturity, and the creditor has the right, any time he chooses, to convert the bond into a fixed number of shares. In addition, when the bond is called, the holder has the choice of converting it or redeeming it at the call price (see, e.g., Brennan and Schwartz, 1992, 453), a feature that ensures that the firm can never call the debt without allowing the bondholder to convert.

Why do firms issue these bonds? One possible explanation is that they help to protect bondholders (via their convertibility) whilst also (via their callability) keeping down renegotiation costs and protecting shareholders against the danger that lenders might veto worthwhile investment projects. A second possible explanation is that they enable levered firms to issue equity 'through the backdoor' in situations where Myers–Majluf (1984) informational asymmetries make conventional equity unattractive (Stein, 1992). A firm that has little debt outstanding can of course always get around this informational problem merely by issuing more debt, and issuing debt also has the attractive of channelling more of the benefits of a good investment project to the (existing) shareholders. However, a firm might not wish to issue more (straight) debt if it already has a considerable amount of it outstanding, and yet issuing equity runs straight into the Myers–Majluf under-pricing issue. It is in these circumstances that a firm with good private information (i.e., one that expects its share price to rise) might issue callable, convertible debt. If a firm issues such debt and its share price subsequently rises, a decision to call the debt will force conversion into equity, and the firm will have effectively managed to issue equity without the adverse stock price reaction of a straight equity issue. At the same time, a firm with poor private information about its future prospects would be loathe to issue such debt because it would not expect to be able to force conversion by calling it – when the share price falls, the holders would take their funds and run – and would merely end up with a bigger debt burden to service. The issue of callable, convertible debt thus allows a firm to get around the Myers–Majluf problem to some extent and exploit good (but not bad) private information about its future prospects.

BANKRUPTCY, LIQUIDATION AND CONTROL

The Nature and Costs of Bankruptcy

As mentioned already, the framework developed here also allows us to motivate default or bankruptcy states where the agent fails to make a specified payment and ownership and control of the firm's assets are transferred to the creditor. In a simple CSV framework, a state of default/bankruptcy is one in which the entrepreneur announces that he cannot make his stipulated fixed payment and the investor has the choice of whether to accept what the entrepreneur claims he can offer or verify his claim and take whatever there is. Verification leads to a transfer of ownership of the entrepreneur's assets from the entrepreneur to the creditor. The states of default and bankruptcy are distinguished in more sophisticated models. In the multi-period CSV model of Chang (1990), for example, *default* is a state where the firm breaks a contractual commitment (e.g., fails to make a coupon payment), but *bankruptcy* is a state where the investor insists on verification which leads to him taking the entrepreneur's assets. More generally, bankruptcy gives the creditor the option to liquidate the firm as a going concern and, in the event there is a secured loan involved, the right to seize the secured asset(s). The creditor who takes over a bankrupt enterprise (or any of its assets) can subsequently dispose of it (or them) as he wishes. If he liquidates (i.e., dismantles) the firm, he will find alternative uses for the firm's assets or sell them; if he chooses not to liquidate, he will try to run or sell the enterprise as a going concern. However, more likely than not, the creditor will have relatively little use for the enterprise itself or its assets and will prefer to sell them.

Bankruptcy also involves the transfer of *control* as well as the transfer of *ownership*. Given that simultaneous joint control by the entrepreneur and investor is inefficient (see, e.g., Aghion and Bolton, 1990, 29), the optimal contract gives control of the firm (and therefore of its assets) to the party with the incentive to make the best use of them. That party is the residual claimant (i.e., the one who bears the bulk of the marginal gains or losses from control decisions). The contract accordingly gives control to the entrepreneur provided the firm is in good financial condition. However, if the return from the project is very low and the firm is unable to pay its debts, the entrepreneur ceases to have any incentive to manage the project properly and the creditor becomes *de facto* the residual claimant. The contract therefore specifies that control should be transferred to the creditor in the event the entrepreneur declares or is driven into bankruptcy (see, e.g., Hart and Moore, 1988; Zender, 1991; Kahn, 1990; Harris and Raviv, 1990). We can thus explain, not only why shareholders lose control if the firm gets into excessive financial difficulties, but also why they have control in the first place in states where the firm is financially healthy.

The costs of bankruptcy follow from what happens (or might happen) when bankruptcy occurs. In the simple CSV model, the costs of bankruptcy are essentially the costs of verifying the borrower's output claims together with the legal and accounting costs that such verification involves. More generally, however, the costs of bankruptcy also include the costs of transferring assets from the entrepreneur to the creditor and selling assets off, and the latter might be substantial if assets (e.g., chattels pledged as secondary collateral assets) have to be sold off quickly at 'firesale' losses in thin markets. In cases where the firm is dismantled but would otherwise have continued to operate as a going concern, there will also be losses from lost profits and the dissolution of organisational capital. Working relationships will be broken up, 'team' knowledge will be lost, employees will suffer (e.g., because they lose their jobs), valuable relationships with customers will be disrupted or destroyed, 'goodwill' will be lost, losses incurred from the transfer of control from a (presumably) experienced entrepreneur to a less inexperienced creditor, and so on.

The empirical evidence also suggests that the costs of bankruptcy are not trivial, though perhaps not as big as one might have expected. To give some illustration of these costs, Warner (1977) estimated that the 'direct' costs of bankruptcy (i.e., the administrative costs, legal fees, and so on) were 5.3 percent of the book value of assets for his sample of railroad companies; Altman (1984) estimated that they were 9.8 percent of assets for larger industrial firms and 4.0 percent for retail firms; and Guffey and Moore (1991) estimated they were just over 9 percent for the trucking industry. Meanwhile, Ang, Chua and McConnell (1982) and Michelle White (1984) estimated that the administrative costs of bankruptcy cases that led to firms being liquidated were about 7.5 percent and 21 percent respectively of the amounts paid out to creditors. Whichever of these estimates one takes, the various 'direct' costs of bankruptcy appear to be considerably smaller than other costs (see, e.g., M. White, 1983), and estimates of the 'indirect' costs of bankruptcy that can be inferred from the risk premium in interest rates – the difference between rates of AAA and Baa bonds, for example – suggest that such costs are perhaps 0.5 percent of GNP (M. White, 1989).

Optimal Bankruptcy Law

The previous discussion also sheds light on what optimal bankruptcy law might look like. The main principles are relatively straightforward. Since bankruptcy itself is costly, the optimal bankruptcy rule will minimise expected bankruptcy costs and, other things being equal, will do so by minimising the probability of bankruptcy occurring. Since the event of bankruptcy in part depends on the actions of the entrepreneur, the law will discourage the entrepreneur from taking actions that lead to bankruptcy (e.g., slacking off or falsely declaring that output was very low) by maximising the penalties imposed on bankrupt entrepreneurs. This is the reason why, in the absence of risk-aversion, the optimal contract frequently calls for the entrepreneur to lose everything in the event of bankruptcy. Indeed, he not only loses all his tangible assets, but also loses the value of the organisational capital, customer and employee goodwill, and so on, which had been built up in the firm as well.

While this 'no mercy' provision might be tough on the entrepreneur *ex post*, it is nonetheless essential to minimise expected bankruptcy costs *ex ante*, and it is important to emphasise that the minimisation of expected bankruptcy costs is in the interests of *both* parties. The greater the *ex post* penalty to which he exposes himself, the more reassurance the entrepreneur can provide the investor, and the better the terms he can obtain on his loan. Since this arrangement minimises the dead-loss of expected bankruptcy costs, the gains from this minimisation can presumably be shared out to make both parties *ex ante* better off than they would have been had the entrepreneur's liability been more limited. The entrepreneur will therefore accept the risk that he might lose everything through bankruptcy, even though he might later regret it.

Should Financially Distressed Firms be Liquidated?

There is however a potential problem. This problem concerns the much-discussed question of whether to give a firm a 'breathing space' if it gets into financial difficulties (see, e.g., M. White, 1989, 1992). In some sense, there needs to be a trade-off between putting 'good' but financially distressed firms out of business, and allowing 'bad' firms to stay in business when it would be better if they were wound up. When a firm is in difficulties, for example, a creditor might wish to press his claim and put the firm out of business even though it might be 'socially' worthwhile for the firm to stay in business. It has therefore been suggested that an entrepreneur in difficulties might be allowed a breathing space to reorganise the firm or otherwise keep his creditors at bay. This kind of argument leads to a preference for a 'lenient' bankruptcy law (e.g., such as Chapter 11 in the USA, which we discuss further below) that in some sense 'favours' entrepreneurs over creditors. On the other hand, there will also be cases where it would be better from a social point of view to put a distressed firm out of business to stop it running up any further losses at its creditors' expense. The firm might have a negative net worth, for example, and the entrepreneur might be inclined to take irresponsible risks with its assets in the hope that the risks might just pay off and restore the firm to financial health. Concern over cases like this would then lead one to prefer a 'harsh' bankruptcy law that in some sense 'favours' the creditors over entrepreneurs. What makes this issue difficult is that individual cases are usually different from each other, and a degree of harshness or laxity that is appropriate in one case will not be appropriate in another. A law that treats bankrupt entrepreneurs in a 'lenient' manner might help to alleviate the problem of 'good' firms being forced to close, but it will do so only by worsening the problems caused by 'bad' firms inappropriately staying in business. On the other hand, a 'harsh' law that ensures that 'bad' firms are driven out of business will only aggravate the problems that occur when 'good' but distressed firms are forced into bankruptcy.

The solution is to give up trying to frame a law that mandates whether financially distressed entrepreneur–debtors should be treated in a lenient or harsh manner; instead, we should frame a law that provides for lax or harsh treatment depending on what the parties themselves have already chosen in their contract. The law should *enable*, in other words, but it should not *mandate*. Provided the parties to each contract are able to recognise, *ex ante*, what kind of treatment would be appropriate in each case, they could make their contracts accordingly. In those cases where they felt *ex ante* that the entrepreneur should be treated leniently (e.g., because he was trusted by the lender), then the parties would ensure that he was treated leniently by giving him the right to a breathing space. The entrepreneur may have to pay for the privilege, but if the right to a breathing space was worth enough to him, he could presumably induce the lender to let him have it. In those cases where they felt the entrepreneur should be treated harshly, he would be, and the entrepreneur would be unable to induce the lender to give him any breathing space. The parties involved would tailor the contract to their circumstances. The optimal outcome results because the parties involved in each case would make the arrangement they think would best suit them, and the law would merely enforce whatever contracts they make. Of course, it may turn out *ex post* that a 'mistake' had been made – an entrepreneur might get into distress and regret the fact that he had not taken out an option to defer payment, or an investor might grant the option to defer payment and wish later that he had not – but the agents involved would have taken the possibility of such mistakes into account when the contract was made and the possibility of such 'mistakes' is part of the optimal arrangement. Whatever is agreed to *ex ante* should therefore be adhered to, and the only[7] purpose of the legal system would be to enforce the previously agreed contract.

An implication of this view of optimal bankruptcy law is that laws that distinguish between different types of 'bankruptcy' are probably indefensible. The classic example is the distinction between Chapter 7 and Chapter 11 of the US Bankruptcy Code. Chapter 7 provides for the liquidation of a bankrupt firm, but Chapter 11 allows a distressed firm the right to suspend repayment of its debt obligations for a certain length of time while it works out a reorganisation plan. Chapter 11 is a good example of the kind of 'lenient' bankruptcy law discussed earlier which gives the entrepreneur the right to suspend debt repayments whilst retaining control of the firm and keeping creditors at bay. This two-fold bankruptcy law seems to be motivated by the legislators' view that

> the role of reorganization [is] one of providing breathing space to save the jobs of supposedly viable firms that are in temporary financial distress ... [but] liquidation is viewed as the process of winding up the operation of firms that are not viable. (M. White (1989, 138)).

Chapter 11 then provides the breathing space, and Chapter 7 provides the 'regular' bankruptcy law covering the transfer of ownership and control, and the liquidation, of bankrupt firms. The basic problem with Chapter 11 should be obvious from the preceding discussion: it mandates a breathing space that will *not* in general be appropriate for *all* cases. Even if an entrepreneur was willing to sign a contract committing him to a 'strict' obligation to repay, the existence of Chapter 11 means that US courts will not enforce that promise. The economic surplus is then lost that would have been reaped had parties been allowed to make such contracts and have them enforced by the courts. The implied inability of the creditor to force a firm directly into 'regular' bankruptcy also undermines the discipline on the entrepreneur (or management) that a debt contract can otherwise provide. It gives an entrepreneur considerable leeway to take risks at the creditors' expense, and even if he does not actually file under Chapter 11, an entrepreneur so inclined can always use the *threat* of a Chapter 11 filing to keep creditors at bay or blackmail them in other ways (e.g., to extract more loans out of them). The existence of Chapter 11 therefore means that too many 'inefficient' firms are allowed to carry on in business, too few firms get liquidated, and assets that should be reallocated by bankruptcy are not.

The Extent of Debtor Liability

The idea that the law should enable rather than mandate also applies to the nature and extent of debtor liability in the event of bankruptcy. There are a variety of possible arrangements to choose from. Under any reasonable arrangement, efficiency considerations require that the entrepreneur should be liable to the extent of his own capital investment in the project, whatever that might be. (Incidentally, this liability also includes any 'uncalled' capital that the entrepreneur has committed himself to invest in the firm, but has not yet actually paid into it.) If his liability is restricted to that investment, so that creditors of the firm have no claims against his own personal wealth in the event the firm goes bankrupt, he has what is known as *limited liability*. If any of his personal wealth is also liable for the firm's debts, however, he has *extended liability*. Should the firm subsequently default and have insufficient assets to pay off the creditor in full, the creditor would have the right to insist that the debtor make up the shortfall out of his own personal wealth, up to whatever maximum he is liable. There are various forms of extended liability. In some cases, the debtor's additional personal liability might be restricted to the value of some particular asset (or assets) that he owns (i.e., he would have a mortgage on the asset(s) concerned), or his personal liability might be tied to the value of his own capital investment into the firm. For example, his personal liability might extend up the value of his capital investment, in which case his total liability would consist of his initial investment plus his personal wealth up to that amount. Since his total liability would then be double his initial investment, this arrangement is usually known as *double liability*. Taking this principle further, his personal liability might extend to twice the amount of his initial investment, so he would have *triple liability*, and so on. Extending this idea even further, the entrepreneur might also accept *unlimited liability* and pledge *all* his personal wealth against the company's debts.

The 'optimal' debtor liability arrangement will generally depend on the specific circumstances of each case. In situations where the debtor is well-off and in a position to pledge his own personal wealth without too much difficulty, it might be appropriate for him to accept some form of extended liability and pledge his personal wealth, to some extent at least, as a guarantee for the debts of the firm. The debtor might be willing to offer such a guarantee if he was reasonably confident about the project outcome and if the guarantee enabled him to obtain a loan on better terms than he could otherwise get. However, it makes sense to limit the entrepreneur's liability in cases where his wealth might be very limited, uncertain or unobservable, or where he might want too much (in terms of reduced interest) for offering the creditor an extended guarantee, or where it might be too difficult or costly to verify or get hold of his wealth in the event of bankruptcy. Faced with a choice between a low-guarantee, high-interest rate loan and a high-guarantee, low-interest one, the costs of providing the high guarantee might be so high that both parties would prefer the low guarantee instead. The best way to ensure that each contract has its own 'optimal' liability structure is therefore for the parties involved to make whatever agreements they consider most appropriate. As with the earlier question of the relative 'leniency' or 'harshness' of the obligation to make debt repayments, the law should simply enforce whatever contract the parties agree to – once again, the law should enable, but it should not mandate.

Extended liability also has implications for the transfer and extent of ownership of the firm. If the shareholder has extended liability but there are no restrictions against transfer of ownership, there is a danger that the shareholder can evade extended liability provisions by selling shares to poor people or to limited liability firms. To stop this evasion, there must therefore either be restrictions on the transfer of shares (e.g., those who buy shares might be required to post a minimum bond) or those who sell their shares must be made responsible for new shareholders. These restrictions then make it costly to trade shares (e.g., because of the costs of posting bonds) and limit the potential market for them (e.g., to those who are rich). These costs may well help to explain why most large firms that have the choice opt for limited rather than extended liability (see, e.g., Carr and Matthewson, 1988, 779–780), but it does *not* follow that limited liability *always* dominates extended liability, and there is certainly no case for imposing limited liability everywhere and preventing entrepreneurs and shareholders from offering extended guarantees if they wish to.[8]

Creditor Credibility in Bankruptcy

We turn now to a somewhat different issue. If a bankruptcy law is to 'work' properly, the agents involved need to come to terms with a serious credibility issue that we have not yet considered. This issue arises right at the heart of the contracting problem between the parties concerned, and is perhaps easiest considered in the context of the simple CSV framework with which we started. In that framework the optimality of the debt-with-costly-bankruptcy contract hinges on the agent A attaching a sufficiently high probability to the principal P verifying him if he declares that output was in the default region. (Clearly, if A believed that P would *not* verify his report, he would have no incentive to report output truthfully. He would therefore always report that output was low and default every time. Of course, P would appreciate that A would always default and therefore never make the contract in the first place. The whole arrangement thus completely unravels.) Before he makes his output declaration, A must therefore be led to believe that he will be verified if he declares a default level of output. (Strictly speaking, he must believe that he will be verified with a sufficiently high probability, but we can abstract from stochastic issues here.) However, if A is made to believe that he will be verified if he defaults, and subsequently does default, then P could reasonably presume that A *was* telling the truth – in which case there would be no point spending resources to verify his report. Yet if A understands that P has no incentive to verify him, then A can rationally expect *not* to be verified. He then has no incentive to tell the truth, and as noted already, if P anticipates that A will not tell the truth, P would not agree to the contract to start with. There is thus a conflict between the requirement that A be made to believe that he *would* be verified if he declares a low output, and P's *ex post* incentive to accept A's report *without* verifying it (see, e.g., Bolton and Scharfstein, 1990, 99, or Kahn, 1990, 2, n.1). If the contract is to 'work', P must somehow provide a credible signal that he would verify low-output reports, despite the incentive after the event not to bother.

The same basic credibility problem can also arise in other models where the lender takes over the firm and any associated collateral in the event of default (e.g., as in Bester, 1990). If the assets taken over are worth less to the lender than to the borrower, or if the process of taking them over is itself costly, the debtor might assume that the lender will forgive him and not enforce bankruptcy if he defaults. The lender's inability to persuade him otherwise might therefore encourage the debtor to default while the firm was still sound, or take excessive risks, slacken his effort or take other actions that increase the probability of default. The inability of the creditor to pre-commit himself to enforce bankruptcy might also lead the debtor to try to 'bounce' him into a situation where he might later feel obliged to renegotiate the loan and forgive some of the outstanding debt.

If he is to avoid these problems, the lender has to find a way to make the borrower take the threat of enforcing bankruptcy seriously – and he cannot do so by merely *threatening* to enforce it, since he may have no incentive after the event to honour any threats he has made. Three different solutions have been suggested, although two of them have serious drawbacks :

- One option is to prohibit renegotiation. As Bolton and Scharfstein (1992, 591) say, the principle behind such a ban is simple:

    'any expected outcome of negotiation in a given future state of nature can be attained directly by rewriting the initial complete contract to include this outcome in that particular state, so that the contract can be made renegotiation-proof in that state. Thus, nothing is lost by banning future renegotiation; and something is gained whenever more efficient outcomes are attained which were impossible to reach with renegotiation.'

    The problem with this argument is that writing up contingent contracts is not costless, and even the most well-designed contingent contract will still lack flexibility (and therefore leave open the possibility that future gains might be foregone). There is also the problem that a ban on renegotiation might not always be feasible if the parties involved feel they have an incentive, *ex post*, to agree to renegotiate anyway.

- The credibility problem could be evaded, at least in some circumstances, by the borrower taking out loans with multiple lenders. The difficulties of getting the lenders to agree on renegotiation then helps to reduce the 'danger' of renegotiation (Berlin and Mester, 1990). To the extent this works, multiple loans precommit the parties involved to verification (or non-forgiveness), and the parties involved can share the benefits that result from the lenders' improved credibility. A problem, however, is that this sort of arrangement lacks credibility and might not even succeed in preventing renegotiation anyway. Having multiple lenders can also create problems of its own, since it involves higher transactions and negotiations costs, problems of co-ordinating monitoring, and the various other forgone benefits of the borrower developing a relationship with a single lender.

- The lender could invest in a reputation for being tough with debtors who default on their payments, but to do so it needs to have an incentive to make that investment and protect it. The only lender who usually has such an incentive is a professional lender (e.g., a bank) who makes loans with many customers and also engages in repeated loan games with them. To the extent the lender is dealing with other borrowers, or expects to deal with the same borrower again, he might have an incentive to force bankruptcy even if the costs of doing so exceeded the benefits in that particular instance, because forcing bankruptcy enhances his credibility in comparable cases in the future: he has an incentive to be tough *pour encourager les autres*. At the same time, the lender always has the option to renegotiate a loan if circumstances suggest that that is appropriate, so this arrangement is flexible as well as credible. As an aside, the benefits of the lender investing in a reputation are another reason why we might expect specialist lenders (e.g., banks) to have an advantage over other lenders and dominate the market.

THE IMPACT OF RISK-AVERSION

What happens if we now relax the assumption maintained so far that both parties are risk-neutral? Perhaps the most reasonable alternative is to assume that the entrepreneur A is risk-averse but the investor P is risk-neutral,[9] bearing in mind that the assumption of lender risk-neutrality is not necessarily as restrictive as it might at first appear. Even if his underlying preferences make him risk-averse, we can still sometimes treat him as if he were (close to) risk-neutral if he has a diversified portfolio of investment projects whose risks tend to cancel out, and this assumption is perhaps particularly appealing if he is a financial intermediary with a large portfolio of loans. In any case, our real interest in the impact on contract form of *differences* between the two parties' attitudes towards risk, and assuming that P is risk-neutral and A risk-averse is merely a convenient way to represent such a difference.

Suppose we go back to the original assumptions set out at the start of the chapter – no costly verification, no moral hazard or adverse selection, and so forth – but assume that the entrepreneur is risk-averse rather than risk-neutral. It is then immediately apparent that the optimal contract – which was previously indeterminate when the entrepreneur was risk-neutral – now requires that the investor bear all the risk and guarantee the entrepreneur a fixed return. The optimal contract is an 'inverse debt' contract in which the borrower–agent gets a fixed payment and the principal-investor gets the residual, a contract that effectively means that A should work for P in return for some preagreed wage. The reason for this contract form is very straightforward: if A is averse to risk, but P is not, the optimal contract should have P bear all the risk, and this is exactly what the inverse debt contract does. The agent's risk-aversion thus leads us to a theory of vertical integration and labour contracting, and the reader who wants to explore it further should turn to the labour contract literature (see, e.g., Hart and Holmström, 1987).

The optimal contract form becomes less clear when we introduce verification or monitoring problems into the picture. If P bears all the risk but cannot costlessly verify the value of output, then the 'inverse debt contract' gives A an incentive to claim the lowest possible level of output and keep what he does not declare. P would always have to verify him, and verification costs would be excessive. The inverse debt contract is therefore particularly ill-suited to situations with costly state verification. Similarly, if output is subject to moral hazard on A's part, the inverse debt contract involves high monitoring costs (if monitoring takes place) or maximises the losses that result from this moral hazard (if monitoring does not take place). The inverse debt contract is therefore ill-suited to hidden action situations as well. On the other hand, the (regular) debt-with-costly-bankruptcy contract has the drawback that it makes the risk-averse party bear the risk. There is therefore a tension between the requirement of the standard debt contract that A bear risk and the consideration that risk be shifted onto P because A is averse to it, and, although we know that debt contracts *can* be optimal in this context (see, e.g., Townsend, 1979), more general solutions to this composite problem are difficult to obtain. However several points do appear to emerge:

● While debt contracts retain the feature that non-verification (or non-bankruptcy) payments to P are fixed, it is no longer the case that the agent pays over everything when verification (or bankruptcy) takes place – A's aversion to risk makes it optimal for him to retain something even in 'bad' verification states (Townsend, 1979; Gale and Hellwig, 1985, section 4). Risk-aversion on A's part thus helps to explain why he might make debt contracts with limited liability. If A is risk-neutral, as assumed earlier, it might make sense for him to invest all his wealth in the project or use all of it to collateralise his loan, since each unit of wealth so used gives the lender more reassurance and induces him to offer better credit terms. But if the agent is risk-averse, he will trade off the benefits of pledging his wealth against the risk of doing so – he will prefer not to put all his eggs into one basket – and will generally leave some of his wealth unpledged (see, e.g., Bernanke and Gertler, 1990). Risk-aversion might also lead the agent/borrower to limit the non-pecuniary penalties (e.g., loss of reputation) to which he exposes himself. The lender's desire for more reassurance must be traded off against the latter's aversion to risk, and provided that debt contracts remain optimal, the logical implication is some cut-off to the penalty inflicted on the borrower in the event of bankruptcy. The borrower might be willing to risk losing his house in the event of bankruptcy, but not to risk a visit by the mafia. We can therefore explain why we don't impose ferocious penalties on bankrupts even though such penalties would prevent some costly bankruptcies from occurring.

- Following on from the previous point, a cut-off to the borrower's exposure to loss in 'bad' states can help make debt contracts acceptable to him that he would otherwise refuse. Since he is risk-averse, he would attach considerable weight to the loss he would suffer in bad states. If that loss can be bounded (e.g., by limited liability), his concern about bad states would be alleviated to some extent and a debt contract made acceptable to him that he would otherwise reject. Provided then that his liability was not *too* limited, such a contract could also be acceptable to the creditor. A debt contract with limited liability provides a compromise that (partially) addresses the borrower's concern about his losses in bad states whilst simultaneously providing incentives that are well-suited to handling verification and monitoring problems (i.e., they provide the 'right' incentives as far as the lender is concerned). These factors perhaps help to explain why debt contracts are so common even though most borrowers seem to be risk-averse.

- The borrower's risk-aversion also affects debt contracts in another way. Risk-aversion increases the non-pecuniary penalties to which he can subject himself, if he should choose to do so. The explanation is that since the borrower's marginal utility rises as his wealth falls, the threat of losing what remains of his wealth translates into a bigger loss of utility, and, hence, a larger non-pecuniary penalty. Knowledge of his aversion to risk (and, hence, of the high non-pecuniary penalties to which he would expose himself) can then reassure a lender and enable debt contracts to be made that the lender would otherwise reject because of insufficient reassurance.

Nonetheless there will be circumstances in which non-debt contracts will be optimal. If agents are uncertain of their individual liquidity needs but interrupting investment is costly, the optimal contract can sometimes involve proportional shares (i.e., 'equity-like' contracts) instead of debt (e.g., Jacklin, 1988; Jacklin and Bhattacharya, 1988) and Jacklin's results suggest that the optimality of these 'equity-like' contracts in these circumstances is robust to agents' risk-aversion. Equity-like contracts can also arise from the costly state *falsification* models of Lacker and Weinberg (1989) and Lacker, Levy and Weinberg (1990). The idea behind these is that the agent has the option of falsifying, at a cost, the publicly observable output level which the principal and agent have agreed to share between them. This framework captures the notion that even though outcomes might be observable, the agent can manipulate observed data in his own interest if he is prepared to pay a cost to do so (e.g., he can keep a secret hideaway, or he can keep two sets of books). With a risk-neutral principal and a risk-averse agent, Lacker and

Weinberg (1989, 1348) find that under a wide variety of falsification cost functions, the optimal contract involves a given amount going to the agent, and any excess over that amount being divided between the two parties in pre-agreed proportions. The contract can therefore be interpreted as an equity-like one, with some agreed amount set aside to cover the agent's fixed 'expenses', and contracts of this basic type are in fact often used in commercial transactions.

CONCLUDING COMMENTS

The optimal bilateral financial contract consequently depends on a variety of factors – the cost of output verification and/or monitoring against moral hazard, the presence of adverse selection, the degree to which wealth constraints bind the parties involved, and the parties' attitudes towards risk – to name only the obvious ones. While the issues involved are certainly complicated, a number of broad 'tendencies' seem to emerge, and it is perhaps helpful at this stage to step back and look at them:

The first and in some respects most important is that verification costs and moral hazard tend to encourage the parties involved to make debt contracts. Debt contracts are often optimal under these conditions because they reduce the impacts of hidden information (since it will often not matter *ex post* that the investor does not directly see the output) and of moral hazard (since debt gives the entrepreneur a strong incentive to work hard). It is clear, then, that there are reasonably plausible circumstances in which debt contracts are optimal, and this point needs to be emphasised in view of the work of Mookherjee and Png (1989) and others which has cast doubt on the optimality of debt contracts. Many economists would presumably find it reassuring that debt contracts are defensible given that they figure so prominently in real-world financial arrangements and have done for a very long time. The literature has also made impressive progress explaining particular features of real-world debt contracts, among them the use of collateral and credit rationing, covenant restrictions of various kinds, the ongoing monitoring and re-financing of loans, and the existence of bankruptcy law. It also helps to explain why so much lending is done by specialist lenders such as banks.

The second broad tendency is that adverse selection over project risk tends to favour equity contracts. Equity contracts dominate debt contracts in the presence of this form of adverse selection because they eliminate (or at least substantially reduce) the possibility of asset substitution by which the entrepreneur could pass expected losses back to the investor. However, the optimality of equity contracts in these conditions is restricted to cases where verification costs (and, sometimes, monitoring costs) are low. If output is costly to verify, the entrepreneur can always announce that output was low, the investor would have to insist on verification to check whether the entrepreneur was lying or not, and 'excessive' resources would be used up on verification. More generally, if the entrepreneur has an information advantage over the outside investor (e.g., about the firm's prospects), then a rational investor would take his potential information disadvantage into account when bidding for shares, and the share price would trade at a discount to reflect this information asymmetry (e.g., as in Myers and Majluf, 1984).

The third tendency is that risk-aversion on the agent's part motivates inverse debt contracts or other arrangements to limit his liability. The explanation is obvious: if the entrepreneur is more risk-averse than the investor, then there is scope for the two parties to trade risk, and the optimal contract will generally allow for *some* risk-sharing, even if it is only a limitation on the agent's liability. The optimal contract will of course also take into account the particular features of the contracting environment within which the two parties find themselves, and some of these might also interact with the agent's risk-aversion to produce unexpected results (e.g., where the borrower's risk-aversion leads to a debt contract because it gives the *lender* sufficient reassurance to sign it).

Nonetheless, there is still a major problem. Results about optimal contract forms are often sensitive to particular assumptions, especially assumptions about the information available to each agent, and yet we often observe broadly similar and relatively simple contract forms operating under a wide variety of conditions. How, therefore, do we explain the popularity of simple contract forms? One possible reason is that it may be costly to verify the events on which payments might otherwise be made contingent. Even if certain events can be *observed* at low cost, what matters as far as the contract is concerned is the cost of *verifying* the event to a third party (i.e., a law court), and verification costs might be much higher than mere observation costs (e.g., Hart and Holmstrom, 1987, 134; Hart and Moore, 1988). A second possible reason is the relative robustness of simple contracts. As Hart and Holmstrom (1987, 91) point out, enlarging agents' choices often reduces the number of feasible contracts by exposing 'complex' schemes to arbitrage opportunities that destroy them. Complex schemes that might be optimal when agents' choices are limited in a particular way then become unworkable, and one has to go for simpler (i.e., more or less linear) schemes that are more robust because they can withstand arbitrage attack. Simple contracts like debt and equity clearly fall into this category, but 'complex' schemes that might be optimal in the idealised environment of some economic model often do not. Part of the reason why exotic schemes are not adopted more often might also be because they are difficult to understand (i.e., because rationality is bounded) or because of computational problems (e.g., Anderlini and Felli, 1994). If economic theorists have difficulty handling complex contracts, then even they might concede that ordinary 'rational' agents could have problems with them as well. Again, the simplicity of observed contracts may also be due in part to informational asymmetries. One party might fear that if payments were made contingent on a particular measurement, then the measurement could be distorted against it (Allen and Gale, 1992). Similarly, the agent who is less well informed about the probability of a particular event might be disinclined to want payments made contingent on that event (Spier, 1992). If the informed party offers a particular contingent clause, the less informed party will naturally discount the offer, and so some contingencies that both sides would cover had they been symmetrically informed are instead left uncovered. Spier gives the example of an athlete negotiating a contract with a particular team. Both parties might otherwise be able to agree an injury clause, but the athlete might not ask for one in case the team manager should think he was more accident prone than most other athletes. Finally, parties might make do with relatively simple contract forms because there are gains from working with standardised securities that people are familiar with (e.g., Gale, 1992a), or they may use them because the possibility of renegotiation makes contracts more contingent in fact than they might appear on paper (e.g., Gale, 1991).

3 Capital Structure and Corporate Financial Policy

Chapter 2 looked at the basics of contract theory in a setting with two classes of agent. This chapter builds upon that discussion by extending the treatment of contracting theory to encompass contracts involving three or more types of agent. Instead of there being just equity-holders and a single class of undifferentiated debt-holders, we now consider cases where there might be equity-holders and two classes of debt-holder (i.e., one with a senior repayment claim on the firm and one with a junior claim), or where the manager of a debt-issuing firm is no longer sole owner, and so we have two types of equity-holder – the inside holder (i.e., the manager) and the outside equity-holder (i.e., the other equity-holder(s)) – as well as the debt-holder. Indeed, we often have situations where there is inside and outside equity as well as junior and senior debt, and we frequently get cases where the firm issues other types of financial instrument as well (e.g., subordinated debt).

These cases differ from the bilateral contracts considered in Chapter 2 in that they give rise to certain interdependencies that do not arise in a bilateral framework with only two agents. The decision of an investor to buy senior debt will depend, not just on the decisions of equity-holders, but also on the decisions of those who cede him a prior claim to the firm's output by accepting more junior debt claims. Similarly, the decision to buy junior debt will depend, not just on the decisions of equity-holders, but also on the decisions of those who buy senior debt and who therefore effectively pay junior debt-holders to shoulder some of the risk they would otherwise have to bear. The decisions of one type of agent now depend on the decisions (or expected decisions) of two or more other types of agent, and we have to go beyond the bilateral framework used previously if we are to understand the interdependencies involved.

There are two basic approaches to explaining multilateral security design and, by extension, the relative amounts of different securities that a firm issues (i.e., its capital structure). The first is the agency approach which postulates that firms issue a variety of securities to reduce the agency costs that arise from conflicts of interest, the main idea being that issuing different securities is a natural way to realise economies from specialisation among investors – some investors will monitor for others by adopting more junior claims in return for higher expected returns, and so on. Agency costs can also explain the firm's capital structure. The basic issue is one of optimal reassurance. Since junior claims provide protection for more senior ones, a firm can reassure senior claim-holders that their investments are safe by maintaining a sufficiently low ratio of senior to junior claims (i.e., by keeping down its *leverage*). The lower its leverage, the safer the firm is as far as senior claimants are concerned. However, since junior claim-holders expect compensation for the greater monitoring responsibility and greater exposure to loss they bear, then lower leverage is also expensive for the firm to maintain. There is therefore a trade-off between the costs and benefits of leverage. A firm whose leverage is too low will be 'excessively' safe, in the sense that it is paying junior investors too much to monitor and bear risk for senior investors. But if the firm's leverage is too low, there is a danger that a shock could occur that leads senior investors to lose confidence. They might then 'run' to liquidate their investments, and the firm might have to borrow at high interest rates to make its repayments, with the high interest reflecting its poor credit-worthiness, or it might suffer 'firesale' losses from having to sell its chattels quickly and at short notice in a desperate bid to raise cash to pay its creditors – and even then the firm might not be able to meet its creditors' demands. A firm that over-extended its leverage could therefore find itself in a state of *financial distress* where it had serious difficulty making contractual payments to creditors. Its managers would normally want to avoid such a state by maintaining the confidence of its investors and keeping down its leverage. From the point of view of financial policy, the principal means of doing so is to maintain its *capital adequacy* – to maintain a cushion of capital large enough to absorb any likely losses and still reassure debt-holders that they will get paid in full.

A different, but complementary, approach to capital structure emphasises the role of asymmetric information. This approach focuses on two issues. The first is how 'informed' parties such as managers can use capital structure to send signals to 'uninformed' parties like outside investors. A good example is given by the Leland–Pyle (1977) model where managers signal their private information about the firm's prospects by means of their own inside equity holdings. The manager of a firm with good prospects can therefore signal his inside information by holding a large inside stake himself, and the manager of a firm with poor prospects would be unwilling to imitate him. The firm's capital structure (and, in particular, the size of the manager's own stake in the firm) then sends a credible signal to outside investors about the manager's own private assessment of the firm's prospects.

The second issue addressed by the asymmetric information literature is how the firm might use capital structure to finance profitable investments that would otherwise be forgone. The seminal work here is that of Myers and Majluf (1984). If investors are less well-informed than managers, they will perceive equity issues as bad news and will respond to equity issues by marking down the share price accordingly. This 'lemons discount' will make equity an expensive source of finance, and a firm that relied on equity finance might be forced to forgo otherwise profitable investment projects because of it. The firm would consequently prefer to finance new investments by alternative means that were less sensitive to the information asymmetry between managers and outside investors (e.g., it might resort to debt finance, provided the market does not see it as too risky, or it might use internally generated funds). The information asymmetry therefore creates a *pecking order* of sources of funding for new investments: A firm will prefer to finance new investments from internally generated funds whose cost is more or less immune to the information asymmetry; if it does not have sufficient internal funds, it will issue debt, and preferably senior debt; and if it cannot any debt at all, it will issue equity as a last resort.

We then consider the issues raised by the firm making payments to its shareholders. As discussed already in Chapter 2, there will typically be some provision to pay equity-holders while the firm is still running normally, and most such payments take the form of periodic dividends to equity-holders in proportion to their equity stake. However, since dividends are discretionary payments authorised by managers, they also give rise to various conflict-of-interest problems between managers, shareholders and other interested parties. We considered the conflict of interest between shareholders and bondholders in Chapter 2, but there is also an important conflict between managers and shareholders. The main idea in this literature is that the managers prefer low dividends to maximise the amount of the firm's funds they can squander on their own perks, empire-building, and the like. Shareholders therefore pressure the management to 'commit' to pay a certain dividend to reduce the funds available for them to squander. Once the firm is 'committed' to a certain dividend, shareholders will regard any subsequent dividend 'cuts' as reflecting badly on management; managers will then be reluctant to make such cuts and actual dividends will show considerable stickiness over time. However, dividend policy can also be used to send signals to uninformed investors about their better-informed perception of the firm's prospects. A good example is the model of Bhattacharya (1979) in which the managers of firms with good inside information commit to pay high dividend levels, and the managers of firms with bad inside information are unable to imitate them because doing so would drain the firm of funds and expose it to financial distress.

The discussion of dividends then takes us to the subject of more general corporate governance. One of the functions of shareholders is to assume the primary responsibility for monitoring management, but shareholders themselves are often too dispersed and unco-ordinated to monitor efficiently, or may have such small shares that they may see little point in monitoring anyway. There is therefore a need for a system of corporate governance that simplifies and specialises their monitoring task, whilst also trying to align managers' interests to reduce the burden placed on the monitoring function. The main institutional device to simplify and specialise shareholder monitoring is to establish a board of directors to monitor management on a regular basis on the shareholders' behalf. The board is effectively a committee consisting of shareholder representatives and other individuals which would have the power to hire and fire senior managers and generally hold them accountable. The board itself would then be accountable to the shareholders as a group at periodic intervals (e.g., at annual shareholder meetings). To reduce the burden placed on the monitoring system, the board would also design senior managers' compensation packages to bring managers interests, as far as possible, into line with those of the shareholders. This package would typically consist of a combination of a salary payment, the prospect of promotion or higher salary in return for good performance, bonus payments related to measures of the firm's performance (e.g., profit-related bonuses), and payments related to the market value of the firm (e.g., the provision of options on the firm's equity).

Corporate governance then takes us to the related issue of the takeover market. Takeovers provide a means by which the ruling shareholder group can be ousted and existing management replaced. The possibility of takeover is useful because it provides a means to replace inefficient or dishonest managers who harm shareholders' interests, and competition among rival management teams both promotes efficiency and helps to channel the economic surplus created by the firm away from managers and towards shareholders. To take maximum advantage of the takeover market, the corporate constitution needs to be designed in ways that encourage 'good' takeovers (i.e., those that increase firm value) as far as possible without leaving management too vulnerable to 'bad' takeovers that do not increase firm value, and this criterion has certain implications for the assignment of voting rights, the proportion of votes needed to take control of the board of directors, and other related issues. The prospect of takeover obviously gives some scope for conflicts of interest between managers and shareholders, but to the extent that such conflicts can be anticipated, the desire of the original owners to maximise the price they can get for their shares should encourage them to design the corporate constitution to contain them as best they can. Firms with better designed corporate constitutions should therefore get better prices for their shares.

The chapter ends with a brief overview of the 'new financial theory of the firm' that emerges from recent work and compares it to the traditional approaches of Modigliani and Miller (1958) on corporate financial policy and Jorgenson (1963) on investment. It then relates this work to recent research on the effects of financial factors on economic activity, and shows how the basic themes of agency costs and asymmetric information can explain, not just observed institutional arrangements, but also some of the main features of real-world economic fluctuations as well.

AGENCY THEORIES OF CAPITAL STRUCTURE

The Basic Conflicts of Interest

We begin with the agency theories of capital structure. Suppose we start with a simple framework with two types of outside claim. We can think of there being outside equity-holders (i.e., non-managerial investors who hold equity claims) and debt-holders. There will of course also be a manager who may or may not hold an equity claim himself (i.e., there may or may not be inside equity). There are now two basic classes of conflict of interest – conflicts between shareholders and managers, and those between shareholders and debt-holders. Conflicts between shareholders and managers can arise in a variety of ways, and the firm will respond to these problems by altering its capital structure accordingly: (1) Perhaps the most obvious conflict is where managers hold less than 100 percent of the residual claim to the firm's output. If managers bear 100 percent of the cost of profit-enhancement activities (e.g., like putting in an effort), but only receive some fraction of the extra profit that such activities create, they will place relatively little value on the extra profit that their effort creates for the outside equity-holders and put in less effort than would be socially desirable. This conflict can be ameliorated by managers increasing their own stake (i.e., by the firm increasing its ratio of inside to outside equity); however, where this might be difficult (e.g., because of limitations on managerial wealth), the firm can also reduce this particular conflict to some extent by increasing its leverage and reducing the ratio of (outside) equity to debt. (2) A conflict of interest can also arise between managers and shareholders because managers over-indulge in activities that give them satisfaction (e.g., playing golf, padding expense accounts, giving jobs to relatives, and empire-building) but that make little contribution to the firm's profits (e.g., Jensen and Meckling, 1976; Jensen, 1986). Again, the problem can be ameliorated by increasing the managerial stake in the firm or issuing debt rather than outside equity. Debt also has the advantage that interest payments soak up the firm's free cash flow and leave managers with less cash to play with (Jensen (1986). (3) There might be conflict because managers want the firm to continue in operation but shareholders prefer liquidation (e.g., Harris and Raviv, 1990). *Ex ante*, this conflict can be eased by the firm issuing debt which gives the debt-holders the option of forcing the liquidation in circumstances in which both parties agree, again *ex ante*, that the firm should cease operating. The relevant conditions can then be written into the contract as covenant clauses, and violation of the covenant would give the debt-holders the right to close the operation down. (4) Similarly, there might be conflict because managers wish to invest and shareholders do not, but this conflict can also be ameliorated *ex ante* by the firm issuing debt which bonds the management and prevents it from investing in bad states (because managers fear the consequences of default), but leaves it free to seek alternative sources of funding in good states.

Conflicts between debt-holders and equity-holders typically centre on asset substitution (i.e., the incentive of the equity-holders to take excessive risks to increase their expected profits at the debt-holders' expense), and we have already discussed this conflict of interest in Chapter 2. The possibility of asset substitution means that firms will often insert covenant clauses (e.g., requirements to observe certain minimum financial ratios) into their debt contracts to protect the interests of debt-holders. The problem of asset substitution can also be ameliorated by firms developing and maintaining reputations that lead them to choose safer investments than they otherwise would (as in Diamond, 1989). Lenders observe a firm's borrowing history, so they encourage firms to build up good reputations by rewarding firms that acquire good reputations, and firms with good credit histories then find it worthwhile to avoid asset substitution. The asset substitution problem can also be ameliorated by tying managerial remuneration to the project's success or failure and downgrading profit-related pay, or by firms rewarding managerial reputation and thereby giving managers incentives to invest in their reputations. If the manager's direct remuneration or reputation depends on the success or failure of the project, with relatively little profit-related pay to make him choose otherwise, then the manager would generally prefer the safe project. Asset substitution can therefore be ameliorated by a combination of covenant restrictions, lenders taking account of firms' reputations, and the provision of incentives to discourage excessive managerial risk-taking and reward managers with good reputations.

Sophisticated Capital Structure

In practice relatively few firms have such simple debt and equity capital structures, and it is very common for firms to issue a variety of different types of securities – mostly debt ones. Indeed, while much of corporate finance theory is devoted to understanding the trade-off between debt and equity, the fact is that firms usually choose debt. As Bolton and Scharfstein (1992, 1) point out, from 1946 to 1987, debt issues accounted for 85 percent of all external financing for US firms, and equity for only 7 percent. Thus,

> if one wants a theory of the composition of external financing, it is potentially much more important to understand the composition of debt financing rather than the choice between debt and equity. (Bolton and Scharfstein, 1992, 1).

We therefore need to explain these more sophisticated capital structures as well as the simple debt-and-equity structure, and recent literature offers a variety of possible explanations. One possibility is that having multiple classes of debt liabilities helps to promote efficient liquidation decisions (Diamond, 1990; Houston and Venkataraman, 1994). Diamond focuses on the liquidation decisions made by creditors when they decide whether to renew credit, while Houston and Venkataraman focus on the liquidation decisions made by management. Suppose that a firm finances a long-term investment project by issuing short-term debt, which it intends to roll over on maturity. When the debt matures, the lenders decide whether to liquidate or extend credit, and Diamond's point is that lenders will be excessively inclined to liquidate because they will not take into account those benefits from continuation that the management cannot properly sign over to them. Projects will then be liquidated that should, from a social point of view, have received continued credit. At the same time, lenders might be reluctant to provide exclusively long-term debt because they want to be able to use the interim information provided by the project to pull the plug on it if they need to. Short-term debt therefore leaves the firm exposed to excessive liquidation risk, and long-term debt is not a viable alternative. The solution is for the firm to issue a *mix* of short-term *and* long-term debt, with the short-term debt having the senior claim. The decision whether to liquidate or not is still made by the short-term lender, but his incentive to liquidate is reduced by the existence of the long-term debt. The greater the amount of long-term debt, other things being equal, the more protection he enjoys, and the less inclined he will be to pull the plug. An appropriate mix of short-term and long-term debt can thus retain the lenders' option to liquidate whilst simultaneously reducing their incentive to liquidate excessively. The Diamond model not only explains why firms might issue different classes of debt claims, but also explains the stylised fact that short-term claims are typically more senior than long-term ones. (The explanation, of course, is simple: if the short-term creditor were junior, he would have even less incentive to continue credit than he would have if all creditors were short-term; the existence of the long-term creditor therefore discourages continuation of credit and exacerbates rather than reduces the tendency to excessive liquidation that exists when there are only short-term creditors.)

In the Houston–Venkataraman model, by contrast, the focus is on the managerial decision whether to continue the project or not when interim information becomes available. As in the Diamond model, an exclusive reliance on short-term debt finance is undesirable because it encourages lenders to discontinue credit excessively, but in this model there is also a danger with long-term finance that managers might decide to continue the project in circumstances where it would be better if the project were discontinued. Short-term debt thus produces a tendency to excessive liquidation, and long-term debt a tendency to excessive continuation. The firm therefore issues a mix of both short-term and long-term debt that appropriately balances these two tendencies and produces, *ex ante*, the right expected balance between liquidation and continuation.

Sophisticated capital structures can also emerge as solutions to the agency and bargaining problems that arise in Hart–Moore-type models over contract renegotiation (see, e.g., Hart and Moore, 1990, 1993; Bolton and Scharfstein, 1993; Berglöf and von Thadden, 1994). The starting point is that debt contracts given creditors the right to force liquidation if the firm defaults, but there can be circumstances where firms default even though their underlying prospects are still good (e.g., because of liquidity problems). Liquidating firms that suffer such liquidity defaults is then inefficient, and both the firm and its creditors will sometimes be better off if lenders agree *ex post* to renegotiate contracts under those circumstances rather than enforce contract terms. Renegotiation therefore reduces the costs of inefficient liquidations. However, the *possibility* of renegotiation also encourages strategic defaults that occur due to management incompetence or other misbehaviour, since any expectation of renegotiation reduces the incentives on managers' part to avoid default. The overall effect of renegotiation on *ex ante* efficiency will consequently depend on whether the former effect (i.e., the effect of renegotiation in reducing costs of inefficient liquidations) is greater than or less than the latter effect (i.e., the effect of the possibility of renegotiation in encouraging strategic default).

A role for debt structure can then emerge as a way of influencing this renegotiation game between the firm and its creditors. In Bolton and Scharfstein (1993), debt structure influences this game by making renegotiation more difficult in cases where it is more important to discourage strategic default and facilitating renegotiation in cases where it is more important to reduce expected liquidation costs. The former case is more likely to occur where the firm is of very poor credit quality (because investors would otherwise be unwilling to lend at all) and also where the firm is of very good credit quality (since liquidity default is then very unlikely). The contract structure would make renegotiation difficult by having many creditors, by giving all creditors identical claims, and by requiring all creditors to agree for renegotiation to take place. The latter case is more likely to occur where a firm is of intermediate credit quality, and the contract structure will facilitate renegotiation by having only one creditor, or by having creditors adopt a seniority structure among themselves and agree to voting covenants that give some creditors the option to force renegotiation. A sophisticated debt structure (as well as other features of observed contract forms) can thus emerge as a means of facilitating contract renegotiation in cases where firms are of intermediate credit quality.

The renegotiation game can also produce more sophisticated debt structures by ameliorating the terms of the trade-off between reducing expected liquidation costs and increasing the costs from strategic defaults (Berglöf and von Thadden, 1994). The basic principle is that having outside investors separate into two types helps to discourage strategic defaults without increasing expected costs from inefficient liquidations. Were there just one outside creditor, and the firm defaulted on a short-term obligation, the creditor might be reluctant to force liquidation for fear of undermining the value of his long-term claim against the firm. The firm's manager would appreciate this reluctance, and this knowledge might tempt him to engage in actions that led to strategic default. However, if investors separate, and one takes a senior short-term claim and the other a junior long-term one, then the holder of the short-term claim is in a better position to take a tough line – since he need no longer worry about the firm's long-term value. The short-term creditor can therefore be expected to take a tough line, and the manager would appreciate that he has this incentive and have more reason to avoid strategic default. (Note, incidentally, that this gives us another reason for the short-term creditor to be senior: seniority gives him a stronger incentive to be tough.) The separation of the two investors thus commits them (or, strictly speaking, one of them, the short-term investor) to take a tough bargaining position *ex post*, and so reduces expected losses from strategic defaults. It also enables the firm to commit itself *ex ante* in ways that would not otherwise be possible, and therefore enlarges the contract opportunity set available to it.

Monitoring Economies and Capital Structure

Capital structures can also arise as means of economising on monitoring costs, and this monitoring-cost story of capital structure is particularly useful because it leads us naturally into the capital adequacy issues which are at the very core of the capital structure problem. To illustrate these economies, suppose we have an entrepreneur with a project requiring the capital investments of two investors, and all parties involved are risk-neutral. If they make the investments, the project yields a return, net of their investments, of Y_e if the entrepreneur puts in an effort, and the lesser return of Y_s if the entrepreneur slacks, but this effort 'costs' the entrepreneur an amount $e > 0$ in terms of tears and toil. We assume that the entrepreneur would prefer to avoid the effort if he could, but it is socially worthwhile for him to put in the effort. Now suppose that each investor can monitor the entrepreneur at some fixed cost m, which is sufficiently low that it is still socially worthwhile for the entrepreneur to put in an effort even if both investors have to monitor him to do so. In the event that the entrepreneur is monitored and found to have been slacking, there is some penalty the monitor can inflict on him (e.g., the monitor might put the entrepreneur on a blacklist) and this penalty is sufficiently high that the entrepreneur would prefer to make an effort to avoid it. Clearly, the social optimum requires the entrepreneur to put in an effort, but he will not do so unless one or other investors monitor him and threaten him with penalties if they find he has been slacking.

One way forward is for the entrepreneur to make identical debt contracts with the investors, with each contract promising to pay the relevant investor an amount D in non-default states. However, such an arrangement does nothing to ensure that monitoring is done efficiently. If each investor thought that the other would monitor, each would decide there was no point incurring monitoring costs himself. Neither would then monitor, the entrepreneur would slack and the return would be Y_s. An inefficient outcome thus results because of insufficient monitoring. However, if each investor thought the other would *not* monitor, then both *would* monitor, and the total output net of monitoring costs would be $Y_e - 2m$. An inefficient outcome again results, but this time because there is *too much* monitoring: both investors monitor, when monitoring by one alone would have sufficed. The only circumstance where the efficient level of monitoring would occur is if one investor independently decided to monitor and the other independently decided not to, but there is of course no reason to *expect* this outcome if the two investors act independently.

The investors therefore have some incentive to co-operate to ensure an efficient outcome, and one way to do so is to alter their contracts to provide appropriate monitoring incentives. Since efficiency requires that monitoring be done only once, the contracts need to be amended to give one party, and only one party, a private incentive to monitor the entrepreneur. The simplest way to create this incentive would be for one investor to accept a junior claim to the firm's assets in the event of default and allow the other investor seniority (see also, e.g., Winton, 1995, 92). Their contracts would be amended to ensure that if the firm defaulted, the senior claimant would have first claim on the firm's assets, and the junior claimant would receive proceeds from the firm's liquidation only when the senior one had been paid off in full. If the firm's proceeds were not enough to pay off the senior claimant in full, the junior claimant would then get nothing at all. This seniority structure would give the junior claimant a stronger incentive to monitor than the senior one, and there will often be cases where the senior claimant can safely decide not to monitor. In the context of our earlier example, the senior claimant need not worry about monitoring if the value of the firm's proceeds in a default state exceeded the value of his nominal claim. The senior claimant would have no incentive to monitor because he would suffer no loss even if the entrepreneur slacked and the firm failed. However, the junior claimant *does* care if the entrepreneur slacks – since he would get whatever is left over after the senior investor has taken his due. The junior investor therefore *has* an incentive to monitor the entrepreneur and ensure that the efficient outcome results. The seniority structure produces an efficient outcome and saves m in excess monitoring costs (which the investors can share among themselves) by having one investor 'internalise' the marginal costs and benefits of monitoring, and one investor can always be induced to become the junior claimant if his promised return is increased appropriately. The most natural way to implement this seniority structure is for the firm itself to offer senior and junior debt, and it is in the firm's own interest to do so because it can presumably expect to reap some of the benefits itself by getting better prices for its debt if it differentiates the debt before selling it. The firm itself therefore differentiates among its debt, and all the investors need do is buy it. Having the investors specialise by adopting an order of seniority among themselves also has the advantage that it reduces bargaining and co-ordination costs, relative to an explicit arrangement between them to pay one to monitor for the rest.

These gains rise with the number of investors involved, and can be particularly important when the number of investors is large. If there are n investors, but one takes junior status and monitors on behalf of all, then $(n-1)m$ can be saved in monitoring costs relative to the case where all investors are identical and all decide to monitor, and there are similar gains in transactions, bargaining, and co-ordination costs as well. Clearly, the greater the number of investors involved, the greater these efficiency gains will be, and the greater the relative advantage of seniority precedence as a means of ensuring that monitoring is done efficiently. Monitoring (and other) cost efficiencies can therefore become very significant as the number of investors gets large. There may also be scope for further efficiency gains. If the costs of monitoring differ among investors (e.g., due to their different expertise), it would make sense not only to specialise the monitoring role, but to have the monitoring done by the investor who can do it at the lowest cost. The specialisation of the monitoring function also creates scope for agents to invest in acquiring monitoring skills that they would otherwise have regarded as unprofitable. Certain investors (e.g., banks) would then be able to exploit the returns that current monitoring technologies allowed them.

The basic principle that there are monitoring cost and related efficiencies to be obtained from differentiating among investors also explains why firms might differentiate among their liabilities in other ways as well. (a) One instance is where firms might issue *subordinated debt* as well as regular debt. Subordinated debt is debt that is automatically converted into equity by certain triggers, usually when some measure of the firm's capital ratio reaches a low point that suggests that the firm needs more equity. Subordinated debt therefore functions as 'regular' debt when the firm's capital position is reasonably strong, but it provides for an automatic recapitalisation of the firm if the firm's capital position should weaken to a critical point. The holder of subordinated debt then becomes an equity-holder and bears the appropriate risks and responsibilities. He therefore has a stronger incentive to monitor the firm than the holder of regular debt, and other debt-holders can trust to that incentive to cut down their own monitoring costs. (b) Another instance is where a firm issues *preference shares* (or *preferred stock*). In some ways, these are rather like a hybrid between ordinary shares and subordinated debt. These are shares which may or may not have voting rights, and which typically 'promise' certain dividends. However, the holders have no right to force the firm into bankruptcy if the promised dividends are not paid, but dividends cannot be paid on ordinary shares until the preferred shareholders have been paid their dividends, and this right to prior payment might also include the right to cumulated past payments due them from previous years in which dividends were not paid (see, e.g., Goacher, 1993, 53). The preferred shareholder therefore has a seniority greater than that of an ordinary shareholder, but less than that of any debt-holder. Other things being equal, he therefore has more incentive to monitor than debt-holders, but less incentive than (ordinary) equity-holders. (c) A third example is where a firm might make a special debt contract to a lender who is better placed to monitor its performance (e.g., a specialist financial intermediary, like a bank). The firm pays the specialist monitor a premium, and issues regular debt contracts (i.e., ones that involve little or no monitoring role) to other investors. The latter then get the benefit of knowing that monitoring is being done, but monitoring is done only once as efficiency demands.

Investor Confidence and Capital Adequacy

Granted that 'outside' investors (i.e., in this context, any investors other than the entrepreneur/manager) adopt a seniority ordering amongst themselves, one might then ask how large their relative holdings should be. To answer this question, let us first go back to the basic capital structure with equity and (undifferentiated) debt. The separation between debt and equity helps to economise on monitoring costs, but whether the seniority ranking implied by these claims actually achieves that purpose will depend, not just on the seniority structure *per se*, but also on the *sizes* of the different investors' stakes. Recall that monitoring efficiency requires that monitoring takes place, but is not needlessly duplicated. All that is normally required to satisfy the first condition and ensure that monitoring takes place is that at least one investor has a strong private incentive to monitor, and the easiest way to provide that incentive is to put his claim at the bottom of the seniority ordering (i.e., in the present context, to make him an equity-holder). Within a certain range, this investor then internalises the marginal social costs and benefits of monitoring, and therefore has the incentive to ensure that monitoring takes place where social optimality requires that it should take place.

However, if senior investors (i.e., debt-holders) are to be sufficiently confident to feel no need to monitor themselves, they generally require, *not only* that equity-holders will monitor for them, but *also* that they have a *large enough* stake that the firm can absorb plausible losses and *still* be able to pay senior investors in full. The junior claimants' investments need to provide a buffer that can absorb firm losses whilst still maintaining the firm's ability to meet its commitments to senior claimants. If the junior claimants provide an adequate buffer, then senior investors can feel reassured that their investments are safe, and the only real 'monitoring' they need do is to check periodically (e.g., by reading newspapers) that junior investors are willing to keep reasonably-sized investments and that nothing untoward seems to be happening with the firm.

A firm that maintains an adequate buffer for senior debt-holders can be said to enjoy their confidence. By and large, we can also say that it is efficient for firms to maintain capital structures that give rise to such confidence because doing so enables investors to keep down their monitoring costs. *Ex ante*, the firm itself also benefits because maintaining its debt-holders' confidence keeps down the cost of inducing them to hold its debt.

The same underlying principles also apply if the firm issues more than two separate types of outside claim. Suppose that a firm issues senior and junior debt as well as equity. Should the firm default, the proceeds of the firm are used to pay the senior debt-holder first; if he is paid off in full, they are then used to pay the junior debt-holder; and whatever is left, if anything, goes to the equity-holder. The senior debt-holders can then be said to be confident in the firm if the more junior claim-holders, the other debt-holders and equity-holders, have a sufficiently large stake that the firm can absorb any plausible losses and still pay them in full, without the senior debt-holders having to engage in a great deal of monitoring. The primary monitoring, as before, would be done by the equity-holder who has most to lose (and gain) from monitoring. The difference, however, is that there is now a third claim-holder, the junior debt-holder, who comes somewhere between the other two. He is like the other debt-holder in that he still relies on the equity-holder to be primary monitor, but he has more at stake than the other debt-holder because of his more junior status. Hence, he feels obliged to put in more monitoring activity than the senior debt-holder. However, if the capital structure is well-designed, he should not feel the need to monitor the way the equity-holder does. His role would not so much be to monitor the entrepreneur, as to monitor the equity-holder. He therefore looks over the equity-holder's shoulder and monitors the equity-holder's own monitoring activity. The junior debt-holder can then be said to have confidence in the firm if he feels adequately protected by the equity-holder's stake and does not feel the need to replicate the equity-holder's own monitoring, although he will of course feel the need to do more monitoring that the senior debt-holder does.

Lack of Confidence and 'Runs'

The benefits of debt-holder confidence can also be seen by looking at what happens when debt-holders lose confidence. The most obvious consequence is that debt-holders would be reluctant to roll over existing debt when it matures. The firm might then have to promise them greater interest to induce them to continue to hold it – to compensate them for the greater risks they were taking by continuing to hold the firm's debt, and to compensate them for the higher monitoring expenditures they felt obliged to undertake. The firm's financing costs would therefore rise, perhaps sharply. Potential investors would also be reluctant to purchase the firm's securities, and would need to be compensated if they did. In more serious cases, debt-holders might want to 'pull out' entirely and redeem their holdings as soon as they can, and the firm might also have difficulty rolling its debt over by persuading others to buy it instead.

The firm would then face a *run*, and a run could be serious. If the firm is fortunate, only a relatively small number of debt contracts would have come due and it would be able to meet the run out if its own reserves or by borrowing elsewhere (e.g., by drawing on previously arranged credit lines). In that case, the firm would be able to meet its obligations at a not-too-excessive cost and survive for the time being. The management would then have to think about how they were going to restore debt-holder confidence and meet their next debt obligations when they come due, but at least they would have some time to sort the firm out. However, even when the firm survives, the loss of confidence can also damage the firm because of the uncertainty it creates: debt-holders who previously presumed the firm to be quite safe are no longer so sure; if they are no longer confident, other relevant parties might also lose confidence, and there will be doubt over the terms on which the firm can get new finance in the future, or whether it can get any finance at all; current and potential customers might also look elsewhere; employees might start looking for other jobs; and so on. The firm therefore loses out, not just because of the 'direct' losses associated with the redemption of its debt and the need to restore debt-holder confidence, but also because the lack of confidence creates uncertainty, which then undermines many of the longer-term relationships on which the firm's well-being depends.

If the firm is less fortunate, there would be too many debt contracts being presented for repayment for the firm to be able to make the payments out of its own or borrowed reserves, and the firm would have to resort to 'emergency measures' to avoid default. It might have to sell off some of its assets, interrupt production to cut down on costs, and so forth, in order to acquire or preserve the funds it needs to meet its creditors' demands. In the former case, it would usually suffer significant 'firesale losses' since the markets for many of its assets would normally be thin and the firm would be unlikely to fetch a good price for them at short notice. In the latter case, interrupting production (e.g., by laying off workers) might save on some of its running costs (e.g., by lowering labour and other input costs), but in most industries interrupting production would be an expensive way to raise cash. Goodwill is lost, delivery deadlines missed, and the like, and a firm would still have to pay many fixed costs (e.g., rent) even if it produces nothing. In addition, in many industries there are significant physical costs of interrupting production (e.g., shutting down a blast furnace is not costless). A firm that is obliged to sell off its chattels for whatever they can get and temporarily close down production to preserve its cash flow is in serious difficulty, and, even if it manages to satisfy its creditors and survive, it does so only at a very significant cost. If the firm is even less fortunate, it will sell off all its chattels and do whatever else it can to meet creditors' demands, and *still* be unable to make its payments. In that case it would be forced to default, and the unsatisfied creditors would proceed with their claims in the bankruptcy court.

Capital Adequacy

Since the loss of debt-holder confidence can have serious consequences, the firm will normally put a high priority on maintaining it. Above all, it must be able to persuade its depositors, and others who would stand to lose if the firm failed, such as regular customers, that the firm is sufficiently strong that they should have no reason to fear its failure. Provided it does so, it can *then* expect to be able to issue new debt and roll over existing debt reasonably easily, at a relatively low cost, and debt-holders will feel confident that they can hold its debt without the need to monitor the firm in any particular depth.

But *how* does the firm maintain debt-holder confidence? Clearly, it helps debt-holders to remain confident in the firm if they perceive it as well-managed, and they will tend to see the firm as well-managed if managers are properly qualified, have a good track record, seem to be the 'right sort of people', and this sort of thing. The firm will therefore have an incentive to get properly qualified, appropriate people, build up a good track record, and so on. However, the firm will also wish to maintain debt-holder confidence by means of its capital structure: issuing more junior claims that are large enough to absorb plausible loss the firm might make and still leave it with enough resources to pay off the senior investors' claims, and whose existence relieves the debt-holders (or the senior debt-holders, at least) of any need to monitor seriously themselves. If the firm uses its capital structure in this way, then any senior debt-holder will not only have confidence in the firm, but will have confidence in it *despite* the fact that he does relatively little monitoring All he really needs to do is check that the more junior investors continue to maintain an 'adequate' stake in the firm themselves. In effect, he decides that if the more junior investors have confidence in the firm, and they have more incentive to be informed about the firm than he does because they get paid only after he does, then he can conclude that his own investment must be safe. He therefore has the relatively simple task of checking every now and then that the more junior investors maintain their stake. Intermediate stakeholders will have more monitoring to do, of course, but even they should feel that they need only monitor the monitor, rather than monitor the firm itself.

The lesson for the firm is then very clear: if it is to maintain the confidence of senior investors, it must ensure that investors with more junior claims maintain an 'adequate' investment. A firm with two classes of claimants, debt-holders and equity-holders, must therefore ensure that its shareholders' stake is adequate (i.e., sufficiently strong) to maintain debt-holder confidence. Since the amount of capital that would be adequate to maintain their confidence will depend, among other factors, on the size of the firm's asset portfolio, it will often be convenient to express the 'adequate' level of capital as a percentage of the value of the firm's assets. The adequate level of capital will of course also depend on various factors specific to the firm's particular circumstances (e.g., the riskiness of the markets in which it operates). The firm will then aim to maintain a capital/asset ratio that exceeds the minimum 'adequate' level, and will normally take remedial action if the capital ratio should fall to levels that threaten its capital adequacy. The same basic principles apply if the firm has more than one class of debt-holder. As far as junior debt-holders are concerned, the firm is capital-adequate if the firm's equity holding is large enough; as far as the senior debt-holders are concerned, the firm is capital-adequate if the shareholders and junior debt-holders *together* provide a sufficiently large stake to reduce the senior investors' expected losses to an acceptably low level. The senior debt-holders will therefore be concerned, not so much about the size of the shareholders' stake, as with the size of the *combined* stakes of shareholders and junior debt-holders, since it is this combined stake that is their 'cushion' against loss. More generally, we can also say that the *firm itself* is capital-adequate if *each class* of creditors regards it as capital-adequate. All classes of creditor then have confidence in it, and monitoring costs are kept to a minimum.

A capital-adequate firm has two attractive features. The first is that it is unlikely to default within the time horizon that relevant parties are working with, and those who deal with it perceive that it is unlikely to default. The firm is therefore 'safe' to do business with, and investors can lend to it, customers can invest in long-term relationships with it, and so forth, in a reasonable expectation that the firm will not inflict losses on them by defaulting. The firm is unlikely to default because the shareholders would lose their stakes if it did default, and any shareholder who felt that the risk of such loss was too high would wish to liquidate his investment while he still could. The very fact that shareholders (or junior creditors) are content to keep their shares therefore indicates that they regard the risk of losing their stakes as low. If shareholders (or junior creditors) are willing to back the firm by staking their own resources on it, other investors can *then* presume that their investments (which have prior claims on the firm) must be safe: if the more vulnerable party involved credibly communicates that he thinks *he* is safe, those who are less vulnerable can reasonably presume that *they* are safe as well. (This financial strength in turn produces a variety of derivative benefits, such as being able to exploit profitable investment opportunities that might arise, e.g., Hart and Moore, 1990, 2, being able to obtain loans easily and at low cost, and so on.)

The second attractive feature of a capital-adequate firm is that the firm's financial structure communicates its safety in a reasonably efficient way, by economising on monitoring costs. Those who deal with the firm naturally want reassurance that the firm is safe, and information is both imperfect and costly. For reasons already discussed, it generally does not make sense to have every investor hold an identical claim, and one of the purposes of having the investors hold separate types of claim is to specialise the monitoring function and thereby economise on monitoring costs. In the simple case of a firm with equity and simple undifferentiated debt – and the basic principles of course apply more generally – such a separation means that the equity-holders take on the (bulk of) the monitoring function, and the debt-holders as it were hide behind the protection of the equity 'buffer' and rely on the equity-holders' self-interest to ensure that the firm is monitored. As mentioned already, the optimal strategy for a debt-holder is to assume that the firm is in good financial health for as long as the equity-holders continue to give it a good financial rating. A typical debt-holder can then dispense with most of the monitoring he might have done had he been, say, a shareholder, and all he need do to is periodically check that the shareholders' confidence continues to hold (e.g., by reading the newspapers). The key point here is that the seniority classification enables the monitoring function to be specialised, and this specialisation reduces the duplication of monitoring activity. Provided the firm maintains its capital-adequacy, the other investors can then normally rest assured that their investments are reasonably safe – and they can do so, moreover, despite the fact that they would typically know less about the firm than the residual claimants.

Debt-holder Dilution

Conflicts of interest can also arise over the issue of debt-holder dilution. Once investors have bought a firm's debt, there may be relatively little to prevent the firm from later issuing *additional* debt which 'dilutes' the value of existing debt-holders' claims. Even if the new debt has the same seniority as the old, its issue can harm the 'old' debt-holders if it causes the price or credit rating of the debt they hold to fall. The damage to existing debt-holders can be particularly severe if the new debt is senior to existing debt. Since the holders of the new debt would have priority claims to the firm's assets in the event of failure, the issue of the new debt would increase the losses old debt-holders expect to bear from the firm failing, and therefore lead to a larger fall in the price and credit rating of the old debt than would have occurred if the new debt had been of the same seniority as the old. The *possibility* of dilution can then harm the firm itself by making investors reluctant to purchase its debt for fear of it later being diluted. Investors might demand higher interest to compensate them for the risk (or expectation) of dilution, or they might refuse to buy it at all. In short, dilution harms existing debt-holders, and the anticipation of dilution harms the firm by making its debt more expensive to issue.

The firm cannot normally solve this problem by merely *announcing* that it will not dilute debt-holders' claims in the future. Whatever it might say now to induce investors to buy its debt, the firm will have them captive once they have bought it, and it might be in the firm's interest to break its promise later and dilute anyway. Rational investors would appreciate that the firm would have no incentive to honour any promise, and any promises it makes would lack credibility. However, a more feasible solution to the dilution problem, and one often used in practice, is for the firm to submit itself to appropriate covenant restrictions. The covenant restrictions in this case would limit the firm's ability to issue subsequent debt. For example, they might stipulate that subsequent higher-priority debt can only be issued if existing debt is upgraded to the same priority, or if the firm satisfies specified minimum conditions of financial health, or they might prohibit subsequent debt issues altogether. In practice, covenants often restrict other forms of subsequent indebtedness as well, particularly contingent indebtedness such as the offer of guarantees to other parties or the signing of lease agreements that have the effect of incurring debt (Smith and Warner, 1979, 136). The trick is to design covenant restrictions so that they deal with the relevant conflict of interest without preventing the firm from engaging in worthwhile activities. For example, a high-net-present-value (NPV) investment opportunity might subsequently appear, and the firm may want to exploit that opportunity by issuing high-priority debt which, if prohibited, might lead to the investment opportunity being forgone. Most covenant restrictions therefore allow the firm *some* flexibility to issue higher-priority debt, but try to prevent it being issued in ways that would harm the interests of existing debt-holders.

ASYMMETRIC INFORMATION THEORIES OF CAPITAL STRUCTURE

We now turn to those capital structure issues that arise from asymmetric information between different parties. The underlying idea is that managers or insiders are assumed to have private information about the firm's return or investment opportunities that outside parties do not share. This information asymmetry can influence capital structure in two quite different ways: first, it can influence capital structure in so far as firms use their capital structure to signal the insiders' private information to outsiders; and secondly, it can influence capital structure in so far as firms use their capital structure to mitigate inefficiencies in the firm's investment decisions that are caused by information asymmetries. We now consider each in turn.

Capital-structure Signalling Models

The first set of models builds on the theme that capital structure can be used to signal insider information to the market, and the seminal paper in this literature is Leland and Pyle (1977). The reader will recall from Chapter 2 that the Leland–Pyle model has entrepreneur–managers with private information about their firms which they can credibly signal to outside investors through the size of their own stake. If entrepreneur–managers have good information about their firms, they will hold a larger stake, and entrepreneurs with bad information will be unwilling to imitate them. Outside investors will therefore regard the size of the inside equity-holding as a signal of the insiders' private information. If the inside information is good, a firm will also increase its leverage (i.e., issue more debt relative to equity) in order to increase the proportion of inside equity and divert a larger share of the anticipated higher benefits to the inside equity-holder(s). Managers who have superior projects can then signal this fact by issuing more debt, and the managers of inferior projects cannot afford to imitate them because of the greater danger that doing so might lead the firm to default and leave them with nothing (see also Ross, 1977 and Heinkel, 1982). The bottom line, then, is that the need to signal their quality leads good firms to have a higher proportion of inside equity and be more highly levered than bad firms.

Firms might also use debt as a signalling device in fights for market share (e.g., Poitevin, 1989). In the Poitevin model an incumbent firm faces potential competition from a new entrant to the market, and each firm's marginal costs are known only to itself. The cost of debt is that it makes a firm vulnerable to predation by rivals (e.g., as in Bolton and Scharfstein, 1990), but the benefit of debt is that it gives a signal that the firm's costs are low. This signal is credible because a firm with low costs can reasonably take the risk of issuing more debt, knowing that its costs are low enough to make its chances of survival sufficiently high to make the gamble worthwhile, but one with high costs cannot. A high-cost entrant will therefore issue only equity. As in the previous models, the Poitevin model implies that the issue of debt is good news, and therefore suggests that firms that issue more debt should have higher market values.

Capital Structure and Efficient Investment

The second strand of the literature stems from the work of Myers and Majluf (1984) and Myers (1984). The underlying idea, which we have touched on already, is that an information asymmetry between the firm's management and outside investors leads to the firm's equity being underpriced by the market. If firms need to finance new projects by issuing equity, this under-pricing may be so severe that outside investors would capture more than the net present value of the new project, so inflicting losses on existing equity-holders and ensuring that the project was never started in the first place. This under-investment outcome can be avoided if the firm can raise funds internally or issue alternative securities that are less under-priced by the market. The implication is that to the extent that its capital structure is driven by investment considerations, the firm will have a *pecking order* of preferred sources of funds (Myers, 1984)). The firm will first seek funds internally; if internal funds do not suffice, it will then seek external funds, and among external sources of funds, it will prefer to issue low-risk debt first and high-risk debt later, and it will only issue equity as a last resort.

The pecking order theory has some important implications. Apart from the relatively obvious implication that new investments will tend to be financed through internally generated funds or the proceeds of relatively low-risk debt, it also implies that the *announcement* of an equity issue will lead the firm's share price to fall. When a firm issues equity, market participants will ask themselves why the firm has chosen to issue equity rather than some other security, and will draw the conclusion that the manager's private information must be unfavourable. (Market participants will reason that the managers would have issued debt if their private information is good, since debt would channel more of the expected benefits to the shareholders. The decision to resort to equity financing in those circumstances therefore constitutes a strong signal of 'bad news'.) The market then discounts the share price accordingly. (As an aside, this 'lemons effect' of an equity issue also helps to explain why equity issues are a relatively small source of funds.) Another implication of the pecking order logic, emphasised by Korajczyk *et al.* (1990), is that the under-investment problem will be least severe just after information releases such as annual reports, the release of auditors' statements, and so on. We should therefore expect many equity issues to be concentrated in the period shortly after such information is released in order to fetch a better price.

However, more recent work has cast doubt on the Myers–Majluf under-investment hypothesis and the 'simplistic' pecking order result to which it gives rise. Brennan and Kraus (1987) and Constantinides and Grundy (1989) each enrich the choice facing the Myers–Majluf firm in slightly different ways; and both find, not only that the firm no longer necessarily prefers debt to equity, but also that the firm can handle the under-investment problem by signalling through capital structure decisions in other ways. In Brennan and Kraus, the good firm issues enough equity to finance its project and retire its existing debt, but the bad firm only issues enough equity to finance its project. Investors perceive firm type correctly, and so the good firm obtains a fair deal on both its debt and equity. Good firms do not imitate bad ones because the bad ones get a poor price for their equity. Bad firms do not imitate good ones because that would mean having to buy back their debt at face value, which implies that they would have to pay more for it than they believe it is worth. The implication is that in equilibrium both types of firms issue equity and invest in positive NPV projects. The Myers–Majluf under-investment result is thus short-circuited and the pecking order result disappears. Instead, we find that the issue of equity *alone* is still a negative signal, but the issue of equity *and* the simultaneous use of the proceeds to buy back debt is a positive one.

While Kraus and Brennan focus on how the firm can resolve under-investment by buying back its debt, Constantinides and Grundy suggest that the firm can also resolve this problem by issuing convertible debt which it uses to finance the investment project *and* buy back some of its own equity. The main idea is that the repurchase of equity removes any incentive for firms to *over*-state the value of the firm – if managers expect the share price to fall, they have no incentive to buy it back – while the issue of a convertible security removes any incentive to *under*-state the value of the firm – if managers expect the share price to rise, they have no incentive to pass the gains to debt-holders by issuing convertible debt. In their model, the costs of over- and under-stating the value of the firm balance exactly and remove any incentive for the firm to misstate its value. The firm can then raise finance without affecting its share value, and the under-investment problem is resolved.

FIRM DIVIDEND POLICY

An aspect of capital structure policy not considered so far in this chapter is the firm's policy regarding payments to shareholders. A firm can make payments to shareholders either by paying dividends on the shares they hold or by buying back its own shares (i.e., repurchasing stock). Of these, dividend payments are very common – in 1985, US firms paid over $83 billion in dividends (Brickley and McConnell, 1992, 691) – while stock repurchases are relatively rare. Most payments to shareholders therefore take the form of dividend payments, and relatively little is lost in practice if we focus on dividends alone.

What determines a firm's dividend policy? A good starting point to consider this question is the Modigliani–Miller framework in which dividend policy is irrelevant. In this framework there are no agency or contracting costs and no information asymmetries, and so shareholders can in effect make their own dividend policy regardless of that pursued by the firm. Suppose that the firm retains and invests its earnings, but shareholders would have preferred to consume a dividend instead. Then all they need to do is sell shares and consume the proceeds, and they can produce an outcome identical to that which would have occurred had the firm actually made a dividend. If the management issues a dividend, it must – other things being equal – issue new stock to finance its investments, so if shareholders prefer to reinvest rather than consume their dividend, they can do so by buying up the new shares with their dividends. Buying up the new shares then undoes the firm's dividend policy and produces an outcome identical to that which would have occurred if the firm had not issued any dividends. Shareholders can therefore costlessly undo any dividend policy that does not suit them and effectively create their own dividend position, and the actual dividend policy pursued by the firm is of no consequence.

Agency Cost Explanations

Any explanation of dividend policy must therefore depart from one or more of the assumptions underlying Modigliani–Miller, and an obvious candidate is the assumption that agency costs are zero. The presence of agency costs can lead to a role for dividend policy for reasons suggested by Jensen's (1986) free-cash-flow model: a firm could commit to higher dividends for much the same reason as it might commit to higher debt repayments – to soak up excess cash flow that might otherwise be dissipated by management. A firm that paid higher dividends would then be perceived as having its excess cash flow problem and, hence, its underlying agency problem, under better control. The reader will also recall from Chapter 2 how agency costs could be ameliorated by the use of dividend constraints incorporated into bond covenants. These would typically aim to prevent under-investment by restricting dividends to come out of current earnings and prohibiting the payment of dividends from working capital, the proceeds of debt issues, or the sale of chattels.

The use of dividends to reduce agency costs is developed further in Rozeff (1982). In this model, firms 'precommit' to pay high dividends to reduce agency costs by reducing managerial 'discretion' to dispose of the firm's assets. The agency costs arise because the firm is less than 100 percent management-owned, implying that management has some incentive to use resources on managerial perks and so forth. Rational outside investors understand this incentive, and take it into account when calculating how much to pay for shares, so managers have some incentive to offer reassurance to induce them to make better offers. Managers therefore 'precommit' themselves by having themselves monitored and posting good behaviour bonds, and one way in which they can post a bond is by 'committing' themselves to pay high dividends which reduce their freedom to indulge themselves with perks. However the commitment to make high dividend payments means that firms will need to seek external finance more often. They will therefore have to bear greater flotation costs, submit to more frequent scrutiny by potential creditors, and so on. A firm that promises higher dividends therefore posts a bond in two ways: directly, by setting a high dividend target which, if not met, might have unpleasant repercussions for the management; and indirectly, by submitting itself to more outside scrutiny that would highlight management failures.

Once firms have 'committed' themselves to certain dividend payments, they are then naturally reluctant to change them. The underlying agency costs do not change overnight, and so firms have little 'good' reason to change dividend levels. If high dividends signal low agency costs, managers will be reluctant to cut dividends for fear that shareholders will interpret the dividend cut as evidence that the firm's agency costs have deteriorated. However, having decided what the longer-term dividend level should be, a firm would also be reluctant to raise dividend level in response to temporarily higher profits in case shareholders perceived the dividend change as 'permanent' and the management was subsequently forced to cut dividends again and incur the penalty for reducing them. The agency models therefore predict that dividends should be sticky, and the stickiness of dividends is perhaps their most striking and definitively established empirical feature (see, e.g., Lintner, 1956).

Asymmetric Information Explanations

The obvious alternative assumption to drop from Modigliani–Miller is the assumption that all agents have the same information. Dropping this assumption can also motivate a role for dividend policy because firms can use dividend policy to signal otherwise private information to outside parties. An early approach along these lines is the model of Ross (1977) in which firms with better prospects pay higher dividends to distinguish themselves from firms with poorer prospects. The underlying idea is that firms with better prospects can better 'afford' higher dividends, and therefore pay them, because they know that weaker firms cannot afford to imitate them without unduly endangering themselves. Outsiders can then evaluate the quality of the firm by looking at the dividends it pays. This theme is developed further by Bhattarcharya (1979) and Miller and Rock (1985). In these models, management has superior private information about the firm's investment projects, and firms with good projects anticipate higher cash flows than firms with poor ones. A firm with good projects can therefore commit itself to pay higher dividends than a firm with bad projects, and the latter will not be able to copy it without risking its cash flow. A policy of 'committing' to pay regular high dividends then leads shareholders to expect higher dividends, and high *expected* dividends are a 'good' signal in they indicate that the management's private information is favourable. Given these expectations, the announcement of actual dividends that are *above* expected dividends is also a good signal, in that it provides 'news' that the firm's investments are better than previously expected. High dividends are thus a good signal regardless of whether they are expected or not.

However, not all models agree that high expected dividends indicate that the firm has good investment opportunities. If firms have private knowledge of their investment opportunities, and are constrained to invest earnings that are not paid out in dividends, then John and Kalay (1985) suggest that high expected dividends might actually be a *bad* signal. Suppose that levered firms have a tendency to under-invest because too many of the gains go to bondholders, as suggested by Myers (1977), and that firms respond to this under-investment problem and reassure investors by committing themselves to minimum levels of investment. If firms differ in the investment projects they have available, firms that lack investment opportunities will only be able to meet minimum investment requirements by forcing themselves to invest in unprofitable projects, which effectively means that they penalise themselves. The strategy of committing to minimum investment levels then works because firms with good investment opportunities will have no difficulty finding suitable investment outlets. The good firms commit to high minimum investment levels by promising *low* dividend payments, and the bad firms feel obliged to promise higher dividends rather than squander their earnings on unprofitable projects. High expected dividends are then a *bad* signal, since they indicate that the firm has relatively few worthwhile investment projects (see also Myers, 1984). However, these results only apply to *expected* dividends, and *un*expected increases in dividends are still a good signal since they indicate that the firm's investment projects are better than previously thought.

CORPORATE GOVERNANCE AND THE MARKET FOR CORPORATE CONTROL[1]

Corporate Governance

We now turn to consider corporate governance. The basic question here is how the residual claimants, the shareholders, ensure that managers protect their (i.e., the shareholders') interests. The answer depends, in part, on the relationship between residual claimants (or owners) and managers, and the precise nature of this relationship varies with the type of firm. The basic types of firm are *proprietorships, partnerships, mutual institutions, non-profit organisations*, and *closed* and *open corporations*. The distinguishing characteristic of a proprietorship is that the roles of owner and manager are vested in the same individual, and so corporate governance issues as defined above do not arise. The distinguishing characteristic of a partnership is that these roles are vested in the same group of individuals. There is therefore no difference between the *collective* interests of owners and managers in a partnership, but governance issues can now arise because there may be a conflict of interest between an *individual* partner and the partners *as a group* (e.g., one partner may slack because most of the benefits of his effort go to others). In a mutual, the residual claim is restricted to customers, so there are obvious governance (or conflict of interest) issues between residual claimants and managers. In a non-profit organisation there is no residual claim at all, and therefore no residual claimants to have conflicts with anyone else. However there is still the problem of ensuring that the firm is run properly, so corporate governance issues still arise, albeit in other forms. A closed corporation is a firm whose shares are held privately (i.e., are not traded on an open market) and whose share ownership is typically concentrated (e.g., among members of a family or managers), while an open corporation is a firm whose shares are openly traded and often widely dispersed. Both closed and open corporations therefore have conflict-of-interest problems between shareholders and managers, but these conflicts are often less severe for closed corporations because their managers frequently have substantial shareholdings in them. By contrast, managers in open corporations rarely have more than very small equity shares. Open corporations therefore exhibit a 'separation' of ownership from management that implies quite stark conflicts of interest between owners and managers (Berle and Means, 1932).

Most large firms tend to be open corporations. If economies of scale are large, the firm must operate on a large scale if it is to operate at all, and that means it must have access to a large amount of investor capital. Unless its investors are particularly rich, which is unlikely, it must therefore find a large number of investors, and it will often be difficult to find the number required unless its shares are openly traded. The free trading of shares that results from the open corporate form also enables outside investors to adopt a more specialised role in the firm (i.e., that of outside investor) without being forced to adopt other roles as well (see, e.g., Fama and Jensen, 1983). This freedom of choice then allows an almost total separation of the risk-bearing and management functions that cannot normally be achieved by other corporate forms (e.g., an investor in a mutual must also be a customer and may not want to buy the product, and so on; cf. Jensen and Smith, 1985). This separation of risk-bearing from other functions further facilitates the transfer of shares, which reinforces the development of an active share market. The existence of the share market then makes it easy for the investor to recover his investment, if he should feel the desire to do so. (By contrast, it can be very difficult, if not impossible, for the individual investor to liquidate his stake in a partnership or closed corporation.) A share in an open corporation is therefore more liquid than residual claims in other types of firm, which is an important consideration for those investors (i.e., the majority) who anticipate that they might need to liquidate their investment sometime in the future. The existence of the share market also facilitates the monitoring process by enabling the firm to use its share price and dividend policy to send signals (e.g., about future earnings prospects) to outside investors in ways we have already discussed, as well as to enable a market for corporate control to operate that serves to discipline, and if necessary, replace incompetent or dishonest management, and we shall have more to say on this market presently.

The Resolution of Problems Between Shareholders

A key concern in corporate governance is that of ensuring that management is adequately monitored when residual claims are dispersed. There are two main problems here. The first is to induce shareholders to monitor properly, a problem that can be particularly acute if there are a lot of shareholders each of whom holds only a small stake in the firm. Since each one bears the full costs of his monitoring efforts but gets only a small fraction of the benefits, he might be tempted to slack on his monitoring and monitor less intensively than he should, or perhaps free-ride on the monitoring that he assumes someone else will do. An individual shareholder might also be discouraged from monitoring on the grounds that his holding is too small to make the management listen to him. The danger is that these factors might result in little real monitoring actually taking place. Many shareholders might not bother going to shareholders' meeting, for example, and even those who do might make little effort to inform themselves properly before they vote.

This problem nonetheless has a natural market solution: If shareholders are too small and dispersed to monitor effectively and make managers or directors listen to them, it is presumably worth someone's while to build up a sufficiently large shareholding to make monitoring worth his while and force managers or directors to listen. If the firm is initially not monitored properly, such an agent could presumably buy up shares at a relatively low price that reflects the current lack of monitoring. The new large shareholder could then institute an appropriate monitoring regime and ensure that he was listened to, and share prices would rise accordingly. The increased concentration of share ownership produces a rise in the value of the firm because it helps to resolve the problems of individual shareholders slacking or free-riding on their monitoring (see also, e.g., Schleifer and Vishny, 1986; Zeckhauser and Pound, 1990). All shareholders would benefit from the higher share prices, but the large shareholder would benefit especially, and therefore have some incentive to buy up a major stake in the first place.

The other problem is that of co-ordinating and delegating the monitoring function. How can an often large and dispersed group of shareholders monitor management to satisfy themselves that their interests are not being sacrificed? To some extent, this problem can be dealt with in the same way as the previous problem, by one shareholder taking a large share that gives him an incentive to adopt an active monitoring role. However it may not always be possible to have a single large shareholder, and even then, there may still be conflicts of interest between him and the other shareholders. A single large shareholder is, at best, only a partial solution to the co-ordination–delegation problem. What is actually required is for shareholders to establish an institutional structure to facilitate their ability to monitor and control what is happening in the firm. Since shareholders are typically dispersed and day-to-day communication between them might be difficult, one obvious arrangement is for them to meet periodically or when crises occur. These *shareholder meetings* would give shareholders an opportunity to discuss the issues that concern them and make appropriate decisions. The meetings could also be used to facilitate communication between shareholders and managers (e.g., by requiring managers to report to them). Since meetings can be costly or inconvenient to those who attend them, and are in any case not always appropriate for certain types of decision, it often makes sense for the shareholders to delegate some of their powers. The shareholders would therefore set up a *board of directors* who could meet on a more regular basis and make the more detailed decisions that are best avoided at general shareholder meetings. The directors could consist of important shareholders and/or outside individuals who were regarded as suitably qualified for the task, and they would act on behalf of the shareholders and be accountable to them. The shareholder-directors would presumably have considerable incentive to ensure that the firm was run in the shareholder interest; the outsider-directors will often be acknowledged experts or respected leaders in the business community who have insight or experience to offer the firm, and, though they may have no inside stake to lose, will often have valuable reputations that could be jeopardised if they were associated with poorly run firms. Both types of directors therefore have some incentive to ensure that the firm is well-managed.

The Resolution of Problems Between Shareholders and Managers

There are of course also serious governance (or conflict-of-interest) problems between shareholders and managers. We have already discussed the problem that managers who bear the full cost of their own effort but receive only a fraction of what it produces have an incentive to put in less effort than shareholders would want. In addition to this choice-of-effort problem, there is also the problem that shareholders' and managers' interests might differ because they have different horizons. Since shareholders have claim to the firm's residual income over its entire lifespan, and the firm's lifespan is indefinite, they normally operate with a relatively long horizon. (This remains the case even if the shareholder plans to sell his shares. The shareholder will want to get the best price he can for his shares, and he will only do so if the purchaser is satisfied that the firm has been managed with an appropriately long-term view.) Yet an individual manager normally operates within a horizon that extends to the end of his career, and is sometimes much shorter. Hence managers will normally take a shorter view and operate with a higher subjective discount rate than the shareholders would want. A third source of conflict of interest arises from their differential risk exposure. An individual shareholder will often be able to hedge his risks, to some extent at least, and the combination of having a portfolio of offsetting risks and having a relatively small investment in each individual stock will make him less concerned about the risk on any particular stock than he would otherwise be. But an individual manager will have often invested a considerable part of his wealth in the firm, in the form of an explicit investment, or in the form of firm-specific human capital, or both, and will not normally be able to hedge that risk away. His greater exposure to the firm's risk might therefore lead him to be more concerned about fluctuations in the firm's value than a typical stockholder would be. To the extent he is, he would take fewer risks than the stockholders want him to take, and the stockholders would lose the expected profits that the foregone risks would have produced.

The parties involved therefore have an incentive to develop a corporate governance structure that helps them to handle these problems, and a key element of this governance structure, which we have touched on already, is the board of directors. One function of the board is to monitor (and if necessary, override) the decisions of senior management on behalf of the shareholders. As Jensen and Ruback write:

> The board of directors in the open corporation is elected by vote of the residual claimants who, while retaining the rights to ratify certain major decisions by shareholder vote, delegate most management and control rights to the board. The board in turn delegates most of its management and control rights to the internal managers while retaining the rights to ratify certain major decisions. Most importantly, the board of directors always retains the top-level control rights, that is, the rights to hire, fire and set the compensation of the top-level managers. (Jensen and Ruback, 1983, 43)

More specifically, the board will supervise important management decisions, and if necessary veto them; it will advise management, where appropriate; and it will appoint and replace senior management, and determine how they should be compensated.

The composition generally reflects a variety of factors. The Chief Executive Officer (CEO) will normally be included on the board, if only to facilitate communication and co-ordination between the board and senior management, but it will often make sense for the board to include firm employees as well as 'outsiders' such as shareholders or respected business leaders. Having corporate insiders on the board gives the board the benefit of 'inside' knowledge of how the firm operates, how competent managers are, what problems they face, and so on. Putting insiders on the board can also give them useful experience (e.g., if they are being groomed for top management) and give the other board members an opportunity to assess them and make more informed appointments (e.g., Weisbach, 1988, 433-434). However, a drawback with insider-directors is that they might merely reflect the thinking of their superiors or lack the will to stand up to them, so if there are too many insider-directors there is a danger that the board will be unable to monitor management or stand up to it effectively. There is therefore an optimal mix between insider-and outsider-directors, and there needs to be a strong enough outside element on the board to ensure that the board is independent of management and able to take on management if it should feel the need to do so.

Apart from monitoring managers, the board of directors can also contain agency problems with management by offering senior management a compensation package that aligns their interests as closely as possible to those of the shareholders. The idea is to design an optimal mix of the three basic types of compensation scheme – salary, schemes that tie compensation to accounting measures of corporate performance (e.g., profit-related bonuses), and schemes that tie compensation to the value of the firm (e.g., stock option and related schemes). The advantage of a salary is that it gives a manager a certain amount of financial security, an important consideration given that a manager will often be dependent on the firm's fortunes because of the investments he himself has made in the firm (e.g., in terms of his human and reputational capital, and perhaps because he owns shares as well). However a salary has the disadvantage that it does little to counter the choice-of-effort problem; it also has the drawback that it can make managers excessively cautious since they have relatively little to gain from taking risks. A partial response to these problems is to promise managers higher salaries in the future to reflect greater effort or successful risk-taking, but that only works, to the extent it does, if the manager still has a reasonable time horizon to work with. A young manager might respond well to that incentive, but one who about to retire may not.

Salary compensation is therefore often supplemented with additional compensation schemes that tie compensation in appropriate ways to measures of corporate performance (e.g., earnings per share) and/or measures of the value of the firm. These schemes give managers more incentive than they would otherwise have to make an effort and take appropriate risks, and otherwise promote stockholder interests (see, e.g., Copeland and Weston, 1989, 666–667). Tying his compensation to a measure of firm performance like short-term profits gives a manager an incentive to optimise firm performance, but also has the drawback that it might do nothing to counter problems arising from managers' operating on a different time horizon to shareholders, and, indeed, could even aggravate them. A manager thinking about leaving might take measures to boost short-term profits (e.g., by forgoing investments with delayed returns) even if the shareholders' interest were better served by taking a longer-term view. There is also the problem that accounting data such as earnings and profits can often be manipulated, and one does not want managers spending their time in such rent-seeking, especially if it is costly (e.g., because managers are distracted, or because accounting statements become less informative). Consequently, accounting-based incentives are often supplemented in practice by schemes that tie managerial compensation to share prices as well. The usual such scheme is a stock option plan that gives managers the option to buy shares over some period at a specified price. Since the value of options rises with the realised share price, managers then have an incentive to take measures that lead the market to increase the valuation of the firm. Stock option plans are therefore a good way to counter any undue aversion to risk that managers might have, but they too have their drawbacks. Since managers already bear a lot of firm-specific risk, they might make managers bear more of this risk than they themselves would prefer, and there is also the disadvantage that a stock option plan might discourage managers from making dividends (Copeland and Weston, 1989, 670). Nonetheless, the fact that empirical studies (e.g., Larcker, 1983) indicate that shareholders react to announcements of such plans by raising the value of shares indicates that such plans can have a useful role to play.

The Market for Corporate Control

However, it is seldom the case that one can rely entirely on internal corporate governance procedures to ensure that a firm is adequately run. Especially in the case of larger firms, it is relatively unusual for managers to own much more than a small share of the firm's equity, and management compensation schemes are often only loosely related to the firm's true performance. Managers in these firms face relatively weak incentives to maximise firm value, and their preferred courses of action may impose significant costs on shareholders. Such firms would then suffer prolonged losses or periods of passed-up opportunities, managers would indulge themselves in perks and empire-building, and the like. As Jensen points out,

> The failure of corporate internal control systems is reflected in the rarity with which large corporations have been able to restructure, reorganize and reorient themselves in the absence of major threat from either product or capital markets ... General Mills is an interesting and well-documented example of a successful restructuring in the absence of external threats ... However, it took 10 years and the sustained efforts of three CEOs to bring about this change. More common is the recent experience of IBM and of General Motors. In both cases the companies failed to take significant action for many years after it was clear they had serious difficulties. Until the companies faced serious product market crises and financial losses, managers and directors failed to take significant actions. This delay is evidence of the failure ... of the internal control systems of these organizations. (Jensen, 1992, 663)

If internal shareholder control provides a relatively weak constraint against self-indulgent or incompetent management, there will often need to be some mechanism to transfer control of the firm from existing management or the currently controlling group of shareholders if the firm is perceived as performing badly. Such a mechanism would serve two purposes. The first and most obvious is that it would allow an inappropriate management (or shareholder) team to be replaced, and so help the firm to cut its losses and put its house in order again. In addition, the existence of such a mechanism should give the existing management (or shareholder) team some incentive to prevent matters deteriorating to the point where control was taken away from them.

This transfer activity takes place in a market for corporate control (or takeover market) where alternative management or shareholder teams compete for the right to manage firms. Takeovers normally take one of three forms: *mergers*, in which the deal is negotiated directly with the management of the target firm; *tender offers*, in which the acquiring firm or group of shareholders buy up a controlling interest, usually at some specified premium over current share prices; and *proxy contests*, in which a dissident group of shareholders, often led by a rival firm or former manager, attempts to take control of the firm's board of directors. Some indication of the importance of the market for corporate control can be gained from the facts that over 35,000 control transactions occurred in the USA in the period 1976-1990, totalling $2.4 trillion in 1990 dollars, and that about 30 percent of US firms were acquired in this market in the period 1976-87 (Jensen, 1992, 657).

The literature on the market for corporate control is based on the idea that self-interested shareholders use their voting power to award the right to manage to the shareholder-management team they judge most likely to maximise the value of their shares. As Jensen and Ruback observe, this literature

> views competing management teams as the primary activist entities, with stockholders (including institutions) playing a relatively passive, but fundamentally important, judicial role. Arbitrageurs and takeover specialists facilitate these transactions by acting as intermediaries to value offers by competing management teams, including incumbent managers ... Stockholders have no loyalty to incumbent managers; they simply choose the highest dollar value offer from those presented to them in a well-functioning market for corporate control, including sale at the market price to anonymous arbitrageurs and takeover specialists. (Jensen and Ruback, 1983, 6)

Relying on the takeover market to discipline management is not without its problems, however. One major concern is that shareholders might respond to a tender offer by refusing to sell their shares in an effort to free-ride on the value created by the acquisition. Such activity would undermine attempts to acquire firms and therefore weaken the discipline the takeover market could impose on management. A possible solution to this problem is to write clauses into the firm charter that allow the bidder to 'dilute' the shares of other shareholders after the takeover has taken place (e.g., by selling the firm's assets to the acquiring firm at below-market prices). The threat of this 'dilution' then gives a shareholder a greater incentive to sell out rather than hold on to his shares. This dilution could also be supplemented by the bidder making a two-tier offer, with relatively generous terms (e.g., a higher price) being offered in the first-tier offer and less generous terms being offered to remaining shareholders in the second-tier offer. Shareholders would then have some incentive to want to sell in the firsttier, which would make a tender offer more likely to succeed.

While an outside team would normally be less familiar about an operation than the incumbent management, there may nonethless be various reasons why it could be better placed to run it. It may be more competent or carry less fat, it may be able to offer a superior strategy for the best use of the firm's resources (e.g., by re-deploying them, changing investment policy, or restructuring the firm), or it may be able to make better use of the firm's resources by combining them with its own in ways that the incumbent team cannot (i.e., it can create synergies with its existing assets). Prospective bidders then evaluate firms and make bids if they believe that they can make a profit doing so; and competition among rival teams *should* ensure that the 'best' team wins (see, e.g., Ruback, 1983). Activity in the market for corporate control should therefore promote corporate efficiency, at least if other things are equal.[2]

The market for corporate control is particularly useful in cases where the most straightforward way of resolving shareholder-management conflicts of interest – for the management to buy up a dominant shareholding – is not possible. The danger of takeover is then 'good' in so far as it gives management some incentive to keep its act together, but also has important implications for firm financial policy. The most obvious implication is that, to the extent that the firm's financial policy influences the outcome of takeover contests, a management team has a clear incentive to manipulate that policy to protect itself against being taken over and replaced. A firm's management might therefore manipulate its capital structure as an anti-takeover device. A more subtle implication is that the possibility of takeover might give other shareholders opportunities to gain at the expense of the competing management teams. 'Passive' investors might therefore use the prospect of takeovers to extract benefits for themselves. We shall now examine each of these implications in turn.

The Use of Capital Structure Policy as an Anti-takeover Device

There are two main ways in which an incumbent management can use the firm's capital structure to discourage takeovers. The first is to use capital structure (and, at a more fundamental level, security design) as devices to discourage takeover attempts, the idea being to maintain a capital structure that makes it more difficult for a rival to take over the firm. A firm's capital structure can be manipulated to discourage takeover attempts in various ways: (1) The firm's by-laws can be amended to require *super-majorities* (e.g., 67 percent) to approve a takeover or merger. Super-majority provisions force a rival to acquire more shares than he would otherwise need to acquire, and thereby raise the cost and difficulty of mounting a successful takeover. (2) The firm's by-laws could stagger directors' terms of office, and so delay the transfer of control and make takeover less attractive to the acquiring firm. (3) The by-laws could require that dismissed managers receive large termination payments (i.e., *golden handshakes*) that compensated replaced managers at the expense of the acquiring firm. (4) Managers could incorporate *poison pill* provisions that inflict penalties on an acquiring firm if it goes through with a takeover, typically by giving the shareholders of target firms the right to buy up the stock of a successor company at a substantial discount. (5) Managers might also make *standstill agreements* with potential acquirers (i.e., agreements that the latter should purchase no more stock). These devices help to protect the incumbent management against hostile takeovers, and are frequently, but by no means always,[3] against the interests of existing shareholders. However, to the extent that they are against shareholder interests, the shareholders themselves have some reason to discourage their managements from adopting them. Indeed, since the use (or possible use) of such devices should be reflected in the share price, shareholders not only have an incentive to discourage management from adopting them, but also to try to commit the firm to avoid adopting them in the future.

The market for corporate control also influences corporate governance in other ways. One important implication of this market is the optimality of simple majority rules to determine the outcome of takeover contests (Harris and Raviv, 1988b, 1989; see also Grossman and Hart, 1988). Other things being equal, this rule is optimal because it ensures that the best team gets elected. If the rival must get more than 50 percent of the votes to take over, the incumbent has an advantage and can sometimes win the contest even if the majority of shareholders see him as the inferior candidate; yet if the rival can win the contest with less than 50 percent of the votes, then *he* has an advantage and might sometimes win against a superior incumbent. A simple majority rule is therefore best because it treats each side symmetrically and maximises the chance of the best team winning. A second important implication is the optimality of a single class of voting shares (i.e., one-share, one-vote). To understand this result, suppose there are two classes of shares, those with high ratios of votes to cash claims, and those with low ratios. To purchase a vote, the inferior candidate must compensate the security holder for the lower cash flow that his inferior management would inflict on him. Since the first class of shares involves low cash claims relative to votes, it would be cheaper for the inferior candidate to purchase votes from this group of shareholders than from the second group. The danger, from the firm's point of view, is that an inferior candidate who gets larger private control benefits than a superior rival (e.g., he might be better at fiddling his expense accounts) might win by buying these 'cheap votes' even though the firm would be better off if he lost. The existence of two classes of shareholders improves the chances of an inferior candidate winning who has greater private control benefits. One-share, one-vote is therefore superior because it ensures that the outcome of the control contest depends more on the relative merits of the two candidates and less on their private control benefits.[4]

Securities can also serve as devices to commit the manager to good behaviour in the face of future takeover attempts. Investors will pay a price for securities that reflects their perception of the agency costs involved. If a firm that is perceived as having serious agency problems when it goes public, the founder-entrepreneur will get a lower price for the shares he sells. He therefore has some reason to design securities *ex ante* that give him little incentive *ex post* to act in ways that harm the outside shareholders. Securities will therefore be designed to enable the incumbent manager to resist takeover attempts by inferior rivals but not superior ones. If he wants to commit *not* to resist attempts by superior rivals to take over the firm, he should therefore maximise the cost of retaining control, whilst not putting a future rival at an 'unfair' disadvantage (e.g., by requiring super-majorities to take over). Hence, the incumbent should retain no voting rights when the firm goes public, and hold securities whose value is as sensitive as possible to who is in control. His lack of voting rights would mean that he would have to buy up voting rights to fight off a rival, which would maximise his private cost of keeping control, and the sensitivity of his securities to who is in control would maximise his incentive to want the best management team in place.[5]

The management's second line of defence is to alter capital structure to protect itself against takeover when a particular takeover threat has manifested itself.[6] Changes in capital structure affect the outcome of takeover contests because of their effect on the distribution of votes more generally, and on the share of votes owned by the manager in particular. An incumbent manager who wishes to fight off a takeover attempt can therefore do so by altering the capital structure to manipulate voting power in his favour. A good model of the issues involved is that of Harris and Raviv (1988a) which focuses on the ability of an incumbent manager to influence the outcome of a corporate control contest by altering the fraction of equity he owns (and hence his voting power). The contest starts when the rival appears. Both parties then buy up whatever shares they wish to at prevailing prices and a vote later takes place to determine who should be in control. Depending on the incumbent's own holding, one of three outcomes can occur: the incumbent's stake might be so small that even an inferior rival takes over; the incumbent's stake might so large that he retains control even if he is of lower ability; or the incumbent's stake might take an intermediate value, in which case the outcome of the contest will depend on the other (i.e., passive) investors' assessment of the relative abilities of the two candidates (i.e., there is a proxy fight). (Incidentally, a proxy fight should normally result in the best outcome for the firm, since it forces both rivals to take account of the wishes of the other shareholders.) When the takeover threat manifests itself, the incumbent then responds by altering his ownership share, and he can do so in one or both of two ways. First, he chooses his shareholding to maximise his expected payoff. As his shareholding rises, he benefits from a greater probability of retaining control, and hence has greater expected control benefits, but if his share is too high, the value of the firm falls and with it the value of his own stake. The incumbent manager therefore trades off the personal benefits he receives from being in control (e.g., his perks) against the capital loss he suffers from the fall in the value of his own stake. In addition, he can also manipulate his ownership share by altering the firm's outside equity stake. If he wishes to increase his share, the firm issues debt to repurchase outside equity; if he wishes to reduce his share, the firm issues equity and retires debt. Given that the private control benefits he receives fall as the firm's debt level rises – if one likes, one can think of higher debt as siphoning off the excess cash flow from which the manager can draw his perks – the optimal debt level (from his point of view) involves a trade-off between the benefits of using debt to retain control and the cost that using debt reduces the benefits of having control in the first place.

Exploitation of Takeover Threats by Passive Shareholders

While Harris and Raviv (1988a) focus on how the outcome of takeover contests can be altered by the incumbent himself altering his share, Stulz (1988) focuses on how the outcome can be affected by the incumbent's share being manipulated by passive shareholders. Since the incumbent is assumed never to sell his shares to his rival, the latter must therefore buy shares from the passive shareholders, and the number of shares he can obtain will rise with the price (or premium) he offers. The greater the incumbent's share, the greater the proportion of the remaining shares that the rival must buy up, and the greater the premium he must offer. Since the rival will only take over the firm if it is worth his while to do so, and control rents (i.e., the benefits from taking over) are assumed to be random, a greater required premium also implies a lower probability of the takeover actually taking place. A greater incumbent share therefore means that passive shareholders get a higher premium if the takeover goes through, but also lowers the probability of the takeover actually going. Passive shareholders want to maximise the expected premium they receive, so they trade off the greater premium they would receive from a higher incumbent share against the lower probability of receiving any premium as the incumbent's share rises. Since the incumbent's relative share can be influenced by the firm's leverage, as already explained, there is therefore an optimal leverage that maximises the passive shareholder's expected premium (or share value).

CONCLUSIONS: CORPORATE FINANCIAL POLICY AND ECONOMIC FLUCTUATIONS

The New Financial Theory of the Firm

It might be helpful to conclude the chapter by sketching out the view of corporate financial policy that emerges from the literature examined here as well as from related work that has not been discussed. This 'new view' is best illustrated by comparing it with the earlier Modigliani–Miller view of corporate policy and the neoclassical theory of investment. The Modigliani–Miller world assumes away all 'frictions' in markets – there are no agency problems, imperfect or asymmetric information, and so on – and so implies that corporate financial policy is not only independent of 'real' decisions (e.g., such as how much to invest), but also quite irrelevant. Real decisions are independent of financial ones because firms can get whatever finance they want at the 'going' rates, and therefore can (and do) always find finance for any worthwhile investment. Financial policy is irrelevant because there is nothing in this world to lead a firm to prefer one form of finance to another.

The neoclassical theory of investment is then a natural complement to Modigliani–Miller. As in Modigliani–Miller, there are no agency or information problems, the firm is not credit-constrained, and the firm takes 'the' interest rate as given. It then keeps borrowing and investing up to the point where the marginal rate of return on its investment has fallen to the same level as the interest rate. If the interest rate falls, it invests more; and if the interest rate rises, it invests less. The amount of investment is determined entirely by the expected marginal productivity of investment relative to the interest rate, and the firm can and will find whatever finance it needs.

The new view throws out the assumptions that there are no agency or information costs. Indeed, at one level, it is no more than a working-out of what happens when those assumptions no longer hold. Once we allow for agency costs, we can no longer presume that managers will always maximise the value of the firm, and it will normally be desirable for the firm to devote some resources to constraining management and aligning managers' interests to shareholders'. The existence of agency costs (as reflected, e.g., in excess cash flow considerations such as those of Jensen, 1986) and/or asymmetric information (which can produce market-for-lemons signalling costs) also means that firms do not have the unlimited access to funds at given cost assumed by Modigliani–Miller and Jorgenson. Firms can then face 'rationing' constraints, and we can no longer assume that they always find the finance for socially worthwhile investment projects even if managers wish to proceed with them. Financial constraints matter, and 'real' decisions can no longer be 'separated' from financial ones as the earlier approaches presumed.

This line of reasoning implies that there will be a difference between the costs of various types of finance, and in particular between the costs of internal and external finance. Certain forms of finance might then be unavailable to a particular firm or only available at a high cost. For example, issuing equity might be seen as a poor signal and lead to a fall in the share price, and this fall in share price might make equity so expensive to the firm that it becomes very reluctant to raise funds in this way. The firm would then be dependent on alternative sources of finance such as retained earnings or issuing debt. Frequently, however, it will also be difficult or costly for the firm to issue debt as well – for example, because of concerns about its credit-worthiness – and so the firm would be almost entirely dependent on raising funds internally. The new theory therefore places considerable emphasis on the availability of internal funds, especially for smaller firms that normally face greater external credit constraints, and the empirical evidence suggests that this concern is well-placed:

> Internal finance in the form of retained earnings generates the majority of net funds for firms in all size categories. The importance of internal finance would be even greater if we were able to include information on depreciation allowances, a source of internal funds roughly equal to retained earnings. Furthermore, the proportion of earnings retained by firms differs substantially by size classes. The average retention ratio is almost 80 percent for the smallest

firms [i.e., those valued at less than $10 million] ...; it drops monotonically as firm size decreases, to a low of about 50 percent for firms with assets of more than $1 billion. (Fazzari, Hubbard and Petersen, 1988, 146–147)

The existence of a gap between the costs of internal and external funds also implies that the availability of internal funds can be a serious constraint on firms' investment policies. A firm might have positive NPV projects, but lack the internal funds to invest in them and be unable (e.g., because of information problems) to obtain external funds at a price that makes it worthwhile to do so – the assumption of the neoclassical model that the firm can always obtain funds to finance worthwhile investments is then clearly vitiated. The prediction that investment is constrained by internal funds is also supported by a large number of recent studies which find that cash flow variables have a significantly positive effect on investment even when investment demand is already allowed for (see, e.g., Fazzari, Hubbard and Petersen, 1988; Gilchrist, 1990; Whited, 1992; Worthington, 1992; all for the US; Hoshi, Kashyap and Scharfstein, 1990, 1991 for Japan; and Devereaux and Schiantarelli, 1990 for the UK).[7] Indeed, these studies may *under-state* the true effect of cash flow variables on investment because they tend to focus on fixed rather than total investment, and Fazzari and Petersen (1993) suggest that the 'true' effect of a cash-flow constraint on investment demand could be considerably greater than results from this type of approach might indicate. In their model, firms need funds to finance both fixed and working capital, but since fixed capital investments involve considerable adjustment costs, firms respond to cash-flow shocks by smoothing fixed capital investments and letting working capital absorb the brunt of the adjustment. To the extent that fixed capital investments are being cushioned in this way, studies that look only at the effect of cash-flow shocks on *fixed* investments lead one to under-state the 'true' effect of cash-flow shocks on *total* investment. One therefore needs a model that looks at the effects of cash constraints on *both* fixed *and* working capital, and Fazzari and Petersen's results using such a model suggest that the effect on investment could be very severe indeed.

Since these financing problems arise from a firm's agency or information costs, it follows that any factor that reduces these costs should ease its financing problems. A particularly important implication of this principle is that an increase in the firm's collateral or net worth should make it easier for the firm to obtain finance, and a decrease should make it harder. Collateral and net worth therefore matter in ways that the Modigliani–Miller or Jorgenson approaches assume away. An increase in net worth should therefore lead to more funds becoming available for investment, which, if investment is constrained to begin with, should lead to a rise in the actual level of investment (see, e.g., Calomiris and Hubbard, 1990), and studies such as Fazzari, Hubbard, and Petersen (1988), Hoshi, Kashyap and Scharfstein (1990), Hubbard and Kashyap (1990) and others suggest that this effect is empirically important. As net worth falls, on the other hand, investment will be increasingly frustrated for lack of collateral, and, unless a firm has the internal funds to proceed on its own, there will come a point where it might become impossible for it to borrow. The ability of a firm to survive in such a financially distressed situation will then depend on its own internal cash flow.

Financial Factors and Macroeconomic Fluctuations

The emphasis of recent models on net worth and financial factors also has a number of important macroeconomic implications, most particularly for the ways in which shocks are transmitted through, and have persistent effects on, the economy.[8] In the models of Bernanke and Gertler (1989, 1990), for example, a positive shock to entrepreneurs' net worth reduces agency costs and leads to greater investment and greater income, and these factors further increase net worth and produce more investment and even higher income. Conversely, a negative shock to net worth can set in motion a downward cycle in which falling investment, falling income and falling net worth all reinforce each other and produce a downward spiral reminiscent of Fisher's earlier 'debt-deflation' process (Fisher, 1933; see also Gertler, 1990). Shocks to borrower net worth can therefore produce persistent investment and output fluctuations in either direction. The sensitivity of lending to net worth also depends on interest rates – if the riskless interest rate rises, banks might not be willing to push up loan rates because of the effect of higher loan rates on their expected default losses, so they decide to cut back lending instead. Given the presence of collateral constraints, a rise in market interest rates can therefore lead banks to cut back on lending, and a sufficiently large rise can lead them to stop lending entirely.[9]

Greenwald and Stiglitz find that the output multipliers associated with equity changes can be very substantial for highly levered economies.[10] Since increased uncertainty raises expected bankruptcy costs, higher uncertainty also causes agents to cut back on risk-taking and reduce investment (e.g., Greenwald and Stiglitz, 1988b, 1993). The Greenwald–Stiglitz model and others like it also generate other notable results:

- Depending on precise parameter values, it can generate macroeconomic cycles – not just macroeconomic fluctuations – that mimic some of the features of observed business cycles. Where cycles occur, output and equity rise together and lead to higher dividends and wages, but these two factors eventually reduce profit and working capital, and equity and output both fall. Wages and dividends fall, profitability is eventually restored, and equity and output start to rise again.
- These models generate a more pronounced change in the demand for capital goods than in the demand for consumer goods (i.e., they generate an accelerator effect). This result is an important one because the existence of accelerator effects is a well-established feature of observed business cycles.[11] An accelerator effect can derive from either or both of two factors: (1) Producer-goods firms could be more constrained in their access to funds than other firms, so a change in demand might imply a more significant relaxation in their collateral constraint. For example, longer time horizons or the greater

complexity of the products may create a bigger information asymmetry between insiders and outsiders. In addition, technology in these industries is typically capital intensive, and since such firms are often highly levered, small changes in their equity can produce large changes in the cost and availability of their funds. (2) An accelerator can also arise because it is natural for managers to cut back disproportionately on more risky activities in the face of a fall in their equity value, and capital investments are more risky than most.

- These models can also be easily extended to explain observed inventory patterns over the cycle. (Inventories tend to rise at the beginning of a recession, but then fall, and inventories only start to rise again on the upswing.) Greenwald and Stiglitz have a simple explanation for this behaviour: firms start the recession by building up their inventories to take advantage of lower production costs, but a point comes where their increased exposure to distress (e.g., higher bankruptcy, credit rationing, and so on) leads them to start cutting back on inventories, and the cutback in inventories is exacerbated by the fall in demand. By contrast, traditional models predict that inventories should be counter-cyclical because interest rates are low during a recession and firms would exploit cheaper costs to build up stock (i.e., inventories serve as buffers to permit production-smoothing). Traditional models therefore explain why stocks should rise at the beginning of a recession, but *fail* to explain why they should fall *before* the recession is over.

- Finally, this basic approach also explains the behaviour of employment, unemployment (including layoffs) and wages over the cycle. The depletion of capital base in a recession reduces the 'net' marginal product of labour – i.e., the marginal product less an allowance for hiring and production risks – because the cost of hiring and production risks rises. The wage rate therefore falls, and workers will prefer to wait out the recession if the wage rate falls below their reservation level (i.e., they choose to become voluntarily unemployed). The Greenwald–Stiglitz story also explains why the reservation wage itself might not fall (and, hence, why wages don't fall further). As Greenwald and Stiglitz observe, there are two problems with lowering current wages, with offsetting increases in future wages, to obviate the effects of a current lack of working 'equity' by the firm.

> First, the commitments of the firm to pay higher wages in the future may not be credible. Second, the individual [worker] in this position is, in effect, a supplier of a kind of equity capital: there is no fixed commitment to repay, even if the firm has the best of intentions. Thus, the usual moral hazard and adverse selection difficulties arise; it is precisely those firms that are in the worst financial position (e.g., Eastern Airlines) that will be most anxious to 'borrow' from their employees, and offer seemingly the most attractive terms. (Greenwald and Stiglitz, 1993, 110)

Unemployment also rises during a recession because working has an element of investment to it, and the high implicit cost of capital facing both workers and firms leads the former to demand a relatively high reservation wage and the latter to be more reluctant to employ. The fact that the erosion of the firm's equity base is only (expected to be) temporary also helps to explain layoff behaviour over the cycle.[12] The shock to the firm's equity reduces the 'net' marginal product of labour and leads the firm to lay labour off, but it re-employs that labour as its equity recovers and the 'net' marginal product recovers (Greenwald and Stiglitz, 1987, 449).[13]

4 Why Financial Intermediaries Exist

The essence of financial intermediation is the use of a third party to facilitate the transfer of information or wealth between two others. Financial intermediaries exist because they improve on unintermediated markets in which the 'ultimate' parties (such as borrowers and savers, or firms and investors) deal directly with each other without the use of any intermediary. An intermediary might be useful in a situation where investors want information about prospective investment projects, but are ill-placed or lack the expertise to collect that information themselves. The intermediary might then be able to provide that information at cost lower than that at which the investors could provide it for themselves. This type of intermediary is known as a broker, and there are many different varieties of brokers, including investment analysts, credit-rating agencies, auditing firms, and various other specialist information services. However, many intermediaries also go beyond the mere provision of information and actually invest on behalf of their clients whom they issue with claims against themselves. These intermediaries can be broadly divided into two types – banks and mutual funds – which are distinguishable from each other by the types of liability they issue. These latter intermediaries might also go beyond providing a conduit for borrowers and lenders to trade with each other, and provide the means of payment or a payments system that agents use to make payments to each other (e.g., by issuing currency).

There is an extensive literature on why financial intermediaries exist (see, e.g., Niehans, 1978, Chapter 9; Santomero, 1984, 577–80; Bernanke and Gertler, 1985; Chant, 1987, 1992; Lewis and Davis, 1987, Chapter 2; Sealey, 1987; Williamson, 1986; and Goodhart, 1989, Chapter 5), but the explanation for why intermediaries exist parallels very closely the explanations we have already given for financial contracts and corporate financial structure. In all these cases, the key is to relax one or more of the assumptions underlying the 'perfect markets' paradigm often used in finance theory. If markets are 'perfect' in the way this approach supposes, then *all* the factors that might plausibly lead to *any* financial structure in the economy – whether contract structure, corporate financial structure, the existence of firms themselves, or the existence of financial intermediaries – have been assumed away, and the economy has no institutional structure at all, including no financial intermediation.

We can therefore explain why intermediaries exist by introducing one or more market 'frictions' and showing how an intermediary can then produce an outcome superior to any that could be obtained without it. Note, therefore, that explaining why intermediaries exist is therefore more than just describing what they do. For example, one often meets the claims that intermediaries exist to pool risks or transform assets, to overcome unspecified information problems, or to issue exchange media, but these claims cannot be complete explanations in themselves because other institutions besides financial intermediaries also pool risks, transform assets and generally deal with information problems, and some of them have even been known to issue currency. More fundamentally, they also fail as explanations for financial intermediation because they do not identify what the intermediary accomplishes that could not otherwise be accomplished. It is therefore one thing to say that an intermediary does something, but quite another to explain *why* it does it.

INTERMEDIARIES REDUCE SEARCH AND TRANSACTIONS COSTS

Two relatively obvious ways in which intermediaries can improve on unintermediated markets are by reducing *search costs* (see, e.g., Chan, 1983; Chant, 1987, 1992; and Goodhart, 1989, 12–13) and *transactions costs* (see, e.g., Benston and Smith, 1976; and Chant, 1987). It will often be the case that some element of search activity must be undertaken if investors are to find suitable investment outlets or if firms are to find suitable sources of funding. Investors or firms could engage in that activity themselves, but it is often worthwhile for them to pay an intermediary to do it for them which can cut out the costs of duplicate searches and reap the economies to be gained from specialising in that search activity. Similarly, if individual contracts involve some element of transactions cost, an intermediary will often enable agreements to be made at lower overall transactions cost than would otherwise be possible. When an intermediary exists, a prospective borrower or lender can go to it instead of engage in an uncertain search for a 'direct' partner, and the intermediary can reduce transactions costs by reducing the total number of transactions required and by offering standardised terms on which it is prepared to do business. It can also reduce search and transactions costs by 'making a market' and being ready to deal on an ongoing basis. Sporadic, dispersed trading would be replaced by a central 'market' created by the intermediary which would be operated on a more or less continuous basis (see, e.g., Goodhart, 1989, Chapter 1). Prospective customers would know where they could trade, and they could be confident of trading on predictable terms at any reasonable time they chose. Duplicated searches would also be eliminated because the intermediary would have no reason to duplicate its own search activities.

The importance of intermediaries especially in reducing transactions costs has been appreciated for some time. Indeed, Benston and Smith (1976) went so far as to argue that reducing transactions costs is the very *raison d'être* of financial intermediation, but it is now clear that this claim is too strong and that the existence of intermediaries cannot be explained by transactions costs alone. As Chant (1987, 5) points out, their notion of transactions costs is vague and the 'assertion that transactions cost explain the existence of financial institutions is not very useful unless the nature of these costs is explained'. Chant then continues,

In the absence of uncertainty, an investor would need to hold more than one asset only to the extent that his portfolio exceeded the scale of the borrowers' needs. With such a mismatch, the number of transactions between lenders and borrowers cannot exceed the sum of the number of borrowers (the number of transactions that would occur with perfect matching) plus the number of lenders (the minimum number of carryovers from one lender to another caused by mismatches). An intermediary would need to make a transaction with each lender and each borrower. Therefore, the number of transactions required with the intermediary equals the number of transactions under the worst mismatching of lenders with borrowers. Financial intermediation, in this case, cannot produce any savings for the economy with respect to transactions costs. (Chant, 1987, 7)

The reduction of search and transactions costs by an intermediary has many dimensions. An intermediary could offer lenders the opportunity to reduce their risks by diversifying their assets at lower cost than they could manage themselves (see also Lewis and Davis, 1987, Chapter 2). Suppose, for example, that there are n investors and m projects. Each of the latter is owned by a separate entrepreneur and the returns to projects are not perfectly correlated. If each transaction imposes a fixed cost b on each person involved, then each investor diversifies his portfolio by investing in every project and faces transactions costs of bm. Total investor transactions costs would then be bmn. Similarly, entrepreneurial transactions costs would also be bmn. Hence, overall transactions costs would be $2bmn$. However, if all transactions were carried out through an intermediary, then each investor and each entrepreneur need carry out only one transaction each, and total transactions costs would be $2b(n + m)$. If transactions costs have any fixed elements, it is therefore cheaper to diversify through an intermediary if there are a high number of investors or investment projects (i.e., if n or m is high), and the cost savings increase as n or m get bigger. An intermediary can thus offer investors 'insurance' against shocks to asset values at lower (transactions) cost than they could otherwise manage.

An intermediary can also reduce the costs of 'insurance' against unexpected consumption demands (e.g., as in Diamond and Dybvig, 1983). If agents cannot predict exactly how much they will want to consume over any future period (e.g., because they may unexpectedly see something they want to buy), then their consumption demands will fluctuate unpredictably, and those who experience positive consumption shocks may want to borrow while those who experience negative ones will have 'spare' funds they could lend. If these shocks are imperfectly correlated, there may be potential for agents to make themselves better off *ex ante* by entering into 'mutual insurance' schemes in which agents agree that those who experience negative shocks lend to those who experience positive ones. If there are n agents and we assume that each such arrangement involves a fixed transactions cost b, then the cost of 'full' mutual insurance – i.e., where everyone 'insures' with everyone else – would be $bn(n - 1)/2$ in the absence of an intermediary. (Each agent would make $(n - 1)$ deals and there are n agents, so there are $n(n - 1)/2$ separate deals. Since each costs b, the total cost is $bn(n - 1)/2$.) If they set up an intermediary, each agent makes only one deal – with the intermediary – and transactions costs are bn. As bn is lower than $bn(n - 1)/2$ for values of n bigger than 3, it is clear that the cost savings from having an intermediary can be quite substantial where n is 'large' and there are many people involved.

Intermediaries can also facilitate trade by providing payments systems. An obvious example is the provision of currency to replace the use of physical commodities or IOUs as payments media. The use of physical commodities to make payments involves storage and portability costs, as well as an opportunity cost that arises because the commodity cannot (usually) be used for other purposes at the same time. The parties involved in trades might be able to reduce the need to rely on physical commodities by using IOUs instead, but the use of personal IOUs raises other problems (e.g., because the party accepting the IOU may not be confident that the other party will honour it). If the party accepting payment trusted a third party, on the other hand, he could accept the third party's IOU instead. An intermediary might also be able to facilitate transfers of wealth in other ways. For example, it might operate a wealth-transfer system that dispensed with the need to use a paper payments medium, or it could certify credit-worthiness and so enable an individual to use his own IOU to make a payment to someone who would otherwise reject the IOU because he did not trust him.

INTERMEDIARIES REDUCE MONITORING COSTS

There are also certain assets whose full values can only be realised by investing a certain amount of time and effort into monitoring their performance, enforcing compliance with covenant and other restrictions, and the like. A good example is where an investor makes a loan to a firm, but once the loan is made the entrepreneur has an incentive to slack because he bears the full costs of his effort but only gets part of the benefits. To maximise his return, the investor (or someone on his behalf) must then invest resources monitoring the entrepreneur to see that he does not slack and that covenant restrictions are complied with. We shall refer to assets that require monitoring to maximise their value as monitoring-cost assets. The existence of such assets gives another reason why an intermediary can sometimes improve on the outcome of an unintermediated market (see also, e.g., Diamond, 1984; Ramakrishnan and Thakor, 1984; and Chant, 1987):

First, an intermediary is often better placed to ensure that monitoring is done efficiently without unnecessary duplication. Where there are many investors, each investor might try to free-ride on the monitoring that he assumes the others will do. Alternatively, no monitoring might take place because each individual investor bears the full cost of his monitoring but gets only a fraction of the benefits, and so he judges monitoring not to be worth his while even though the investors as a group would benefit if some monitoring took place. In any case, even where an individual investor does decide to monitor, he might monitor less intensively than would be desirable. There is a danger, then, that monitoring might take place cursorily, or not take place at all. There is also a danger that there might be too much monitoring. Such an outcome could occur if a number of investors individually decided that others were not going to monitor, and if they each calculated that it was worth their while to monitor even though many of the gains from their monitoring would accrue to other investors. In this case we get productive efficiency – the entrepreneur is induced not to slack – but that productive efficiency is only obtained at an excessive monitoring cost. The point is, of course, that an intermediary can generate an improved outcome by ensuring that monitoring is done, but not duplicated needlessly.

The issues involved can be illustrated with a simple example. Suppose there are n investors in a project which yields each investor a return of unity if it is monitored, and $(1 - m)$ if it is not, and that it costs c to monitor. Suppose also that $mn > c$, so that it is socially worthwhile that at least some monitoring is done. If $c > m$, no individual investor would choose to monitor because it would cost him more to monitor than he would recover in terms of his own improved payoff – even though his monitoring would improve the payoff to everyone else as well and it is worthwhile that some monitoring be done. The aggregate return would then be $n(1 - m)$. However, if the monitoring were done by an intermediary who only needed to monitor once, then the aggregate return would be $(n - c)$, which would be substantially larger than $n(1 - m)$ for large values of n. The difference – $(nm - c)$ – represents the inefficiency of the unintermediated outcome relative to what an intermediary could achieve. If $c < m$, on the other hand, then everyone would monitor, assuming that no one tried to free-ride, $(n - 1)c$ would be needlessly wasted on duplicated monitoring, and the market would still be inefficient relative to the intermediary. The only situation where an efficient outcome would arise would be where one investor decided for some reason to monitor and the others all decided not to, but there is no particular reason to expect such an outcome if the investors' actions are uncoordinated. The unintermediated outcome would normally be inefficient, and an efficient outcome could arise only by chance. By contrast, the intermediary could deliver the efficient outcome every time.

Second, an intermediary is better placed to exploit the benefits of specialisation in the monitoring industry. Individual investors will typically lack specialist expertise in monitoring, and part of the reason they lack such expertise is that they have relatively little incentive to invest in acquiring it. A typical investor does not rely on monitoring to make a living; he therefore has little incentive to acquire any but relatively basic monitoring skills. In the absence of professional monitors, many of the potential gains to be achieved from monitoring activity would therefore never be reaped. Since many of the skills involved in monitoring require considerable effort and resources to obtain (e.g., a good monitor might need to know a lot of technical information about the activities of the firm he is monitoring), it is unlikely that a typical 'casual' investor would be willing to make the investments involved. The losses from having relatively inadequate, amateurish monitoring could then be quite high. What is required is for an intermediary to become a professional monitor who can reap the gains from investing in the acquisition of monitoring skills.

INTERMEDIARIES REDUCE VERIFICATION COSTS

It is often the case that the value of an asset to its owner depends on private information which he has but cannot pass on costlessly to someone else.[1] This information gap then drives a wedge between the value of an asset to its holder, and its value to anyone else. Imagine that an asset has a value of p, but the information that enables one to value the asset can only be transferred at some verification cost $c \leq p$. (If $c > p$ the information is of course effectively untransferrable.) If a purchaser wants its value verified before purchasing it, the act of sale is bound to involve the expenditure of c on verification, and the resale value of the asset is only $(p - c)$ regardless of who actually pays for verification. (If the purchaser is to pay for it to be verified, he will only be willing to pay $(p - c)$ for it. If the holder pays for it to be verified, he could charge him p but his net return would still be $(p - c)$.) Alternatively, the asset may be sold without verification, but at a discounted 'pooling' price p^* that reflects the market's inability to distinguish the asset from superficially similar assets, along lines similar to those of the market for second-hand cars in Akerlof (1970). Whether or not the asset would be verified would then depend on whether or not the pooling price p^* was bigger than the verification (or non-pooling) price $(p - c)$. The resale price of the asset would be max $[p^*, p - c]$ and the holder would suffer a resale loss of min $[p - p^*, c]$.

Since verification costs make an asset expensive to sell, an agent would buy these verification-cost assets only if he had some confidence about being able to hold them to maturity, other things being equal. A financial intermediary then has a potentially useful role if agents face consumption 'shocks' similar to those we discussed earlier – and even if there are no transactions costs. An agent who experiences a large consumption shock might find himself 'forced' to sell assets which he had earlier expected to hold, and if those assets involved verification costs he might have to sell at a loss. If these consumption shocks are imperfectly correlated across different agents, the parties involved can make themselves better off by forming an intermediary to provide them with 'insurance' against the contingency that they might have to sell assets at a loss. The larger the number of agents involved, the more accurately they can predict the average *per capita* consumption shock, and the lower their expected verification costs from having insufficient reserves. Indeed, if the group is very large, then it may be possible to diversify the individual consumption shock completely, and the group could ensure that verification costs were never incurred. If agents can (somehow) pool their resources, they can therefore 'insure' themselves against consumption shocks by reducing or even eliminating the expected costs of liquidating assets at a loss. Forming an intermediary is then an ideal way to make pooling operational. Instead of individuals buying verification-cost assets themselves, they would form an intermediary which would buy the verification-cost assets on their behalf, and it would do so by selling claims against itself to the investors and using the proceeds to buy the assets. The intermediary would be able to predict fairly accurately the average consumption shock experienced by its investors, and it would hold an asset portfolio that enabled it to meet expected demands for early redemption of its liabilities without having to experience significant verification costs itself. It could then pass the savings to its investors, offering them the option of early withdrawal to meet unexpected liquidity demands without incurring the verification costs they would have to pay if they invested on their own. An intermediary that invests on investors' behalf is thus an ideal way for agents to invest in verification-cost assets whilst simultaneously obtaining insurance against the verification losses that would otherwise arise from their own uncertain liquidity needs.

5 Broker Intermediaries

A broker is an intermediary who sells information, but does not purchase financial assets from his clients or issue financial assets to them (see, e.g., Ramakrishnan and Thakor, 1984; Chant, 1987, 3, 11, 21–2; Lewis and Davis, 1987, Chapter 2; and Allen, 1990). There are many different kinds of brokers – search specialists who bring buyers and sellers together, insurance brokers, credit-rating agencies, forecasting units, financial consultants, investment analysts, accounting firms that provide specialist advice and auditing services, and others – but they all sell information without taking a direct stake in it by buying the assets on which they report; other intermediaries also provide information, but a broker does *no more* than provide information.

Perhaps the most common reason for using a broker is that he can provide clients with information at a cost (or inconvenience) lower than that at which they can provide it for themselves. While individual investors might have difficulty assessing a prospective investment outlet, a broker with the relevant expertise could do the assessment for them and charge them accordingly. A good example is where an individual is interested in buying property, but cannot assess the property's state of repair. He therefore employs an expert surveyor to provide him with a report. Similarly, an individual investor might be considering a particular investment, but does not have the expertise or information to assess the investment properly, so he employs an expert who can assess it for him.

Apart from providing information at lower cost, a broker can also be useful in coordinating search activity to ensure that information searches are not needlessly duplicated. If a large number of investors are thinking about investing in a firm, there could be considerable replication of search activity if each investor felt obliged to screen the firm himself. This replication could be avoided by employing one party to collect the relevant information on behalf of the others (see, e.g., Ramakrishnan and Thakor, 1984, 416). Since there are obvious problems co-ordinating investors – investors are typically dispersed and unaware of each others' locations – a firm will often hire the intermediary to collect the information and publish the results to all who might be interested. In this way one search is done, but all potential investors get the benefit, and the firm can recover the cost of the search by charging its clients later. Another example is where the shareholders (or potential shareholders) of a firm want reassurance that their investments are (or would be) in good hands, but auditing the firm's statements is costly, and, perhaps for some shareholders, effectively impossible. There is also a problem of co-ordinating the monitoring efforts of different investors. The firm therefore responds by hiring an independent auditor to produce a report on behalf of all the shareholders. Once again, a single search is done, but all interested parties benefit.

THE LIMITS OF BROKERAGE

The Reliability Problem

A major problem with brokerage is to ensure that the information the broker sells is reliable. If clients are to commission him in the first place, they must be reasonably confident that the information he would produce would be sufficiently reliable to make his services worth their price (see, e.g., Hirshleifer, 1971; Allen, 1990). The solution is for the broker himself to take some sort of stake in the reliability of the information he sells (i.e., to post a bond of some sort). An obvious way to post a bond would be for him to take a direct stake in the information he provides – if he provided information about investment opportunities, he could promote clients' confidence in his judgement by himself investing in those projects he claimed were best – and many intermediaries do exactly that (see, e.g., Leland and Pyle, 1977; Campbell and Kracaw, 1980). However an intermediary who took such a direct stake would cease to be a broker as such and become a mutual fund or a bank instead. By definition, a broker must provide reassurance in a different way.

If he cannot buy directly into the product or asset about which he provides information, he can often provide reassurance using his own wealth to guarantee that his product will satisfy certain measurable standards of quality. For instance, a lawyer might take legal liability for a service he provides, and a dissatisfied client can sue him later if he has reason to suspect malpractice. The lawyer's own wealth then stands as surety to the service he sells. The same principle is at work with accounting companies that guarantee the quality of their audits with the personal wealth of their partners. The operative principle in both cases is that the seller uses his own wealth to guarantee that his service comes up to some objectively verifiable standard, but its application in practice is to some extent limited by the broker's wealth. The lower the broker's personal wealth, or the lower the net worth of the brokerage firm, the weaker that guarantee will be. The value of the guarantee is also constrained by the fact that it might be necessary to go through a perhaps difficult and costly verification process to determine whether malpractice has actually taken place.

Because of these limitations, brokers in practice often offer guarantees of a slightly different sort. Instead of pledging their relatively limited current assets, they seek to pledge their future brokerage income by cultivating a 'good' reputation which can then be offered as a hostage to guarantee their performance. Since clients want to distinguish 'good' brokers from 'bad' ones, every broker will want to appear to be 'good' – the genuinely good ones to distinguish themselves from the bad ones, and the bad ones to imitate the good ones so that the public cannot tell them apart. The good ones therefore seek a means to distinguish themselves in a way that makes it as difficult as possible for the bad ones to follow them, and one way in which they can do so is by building up reputational capital (i.e., a good reputation) that would be jeopardised if they were to exploit their clients. Clients can then have some confidence in the broker based on the knowledge that a broker who misbehaved would damage his reputation and thereby reduce his own future income (see, e.g., Ramakrishnan and Thakor, 1984). The greater the broker's reputation, other things being equal, the more he has to lose from misbehaviour, and the more confidence a potential client can have in him. Since he could only build up a good reputation by abstaining from misbehaviour or incompetence, a bad or incompetent broker would be reluctant or find it difficult to imitate him. A good reputation then sends out a credible signal of the broker's true quality, and a client who wants a good broker need do little more than make sure he chooses a reputable one. He would therefore choose a broker on the basis of a personal recommendation from someone he trusted, or pick one who had a good measurable track record (e.g., an investment analyst with a knack for picking winners), had himself frequently monitored (e.g., by an independent auditor), or was unlikely to disappear suddenly because he had been around for a long time and had made a clear commitment to the local community.

Many sellers of information go further and establish their own professional associations to stipulate acceptable standards, monitor individual brokers' performance and identify those who do not come up to par. The good brokers would naturally want to join such an association, and the bad ones would feel obliged to. Minimum standards, policing arrangements, punishments, and grievance procedures would be set by the association itself and its primary task would be to protect the reputation of the members as a group by publicly identifying those that did not meet its standards. One of the strengths of such a club is that the good brokers can effectively call the shots because the bad ones would be afraid of exposing themselves. The latter would come under pressure to meet minimum standards that they secretly oppose but cannot prevent, since either of the alternatives – leaving the association themselves, or letting the good brokers form their own more stringent association – would expose them to the general public. All brokers who wish to appear reputable would have to join, but once they have done so, the threat of expulsion would limit the extent to which they can exploit their customers or act in ways that bring the profession as a whole into disrepute. The net gain, from the public's point of view, is an increase in the average quality of brokerage services provided by members, on the one hand, and the public identification of bad or incompetent brokers, on the other.

The Resale Problem

The other serious problem with brokerage is that of preventing resale. The problem is that once a broker has sold information to a client, the client can sell the information himself and thereby undercut the broker's market. Competition between the broker and his former client can then drive down the resale price of information to a very low level and often mean, in effect, that the broker can only sell his information once. If it is to be worthwhile for him to provide the information in the first place, the broker must then charge a price high enough to make a reasonable profit on the first sale. The price of his information might then be considerably higher than it would otherwise have been. Indeed, in some cases it might be so high that no one would buy it and there would no longer be any point in the broker collecting it in the first place. The problem of preventing resale can therefore drive up the price of information or even destroy the market for it altogether.

A natural solution is for the intermediary to invest in the assets about which it collects information. As Allen (1990) points out, while a broker can only capture part of the surplus created by the information he provides, an asset-holding intermediary can capture all of it (e.g., by buying up the whole of a debt issue). However, investing in the relevant assets is not the only answer, and as already explained, a broker cannot do so and still remain a broker. An alternative solution is for one party buy the information on behalf of all. Instead of selling information to individual investors, and thereby running into resale problems, a broker can sell the information to the firm in whose debt the investors are interested. The firm would then make the information freely available, and the issue of resale would never arise. It is also sometimes possible to circumvent the resale problem by raising the cost of passing on the information. For example, a software producer can destroy the market for copies of his work by copy-protecting the disks he sells so that those who want them have to buy from him. In other cases, the resale market can be undermined by alternative institutional arrangements. A professional association might require its members to refrain from trading in the second-hand market and expel those who were found to have done so. Alternatively, the initial seller could insist on copyright protection and certain rights of inspection. A computer producer might insist as a condition of sale that he has the right to inspect institutions that use his hardware (e.g., educational establishments) to check that any software being used on those machines had been legally obtained. The fact that he might not be able to spot pirated copies being taken would then be less of a problem if he had the means to catch those who are using it and sue them for damages.

TYPES OF BROKERS

Despite these limitations, there are many situations where we would expect to see brokerage taking place. Almost by definition, brokerage is best suited to situations where parties want to buy information, but do not want any further involvement from the party who sells that information. An investor might hire a broker to provide him with information about a firm, but might not want the party he hires to invest funds on his behalf, or a firm might want a broker to help find investors, but might not want to obtain funds directly from a mutual fund or bank. If brokerage is to 'work', there needs to be some reassurance about the reliability of the information provided, but there are various ways in which brokers can provide that reassurance – by providing guarantees of (measurable) standards of service, by cultivating valuable reputations that they can lose if their service deteriorates, by accepting liability for deficiencies in the information they provide, and by joining professional associations that can enforce standards and punish those who fall short of these standards. We can therefore explain why purveyors of information like accounting firms are so concerned about their public reputations, why they are concerned about professional standards and associations, why they take the form of unlimited liability partnerships, and the like. For brokerage to thrive, there also need to be ways to prevent the profitable reselling of the broker's information. The desire to circumvent the resale problem then helps to explain why brokers are so often commissioned by the firms that issue debt rather than by the investors who buy it; it also helps to explain why so much brokered information is either client-specific information that has little resale value or else is information that can easily be detected if illicitly passed on.

Rating Agencies

Before ending the chapter, it might be useful to give some more detailed examples of real-world brokerage. One important form of brokerage is a *credit-rating* agency. If debt is to be priced appropriately, market operators need to assess the credit-worthiness of the issuer, and rating agencies provide them with the information to do so:

> The credit rating is an expert opinion of the likelihood that a debt issue will pay principal and interest on time. The rating is provided by a rating agency, an independent company which provides expert financial analysis and opinion to the markets. (Blitzer, 1992, 537)

Ratings are provided on new issues of fixed income securities such as corporate bonds, commercial paper, municipal and government debt, Eurobonds, bank certificates of deposit, preferred stock, and a variety of other debt instruments (see, e.g., Cantor and Packer, 1994, 3). They are also provided on existing security issues through to maturity.

Rating agencies in their modern form initially developed in the nineteenth century, but the industry has grown very rapidly over the last twenty-five years. The best known rating agencies in the US are Standard and Poor's Corporation and Moody's Investors Services, but other agencies have established themselves more recently as additional major players in the US rating industry. There are also specialist agencies that focus on particular sectors such as banks or insurance companies, as well as major rating agencies in Britain, Canada, and Japan. Rating agencies

> maintain large staffs of professional financial analysts with extensive training and experience in credit analyses of issuers and their bonds ... Typically, the agency will examine publicly available data such as prospectuses, annual reports and regulatory filings. The agency staff will meet with the debt issuer to review the issuer's financial condition and recent business developments.

Information discussed at these meetings is confidential. After these issuer meetings and further internal review, the rating agency publishes the rating and, usually, its analyses. In some rating agencies, the debt issuer is advised of the rating and may ask for a second meeting to offer additional information or to argue for a better rating. At the conclusion of this 'appeal' process, the rating is published. (Blitzer, 1992, 537–538)

The rating agency's opinions are summarised by 'rating' a debt issue according to some scale. For example, Standard and Poor use a scale ranging from AAA at the top, followed by AA, A, BBB and then finally D, and ratings may be refined further by the addition of a '+' or '−' after the letter scale. The higher ratings – in Standard and Poor's case, any rating equal to or above BBB– – are regarded as 'investment grade', and anything lower as 'speculative' or 'junk' grade. The lower the grade, the lower the probability of timely repayment, and the greater the perceived risk of the issue. Since the rating gives a signal of the default risk of the issue to the investor, investors usually respond to the signal by charging an appropriate premium or, in more serious cases, by refusing to buy the debt at all or selling what they already hold (e.g., many institutional investors are bound by fiduciary requirements that restrict them to buy only investment grade debt). The rating therefore affects the cost of issuing debt, but can also affect the availability of funds as well.

Traditionally, rating agencies would receive payment for their work by charging for publicly issued reports, but their ability to earn profits in this way was severely limited by a resale problem: once a report was out, people could copy it fairly easily and thereby undermine an agency's ability to profit further from it. Agencies responded to this problem by increasingly charging the firms they rated, with the fees involved being agreed before the firm is rated. Firms will often agree to pay for rating because rating would influence the cost of their borrowing. A good firm would willingly pay for rating because it would expect to receive a rating that reduced the cost of issuing debt and more than paid for the cost of the rating itself. Given that good firms would signal themselves by paying for ratings, rational investors could assume the worst of any firm that did *not* have itself rated and punish it accordingly (e.g., by charging high risk premiums). The desire to avoid this punishment would then give any firms other than the very worst ones an incentive to have themselves rated. Most firms would therefore agree to be rated, and investors could by and large ignore those that did not.

The key to the rating business is credibility. Firms will pay for ratings only if they believe that investors will respond to them, and investors will only respond to them if they are credible. A rating agency's overriding object must therefore be

to maintain a reputation for high-quality, accurate ratings. If investors were to lose confidence in an agency's ratings, issuers would no longer believe they could loser their funding costs by obtaining its ratings. As one industry observer has put it, 'every time a rating is assigned, the agency's name, integrity, and credibility are on the line and subject to inspection by the whole investment community' ... Over the years, the discipline provided by reputational considerations appears to have been effective, with no major scandals in the ratings industry of which we are aware. (Cantor and Packer, 1994, 4).

The incentive to maintain standards is also reinforced by other factors. One of these is the ability of other analysts to monitor rating agencies – in particular, to rank their relative performance and highlight their mistakes; the desire to avoid damaging publicity then provides a very strong incentive to avoid rating mistakes. In extreme cases, a rating agency also faces the threat of court action by injured parties, and such action could be very damaging to the agency's reputation even if the plaintiff is unable to prove malpractice or incompetence on its part. Finally, incentives to maintain standards are typically reinforced by ownership structures that avoid serious conflicts of interest: rating agencies tend to be either independently owned or owned by financial companies.

Security Analysts

Since they do no more than assess default risk, rating agencies provide only part of the information that investors might want before making investment decisions. A measure of default risk is not sufficient to determine whether a particular debt issue is a good investment or not, and measures of the riskiness of various debt issues are in any case of little help to investors considering other securities such as equity. Investors therefore need all sorts of other information and advice that ratings agencies do not provide. There is thus a need for *security analysts* to provide this more heterogeneous information about security issues, provide independent assessments of firms' prospects, and advise clients on their investment decisions:

> Few individual investors have the time or skill to determine the true worth of large publicly available corporations. However, all are forced to make far-reaching personal investment decisions. Consequently, when investors trade securities, many rely on outside counsel. Usually, their premier concerns are safety of principal and freedom from administrative hassle. People want to avoid costly mistakes but they would also like to receive a 'fair' return on capital. (de Bondt, 1992, 435)

The same writer continues a little later,

> In any event, much financial information and advice is sold, directly or indirectly, by security analysts employed by brokerage houses. Further, large institutional investors, money management firms and investment banking companies employ analysts in-house. The analysts prepare detailed studies of individual stocks and bonds, make careful comparisons between companies

(resulting in industry reports) and form expert opinions on their likely future earnings and investment performance. (de Bondt, 1992, 435)

Similar issues of credibility and reputation arise with security analysts as with rating agencies. Analysts are acutely concerned about their reputations and try to provide reassurance to clients and potential clients in much the same ways as rating agencies do.

Auditors

Another important brokerage function is *auditing* (i.e., verifying management reports). Audits are a useful means of dealing with the agency problems that arise between shareholders and managers (see, e.g., Watts and Zimmerman, 1983; Antle, 1984; and Ball, 1989). Apart from slacking off by managers and other forms of moral hazard, agency problems can also be reflected in managers distorting the information they provide to shareholders. If they can get away with it, managers that are so inclined can use distorted reports to provide a smokescreen that allows them to pursue their own inclinations at the expense of the shareholders whom they are nominally supposed to serve. The purpose of auditing is therefore to verify management claims and to report on any irregularities the auditors find. The prospect of being caught out by an audit then helps to keep a potentially dishonest or incompetent management in line.

The origins of auditing go back a long way. The historical evidence of Watts and Zimmerman (1983, 615) suggests that 'audits were common in early English business corporations, the medieval craft and merchant guilds, and regulated and early joint-stock companies'. Their work also suggests that auditors had strong incentives to be independent. For example, the medieval auditor

> could be heavily fined for not completing the audit in due time. In addition to that cost, lack of performance and independence affected the auditor's reputation and, in the extreme, caused loss of his guild membership and his share of the guild's monopoly profits. In one case, at least, the guild auditors had to own property. Presumably this requirement made it easier to recover damages against them if they breached the contract, thereby providing the auditors with further incentives to report a breach, if one occurred. (Watts and Zimmerman, 1983, 618–619)

The incentives of medieval auditors were strengthened further by the use of audit committees rather than a single auditor, a practice that encouraged auditor performance and made collusion between management and the auditors more difficult. As Watts and Zimmerman (1983, 625) observe, 'The survival of the committee of auditors for six hundred years strongly suggests that it was an efficient monitoring device'; it also flatly contradicts those historians who 'argue that the method was inefficient on the basis of the frauds which occurred in the seventeenth to nineteenth centuries' and draw the conclusion that effective corporate control required government regulation. In the words of the historian R. W. Scott, writing in 1912,

> the methods of control and of internal organization were far from perfect, [but] they were much better than might have been expected, considering the times ... Despite some instances of fraud, carelessness and profligacy on the part of agents abroad, numerous instances can be quoted of a remarkable devotion to duty, whilst among the directors ... there was a large-hearted disinterestedness, united to a careful supervision of business, which is highly commendable. *It is noteworthy that out of the great number of companies, whose officers have been investigated in this work, the allegations of fraudulent management are comparatively rare.* (quoted in Watts and Zimmerman, 1983, 625–626, his emphasis)

The fact that auditing survived so long in the absence of legal restrictions compelling its use is thus strong evidence of the role it plays in effective corporate governance.

In the nineteenth century, the older form of auditing by directors or shareholders gave way to auditing by professional auditors brought in from outside, but the use of professional auditors had already become widespread well before the passage of legislation making their use mandatory. Later legislation on compulsory auditing must therefore be interpreted as enforcing what was already standard practice. Watts and Zimmerman suggest that the switch to professional auditing can be explained by two principal factors. The first was an increased demand for auditing services arising from the increasing number and complexity of firms, and the latter in particular presumably meant that the old amateur auditing procedures were proving less effective. The second factor was the growth of professional accountancy which provided a low-cost means of certifying auditor competence and independence. Professional accountancy associations originally arose to provide information that enabled people to choose reputable accountants as bankruptcy trustees. These associations soon adopted their own entry requirements, codes of behaviour, disciplinary procedures, and qualifications, and in so doing provided the public with valuable information about the competence and integrity of their members. Once professional accountancy associations had been set up to enable members to handle trustee cases, it was then relatively easy for the same associations to certify their members' suitability for auditing as well. The rise of professional auditors was thus, in part, a natural outgrowth of the development of professional accountancy.

6 Mutual-fund Intermediaries

A mutual fund can be defined as a financial intermediary that issues its own liabilities and uses the proceeds to buy income-earning assets, but issues only one kind of liability (see, e.g., Glasner, 1987; Cowen and Kroszner, 1989; and Wicker, 1988). A mutual fund therefore differs from a broker in that it holds assets and issues liabilities as part of its intermediary function; it also differs from a bank in that it issues only a single class of liability – which, since it is a claim to the fund's residual income, can usually be regarded as a form of equity – while a bank issues at least two types of liability, namely, debt and equity. Alternatively, a mutual fund can be defined as an investment company that invests deposited funds in a portfolio of investments, but is set up in such a way that shareholders (or residual claimants) and depositors are identical (see, e.g., Ippolito, 1992, 831).

Mutual funds are an important part of modern financial systems and have grown spectacularly in the last two decades. They include not only the institutions that go by that name in Canada and the USA, but also many thrift and similar institutions in those countries, as well as the unit trusts, investment trusts, building societies and friendly societies found in the UK (see, e.g., Goacher *et al.* 1987). Mutual funds date from the early nineteenth century and were typically formed to enable groups of small investors to profit from diversification opportunities that would otherwise be unavailable to them (Brauer, 1992, 375). Given the search, transaction and other fixed costs of making investments, the only investors that could effectively diversify their portfolios before mutual funds came along were institutional investors or rich individuals. The typical small investor had to make do with a relatively undiversified portfolio and bear the corresponding risk. Mutual funds gave such investors the opportunity to pool their funds and invest in a diversified portfolio that none of them could invest in on their own:

> Funds usually specialize in certain types of investments, including growth stocks, income-producing stocks, small-firm stocks, short- or long-term bonds, tax-exempt bonds, precious metals, international stock, and the like ... Individuals can also invest in a money market fund which specializes in high-grade, short-term securities that offer market returns on cash-equivalents, and permit cheque-writing privileges. (Ippolito, 1992, 832)

Apart from thrift and related institutions that went by different names, there were about 100 mutual funds operating in the USA by the end of the 1920s. However, most were wiped out in the 1929 crash and they only started to become prominent again in the 1970s (Brauer, 1992, 375). They then grew very rapidly in the 1980s and by 1984 there were 1247 funds operating in the USA with a total of $370 billion in assets. By 1989, the number of such funds had grown to 2918 and their assets to $970 billion (Ippolito, 1992, 832).

Early funds were usually run on a trustee basis, which meant that a fund's investment portfolio was more or less fixed and little else was required once the fund was set up but for trustees to ensure that procedures were followed and payments made on time. Later on, funds began to allow more scope for investments to be changed in response to changing opportunities and funds employed managers to make investment decisions for them. The older trustee fund then largely gave way to the actively managed fund, and a modern mutual fund in the USA will often have a turnover of 50 percent a year or more. Since turnover itself imposes a drag of perhaps 0.5 percent a year on the fund's net worth, and the personnel and related costs of active management usually come to between 0.5 and 1 percent of the fund's worth each year, actively managed funds must perform significantly better than alternatives such as trustee funds or indexed securities if they are to be competitive (Ippolito, 1992, 831).[1]

OPEN-END AND CLOSED-END MUTUAL FUNDS

Mutual funds can be divided into *open-end* and *closed-end* funds (or, to use UK jargon, *unit trusts* and *investment trusts*). An open-end fund is one in which the fund itself stands ready to buy and sell its own shares each trading day at the going market rate. The price of the share, in turn, is equal to the value of the fund's assets *minus* allowable costs (e.g., for management), all divided by the number of shares outstanding. The number of shares thus varies directly with the public's demand for them. On the other hand, with a closed-end fund, the number of shares is fixed and the fund itself neither buys nor sells its own shares. If an investor in a closed-end fund wishes to get rid of his shares, he cannot therefore sell them back to the fund that issued them. Instead, he must sell them on the market for whatever he can get. Most funds tend to be open-end, but there is still a substantial minority of closed-end ones.

Open-end Mutual Funds

When a fund is open-end, it must buy and sell shares on demand according to a specified exchange rule. Since a share is a claim to a proportion of the fund's assets, the fund will respond to a demand to redeem shares by selling off an appropriate proportion of its assets and handing over the proceeds to the investor who demands redemption. The size of the fund then shrinks to reflect the lower public demand for its shares. When a member of the public asks to buy shares, on the other hand, the fund simply issues him with new shares and invests the proceeds by purchasing additional quantities of the assets in its portfolio. If the fund initially has 100 shares and has an asset portfolio consisting of x amount of asset one, y amount of asset two, and so on, the fund would use the proceeds to buy $x/100$ of asset one, $y/100$ of asset two, and so on. In other words, the fund would simply scale up the size of its asset portfolio, keeping the composition of that portfolio (substantially) unchanged.[2] The size of the fund's asset portfolio (and, hence, the size of the fund itself) would therefore change *pari passu* with changes in the demand to hold the fund's liabilities.

It is easy to show that the fund should set the price of its shares equal to the net value of the fund's assets divided by the number of shares. Suppose the fund set the share price higher than this value. If there are n shares outstanding and the net value of the fund's assets is $A, the fund would then be ready to buy and sell its shares at a price of $(A + \varepsilon)/n$, where $\varepsilon > 0$. Since the total share value (i.e., $(A + \varepsilon)$) exceeds the value of the fund's assets (i.e., $A), a rational investor would appreciate that the fund could not buy back all its shares at this value. He would also appreciate that if he redeemed at this rate, he could convert his proportionate share of the fund's assets (i.e., A/n) into cash or some equivalent asset worth $(A + \varepsilon)/n$, and make an arbitrage 'profit' of ε/n. He would also realise that doing so would leave the fund with $[(A - \varepsilon)/(n - 1)]/n$ assets left per remaining investor, so there would be even less left in the fund, per investor, than there was before. The next investor would therefore have a stronger incentive to redeem, the one after him an even stronger one, and so on. Because the fund had over-priced its shares, it would be using up the assets implicitly 'belonging' to those shareholders who do not redeem to pay off the over-valued claims of those shareholders who do. The assets left per investor would fall with each redemption, and if redemptions continued the fund would eventually run out of assets even though it still had shareholders who had not yet been paid off. Faced with this prospect, our rational investor would decide to redeem his share as quickly as possible. Other shareholders would naturally do the same, and the fund would face a run that led to the loss of all its assets.

If the fund priced its shares too low, on the other hand, it would face an unlimited demand for its shares. Imagine that the fund stood ready to buy and sell shares at a price of $(A - \varepsilon)/n$. An investor who held the actual portfolio held by the fund but was not a fund shareholder could then sell his portfolio, use the proceeds to buy fund shares that were a claim to exactly the same portfolio, and make a profit in the process of ε/n. Investors would therefore sell their direct holdings of the asset portfolio and convert them into fund shares which were an indirect claim on the same portfolio. By selling shares at too low a price, the fund is giving away the wealth of its initial shareholders to everyone who buys new shares, and investors would clamour for new shares and continue to do so for as long as the fund's shares were underpriced.

The fund therefore has little choice but to set its share price equal to the net value of its assets divided by the number of shares (i.e., A/n). This pricing rule then implies that share prices should be marked up or down in accordance with changes in the value of the fund's asset portfolio. If the value of the fund's assets rose by 50 percent, the fund would automatically increase the price of each share by 50 percent. If the value of the fund's assets fell by 50 percent, the fund would automatically mark down its share price by the same proportion. All gains or losses on the fund's portfolio would be passed directly (and immediately) to shareholders by appropriate changes in the share price.

The actual equilibrium market price of fund shares must then be equal to the price at which the fund itself stands ready to buy them. Were the market price to be greater than the fund price, agents could make arbitrage profits by buying shares from the fund and selling them on the market. The supply of fund shares on the market would rise, and the market price would fall. Since arbitrage profits could be made for as long as the market price exceeds the share price maintained at the fund itself, and the latter is given by the fund's pricing rule, the exploitation of arbitrage profits would drive down the market price to the price maintained by the fund. If the market price were less than the fund price, there would be arbitrage profits to be made from buying up fund shares in the market and selling them to the fund, and such operations would drive up the market price to the fund price. The only equilibrium price on the market is the price at which the fund itself stands ready to buy and sell its shares.

The actual size of the fund is then determined by the public's demand for fund shares, which is determined by investors' perceptions of the expected return, risk and perhaps other characteristics of the fund's portfolio relative to the relevant characteristics of other investment opportunities. Should the fund's portfolio become more attractive than alternative investments – because the expected return on the fund's portfolio rose relative to expected returns elsewhere, say – the demand for fund shares would rise. Members of the public would demand more shares from the fund over the counter, and the fund would issue them with shares as demanded at the prevailing price. The number of shares would rise, and the fund would use the proceeds to scale up the size of its investment portfolio. Should the demand for fund shares fall, the fund would face shareholders demanding that their shares be redeemed. The fund would respond by selling off appropriate quantities of fund assets – one can think of fund tellers sitting at computer terminals sending 'sell' orders to market traders for each shareholder who demands redemption – and using the proceeds to meet redemption demands. The size of the fund's asset portfolio would then fall along with the number of outstanding shares. The size of the fund's portfolio and the number of fund shares thus vary directly with the public demand for fund shares. Competition among fund managers should then ensure that funds provide the portfolios – the 'right' balance of risk and return, and so on – that the public want.

Closed-end Mutual Funds

Closed-end mutual funds differ from open-end ones in that they do not buy and sell their own shares once the funds themselves are up and running. The economic forces that determine the value of the shares of closed-end mutual funds are therefore somewhat different from the forces determining the prices of the shares of open-end funds. If markets were perfectly frictionless with zero search and transactions costs, 'perfect' information, and the like, it is immediately apparent that the price of a mutual fund share – the price of a share in a closed-end fund as well as the price of a share in an open-end one – must be the same as the price of the security bundle to which each share is an implicit claim: if there are n shares and the fund has assets worth $\$A$, the fund's share price must be $\$A/n$. If the price were higher or lower than $\$A/n$, investors would make arbitrage profits by converting their indirect claims on the fund's security bundle into direct claims, or by doing the reverse, and these arbitrage operations would return the price of fund shares to its par value of $\$A/n$. In practice, of course, markets are not without frictions, and mutual funds would have no reason to exist if they were. Once we allow for 'frictions', we must also allow for the possibility that the actual fund price might deviate from the 'par' price – remember that with closed-end funds, there is no redemption mechanism either, and so investors cannot force the price back to par by redeeming or buying shares at the fund itself. The empirical evidence suggests that these deviations exist and can sometimes be quite substantial. For example, Brauer (1992, 375) reports that US share price deviations from par for closed-end mutual funds ranged from a premium of more than 35 percent in one case to a discount of more than 25 percent in another, and Matatko (1992, 526) reports that investment trusts in the UK usually have share prices trading at a discount relative to par.

MUTUAL FUND LIABILITIES

The fact that a mutual fund by definition issues homogeneous liabilities has important implications, perhaps the most important of which is that it makes it difficult (and, in the case of open-end funds, extremely difficult) for the fund to issue debt. If a fund issues debt, then it must issue *only* debt, since its liabilities are homogeneous. If the fund is open-end, there can be no difference, in equilibrium, between the value of the fund's assets and the value of its liabilities, and so the fact that the face value of its liabilities is predetermined means the fund must choose assets whose nominal values are also predetermined. Indeed, it must choose assets whose nominal values are not only predetermined, but whose total nominal value is actually the *same* as the total nominal value of its liabilities. It is very difficult to see how a fund could find an asset portfolio that satisfied this condition: virtually all assets have some risk, and the fund could only hold risky assets to the extent that the risks perfectly cancelled out and left the portfolio itself riskless. Should there be any portfolio risk, the fund would be open to a run if it suffered losses on its portfolio, and to potentially infinite demands for shares if its portfolio increased in value. A open-end fund that issued debt would therefore be highly unstable and unlikely to survive (see also McCulloch, 1986a, 80, n. 1). These speculations are borne out by the experience of a number of funds which faced runs once they tried to make their liabilities more fixed in nominal value and news arrived that they had suffered losses on their assets. This happened to the Provident Institute in the UK in April 1986, for example, and Mervyn Lewis reports similar cases in Australia (see Goodhart, 1989, 186, n. 1).[3]

A closed-end fund that issued debt would still have difficulties, although it would not be open to the same arbitrage attack as its open-end counterpart. In the absence of the fund trading in its own liabilities, there is no real mechanism to make the fund's debt trade at par, and so the most likely response to any major shock to its asset values would be an alteration in the market price of its debt. For example, if the fund's asset value rose through the roof, there would be a strong incentive for someone to try to buy up a controlling interest in claims against the fund so that they could get their hands on the fund's capital gains, and the result would be a rise in the price of fund debt. If the value of the fund's assets plummeted, on the other hand, there would be a strong incentive to ditch fund debt, and the price of fund debt would fall. However, one must bear in mind that the ability of fund debt to trade at non-par prices is limited, and a major negative shock could occur that left the fund unable to repay its debts, and therefore left fund debt effectively worthless. Even a closed-end fund would therefore have difficulty issuing debt. Nor is it obvious why it would want to, or why investors would be willing to buy debt from it.

OPEN-END MUTUAL FUND ASSETS

Regardless of whether they issue debt or equity liabilities, open-end mutual funds also have difficulties holding imperfectly marketable assets. Assets are imperfectly marketable if they can only be sold at some loss. The most obvious example is where there is a verification-cost problem as in Akerlof's market for second-hand cars (Akerlof, 1970). In this kind of situation the seller of an asset has more information about the asset's quality than a buyer, so resources must be spent to verify the seller's claims or else the asset will sell at a pooling price reflecting the market's perception of the average quality of similar assets trading on the market. Either way the asset can only be sold at a loss relative to its 'true' value. Resale costs can also include the costs of the time and effort involved in finding a buyer and negotiating with him, and these costs are particularly important for heterogeneous assets whose 'true' values might not be immediately apparent. The principle that mutual funds should avoid imperfectly marketable assets also makes it difficult for a fund to hold monitoring-cost assets unless a relatively cheap means is found to share the monitoring cost burden among the different investors. If the fund itself does the monitoring but other investors hold similar claims against the firm being monitored, then those other investors would have an incentive to free-ride on the fund's monitoring and the fund would find it difficult to compete.

There is also the problem of how to handle losses arising from investors' demands for redemption. Imagine that a fund only holds assets that can be sold at a loss, but an investor wishes to redeem his shares. The fund therefore has to sell off assets at some cost, but who should bear the cost? If the fund passes the loss to the shareholder, the latter would regard his shares as illiquid, because of the cost of redeeming them. If he values liquidity, he would often be reluctant to buy the shares in the first place. Why buy illiquid shares, when he can presumably invest in other mutual funds or banks that offered more liquid investments? The alternative is for the fund itself to absorb the loss, but then the fund effectively over-prices its shares and we run into the earlier problem of losses being passed back to other investors, thereby inducing them to run to escape 'their' share of the losses. To some extent, the fund can respond to this dilemma by holding liquid assets in its portfolio – if fund managers can predict redemption demands accurately, they can then avoid losses by holding liquid reserves to meet such demands. However, the underlying problem still does not go away. Even if fund managers can predict the proportion of investors who experience liquidity shocks that lead them to demand redemption, there is still the danger that the other investors (i.e., those who do not experience liquidity shocks that force them to redeem) might 'panic' and decide to demand redemption as well (see, e.g., Diamond and Dybvig, 1983, and Chapter 9 in this volume). The prospect of losses resulting from a high number of redemption demands could trigger fears that actually brought about a high number of redemption demands, exhausted the fund's liquid assets, and led to losses from the need to sell less marketable assets.

The only way to avoid this problem entirely is for the fund to hold *only* marketable assets. The much-vaunted 'transparency' of the assets of open-end mutual funds is therefore a reflection, not of any intrinsic advantage on the part of such funds, but of their inability to hold other assets. This transparency is a symptom of their weakness, not of their strength, and it is misleading to argue, as mutual fund enthusiasts sometimes do, that open-end funds are superior to banks because they have a transparent asset structure and banks usually do not. Banks hold imperfectly marketable assets in their portfolio because they are able to cope with the problems such assets pose and still find it worthwhile to hold them. A bank *could* restrict itself to holding marketable assets and thereby enjoy the benefits of transparency, but it usually *chooses not to*. An open-end fund has little choice but to avoid imperfectly marketable assets and make the best of its enforced transparency.

STABILITY OF OPEN-END MUTUAL FUNDS

Granted that they do not hold assets that expose them to resale costs, open-end mutual funds can then accommodate even large shifts in public demand without causing major disruptions. One of the attractions of mutual funds to its proponents is that they can accommodate large shifts in public demand whilst largely avoiding the external effects commonly attributed to a falling demand for bank liabilities (e.g., Cowen and Kroszner, 1989; Glasner, 1987). If a fund experiences a large fall in demand, it simply sells off the appropriate proportion of its assets and scales down its size accordingly. Provided their assets are fully marketable, there are no losses involved and open-end mutual funds are more or less run-proof. To see why, suppose there are n investors, each holding a claim worth $\$A/n$. If one of them redeemed and fund assets were sold off at no cost, there would be $\$(A - A/n)$ assets left in the firm, and so each remaining shareholder would have a claim to

$(A - A/n)/(n - 1) = \$A/n$ assets. The remaining shareholders would therefore be unaffected by the first one selling out. By induction, they would also be unaffected by two or more shareholders selling out. A shareholder would therefore have no reason to run to demand redemption because he sees others demanding redemption or because he thinks that they might do so in the future. The fund is therefore run-proof.

Open-end mutual funds are also stable in another sense. If we assume that asset markets are efficient and reflect available public information, then the prices of fund assets should adjust to new information almost immediately it becomes known. The funds' share-pricing rule ensures that the prices of fund shares should also adjust rapidly, and fund investors would have no incentive to sell fund shares merely because fund assets have fallen in value – they cannot avoid the losses by selling fund shares. Asset market efficiency therefore eliminates any 'arbitrage motive' for running on a mutual fund. A second possible source of a run – shareholders' fear that fund managers have private information which they will use against them – is also substantially eliminated because the transparency of funds means that managers should have little or have no private information to use anyway. Shareholders might still demand redemption for other reasons – they might have liquidity needs, or change their risk-return preferences, or lose confidence in the fund manager – but funds should be substantially immune to runs driven by arbitrage or shareholders' lack of information.

In this respect funds are very different to weakly capitalised banks. If such a bank suffered losses on its asset portfolio, the fall in its net worth could lead depositors to fear that the bank might be unable to redeem their deposits in full. If a bank operates a first-come, first-served rule to redeem deposits, then a signal that the bank is in difficulties can provoke a run as depositors scramble to beat each other to recover their investments. By contrast, open-end mutual funds are immune to this danger provided they hold marketable assets, because the observation that the fund has experienced losses on its assets gives fund shareholders no reason to demand redemption. With mutual funds there is 'no "bonus" to being first to withdraw' and so

> random noise will not induce runs on mutual fund 'banks' ... those who needed to withdraw would take a loss rather than imposing losses on all parties through a suspension and possible liquidation. (Cowen and Kroszner, 1988, 14–15).[4]

WOULD MUTUAL FUNDS ISSUE EXCHANGE MEDIA?

Another controversial question is whether open-end mutual funds would issue exchange media:

> If mutual funds really could provide payments services efficiently, it would be natural to expect money market mutual funds ... to begin announcing bilateral

or multilateral arrangements to permit check writing in any amount for purposes of transferring wealth to accounts in participating funds. By this service, each participating fund would enhance the spendability and hence desirability of its shares relative to nonparticipating shares and demand deposits. (L. H. White, 1984b, 708)

This naturally leads one to ask what obstacles exist, if any, to prevent the emergence of a payments system based on mutual funds? Several obstacles have been suggested:

The first is that people prefer to write cheques on deposits of predetermined value, and the value of claims on mutual fund investments cannot normally be predetermined.[5] When an individual hands over a cheque, it must have a fixed nominal value, but the mutual fund share on which the cheque is a claim will vary in value. This means that unless an individual constantly monitors his balance – which itself imposes costs – then he will have to write cheques on a balance whose value is unknown to him. If the value of his balance is lower than he expects, he might write too many cheques and overdraw his account. If the mutual fund has a policy of refusing to honour overdrawn accounts, he will be forced to hold larger balances to be confident of his cheques being honoured, and he may prefer a fixed-value deposit with a bank instead. A mutual fund could of course monitor accounts and grant temporary overdrafts, but in doing so the fund would be acquiring non-marketable assets and accepting the associated monitoring problems that mutual funds are supposed to avoid.

A second problem arises in the clearing of mutual fund cheques. There will be a delay between the writing of a cheque of any given value and its clearing, and the value of the portfolio of assets on which the cheque is drawn will typically change in the interim period. The possibility of such a change means that someone has to accept a risk – a risk that typically does not arise when cheques are drawn against accounts at banks. If the person taking the cheque were to accept the risk, then he would presumably charge a risk-premium to cover it. Apart from making it more expensive to write cheques against mutual funds, the required risk-premium would probably vary with the individual and the mutual fund on which the cheque is drawn. This would make it difficult to agree on prices at which trade could take place, and therefore discourage trades from taking place with mutual-fund exchange media. The exchange media issued by banks would therefore be generally more acceptable than those issued by mutual funds.[6]

CONCLUSIONS

Mutual funds have certain attractions. They enable small investors to benefit from diversified portfolios that might otherwise be unavailable to them. Mutual funds can offer investors a large variety of portfolios tailored to their individual risk-return preferences, and competition among funds will keep their operating costs down. To the extent that they avoid imperfectly marketable assets, open-end mutual funds can also avoid some of the instability problems to which regular banks are sometimes exposed. Indeed, provided they are properly designed, open-end funds are effectively run-proof.

Nonetheless, mutual funds are also subject to serious limitations relative to banks, and these mean that there is little reason to expect them ever to displace banks as the dominant form of financial intermediary: (1) They are ill-suited to meet the very large demand among investors for debt-type investments. (2) Open-end funds have difficulty holding imperfectly marketable assets. If funds wish to hold such assets, they need to forgo redeemability and be closed-end funds, but that means that their shares must be fairly illiquid. A mutual fund can *either* issue redeemable (and therefore liquid) liabilities *or* it can hold imperfectly marketable assets, but it cannot do both. Yet banks *can* do both, and often specialise in doing so. (3) The fact that mutual funds' liabilities typically vary in value puts them at a disadvantage relative to banks in the provision of exchange media.

7 Bank Intermediaries

DEFINITION AND CHARACTERISTICS OF BANKS

A bank is a financial intermediary that holds assets and issues liabilities, but issues at least two classes of liability – typically, forms of debt and equity – with differing claims to its assets in the event it defaults.[1] A bank is like a mutual fund in so far as it is a financial intermediary that invests on its own account, and issues claims against itself to the 'ultimate' investors who provide the funds it invests. However, a bank is unlike a mutual fund and like most other large firms in capitalist economies and in so far as it has a capital structure consisting of two or more distinct classes of liability. Indeed, one can think of a bank simply as a debt-and-equity-issuing firm that is engaged in the business of financial intermediation, in a manner analogous to the way in which, say, a typical steel-producing company is a debt-and-equity-issuing company engaged in the business of making steel.

Banks are (and always have been) the dominant form of financial intermediary. In their comparative study of international banking, Frankel and Montgomery observe that

> Banks have consistently provided over half of net external finance in both [Germany and Japan] ... [and] continue to provide more than twice the funds that direct securities markets provide. Data for Britain, while less stable than for Germany and Japan, show that there too banks dominate the provision of external financing. (Frankel and Montgomery, 1992, 266, 268)

Banks are particularly dominant in the provision of short-term finance, and in all major countries bank loans are still much greater than the next largest source of short-term commercial and industrial finance.

The institutions we recognise as banks have five notable empirical characteristics. The first is that they have a high ratio of financial to 'real' assets, relative to firms whose principal business is non-financial (Lewis, 1992b, 121). Virtually all firms hold both financial and 'real' assets, but a non-financial firm typically holds mostly 'real' assets (e.g., factories) while a bank mainly holds financial ones such as bonds, loans or equity. A bank's real assets mainly consistent of its own offices and equipment, and these are only a fraction of its total assets. This first characteristic therefore merely reflects the fact that a bank's main line of business is financial intermediation. The second empirical characteristic is that bank liabilities tend to be much more liquid than the liabilities of most other firms. To give an illustration, Lewis (1992b, 121) notes that over 80 percent of bank liabilities in the UK are either redeemable on demand or on seven or less days' notice. The reasons for the liquidity of bank liabilities will be explained presently.

The third characteristic, related to the second, is that many bank liabilities are transactable, i.e. are used as media of exchange. Obvious examples are banknotes and cheques drawn against chequable deposits. The fourth characteristic is that banks' assets usually have much longer terms to maturity than their liabilities, and are therefore generally less liquid. Banks thus 'transform' relatively illiquid longer-term assets into relatively liquid short-term liabilities. Finally, banks are more highly levered than other firms. For example, US banks had a capital – asset ratio of 12 percent in 1926 while non-financial firms had a ratio of 60 percent; in 1986, the US banking industry had a ratio of well under 10 percent – and in fact even lower, after allowing for measurement problems – while non-financial firms had an average ratio of 26.1 percent (Kaufman, 1992, 386–387). The banks' lower capital asset ratios might reflect a perception that the banking industry is safer than most other industries, and therefore has lower capital adequacy requirements; however, it also appears, especially in the USA to reflect regulatory policies that have encouraged banks to run down their capital and rely for their safety on deposit insurance guarantees or expectations of central bank bailouts, but we shall have more to say on these issues in due course.

Banks Compared to Mutual Funds

Banks are like mutual funds in that their main line of business is to accept investments from large numbers of (often relatively small) investors and lend out these funds to large numbers of borrowers. However, banks differ from mutual funds in offering their investors more than one choice of investment contract; they can therefore exploit the various economies that arise from specialisation *among* investors. In the simplest case, a bank might issue two sorts of liability. The first is a debt instrument that would promise specified payments to its holders in non-default states and give them first claim to the bank's assets in the event of default by the bank. The second would be an equity claim whose holders would be the claimants to what is left of the bank's assets after debt-holders have been paid. Since an equity share is a claim to what is left over, and the left-over is usually unpredictable, the equity-holders would therefore be residual claimants whose claims would absorb any shocks in the bank's net value.

There are a number of reasons why the debt–equity distinction is important for banks; these reasons very much reflect the capital structure issues discussed in Chapter 3:

- If investors differ in their attitudes towards risk, then issuing liabilities with differing risk-characteristics is generally Pareto-superior to a issuing single liability because it allows investors to exploit the gains from trading risk.
- Issuing debt and equity helps to economise on monitoring costs by specialising the monitoring function between different investors. Since equity-holders are residual claimants, they have considerable incentive to inform themselves and monitor the bank management. If equity-holders are still willing in those

circumstances to bet that their claims are safe (i.e., by continuing to hold them), then debt-holders can credibly conclude that their own claims are reasonably safe as well, without so much need to monitor themselves. Debt-holders can therefore rely on equity-holders to much of the monitoring for them.

• If equity-holders are residual claimants and primary monitors, it is also generally efficient to give them overall control of the way the bank is run. Provided that the bank meets its debts, they would get most of the marginal gains from any increase in the surplus created by the bank, but they would also suffer most of the loss from any bank inefficiency they tolerated. Debt-holders on the other hand have relatively little interest in the bank beyond wishing to ensure that it can meet their claims. It therefore makes sense to give the share-holders overall control, though their freedom of operation would naturally be subject to the constraints implied by the contracts the bank has made with other parties. Equity-holders would therefore be responsible for the appointment of management, the contracts under which management operates, and the monitoring of its activity. In practice, there are also economies to be gained from specialisation among share-holders and from the delegation of some of their monitoring to shareholder representatives (e.g., a board of directors).

• Lastly, if equity-holders maintain an adequate capital buffer, the bank can always be confident of being able to meet unexpected contingencies by issuing more debt, if it should need to do so; the bank can then hold imperfectly marketable assets (i.e., assets that can only be sold at a loss) without having to worry unduly about being forced to sell them before they mature. The bank could also buy assets that needed to be monitored without being pressured to reveal the information obtained from its monitoring; the bank could then develop relationships with borrowers where it could protect their confidentiality without alarming debt-holders who were not privy to the bank's 'private' information.

Banks Compared to Other Debt–Equity Firms

It is also useful to compare banks to other (i.e., non-financial) firms that issue debt and equity. The traditional banking literature tends to overemphasise the difference between banks and non-financial firms, and therefore overlooks important similarities between them. As Sealey asks,

> what distinguishes the operations of banks from those of other firms? All firms transform assets. GM transforms human capital, physical capital ... etc., into automobiles. Consumers prefer the transformed package put together by GM to the one they can put together themselves. Keep in mind, as well, that the transformation need not be physical as in the case of automobile production. A refrigerator bought at the factory by a wholesaler and sold to the ultimate consumer, although physically unaltered, is nonetheless transformed in a production sense. Moreover, all firms are two-sided in their

operations (or more accurately, multi-sided) in that they buy and sell in a number of markets ... In fact, financial intermediaries, particularly banking intermediaries, have more in common with GM than with the commonly assumed financial market agents such as [money market] mutual funds who are assumed to have unlimited ability to arbitrage, short sell, and otherwise costlessly transact. (Sealey, 1987, 427)

Banking firms are also similar to other firms in that they use up substantial amounts of real resources. The banking literature has traditionally disregarded this aspect of banking, on the (often implicit) presumption the 'real resource' aspects of banking and the 'financial' or 'portfolio' aspects, on which most of the existing literature concentrates, can somehow be separated' (Baltensperger, 1980, 2). This disregard of the 'real resource' aspects of banking has combined with the tendency of researchers in other fields to disregard the 'finance' aspects of other businesses to reinforce the widespread but misleading view that banking is somehow intrinsically 'different' from other businesses. In practice, the real difference is mainly one of emphasis: all firms hold financial as well as real assets, but as befits their role as financial intermediaries, banks differ from non-financial businesses in having a much greater ratio of financial to real assets.

In other respects, banks face much the same qualitative problems as other debt-and-equity firms – they hold many imperfectly marketable assets, they seek to maintain capital adequacy and keep their debt-holders' confidence, they seek to protect their liquidity, and so on. Banks do of course face the constraint that their liabilities are usually redeemable on demand or at short notice, but other firms also face the problem of ensuring that debt-holders continue to hold their debt, and the difference between banks and other firms in this regard is again primarily a difference of degree. Any firm that lost its debt-holders' confidence would lose its ability to raise further credit, and its existing debt-holders would seek to redeem their holdings as soon as they could (i.e., they would run). (Share-holders might also try to sell out while they still have the chance, in which case the firm's equity value would also collapse, and in so doing give debt-holders even more inducement to run.) The main difference between a bank and a typical non-financial firm in this regard is that a bank run would be more or less immediate, but the debt-holders of other firms can only run when the debt instruments they hold actually mature. But even this difference might not matter much in practice because the loss of a firm's credit-worthiness will usually be enough to drive it to default and/or lose see its share value collapse anyway.

BANK PORTFOLIO MANAGEMENT IN GENERAL TERMS

Bank Liability Management

Before getting into more specific issues, it would be helpful to examine bank portfolio management in general terms, and we begin with bank liability management. The key issue here is of course the bank's balance between debt and equity. The bank capital issue has always been regarded as extremely important by banking analysts and more 'traditional' academic treatments of banking (see, e.g., Benston *et al.*, 1986; Benston and Kaufman, 1988; Kaufman, 1987; and Gardener, 1989), but has received remarkably little attention in the more formal theoretical literature. In his 1980 survey, Baltensperger observed that it has been 'almost completely disregarded in most analytical models of bank behaviour. Often, it is not mentioned at all, and in the remaining cases it is usually treated as exogenous and does not perform any meaningful role in the model' (Baltensperger, 1980, 10; see also Pringle, 1974, 779–80).[2] Relatively little has changed since then, as the survey of the recent theoretical literature in Chapter 9 will make clear. It is ironic, too, that theoretical treatments in *other* areas than banking have also emphasised the importance of capital. The reader will recall from earlier chapters the extensive literature on how 'insiders' could use capital to post bonds to reduce agency costs and reassure 'outsiders' that their investments are safe (e.g., Jensen and Meckling, 1976; Leland and Pyle, 1977; and Bernanke and Gertler, 1985, 1987, 1989; and many others); yet, with the exception of a relatively small number of papers (e.g., Gorton and Haubrich, 1987; Dowd, 1988c, 1993b; Eichberger and Milne 1989) and Bond and Crocker, 1993), the insights of this theoretical work have yet to be applied specifically to banking. We therefore have the rather peculiar situation that the traditional 'informal' literature on banking has always recognised the importance of bank capital, and economic theorists have recognised for some time the importance of capital issues more generally, but there has been relatively little attempt to incorporate the insights of this work into the theoretical banking literature as such.

The basic analysis of the breakdown of the bank's liabilities between equity and debt closely parallels the debt–equity discussions of Chapter 3. An investor has to choose whether to hold debt or equity, and holding debt gives him three potential advantages: it imposes on him a less costly monitoring problem than holding equity; it keeps down his expected losses from bankruptcy, assuming bankruptcy costs are non-trivial, because these costs can only be passed on to him after the firm has gone bankrupt and the share-holders' resources have been exhausted; and if he is risk-averse, debt also has the advantage of a more certain return. It follows, then, that the return anticipated by an equity-holder must exceed that promised to a debt-holder by a sufficient margin to compensate equity-holders for these factors.

However, it does *not* follow that it is always cheaper for a bank to issue debt than to issue equity, because a bank that issued an 'excessive' amount of debt relative to its equity base would erode debt-holders' confidence that it could honour its obligations. The greater the bank's leverage, other things being equal, the less likely is the bank's capital buffer to withstand shocks that might hit it and the greater the expected bankruptcy costs faced by debt-holders. If the bank was excessively levered, it would have to offer debt-holders a higher interest rate to compensate them for their increased expected bankruptcy losses and the increased monitoring they consequently felt obliged to undertake. If they were risk-averse, the bank would also have to compensate them for the greater risks they were taking by continuing to hold the bank's debt. The 'true' marginal cost of issuing debt would therefore start to rise, and a point may even come where no amount of promised interest would induce the public to continue to hold the bank's debt. Its debt–equity ratio would have risen so high that its equity was no longer sufficient to give debt-holders the reassurance they want. The debt-holders would have lost whatever confidence they previously had, and the bank would face a run and probably be driven out of business. If the bank is sensibly run, however, its managers would appreciate these consequences and take steps to increase their equity before the bank's debt rose to manifestly harmful levels.

The value of the bank can also fall when the debt–equity ratio gets too low. A very low debt–equity ratio implies an 'excessive' proportion of equity-holders and, hence, an 'excessive' amount of shareholder monitoring. Since the bank has to pay for this monitoring by offering equity-holders higher expected returns, a bank that was excessively capitalised could increase its value by a debt–equity swap that retired equity for debt and reduced unworthwhile shareholder monitoring and, hence, the bank's payments for such monitoring. If equity-holders are risk-averse, a debt–equity swap might also raise the bank's value by reducing the payments the bank makes to equity-holders to compensate them for the risks they are bearing.

As with any other firm that issues debt and equity, there is therefore an optimal debt–equity ratio somewhere between these extremes. For banks especially, this ratio will be one low enough to ensure that debt-holders' claims are relatively safe without debt-holders having to do much monitoring, and at the same time high enough to avoid the costs of excessive monitoring or risk-bearing by bank equity-holders. Should the debt–equity ratio deviate become too high, the bank would intervene at some point to bring it back down, and if it should fall too low, it would intervene to bring it back up again.

Bank Asset Management

We turn now to the asset side of the bank's portfolio management problem. Following on from our discussion of the debt–equity decision, we can safely assume that the bank maintains a capital buffer sufficiently high to convince debt-holders that its debt is safe. The essence of the bank's asset management problem is then to maintain an appropriate balance between marketable and imperfectly marketable assets. Marketable assets can be bought and sold continuously at a zero or near zero trading cost; imperfectly marketable assets cannot be traded at zero cost, but promise higher expected returns than marketable assets. (If they did not, the bank would of course never choose to hold them.) However, given that it cannot predict redemption demands perfectly, a bank that held only imperfectly marketable assets would frequently find itself embarrassed by redemption demands that it could not immediately meet. Since each such embarrassment would have a cost (e.g., a legal fine, or the cost of a lawsuit, or just bad publicity), the bank wish to avoid at least some of these costs by holding reserves of appropriate media to meet redemption demands. These reserves would consist of 'till cash' in some form, or whatever else the bank uses to pay off debt-holders when they demand redemption. Given that this primary reserve will often yield a low return – 'cash', for example, would yield no return at all – the bank might also to supplement its reserves of redemption media by a secondary reserve of other marketable assets. These would yield a higher return than its redemption assets, but would give it additional reserves on which it could draw if the need arose, without having to sell its imperfectly marketable assets at a loss. The bank's own experience would then give it some indication of the optimal trade-off between these three types of assets.

The upshot is that a bank would normally hold three different classes of assets. The first class would be imperfectly marketable assets that could only be sold at some cost, but which promise relatively high returns if held until maturity. The degree of illiquidity will vary considerably, and may range from assets that have no resale value at all, at one extreme, to nearly liquid assets that can be sold off at relatively low cost, at the other. The banker's intention would be, as far as possible, to hold these assets until maturity to realise their high returns. In order to help him to do so, given the unpredictability of demands for redemption, he would also hold marketable assets that could be used to satisfy such demands at little or no cost. These marketable assets would not bear the high returns expected of the other assets, but they would have the compensating advantage of enabling the bank to meet redemption demands at lower cost than would otherwise be the case. The bank's holdings of marketable assets can then be subdivided into primary and secondary reserves. The primary reserve is its holdings of redemption media, that is to say, its holdings of whatever assets it can use to satisfy redemption demands directly (i.e., by literally handing them over to meet redemption demands). For example, if the bank's contract with its debt-holders specifies that the bank will redeem its debt with gold coins, the bank's primary reserve will consist of its holdings of gold coins; if the bank's contract specifies that the bank will redeem its debt with gold coins or the notes of specified other banks, its primary reserves would consist of its holdings of gold coins and the notes of those other banks; and so on. In addition to this primary reserve, a bank will also hold a secondary reserve consisting of other marketable assets that yield higher returns than the primary reserve, but can be liquidated if necessary to meet redemption demands.

The actual assets to be used as redemption media would be specified in the contracts the bank makes with its debt-holders. For example, if IBM shares were the redemption medium, and the dollar was the accepted medium of account, the bank would hand over $1-worth of IBM shares for each $1 note presented to it. Under *laissez-faire* conditions, a bank could offer the public any redemption medium it liked, but a bank that offered one that the public did not want – like bricks, perhaps – would risk losing its market share to competitors who were willing to provide the public with the redemption media they wanted. The competitive process should therefore ensure that banks would converge on the public's most preferred redemption media.

For banks other than the largest ones, the most likely redemption medium would almost certainly be the debt of another bank (e.g., a small town bank would offer as its redemption medium the notes of or cheques drawn against a big city bank), but it is likely that the biggest banks in the system would want to use some 'outside' redemption medium. Physical commodities are one possibility, but involve considerable storage, handling and portability costs, and barring sentimental reasons (e.g., nostalgia for gold), it is arguable that they would be unlikely to survive as redemption media in a competitive market. The alternatives to physical commodities are financial instruments, but not all 'outside' financial instruments would be equally suitable as redemption media. An ideal redemption medium would have an easily recognisable value, impose minimal obligations (e.g., monitoring obligations) on its holder, bear a 'reasonable' expected rate of return, and have a stable value. A bank might also want an instrument which it could buy or sell reasonably quickly and easily, if it needed to, so the redemption medium would also need to be traded on a fairly active market. However, in practice, a bank might not be able to find an 'ideal' redemption medium that satisfied these conditions, and would therefore have to make do with the next best medium (or media) available (e.g., it might have to accept a redemption medium with a low expected return).

SPECIFIC ISSUES IN BANK LIABILITY MANAGEMENT

The Redeemability of Bank Debt

Having set out the bank's portfolio management problem in general terms, we can now address various specific issues in more detail. We therefore return to the liability side of the bank's balance sheet, and begin with the issue of the redeemability of bank debt. The process of issuing debt involves a commitment undertaken by the issuer to redeem (or buy back) the debt at a specified future time (or at some time over a specified period) for a redemption medium of specified nominal value. This contract might take one of two basic forms. The first is one that requires the holder to wait a certain period of time before he obtains his funds. The contract therefore has a maturity period of positive length (e.g., as a bond does), or else requires the holder to give prior notice of his intention to withdraw his funds (e.g., as with a term deposit). The second is debt that gives the holder the right to demand his funds at any time, without prior notice. Such debt is *redeemable on demand* (or *demandable*). The most obvious example is a demand deposit, but in the past banknotes were often demandable as well. The reader will recall that most bank debt is demandable or redeemable at very short notice, and the liquidity of their debt is indeed one of the principal empirical characteristics of real-world banks as opposed to other debt-issuing firms.

So why is so much bank debt demandable or near-demandable? The answer relates to the cost of providing demandability being low, on the one hand, and to demandability providing certain benefits to debt-holders, on the other:

The Cost of Demandability

The main cost of demandability is the cost of the extra (i.e., precautionary) reserves that a bank must maintain to be able to meet unexpected demands for redemption. If a bank issues debt that requires notice of withdrawal, by contrast, it can use this notice to predict its redemption demands and then make provision to meet them, *without* any need to maintain precautionary reserves to meet uncertain redemption demands (see also Goodhart, 1989, 61, n. 3). The cost of demandability is consequently the cost of the precautionary reserves held by a bank that issues demandable debt.

Nonetheless, there are reasons to expect the cost of the additional reserves required by convertibility to be very low:

- Provided that demands for redemption are independently distributed – a reasonable assumption under most circumstances, assuming there are no undue concerns about the bank's soundness – the central limit theorem implies that the variance of aggregate demands for redemption will fall as the bank grows in size, and so aggregate demands for redemption will become increasingly predictable. The larger the number of bank customers, the more predictable aggregate redemption demands will be, and, hence, the lower the cost of offering demandability. In the limit, indeed, demands for redemption would be as predictable with redeemability on demand as they would be if the bank's debt required notice, and the cost of demandability would fall to zero.

- The bank need only concern itself with redemption demands that might occur sufficiently soon that there would not be time to obtain reserves from elsewhere. It is arguable, therefore, that the only reserves the bank really needs are the 'till reserves' to see it through the length of time it would take to get more reserves in. If matters got desperate (e.g., because a customer came in with an extremely large demand for redemption), the bank can always resorting to time-honoured delaying tactics such as paying out in small coins, while a courier went off post haste to fetch more reserves. Provided it has suitable credit available, a bank can usually operate quite safely with very low reserves in its tills.

- The evidence suggests that free banks could operate safely on very low reserve ratios, and therefore with very low reserve-holding costs. For example, Munn (1981, table 25) presents data for a sample of Scottish free banks in the 1820s and 1830s which indicate that these banks' specie holdings were in the region of 1 percent of their demand liabilities. If we take the opportunity cost of holding reserves to be 5 percent, then the cost of holding reserves equal to 1 percent of liabilities would be 0.05 percent of the aggregate value of liabilities. Bearing in mind that the bank would still have to hold *some* reserves even if it offered only non-demandable debt, the cost to the bank of offering demandability would therefore be even lower. If Scottish banks could operate on such low reserve ratios so long ago, the various technological and other improvements that have taken place since then suggest that modern free banks ought to be able to operate on even lower ones. Reserve-holding costs might also be lowered further under *laissez-faire* conditions because banks have an incentive to use income-earning assets as reserves and redemption media rather than 'sterile' assets such as gold coins or the (non-interest-bearing) notes of other banks. The opportunity cost of holding reserves could then be considerably less than the gross return on alternative assets, and total reserve-holding costs would be even lower. The costs to the banks of offering demandability thus appear to be very small indeed.

Demandability Can Reduce Monitoring Costs

Demandability also provides certain benefits. One benefit, emphasised by Calomiris and Kahn (1991), is that demandability reduces debt-holders' monitoring costs. In their model bankers have a comparative advantage in making investments, but if depositors are to have the confidence to make deposits with them, some means must be found to control the agency problems that arise between the bankers and their depositors. (We can think of a certain amount of monitoring already being done by bank share-holders, but some additional monitoring also needs to be done by depositors as well if these agency problems are to be properly controlled.) The bankers therefore need to pre-commit themselves to a contract structure that gives the debt-holders maximum protection, and the contract structure that provides the most protection is one in which debt-holders have the right to withdraw at will.

The ease with which banks may be forced into liquidation, far from being an unfortunate consequence of the contracting structure, [thus] turns out to be central to [it], since it gives the depositor or note-holder the right to reclaim his assets at any time and put them beyond the banker's reach (Calomiris and Kahn, 1991, 498).

The banker then faces the ever-present threat of a run and can only stay in business if he can maintain the confidence of a sufficient number of his debt-holders. The demandable contract thus gives a banker a means he would otherwise lack to pre-commit himself not to 'misbehave'. It follows, then, that while demandable debt can sometimes lead to costly liquidation *ex post*, it is often Pareto-superior *ex ante* because it creates investment opportunities for depositors that would not otherwise exist.

The demandable contract also gives the depositors appropriate monitoring incentives. Since a depositor has the right to redeem at any time, there is some incentive for depositors to monitor frequently to see if any information comes to light that might lead them to believe they would be better off withdrawing. However, one of the problems with multiple monitoring is that some depositors might feel tempted to free-ride on the monitoring done by others, and if monitoring is to take place at all, there must be some private incentive for some depositors to monitor even if they believe that others will not. The demandable contract resolves this problem, at least partially, by means of the *sequential service constraint* – that is, the first-come, first-served rule – that demandability necessarily implies. The incentive to invest in monitoring is that one becomes aware of a problem with the bank before other investors do, and so one can rush to the bank to be first in the queue to redeem one's deposit. Other depositors can free-ride if they want to, but if they do so, they take the risk that they end up at the back of the queue, and those at the back of the queue are the ones most likely to lose their deposits. There is thus a three-sided relationship:

> The monitors pay the costs of vigilance but receive the benefit of knowing that they will be 'first in line' (and thereby receive a higher payment than other depositors) should it become necessary to withdraw their funds from the bank. The depositors who do not monitor are willing to pay the price of being last in line in 'bad' states, because they receive a benefit in return: the active monitors keep the banker in line and thereby provide a benefit to the passive depositors. Depositors need not reveal whether they are active or passive; the same contract works for both types. (Calomiris and Kahn, 1991, 500)

The bank is consequently monitored by debt-holders, but in a way that does not force every debt-holder to pay monitoring costs – the demandable contract reduces multiple monitoring whilst providing bank managers with appropriate incentives to behave themselves.

The Provision of Liquidity

A second benefit is that demandable debt is highly liquid to its holder. Liquidity in this context refers to the ability of a debt-holder to redeem the debt he holds in the event he has an unanticipated desire or 'need' to spend. Should the holder of such debt find that he needs to spend, he could 'cash in' his bank note or deposit without having to give the bank notice or pay a penalty for premature withdrawal. The bank debt is therefore liquid to him, even though the bank's assets might be largely illiquid.

The basic principles behind this bank provision of liquidity are very straightforward (see, e.g., Diamond and Dybvig, 1983). Many 'ultimate' investment assets are imperfectly marketable, in the sense that they can only be sold at a loss, but are otherwise attractive investment assets. Individual investors *could* directly invest in such assets on their own, but if they did so they would take the risk that they might have to sell their assets at a loss if caught short by some unexpected future consumption 'need'. These individual consumption shocks are unpredictable, but if they are independent of each other and their distribution can be observed, it should be possible to predict the *proportion* of individuals who will get caught short even one cannot predict the *particular* individuals involved. Since the shocks are independent, individual shocks will offset each other to some extent and the variance of the proportion of agents who need to consume early will fall as the number of agents involved gets larger. In fact, as the number gets very large in the limit, this variance will go to zero and the proportion of agents demanding early consumption will become perfectly predictable. The point, therefore, is that a banker who takes in agents' funds as deposits and invests them on their behalf can easily predict the aggregate number of redemption requests and hold appropriate quantities of reserve assets to meet them. The remainder of its asset portfolio can then consist of high-yielding illiquid assets which the bank can hold with the reasonable expectation that it will not be forced to sell them prematurely to meet redemption demands. In short, the bank can hold an asset portfolio consisting of mostly imperfectly marketable assets, issue demandable liabilities against those assets, *and* be confident of not having to sell those assets at a loss to meet redemption demands. The bank 'transforms' imperfectly marketable, longer-term assets into fully marketable, short-term liabilities, and in the process provides its debt-holders with 'insurance' against the contingency that they will be caught short by an unexpected liquidity 'need'.

The Provision of Media of Exchange

The liquidity of many bank liabilities leads in turn to their transactability. The agents who hold them can therefore use them as exchange media as well as just investment assets. Demandable debt instruments have many of the characteristics of a good medium of exchange – they have an easily ascertainable face value; they are divisible; they can be structured so that ownership is easily transferable; and they are safe (e.g., in the case of bank notes) or can be made safe (e.g., by issuing a guarantee card to be used when writing cheques), so that those who accept them need have few worries about losses. A related point, stressed by Calomiris and Kahn (1991, 509) is that demandable debt is attractive to hold, and therefore attractive as a medium of exchange, because a bank that issues demandable debt usually has its agency problems under better control than one that does not.

All these factors mean that demandable debt can be made transactable at relatively little cost and then used as an exchange medium. As Mervyn Lewis puts it, by the time a bank has made its debt demandable, it

> has then gone a long way towards creating a claim which can serve not just as a store of value but as a medium of exchange and payment. (Lewis, 1992a, 217).

Banks will therefore issue notes in convenient small amounts, provide cheque-writing facilities against demandable deposits left with them and issue cheque guarantee cards to facilitate their use, build cash-point machines – ATMs, to use the American terminology – in convenient places to facilitate withdrawals from and deposits into people's accounts, and so on. A bank that makes its demandable debt transactable increases the demand for its debt, and presumably increases its market share and its profits. Competitive forces should then ensure that banks provide the transactable media that the public demand, and we can explain why banks play such a major role in the provision of exchange media and payment services (see also Lewis, 1992a, 217).

As an aside, it should now be apparent why mutual funds tend to be relatively marginal providers of liquidity and exchange media. A mutual fund faces a dilemma. If it tries to make its liabilities debt-like and fixed in value, then it has no way to absorb shocks to the value of its assets and maintain the value of its liabilities. It would therefore be acutely unstable, and it is difficult to see how it could survive for long, especially in the presence of banks that could provide the genuinely safe assets that most members of the public presumably want. On the other hand, if the fund issues equity claims, the value of its shares will generally fluctuate and investors will often prefer the greater liquidity and safety of bank debt instead. Shares are also ill-suited to function as exchange media, if only because of the difficulties of keeping track of share values to determine what an exchange medium issued by a mutual fund is actually worth (see also Chapter 9 below). It is therefore not surprising that most liquidity and most exchange media are provided by banks.[3]

The Possibility of Option Clauses

Nonetheless, it is conceivable that the demandability of bank debt might be qualified in some way to give a bank an option to defer redemption under certain circumstances. The simplest kind of 'option clause' would give bank the option to defer redemption of its debt for some specified period, on condition that it subsequently pays (prespecified) compensation to those debt-holders whose demands for redemption have been deferred. The attraction of an option clause is that it provides a bank with a means of enhancing its liquidity. For example, suppose that note-holder or depositor redemption behaviour is very volatile, and so a bank cannot easily predict its redemption demands. If it is also difficult or costly for a bank to replenish its reserves of redemption media, the bank might have to hold relatively large reserves to keep down the probability of its defaulting to an acceptable level. However, if it inserted an option clause into the contract, it could cut down on its reserves and thereby reduce its reserve-holding costs – and do so, moreover, without necessarily making its creditors any worse off. It might also relax the constraints that redeemability imposes on the bank's choice of assets, and thereby enable the bank to hold less marketable assets or longer-term assets than it otherwise would (see, e.g., Dowd, 1991c, 723-724). The option clause thus offers a bank the chance to cut down on the costs of maintaining its liquidity, and banks under *laissez-faire* might choose to avail themselves of it.[4]

The option clause can also help to protect banks by defusing any potential for speculative demands for redemption and the movements in interest rates and asset prices associated with such demands. When banks operate on a fractional reserve, it is at least conceivable that 'self-fulfilling' bank runs might occur in which agents run because they fear that others will run and because they know that the bank cannot meet all possible redemption demands simultaneously, or because they see queues at the bank and assume that those in the queue know something about the bank that they themselves do not. Option clauses have the advantage that they discourage debt-holders from behaving in this way, *should* the possibility of such behaviour be seen as a problem. Should the demands for redemption reach a point where the bank was being seriously undermined by the need to sell assets at firesale losses, the clause enables the bank to put a stop to these losses by suspending redemption. The bank can then use the time 'bought' by the option clause to reassure debt-holders and calm them down, or else it could build up its reserves by liquidating assets at a more leisurely pace or seeking out a credit facility on which it could draw if it needed to.

The existence of an option clause can also discourage speculative redemptions in another way. Without the option clause, debt-holders will often perceive a gain from being first to go to the bank to demand redemption; the option clause however creates some incentive *not* to join the queue, since those who have not already withdrawn will get compensation if the bank invokes the option to suspend:

> With the option clause ... those noteholders who failed to be first in line would lose nothing by the suspension of convertibility, provided only that the solvency of the bank was not called into question. In fact, they would actually gain if the bank suspended [i.e., invoked the option clause] and then had to pay them compensation. At the margin, a noteholder would be *less* likely to run if he thought others might run – the prospect of compensation would encourage a noteholder to *defer* redemption in the hope that others would force the bank to suspend. This discourages redemption and makes suspension less likely. Hence, the option clause helps to convert speculative demands for redemption ... [into] a stabilizing force that protects the banks' reserves when they are run down. (Dowd, 1991a, 764)

Without the option clause, it is also possible that a group of banks might feel obliged to fend off a drain on their reserves by raising their deposit or other borrowing rates, and if speculators are so inclined, interest rates might rise, and asset prices might fall, in a speculative bubble that could undermine the net worth of the banks and otherwise destabilise the financial system (see Dowd, 1988d, 326–327). But if banks have the option clause, there would come a point, as interest rates continued to rise, where it would be worth the banks' while to invoke the option and suspend redemption, and this bank 'intervention' would help to stabilise interest rates and bring the speculative bubble to an end. More importantly, since the banks' intervention would be predictable, it would take a rash bear speculator who would bet on further falls in asset prices when all involved can anticipate that the banks are about to intervene and that their intervention would prevent any further price falls. Faced with the prospect of the banks' intervening, bear speculators would generally decide to stop selling assets and start buying them, and their behaviour would itself reverse the speculation and ensure that interest rates never rose to the point where the banks actually *did* intervene:

> In these circumstances, the banks' *anticipated* intervention when bill prices hit the threshold point ought to be more than sufficient to break the price fall. The

bear speculators would almost certainly cut and run before the banks intervened, and the price of ... bills would [rise] to normal. It would be the *threat* of intervention [i.e., the invocation of the option clause], rather than the intervention itself, that would stabilize the market. This shows how effective option clauses can be even if they are never invoked. (Dowd, 1991a, 765)

In short, the *knowledge* that the option exists would discourage speculative runs, so banks with the option clause should be less vulnerable to runs driven by self-fulfilling expectations of bank defaults.

However, any bank that introduced the option clause must persuade its debt-holders that the clause will not make them worse off – if it failed to do so, it might lose its market share to rivals that continued to offer unqualified redemption on demand – and the public would naturally be concerned that the clause might be used, not to protect a 'good' bank's liquidity, but to suspend the market discipline that would otherwise enable a 'bad' bank to be rapidly driven out of business. An option clause used under such circumstances would merely give a 'bad' management more time to squander their debt-holders' resources, and the existence of the option might also discourage the debt-holder monitoring on which efficient resource management to some extent depends. Nonetheless, there are circumstances where option clauses could clearly be useful:

- Option clauses might be useful where these agency problems were already under reasonable control (e.g., because bank share-holders were wealthy and had unlimited liability) and liquidity problems were paramount. A good example is where a bank might face bankruptcy proceedings if one of its branches failed to honour a single note, and yet there is always a positive probability that could face a freak demand for redemptions so high that a branch ran out of reserves. A bank might respond to this possibility by increasing its reserves 'just in case', but there are limits to how much it would be willing to increase its reserves to protect itself against an eventuality that would almost certainly never occur, and, in any case, doing so merely reduces rather than eliminates the probability of 'accidental' default. The obvious solution is a very short-term option clause. The small print on the back of the contract could say that in the unlikely event of a branch running out of reserves, the branch could retain the right to 'stamp' notes or do the electronic equivalent to deposits, promising to redeem them in a day or two's time and pay generous compensation to those whose demands for redemption were deferred. The bank would then be under less pressure to keep reserves to meet 'freak' demands for withdrawal and, given that the agency problems mentioned earlier do not really come into play, it is difficult to imagine the public objecting to the option clause if the promised compensation was generous enough.[5]
- If agency problems were regarded as the major obstacle to the introduction of option clauses, they could presumably be dealt with by making the exercise of an option contingent on some other measure designed to mitigate agency costs

and reassure debt-holders that the option would not be exercised to harm them. The basic idea would be to require that the exercise of the option trigger an automatic re-capitalisation of the bank that would give the management greater incentive to be prudent, and this increased incentive to be prudent would offset any agency problems arising from the exercise of the option itself. This re-capitalisation could take the form of a call on share-holders (i.e., negative dividend), an automatic conversion of subordinated debt into equity, or an extension of shareholder liability. Debt-holders would get the reassurance they would want, and the recapitalisation should take care of any agency problems. If the option clause was really worthwhile, share-holders would presumably be willing to accept greater contingent liability to get it, or pay subordinated debt-holders to do so, and the public would have relatively little reason to object.

SPECIFIC ISSUES IN BANK ASSET MANAGEMENT

We now leave liability issues and consider the asset management side in more detail. The first point to keep in mind here is that many of the issues faced by banks in their capacity as lenders apply to lenders generally, and not just to banks alone. We can therefore take for granted much of what was said earlier in Chapters 3 and 4 about lending issues in general. Like other lenders, banks need to formulate appropriate lending policies – they need to decide to whom they should lend, what interest rates to charge, whether and how to ration credit, the collateral or other guarantees to require, and so on.

There are nonetheless some important differences between banks and other lenders. Whereas most other lenders are relative amateurs who lend now and then, and most often as a sideline to their main line of business, banks are professional lenders whose main incomes come from lending. They lend to large numbers of borrowers, and often repeatedly and over long periods of time. Banks are therefore in a position to benefit from economies of scale – for example, economies of diversification and specialisation (e.g., in monitoring) – and economies of repetition that other lenders cannot reap. Competence in these activities requires specialist knowledge and skills, and a bank – unlike an occasional amateur investor – would be able to recover the investments needed to acquire them. A bank also has the advantage, over some other lenders, that it has an incentive to maintain a good reputation, both as a lender and as a borrower. As Chapters 2 and 3 made clear, there are many situations where time-inconsistency problems arise which lead to one party being unwilling to place himself in a position where he could later be exploited by the other, but these problems can often be ameliorated if one party builds up a valuable reputation which he then offers as hostage for his future good behaviour. A good example is where a loan customer takes out a short-term line of credit to make a long-term investment, but is afraid that when he comes to renew it the lender might use his 'monopoly power' to impose unfavourable terms on him. A non-bank lender might not be able to do much to reassure his prospective client, but a banker might reassure him by pledging his own reputation as an implicit guarantee that he will not take undue advantage when loan terms come up for renewal. The borrower would be more inclined to 'trust' the banker because he would appreciate that the banker's own future income depends on his reputation for good behaviour, and his desire to maintain his reputation will therefore discourage him from abusing his clients. Finally, banks differ from other lenders (and, more generally, other investors) in that they engage in a variety of lending-related (and, more generally, investment-related) activities that others do not normally engage in. The very fact that they are specialist lenders (or investors) means that they have expertise and information that can be used to provide other services in addition to 'regular' loans or investments (e.g., they can provide monitoring services without making loans to go with them, they can offer various guarantees and underwrite security issues, and they can draw on their customer base to 'make markets' in swap derivatives). Banks therefore predominate in these activities and drive out competitors because of the competitive advantage they obtain from lending-related (or investment-related) economies of scope.

Bank Lending, Credit Rationing, and Collateral

Banks are the dominant suppliers of commercial, industrial and consumer loans in modern economies. Some indication of the amount of lending they do is given the observations that, as of 31 December, 1989, insured commercial banks in the USA held $616 billion in commercial and industrial loans and $375 billion in consumer loans (Sinkey, 1992, table 18.1, table 19.1). Since their total assets at that date were $2.862 trillion, their loans therefore amounted to well over a third of their total asset portfolio (Sinkey, 1992, table 18.1). The importance of bank lending to the corporate sector can also be gauged from the observation that, between 1977 and 1986, bank loans represented some 46 percent of all debt financing by US non-financial corporations (James and Wier, 1988, 49). Banks are therefore not only the dominant source of loans, but bank loans are also the dominant source of finance in general.

A good way to handle bank lending is to recapitulate briefly the discussion of lending in earlier chapters, but expand upon this discussion in places particularly relevant to banks. Let us therefore go back to the basic lending problem. The reader will recall from Chapter 2 that what makes this problem difficult is the possibility of default. If repayment could be taken for granted, the bank would simply lend out what it could at the highest possible interest rate. The market for bank loans would always clear, in the sense that a borrower could always get the loan he wanted if he were prepared to pay the going rate of interest (i.e., there would be no credit rationing), and there would be no need for collateral or other forms of guarantee.

Unfortunately, repayment *cannot* be taken for granted and a bank must frame its lending policy to take the possibility of default into account. Roughly speaking, the bank's profit-maximisation problem then requires that the bank charge what interest it reasonably can whilst trying to keep its expected default losses under adequate control. Apart from monitoring the borrower – and we shall discuss monitoring issues presently – the bank also has two other instruments it can use to control these losses:

Credit Rationing

One instrument is to ration credit. But why would a bank faced with an 'excess demand' for loans ever ration credit instead of raise the interest rate to 'clear the market'? The answer is that a bank faced with an excess demand for loans will raise its interest rate only if doing so increases its expected profit, and it does not always do so. The expected profit from a loan depends, not just on the promised interest, but also on the perceived probability of default. A higher interest rate will certainly increase the promised return, but it can also increase the probability of default and, if the latter effect is large enough, *decrease* expected profits overall.

A clear example of this possibility is given by Williamson (1986, 1987, 1988). Suppose that there are large-scale, increasing return investment projects in a costly state-verification environment. If there are many small investors, Williamson shows that the optimal arrangement is for a bank intermediary to accept deposits from the investors, and lend out the funds it obtains to the entrepreneurs so that they can invest in their projects. In this environment the bank could respond to an excess demand for credit by increasing the interest rate on its loans, thereby increasing its return in non-default states, but an increase in its interest rate would also raise the probability of default and thus increase expected verification costs. The net effect of an increase in interest on the bank's expected profit is therefore ambiguous, and if the net effect is to reduce the bank's expected profits, the bank will respond to an excess demand for loans by rationing credit. Since there are large economies in the investment projects, it makes little sense for the bank to give an entrepreneur a small amount of credit, so the bank must either give an entrepreneur a large loan or give him no loan at all. The bank could find therefore find itself in a situation where it faced identical demands for loans and chose to respond by giving loans to some and not to others. Those who were denied loans would be credit rationed, but this credit rationing would be an equilibrium phenomenon in the sense that there would be no way those denied credit could induce the bank to give them the credit it was giving to others.

A rise in interest rates might also cause expected profits to fall, and therefore lead a bank to ration credit, for two other reasons that have been much discussed in the literature – adverse loan selection and borrower moral hazard. Suppose there are two types of borrowers: 'good' borrowers who intend to pay back, and 'bad' borrowers who do not (or more generally, intend to pay back with a lower probability), but the bank cannot tell these borrowers apart when they apply for loans. If interest rates rise, 'good' marginal borrowers will be priced out of the loan market, but 'bad' borrowers won't be bothered as they had no intention of repaying anyway. An increase in interest rates therefore causes an increase in the proportion of 'bad' borrowers (i.e., adverse selection) and reduces the average probability of repayment (Jaffee and Russell, 1976; Keeton, 1979; Stiglitz and Weiss, 1981). Adverse selection can then lead to a credit rationing equilibrium which the 'good' borrowers prefer to a non-rationing equilibrium because it involves lower interest rates. The rationing equilibrium comes about because the 'good' borrowers demand it and the 'bad' borrowers have to mimic them if they are not to reveal themselves to the bank (which of course would then solve the bank's problem of telling loan applicants apart).

The probability of default could also rise because higher interest leads borrowers to take more risks which the bank cannot monitor. This is the moral hazard explanation for a greater probability of default (see, e.g., Keeton, 1979; Stiglitz and Weiss, 1981). Assuming he can, an entrepreneur will choose a level of risk that provides an appropriate balance, to him, between the upside and downside consequences of the risk he takes, but the point is that this balance also depends on the interest rate. If the interest rate then rises, the bank takes a greater slice of whatever return is made, but the rise in interest has a *proportionately greater* effect on the entrepreneur's return if he plays safe. The entrepreneur's previous privately optimal degree of risk is now too low, and he can make himself better off by taking more risk. He therefore does so, but the additional risk increases the probability of default and hence the expected losses that default would impose on the bank. If this effect is sufficiently strong, these expected losses can rise by enough to reduce the bank's expected profit overall, despite the fact that higher interest raises the bank's return in non-default states, and the bank would prefer to ration credit instead of letting interest rates rise to 'clear the market'.[6]

Collateral

The other instrument a bank can use to control its lending risks is collateral policy. A bank can require collateral or other guarantees from borrowers to ensure that they have some stake in the success of their projects, and give the bank some protection and reduce its losses in the event that default occurs. The practice of insisting on some form of security is very common, and nearly 70 percent of commercial and industrial loans made in the US are made on a secured basis (Berger and Udell, 1990a, 21). If borrowers could provide *any* amount of collateral, the bank could of course avoid any default losses at all by setting collateral requirements at a level high enough to ensure that the bank was always repaid in full, along with any incidental expenses (see, e.g., Bester, 1985, 1987; Bernanke and Gertler, 1989, 1990). The bank would then be guaranteed against loss and, since it would no longer have any reason to care about default, could offer borrowers whatever credit they wanted at the going interest rate. However, more often than not, borrowers cannot provide 'perfect' guarantees because their collateral is limited, and even collateralised bank loans are then risky.

The limited amount of collateral also makes bank collateral policy more difficult. Collateral can be used in one of two ways, each of which gives rise to its own distinct testable hypothesis. The first hypothesis is that bankers design collateral requirements on the basis of *their* assessment of the risk that a particular loan poses. The more risky they perceive the loan to be, the more collateral they will require, which yields the prediction that *observably more risky* loans should be associated with greater collateral requirements. The other hypothesis is that borrowers who have private information that they are safer than average would offer more collateral than the average borrower, and thereby reveal themselves to the bank in a way that less safe borrowers would be reluctant to emulate. This hypothesis predicts that greater amounts of collateral should be associated with loans to borrowers who had private (i.e., *un*observable) information that they were *relatively safe*. The first hypothesis is favoured by the 'practical' people who know the industry, and receives strong empirical support; while the second is favoured by academic theorists who frequently do not know the industry, and is empirically rejected (Berger and Udell, 1990a, 40–41). The evidence thus indicates that banks use their assessment of individual borrower risks to require that observably risky borrowers post more collateral.

If borrowers' collateral constraints 'bind', it also follows that changes in the amount of collateral they can offer should influence the amount of bank lending they obtain. Should their collateral constraints relax – say, because their net worth rises, or because their prospects improve and so their collateral is worth more – their credit-worthiness will improve and banks will give them more credit (see, e.g., Bernanke and Gertler, 1987, 1989, 1990; Gertler, 1990; Schreft and Villamil, 1990; and Calomiris and Hubbard, 1990): bank credit and investment consequently increase as the borrower's net worth rises relative to his liabilities. A strengthened balance sheet also means that a borrower has more resources available to invest directly in a project himself. The 'inside stake' therefore increases, which will further reassure the banker and encourage him to lend more.

There are a number of variations on this basic theme that bank lending rises with borrower net worth: (1) In the Schreft–Villamil model, borrowers have private information regarding their future ability to repay, and imperfectly competitive lenders know the distribution of future repayment abilities but are unable to identify the repayment abilities of specific individuals. Lenders therefore offer agents a variety of loan-size–interest-rate packages to encourage borrowers to self-select, and this set of contracts leads to loan-size constraints which become more binding as the future ability to repay falls. (2) In the Calomiris–Hubbard model, a borrower with low net worth faces credit rationing similar to that of Stiglitz and Weiss. If his net worth improves, the borrower can escape credit rationing if he can provide marketable assets as security, but not if he provides non-marketable ones. If his net worth improves further, he can then escape credit rationing even if he provides non-marketable assets as security. Shocks to net worth can therefore have a major impact on the economy through induced changes in credit rationing, and a major negative shock can even cause lending to particular sectors to dry up entirely (e.g., Mankiw, 1986; Calomiris and Hubbard, 1990; Bernanke and Gertler, 1987, 107–108. (3) Changes in other variables such as interest rates can produce very different effects on lending to different classes of borrower because of their differential impact on their credit-worthiness. For example, Mishkin (1990, 4) suggests that a rise in the riskless interest rate might have relatively little impact on 'quality' borrowers for whom the lending bank has reliable information, and perhaps collateral, but other borrowers might face severe credit rationing and/or face a large rise in the risk premium charged by their bank (e.g., because the rise in the interest rate would undermine the value of their collateral, worsen their prospects, or aggravate adverse selection or agency problems). The rise in the riskless interest rate might thus produce an increased spread between the rates charged to different borrowers, with the riskier borrowers facing increased credit rationing as well.

Bank Monitoring

Banks as Delegated Monitors

Many of the assets a bank might hold are ones whose full values can only be realised by investing resources into monitoring them. As discussed already in Chapter 4, an unintermediated group of investors could have difficulty handling the monitoring 'externalities' that arise with such assets, and one way to handle this problem is for someone to set up a financial intermediary to carry out the monitoring on investors' behalf. This intermediary arrangement provides a means of delegating the monitoring function, but resources will usually need to be spent to ensure that the arrangement 'works'. In the Diamond (1984) model of the financial intermediary as delegated monitor, the optimal contract structure (i.e., the one that minimises the delegation cost) is then a 'two-sided' debt contract in which the borrowing firms issue debt to the intermediary, on the one side, and the intermediary issues debt to the investors, on the other. The fact that the intermediary issues debt to its investors means that it gets the maximum return from its monitoring activity and gives it the appropriate incentive to monitor. At the same time, the fact that they have senior claim to the intermediary's income flow (i.e., are debt-holders) gives the investors some degree of protection against fluctuations in the intermediary's return and reduces the pressure on them to monitor the intermediary themselves. The two-sided contract consequently ensures that borrowers are monitored by the intermediary, but in a way that minimises the need for investors to monitor the intermediary themselves.

The potential drawback of this arrangement is that if the project return has any random element, a low return might force the delegated monitor to default and impose losses on the debt-holders. The costs of delegation therefore include the intermediary's expected bankruptcy costs as well as the costs of his own monitoring activity. The key to the Diamond model is that these delegation costs get smaller as the intermediary diversifies its holdings – as the intermediary diversifies, the probability that its average return falls in the extreme lower tail of its distribution gets smaller, and the probability of bankruptcy, and hence, expected bankruptcy costs, fall. In Diamond's model, if the returns to projects are independent, the probability of the intermediary defaulting, and, hence, expected bankruptcy costs, will in fact go to zero in the limit. Diamond could therefore show that the expected delegation cost per entrepreneur monitored by the intermediary gets arbitrarily small as the number of monitored entrepreneurs grows without limit. The total cost per entrepreneur of providing monitoring services then falls to its lowest possible level, the physical cost of monitoring (Diamond's Proposition 2).

This proposition has the important implication that, since the bank's lending risks to some extent cancel out, depositors might be confident about the safety of their investments even if the bank's capital buffer is relatively small. The Diamond model – and models like it, such as that of Krasa and Villamil (1990), which does not rely on such restrictive assumptions – indicates that a bank can be highly levered and still quite safe, and this in turn indicates that depositors can be confident about obtaining their return without (at least in this class of model) necessarily having to monitor the monitor. A further implication is that there is no need for the intermediary to inform them of the results of his monitoring activity. The only reason depositors might want information about investments is because they are concerned about the safety of those investments; provided the bank can reassure that their investments are safe, they will have no need to know anything about specific investments as such. A monitoring bank can therefore respect the confidentiality of commercially sensitive information at virtually no extra cost.

Haubrich (1989) provides an interesting extension to the Diamond analysis to consider the impact on it of enduring relationships – 'repeat buying'. His essential point is that repeated lending allows a bank to produce information and enforce contract compliance in a less costly way than direct monitoring. Since it is less costly to monitor a net outcome (such as a borrower's payment history) over time than to monitor compliance with complicated covenant clauses and the like, as in the Diamond model, it makes sense for the bank to establish a long-term relationship with the borrower and focus on the net outcome instead. (As an aside, the Haubrich model thus helps to explain why a borrower might enter into a long-term relationship with a bank – a long-term relationship facilitates cheaper monitoring by the bank from which both parties can benefit.) As already discussed in Chapter 2, if the net outcome is not satisfactory, the lending bank will then impose some penalty such as suspending credit to the offending borrower. A bank can therefore make loans to firms who each period announce their output and make a repayment to the bank that depends on their declared output value. The bank monitors the net outcome over time and punishes those firms that appear to be cheating by depriving them of credit for a while. If punishment and trigger periods are appropriately chosen, cheating firms should be continually without loans, and honest ones would be constrained only occasionally. These occasional errors could admittedly be avoided by (more expensive) continuous monitoring, but a firm would often prefer the risk of occasional errors because a bank that monitored only the net outcome could charge lower service fees or lower loan interest rates than one which monitored intensively all the time.

Corporate Demand for Bank Monitoring

While the previous models focused on how *investors* might want banks to monitor firms on their behalf, the *firms themselves* can also demand to be monitored. Firms might demand to be monitored if the public observation that they were being monitored helps them to transmit favourable information to potential lenders or other investors, and thus reduce their cost of funds. One obvious and important reason a firm might demand monitoring services is simply to reassure a lending bank and ensure that the bank gives it access to funds on favourable terms. Should a promising investment opportunity arise, the bank would be more willing to make funds available because it was better informed, and the firm's investment spending would be less constrained by cash-flow considerations. The importance of this reason for demanding monitoring is borne out by James and Wier's estimate (1988, 49) that over three-quarters of debt is 'inside' debt which involves the borrower giving the lender access to private information about itself that is not publicly available. The claim that the presence of a monitoring bank gives a firm greater security against the vagaries of its cash flow is also borne out by various empirical studies that suggest that the investment behaviour of firms with close ties to banks shows little sensitivity to cash flow, but the investment of firms without such ties is much more sensitive to it (e.g., Hoshi *et al.,* 1990, 1991; Morgan, 1991; and Chirinko, 1989).

However, a firm might also want to be monitored by a bank even though it wishes to obtain finance elsewhere. For example, a firm might wish to raise finance in the capital markets but want a public signal of having been monitored by a bank to get better terms when it does so. The firm might therefore go to a bank to take out a credit facility, publicly announce the fact that it had obtained the facility, and then go to the capital market. The announcement that it was worthy of bank credit would improve its public credit rating, and the firm would presumably hope that the resulting cheapening of its cost of credit in the capital market would more than cover the cost of the credit facility with the bank. Another example is where firms wish to issue equity, but equity is under-priced in the market because of asymmetric information between the firm and investors (as in Myers and Majluf, 1984). A firm can then reduce the underpricing of its equity by establishing a borrowing relationship with a bank, and the empirical evidence of James and Wier (1990, 151) suggests that firms with established borrowing relationships do in fact face significantly less under-pricing on initial public offerings of equity than other firms.

The point of demanding to be monitored in these circumstances is to use the bank to convey private information (or some of it, at least) to those otherwise uninformed parties from whom one intends to seek finance – the bank's willingness to hold inside debt sends a signal to less-informed investors about the borrower's financial condition (see Fama, 1985; Gorton and Haubrich, 1987, 291–297). This signal helps to reduce the information asymmetry between the firm and the public, but does so in a parsimonious way that indicates that the firm is worthy of credit without revealing the specific information on which the purchaser of the 'inside' debt made the decision to grant credit. Relatively uninformed investors then get a simple signal of the firm's credit-worthiness without being swamped by lots of specific information that may be difficult or at least inconvenient to process. At the same time, the firm can raise finance from them without having to make public information that it would rather keep secret. If a firm wanted to raise finance on the capital markets for an investment project, for instance, but did not want its rivals to know what it was planning, it could obtain a standby credit facility from a bank and then approach the capital markets. The bank would know of its plans, but the public and, in particular, its rivals, would not.

The strength or credibility of this signal depends on the bank's presumed risk of loss, which itself depends on the size of the credit facility and the seniority of the bank's claim in the event the firm defaults. The more the bank has to lose by mistakenly lending to the firm, the stronger the signal implied by the bank agreeing to make the loan, and hence the stronger the effect on the firm's public credit rating. The strength of the signal also depends on the seniority of the bank's claim in the event of default. If the bank is first in line for the firm's assets in the event of default, the fact that the bank is willing to extend credit on that basis might give relatively little reassurance to those outside investors who would stand further back in line if the firm defaulted; the effect of the bank credit facility on the bank's public perception of its credit-worthiness might then be fairly muted. If the bank accepted junior status, on the other hand, a rational outside investor would conclude that the 'inside' information to which the bank is privy must be fairly upbeat about the firm's prospects. (Were it otherwise, the bank would never make a loan and accept the status of junior claimant.) The lower the bank's priority in the event of default, the stronger (and more credible) the signal provided by the bank's willingness to advance credit. Clearly, the best signal is a large credit facility from a bank that accepted the most junior claim to the firm's assets.

Since a bank decision to offer a firm a credit facility sends a credible signal to less-informed agents that lending to the firm is reasonably safe, it reduces the need for other investors to collect information themselves or to expend their own resources monitoring the firm or verifying its claims. As Fama puts it,

> Positive renewal signals from a bank loan mean that other agents with higher-priority fixed payoff claims need not undertake similar costly evaluations of their aims. Bank signals are credible since the bank backs its opinion with resources, or by declining resources. (Fama 1985, 36)

Fama's analysis therefore explains why a firm might apply for bank credit even though it had no intention of ever drawing upon it, and also explains why banks can survive in the loan business even though bank loan rates are frequently higher than alternative sources of credit. Bank credit *appears* to be expensive because the bank is really providing a joint product – it is providing bank credit (or a bank credit facility) *and* a public signal of credit-worthiness – whereas other forms of credit typically come without the public signal.

Fama's hypothesis is consistent with empirical evidence on the effects on stock prices of announcements that firms had secured or renewed bank credit. The idea is that if bank credit facilities provide a positive signal to the market, as Fama suggests, then announcements of loan facilities should lead to higher stock market valuations, and the work of Mikkelson and Partch (1986), James (1987) and James and Wier (1988) suggests that this prediction is borne out empirically. As James and Wier (1988, 47) put it,

> announcements by public firms of new bank lending agreements elicit, on average (and in a very strong majority of cases) a significantly positive reaction from the stock market, [a finding that] offers a pointed contrast to the neutral to negative responses that have recently been found to accompany almost all other kinds of securities offering.

The results of James (1987, 226) also suggest that there is no difference between the effects of credit facility announcements that indicate immediate borrowing will take place and the effects of announcements in which no immediate borrowing is indicated, a finding that is very much in the spirit of the Fama hypothesis because it indicates that it is the *availability* of credit that matters, not so much the loan *per se*. Further support for the Fama hypothesis is also provided by the significantly negative effect on stock prices associated with the announcement of private placements to repay bank loans and thus dispense with the bank credit signal (James, 1987, 217).[7]

Fama's hypothesis about bank monitoring also explains why many firms will submit themselves to regular bank scrutiny by taking out short-term credit facilities. If a firm needs to raise funds regularly from capital markets, it might make sense for it to seek bank 'validation' before each capital market visit, and the most obvious way to obtain that validation would be to take out a sequence of short-term credit facilities and time the periodic credit renewals to have maximum effect on its capital market standing. Apart from indicating that the firm will submit itself relatively soon to another bank monitoring process, the provision of a short-term credit facility also indicates that the management of the firm concerned have relatively little to hide. If management have 'good' private information, they also have an incentive to issue short-term debt to obtain better refinance terms once the improvement becomes public knowledge. A firm's decision to commit itself to these periodic reviews therefore provides both a positive signal about the its earnings prospects as well as a discipline against management 'misbehaviour', a point apparently confirmed by the evidence of James and Wier (1988, 52) that debt issues with longer maturities tended to produce a worse stock market reaction than issues of shorter-term debt. Fama's approach thus helps to explain why so much bank credit has a very short-term to maturity. (James and Wier, 1988, 53, n. 9, for example, report that only 13 percent of commercial bank loans in May 1987 had a maturity of more than a year.) According to this view, bank credit is often short-term because the *borrowers* want the reassurance signals it provides to less-informed investors.[8]

Loan Syndicates

We began by examining how banks issued loans and monitored them through to maturity, and how in the process they implicitly guaranteed those loans to their depositors by maintaining an equity buffer that could absorb loan losses. In such cases, banks would not only issue (or to use the jargon, *originate*) loans, but would also *hold* them to maturity, *monitor* them until they matured, and *guarantee* them as well. However there is no reason why a bank must necessarily originate, hold (and therefore fund), monitor *and* guarantee every loan with which it is involved, and it sometimes makes sense to separate these functions. In the last section, we then discussed why lenders might seek bank credit facilities, not necessarily because they want bank credit *per se*, but because they want the public signals that the availability of such credit would give them in order to obtain credit elsewhere. The bank would therefore provide a guarantee, and perhaps ongoing loan services such as monitoring, but not provide the finance itself.

In this section we pursue this separation-of-functions idea further and examine the phenomenon of bank syndication – arrangements by which loans are financed by a group of banks rather than by one individual bank. Alternatively, we can think of a syndicate as an arrangement by which a bank 'sells' part of a loan to other banks. One bank, the lead bank, typically organises the loan and arranges monitoring, but all banks, including the lead bank, contribute to the finance. Syndicates are very widely used in wholesale banking, and often involve large numbers of banks (see, e.g., Lewis and Davis, 1987, 105–107, 346). They enable banks to specia lise in their various loan functions. A bank might have a particular expertise in monitoring loans to a particular industry, or finding loan customers, and so a syndicate enables it to 'share' that expertise with other banks. Syndicates also give banks a means of benefiting from economies of scale such as greater diversification. A bank that lends by participating in loan syndicates can spread its risks more than one that does not. Syndicates can also be useful for very large borrowers whose loans might be too large for a single bank to handle safely. Without a syndicate, the borrower might be unable to obtain a loan on the desired scale, or it might have to arrange multiple loans with a number of different banks. A syndicate enables him to take out a single large loan, and also cuts down on transactions costs and avoids the various co-ordination problems (e.g., over monitoring) that might arise if it took out a number of smaller loans.

The main problem with syndicates is to ensure that the lead/monitor bank has sufficient incentive to find good borrowers and monitor them appropriately. Since the lead bank bears the costs of screening and monitoring customers, but shares the benefits with the other participating banks, there is a concern that it might not put the socially optimal amount of effort into screening and monitoring borrowers. One possible solution is for the lead bank to take a more junior claim on the borrower, but accepting a junior claim makes the loan more risky – possibly much more risky – and undermines the risk-diversification benefits that are one of the main incentives to enter into syndicates in the first place. A more helpful solution is for the lead bank to keep a sufficiently large participation itself. The larger its stake, the more it has to lose if the loan defaults, and hence the stronger its incentive to screen the borrower before arranging the loan and monitor him afterwards. The analysis here very much parallels the inside equity discussion of Chapter 2: the bigger the inside equity stake, the stronger the signal of the quality of the investment (as in Leland and Pyle, 1977 and Campbell and Kracaw, 1980), and the stronger the incentive of the insider, in this case, the lead bank, to monitor the borrower (as in Berger and Udell, 1990a and Bester, 1990). In practice, the inside stake solution can also be complemented by a reputational solution of the sort we have already met a number of times before: a bank might invest in a reputation for leading loan syndicates; its future business therefore depends on it keeping its reputation by screening customers and monitoring them well; and so other banks feel reassured about entering a syndicate because they know that the lead bank wishes to maintain its reputation.

Loan Sales

The natural extension of a bank taking the lead role in a loan syndicate, in which a bank effectively sells *part* of a loan, is a 'proper' loan sale in which it sells *all* of it. A loan sale – sometimes referred to in the literature as *securitisation* – is a contract between a bank and some other party, the beneficiary of the contract, in which the bank sells the beneficiary the cash stream from one of its loans. The bank that sells the loan may or may not offer the beneficiary some guarantee. If the bank does, it must make up any loss that the beneficiary would otherwise suffer from the borrower defaulting on the loan. More usually, however, a bank does *not* guarantee the loan it sells, and so the beneficiary has no recourse to the bank in the event that the borrower defaults. (In this latter case, there is an obvious potential agency problem in that a bank that sells a loan without guaranteeing it might have little incentive to monitor it properly, but we shall come back to this problem shortly.) A loan sale enables a bank to separate out entirely the services associated with bank lending, such as monitoring and risk evaluation, from the actual funding of a loan. It is therefore a natural way for banks to exploit differences among themselves (e.g., where one bank might be better-placed to originate a loan, but another to fund it).

Consumer Loan Sales

Bank loan sales are of one of two main types. The first are sales of consumer loans such as mortgages, car loans and credit card loans, and sales of such loans grew from virtually nothing a few years previously to about $50 billion by 1989 (Gorton and Pennacchi, 1992, 4). Consumer loans tend to be highly standardised loans for small amounts that are governed by relatively straightforward contracts. Once a borrower has been screened and approved for the loan, a consumer loan also tends to be straightforward to monitor, so such loans can be serviced easily at comparatively low cost (see, e.g., Berlin, 1992, 434). These characteristics mean that the cash flows they generate can be predicted relatively easily if the loans are sold in large bundles (as they typically are) in which individual loan risks largely cancel out. The fact that loans are standardised and easy to service also implies that there are relatively few agency problems from having the bank service the loan despite the fact that it is the loan purchasers who benefit from the servicing. Consumer loan bundles are therefore easy to rate, and are usually rated by credit agencies and guaranteed or insured by some other party. Consumer loans are consequently ideally suited to permit a radical unbundling of some of the functions that banks have traditionally combined, as Berlin illustrates:

> Consider the securitization of home mortgage loans. In a typical transaction, the mortgage loans may be originated by a bank or a finance company ... These mortgages are then sold to a special purpose vehicle, a trust or corporation whose sole function is to hold this particular type of security. With the aid of an investment banker, the vehicle then sells securities, backed by the pooled cash flows of many individual mortgages. These securities usually receive a credit enhancement in the form of a guarantee from a bank or insurance company, thus permitting the securities to receive an investment grade rating from a public rating agency. Often, the underlying cash flows will back securities of various maturities (tranches) tailored to the needs of particular types of purchasers ... The collection and distribution of the cash flows from the underlying mortgage loans may be performed by a commercial bank, a savings bank, an investment bank, or a nonbank processing specialist. (Berlin, 1992, 433)

Thus, as Berlin notes, there are at least three separate parties involved – the originating bank, the guarantor, and the rating agency – as well as the purchaser himself, each of whom can then specialise in the function in which he has a comparative advantage.

Commercial and Industrial Loan Sales

The other type of loans sold are commercial and industrial loans. As compared to consumer loans, these tend to be very large and idiosyncratic and tailor-made to each borrower. They also tend to require considerable servicing (e.g., monitoring) since the holder faces potentially serious asymmetric information and agency problems *vis à vis* the borrower. Their returns are therefore more difficult to predict than the returns from consumer loans, and are also subject to greater information and agency problems. As a result, they do not lend themselves to being sold in packages, and are normally sold individually. Sales of commercial and industrial loans are not new, but have only recently become prominent. Indeed, prior to 1983, they were not even reported to the FDIC because the amounts involved were regarded as too small to be significant (Gorton and Pennacchi, 1989, 126). They subsequently grew at an enormous rate – with many of these being sales among banks – to peak at over $250 billion in 1989, and then fell to under half their peak value three years later (Haubrich and Thomson, 1993, figure 2):

> Commercial and industrial loan sales [in the US] grew tremendously during the 1980s ... [T]he outstanding amount of commercial and industrial loan sales increased from approximately $26.7 billion in the second quarter of 1983 to a peak of $290.9 billion in the third quarter of 1989. This growth has been accompanied by signs of a developing market. In the early stages of the market, the loans sold were very short maturity claims on the cash flows of loans to well-known firms. However, as the loan market has grown, the loans sold have increasingly represented claims on riskier firms. Now less than half the loans sold are the obligations of investment-grade firms. There is also evidence that the maturities of loan sales have increased. In 1985, 80 percent of the loan sales had maturities of 90 days or less, while by mid-1987, over half had maturities exceeding one year. (Gorton and Pennacchi, 1990, 1)

The growth in sales of industrial and commercial loans is not easy to explain, particularly since most loan sales do not involve recourse, explicit or otherwise (see, e.g., Gorton and Pennacchi, 1990, 23, 28), and the loan sales contract does not normally require the bank to keep *any* part of the loan. (The reader might recall here the signalling cost arguments of Chapters 3 and 4 which would have led us to expect that banks might have agreed to keep *some* proportion of the loan to reassure potential purchasers that they still had some stake in it.) The phenomenon of commercial and industrial loan sales of the type we observe is therefore something of a puzzle. As Gorton and Pennacchi put it,

> The existence of this new market challenges recent theories of financial intermediation which would predict that loan selling would be a 'lemons' market. Loan sales also contradict the presumption that bank loans are illiquid, which is the underlying rationale for much of bank regulation and Central Bank policy. (Gorton and Pennacchi, 1990, 1)

They elaborate a little later:

> Loan sales appear paradoxical because commercial bank lending is thought to involve the financing of non-marketable assets. The theory of financial intermediation explains that the (publicly unobserved) credit evaluation and monitoring services provided by banks require, for incentive compatibility, that the bank hold the loans it creates. Holding loans until maturity insures [*sic*] that the bank has incentive to effectively evaluate and monitor borrowers. If loans were sold, then the bank would lack the incentive to produce an efficient level

of credit information and monitoring since it would not receive the rewards from this activity. Loan buyers would recognize this lack of incentive and value the loan lower than otherwise. (Gorton and Pennacchi, 1990, 2)

These loans should therefore be imperfectly marketable, and hence difficult to sell. How then do we explain the large market in them, as well as its rapid growth and subsequent retrenchment?

- Loan sales may have developed to circumvent regulatory constraints. Selling loans without recourse can help to avoid capital adequacy constraints by getting the loan off the bank's asset portfolio; since loan sales also liquidate the corresponding liability item in the bank's balance sheet, they help to avoid reserve requirements as well (see, e.g., Pennacchi, 1988). Pushing this line of argument further, loan sales could then be viewed as ways of getting around regulatory constraints on leverage, perhaps to maximise the implicit subsidy that federal deposit insurance provides to those who hold deposits, and indirectly to the banks who provide them. They might also be viewed as a way of getting around constraints on bank aggregation such as the anti-branch banking restrictions in the USA. A bank in a region that was rich in investment opportunities but poor in savings might therefore originate the loan, but sell it to a bank in a region that was flush with savings but poor in investment opportunities. A weakness of this 'regulatory' explanation, however, is that it fails to explain why the pattern of loan sales. If these factors account for loan sales, why were there so few sales *prior* to the 1980s?
- Loan sales might reflect the fact that banks that have a comparative advantage in originating and servicing loans might not have a comparative advantage in loan funding or in interest rate risk management (e.g., Flannery, 1989). Securitisation therefore occurs when banks with a comparative advantage in originating loans come across 'good' investment projects which they originate but then securitise because they have no particular advantage in financing them. But again, if this explanation is enough, why were there so few loan sales prior to 1980?
- Loan sales might have developed because the purchasers of loans do not require the information production and monitoring services that banks have traditionally provided (Gorton and Pennacchi, 1989, 127). However, this logic suggests that loan sales should be restricted to those of well-known companies such as those that already have access to the commercial paper (CP) market. How then do we explain the fact, pointed out by Gorton and Pennacchi (1989, 128), that by 1985 a third of loan sales involved the loans of firms that did *not* have access to the CP market?
- James (1988) suggests that loan sales can mitigate an under-investment problem of the sort identified by Myers (1977). Suppose a bank with risky debt outstanding has the opportunity to invest in a positive NPV project. The problem identified by Myers was that the firm – in this case, the bank – might pass up the investment because too many of the benefits would accrue to the bank's debt-holders in the form of reduced expected bankruptcy costs, rather than to the

bank's share-holders as higher expected profits. To avoid this problem, some means must be found to channel more of the benefits to the bank's share-holders, and the bank does so by issuing debt collateralised by the project in which it wants to invest. (How does this benefit the bank's share-holders? The holders of the collateralised debt would be better off holding that debt than holding uncollateralised debt because it gives them a specific first-priority claim on the investment itself *as well as* a more general claim on the rest of the bank's assets. The bank can then charge more for the collateralised debt and channel the profit to its share-holders.) The issue of secured debt consequently allows a bank to appropriate to its share-holders some of the benefits that would otherwise be 'dissipated' to outstanding debt-holders, and thus enables the bank to solve its under-investment problem. The issue of secured bank debt is illegal in the USA, but the issue of standby letters of credit (SLCs) and secured loan sales are a good substitute for them because they enable a bank to sell the cash flows associated with a new investment. The James model predicts that loan sales and (SLCs) are more likely to be used for low-risk loans (i.e., loans that require less servicing, and therefore involve lower agency costs), for banks for which regulatory constraints are more binding, and for banks that are more risky themselves, and his empirical evidence is consistent with these predictions (James, 1988). However, the James story is limited in that it only refers to *guaranteed* loans sales and *not* to loan sales without recourse (i.e., the majority of them). Along with most other explanations, it also fails to explain why loan sales are a relatively recent phenomenon.

● It may be that the information asymmetry that used to exist between a bank and the purchaser of a loan has been eliminated, or at least, greatly reduced, due to technological change (Gorton and Pennacchi, 1990, 1992). Developments in information technology now make it possible for other investors to acquire information at much lower cost than they could in the past, and these developments suggest that the banks' traditional comparative advantage in the acquisition and production of information should have fallen. Even if other agents could not directly acquire low-cost information about certain borrowers, they might still be able to verify the bank's information at relatively low cost, and banks in particular might be well-suited to verify information provided by other banks (which, incidentally, would explain why so many loans sales are from one bank to another). Since loan sales might be feasible now that were not feasible even a relatively short time ago, we can therefore explain the growth in loan sales in the 1980s. This explanation does *not* however account for the large fall in loan sales since 1989.

'OFF-BALANCE-SHEET' ACTIVITIES

Then there are various activities that do not appear in banks' balance sheets, or else only appear as notes attached to the balance sheet. The essence of these activities –

and the reason they do not appear on the balance sheet, at least in the conventional manner – is that they involve the issue of contingent liabilities or the acquisition of contingent assets. For example, a bank might issue a liability that requires it to make a certain payment if a certain event should occur, but not otherwise, and the contingent nature of this liability prevents it being included 'on' the balance sheet in a conventional sense. These 'off-balance-sheet' activities are of very considerable importance to modern banks. Even for retail banks whose off-balance-sheet positions are relatively less important, the gross size of their off-balance-sheet position is still typically much greater than the size of their total consolidated balance sheet assets, and banks that specialise in such activities – such as the UK merchant banks, and the investment and money centre banks in the USA – often have off-balance-sheet positions that are many times their consolidated assets.

Bank off-balance-sheet activities cover four main areas, and we shall consider each in turn: (1) loan commitments; (2) underwriting activity; (3) acceptances; and (4) bank activities in derivatives markets.

Bank Loan Commitments

A *bank loan commitment* is an obligation by the bank to give a particular borrower a loan of up to a certain amount, at any time over a specified period, on pre-arranged terms (e.g., regarding the interest to be paid, or the borrower's financial health). Loan commitments are pervasive in modern banking, with over 75 percent of commercial and industrial loans in the USA being take-downs of earlier loan commitments (Veitch, 1992, 605). Loan commitments include not only 'formal' loan commitments, but also overdraft facilities, credit lines of various sorts (e.g., revolving lines of credit), repurchase agreements (i.e., agreements to sell a security and then repurchase it again later at a given price), and standby letters of credit (i.e., loan commitments issued to support a customer's potential obligation to another party). The extent of the bank's commitment varies with the precise obligation it makes. For example, a 'formal' loan commitment normally leaves the bank legally committed to make the loan unless it can show that the customer's financial health has deteriorated in an adverse material way, but other commitments are looser and can be terminated more easily (e.g., an overdraft agreement). Banks earn a return from loan commitments by charging for the commitment itself, and also by charging interest on the amount of the loan actually taken down.

There are a number of possible explanations for the issue of bank loan commitments. One is that they give the borrower insurance against a possible future deterioration in the terms on which he can obtain credit (Thakor, Hong and Greenbaum, 1981). For example, a borrower concerned about the prospect of a rise in interest rates might want a loan commitment to insure himself against higher interest rates, and the commitment can make both parties better off if the bank is better able to bear interest rate risk than he is. However, since a borrower's financial health can deteriorate in the period between obtaining a loan commitment and taking down the loan, a bank will normally protect itself by insisting that the commitment be conditional on the customer maintaining a minimum level of financial health.

Besides providing insurance against liquidity risk, loan commitments can also counter borrower moral hazard and adverse-selection problems, and thus complement the bank's collateral and credit rationing policies. If firms were to borrow on the future spot market, there is a danger that high future interest rates could lead firms to take more risks than the bank would desire. The bank therefore responds to this moral hazard by offering a commitment to keep interest rates relatively low, and the low interest rate encourages the borrower to keep down his risk-taking. Since this commitment by the bank would otherwise earn it a negative profit, the bank then charges a commitment fee to make the package worthwhile to it (Boot, Thakor and Udell, 1987). Similarly, banks can use commitments to counter adverse selection by designing fees and interest charges to encourage borrowers to self-select. The bank can then classify its customers and charge them appropriately (Kanatas, 1987).

Another explanation, and one that also explains why *banks* (as opposed to anyone else) provide loan commitments, is that banks can provide commitments with a credibility that other potential lenders cannot match (Boot, Thakor and Udell, 1991). The credibility issue arises because of the concern that when a borrower comes to take down his loan, the lender might renege on the deal by claiming that his financial condition has deteriorated, which would then relieve the lender of his obligation to lend. (Why? The decision to take down the loan implies that the committed loan is cheaper than alternatives. If the lender can invalidate the agreement, it can force the firm to take out a more expensive spot loan, or at least free itself from a commitment to provide a loan at less than 'market' rates.) If the agreement is to be credible, there therefore needs to be some way to discourage the lender from reneging on the deal. (The alternative is of course to remove any fuzzy qualifier clauses, but this makes the contract inflexible and discourages the lender from making any commitments at all.) The solution is for the lender to invest in a reputation and then reassure the borrower by offering his reputation as hostage, and a bank is better placed to implement this solution than other lenders (e.g., because it lends repeatedly, and so much of its income depends on lending).

One particularly important type of loan commitment is a *standby letter of credit* (SLC). As noted already, an SLC is a loan commitment issued to support a client's obligations to some other party. For example, the client firm might wish to issue commercial paper, but be concerned that the market's lack of information about its financial condition would lead to its paper selling at a discount. The firm might therefore take out an SLC to support its commercial paper issue, and the SLC would commit the bank to honour its client's debt if the client himself failed to do so. Once the bank has guaranteed the issue, the firm's paper would trade at the same price as the bank's own debt and the information discount would be eliminated.

The use of SLCs has grown considerably over the last two decades or so. SLCs grew from less than 0.5 percent of US bank balance sheet assets in 1973 to $140 billion or more than 5 percent of bank balance sheet assets by 1985, a growth rate of over 24 percent a year (Benveniste, 1992, 530). Their use can be explained by one or more of three factors: The first is that they offer banks a useful way to circumvent regulatory taxes. Since SLCs do not appear on the balance sheet, a bank can issue substitute loans by means of SLCs without adversely affecting its key balance sheet ratios, and in so doing avoid the 'regulatory tax' that a normal loan would imply. A second possible explanation is that investor might prefer SLC-backed loans to loans funded by deposits because of the greater security that SLC-backed loans give them in the event that the bank should fail. If they invest their funds in the bank and the bank fails, then their only claims are general creditor claims against the failed bank; but if they lend their funds directly to the firm and have the firm take out an SLC, they still have a claim against the firm if the bank fails. Other things being equal, investors would therefore prefer SLC-backed loans to regular bank loans. The third explanation is related to the second. If investors prefer SLC-backed loans to regular bank loans, they will pay more for the former than for the latter. Firms can then charge more for SLC-backed loans, and in so doing appropriate some of the gains for their share-holders. SLC-backed loans are therefore a better way to handle Myers-type under-investment problems that occur when a firm has positive NPV investment projects, but chooses not to invest in them because too many of the benefits go to existing debt-holders in the form of reduced expected bankruptcy costs. SLC-backed loans effectively offer a firm the chance to collateralise the project and thereby channel more of the surplus it creates away from existing creditors and towards share-holders (see, e.g., James, 1988).

Bank Underwriting

There are also the related questions of bank *underwriting* and *acceptance* activity. In its broadest sense, underwriting relates to a bank's supporting the issue of private sector financial instruments. Such support often involves giving advice to the issuer and placing the issue, but it can also involve recommending shares to investors and guaranteeing the issue as well (i.e., underwriting the issue in a narrower sense). Banks can underwrite both debt and equity instruments, and they can do so in various ways. In a *firm commitment* underwriting, the bank agrees to purchase the whole security issue for a specified price and then sell the securities itself. A bank can also engage in *standby underwriting*, according to which it undertakes to buy up for a specified price that portion of a security issue that the firm cannot sell on the market. There is also *'best effort'* underwriting, according to which the bank merely promises to use its best efforts (and, implicitly, its good name) to sell the shares on behalf of the issuer, but does not actually guarantee the sale in the way it does with other forms of underwriting. These three types of underwriting differ principally in the way in which they allocate the risk relating to the price the securities will fetch on the market. With firm commitment underwriting, the bank absorbs all the market price risk and in effect insures the issuer against it. The bank then makes the issuer pay for that insurance by paying him a lower price for taking the issue off his hands. Standby underwriting generally involves some degree of risk-sharing between the two parties, while best effort underwriting allocates the market price risk to the issuer.

The existence of fixed commitment and standby underwriting can largely be explained by the combination of information asymmetry and agency costs. The information asymmetry is what leads the issuer to approach the bank in the first place – he will be concerned that the public's lack of information will lead them to offer him a low price, which then creates a Myers–Maljuf under-investment problem – but the bank will only be able to ameliorate the information asymmetry if the public can be confident that it will do a good job assessing what the issuer has to offer. There is therefore an agency problem as well as information one. A natural solution is for the underwriting bank to assess the debt or equity involved, but to make its assessment credible by itself taking a direct stake in them, and it can do so by buying up or guaranteeing all or part of the issue to be underwritten. The bank would therefore offer fixed commitment or standby underwriting, and the agency problem would be largely solved because the bank would internalise the costs and benefits of its own effort (see, e.g., Baron, 1982; Raviv, 1987).

How then do we explain cases, such as 'best effort' underwriting, where the bank takes little or no 'direct' stake in the underwritten issue? One explanation, suggested by Booth and Smith (1986), Beatty and Ritter (1986), and Chemmanur and Fulghieri (1994), is that best effort underwriting may 'work' – and therefore ameliorate imperfect information problems – because the bank stakes its own reputation on it, and hence uses its reputation as a hostage. A firm can do relatively little to solve a Myers–Maljuf problem by trying to post its own reputation as hostage (e.g., because the public will typically have little idea of when it will next go to market, and hence be unsure about how they can extract revenge if the firm misleads them), but a banker would be better placed to do so, especially if he specialises in underwriting activity and therefore has a strong-incentive to protect his reputation by ensuring that he avoids underwriting poor-quality issues. The bank's 'certification' would therefore have some credibility, and the firm's under-investment problem would be reduced in a way that the firm itself could not have done. This solution works because investors judge the banks by their past performance. A banker who does his homework well will get less immediate business, since there will be fewer firms whose shares he can 'recommend', but over time he will get a better track record and, hence, more credibility. Having established the credibility of his reports, he can then charge higher fees to those client-firms whose business he takes on. A banker who adopts less stringent standards will get more immediate business, but his ratio of misses to hits will be worse and he will not be able to command such high fees in the future. We can thus explain why so many firms have their share issues underwritten – Smith (1977), for example, reports that 90 percent of seasoned share issues were underwritten – despite the costs of doing so. The answer is that is that all firms prefer underwriting in the presence of asymmetric information – because they get the benefit of the banker's reputation behind them – and the only firms that do not underwrite are those without significant asymmetric information problems or those judged to be sufficiently poor risks that no investment bank will take them on. We can also explain why more reputable bankers are able to fetch higher prices for the issues they underwrite – they do so because they reduce the degree of Myers–Maljuf under-pricing – as well as the related observations that more reputable bankers deal with lower-risk clients and charge more for the services they provide (see, e.g., Carter and Manaster 1990).

Bank Acceptances

Bank acceptance activity is similar to bank underwriting, but the instruments involved are not the liabilities of the bank's client firm, but the liabilities of the client firm's own clients, issued as part of a commercial transaction between them. One firm might purchase goods from another, but the firm that purchases the goods wishes to pay on credit, and does so by issuing a bill drawn upon itself, which obliges it to pay at some specified future date. (Such arrangements are common in international trade, for example, and give the purchaser three or six months to pay.) However, the firm that accepts the bill might want immediate payment and, though it could sell the bill, it would run into the problem that, unless its client is very well-known, the bill would sell at a discount reflecting the market's lack of knowledge about the firm on which the bill is drawn. One way to deal with this problem is to have the bill *accepted* (i.e., guaranteed) by a bank. The bill would then be regarded in the market as equivalent to the bank's own debt, and the asymmetric information discount would disappear. Bank acceptances thus involve four parties – the two initial firms, the bank, and the ultimate investor who buys the bill. (In some cases, the ultimate investor and the bank might be the same, in which case the bank discounts the bill and not just accepts it.) The bank's client gets immediate payment, the client's client gets a period of credit, the investor provides that credit, and the bank by accepting the bill enables the investor to provide that credit without the discount that the investor's lack of knowledge would otherwise imply. The bank will charge a fee for accepting the bill, and, in practice, will often give its clients acceptance facilities by which it agrees to discount bills up to a certain limit, with the client being charged for the facility as well as for each bill it accepts (see, e.g., Goacher, 1993, 46–47).

The interesting issue with bank acceptances is why the bank should be in a better position than anyone else to accept a bill. Two possible reasons suggest themselves:

- A bank might have a better knowledge about the firm on which bills are drawn than the average outside investor. It could therefore judge bills better, and hence be better placed to avoid accepting poor-quality bills. As Fletcher points out, success in the accepting business requires 'an intimate knowledge of the various trades in which bill finance [is] employed and the acquisition of a "nose" for a bad name on a bill' (Fletcher, 1992, 673). Banks therefore invest in acquiring information about these firms, and the income they get from their acceptance business can be regarded as their return from these investments. One may then ask why *banks* should have an advantage in acceptances, as opposed to other forms of specialist acceptance firms that might make similar investments in information, but the point is that banks will often be able to acquire this specialist information at lower cost, as a by-product of their other activities, and therefore have a competitive advantage over other acceptance firms. We can thus explain, not just why acceptance business exists, but also why it is typically provided by banks.

- The other reason why banks might be better placed to deal with acceptances is because they can use their relationships with their clients to sift out bad bills. If a bank repeatedly makes losses from accepting bills presented to it by a particular client, it will eventually respond by refusing to accept any more bills for it. These repeated losses might also lead the bank to question the commercial judgement of the management of its client firm, and therefore lead it to curtail its credit as well, and a client's desire to avoid this punishment gives it an incentive to avoid passing low-quality bills to the bank. A bank's relationship with its client thus gives it some leverage over it, and it can use this leverage to ensure that the client only asks it to accept good-quality bills.

Bank Activities in Derivatives Markets

Finally, banks are heavily involved in the various derivatives markets. Derivatives are financial instruments that are based upon, or derivative of, the 'basic' financial instruments such as debt or equity. The main derivatives are forward and futures contracts, options and swaps, but these contracts themselves come in many different forms, and there are also more exotic derivative contracts that are effectively derivatives of derivatives (e.g., options on interest rate futures). A *forward contract* is a contract that calls for a future delivery to be made, at a price agreed now but to be paid on delivery. (It therefore differs from 'ordinary' or spot contracts in that the price is preagreed, and not negotiated at the same time as delivery and payment.) A *futures contract* is similar to a forward contract, but differs in that the commodity or instrument to be delivered is standardised and the deal is made with a central exchange rather than a 'private' counterparty and involves 'margin' payments that forward contracts do not. An *option* is a contract that gives the purchaser the right to buy or sell a particular commodity or instrument at a particular price over some period of time (in the case of 'American' options) or at a certain date in the future (as in 'European' options). Options themselves come in two main forms – *call* options that give the purchaser the right to *buy* at a particular price, and *put* options that give him the right to *sell* at a particular price. Finally, a *swap* is a contract to exchange streams of cash flows between the parties involved, the most important examples being interest rate swaps involving the exchange of interest-payment obligations, and foreign currency swaps involving the exchange of obligations to make payments in different currencies. The use and variety of derivative products has increased very rapidly since the early 1970s. Of these, the banks are particularly involved in swap markets, and in interest rate swaps most of all, which have gone from being negligible in the early 1980s to grow to a staggering notional principal of over $2 trillion within a decade later (Wall, 1992, 445).

Agents can benefit in various ways from trading in derivatives. The first and perhaps most obvious benefit is that it helps them to manage their risks. Managing risks usually means hedging them – that is, taking out a counterbalancing transaction to protect oneself against a particular exposure – and firms can use derivatives to hedge individual transactions or hedge their overall balance sheet positions. For example, if a firm was concerned about a possible rise in the future spot price of some commodity it intends to buy, it might hedge itself by taking out a forward contract that specified the price it would have to pay in advance or it might take out a call option on the commodity which would give it the right to buy the commodity at a specified price. Alternatively, if the firm was concerned about a possible fall in the future price of a commodity it intended to sell, it might hedge its risk by selling forward or by taking out a put option that gave it the right to sell at a particular price in the future. These are both cases of hedging particular transaction risks, but firms can also hedge their overall portfolio. The most obvious case is where a firm that is a net debtor is concerned about the possibility of a rise in future interest rates, so it purchases an interest futures contract or an interest rate cap, a form of interest rate option, which would cap the future interest it would have to pay.

Trading in derivatives also helps firms to 'unbundle' the different characteristics of financial instruments. One reason why firms might wish to do so is to exploit the 'gains from trade' from differences in their comparative advantages in obtaining finance. Suppose that one borrower wishes to obtain a fixed-rate loan, but can only obtain such a loan at high rate of interest because of its poor credit rating, which means that it has a comparative advantage in obtaining floating-rate finance. Suppose also that there is another firm with a good credit rating, and, hence, a comparative advantage in obtaining fixed-rate finance, but this firm wants a floating-rate loan. Instead of the first firm making do with a floating-rate loan, and the second one with a fixed-rate one, both firms can make themselves better off if they each take out these loans and then swap the interest payments. In addition to helping firms exploit arbitrage profits from differences in their costs of funds, swaps can also help firms to engage in duration matching. A firm with variable-rate assets and fixed-rate debts is exposed to risk if interest rates fall, while one with fixed-rate assets and variable-rate debts is exposed to risk if interest rates rise. A fixed-for-floating interest rate swap would then leave the first firm with variable-rate assets and variable-rate liabilities, and the second with fixed-rate assets and fixed-rate liabilities, and thus reduce *both* firms' exposure to interest rate risk. Finally, interest-rate swaps can help firms to get around other constraints. For example, a firm might have issued long-term debt that it would like to retire, but cannot because the debt is not callable. To get rid of its long-term obligations without formally retiring the debt, the firm could then swap its long-term interest obligations for short-term ones, and thus effectively pay off its debt earlier.

The question then arises as to why *banks* trade derivatives. Part of the reason why banks trade derivatives is to manage their own risks. Again, these risks can be at the 'micro' or 'macro' level. At the micro level, a bank might wish to hedge itself against *specific* transaction risks to which it had exposed itself. For example, when a bank issues a loan commitment, it faces a risk of loss if interest rates rise and might wish to hedge this risk by taking out a put option on a debt instrument. If interest rates subsequently rise, the price of the debt instrument falls and the bank can make a profit by selling the debt instrument at a price above the prevailing spot market price. This profit would then compensate it for the loss on the exercise of the loan commitment and so hedge the bank against the interest rate risk implied by that commitment. At the 'macro' level, a bank might also trade derivatives to hedge the risk attached to its overall balance sheet position. The main risk here is interest-rate risk attached to the difference between the 'duration' of its assets and liabilities, or duration risk for short. Changes in interest rates have a greater effect on the value of a security the longer its term to maturity, or duration. Since banks' assets have longer durations than their liabilities, the value of their assets is more sensitive to changes in interest rates than the value of their liabilities. Their net value is therefore vulnerable to changes in interest rates, falling when interest rates rise and rising when interest rates fall, and banks might wish to hedge this risk by taking out suitable derivative contracts like interest caps (see, e.g., Sinkey, 1992).

Banks might also trade derivatives because they find it worthwhile to intermediate in derivatives markets. In the simplest case, a bank might be well-placed to 'make a market' in derivatives because its existing customer base enables it to find buyers more easily than other institutions could find them. Someone who wanted to make a swap, say, would go to the bank which would then search through its customer base for a suitable counterparty (Brown, 1992, 619). However, once the bank had started to make a market, its role would soon expand beyond that of mere broker (see, e.g., Lewis and Davis, 1987, 334–336). For example, since the trade in derivatives would be limited by agents' concern about possible default by their counterparties, the bank might guarantee the trades in which it deals by buying and selling them on its own account, an arrangement that also has the advantage of preserving counterparty anonymity. Furthermore, since trades would otherwise be limited by coincidence of wants problems, banks might expand the market by 'warehousing' contracts – making a contract with one party without having lined up a suitable counterparty to balance the trade. The bank would then offload the contract later when a suitable counterparty turned up. Warehousing contracts also enables banks to accommodate their customers' needs more easily and widen the choices they can make available to them. To give another example: if a customer wants a fixed-rate loan, but the bank is only willing to provide a floating-rate one, the bank might offer it a combination of a floating-rate loan and a fixed–floating interest-rate swap, and then warehouse the swap. The customer *de facto* gets the fixed-rate loan he wants, but the bank is free of any commitment to provide a fixed-rate loan once it has sold the swap it has warehoused. Warehousing also opens to way to various forms of repackaging. For instance, a bank that wished to get rid of fixed-rate bonds but did not want to lower their price might repackage them as floating-rate bonds instead. Such arrangements enable banks to tailor-make financial packages to suit the need of particular clients, but they also increase the clients' options by giving them access to markets (e.g., the fixed-bond market) that they might otherwise lack. In short, a bank can provide genuine intermediation services in derivatives markets, particularly swap ones, because of economies of scope related to its other lines of business, but can also use derivatives to increase the range of services it can provide for its customers. In addition, since risks within the bank's warehouse will to some extent cancel out, a bank that runs its own 'book' is also better able to bear the risks associated with derivatives trading than other agents (Campbell and Kracaw, 1991). We can thus explain, not only why banks trade derivatives on their own account, as it were, but why they go further and provide intermediation services in derivatives markets as well.

BANKING STABILITY AND INSTABILITY

Bank Runs

We turn now to consider various issues relating to banking stability and instability, and a good place to start is with the issue of bank runs. The reader will recall from our earlier discussion that bank liabilities are generally more liquid than bank assets. Most liabilities are in fact demandable, but a large proportion of a bank's assets typically consists of assets that not only take time to mature, but can be liquidated before they mature only at a loss. This mismatched balance sheet makes a bank vulnerable to runs in which a large proportion of its debt-holders demand redemption. We therefore need to consider runs in some detail, and there are three main cases we need to consider.

A Run on a Weak Bank

The first is where there is a run on a weak bank. If the bank is genuinely weak, the chances are that its weakness would be publicly known or at least suspected – indeed, it would normally be a public signal of its weakness that sets off the run in the first place – and so the bank would have considerable difficulty obtaining credit with which to meet its redemption demands. It would therefore be dependent on meeting the run out of its own assets, but would rapidly run out of reserves and other marketable assets and, as the run continued, would have to sell less marketable assets at increasing 'firesale' losses. These losses would erode its financial condition even more and further encourage any remaining debt-holders to run, and the bank would almost certainly be forced into default. Bankruptcy procedures would then come into play, the management would lose control, and the bank's remaining assets would be sold to satisfy its creditors. The faster or more alert depositors would have recovered their deposits in full, but other depositors would lose at least some of their deposits and the share-holders would be lucky if they recovered anything at all.

This outcome is hard on the later depositors and share-holders, but the arrangement under which this *could* happen nonetheless has much to commend it. The implicit contract calls for share-holders to be residual claimants, and thereby provide some degree of protection for the debt-holders, in return for being granted conditional control rights. It follows, therefore, that they *should* lose their investments if they fail to monitor their management properly, and it is the *threat* of losing their investments that provides them with much of the incentive they need to carry out their monitoring and control duties properly. The losses faced by depositors and note-holders are also appropriate because the desire to avoid them gives them some incentive to monitor the bank themselves. Those debt-holders who monitor the bank more closely would get to the bank early to demand redemption and recover their funds in full, and hence get the reward for their diligence; while the losses suffered by the slower debt-holders who get to the bank later are the penalty they must pay for neglecting their monitoring.

In this context, the desire of individual debt-holders to beat each other to the bank serves a useful function because it ensures that the bank is driven into default very quickly. Once it becomes clear that the bank is terminally ill, it is important that operational control of the bank be quickly taken away from managers who no longer have any real incentive to look after its remaining resources properly, and who might otherwise squander them (e.g., by selling off assets in a hurry, at lower prices than would otherwise be obtained) A bank run accomplishes this purpose by driving the bank to default more or less immediately. Far from being undesirable, the (apparently) 'panicky' behaviour of depositors and note-holders who race each other to the bank to demand redemption is in fact an essential feature of the bank's efficient liquidation.

A Run on a Strong Bank

If the bank is genuinely strong, it should be able to meet the run out of its own reserves or by obtaining reserve media from elsewhere. Initially, it would respond by drawing down its own reserves. If its reserves did not suffice – or more accurately, did not look at though they would suffice – the bank would then try to obtain them elsewhere, and it could do so either by borrowing or by selling its own assets. Should it need to borrow, it would presumably need to do so at short notice, and it would also need to know *ex ante* that it could do so. A typical bank would therefore take the precaution of taking out one or more lines of credit on which it could draw if the need arose. These facilities might also be backed up by other arrangements, such as 'implicit' understandings with other banks to help each other out, or, conceivably, the establishment of an institutional apparatus (e.g., a bankers' club, see Chapter 9 below) to provide emergency loans in a hurry. A bank that wanted a loan could then apply to the bankers' club, which would vet the application quickly and grant the loan if it felt that it was sound. There are thus a variety of reasons to believe that a sound bank would have little difficulty obtaining emergency liquidity if it needed it. A bank might also replenish its reserves of redemption media by selling assets, but – given that it could normally expect to be able to borrow – a sound bank would only sell marketable assets. There is after all no point a bank selling assets at a loss to replenish its liquidity when it can obtain liquidity on reasonable terms simply by borrowing it. In short, the likely outcome is that a sound bank would meet a run by borrowing, perhaps supplemented to some extent by selling marketable assets, but precisely because it is sound, it should have little difficulty persuading other banks to lend to it. A sound bank could therefore meet the run without any serious danger.

Indeed, it is most unlikely to face a run *precisely because* it *could* withstand one: debt-holders have no reason to run on a sound bank that can withstand a run. The bank's ultimate line of defence is therefore the maintenance of its financial health. A bank must build up its financial strength to reassure debt-holders that it has the resources to pay them off in full even if it suffers some losses on its loan portfolio, and the bank must provide this reassurance in a variety of visible ways – it must maintain its capital adequacy (i.e., keep down its leverage to patently safe levels); it must keep a reasonable quality loan portfolio, and as far as possible, communicate that fact to its debt-holders; it must maintain its liquidity, and be seen as being able to meet unexpected demands for redemption should they occur (e.g., by taking out back-up lines of credit, and by having marketable assets it could sell); it should employ competent and honest management; it should regularly provide debt-holders and other investors with the information they need to monitor its performance; and it should submit itself to regular auditing by independent outside experts to give debt-holders and other investors confidence that the information it offers them is reliable.

A bank that pursues such policies then has little to fear. Should a large demand for redemptions occur for some reason, the bank should be able to meet those demands very easily. But, more fundamentally, the very fact that it could meet the run easily would mean that it was most unlikely to face a run in the first place. A typical debt-holder would appreciate that the bank could easily pay its debts, and would therefore have no reason to demand redemption out of fear that the bank was about to become insolvent. Others would think like him, and the only redemptions the bank would face would be the everyday ones that occur when a customer needs liquidity unexpectedly, when more cheques are drawn on the bank than are deposited with it, and so on. The irony is that it is precisely because the bank *could* face a run that a run does not *actually* occur. A sound bank could face a run, but has little reason to expect one.

Systemic Effects of Bank Runs

Bank runs can also have important ramifications for the rest of the banking system. A depositor who withdraws his funds from his bank out of fears for their safety must then decide what to do with them. He will usually wish to invest them elsewhere, and his basic choice is between investing them in another bank and investing them in non-bank form (e.g., stuffing them in the mattress). *Unless* he has reason to fear that other banks are in danger as well – a possibility we shall discuss shortly – he will usually want to invest his funds in another bank for much the same reasons that he chose to make an initial bank investment in the first place. He will then purchase the debt of another bank, and so will others like him. Most of the funds (or more precisely, redemption media) withdrawn from the first bank will therefore be presented to other banks as demands for more banknotes or new deposits, and the run on the first bank results, for the most part, in a transfer of debt-holdings, and the reserve media that go with them, to other banks. If the bank experiencing the run was sound, the other banks would lend it many of the reserves deposited with them, and the run would produce little more than a certain amount of recycling of debts and reserve media within the financial system. However, if the bank experiencing the run was weak, the run would normally put it out of business, but the funds withdrawn would still largely return to the banking system and the 'gap' created by the failure of the weak bank would soon be filled by the other banks. Either way, a run on an individual bank should have little major detrimental effect on the rest of the banking system.

But what would happen if there was a run on a significant group of banks, or even a run on the banking system as a whole? *If* such a run *did* occur, the system would have much less ability to absorb the run by merely recycling reserves or deposits from one bank to another. There would be a large *aggregate* fall in the demand for bank liabilities, and the system would have to find the reserve media to meet this fall. Yet even then, the banks, if they are sound, should still be able to borrow from elsewhere (e.g., from foreign banks), and banks can also to some extent meet the fall in demand for their liabilities by selling assets. The system's response to a run would therefore be similar to the response of an individual bank facing a run – it would borrow, and perhaps sell some assets – but it should have no fundamental difficulty meeting the run provided it is sound. However, as is the case with an individual bank, there is also the more fundamental point that the public have no reason to run on the banking system in the first place if they perceive it to be sound. Each individual member of the public faces the decision whether to run on his own bank, and he will not run on his own bank if he believes it to be sound. Hence, if the banks are sound, as a system, then each individual bank will continue to enjoy the confidence of its customers, and no bank will face a run. There will therefore be no run on the system either.

There is also a further reason why we would not expect to see a run on the banking system as a whole, as distinct from runs on individual banks. The competition for market share gives the better banks an incentive to distinguish themselves from the weaker ones in order to win their market share, and they will do so by positioning themselves in a way that encourages the customers of weaker banks to transfer their business to them. Suppose for the sake of argument that one bank perceives another as pursuing questionable policies that undermine the latter's financial health (e.g., the latter might be over-extending its leverage or making an excessive proportion of its loans to one potentially risky sector of the economy). The weaker bank would make easy profits at first, but in time the underlying economic fundamentals would reassert themselves, its financial health would deteriorate, the public would become aware of at least some of its problems, and at some point an adverse development (e.g., the revelation of a bad loan) would trigger off a run. This course of events would be predictable, and so the strategy of the good bank would be to anticipate it and place itself in a position where if could win over the customers of the weaker bank once they lost confidence in it. When that happened, the strong bank would induce them to switch over by pointing to its own demonstrable financial strength. Indeed, it would positively *encourage* the customers of the other bank to run. The weaker bank would then lose much of its market share, and might even be driven out of business altogether. The basic strategy for the stronger or more far-sighted banks is thus very simple: they would adopt a longer-term game plan; they would build up, or at least, maintain, their financial strength, and resist the siren calls of easy short-term profits; and, when the crisis came and the weaker banks found themselves on the edge of the abyss, they would give them a push and launch an all-out attack for their market share.[9] This market share-competition argument makes a run on the system as a whole unlikely because the whole point of market share-competition is to encourage the customers of weaker banks to transfer their business to the stronger banks, and not to simply to withdraw from the system. Any tendency of weak banks to start going off the rails would be met by the strong banks becoming, if anything, even stronger, with the end result being a run on the weaker part of the banking system, but no run on the system as a whole.

Bank Run Contagion

Part of the still widespread fear attached to bank runs no doubt arises because of a belief that bank runs are contagious, that is to say, that a run on one bank can trigger off runs on others. According to this view, bank runs are like infectious diseases or forest fires. They are dangerous, not so much because they might force an *individual* bank to default, but because they might shatter confidence in the banking *system* and provoke a system-wide run. The bank run contagion hypothesis is very widely accepted – in the words of Kaufman (1987, 10), 'Most writers do not seriously question that it occurs almost automatically and have accepted it as a matter of faith' – in part because they (incorrectly) believe that bank run contagion is a major feature of the historical record. It also plays a large part in the widespread fear of bank runs and the belief associated with that fear that bank runs are an evil to be avoided at virtually any cost:

> It is accounts of systemwide contagious bank runs that appear to underlie the traumatic – almost psychotic – fears of bank failures and of the severity of their damage on overall economic activity. Such fears remain widespread today. In defending his action in rescuing the Continental Illinois National Bank in May

1984, Comptroller of the Currency C. T. Conover (1984) testified that 'In our collective judgement ... had Continental Illinois failed and been treated in a way in which depositors and creditors were not made whole, we could very well have seen a national, if not an international, financial crisis the dimensions of which were difficult to imagine. None of us wanted to find out'. (Benston *et al.,* 1986, 50–51).

The most plausible argument for bank-run contagion is that debt-holders might run on their bank if they observe a run at another bank that leads them to believe that their own bank is no longer safe. A depositor will be imperfectly informed about the true state of his bank's financial health, and, if he is rational, will use all available information when trying to assess that state and decide whether to keep his deposit at his bank. The observation that another bank is in difficulties might then cause him to revise his assessment of the financial health of his own bank, particularly if the other bank is similar to his own. Whatever is causing the difficulties of the other bank might also affect his own bank as well, and he will have to decide whether the 'news' about the other bank should lead him to downgrade his estimate of his own bank's financial health by a sufficiently large amount that his deposit becomes endangered. If the two banks are sufficiently similar and the news about the other bank is sufficiently bad, he may therefore decide to withdraw, and if others think like him, the bank will face a run. The run on the first bank could then be described as contagious.

However, the second bank must be fairly weak already if the run on the first bank is enough to triggers off a run against it. The bank run contagion scenario is therefore limited because it can only really explain contagion from one weak bank to another. The most a strong bank has to fear is that the observation of a run at a weak bank might lead share-holders to mark down its equity value, but it should be able to absorb such a reduction precisely because it *is* strong. In any case, as discussed a little earlier, good banks do in fact have an incentive to distance themselves from bad ones and place themselves to take over their market share when their difficulties become apparent. Far from leading to the strong banks facing a run themselves, the most likely result is that depositors at the weaker banks transfer their deposits to them instead. Indeed, to the extent there *were* any problem of potential contagion, the stronger banks would have an incentive to strengthen themselves further to reinforce public confidence in them. If they felt that the failure of a weak bank *could* produce a shock wave that might hit them too, then they have an incentive to strengthen themselves for when the shock comes. The *prospect* of contagion might therefore make the strong banks stronger than they would otherwise have been, and thereby ensure that contagion does not *actually* occur when a weak bank fails. It follows that the only banks that would have any real reason to fear contagion would be other weak banks, particularly those that were similar to any weak bank that failed, but the underlying problem would then be their weakness rather than contagion as such, and there is a good case that they *should* be put out of business anyway.[10]

Empirical Evidence on Bank Runs and Bank Failures

These theoretical conjectures are also consistent with the empirical evidence. The historical experiences of free (or nearly free) banking in Australia, Canada, China, Scotland, and various other countries indicate that bank runs and failures were rare events affecting only very limited numbers of banks (see, e.g., the case studies in Dowd (ed.), 1992). Runs were usually triggered off by revelations that a particular bank had suffered major loan losses. They were also restricted to the bank that suffered the loss and to other institutions that depended on it, and other banks were either not adversely affected by the run or, if they were, managed to absorb the shock relatively easily. The evidence also indicates that these runs were not random, unpredictable events, but rational and to a certain extent predictable responses to the news of the difficulties of a particular bank or banks.

The relative rarity of runs and failures under free banking is also apparent from comparisons of free banking systems with their more regulated counterparts. One comparison is that between the Scottish banking system during the late eighteenth and early nineteenth centuries, which was largely free, and the contemporary English banking system, which was subject to significant legal restrictions. The Scottish system experienced fewer runs and was better able to weather those it did experience. In 1793, for example, a major crisis shook the English financial system, and at least 100 banks failed and many more were badly shaken, but in Scotland only two banks failed and even these met their claims in full (L. H. White, 1984a, 45). Four years later, the landing of French troops in Wales triggered off large-scale runs in England that culminated in the Bank of England suspending the convertibility of its notes, but in Scotland the banks 'confronted only a minor internal drain' (L. H. White, 1984a, 46). When a third crisis hit the British financial system in 1825–1826, almost the entire English banking industry asked the Bank of England for assistance and a very large number of banks failed. In Scotland, in comparison, only two small banks failed and at least one of these subsequently paid its liabilities in full (L. H. White, 1984a, 47). The very considerable confidence that free banks commanded is also indicated by the evidence that Scottish bank notes circulated widely in northern England during this period, but English notes did not circulate in Scotland, and by other evidence that the English preferred Scottish notes to the notes of their own banks. Scottish banks were thus subject to fewer runs than English banks, and their notes were regarded as safer. This difference between the two banking systems was due in large part to the difference between the restrictions under which the English banks had to operate, and the relative freedom of the Scottish banks. That the Scottish banks were safer – and therefore less liable to fail – than their more regulated English counterparts also comes across in the figures for debt-holder losses. L. H. White (1984a, 41) reports a contemporary observer who estimated that the total loss to the Scottish public up to 1841 from the failures of Scottish banks was only £32,000 – a figure that is over twice the losses to debt-holders from the failures of London banks in the previous year alone.

Banks were also highly stable in the *antebellum* USA. Recent reassessments of banking during this period have made it plain that, far from being a failure, as had been widely believed, banking during this period was in fact highly stable, and such failures as there were can often be related to the combination of legal restrictions such as bond-collateral requirements and unstable fiscal (i.e., political) factors. There is considerable evidence to link 'free bank' failures with capital losses, and these losses can in turn be linked to the fiscal instability that certain states experienced at particular times (see, e.g., Rolnick and Weber, 1982, 1983, 1984, 1985; Economopoulos, 1988; and Dowd, 1992a). In the final analysis, the losses that put so many of the 'free banks' out of business were ultimately caused by the combination of legal restrictions and fiscal factors, and hence, at an even more basic level, by political factors. It must also be borne in mind that the 'free banks' discussed here are not so much banks operating under *laissez-faire* conditions, as banks that operated under laws modelled on the free-entry, bond-collateral legislation enacted in New York in 1838. (This type of law – frequently though misleadingly described as a 'free banking law' – allowed free entry to the industry *on condition* that banks provided collateral of approved bonds, usually state bonds, with the state authorities.) These 'free banks' co-existed with other types of banks, including banks that operated in systems that were even less regulated than New York-style 'free banks'. The banks of Massachusetts and South Carolina, for example, operated under very liberal regulatory regimes and were both highly stable, and Massachusetts had very few 'free banks' and South Carolina none at all. As far as I can tell, genuinely free banks were more successful than those banks that operated under New York-style 'free banking' laws, and the assessments of Rolnick and Weber, Economopoulos, and others of 'free banking' therefore provide a somewhat *under-stated* impression of the relative success and stability of banking *laissez-faire* in this period (Dowd, 1992a, 225–228).

By modern standards, the US banking system was still relatively free even after the Civil War and the introduction of the legislative restrictions of the National Banking System. There was still no central bank and no federal deposit insurance system to guarantee banks' liabilities. The threat of a run was consequently very real for a bank that lost the confidence of its debt-holders, and this threat was a strong inducement for a bank to maintain its financial health. Runs were therefore relatively infrequent, and many of those that did occur during this period can be traced to the effects of economic recession (see, e.g., Gorton, 1986) or the effects of legal restrictions that provoked scrambles for liquidity and then prevented banks from meeting those demands (see, e.g., Dowd, 1989, Chapter 5). The average annual bank failure rate for the period 1875–1919 was well under 1 percent, which was lower than the corresponding failure rate for non-financial firms (Benston *et al.,* 1986, 58). The failures that did occur also tended to be concentrated in particular areas, and to involve relatively small banks:

Almost all the banks that failed in the 1920s were small banks in rural areas, particularly in the central and western grain areas and the southwest. Almost 90 percent had capital of less than $100,000 ..., more than 90 percent had loans and investments of less than $1 million ..., 60 percent were located in towns of less than 1,000 in population, and 90 percent were in towns of less than 5,000. The average failed bank was less than one-half the size of all banks. (Benston *et al.*, 1986, 61)

Indeed, no national bank with capital in excess of $5 million failed at all during this period (Benston *et al.*, 1986, 61). Even in the 1930s, when bank failures were most prevalent,

> banks that failed tended, on the whole, to be the smaller banks. The proportion of total bank deposits held in banks that failed was considerably less than their proportion of the number of banks. Deposits at failed banks averaged only 2 percent of total deposits in 1930 and 1931, 1 percent in 1931, and 12 percent in 1933. Thus, it is likely that many banks continued to fail primarily because of adverse local business conditions rather than because of spillover from other failed banks outside their market areas. (Benston *et al.*, 1986, 62)

Runs were not the problem that late twentieth-century economists – brought up to take the 'need' for federal deposit insurance or a lender of last resort for granted – presume they must have been. To quote Kaufman again,

> a study for the American Bankers Association in the late 1920s was summarized by a reviewer as relegating 'the run as a real reason for [bank] suspensions ... to a position of minor importance. It is found to be an effect of banking difficulties rather than a cause as a general proposition which is contrary to the fixed ideas of the public and even many bankers'. The evidence also suggests that the primary direction of causation was from problems in the real sector to problems in banking and not the other way around. That is, both bank runs and bank failures were the effect and not the cause of aggregate economic contractions and hardships. This suggests that almost all bank runs ... [involved] either direct or indirect redeposits. They did not develop into runs on the system. (Kaufman, 1987, 13)

The comparative infrequency, if not rarity, of bank runs under the relatively competitive conditions of the past seems to be due to the combination of market discipline – much, though not all of it due to the threat of runs – and to the public demand for sound banks. Banks *had* to be strong to remain in business, and their strength comes out very clearly from the historical data on bank capital ratios. For example, the capital to assets ratio of US banks was well over 40 percent (!) for most of the 'free banking' period when there was no significant federal involvement in banking. It fell in subsequent years, but was still over 14 percent in 1933 on the eve of the establishment of federal deposit insurance (Salsman, 1990, 95, 46). These figures are much higher than modern figures, and yet actually *under-state* banks' true capital ratios because they ignore the fact that most bank share-holders in the past had double liability.

The greater stability of free banking also comes across from a comparison of the US and Canadian banking systems in the later nineteenth and early twentieth centuries. The Canadian banking system of the time was less unregulated, and free of the recurrent systemic crises that plagued the USA. Again and again – 1857, 1873, 1883, 1890, 1893, and 1907 – the US banking system experienced crises involving runs on weaker banks, spikes in interest rates, and sometimes suspension of specie payments. These crises were largely home-grown in the sense that they were usually triggered by domestic shocks but seriously aggravated by the various restrictions under which US banks had to operate. The Canadian system inevitably experienced the ripples of the American crises, but runs in Canada were extremely rare and Canada largely escaped the consequences of the US crises without serious damage. As with the Scottish banks, the greater confidence enjoyed by Canadian banks was also reflected in the widespread use of Canadian banknotes south of the border, the widespread admiration of the Canadian system in the USA, and the fact that many US bankers wanted to imitate it.

Empirical Evidence on Bank Run Contagion

Then there is the issue of bank-run contagion. The various episodes of relatively free banking systems in the past showed little or no evidence of bank run contagion. Runs were infrequent, but when they did occur, were associated with news that particular banks had suffered major losses, and the funds withdrawn were usually redeposited in stronger banks.

One could give many examples of this sort of outcome. For example, the run on the Ayr Bank in 1772 was not contagious, and merely led the stronger Scottish banks to increase their market share. The suspension of specie payments by the Bank of England in 1797 produced only a relatively minor drain in Scotland, and the banking crisis that shook the English banking system to its foundations in 1825–1826 more or less stopped at the Scottish border. Nor is there any clear evidence of contagion in the most severe banking crisis to have occurred under relatively free conditions, namely, that which occurred in Australia in the early 1890s. The banks most affected by the loss of confidence in the public were the newer 'fungoid' banks that had grown up in the previous decade primarily to finance the land boom. When they started to face runs in the early 1890s, the trading banks still enjoyed public confidence. The trading banks only started to face runs themselves when bad news was released about loan losses, and even then the runs were restricted to the individual banks concerned. The crisis peaked in early 1893, at which time the biggest trading banks experienced massive inflows of funds – fund inflows were so large, in fact, that two of the banks concerned were positively embarrassed by them. Despite various government attempts to encourage the banks to suspend, the two biggest banks remained open and enjoyed full public confidence throughout the crisis (see, e.g., Butlin, 1961, 305; Dowd, 1992b, 60–65).

The bank run contagion issue has been most widely researched in the context of the USA, but little or no hard evidence of contagion has actually been found. For the *antebellum* period, Rolnick and Weber found that bank failures tended to be clustered, and that clustered failures in the different states – such as in New York in the early 1840s – were associated with shocks that were specific to particular groups of banks, with little tendency for banking problems in one state to spread to other states (see, e.g., Rolnick and Weber, 1985, 5–8; 1986, 885–887). Rolnick and Weber also looked for evidence of intrastate contagion in this period and found little sign of that either (1986, 887, n. 7).[11]

For the period after the Civil War, Benston *et al.,* (1986, 59) suggest as a rule of thumb that contagious runs should be associated with increases in the public's currency/deposit ratio and a decrease in their deposit holdings, and these events occurred in only three crises – 1873, 1893, and 1908 – in the period between the Civil War and the 1930s. They therefore conclude that '[s]ystemwide contagious bank runs *may* have occurred in these periods' (1986, 60, my italics), but this conclusion implicitly concedes that contagious runs did not occur at other times and still does not establish that contagious runs *did in fact* take place during these three crises. They go on to point out that less than 1 percent of the total number of banks actually failed even in the severe crisis of 1908 (Benston *et al.,* 1986, 60). If any of these failures *were* contagious, the contagion must have been extremely limited.

There is also evidence that the widespread interpretation of the bank collapses of the early 1930s as waves of contagious bank failures is, to say the least, exaggerated. The work of Wicker (1982) concluded that the initial impact of the 1930 crisis was confined almost entirely to readily identifiable local economies, and had no discernible influence on the economy as a whole, and that of Eugene White (1984) suggests that the wave of bank failures in 1930 was primarily caused by the downturn in economic activity. Contemporary accounts also lead one to believe that later writers have, to say the least, exaggerated the role of contagion in the 1930s. None of the papers or discussants at the 1931 AEA meeting on the banking situation stressed the bank contagion issue or even saw it as a significant factor in the banking crisis (Benston *et al.,* 1986, 67–68). Contemporary discussion of contagion only really began in 1933, but even then the events of late 1932 and 1933 that some writers saw as instances of contagion can also be explained in other ways. The increasing resort to state-declared banking holidays would have provoked scrambles for cash in states where banks were still open, especially if people felt that such holidays increased the probability of their own banks being closed as well, and these scrambles for liquidity could easily be misinterpreted as contagious bank runs. Similarly, the election of Franklin Roosevelt in late 1932 fuelled expectations of a devaluation of the currency as well as expectations of a nation-wide banking holiday – both of which subsequently occurred – and both of these would have encouraged pre-emptive demands for cash that might easily be mistaken for bank run contagion.

The Costs of Bank Failures and Bank Distress

Bank failures involve various types of cost. Perhaps the most obvious are the 'direct' costs such as the losses to debt- and equity-holders when a bank fails and they lose some or more of their investments, but there are also other costs such as the costs borne by bank customers and employees – some of which are borne when banks become distressed, and not just when they fail – and as well as certain costs to local communities and to the economy more generally.

The 'Direct' Costs of Bank Failures

The available evidence on 'direct' note-holder and depositor losses under relatively unregulated banking systems suggests that such losses are very small, and we have already discussed the low costs of bank failures in free-banking Scotland relative to the costs of bank failures in the more regulated English system of the time. The low costs of Scottish bank failures are also apparent from the reaction of the citizens of Cumberland and Westmoreland when it was proposed to prohibit the circulation of Scottish bank notes in England. They responded by petitioning Parliament against the proposal and noted how the greater freedom of the Scottish banks gave

> a degree of strength to the issuers of notes, and of confidence to the receivers of them, which several banks established in our counties have not been able to command. The natural consequence has been, that Scotch notes have formed the greater part of our circulating medium. (quoted in L. H. White, 1984a, 42)

They went on to add that they had, with one exception, never suffered *any* loss from accepting Scottish notes over the last fifty years,

> 'while in the same period the failures of banks in the north of England have been unfortunately numerous, and have occasioned the most ruinous losses to many who were little able to sustain them'. (1984a, 421).

The losses suffered by bank creditors during and after the National Banking System were also relatively small. Benston *et al.,* (1986, 63–64) report loss annual estimates from bank failures over the period 1865–1933 equal to 0.21 percent of the value of deposits, and the losses averaged only 0.78 percent of deposits even in years identified as years of crisis. Their figures also indicate that even in the worst crisis, that of 1930–1933, depositor losses were still only 0.81 percent, and there is reason to believe that even this figure is an over-estimate because the FDIC study from which it came ignored some of the assets subsequently recovered when the banks in question were finally wound up.

This conclusion is also consistent with the estimates of Gendreau and Prince (1986) for the direct, out-of-pocket expenses to stockholders and debt-holders of national bank failures between 1872 and 1904, and 1929 and 1933. They estimated that total receiver and legal fees for handling bankrupt banks averaged between 3 and 6 percent of the value of bank liabilities (Gendreau and Prince, 1986, 9–11), but also found that these bankruptcy costs were considerably lower for larger banks – for the big banks in their sample, they were only 1–2 percent of the value of liabilities – and concluded that though direct bankruptcy costs were 'fairly large' relative to the value of small banks, they were 'negligible' in relation to the value of larger ones (Gendreau and Prince, 1986, 13). Since anti-branching laws kept banks artificially small in the USA, the Gendreau–Prince estimates would lead one to expect these losses to be more or less negligible under a more liberal regulatory environment that allowed banks to grow to their optimal sizes. In any case, one might also note that these figures – *despite* the fact that they are pushed up by regulatory restrictions – are *still* generally lower than the comparable figures reported for non-financial firms by Warner (1977) and Altman (1984). The widespread idea that bank failures impose larger losses on creditors than the failures of other types of firm thus appears to be mistaken.

One reason why these losses were so low is that the public demand sound (i.e., highly capitalised) banks and, where they are allowed to do so, market forces ensure that they get them; if banks are highly capitalised, bank failures should then be relatively infrequent and the losses involved should be correspondingly low. A second reason is that banks hold mainly financial assets and, while these can often only be sold at a loss, the loss is small relative to that faced by a firm with real assets such as equipment, fixtures, furniture, perishable inventory, and similar assets. Banks' portfolios are usually also more diversified than the portfolios of other firms, and are therefore less likely to collapse in value overnight. Since a bank run provides a means of putting a weak bank out of business very quickly, there is relatively little prospect, at least where market forces are allowed to operate reasonably freely, of a weak bank building up a large negative net worth and simultaneously managing to stay in business. Free banks tend to be driven out of business *before* they can accumulate very large losses.

The 'Indirect' Costs of Bank Failure and Bank Distress

There are also various indirect costs of bank failures. A bank failure at the very least disrupts a borrower's relationship with the bank that lends to it. If the bank is wound up rather than just taken over, the capital invested by both bank and borrower in their relationship will often be completely lost. Many borrowers depend on an 'understanding' with their bank that they can normally expect their credit to be renewed when the time comes to review their position, but that 'understanding' is the product of both sides' investing time and other resources to maintain the relationship. Both sides then lose if the relationship is severed. The bank loses because the relationship represents an asset whose value to the bank depends on accumulated knowledge that can only be transferred to someone else at some cost. The borrower loses because he would have to build up another relationship with a new lender and, perhaps more importantly, because his credit is suddenly cut without any warning. His 'shadow price' of credit suddenly rises, and this rise in the cost of credit could be highly damaging if he had depended on the continued availability of credit. A loan-customer might be forced to default himself or at best forgo profitable investment opportunities that he could have undertaken had the bank credit still been available. Depositors will also have to establish new banking relationships and

> will also likely be denied access to their funds until their claim against the closed bank is settled. For uninsured depositors, this delay could be quite long. Although bank receivers are required to liquidate a bank as quickly as possible, it is not uncommon for a bank liquidation to take over a decade. (Gendreau and Prince, 1986, 5)

Bank employees will usually suffer as well. Those who are lucky will retain their jobs if their bank is taken over and the acquiring bank decides to keep them, but in many cases the branch in which they work will close down or jobs will be cut even if the branch itself remains open.

There are also various costs of involved when a bank becomes financially *distressed*, even if that distress does not actually lead the bank to *fail*. Firms that are financially distressed – banks as well as other firms – tend to experience difficulty hiring and keeping employees. Employees and prospective employees can often perceive the firm's difficulties and realise that their positions are not (or would not) be safe, and therefore look around elsewhere for jobs. Customers would think the same way. A bank in financial distress could therefore find its loan customers deserting it and its creditors demanding payment. Loan customers could also lose because a bank in financial distress might cut back its lending. Moreover, as Gale (1992b, 2–3) points out, this retrenchment can often work in perverse ways. Since such a bank would want to retrieve what it has loaned out, it might cut the loans of those customers who are in a position to repay, and thereby inflict a disproportionate share of the cuts on the bank's more 'worthy' customers. The bank itself would also experience difficulties obtaining credit, or would only be able to obtain credit on relatively unfavourable terms reflecting the outside perception of its weakness. Apart from the obvious risk that it might face a run it had not the reserves to meet, this disruption to its own credit supply would also mean that the bank would be unable to take advantage of investment opportunities that it could have taken up had it been financially healthy.

Another indirect cost of a bank failure is the effect on the local community. The evidence on this issue suggests that a bank failure has a relatively limited effect comparable to the effect of the closing of other local businesses:

> A recent article in the *American Banker* analyzed the effects on communities of the closing of their only banks. According to the author, the communities that lost their only local source of banking services in recent years were generally very small towns with populations of under 300 persons. These towns tend to

be too small to support another independent bank or even a branch of a distant bank. The only bank's departure was both an inconvenience and led to reductions in revenues and even to the closings of neighboring business firms, generally retail shops. Consumers had to travel to nearby cities to obtain personal banking services and those who used to bank locally shopped less frequently at nearby shops. They transferred some of their business to shops nearer to their new banks. But these effects are hardly very different from the repercussions of the loss of a community's only movie theater, department store, or even supermarket. (Kaufman, 1987, 31)

Other empirical work also suggests that the effects of bank failures on local communities are limited. Benston *et al.* state that

The evidence from most of US history indicates that, contrary to general belief, the adverse effects of bank runs and bank failures on the community have, for the most part, not been much greater than the effects of financial difficulties of most other business firms of comparable relative size and importance in the community, and may often be considerably less. (Benston *et al.,* 1986, 74)

This conclusion is also consistent with the empirical work of Gilbert and Kochin (1987, 1989) on the impacts of bank failures on local communities. These studies found that bank failures in rural counties either had no, or at most, limited, effects on economic activity in the communities in which they occurred. Furthermore, as Benston and Kaufman point out,

bank failures generally do not leave communities without banking facilities. Rather, customers are likely to face banks under different managements and ownerships. This may cause some hardships, but these should not be overly severe. Deposit customers will be affected only to the extent that the new bank charges different service fees and pays different deposit rates. These changes are as likely to be favorable to the customers as unfavorable. The hardships may be more substantial for loan customers. The new banks could have different loan standards and loan officers, and long-standing bank-customers relationships may have to be reestablished. But it is unlikely that changes in bank management will result in changes of all or even most loan officers so that the continuity of the personal relationship may well be unaffected. Indeed, strong bank-customer relationships are valuable intangible assets that are readily marketable to other banks. If a bank failed because of poor loans, it may be possible that new banks will be reluctant to assume the failed bank's commitments not in default because of distrust of its credit judgement and/or probity. But, rather than reject all commitments, it is the acquiring bank that will benefit from screening the failed bank's loan portfolio and assuming those loans that are consistent with its own lending standards. Thus, those loan customers who are inconvenienced are likely to be those who should not have been granted bank loans to begin with. (Benston and Kaufman, 1988, 14)

Then there are the effects of bank failures on the wider economy. Many economists still believe these effects are very large, but this belief is in some way another lingering folk-memory of the peculiar events of the 1930s, and more recent work by Benston *et al.* (1986), Kaufman (1987, 1988) and other suggests that these effects are considerably smaller than was previously thought. (Grossman, 1989 however disagrees, but his simulation results about the effects of national banking system crises are somewhat extreme and inconsistent with reported changes in economic activity.) Benston *et al.* (1986, 53) conclude that, with the exception of failures brought on by fraud, bank failures

> inflict about the same damage on the local or national economies, beyond that already contributed by the forces that brought about the failures, as do the failures of nonbank firms of equal size and relative importance.

In any case, 'The main direction of causation is likely to run from the economy to bank failure and not the reverse' (Benston *et al.* (1986, 53), so bank failures are not only limited in their impact on economic activity, but cannot even be said to be the *cause* of the economic disruption often associated with them (see also Tallman, 1988).[12]

8 The Structure of the Banking Industry*

This chapter considers the scale of operation of the banking firm. We focus on two key issues. The first is whether the banking industry shows sufficiently large economies of scale that only one firm survives in the competitive equilibrium, i.e., we consider whether banking is a *natural monopoly*. This is an important question because arguments that banking is a natural monopoly have sometimes been used to justify government intervention into the banking industry, or else to make the case that there is no point deregulating banking because the industry – or, more specifically, some aspect of it, such as the note issue – would be a monopoly anyway even under *laissez-faire*. Our discussion suggests that the claim that banking is a natural monopoly is theoretically weak: theory suggests that banking is subject to scalar economies, but these economies are not sufficiently pronounced to make banking a natural monopoly. The theory is also confirmed by the empirical evidence, and there is in fact no evidence at all that banking is a natural monopoly.

A second issue then arises once one grants that banking is not a natural monopoly. This is the 'banking club' issue: whether banks might usefully form an interbank organisation to which they might delegate certain functions – like economising on reserves, providing emergency loans or dealing with possible bank run 'contagion' – while still retaining some degree of independence. This issue is important, since a number of economists have recently argued that these club 'regulations' provide a justification for the regulations imposed by modern systems of central banking. According to this argument, the regulations imposed by modern systems of central banking merely do what a private banking club would do anyway. There is therefore little point establishing free banking, because institutions with central bank functions would evolve again from it. We review these arguments in some detail, but end up rejecting them. One problem with them is that there is no reason to believe that the 'regulatory' structures of banking clubs – if the clubs and their 'regulations' even exist at all – would be qualitatively similar to those imposed by present-day systems of central banking. Modern central banking is a very different animal from any conceivable private banking club. Furthermore, since the benefits that regulation can bring are essentially economies of scale – economies external to individual firms, but internal to the industry – these arguments for 'spontaneous regulation' would appear to be tantamount to claims that banking is a natural monopoly. Yet the empirical evidence clearly indicates that banking is not a natural monopoly. Arguments for spontaneous regulation are

*Parts of this chapter appeared as 'Is Banking a Natural Monopoly?', *Kyklos*, 45(3) (1992), pp. 379–392, and also as 'Competitive Banking, Bankers' Clubs and Bank Regulation', *Journal of Money, Credit and Banking*, 26(2) (May 1994), pp. 289–308.

also refuted by the evidence that the historical banking systems that were relatively close to *laissez-faire* developed little or none of it, and there is a plausible argument that the nineteenth-century US cases often cited as examples of 'private' regulation only developed such 'regulation' as a response to branching and other restrictions that prevented a more explicit appropriation of scalar economies.

NATURAL MONOPOLY

An industry can be said to be a natural monopoly if the average production cost is lower for one firm than it would be for two or more firms, and this condition requires that the production technology exhibits increasing returns to scale to the point where all market demand is satisfied. These increasing returns might arise from falling fixed costs or falling variable costs of production. In banking, the former might arise from falling expected bankruptcy costs, and the latter from transaction-cost economies or economies of reserve-holding or diversification. Should there be two or more firms in an industry characterised by natural monopoly, then both firms would have higher average production costs than would be the case if either supplied the market on its own. These higher costs would presumably indicate scope for one firm to 'eliminate' the other in a mutually profitable way (e.g., bribing it to leave the market, or taking it over and closing down production facilities). It follows that while we *might* observe more than one firm in an industry characterised by natural monopoly, we would not normally expect that state of affairs to *persist*. Most of the time, an industry characterised by production taking place under natural monopoly conditions should only have one firm actually operating in it.[1]

Returns to Scale in Banking

Economies of Scale in Reserve Holding

There are several reasons why banks might face increasing returns to scale that might conceivably lead to natural monopoly. One source of increasing returns is the economies from reserve holdings. The underlying idea goes back to Edgeworth (1888) and has since been developed in a number of places (e.g., Porter, 1961; Niehans, 1978, 182–184; Baltensperger, 1980, 4–9; Sprenkle, 1985, 1987; Glasner, 1989b). These economies are based on the well-known result that, subject to certain plausible conditions, a bank's optimal reserves rise with the square root of its liabilities, a condition that implies that the bank's optimal reserve ratio falls as the bank gets bigger. Given that reserves are costly to hold, a larger bank therefore faces lower average reserve costs than a smaller bank, and one might be tempted to conclude, as Laidler (1990, 109) does, that banking is a natural monopoly.

To illustrate these economies more formally, suppose, following Baltensperger (1980, 4–9), that a bank has N $1 notes outstanding. Each note i is either held or presented for redemption during a given planning period. In the former case, X_i realises a value 0; in the latter case it realises a value 1. Each X_i is assumed to be independent, and total withdrawals $X = \sum_{i=1}^{N} X_i$. The bank holds reserves R at the start of the planning period, and each \$1 held in reserves bears an opportunity cost r. However, the bank also has to pay a penalty p for each redemption demand in excess of its reserves. The bank's decision problem is then to choose R to minimise the sum of its reserve opportunity costs (i.e., rR) and the expected penalty costs if withdrawals exceed R (i.e., $p \int_R^N p(X - R)f(X)dX$, where $f(X)$ is the density function for X). Optimisation with respect to R yields the first-order condition:

$$r = p \int_R^N f(X)dX . \tag{8.1}$$

Assuming that $f(X)$ is approximately normal, optimal reserves are:

$$R = b\sigma_X \tag{8.2}$$

where $b \equiv r/p$. Noting that $\sigma_X^2 = N\sigma_{X_i}^2$, (8.2) can be rewritten as

$$R = b\sqrt{N}\,\sigma_{X_i} \tag{8.3}$$

and optimal reserve holdings rise with the square root of the size of the bank's liabilities. The average reserve/liability ratio therefore falls as the bank gets bigger, and so increasing scale reduces the average reserve cost. To see the size of the economies involved, two banks with liabilities of N each would hold combined reserves of $2b\sqrt{N}\sigma_{X_i}$, but if they united to form a single bank, their reserves would only be $\sqrt{2}b\sqrt{N}\sigma_{X_i}$. The difference (i.e., $(2 - \sqrt{2})b\sqrt{N}\sigma_{X_i}$) is their saving in reserves from operating as one bank instead of two. This saving is a scalar economy, but this economy also diminishes with the size of the bank as proxied by N. However, if we differentiate this gain by N, we also see that the marginal return to scale (i.e., $[(2 - \sqrt{2})/(2\sqrt{N})]\sigma_{X_i}$) falls as N gets larger, and approaches zero in the limit. Returns to scale are always increasing, but they increase at a decreasing rate, and the marginal return to scale diminishes in the limit to zero.

Simple simulation results also suggest that these economies are likely to diminish rapidly in practice. As Glasner writes:

A simple numerical example will demonstrate how trivial savings on reserve costs are as a source of natural monopoly. Suppose the rate of interest is 10% on short-term liquid securities that are the alternative to holding non-interest-bearing reserves. And suppose that if a bank issued just \$1 of money, its optimal reserve would be exactly \$1 of non-interest-bearing reserves, which would imply a yearly interest cost of 10 cents per dollar issued. If the bank increased its deposits or notes a hundredfold, the square-root rule tells us that the bank would have to increase its holdings of non-interest-bearing reserves only tenfold. The annual interest cost would be only. 1 cent per dollar – a reduction of 90 percent in reserve costs. If it increased its deposits or notes another hundredfold, the bank would reduce its interest cost to only .1 cent per dollar – a reduction of 99 percent of its original cost. In other words, a bank with only $10,000 of liabilities would exhaust 99 percent of the possible savings in holding reserves ... there are virtually no further economies of scale in holding reserves. (Glasner 1989b, 7)

This argument is very plausible. Nonetheless, there are several reasons to believe that Glasner actually *exaggerates* reserve-holding costs and thereby *over-states* the potential gains from banks' merging:

- Glasner's scenario implicitly assumes that redemption media are non-interest-bearing. If we relax this assumption – and banks have an interest in holding reserves that earn a return in preference to reserves that do not – then the opportunity cost of holding reserves would be less than the interest rate, and Glasner's argument would over-state the cost of reserve holding and exaggerate the gains from merger. However, this qualification merely reinforces the point he is making.
- It might be that larger banks involve larger average transactions, but if this is the case, then a larger bank's optimal reserves will be higher than suggested by (8.3). (8.3) would then lead us to over-state the reserve-holding economy of scale and hence bias our analysis towards the claim that banking is a natural monopoly. We thus have a second qualification that reinforces Glasner's main point.
- Glasner's example also over-states the advantage of a large firm over a smaller one because of the possibility that smaller firms might be able to appropriate some of the benefits of returns to scale without explicitly merging. For example, two banks might agree to pool their reserves (and thereby economise on them) but continue to operate as otherwise separate institutions. Such an arrangement is not without its difficulties – reserves would presumably need to be monitored, and there may be a moral hazard problem which would be costly to keep under control – but the point is that merging is not the only way to obtain the benefits of economies of scale. The existence of these alternatives implies that we need to distinguish between the benefits of scalar economies *per se* and the benefits of merger as a means of obtaining those scalar economies. The existence of such alternatives means of realising scalar economies also means that the benefits of merger will often be less than the scalar economies themselves. Consequently, Glasner's estimates of scalar economies might over-state the benefits of merger and again bias us towards the conclusion that banking is a natural monopoly.

So while there are always increasing marginal returns to scale in reserve holding, these increasing returns provide a weak basis on which to argue that banking is a natural monopoly. These returns seem to diminish very rapidly, and once a certain point is passed the gains from further expansion become negligible. In any case, as Selgin argues,

For a bank to gain a monopoly of note issue [or deposit issue, for that matter] it is not sufficient that banking involve substantial fixed costs, with relatively small marginal costs, from *issuing* additional notes. The bank must also take steps to improve the popularity of its notes relative to [substitutes], or it must suffer the expense of redeeming them soon after their issue. If the costs to the bank of *extending* the market or of redemption rise rapidly enough at the margin, its average costs per unit of outstanding currency will rise above the minimum level long before the point at which it would saturate the demand for currency. In this case the industry cannot be considered a natural monopoly. (Selgin, 1988a, 151, his emphasis)

Economies of Scale from Diversification

A second source of a possible natural monopoly is scalar economies resulting from a larger bank's increased diversification of its assets. In earlier chapters we discussed various factors that might make it more costly for a small bank than for a large one to diversify its assets. If transactions costs have a fixed element, for example, then it will be relatively more costly for a small bank to achieve a given degree of diversification than for a large bank. Also, if monitoring each project involves a fixed cost, the analysis of Diamond (1984) suggests that a large bank can reduce average delegation costs. The Diamond argument is that as the bank increases the number of loans it makes to projects whose returns are independent, then the probability that it will incur the deadweight penalties implied by very low average returns (i.e., bankruptcy) will fall, and this lower probability of bankruptcy implies a lower average delegation cost. To quote Diamond:

the delegation cost for N projects monitored by a single intermediary is less than the sum of the delegation costs for monitoring proper subsets of them by several intermediaries. *Increasing returns to scale from delegation cost savings is a very general result.* The assumption of independence allows a stronger result. The expected delegation cost per entrepreneur monitored by the intermediary gets arbitrarily small as N ... grows without bound. This implies that the total cost (per entrepreneur) of providing monitoring converges to K, the physical cost of monitoring. (Diamond, 1984, 401, emphasis added)

These reductions in transactions and delegation costs mean that larger banks will be safer – and perceived to be safer – than smaller ones, *ceteris paribus*. This greater safety then enables a large bank to obtain certain other benefits for itself and its customers:

• A large bank can economise on confidence-building expenditures and still be safer than a smaller bank. For example, it can reduce its capital ratio and increase its expected rate of return on capital. A large bank can thus convert some of its greater safety into a higher rate of return for share-holders.
• There may be less pressure on liability-holders to monitor a larger bank, and so

they can reduce their monitoring expenditures. If it wanted to, a large bank might also capitalise on the greater public confidence in its liabilities by reducing the interest it pays on its deposits.

- A large bank can provide borrowers with more assurance that their credit will not be curtailed in the future provided they honour their present commitments, and this greater likelihood of future credit will increase the value to them of their relationships with the bank. The bank can then increase its lending interest rates or its charges for associated services.

- A large bank may be under less pressure to reveal its books to outsiders, and therefore be better placed to maintain client confidentiality. They will then 'trust' the bank more readily with sensitive information, and this increased 'trust' will translate into lower monitoring costs. This increased client-protection might also be an additional reason why a large bank could charge more for credit.

Yet there is *still* no reason to suppose that these economies are large enough to make banking a natural monopoly. As with the earlier economies of reserve-holding, the mere existence of these economies does not suffice to establish that they are large enough to produce a natural monopoly. For example, Diamond's monitoring economies arise from diversification and therefore diminish as the bank gets large and ultimately disappear in the limit. Once a bank has reached a certain size, the economies from further growth are negligible.[2]

There is also the problem that even if economies were large, a merger might not be the most appropriate way to realise them. There are several ways in which banks could reap the benefits of these economies without merging. They could form a banking club that can act as a bankers' bank and be large enough to appropriate the scalar economies that the smaller banks cannot reap. We shall discuss this possibility in detail in the second half of the chapter, but banks can also reap scalar economies by forming *syndicates* or *correspondent relationships*. If a group of banks wished to make loans on a larger scale than they could manage individually (e.g., to cut down on fixed costs or reap diversification benefits), they could form a syndicate and act as a group for the purposes of those loans. One bank could take the lead role in the syndicate and organise and manage the loans, and the other banks would reimburse it for their share of the costs involved. Alternatively, banks could form *correspondent relationships* in which one bank would provide others with services that the other(s) could not provide for themselves, or could only provide at greater cost. The bank might provide them with access to a clearing system or provide them with specialist service or access to new lending opportunities. It follows, then, that even if we could be confident that banking exhibits 'extreme' economies of scale – and there is no reason to suppose that it does – it still does not follow that merger is always more efficient than the next-best means of obtaining those benefits. Until we are confident on *both* these points, there is no basis on which we can safely predict that banking should be a natural monopoly.

Some Spurious Arguments for Natural Monopoly

There are also some common but spurious arguments for natural monopoly.

The Argument That Competitive Note Issue Leads to Hyperinflation

The first argument is based on the gap between the marginal private cost of printing notes and the marginal social cost of putting those notes into circulation (see, e.g., Johnson, 1968). The argument goes as follows: the private marginal cost of issuing a note is just the cost of the paper and ink needed to print it, and this cost is virtually nothing. The marginal revenue of issuing a note is the value of the goods that can be bought with a note, which is usually much greater. Under conditions of private competition, issuers of banknotes will therefore find it worthwhile to keep on issuing additional notes until the marginal revenue is brought down to the marginal cost, and this can only mean that so many notes are issued that they become virtually worthless (i.e., there would be a hyperinflation). The problem with private competition is that each issuer of notes fails to take into account the effect of his notes on the value of the notes issued by others – that is, the private cost of a bank note is less than the social cost – and it is this discrepancy between private and social costs that leads to the excess of notes and the resulting hyperinflation. The 'solution' is to make the issue of notes a legal monopoly which is then usually entrusted to the government or a central bank.

A key problem with this argument is that it is not really a natural monopoly argument at all, although it is often presented as such. Recall that a natural monopoly argument maintains that an industry can produce at lower cost with a single firm. The argument considered here cannot be a natural monopoly argument in any conventional sense because it relies on no such claim. It is really an 'externalities argument' based on a distinction between the private and social costs of printing 'money'. Yet it is still weak even as an externalities argument. The source of its weakness is that it identifies the costs of *issuing* a note and *keeping it in circulation* with the cost of *printing* it, and these costs are the same *only* if notes are inconvertible. As made clear in earlier chapters and elsewhere (see, e.g., Selgin, 1988a, Chapter 10 or Dowd, 1989, Chapter 1), unrestrained competition would force banks to issue convertible notes, and the cost of issuing a convertible note and keeping it in circulation is much more than the cost of merely printing it. A convertible note is an evidence of debt, and a large part of the cost of issuing any debt is the obligation to repay – a cost that dwarf the cost of printing the document. Once we acknowledge this point, there is no longer any reason to suppose that a gap exists between the private and social costs of issuing notes, and certainly no reason to believe that competitive banks would issue virtually unlimited quantities of notes and produce a hyperinflation. Put another way, the argument that competitive note (or deposit) issue would lead to hyperinflation is only valid if there is already an inconvertible currency, but the existence of an inconvertible currency presumes that competition in the note issue has already been suppressed, and, as Selgin (1988a,

151) observes, to 'assume the existence of a monopoly in currency supply in order to explain its "natural" occurrence obviously begs the question'.

Economies of Standardisation and Natural Monopoly

A second argument claims that banking is a natural monopoly because everyone in a community (typically) uses the same unit of account, but this argument is invalid because it is based on a confusion between economies of standardisation (or economies in use) and economies of production (see also, e.g, Vaubel, 1984). Economies of standardisation arise where we find it convenient to adopt certain social conventions. For example, we usually find it convenient to use the same language, drive on the same side of the road, and post prices in terms of the same unit of account. But the point is that a convention simply *exists*, and it is (usually) meaningless to say that the user of it produces more of it merely by the act of using it. The English language exists, and I can use it or not as I choose, but if I use it, I would not (normally) be described as producing more of it in the process. The fact that an individual *uses* a convention does not imply that he *produces* more of it, and our use of a common unit of account implies *nothing* about the production of 'money' or anything else. However, a natural monopoly argument is by definition an argument about production, and it therefore cannot apply to a situation where there is no production. The production of bank notes may or may not be a natural monopoly, but at least it makes sense to discuss whether it might be. The use of a pre-existing social convention like a unit of account on the other hand does not involve production in any relevant sense, and so arguments about production *cannot* apply to it. There are thus two separate issues,

> one being whether the market tends to adopt a single unit of account (e.g., an ounce of gold or a pound of silver) and the other being whether the production or issue of *material representatives* of this standard unit is most efficiently undertaken by one or several firms ... The relation between the monetary unit and actual money – its material representatives – can be likened to that of a standard unit of length, such as the yard, and its material embodiment, the yardstick. The yard is a standard unit of measurement throughout the USA; one can call this a 'natural monopoly' if one likes, but such a label would be irrelevant since yards are not objects of production or exchange, and what is not produced or exchanged cannot be produced or exchanged inefficiently, by a monopoly or otherwise. The same is true of other standards – such as shoe sizes and rules of spelling. Only when it comes to material embodiments of these standards, namely, yardsticks, shoes and dictionaries – does the question of natural monopoly arise. (Selgin 1988a, 153, his emphasis)

'Confidence' as a Natural Monopoly

A third type of spurious argument is that banking is a natural monopoly because of economies of scale in building public 'confidence'.[3] A well-known version is the

Klein–Melvin (1982) argument that public confidence in the value of a currency depends on confidence-building expenditures that involve certain fixed costs, the presence of which implies that one bank could always produce confidence more cheaply than two or more could. Klein and Melvin go on to suggest that the government would have an advantage in providing this confidence because its ability to tax implies that it does not need to hold reserves to maintain confidence as private banks would.[4] There are a number of problems with this argument:

- It depends on the assumption that competitive banks would issue inconvertible currencies, but competitive issues would actually be convertible, as discussed already, and convertibility undermines the whole thrust of the Klein–Melvin analysis (see also Vaubel, 1986, 932). If competition leads to a credible convertibility guarantee, there should be no lack of public confidence regarding the value of the currency, and the problem that Klein and Melvin discuss does not arise.
- If their argument is valid, it proves far too much (Selgin, 1988a, 153). The logic of the Klein–Melvin argument applies to deposit banking as well as the note issue. Why therefore do they restrict the monopoly to the note issue only, and not apply it to deposit banking as well? And why restrict the monopoly to banking? Furthermore, since many other industries also exhibit similar features (e.g., insurance), the Klein–Melvin argument presumably implies that they should be monopolised too.
- To put it mildly, it is very difficult to make out a serious case that government intervention in the monetary system has helped promote confidence in the currency. The very problem that Klein and Melvin discuss – the question of confidence in an inconvertible currency – only arises in the first place because governments have suppressed the convertibility 'guarantee' of the value of the currency that private competition would have provided. Far from providing the public with currencies in which they could have confidence or promoting public confidence in private currencies, government policy has often been designed to *compel* the public to use currencies in which they had *little or no* confidence. To quote from Selgin again,

> government monopolies in money production have everywhere been achieved by coercion: governments have outlawed private coinage, passed forced-tender laws, restricted private and incorporated banking, prohibited branch banking and note exchange, taxed bank notes out of existence, passed bond-deposit legislation, refused to enforce redemption contracts, and imposed exchange controls. All of these measures discouraged private, competitive production of money while encouraging production by governments. Most were undertaken to aid the monetization of government debt, which means they were undertaken precisely because confidence in governments was too *low* to allow them to obtain funds through normal channels. (Selgin, 1988a, 152, his emphasis)

The historical record thus gives no support to the claim that governments promote confidence. It suggests, on the contrary, that they tend to destroy it.

• It is doubtful anyway that the government's power to raise taxes actually does promote confidence. Real confidence is about ultimately about how secure people feel about their property, and the power to tax is essentially a power to seize private property for whatever purpose the government wishes. The less restrained the power to tax, the less secure people will be, and the lower their confidence. But the Klein–Melvin confidence argument is still unconvincing even if one accepts the general principle that the government's power to seize private property somehow promotes confidence. Klein and Melvin suggest that the power to tax enables the government to dispense with reserves that private issuers would need to hold, but the counter argument is that it is not reserves as such that maintain confidence, but the performance bonds that private issuers pledge when they enter into contracts with note- and deposit-holders. A bank only holds reserves to satisfy relatively immediate demands for redemption – as would a government bank, if it issued a convertible currency – but as Chapter 7 made clear, public confidence in a bank is based primarily on the bank's capital adequacy and the public's knowledge that the bank can obtain more reserves if it needs them, and not on the bank's reserves as such.

The Empirical Evidence on Returns to Scale and Natural Monopoly in Banking

We turn now to the empirical evidence. One source of evidence is the experience of relatively unregulated banking in the past. These experiences all suggest that there are some economies of scale in banking, but no tendency towards natural monopoly. White's assessment of Scottish 'free banking' is typical:

> The rise of nationally branched joint-stock banks and the decline of local banks in Scotland during the heyday of free banking (1775–1844) indicates that there emerged substantial economies of scale in producing bank note services ... But these economies were always limited. Thomas Kinnear, an Edinburgh private banker who also served as director of the Bank of Scotland, testified ... that the Bank of Scotland had been forced to abandon some of its branch offices due to competition from local banks. No one bank could serve the entire market so cheaply as to exclude others. Scottish experience offers no reason to suppose that there exist 'natural monopoly' characteristics in the production of convertible currency. (L. H. White, 1984a, 36)

Studies of relatively free banking in Australia (Dowd, 1992b); Canada (Schuler, 1992a); China (Selgin 1992b); Colombia (Meisel, 1992); France (E. N. White, 1991); Nataf, 1992; Sweden (Jonung, 1989); Switzerland (Weber, 1988, 1992); the USA (see, e.g., King, 1983, 154; Dowd, 1992a), and various other countries (see

Schuler, 1992b) all suggest that the experience of other countries is broadly consistent with that of Scotland: *in every case there were some economies of scale but no natural monopoly*. Nor is this conclusion contradicted by the fact that in country after another a single bank was able to secure for itself a monopoly of the national note issue. In every case without exception, the establishment of a single note issue was due to government intervention which gave one bank monopoly privileges over the note issue (see, e.g., Selgin, 1988a, Chapter 1 or Dowd, 1989, Chapter 5), and there is no reason to suppose that any of these banks would have been able to establish itself as a natural monopoly in the absence of the restrictions against its competition.

The conclusion that there are economies of scale but no natural monopoly is also supported by the extensive empirical literature on returns to scale in modern banking. There are three surveys of this literature and they come to similar conclusions.[5] Gilbert (1984) and Lewis and Davis (1987, 202–209) between them surveyed well over 20 studies of varying age and methodology. The general finding is that banking does exhibit increasing returns to scale, and the more recent (and presumably more sophisticated and more reliable) studies also indicated that these economies are limited.[6] The third survey (Clark, 1988) covered an additional 9 studies and concluded that the 'empirical evidence appears to support a conclusion of significant overall economies of scale only for depository institutions of relatively small size – less than $100 million in total deposits.' (Clark, 1988, 26). The conclusion that returns to scale exist but are limited is thus robust to the types of institution covered (i.e., commercial banks, savings and loan institutions, and credit unions), the data sets used, the product and cost definitions, and the general methodology. There is some disagreement over precisely how limited these economies are, but *no* study suggests that banking is a natural monopoly.

THE THEORY OF BANKING CLUBS

Granted that there will be more than one bank in the competitive equilibrium, we might then ask how the banks would relate to each other. Would they relate to each other purely on a 'market' basis, where every deal was negotiated separately? Or would they find it useful to form an interbank organisation – a banking club – to which they could delegate certain functions, and which would then co-ordinate at least some interbank activity by central 'command'? If the banks do form a club, which functions would they delegate to it, and what powers would it have over member-banks?

Why might Banks Prefer a Club?

Leaving aside any issues relating to banks forming a clearing-house, which were discussed in Chapter 7, there are three possible factors that might lead banks to prefer some sort of club.

Reducing Transactions and Monitoring Costs for Interbank Loans

One possible reason is to minimise the transactions and monitoring costs of banks' lending to each other. Each bank faces a stochastic net demand for reserves from the public which implies that its reserve position will fluctuate randomly from day to day. Some banks will experience reserve shortages at any given time and wish to borrow, and others will be flush with reserves and be willing to lend. Banks will therefore participate in the market for reserves, and they might even form a special interbank reserve market if the transactions or information costs are lower for interbank transactions than for those involving other parties. It may be that bank co-operation goes no further than participation in the market for reserves – if banks' demands for reserves are relatively small, or if there is only a small number of banks that know each other well and have an 'informal' understanding to help each other out, there might be little scope for a mutually beneficial interbank organisation and the 'unassisted' market will suffice without any 'hierarchy' to support it.

Nonetheless, it is conceivable that the transactions and monitoring costs of arranging interbank loans might make a bankers' bank attractive to the banks for much the same reasons that individual borrowers and lenders often prefer to deal with each other through an intermediary (see, e.g., Chant, 1992). In the absence of a bankers' bank, each bank wanting a loan would have to transact with each of its potential lenders, and a bankers' bank can cut down these transactions costs by arranging loans centrally. A bankers' bank can also co-ordinate monitoring and eliminate unnecessary monitoring costs where there are multiple lenders. It can therefore circumvent banks' trying to free-ride on each other's monitoring costs, on the one hand, and duplicating each other's monitoring, on the other. Since it is both difficult and time-consuming to ascertain banks' values, the bankers' bank would not necessarily try to assess a bank's value *de novo* each time it applied for a loan. Instead it might monitor borrowers on an ongoing basis to be able to handle loan applications quickly. Since they would hope to be able to obtain loans, its customers would have an interest in keeping it suitably informed, but much of this information would be commercially sensitive information that they might want kept secret from rivals. The banks' sensitivity regarding their accounts also implies that an independent outfit would normally be better placed to monitor member-banks than one of their own number. A bankers' club run by its own independent management is therefore likely to be more effective than a club in which a member-bank takes on the monitoring and management roles. The effectiveness of the club can be further enhanced by officials accepting contracts which give them an incentive to preserve their independence and honour the confidentiality of their work, and which provide for penalties in the event of perceived lapses from duty.[7]

The 'Reserve Externality' Argument

It is sometimes claimed, e.g., by Goodhart (1988, 53–55), that a banking club (or some other means of assisting bankers) is needed because banks have insufficient private incentive to hold the 'socially optimal' level of reserves. According to this argument, each bank holds reserves to equate the marginal private benefits of reserve holdings to their marginal private costs – the former are the expected benefits of not having to go to market or declare bankruptcy in the event a customer demands redemption of bank liabilities, and the latter are the opportunity costs of having to hold redemption media that yield a lower return than some alternative assets. The problem is that the bank ignores the 'external' benefits that *its* reserve holdings confer on *other* banks. These external benefits arise because the greater a bank's reserves, the more likely it is to be able and willing to lend to other banks should they desire a loan. The other banks then derive the benefit that the reserve-supply curve they face has shifted to the right. The argument, therefore, is that the unassisted market outcome could be improved upon if all banks could be induced to hold more reserves than they would otherwise choose to hold, because they would all benefit from the 'external' effects of the higher reserves held by the others.[8]

Banks could try to appropriate these 'external' benefits by making an agreement to hold higher reserves than they would otherwise have chosen to hold, but if such an arrangement is to be viable, it is necessary to find some means of restricting the benefits that go to non-members – if non-members get the same benefits as members, then each bank would prefer to 'free-ride' on the others' higher reserves and the scheme would never have any members. A solution would be for member-banks to pledge a certain proportion of their reserves to be loaned to each other, presumably on more favourable terms than could be obtained 'on the market', but to be loaned to non-members at a penalty rate of interest, if at all. This discrimination against non-members would give the latter the incentive to join that was previously lacking. To make these arrangements operational the bankers could establish a club to which they delegated the power to impose reserve requirements and lend (a proportion of) member-banks' reserves. Alternatively, if a clearing-house already exists, they might prefer to delegate the appropriate powers to the clearing-house which would then function as the bankers' club.

Bank 'Contagion'

A third rationale for a banking club – and one that has received considerable emphasis in the literature (e.g., Guttentag and Herring, 1983; Gorton and Haubrich, 1987; Donaldson, 1988; and Goodhart, 1988) is the prospect of 'contagious' bank runs, or 'contagion'. Contagion occurs when the observation that one bank is facing a run (or some other serious difficulty) leads those who have notes and deposits issued by other banks to demand redemption themselves. Since redemption imposes costs on note- and deposit-holders (e.g., it takes time and effort to go to the bank and queue there, and in the case of deposits, it involves the liquidation of a valuable relationship with the bank), an individual will usually only demand redemption if he is sufficiently apprehensive that his bank will default on its obligations to him. If he were, he would demand redemption to avoid the capital losses that could be inflicted on those who continued to hold his bank's debt. Others would think like him, and the bank would face a run. The danger is then that a shock to one bank could raise the public's apprehension about other banks to a level where they faced runs as well. Contagion is thus a negative potential externality that banks might impose on each other, and the claim is that banks could handle these externalities by forming a club.

The most obvious arrangement would be an emergency lending procedure designed to pre-empt any contagion problem. If a bank got into difficulties, the club would make a decision whether to assist it. If the bank qualified for help, the resources of the other banks would be pledged to keep it open, public confidence in it would be restored, and the run on that bank should subside without infecting the other banks. Alternatively, the bank could be refused assistance, and the banking club would try to prevent contagion by 'distancing' its members from the bank in difficulties (e.g., by publishing collective balance sheets to emphasise their soundness). The refusal to assist it would then send out a strong signal of its weakness and encourage the public to run on it and put it out of business. The club would thus assist the healthy banks and throw the sick ones to the wolves, and either way, ideally, there should be no contagion from the first bank to the rest.

The 'Regulatory' Role of Clearinghouses

We have seen that there are two or three reasons – the minimisation of transactions/ monitoring costs, the 'reserve externality' argument, and, more dubiously, the possibility of contagion – why banks *might* want to establish a club that would provide a bank in difficulties with loans that would be more expensive or even unavailable on the 'unassisted' market. However, the existence of the club creates a moral hazard problem for member-banks because they are now effectively co-insuring each other. A typical bank will have an incentive to take additional risks on the grounds that it will get all the benefits if the risks pay off but it can offload some of the losses to other banks if they do not. The other banks face the same incentive, and the result will be socially 'excessive' risk-taking that would leave each bank worse off on average than it would have been if *all* banks could somehow agree that *no-one* would take any extra risks. The solution, if it is feasible, is for a club to impose controls on 'excessive' risk-taking by member-banks. These controls might include minimum capital–asset ratios and restrictions on the quality of assets that member-banks are allowed to hold. They might also impose restrictions on deposit rates to prevent the more aggressive banks bidding up deposit rates to obtain the funds with which to take additional risks, and the clearing-house would also have to increase its monitoring capability to ensure that the new regulations were obeyed. In a nutshell, the clearing-house faces a *moral hazard problem* that might lead it to acquire *extensive 'regulatory' powers* over member-banks and establish some form of *'hierarchy'*.

It is important to emphasise why individual member-banks might choose to submit themselves to these 'regulations'. Joining a club gives a bank more access to emergency loans and can also increase public confidence in it. The public would appreciate that a member-bank is better placed to meet a reserve drain than a comparable non-member bank because of its greater access to emergency funds. If the club can control members' risk-taking effectively, the public would also appreciate that the potential moral hazard problem arising from the bank's membership of the club would be under adequate control. A typical member of the public might then conclude that the member-bank was safer than a comparable non-member-bank and be less likely to demand redemption. Note that this increased public confidence is a rational response to the greater perceived safety represented by club membership, and not a 'free good' which can be conjured up out of thin air. It depends in a vital way on the ability of the club to control its risks. If a club could not control its risk at an acceptable cost, then the underlying moral hazard could undermine confidence and lead the more conservative banks to pull out to avoid liability for the risks being taken by their more aggressive competitors, and the club would collapse. The irony is that while banks might not 'like' obeying club 'regulations', those very 'regulations' help to increase public confidence and thereby make club membership potentially attractive in the first place.

It is interesting to compare these club 'regulations' with contemporary financial regulations. They share one key feature – those to whom they apply will usually perceive them as 'binding' constraints that prevent them doing what they would otherwise prefer to do, and so resources have to be devoted to monitoring and supervision to make sure the rules are obeyed – but they differ in important respects:

First, these 'regulations' would not imposed by some comparatively unresponsive 'outside' body. They would be imposed by the banks themselves and be 'voluntary' in a sense that contemporary regulations are not. Club 'regulations' should be thought of as part of the 'price' of membership, but membership itself would be voluntary. While each bank would prefer the benefits of membership and the freedom to do as it wished, the club can only be viable if those who choose to become members are made to obey the rules. It follows that the choice facing an individual bank is *not* whether it wants to follow the rules, *ceteris paribus*, but whether it wishes to be a member and accept the constraints that go with membership, or whether it wishes to retain its freedom of action and forgo the benefits of membership.

Second, club regulations would be imposed by officials whose powers and contract structures would be determined by the banks whom they serve. Since the banks would not allow their own freedom of action to be restricted for no good reason, the banks would ensure that the powers of club officials were restricted to areas where a clear case has been established for them. The fact that their powers would be delegated also means that club powers would tend to reflect the 'minimum common denominator' – i.e., what a substantial majority, if not everyone, can agree upon – and those who would want a 'stronger' club would generally have to defer to those who want a 'weaker' one. A minority might acquiesce in *some* features that they would prefer to avoid, but if a majority insisted on too many features that they oppose, then it would no longer be worthwhile for the minority to continue as club members. The threat of leaving would therefore keep the powers of the club down to a level that the most 'independence-minded' members are (just) willing to live with. Finally, since the member-banks would bear the consequences of club actions, the banks would ensure that club officials were effectively monitored and held to account to them. By contrast, 'official' regulators are typically accountable to government or government-sponsored banking authorities rather than to commercial bankers, and their regulations frequently reflect political considerations. In addition, since their powers derive from the political process rather than a mandate from the commercial banks, these regulators frequently have greater powers and discretion than club officials and less incentive to respond to bankers' demands. The consumer sovereignty enjoyed by banks *vis à vis* their club is destroyed and, indeed, reversed, and the banks end up taking orders from their regulators instead of giving orders to them.

Following on from this last point, 'official' regulation has generally had a much broader coverage than any regulation that a private banking club would impose. To anticipate our later discussion, the historical evidence indicates that under conditions 'close' to *laissez-faire*, clearing-house powers were usually confined to minor matters such as organising clearing and dealing with counterfeits. (US banking clubs often had much broader powers, but for reasons explained later in this chapter, they are not typical of *laissez-faire* clubs.) 'Official' regulations were much wider-ranging, even in the nineteenth century, and included, *inter alia*, restrictions on the issue of notes and deposits, restrictions on asset holdings, amalgamation restrictions, reserve requirements, and subjection to requisitions and 'moral suasion'.

The system of 'regulation' imposed by a particular club would also have to prove itself viable under competitive conditions, and those regulations would have to satisfy certain obvious constraints that 'official' regulators can take less seriously or even ignore altogether. If the club set a deposit interest ceiling, for example, then it ought to be set no lower than the level that non-member-banks are paying, or else member-banks will tend to lose business. By contrast, 'official' regulators can often avoid this problem by imposing interest ceilings on all banks, regardless of whether they want to be members or not. Another constraint is the threat that member-banks would withdraw (or set up or join a rival club) if they found club rules too irksome. Such an event might occur, for instance, if a group of banks hijacked the club to pursue some sectional interest. The threat of withdrawal would restrict the ability of any one club to abuse its power by making excessive demands of its members, and it would operate even if the market for club services could only support one club in a region.[9] The club would always have to reckon with the danger that it might have to deal with a rival (i.e., the market would still be contestable). Again, 'official' regulators can avoid all these problems by making club membership obligatory.

In addition to constraining a club, competition would also provide it with information about the success or failure of alternative product–price mixes, and an incentive to experiment with new ones to cut costs or obtain a competitive edge.[10] By contrast, contemporary regulations are typically imposed regardless of their underlying economic viability, and the inhabitants of that region are usually prohibited from adopting other sets of regulations or from opting out from regulation altogether. Since they are shielded by legislated privilege, our banking authorities therefore have less incentive to experiment with new regulations or adopt foreign regulatory practices that might have proven successful.

Clearinghouses and Scalar Economies

It is perhaps helpful at this point to recapitulate our discussion of banking clubs. One reason for forming a club was to enable banks to minimise the transactions and monitoring costs of arranging interbank loans; another was to internalise putative externalities from reserve holdings; and a third reason was to combat possible bank run contagion. A club enabled banks to internalise these benefits, but it also created a moral hazard problem that could only be overcome at the price of monitoring and 'regulation'. If these benefits were high enough, banks *might* then be prepared to pay this price and form a club to appropriate them.

But whether they *would* is another question. Unless there is a large number of banks, the transactions cost savings would be relatively low, and there are often alternative ways around the monitoring problem (e.g., loan syndicates). The historical evidence also suggests that banks did not form clubs for the reasons suggested by the banking club literature. Some banks established clubs for clearing purposes, and, though some clearing-houses did lend to member-banks, at least on occasion, the fact that banks frequently set up no multilateral outfit at all suggests that they perceived whatever gains could be obtained from doing so to be outweighed by their set-up and operating costs (Schuler, 1992b, 17). Also, as Schuler notes, since historical free banking systems

> often had just a handful of banks, so multilateral clearing had little advantage over bilateral clearing. The author of a handbook for Canadian bankers stated near the turn of the century that there was little gain to be had from establishing clearing-houses in cities with fewer than seven banks ... Branch banking combined with regular bilateral exchange was often a satisfactory alternative to a clearing-house. (Schuler, 1992b, 17)

Nor is it clear that there would be large benefits from dealing with 'reserve externalities'. The earlier discussion suggested that these economies are very limited beyond a certain point, but even leaving these arguments aside, these economies will also be small because the empirical evidence suggests that 'free' banks can operate safely on relatively low reserve ratios anyway. For example, figures provided by Cameron (1967, 87–88) indicate that Scottish banks of the late eighteenth and early nineteenth centuries usually operated with specie reserves less than 5 percent, and often less than 1 percent, of liabilities. The costs of holding reserves would be correspondingly low, and so too would the costs of any 'lost' reserve externalities.[11]

We are left then with the contagion argument, and it is not obvious that contagion would lead to a banking club either. As Chapter 7 made clear, bankers are usually aware of the possibility of runs and the damage they can do, and this awareness gives them an incentive to invest in confidence-building measures to pre-empt runs. These measures would include the maintenance of an adequate capital ratio and the pursuit of sound lending policies to reassure debt-holders that their funds are safe. But if banks engage in such measures, there is no particular reason to expect one bank's difficulties to 'infect' another unless the second bank was already seriously weakened. Contagion would be likely only among banks that were already weak, but in that case the real problem would be the banks' underlying weakness rather than the shock that sparks off the contagious runs. We should not blame the straw for breaking the camel's back. 'Good' banks would also try to prevent contagion by distancing themselves from 'bad' ones. While such measures could not normally provide 'perfect' reassurance – depositors would normally still know less about the state of the bank's financial health relative to management, and so on – the evidence nonetheless indicates that the public did look at factors such as these to discriminate in favour of well-capitalised, prudently managed banks (see, e.g., Kaufman, 1987, 15–16, 1988, 568–9). When financial crises occurred, those who withdraw funds from a bank they perceive as weak seldom choose to keep them at home 'under the mattress'. They look instead for safe investment outlets, and usually re-deposit their funds with other, safer, banks. If other banks are perceived as sound, they would – and do – experience inflows of funds during crises (see, e.g., Kaufman, 1987, 7–9). The usual result was thus a 'flight to quality' in which the public would transfer their accounts from weaker to stronger banks,[12] and there is little convincing evidence of contagious runs in which the public ran indiscriminately against all banks regardless of their specific circumstances (see, e.g., Benston *et al.*, 1986, 53–60, 66). The evidence thus indicates that sound, reputable banks had little to fear from the difficulties of weaker competitors. The contagion argument therefore provides a doubtful basis for a banking club.

These arguments for a banking club are also open to another objection. The various factors isolated as possible reasons for forming a club can each be considered as economies of scale external to the firm but internal to the industry, and the point of the club is to 'internalise' these economies. Yet, if the benefits are high enough to make a club worthwhile, one has to explain why the banks prefer to internalise those benefits by forming a club instead of by merging to form a single firm. We need to explain why the 'partial' hierarchy of a club is superior to the 'full' hierarchy of a single firm. None of the 'advocates' of banking clubs has yet provided any answer to this question. The existence of scalar economies merely suggests that banks would grow to a size where they can reap their benefits; if scalar economies exist but are limited, as the evidence suggests, then we would expect there to be more than one 'large' bank in the resulting equilibrium. But whether they are limited or not, the mere existence of scalar economies does *not* explain why banks would want to form a club.

The claim that there is little scope for clubs under *laissez-faire* also seems to be borne out by the experience of less regulated banking systems in the past. The historical record of relatively unregulated banking systems outside the USA – in countries such as Australia, Canada, Ireland, France, Scotland, Sweden, Switzerland, and many others – indicates that (relatively) 'free' banks had little use for banking clubs with extensive regulatory powers. In apparently all such cases, bank co-operation seemed to consist of little more than an arrangement for clearing notes and deposits with occasional ad hoc measures to deal with particular problems as they arose. Apart from clearing itself, clearing-house policy dealt mainly with minor matters of mutual concern such as procedures to handle out-of-town cheques and efforts to detect fraud (Schuler 1992b, 18)). Only relatively rarely did free banks co-operate for more ambitious purposes (e.g., to provide emergency loans), and even then they did so with little formal power other than that to deny loans to applicants who did not co-operate.[13]

In the USA, on the other hand, banks did form 'private' clubs which exercised quite extensive regulatory powers. One of these was the Suffolk system which arose out of the attempts of the Suffolk Bank of Boston to counter the Boston circulation of the notes of out-of-town ('country') banks. Branch-banking restrictions had made it difficult to redeem these notes, and they consequently circulated at a discount. In 1819 the Suffolk started buying them at their Boston discount, and it gave the issuers the option to redeem them at the price the Suffolk paid for them provided they maintained (non-interest-bearing) deposits at the Suffolk. In 1824 the Suffolk began to allow participating banks the benefit of overdraft facilities, and since it was now extending credit, started supervising them to ensure they were soundly run. Its position as manager of the system gave it the information to carry out that supervision effectively – any bank that followed a policy of systematic over-expansion would rapidly develop a persistent adverse clearing balance that would reveal what it was doing. The usual response of the Suffolk to a delinquent bank was 'moral suasion' – lecturing offending banks on the importance of correcting their policies – but it could also limit its overdraft or send its notes for redemption. In the final analysis, it could also expel it from the system, and the threat of expulsion was a potent sanction because it provided a clear signal to the public that the well-informed Suffolk did not consider the bank to be a good credit risk. The Suffolk system was thus a banking club in which the Suffolk both set the rules and enforced them. The 'price' of membership was the deposit that members were required to keep and the obligation to obey the club rules. In return, members enjoyed increased public confidence resulting from the widespread par acceptance of their notes and the vetting and support services provided by the Suffolk. Its readiness to lend to member-banks made its vetting of their policies credible to the public, and the credibility of its assessment reduced the pressure on the public to vet a bank themselves. Since non-member banks enjoyed less confidence, banks felt under pressure to join even though they found the Suffolk's conditions irksome.

The other US clubs were the clearing-house associations in the period from the mid-nineteenth century to 1914. They were first established to facilitate the return of notes to the banks that issued them, but in the 1850s the New York

Clearinghouse Association began to issue certificates to member-banks which they could use to settle clearing debts, and which economised specie and relaxed the impact of legal restrictions against the note issue (Sprague, 1910; Timberlake, 1984, 1993; Horwitz, 1990, 1992). These benefits were especially useful during panics when notes and coins were scarce and legislative restrictions particularly binding. In later panics, clearing-houses issued certificates that banks could use to meet redemption demands by the public. These certificates were claims against the clearing-house and enjoyed public confidence because they were free from the default risk attached to individual banks. They were retired after each crisis and members of the public who accepted them suffered no losses. In the end, clearing-houses were effectively issuing hand-to-hand emergency currency that the public readily accepted even though it was illegal (Timberlake, 1984, 6–7). Clearinghouse associations also developed a formal apparatus to provide banks with 'last resort' lending, and they developed a regulatory apparatus to accompany it. Banks had to satisfy capital requirements and submit to auditing and the requisitioning of their reserves when required to. Banks that failed to satisfy these conditions were disciplined, and the penalty for extreme violations was expulsion.

To summarise, the claim that there is little useful scope for clubs under *laissez-faire* appears to be broadly consistent with the historical evidence. Historical experiences outside the USA suggest that banks had little need for clubs other than to arrange clearing and settle minor issues of mutual concern. The USA experience is different, but there is reason to believe that the 'strong' clubs that arose in the US were a response to the unique legislative restrictions under which US banks had to operate (see also, e.g, the work of Horwitz referred to above). These restrictions – the most significant being those against branch-banking – deprived US banks of many scale economies that banks elsewhere appropriated by merging. Forming a 'strong' club was therefore a means to appropriate scale economies where the most straightforward method was prohibited by law, and there is relatively little evidence of 'strong' clubs in permissive legal environments.[14]

Gorton and Mullineaux's Analysis of Clearinghouse Associations

We end the chapter by considering several alternative treatments of banking clubs to be found in the literature. One of these is that of Mullineaux (1987) and Gorton and Mullineaux (1987). Their argument goes as follows. The public use two types of bank liability in their everyday exchanges – bank notes and deposits on which they can write cheques – and these liabilities differ in an important respect. In deciding whether to accept a note, a member of the public needs information only on the bank that issues the note. To be reasonably confident that he will not suffer any losses, it generally suffices for him to know that the bank that issues the note is in a position to honour it. However with cheques he needs to know not only that the *bank* has the resources to honour the cheque, but also that the *agent* on whom the cheque is drawn has sufficient funds in his account to honour the cheque. Since all notes issued by a bank are effectively alike, a secondary note market can then develop relatively easily, and this secondary market gives the public information about the underlying value of the bank. However, a secondary market does not develop in cheques because agents would need information on specific bank accounts as well as the soundness of the bank on which the cheques are drawn, and these information requirements make the operation of a secondary cheque market (typically) too expensive to be worthwhile.

As the monetary system evolved, the public's desired note/deposit ratio gradually declined. Gorton and Mullineaux argue that the secondary note market became less informative about the value of the bank itself, and a public 'information gap' gradually developed. They then argue that this information asymmetry made the public more inclined to 'run' on the banks: In the past, a shock to a bank's value (e.g., the revelation of a bad loan) would have been reflected in an increase in the discount on banks' notes in the secondary note market, and the public would have had a clear signal of the worth of their note holdings after the shock had hit the bank. But when deposits supplanted notes there was no secondary cheque market on which the new bank value can be reflected. The public was then more inclined to 'panic' and demand redemption because it was deprived of information that it would previously have had about the bank's value. Clearinghouses therefore arose to protect the banks against these panics to which they were now more prone. The clearing-houses would be delegated various powers over member-banks – among these the powers to set minimum reserve and capital ratios, the rights to monitor member-banks' accounts, and the power to requisition member-banks' reserves – and the incentive to submit to these rules was the greater likelihood of clearing-house support in an emergency. When a run then occurred, the clearing-house would assess whether the banks experiencing the runs were sound or not. If they were deemed to be sound, the clearing-house would use the resources of other member-banks to guarantee their liabilities, and this measure would usually suffice to reassure the public and dissuade them from continuing to run. If the banks were considered bad risks, on the other hand, the clearing-house would say so and give the public a clear signal to continue the run and put them out of business.

One problem with this argument is that it implies that the most direct solution to the banks' problems is for them to merge – that is, it appears to predict that banking should be a natural monopoly – and yet the evidence indicates that this prediction is falsified. But even if one leaves aside this problem, there are others:

- The argument ignores the role of equity market in signalling a bank's net worth. As discussed already in a number of places, one of the functions of equity-holders is to provide a 'buffer stock' to reassure liability-holders that they have little reason to fear losses. The credibility of this buffer-stock signal arises from the fact that the stock-holder is a residual claimant who only gets paid once other creditors have been paid off. The very fact that the stock market gives a bank a positive value then indicates that the bank can pay off all its note- and deposit-holders and still have resources left over, and so the liability-holders should have little to fear. Instead of looking at discounts on a secondary note market, liability-holders need only check that it has a sufficiently positive stock market evaluation to absorb any likely losses that the bank might suffer. We would therefore expect liability-holders to run on a bank under *laissez-faire* conditions only if its stock market value had already fallen to some 'danger' level where there was some significant likelihood that losses would be passed on to them.

- The Gorton–Mullineaux argument exaggerates the information provided by the secondary note market. L. H. White (1984a), Selgin and White (1987) and Selgin (1988a) have argued forcefully that banks would agree to accept each other's notes at par, and par acceptance leaves very little room for bank note discounts to deviate from zero. (The only exception is where a bank lost its 'good standing' at the clearing-house. Discounts would then rise to reflect the inconvenience of being unable to redeem at par at other banks. They might also reflect the public's anticipation that the bank cannot honour its liabilities in full. Only in this case does the Gorton–Mullineaux mechanism come into play, but we would only expect a bank to lose its good standing if it was in serious difficulties, and such a bank would be unlikely to survive for long.) It follows that in normal circumstances the *only* information provided by the secondary note market is that the bank is still considered to be of good standing, and (therefore) that its notes and deposits are likely to continue to be redeemed at par. A corollary is that there is no obvious difference in the information provided by notes and cheques. 'Good' cheques (i.e., cheques drawn on accounts with the funds to honour them, or supported by overdraft facilities) will trade at par for the same reasons that notes will trade at par, provided that the bank involved maintains its good standing. The 'replacement' of notes by deposits makes no significant difference to public information about the bank.
- Even if notes and cheques *did* convey different information about the bank on which they were drawn, the extra information provided by notes would *still* be publicly available as long as there is *some* demand for banknotes. It is not the *size* of the secondary note market that matters, but the fact that it still *exists*. It then follows that a fall in the public's desired note/deposit ratio would not create an information gap, unless that ratio went to zero, and it did not go to zero in the historical banking systems that Gorton and Mullineaux try to explain.
- Finally, the Gorton–Mullineaux analysis makes predictions that are empirically falsified. They deal with how a *laissez-faire* banking system would evolve a system of 'endogenous' regulation to deal with a particular information asymmetry problem that is reflected in a declining public currency/deposit ratio. However, all relatively 'free' historical banking systems apparently experienced falls in the currency/deposit ratio but none of them evolved endogenous regulation along the lines Gorton and Mullineaux predict. The case they emphasise – the late nineteenth century USA – was characterised by extensive legislative restrictions, and the most plausible explanation for the clearing-house

system is that it arose to enable banks to circumvent these restrictions. In short, relatively unregulated banking systems in the past did not experience the banking structures predicted by Gorton and Mullineaux, and the case that they focus on was characterised by important and very relevant legal restrictions.

Goodhart's Analysis of Banking Clubs

Charles Goodhart (1987, 1988) presents an alternative treatment of banking clubs.[15] His analysis begins with an information asymmetry between banks and their liability-holders. The management of a bank is better informed about the value of the bank than its liability-holders, and there is no costless and credible way in which management can pass on their information. A situation can therefore arise in which a bank is sound but the management cannot easily persuade its customers of the fact. A simple announcement that the bank is sound will be insufficient because the public would appreciate that the management has an incentive to paint a healthy picture regardless of the true state of the bank's finances. The management could presumably call in outside monitors (e.g., auditors) who could inspect the books and verify that the bank was sound, but such inspections can be expensive and time-consuming, and the public would need reassurance that they could believe the monitor. There can therefore be no guarantee that the monitor could provide the public with the reassurance they want in the time available. The public might then choose to 'play safe' and redeem their holdings of bank liabilities, and the bank would face a run.

The problem is that bank runs cause real damage. When a bank redeems one of its liabilities, it must either reduce its asset-holdings or issue more of some other liability. A bank will hold many non-marketable assets (e.g., consumer loans) which it cannot liquidate to meet demands for redemption or which it can only liquidate at considerable cost. Alternatively, the bank can meet demands for redemption by issuing more liabilities (i.e., by borrowing), but it must be able to reassure its potential creditors that it is still sound. As it continues to borrow, potential creditors will doubt its soundness and the cost of further borrowing will rise. A bank thus faces increasing marginal redemption costs regardless of whether it tries to meet redemptions by running down assets or issuing more debt, and these redemption costs imply that runs can impose real damage to the banks involved.

Goodhart suggests that bankers might establish a club to help them handle the problems that runs pose. However, he also maintains that there are a variety of reasons why banks cannot achieve the best outcome on their own, and he infers from these that a bankers' club needs some sort of 'help' from an 'outside' source (i.e., the state). The reasons he gives fall under three broad headings:

First, he claims that there are certain general problems in the structure of private banking clubs that a system of central bank regulation could presumably be expected to overcome. One problem is that the rules can be rigged to restrict new entrants or benefit those in charge of key committees (1988, 71). Another is that one cannot always take the independence of club managers for granted, and he cites as an example the refusal, essentially for sectarian reasons, of the New York Clearinghouse Association to assist the Knickerbocker Trust in 1907 (1988, 38–39). He also maintains that it 'may well be impossible to check whether club members are obeying the regulations without spot checks, close monitoring, etc.' which he believes would 'be intolerable between competing members' (1988, 71). Finally, he suggests that heterogeneity among the members might make it difficult for private clubs to maintain their cohesion, and that government-imposed rules might therefore be required to protect the club's integrity (1988, 71).

Second, Goodhart suggests that a private club would be unsuited to carry out rescue operations. The

> usual circumstances of a rescue, at very short notice under conditions of severely limited information, make it more difficult for commercial banks to act conclusively than for an independent Central Bank to act swiftly and decisively. (1988, 102)

This difficulty in mounting operations is partly due to the influence of commercial rivalry (1988, 43–44), partly due to the consideration that crises require 'leadership' which can only be provided by a 'noncompetitive, non-profit-maximizing body' which is 'above the competitive battle' (1988, 45), and partly due to differences about the appropriate level of support leading to support being watered down to the level of the 'lowest common denominator' (1988, 45).

Third, Goodhart argues that only some form of external control can dampen down the cycles to which the banking system is otherwise prone.[16] He cites approvingly an old argument that

> competitive pressures would drive the banks to seek to maintain and expand market shares during normal (i.e., noncrisis) periods ... [and that] during such periods ... the more conservative banks would lose market share. With the public often being poorly informed, or incapable of discerning whether slower growth was due to conservative policies or lack of managerial effort and efficiency, there was no guarantee that the more conservative banks could recover during panics ... the market share lost in good times. (1988, 47–48)

Assuming that these cycles pose a problem that needs to be dealt with, one might then ask why a 'private' bankers' club could not deal with them. Goodhart's position seems to be that such a club could not be expected to match the independence and leadership that a central bank could show. He goes on to suggest the LDC debt crisis as an example of the way that profit-maximising commercial banks can get themselves into this kind of trouble:

> The recent history of the rapid expansion of international bank lending to sovereign LDCs during the 1970s, the resulting crisis, and the subsequent cessation of further voluntary lending would appear to provide an excellent example of this syndrome. Competitive behavior seemed to force all the major

banks to take part in an undue expansion of lending, ... the evidence seems incontrovertible that without the intervention of the IMF, and the support of national Central Banks, the crisis in, and after, 1982, arising from these events, would have been contagious, far-reaching, and probably disastrous on a massive scale. (1988, 48–49)

These arguments need to be considered closely. But before doing so, we should first note that Goodhart's theory of clubs shares the same sort of weakness as the previous one, in that if moral hazard exists between member-banks who form their own club, as Goodhart suggests, then the obvious solution is presumably for them to merge into a single big bank. If economies of scale were sufficiently large, we should therefore expect a natural monopoly; if economies of scale were smaller, on the other hand, we would expect a group of smaller independent banks, but neither way would we expect a banking club.

Leaving aside this issue, one can also make a number of other objections. Consider first his arguments about the general unsuitability of private clubs. It is true that club rules can be rigged and that club members may use their positions on key committees to pursue their own ends; it is also true that one cannot take the independence of club managers for granted. But the basic answer to these points is that setting up and running a bankers' club, like any other club, is a non-trivial principal–agent problem, and all we can really say is that the incentive is there for the principals to do the best they can. Club members will generally try to minimise anti-social behaviour on the part of club officials because they would expect to bear the costs of it. They will therefore write contracts with officials that encourage propriety and independence, and they will usually have their activities monitored. The argument about founder-members rigging the rules against later banks is also difficult to substantiate in any depth,[17] and there is in any case the plausible counter-argument that founder-members will be aware that the benefits of a bankers' club tend to rise, and fixed costs per member fall, with the number of members – reasoning that suggests that the club will often find itself trying to attract new members instead of trying to keep them out. In short, the members will never manage to eradicate anti-social behaviour in the club, but they have an incentive to minimise the damage it does, and we must expect that they will do so. Goodhart suggests that member-banks will find monitoring by fellow-banks intolerable, but the solution is surely to delegate the task to clearing-house officials and give them an incentive to maintain their independence and respect confidentiality. Member-banks might still not *like* being monitored, of course, but they will appreciate that if they refuse to submit to monitoring then loans will be more difficult and possibly more expensive to obtain. Finally, as for the argument about the cohesion of clubs, it is not clear why cohesion should be an end in itself. A club can only be said to benefit its members when they join voluntarily. If individual banks perceive their own interest correctly and choose not to join, then they regard the costs of membership as exceeding the benefits and we should not force them to join against their will. We cannot be confident that a club will benefit its members unless they join voluntarily. The bottom line, then, is that Goodhart gives no reason to presume that clubs among bankers are an exception to the general result from club theory (e.g., Helsey and Strange, 1991) that competitive clubs produce optimal outcomes.

Then there is the issue of whether a private club can handle a crisis. It is true that a group of banks might find it difficult to act decisively and in concert in a crisis, and there might be some tendency for the level of support to sink to the level of the 'lowest common denominator', but it is precisely because of factors like these that we would expect members to delegate crisis-handling to a clearing-house in advance. We would not expect the banks to wait for a crisis to find out the benefits of decisive action and leadership. They would anticipate the way in which a crisis should be handled and delegate appropriate powers beforehand to the clearing-house. In this they are much like Parliamentary systems of government which anticipate that certain types of situation are best handled by delegating 'emergency powers' to the executive. One must also bear in mind that there needs to be some mechanism to restrict the abuse of emergency powers, and the best way to prevent abuse of any powers is for member-banks to make the rules and hold clearing-house officials responsible for their actions. 'Leadership' has its uses, but it needs to be circumscribed to prevent its over-use. This is why parliaments typically hold their executives to account for the way their emergency powers have been used. The danger with the leadership provided by Goodhart's central bank is that the commercial banks cannot easily restrain it or hold it to account. If clearing-house leadership corresponds to parliamentary government, the leadership of a central bank is more like a dictatorship which has a tendency to provide too much 'leadership' and be unresponsive to the desires of those it is meant to serve.

Lastly, there is the argument that competitive behaviour would lead banks to engage in 'excessive' cycling, but this argument also has its problems. A bank that engages in a policy of aggressive expansion will tend to experience a deterioration in the average quality of its loans, its portfolio may become unbalanced, it may have to bid more for deposits, and so on, and these factors undermine its longer-run solvency and increase the chances it will face an eventual run. It is not obvious why the bank would want to pursue such a policy unless it believed that it could pass off some of the costs onto others, and it is doubtful that it could do so under competitive conditions. It would only be able to count on assistance from a private clearing-house to the extent that it could persuade the clearing-house that its policies were sound, which is tantamount to its being able to 'fool' clearing-house officials. More likely, clearing-house officials would detect the drift of the bank's policies and eventually cut off its credit. The clearing-house action would then send a signal to other actual or potential creditors, and they would cut back their exposure as well. When the crisis occurs, the 'good' banks would have distanced themselves from the 'bad' one, and the latter would be left alone to face the consequences of its own earlier actions. Nor could is there any reason to believe that a 'bad' bank could force more conservative banks to go along with a more aggressive policy. It could probably expect to earn some 'easy profits' in the short term, but if they are willing to forego the lure of quick profits the more conservative banks could expect to increase their market shares in the longer run when the aggressive bank runs into difficulties. In the final analysis, the public want stability from their banks, and the banks that provide stability will eventually win out over the cowboys who aim for quick profits. Goodhart might still claim that this is not what happened with the LDC debt crisis, but the debt crisis can hardly be considered an example of what banks will do under *laissez-faire* conditions. While there was certainly a great deal of competition among the banks, many national authorities were actively 'encouraging' commercial banks to provide loans to the Third World, and the banks could reasonably expect a bailout from their central banks (and perhaps the IMF) if their loans turned sour. Why else would they choose to expand to a point where they put themselves in such serious danger? The over-expansion of bank lending can therefore be plausibly attributed to various forms of state intervention, and there is no reason to believe that a crisis as severe as this one would have occurred had the banks had to rely only on their own resources.

9 Recent Models of Banking Instability

We end our present treatment of banking by considering some recent theoretical work on banking instability. This work has attracted considerable attention, and purports to provide rigorous theoretical justifications for government deposit insurance and other features of modern central banking. The key paper in this new literature is Diamond and Dybvig (hereafter DD, 1983). This paper posed two questions that have dominated the subsequent literature. First, why are financial institutions subject to instability and, as a subsidiary question, why is this instability damaging? Second, what, if anything, should the government or central banking authorities do about this instability? DD suggested that the instability arises because depositors' liquidity demands are uncertain and banks' assets are less liquid than their liabilities, and they suggest that the instability is harmful because it ruins risk-sharing arrangements and damages production. They also argued that this instability creates a need for government deposit insurance or a lender of last resort to provide emergency loans to banks. Later literature in the DD tradition develops these answers further and has been used to justify additional policies such as interest-rate ceilings (e.g., Anderlini, 1986b; Smith, 1984) and reserve requirements (e.g., Freeman, 1988).

However, the basic problem with this literature is that it has little to do with real-world financial institutions. It talks about 'banks', 'demand deposit' contracts, and the like, but the institutions and contracts that go by these names are quite unlike their real-world counterparts. The 'bank' that dominates this literature is not a bank at all, but a peculiar kind of mutual fund that issues investors with identical contracts that are neither debt nor equity, and do not exist in the real world. The 'demand deposit' contract is therefore not even a debt contract, let alone any form of bank deposit in the accepted meaning of the term. The financial intermediaries that arise in the DD world are subject to instability – in particular, investors might run if they fear that other investors will run – but this instability is easily dealt with by establishing banks in the proper sense of the term. As explained already, bank share-holders remove the incentive of depositors to run by pledging their own capital as reassurance. The DD intermediary is therefore subject to instability because it has no share capital and no alternative means of providing the reassurance that shareholder capital could provide. The fact that they can provide such reassurance then gives banks an advantage over the DD intermediaries, and also helps to explain why we observe banks in the real world and do not observe the peculiar institutions predicted by DD. Far from explaining why we need deposit insurance, a lender of last resort,

Large parts of this chapter appeared as 'Models of Banking Instability: A Partial Review of the Literature', *Journal of Economic Surveys*, 6(2) (1992), pp. 107–132.

and other features of modern central banking, the DD literature actually has relatively little to say about real-world banking. Its attempts to explain financial intermediation and justify the need for central banking are therefore failures.

To examine this literature more formally, we need first to establish criteria by which to assess it. As it has evolved, the literature has gradually developed the yardstick that if it is to explain banking instability and motivate a role for the government in the banking system, the models involved must also explain why financial intermediaries exist in the first place. Financial intermediation should therefore be 'properly motivated' in the sense that the intermediated outcome is superior in some sense to the unintermediated one. One reason for using this criterion is to weed out explanations of banking instability or analyses of government intervention in the banking industry that are unconvincing, either because they attempt to discuss an industry that the models themselves predict should not exist, or because those models also have alternative, unintermediated outcomes that match the optimal intermediated ones. In addition to explaining the *mere existence* of intermediation, it would also seem reasonable to expect (or at least hope) that our models could say something about the characteristics of *observed* financial intermediation. The most basic characteristics to be explained would seem to be the types of claims that financial intermediaries issue and hold, the fundamental types of claim being obviously debt and equity. In short, we need to explain why financial intermediaries exist in the first place, but we also need our intermediaries to issue debt and/or equity claims as well, and thus correspond to real-world banks and/or mutual funds.

THE DIAMOND–DYBVIG MODEL WITH NO AGGREGATE CONSUMPTION RISK

We now begin with a benchmark model suggested by DD (1983). This model is based on the following assumptions:

- There are three periods $(T = 0, 1, 2)$ and a single good.
- Everyone has access to an identical production technology which converts each unit invested in period 0 to one unit output if liquidated in period 1, and $R > 1$ units of output if left until period 2. These assumptions are meant to capture the idea that interrupting the production process is costly, and these costs can be interpreted as the costs of physical interruptions to the production process[1] or (as in Freeman, 1988, 47–48) as resale costs).[2] All investments are perfectly divisible, and R is assumed to be certain.
- Agents have access to a private storage technology which enables them to store the good without being observed, and the storage technology yields a zero net return.
- There is a continuum of agents whom we can think of as distributed along a unit line. They are identical in period $T = 0$ when each agent is endowed with one unit of the good.

- In period $T = 1$, each agent is revealed to be one of two types. Type 1 agents die at the end of $T = 1$ and type 2 agents die at the end of $T = 2$. The probability of being type 1 is t, and t is initially assumed to be known in $T = 0$. These assumptions are meant to capture the idea that agents have unpredictable consumption 'shocks' that may lead them to want to liquidate their investments before they have matured. Their preferences are assumed to take the form

$$\mu(c_1, c_2, \theta) = \theta u(c_1) + (1 - \theta)\rho u(c_2) \qquad (9.1)$$

where c_T indicates consumption in period T, θ is a random variable taking the value 1 if the agent is type 1 and 0 if he is type 2, and r represents the time preference rate which satisfies $1 \geq \rho > 1/R$. These assumptions imply that type 1 agents will only consume in period 1, and type 2 agents will only consume in period 2 (i.e., agents have 'corner preferences').[3] We also assume that the utility function satisfies the Inada conditions, and that the coefficient of relative risk-aversion is greater than one.

- At $T = 0$, and given that $E(\theta) \equiv t$, then agents are assumed to maximise the expectation of their (state–dependent) utility function

$$E(\mu(c_1, c_2, \theta) = tu(c_1) + (1 - t)\rho u(c_2). \qquad (9.2)$$

- At $T = 1$ each agent learns his own type only. He has no credible way of directly revealing his type and he does not know what type others are.

These assumptions imply that all agents will make investments in $T = 0$, but type 1 agents will want to liquidate their investments in $T = 1$ while type 2 agents will consume their investments when they mature in $T = 2$. If agents decide to invest autarkically, they are guaranteed returns of 1 if they turn out to be type 1 and choose to liquidate their investments in $T = 1$, and R if they turn out to be type 2 and keep their investments until $T = 2$. However, since they are risk-averse and know the proportion of types, there is presumably scope for mutually beneficial risk-sharing against the 'unlucky' event of turning out to be type 1. If we let $c_{j,i}$ represent the consumption of a type i agent in period j, this 'insurance' would involve $c_{1,1} > 1$ and $c_{2,2} < R$, and Diamond and Dybvig show that an optimal insurance contract exists and satisfies:

$$c_{1,2}{}^* = c_{2,1}{}^* = 0; u'(c_{1,1}{}^*) = \rho R u'(c_{2,2}{}^*);$$
$$tc_{1,1}{}^* + [(1 - t)c_{2,2}{}^*/R] = 1 \qquad (9.3)$$

(where the * denotes optimal quantities). The first condition comes from noting that type 1 households derive no utility from consumption in period 2, and vice versa; the second indicates that marginal utility is in line with marginal productivity, and the third is the resource constraint. Note that $\rho R > 1$ and the second condition in (9.3) imply that $c_{1,1}{}^* < c_{2,2}{}^*$. It follows that the optimal outcome satisfies the self-selection constraint that no agent has an incentive to misrepresent his type – type 1s have no incentive to represent themselves as type 2s since $c_{1,1}^* > 1 > c_{2,2}^* = 0$, and type 2s have no incentive to misrepresent themselves since $c_{2,2}^* > c_{1,1}^*$.

The DD Intermediary

The problem is to find a way to implement this contract. A conventional mutual insurance scheme (i.e., one where agents just announce their types) is ruled out because each agent would claim to be type 1 to get the insurance handout and there would be no way to distinguish truthful claims from false ones. DD suggest agents might be able to implement the optimal contract by establishing an intermediary that would take in deposits and invest them in the production process, but promise depositors a reasonable return if they withdrew their deposits in period 1.[4] They therefore suppose that this intermediary would offer a contract that promises to pay $r_1 = c_{1,1} > 1$ for each deposit withdrawn in period 1 provided that the intermediary still has assets to liquidate. Demands for withdrawal arrive at random times at the intermediary, which deals with them as they come until it runs out of assets. If it has any assets left, they are liquidated in period 2 and divided *pro rata* among remaining deposit-holders. More formally, if V_i is the payoff in period i for each unit deposited, f_j is the number of withdrawers' deposits serviced before agent j as a fraction of total withdrawals, and f is the proportion of deposits withdrawn in $T = 1$, then the return to a depositor is given by

$$V_1(f_j, r_1) = r_1 \text{ (if } f_j < 1/r_1 \text{) or } 0 \text{ (if } f_j \geq 1/r_1\text{)}$$

and

$$V_2(f, r_1) = \max\left[R(1 - r_1 f)/(1 - f), \, 0\right] \tag{9.4}$$

(see DD, 1983, 408).[5] The assumption that demands arrive randomly and are dealt with sequentially is meant to capture the notion that depositors withdraw at different times through period 1, and DD justify it as allowing them to 'capture the flavor of continuous time' in a discrete model (1983, 408) and to represent intermediary services that they do not explicitly model (1983, 414). This sequential service constraint (SSC) means that the intermediary does not – and, for reasons that are not spelt out, presumably cannot – simply cumulate requests for withdrawal and then make payments contingent on the total number of withdrawal requests. The SSC also means that an agent's return can depend on his place in a queue. The SSC turns out to be very significant and we shall return to it shortly.

One should also note the form of the contract between the intermediary and its depositors. DD (and much of the subsequent literature) refer to this contract as a 'demand deposit contract'. This label suggests that it is some sort of debt, but is misleading because the contract does not specify (as 'proper' debt contracts do) a fixed return for deposits withdrawn in non-bankruptcy states. Those who withdraw in $T = 1$ are promised a fixed return provided the intermediary still has funds, but those who withdraw in $T = 2$ are residual (or equity-like) claimants rather than debt-holders *per se*. As noted already, the term 'debt' is normally understood to refer to an asset whose promised return is pre-specified outside of default by the issuer. The DD contract is a kind of debt–equity hybrid which looks like debt to those who withdraw in $T = 1$ and looks like equity to those who withdraw later, but there is no debt–equity distinction as such because all claims issued by the intermediary are identical. The identical nature of its liabilities also means that the intermediary is a mutual fund rather than a bank as such, since banks issue both debt and equity, whereas a mutual fund issues only one type of liability. However, the debt–equity 'hybrid' liabilities issued by the DD mutual fund also differ from the equity usually issued by conventional mutual funds, so the DD intermediary is something of an unconventional mutual fund. We shall come back to these points later as well.

The Problem of 'Runs' and the DD Solution

DD show that their contract can support the optimal insurance contract as a Nash equilibrium, but the equilibrium is not unique and there exists an alternative 'run' equilibrium in which all the intermediary's assets are liquidated in period 1. This equilibrium occurs when type 2 depositors 'panic' and withdraw their deposits because they anticipate that the intermediary will run out of assets, and this possibility exists because the intermediary's potential liability in $T = 1$ is r_1 which is greater than what it could recover from its assets if they were all liquidated then (i.e., unity). It is a worse outcome for both types of agent than the initial 'autarky' equilibrium because certain returns of 1 and R for each type are replaced by uncertain returns of mean unity. Runs are damaging because they ruin the risk sharing between agents and take a toll on the efficiency of production because all production is interrupted at $T = 1$ when it is optimal for some to continue until $T = 2$' (1983, 409).

The occurrence of the run equilibrium hinges on the beliefs type 2 agents have about each other. If a type 2 agent believes that other type 2 agents will not demand redemption, then he has no reason to demand redemption either because his investment would yield him a greater return if it were liquidated the next period. But if he believed for whatever reason that other type 2s *would* demand redemption, then he would demand redemption because he would expect the intermediary to have no assets left the next period. If other type 2s think like him, they will all run and the intermediary will be run out of business. There is therefore a sense in which runs are self-fulfilling: once they have deposited, anything that causes [depositors] to anticipate a run will lead to a run' regardless of whether it has anything fundamentally to do with the soundness of the institution's condition or not (DD, 1983, 410; see also Azariadis, 1981 and Waldo, 1985, 273, n. 7). The implication drawn by DD is that the 'good' equilibrium is fragile and the intermediary will be acutely concerned with maintaining depositor confidence.

Having established that runs are possible, Diamond and Dybvig nonetheless have difficulty explaining why they should occur. The problem of determining which equilibrium actually results when there are possible multiple equilibria is common in forward-looking rational expectations models, but DD do not provide the plausible story needed to reduce the possibility of multiple equilibria to a single determinate outcome. They merely suggest that one could occur

> if the selection between the bank run equilibrium and the good equilibrium depended on some commonly observed random variable in the economy. This could be a bad earnings report, a commonly observed run at some other bank, a negative government forecast, or even sunspots. (DD, 1983, 410)

The problem is that none of these factors is in their model. They cannot rely on a bad earnings report because their model has no uncertainty regarding the returns to production; they cannot rely on a run on another institution because they would then have to explain how that run got started; and they cannot rely on a report by the government or anyone one else because it is not clear what there is in the model that they could report on or why the report would matter anyway. DD end up relying on extraneous uncertainty (i.e., sunspots) to generate expectations, but this explanation is incomplete because they fail to explain why rational agents would form their expectations in this way (see also Webb, 1986, 180). The DD story still fails to explain whether runs *would* actually occur or not.[6]

Be this as it may, DD then show that the 'bad' equilibrium can be eliminated by a simple modification of their contract. Since it knows what t is, the intermediary can predict exactly how many type 1 agents there will be, so it promises to redeem on demand in $T = 1$ until that number of agents has been dealt with, and then refuses to redeem any more deposits until $T = 2$. This 'suspension of convertibility' version of the DD contract specifies the following returns to type 1 and type 2 agents:

$$V_1(f_j, r_1) = r_1 (\text{if } f_j \leq t) \text{ or } 0 \ (\text{if } f_j > t)$$
$$V_2(f, r_1) = \max \left[R(1 - r_1 f)/(1 - f), R(1 - r_1 t)/(1 - t) \right] \quad (9.5)$$

(see, e.g., DD, 1983, 411). The $T = 1$ payments are set so that type 1 agents get their optimal return, and no type 2 agent will wish to withdraw in that period because he is confident of getting his optimal return if he leaves his investment until $T = 2$. The 'suspension of convertibility' contract then guarantees optimal returns and eliminates the possibility of a run.[7]

Equity Contracts, Agents' 'Isolation', and the SSC

A problem with this analysis is that the DD contract is not the only one that can deliver the optimal outcome. An alternative, suggested by Jacklin (1987, 30–31), is for agents to invest in a mutual fund that invests its deposits in the production process and issues investors with equity claims in $T = 0$. The intermediary also promises in $T = 0$ to pay a fixed dividend D at $T = 1$ – the intermediary has to announce the dividend in $T = 0$ since individuals would no longer be able to agree on dividend policy if they waited till $T = 1$ when they knew their types (Jacklin, 1987, 31) – and the residual (i.e., $R(1 - D)$) to those share-holders who remain at $T = 2$. When $T = 1$ arrives, individuals receive their dividend D and learn their types, and the type 1s sell their shares to type 2s for additional period 1 goods. If D is set at tr_1 and the market clears, then the price of shares in $T = 1$ is $(1 - t)r_1$ and the optimal outcome results. Type 2s will buy at this price because the return they would get from those shares is greater than the market price (i.e., $R(1 - D) = R(1 - tr_1) > r_1(1 - t)$). The type 1s will sell at this price because future dividend payments are no use to them. The total return to type 1s is then equal to their $T = 1$ dividend (i.e., tr_1) *plus* what they get for their shares (i.e., $(1 - t)r_1$). Their return is therefore equal to r_1 which is optimal if r_1 is set to $c_{1,1}^*$. It is then easy to show that the return to type 2s is equal to $R(1 - c_{1,1}^*t)/(1 - t)$ which is the social optimum by (9.3). The Jacklin equity contract consequently delivers the same (optimal) outcome as the Diamond–Dybvig contract, but relies on a market instead of a suspension mechanism to do it.[8]

A more serious problem is that the assumptions so far imply that an intermediary is not even necessary to achieve the social optimum. Each individual could issue shares in his own 'back yard' project, and everyone could buy shares in all the projects. All shares would be identical because the underlying projects are identical, and each share contract would have the conditions specified in the Jacklin equity contract just outlined. However, in this case there would be no intermediary. Individuals would trade shares that were 'direct' claims to project outcomes instead of 'indirect' claims on an intermediary, but the earlier Jacklin argument can then be adapted to show that this direct investment process would yield the same outcome as financial intermediation would. It follows, then, that financial intermediation does not improve on the best unintermediated outcome, which in turn means that financial intermediation is not properly motivated. Far from being able to say what intermediaries would do, and what problems they would face, we have no reason yet for intermediaries to exist in the first place.

If we are to have properly motivated intermediation, there must therefore be some market 'frictions' that the intermediary can overcome. One possibility, suggested by Wallace (1989, 9), is to assume that agents in period $T = 1$ cannot trade because they are 'isolated' from each other:

> Although this isolation assumption may seem extreme, it is consistent with the notion that people hold liquid assets because they may find themselves impatient to spend when they do not have access to asset markets, in which they can sell any asset at its usual market price. (Wallace (1989, 9).

The important point is not that trade between $T = 1$ and $T = 2$ is prohibited, but that it is sufficiently costly that agents would prefer to deal with an intermediary instead, and the prohibition of trade between these periods is only an extreme means towards that end. Wallace (1989, 9) also notes that this isolation assumption is consistent with the notion that 'liquid' assets 'provide the holder with the possibility of spending at any time, if not also at any place, a notion which implicitly assumes that not all people are together'.[9] Since the isolation assumption prevents agents meeting together in $T = 1$, it effectively rules out both the Jacklin intermediary-share market and the 'private' credit market in $T = 1$. Apart from 'pure' autarky, the only remaining option is then an intermediary such as the one originally suggested by Diamond and Dybvig, but with the difference that the SSC now plays a much more explicit role than it did in their original formulation.

THE DIAMOND–DYBVIG MODEL WITH STOCHASTIC AGGREGATE CONSUMPTION

Stochastic Aggregate Consumption Makes DD Contracts Suboptimal

Suppose we now relax the assumption that t is determinate and known, and suppose instead that t is random with a known density function. No-one can now predict how many agents will turn out to be type 1s, and none of the earlier DD contracts can be relied on to achieve the previous optimum. Since the optimal payment is contingent on t but t itself is no longer known, the intermediary would not know what to pay out until all requests for withdrawals had been dealt with. If the intermediary is to ensure that the optimum is attained, it would need some way to contact those who had already withdrawn to top up the earlier payments it had made to them if the earlier payments had been too low, or to recover part of the earlier payments if they had been too high. However, if the intermediary had the means to recover payments in this way, it would effectively nullify any 'isolation' between agents at $T = 1$, and if there is no isolation, as we have just seen, the intermediary itself would have no reason to exist. If we are to take isolation seriously, it would also seem to follow that the intermediary cannot offer contracts contingent on actual, as opposed to expected, t. The optimal feasible contract must take this constraint into account and the DD 'optimal' contract does not.

A stochastic t also exposes the DD contracts to an additional problem. As we have seen, the contract must have a suspension clause if it is to prevent runs, and a suspension clause requires that the intermediary select as part of its contract (and, therefore, *before* t is realised) a threshold level of withdrawals at which it will suspend payments. But if the suspension threshold is set too low (i.e., if f' is less than the maximum possible realisation of t) then outcomes are possible which would be inefficient *ex post* because some type 1 agents would be unable to withdraw when they wanted to. The only way to avoid such an outcome would be to set f at the upper bound of t's distribution (i.e., unity), but in that case the intermediary would only suspend when it had nothing left, and the suspension would serve no purpose. A threshold that high would therefore be tantamount to having no suspension facility at all, and the contract would be vulnerable to runs again. If there is to be an effective suspension facility, type 1 agents must therefore run the risk that they might be unable to withdraw in $T = 1$. A final problem, noted by Anderlini (1986c) and Engineer (1989), is that if agents have a longer time horizon than two periods and they discover their types over time, then the DD-type suspension contract might not be able to rule out runs anyway.[10]

A Case for Government Intervention?

The question then is whether the outcome could be improved if some outside agency (i.e., the government) were to intervene, and DD suggest that it could. Suppose that there exists a government that could tax (or subsidise) those agents who withdraw in $T = 1$. Suppose also that the government could assess taxes after all withdrawals have taken place in $T = 1$, so it could base the amount taxed on the realised total withdrawals and hence, in the absence of panic, on the realised value of t. DD then show that a tax-subsidy policy exists which enables the earlier socially optimal outcome to be achieved (Proposition 2, 1983, 414–45). One can think of this policy as a deposit insurance scheme or as a central bank bailout rule to help illiquid intermediaries, and it operates as follows:[11] when $T = 1$ arrives, those who wish to withdraw queue up at the financial intermediary which redeems their deposits on the basis of some expected value of t. (Remember that the intermediary does not yet know the true realisation of t.) Assuming that only type 1s desire to withdraw in $T = 1$, the government infers the realised value of t after all requests for withdrawal have come in and then implements a tax-subsidy policy to ensure that type 1s receive their optimal consumption bundle contingent on the realisation of t, as given by (9.3).[12] This policy means that type 1s receive a subsidy or tax assessment after withdrawals have taken place but before they have consumed in $T = 1$. The tax-subsidy is assumed to be costless to operate, so a DD contract would give the type 2s their optimal consumption as well (again, see (9.3) above). Since the returns are guaranteed contingent on t, the earlier self-selection constraint is satisfied, and there is no incentive for type 2s to withdraw in $T = 1$. The 'bad' run equilibrium is then eliminated and the only equilibrium left is the 'good' one where agents receive their optimal bundles.

However, the state intervention might also create moral hazard problems that can only be dealt with by further intervention. Since the expected value of the bailout to any individual banker rises with the probability of default, and the probability of default rises with the promised return to withdrawals in $T = 1$, the latter would rise as each individual banker attempted to maximise the value of his bailout-subsidy, so the bailout facility might encourage competitive intermediaries to bid more aggressively for deposits by raising deposit rates paid to those who withdraw in $T = 1$. $T = 1$ deposit rates would then rise indefinitely, and a point would come where the anticipated returns to $T = 2$ withdrawals had fallen so low that there was no point keeping deposits beyond $T = 1$. Type 2 depositors would then run and trigger off the bailout mechanism (Anderlini, Proposition 4, 1986b, 25; see also Smith, 1984, 305–308; and Freeman, 1988, 61–2). Anderlini draws the conclusion that the bailout rule needs to be supplemented with 'regulation' – in this case, a deposit interest ceiling – and proves (Proposition 5, 1986b, 28) that an appropriate combination of a bailout facility and an interest-rate ceiling can eliminate the bankers' moral hazard and achieve the optimal outcome.[13] If production is irreversible (e.g., as in Freeman, 1988), moral hazard might also manifest itself in a tendency to hold too few reserves, so reserve requirements might be necessary as well.

These 'improvements' to the *laissez-faire* outcome however turn out to violate the 'isolation' assumption made earlier (see also Wallace, 1989, 13). The private sector is assumed to lack the means to overcome isolation in $T = 1$, and this isolation is the reason why a private intermediary cannot 'get back' to agents after they have withdrawn in $T = 1$ to top up their payments or retrieve what it has already paid out. The problem is that the assumption that the government has the means to tax or subsidise agents in $T = 1$ after agents have withdrawn (i.e., when it is in a position to infer what the realisation of t was) is tantamount to assuming that the government has *access to the very technology the private sector is assumed to lack*. It is therefore hardly surprising that DD find the SSC does not 'bind' their social optimum. They obtain that result because they implicitly assume that the government has the means to overcome the SSC to which the private sector is subject. Imposing that constraint on the private sector alone makes no difference to the socially obtainable outcome if the government can overcome the constraint itself.

Furthermore, if the technology exists, one also has to explain why the private sector lacks it *and* why the private sector cannot simply hire out the government's technology as it might hire out any other service. Indeed, if the technology exists to overcome isolation, one must also explain why intermediaries exist at all given that the absence of isolation implies that the intermediary contract is undermined by arbitrage at $T = 1$. Yet, if the technology does not exist, then the government tax-subsidy scheme is not feasible because the government has no way to 'get back' later to those who have already withdrawn in $T = 1$. In the context of the model itself, the government scheme would therefore appear to be either unnecessary or unfeasible, and neither way would it generate a superior outcome to *laissez-faire* (see also McCulloch and Yu, 1989).

Many economists nonetheless reject this conclusion and argue that the government's unique legal powers give it the necessary 'technological superiority' over the private sector to justify at least some of its interventions into the banking system. Many of these arguments hinge on the government's power to tax. DD themselves argue (1983, 413–414, 416) that private insurers would have to hold reserves to make insurance promises credible, but the government's power to tax enables it to offer credible insurance without reserves. They also argue that private agents might lack the necessary resources anyway, but the government should not lack them because it can always obtain them through taxation. Anderlini (1986b, 8–9), Bryant (1980, 341) and DD (1983, 413) also argue that the government has an advantage in that it can make use of inflation to finance the cost of its bailouts or deposit insurance, but the private sector cannot. In addition, there are arguments that intervention might be required because banks are too small to diversify away individual consumption risk (e.g., Bhattacharya and Gale, 1987; Chari, 1989) or because intervention can help to overcome banks' vulnerability to contagious runs (e.g., Smith, 1991; Park, 1991; Bougheas, 1994). Finally, one occasionally meets arguments that the government might not be able to rent out its 'superior technology' or that the bailout or lender of last resort facility is some sort of public good that the private sector is (allegedly) incapable of providing.

These arguments are highly dubious. It is not reserves as such that private insurers need to offer credible insurance but adequate wealth on which they can draw if the need arises (i.e., they need adequate collateral) and, as many Lloyds' names appear to do, individual insurers can offer that guarantee with few liquid reserves. The argument that individuals lack the necessary wealth is implausible in view of the immense wealth of modern economies, but it is also logically flawed because the government's own resources must come from the private sector – if the private sector lacks the necessary resources, then the power to tax is of no avail anyway because the resources are simply not there to take. The inflation-tax argument is also questionable: if banking were free, we would expect that competition would force the banks to make their liabilities convertible, and convertibility would deprive the government of the use of an inflation tax. Furthermore, since the government can only use that tax if it intervenes (e.g., by setting up a fiat currency), the very existence of the inflation tax would seem to presuppose that the government has *already* intervened, and so the argument does not apply to a genuine *laissez-faire* economy. There is in any case very considerable evidence that inflation is an inefficient and undesirable form of taxation even if the alternative is to levy other taxes that distort economic activity (see, e.g., Chapter 14 in this volume). The arguments that intermediaries are too small to diversify risk or are vulnerable to contagion are open to the objection that the relevant problems can be dealt with by the intermediaries combining to form a single firm, and the latter argument is in any case also open to various objections made in Chapter 7. The remaining arguments – that the government cannot rent out its superior technology and that government must provide the bailout facility on public goods grounds – are also unconvincing and need in any case to be developed. Even if the government has a natural monopoly in the provision of law and order – which, in any case, is dubious – all that seems to be required to undermine the case for the government bailout facility is that private agents have access to the government legal system to make contracts with each other. Nor is it obvious what public good is provided by a bailout facility or why the private sector cannot provide that public good itself. Lastly, and by no means least, the models themselves imply that the very technology that is used to justify government intervention also undermines the need for intermediation itself, and therefore violates our requirement that intermediation should be properly motivated. If we stick strictly to the models, the motivation for financial intermediation makes the government intervention unfeasible, and making government intervention feasible destroys the motivation for financial intermediation; we cannot have properly motivated financial intermediation *and* properly motivated government intervention.

BANKING INSTABILITY WITH UNCERTAIN RETURNS TO PRODUCTION

We consider now what happens if the returns to production are uncertain. Production uncertainty is not especially significant on its own, but it becomes significant if some agents have interim information about production returns on which they might act. As Jacklin observes, production uncertainty can be of importance

> only if there is interim information about the underlying asset returns that becomes available at $T = 1$. ... If one re-examines the [earlier] arguments ... it is clear that they do not rely on the riskless nature of R, as long as none of the uncertainty regarding R is resolved prior to trade taking place at $T = 1$. Thus, ... the underlying asset returns are not only assumed to be uncertain, but individuals are assumed to be asymmetrically informed about the returns before trade takes place at $T = 1$. (Jacklin, 1988, 14–15)

The combination of uncertain returns and asymmetric information makes formal analysis difficult, not surprisingly, but a few relatively disparate models have made some progress with the problem. One is Jacklin (1988). In his model each unit invested in $T = 0$ yields a return of 1 if the investment is liquidated in $T = 1$, and a random return of R if it is left until it matures in $T = 2$. The expected value of R exceeds unity and investors have corner preferences. Some type 2 individuals are then given private information about R in $T = 1$ which helps them to decide whether to liquidate their investments in that period. (Note that the corner preference assumption implies that private information about R is of no use to type 1s since they would liquidate their investments anyway.) There are no restrictions against trading assets in $T = 1$, so there is no sequential service constraint. Jacklin then constructs an example where an equity contract achieves the optimal allocation provided that the aggregate consumption shock t is non-stochastic. The equity contract is optimal because the share price fully reveals the private information about the random variable R in the absence of other shocks. However, if t is stochastic as well as R, the share price will reflect both shocks, and the equity contract will no longer give a noiseless signal about R. Jacklin demonstrates by means of an example that the equity contract can then be suboptimal even though the DD contract cannot achieve the DD social optimum and the possibility of panics still remains. He thus gives some insight into why demand debt-type contracts have arisen that promise liquidity in $T = 1$ and a return that is fixed over a range of project outcomes, and why they have arisen instead of equity ones even though they might be more subject to runs. As he observes, demand debt arose not only to provide liquidity transformation, but also to provide

> transformation using illiquid assets with underlying values that are both *uncertain* and about which there is the *potential for great asymmetry of information* with respect to the uncertainty. (Jacklin, 1988, 3, his emphasis)

When there is a credit market at $T = 1$ demand debt is no more liquid than equity, but

> demand debt [by which Jacklin means the DD contract] has the benefit of being relatively insensitive to informational asymmetries about the underlying portfolio values. On the other hand, demand equity is not subject to runs but is very sensitive to informational asymmetries about underlying portfolio values. (Jacklin, 1988, 5)

There is, in short, a trade-off between the problems caused by the potential for bank runs which might lead one to prefer equity and the problems caused by information asymmetries which might lead one to prefer debt or DD-type contracts instead.

More insights into these issues are provided by Jacklin and Bhattacharya (JB) (1988). They have the same production technology as Jacklin (1988) but a return of zero instead of unity if investment is liquidated in $T = 1$. (This irreversibility assumption captures the idea of a 'readily discernible cost' to early consumption. One can think of the crop being destroyed before the harvest is ripe.) JB also differ from Jacklin (1988) in so far as investors are assumed to have smooth rather than corner references, but as in Jacklin, agents' types are revealed in $T = 1$ and some type 2s receive a signal about R later in the same period. JB then show that the DD contract is subject to runs while the equity contract is not, but the value of a DD asset is unaffected by news about the underlying project return, except if the news is very bad, while the value of equity is affected by any information about the return to production. The underlying idea is that the DD contract insulates the investor against small gains or losses on production, but large losses (i.e., ones that make the intermediary insolvent) have to be passed back to him. There is therefore the same trade-off as in Jacklin (1988), and the implication is that the DD contract would be preferred where the risk of runs was relatively small (e.g., in financing low-risk projects), but the equity contract would be preferred otherwise. Unlike DD, JB obtain a unique equilibrium, and they explicitly address the factors (i.e., bad interim information) that could trigger runs. Runs are now 'systematic' events triggered off by movements in economically relevant indicators (e.g., bad earnings reports). They are no longer purely random events triggered off by variables like sunspots which are in themselves economically irrelevant but which for some reason trigger off self-fulfilling expectations of a run.

While Jacklin and Bhattacharya focus on the relationship between choice of contract and the riskiness of an institution's assets when some agents are informed about the value of those assets, Chari and Jagannathan (1988) examine the implications of the converse problem of how *uninformed* agents infer private information about project values from the behaviour of other depositors who are more informed. They have a model in which some individuals might withdraw in $T = 1$ because they have private information that the future return to production will be low, while others withdraw for other reasons (e.g., due to liquidity needs). The uninformed consequently face a signal extraction problem in which they try to infer the private information they do not have from the size of the queue at the bank, and when they observe a long queue they are more likely to conclude that the bank is in difficulties and decide to run. A run could then damage the bank by forcing it to liquidate its assets at a loss. In their model, investments are made in $T = 0$, and returns are random but expected to be high if the investments are left until $T = 2$. The return takes one of two values: H (high) or L (low), and $H > L$. If the investment is liquidated in $T = 1$, however, the return to the bank depends on how many wish to liquidate their investment. If only a small number wish to withdraw, the return per unit deposit is one, but the return is smaller (reflecting resale losses) if a large number wish to withdraw. All agents are risk-neutral and each is endowed with one unit of the consumption good in $T = 0$. Types are revealed in $T = 1$, and the proportion of type 1s (i.e., t) is random. Type 1s care only about $T = 1$ consumption while type 2s care about consumption in both $T = 1$ and $T = 2$. Also in $T = 1$, a random fraction a of type 2s receive (perfect) private information about prospective returns in $T = 2$, where $0 \le a < 1$, and no individual can predict whether he will be informed or not. The only public information in $T = 1$ is the fraction of the population that decide to liquidate their investments (i.e., the queue at the bank), but no-one observes the reasons that lead others to decide to withdraw their investments. (There is however nothing in the model to show why agents prefer to borrow and lend through an intermediary instead of dealing with each other directly.) When the 'private' information is given out in $T = 1$,

> All uninformed type-2 agents will realize that the equilibrium value of [the aggregate $T = 1$ investment] is correlated with the signal received by the informed agents and hence 'reveal', albeit imperfectly, their signal. It is important to realize that the aggregate investment could be low *either* because the value of t is high *or* because some type-2 agents have received information that prospective returns are low. It is this confounding that is crucial. (Chari and Jagannathan, 1988, 753)

They then show that a unique rational expectations equilibrium exists, but depending on the realisations of the stochastic variables, this equilibrium could involve a panic in which everyone withdraws even though no-one receives any negative information about R. One should note, however, that the contract form is assumed, and Chari and Jagannathan fail to show why – given that there is no SSC in their model – the bank does not simply condition contractual returns on the verifiable information the informed depositors receive. The run would then be short-circuited, and the losses it could cause avoided.

Williamson (1988) provides in some ways a more satisfactory analysis. As in DD, he has agents whose random preferences generate a demand for assets that are liquid in the short term, but his agents are risk-neutral rather than risk-averse and their risk-neutrality implies that there is no risk-sharing benefit from financial intermediation. There exist primitive short-term and long–term assets, but trade in claims to these assets is hampered by the difficulties potential buyers face in distinguishing claims to 'good' assets and claims to 'bad' ones. An individual who held direct claims on the production process might then find himself unable to meet unexpected liquidity needs without having to liquidate 'good' assets at a loss that reflected the market for lemons problem in the capital market. However, a bank-type intermediary could exploit the fact that individual liquidity shocks tended to cancel out in large numbers and issue claims that enabled individuals to invest in the underlying production process while simultaneously holding assets that could be liquidated at little loss in the short run (see also Freeman, 1988). In Williamson's model, banks generate superior outcomes to unintermediated markets in some states of the world, and the same outcome in others, so it always makes sense *ex ante* for agents to invest in a bank rather than invest directly themselves in the primitive assets. Banks are therefore properly motivated, but should a state occur where the bank does not improve on the unintermediated outcome, Williamson suggests that the bank might agree to dissolve itself and leave investors holding the underlying primitive assets, and he interprets such occurrences as bank 'failures'. However, his explanation is unconvincing because there is no reason in his model for the bank to dissolve rather than remain as it is, and his treatment is also unconvincing in so far as it implies that the act of bank failure *per se* is costless and, indeed, economically irrelevant.

A final analysis of how 'noisy' indicators can lead to runs is Gorton (1985). His model has banks that finance two-period investments with deposits and equity. Depositors derive utility from consumption in both periods, and they have an initial investment in $T = 0$ which they choose to invest between bank deposits and an alternative store of value. The initial amount of bank equity is chosen to equate the expected return on bank equity with the (exogenous) expected return on equity elsewhere, and the bank obtains additional funds by issuing deposits to the public. The deposit contract then offers depositors specified returns in each of the two periods provided the bank remains solvent, and it gives depositors first claim to the bank's assets if the bank defaults. Depositors also have the right to demand liquidation in $T = 1$. The return on the alternative (i.e., non-bank) asset and the return to the bank's investments are each subject to shocks in $T = 1$, and the latter shock is assumed to be private information to the bank. There is an implicit sequential service constraint by which depositors wishing to withdraw are served sequentially in the (presumably random) order in which they arrive at the bank, and the bank continues to meet demands for redemption until it runs out of assets and defaults.

If we initially assume that depositors perceive the state of the bank's investments correctly, the depositors' decision whether to withdraw or not depends on a straight comparison of the expected rates of return on the two stores of value. They will keep their deposits if the expected return on deposits is at least as high as the return on the alternative store of value, and they will liquidate them otherwise. In the latter case the bank would face a run and lose its deposits, but the outcome in either case is Pareto-optimal. If depositors are imperfectly informed about the bank's state of the investments, on the other hand, they will have to make their decisions on the basis of 'noisy' indicators of those investments, and they can make decisions that turn out to be worse than the decisions they would have made had they been better informed. Two sorts of 'mistakes' of this nature are then possible. Depositors can over-estimate the value of the bank's assets and as a result mistakenly keep their deposits in the bank and earn a lower return than they would have obtained had they withdrawn their deposits. Or, alternatively, they can under-estimate the value of the bank's assets and run on the bank in the mistaken belief that they could earn a higher return by withdrawing their deposits and investing them elsewhere, and in the process they bring about inefficient liquidations. The deposit contract can no longer be relied upon to deliver an outcome that is optimal *ex post*.

Gorton then suggests that the *ex post* optimum could be achieved by inserting a suspension clause into the deposit contract. His argument is that if the 'true' state of the bank could be revealed to depositors at some verification cost – one can think of this cost as the cost of bringing in outside auditors to go over the bank's books – the bank would make an agreement with its depositors that it could suspend on condition that it submit to a verification, the cost of which was to be borne by the bank's share-holders. (The assumption that share-holders are in a position to pay this cost is not trivial. The most natural interpretation of this arrangement is to think of the payment as coming out of bank capital, but then the latter must be at least as great as the verification cost.) Gorton argues that the verification-suspension clause is incentive-compatible in that the bank would only have an incentive to use it to reassure depositors who had underestimated the bank's true worth, and he suggests that this arrangement would be in the interests of both the bank and its depositors because it would protect them both against the losses they would each suffer if depositors ran while the bank was still sound. However, Gorton fails to explain why the bank does not reassure depositors by posting a bond of some sort (e.g., by augmenting bank capital). Since the share-holders know the bank is sound, they would then have no reason to fear losing their investment, and augmenting bank capital has the advantage that it avoids the verification cost. Verification/suspension is therefore dominated by posting a bond of some sort (e.g., by share-holders subscribing more capital or extending their liability).

CONCLUSIONS

Leaving aside the point that this literature predicts that financial institutions should be unstable, and the evidence clearly suggests they are not (see, e.g., Gorton, 1986, and Chapter 7 above), perhaps the most obvious point that stands out from this literature is that relatively little of it deals with institutions that have much resemblance to real-world banks. As discussed already, the financial institutions we observe in the real world for the most part distinguish between creditors who hold their equity and those who hold their debt. Their equity liabilities are residual claims that also make the holders owners of the institutions in a legal sense. The debt liabilities, by contrast, promise pre-specified returns in all non-default states, and first claim to the institution's assets if it defaults. When we refer to 'banks' it is these institutions we normally have in mind, and the substantive issue is that it is these institutions – whatever we may call them – that we are mostly interested in, and yet this literature has very little to say about them. The other financial intermediaries we observe are genuine mutual funds whose liabilities are equity-claims on its assets, but these too are not (usually) predicted by this literature, and nowhere do we observe the peculiar mutual fund intermediaries that the literature *does* predict.

Furthermore, while the literature talks about 'debt' and debt-like instruments such as 'demand deposits', the instruments labelled in this way are usually not debt at all, or at least not 'debt' as defined above. The so-called 'demand deposit' contract in much of this literature typically specifies a fixed non-default payoff in $T = 1$, and a residual payment in $T = 2$ for those who leave their investments till then. Such an instrument might resemble debt if one looks at the $T = 1$ payment, but a real debt contract would have specified fixed payments in both $T = 1$ and $T = 2$. Again, the issue is not merely semantic. Whatever we choose to call them, the instruments I have labelled debt play an important role in real-world financial intermediation, and our theories ought to be able to predict them – and predict equity too, for that matter. I suspect that part of the problem is that the literature focuses on the wrong question by asking whether a representative investor would want to hold a residual claim-type asset or one that has some 'fixity' in its payoff which it (dubiously) identifies as 'debt'. This approach ignores the symbiotic relationship between the two types of assets – if someone is to hold debt, someone else usually has to be the residual claimant who absorbs the gains or losses to the project value and ensures that the return to the debt-holder is fixed outside bankruptcy – but we then need a framework that enables us to study the simultaneous demands for both assets, and we cannot motivate such a framework if we start off by asking which asset(s) a *representative* agent will hold. We need to explain why *some* individuals choose to hold debt while *others* choose to hold equity, and it is not clear how we can provide that explanation using a framework that maintains that all agents are identical when they make their investment decisions.

The issues involved here can be illustrated using an example. Suppose we go back to the initial DD framework with corner preferences and a stochastic t, and suppose too that we ensure that an intermediary has a role to play by making an explicit isolation assumption along the lines suggested by Wallace (1989). Now introduce a new agent with K units of capital who knows in $T = 0$ that he will get utility only from consumption in $T = 2$. (We can think of this agent as someone with capital to invest who does not have to worry about short-term liquidity.) One way to invest his capital is to set up a bank. If he does so he would capitalise the bank with his endowment of capital and take in deposits from the public. The bank's capital and deposits would then be invested in the productive process, and depositors would be promised fixed returns for withdrawals in both $T = 1$ and $T = 2$ as well as the option to withdraw on demand. Denote these returns by r_1 and

r_2 respectively. Suppose also that the bank would pay each depositor-type his 'optimal consumption bundle' as specified by (9.3), i.e., $r_1 = c_{1,1}^*$ and $r_2 = c_{2,2}^*$. Depositors would then obtain returns at least as good as they could obtain if they set up their own intermediary along the lines suggested by DD, so they would prefer the new bank to DD's intermediary. Letting E be the value of the bank when it is wound up after all deposits have been repaid, and assuming that type 2 investors do not withdraw in the first period, then it can readily be seen that

$$E = KR + [t + (1 - t)R] - [tr_1 + (1 - t)r_2]. \tag{9.6}$$

The first term is the return on the investor's own capital, the second is the return on its deposits, and the third is (the negative of) its deposit liabilities. Assuming that he expects depositors to satisfy the self-selection constraint – and it can easily be shown that they will – our investor will expect to make a profit from the bank if t is less than some threshold level. He would therefore go ahead and establish the bank if he expected t to be sufficiently less than this level to compensate him for doing so (see, e.g., Dowd, 1993b).

The differences between a bank and the DD mutual fund now become apparent. The possibility of bank runs arises with the DD intermediary because each type 2 depositor is aware that he would suffer capital losses if sufficiently many others withdrew their deposits, and the prospect of these losses arises because the intermediary has insufficient capital to redeem all its deposits in $T = 1$ at the rate of r_1 per deposit. However, if the bank had sufficient capital to meet this liability, the public would have no reason to fear capital losses and therefore no reason to run. The bank could provide such assurance by ensuring that its capital was adequate to cover its losses in the 'worst case scenario' when everyone withdraws in $T = 1$, i.e., by ensuring that K satisfies

$$K \geq r_1 - 1 \tag{9.7}$$

where $(r_1 - 1)$ is the loss the bank makes on deposits withdrawn in period 1. If this condition holds, the self–selection constraint would be satisfied, no type 2 depositor would withdraw in period 1, and there would be no bank runs. Runs arose in the DD model precisely because the zero value of K meant that this condition could not hold. The key point, therefore, is that an adequately-capitalised bank can use its capital buffer to prevent runs by reassuring potentially nervous depositors, but a DD mutual fund is vulnerable to runs because it cannot provide that reassurance. Genuine banks are therefore more stable than the mutual funds predicted by the DD literature, and we should be careful drawing inferences about the stability of the former from the peculiar problems faced by the latter.

The last main point that emerges from this literature on 'banking' instability is the shakiness of the foundations on which arguments for government intervention into the financial industry are based. Most of the arguments for intervention to be found in this literature are based on the premise that the government has access to a technology for overcoming 'isolation' between individuals that the private sector is assumed to lack. The assumption of such a governmental technological superiority is surely far-fetched, but even if one accepts it, the first-best outcome could still be achieved in these models provided the government gave the private sector access to its own superior technology. The advocates of intervention therefore have to explain why an interventionist policy is to be preferred to the government simply renting its technology out. Even if such an explanation is provided, the government's own technology would make financial intermediation redundant anyway by destroying the 'isolation' friction that gives rise to intermediation in the first place. The other arguments for intervention are also highly questionable. The DD argument that a case for intervention might be based on the government's monopoly of the currency is open to the objection that the currency monopoly is itself the product of intervention, and the arguments for a legislated currency monopoly have been pretty much discredited. The proponents of intervention then have to rebut the argument that the first-best outcome is *laissez–faire* in banking, *including* an end to the currency monopoly. There is, finally, the argument that policy might be required to enable firms to exploit economies of scale, but one would then need to explain why firms are not exploiting economies of scale in the first place. If it is because they are prevented by legal restrictions, as US banks are sometimes prevented by anti-branching laws, then the obvious response is that these restrictions should be removed; if institutions are not prevented by legal restrictions, on the other hand, one has to explain why banks are failing to pursue their own self-interest. *Laissez-faire* is optimal, again.

10 Media of Exchange and Payment Systems

This chapter addresses various issues related to exchange media and payment systems. We begin with the media of exchange issues. A medium of exchange (MOE) may be defined as any object which is taken in exchange, not to be consumed or used up by the receiver, but with the intention of being exchanged for something else at some point in the future. The first issue is therefore to explain the development of a commonly or generally accepted MOE. Economists broadly agree over how a commonly accepted commodity MOE can arise spontaneously from initial conditions of barter, but what happens next is more controversial. The controversy centres on the claim made by Kiyotaki and Wright (1989), and others, that commodity currency would then directly give way to *fiat* or *inconvertible* paper currency. However, such a development is in fact most unlikely. The commodity currency actually would give way to *convertible* paper currency and that the currency would remain convertible thereafter. Convertibility arises and then persists because the public demand it, and they demand it because of the reassurance it provides them regarding the value of their currency. An implication of this position is that real-world fiat currencies did not arise spontaneously, but because of government intervention to suppress the convertibility guarantee.

We then examine two other issues that have received considerable recent attention in the New Monetary Economics (NME) literature (e.g., Wallace, 1983; Cowen and Kroszner, 1994) – the legal restrictions' theory that maintains that currency would disappear under *laissez-faire* conditions, and the 'monetary separation' hypothesis that maintains that the MOE and medium of account (MOA) would 'separate' from each other under *laissez-faire* (i.e., that people would use MOE denominated in units that fluctuated in value against units of the MOA). I suggest that both claims are theoretically questionable and empirically falsified. *Laissez-faire* would lead neither to the disappearance of currency nor to the 'separation' of the MOE and MOA. A *laissez-faire* system is therefore 'closer' to present-day systems than advocates of the NME in particular have suggested.

The second half of the chapter deals with issues relating to payment systems. Perhaps the easiest way to come to grips with these is to go back to an early stage in the economy's evolution and use a conjectural history to explain how the payment system would arise. Every transaction initially involves an exchange of goods and/ or services, but over time barter gradually gives way to monetary exchange in which transactions are carried out via a tangible MOE. There then develop systems of payment – McCallum (1985) refers to them as accounting systems of exchange – that principally involve the transfer of bookkeeping entries and do not use an MOE as such. At this point, we can now explain how payment systems work. The central problem with them is that of systemic risk – in particular, the risk that the failure of a participant in a payment system might make it difficult for other participants to meet their settlement obligations, and perhaps lead them to fail as well. This problem is potentially serious, but there are various ways of dealing with it. We then go on to discuss whether accounting systems are likely to displace monetary systems entirely – another issue that has been given considerable prominence by the NME – but conclude that such an outcome is unlikely. Finally, we end the chapter with a brief review of some of the arguments for government intervention in payment systems.

EXCHANGE MEDIA

The Development of Commonly Accepted Exchange Media

The development of a commonly accepted MOE can perhaps best be understood using the invisible hand story set out by Menger (1892). Individuals start off in a state of barter, but have to cope with the coincidence of wants and coincidence of timing problems that barter involves. At some point, one or more individuals realise that they can accomplish the trades they want more quickly or more easily by resorting to indirect exchange – exchanging their goods for goods that they do not wish to consume, but which they believe would be more acceptable to individuals with the goods they are looking for. The practice of indirect exchange would then gradually spread as other individuals became aware of its benefits. Over time, certain already relatively saleable goods would become the preferred media for indirect exchange, the growth of demand for them for the purposes of indirect exchange would make them even more saleable, and their increased saleability would make them even more desirable as intermediary goods, thereby further reinforcing the adoption of indirect exchange. Indirect exchange would displace barter, and in the end a single good (or perhaps small number of goods) would become the commonly accepted medium (or media) of exchange.

While this invisible hand story is intuitively very plausible, economic theorists have had great difficulty trying to model the process formally. For example, the overlapping generations and cash-in-advance models that are used so often in other areas of monetary economics are useless for analysing this sort of issue. In the words of Kiyotaki and Wright,

> Overlapping generations models basically ignore the medium of exchange role, concentrating on money's store of value function. Cash-in-advance models simply impose the medium of exchange role by an *ad hoc* restriction that goods can be acquired only using money. These approaches are useful when we are interested only in getting money into the system so that we can proceed to analyze some substantive economic issues, but they have no hope of explaining endogenously either the nature of money or the development of monetary exchange. (Kiyotaki and Wright, 1989, 928, n. 1)

The most promising approach is that pioneered by Jones (1976) and developed further by Oh (1989) and Kiyotaki and Wright (1989). These studies model the development of monetary exchange by examining the trading strategies of agents who are endowed with different goods and who meet each other more or less randomly. We can think of them bumping into each other by chance in the jungle. There are no markets as such and no auctioneer or any similar construct to organise trades. Nor can individuals avoid the problems of barter by issuing IOUs, since they cannot count on meeting each other again. There is no 'trust' between individuals, and no institutions that individuals can 'trust' to provide credit that might otherwise overcome barter problems. Each individual develops a trading strategy to obtain the consumption good he wants at the minimum expected trading cost. The essence of this strategy is never to pass up the chance to exchange a less saleable good for a more saleable good, even if one does not wish to consume the more saleable good. Indirect exchange then dominates barter for all transactions other than the comparatively few in which a double coincidence of wants occurs and two individuals meet who each want to consume the other's goods. The result is an equilibrium in which most trades are carried out using a commonly accepted medium of exchange, but a small number of trades are carried out through barter.

Kiyotaki and Wright (1989) develop this approach further by showing that the resulting equilibrium can depend, not only on the intrinsic properties of the good(s) chosen as MOE, but also on agents' expectations of each other's trading strategies. They find that the properties of the goods selected as exchange media matter – individuals prefer to use intermediary goods that involve low storage costs, other things being equal – but a multiplicity of equilibria can also arise because of the dependence of an individual's behaviour on he expects others to do. One possible equilibrium is that in which each individual adopts the strategy of accepting a good with a low storage cost until he finds a trading partner with the good he wants to consume – the low-cost good emerges as the preferred intermediary good. However, if individuals expect each other to adopt an intermediary good that involves higher storage costs, we might end up with an alternative equilibrium in which a high-cost good emerges as the medium of exchange (Kiyotaki and Wright, 1989, 934–935). Expectations can be self-fulfilling, and there is no guarantee that the good with the lowest storage cost will actually be chosen as medium of exchange.

These last two points need emphasising. To some extent, each individual agent has an incentive to go along with the choice of indirect exchange medium that he believes others will choose themselves. The more he expects his trading partners to choose a particular indirect exchange medium, he more incentive he has to choose that commodity himself as his own preferred medium of indirect exchange. The individual decision whether to use a particular commodity as a medium of indirect exchange consequently depends on how many others he expects to choose the same commodity (i.e., it is subject to network externalities), in much the same way that the decision whether to learn a new language or install a telephone depends on how many others are already in that network by virtue of speaking that language or having a phone. Expectations can therefore be self-fulfilling, in that anything that leads agents to *expect* that a particular medium will be chosen could lead to that medium actually *being chosen*. There is then no guarantee that the selection process will converge on the commodity that would be regarded as the technically most efficient one in the absence of network externalities. As Wärneryd puts it in the context of language externalities, Esperanto might be a 'simpler and more logical language', but learning it 'does not pay off if the person you are speaking to does not know Esperanto' (1989, 614). The apparently inefficient equilibrium persists because there is no way to coordinate a move away from it.

The other point is that our notion of a MOE is a very subjectivist one – a MOE is whatever a typical individual can reasonably expect others to accept in exchange. This notion is very different from the still standard textbook view that tends to define a MOE (or, more often, the much-abused and vague term 'money')

> in, on the one hand, the property of being legal tender, and, on the other, certain physical attributes of a good, such as its divisibility, storability, transportability, etc. While these attributes are often present, what serves as a CAMOE [i.e., commonly accepted MOE] in a particular society at a particular time cannot be identified by looking for the good that satisfies a list of physical criteria best. Again, a CAMOE is *whatever* is commonly used for indirect exchange. (Wärneryd, 1990, 121, his emphasis)

The (Non-) Emergence of Fiat Currency

It cannot be stressed too strongly that these models only provide an explanation for the use of a *commodity* MOE, and – despite attempts to do so – they *cannot* be used to explain the widespread use of *inconvertible fiat currency*. The most well-known attempt – that of Kiyotaki and Wright (1989, 941–947) – essentially boils down to the argument that if goods are costly to store, and therefore costly to use as media of exchange, then agents would be prefer to use some costlessly produced, intrinsically worthless asset as MOE instead – *provided* they expected each other to accept this asset as MOE *and* they had confidence that it would retain its exchange value. They then identify this asset as 'fiat money' and claim to have a theory for the widespread use of fiat currency (Kiyotaki and Wright, 1989, 929), and they also claim that this fiat-money equilibrium is more efficient than an equilibrium with a commodity MOE because it saves on the storage costs of holding monetary reserves of the commodity involved.

However, this story does *not* provide a convincing explanation for the emergence of real-world inconvertible currency. One obvious problem is that fiat currency only 'takes off' in this model if agents have 'faith' in the fiat currency and expect it to be generally accepted, but there is nothing in the model to give them that faith or make them expect each other to accept the fiat currency. Nor do Kiyotaki and Wright provide any reasons why agents would find it *individually* rational to accept intrinsically worthless paper for their goods; they merely demonstrate that under certain conditions individuals would be *collectively* better off if they expected each other to accept it.[1] Indeed, there are very good reasons why agents would *not* accept an intrinsically worthless asset. If an individual can produce such an asset at zero cost, he would always prefer to produce such an asset and hand it over in exchange for real goods. Everyone would therefore wish to do so, and we would get the 'wallpaper money' scenario of Friedman (1960) and Johnson (1968) in which individuals produce their own inconvertible 'currency' but have no incentive to limit their issues or otherwise maintain their value. Currency issues would become worthless, and the only equilibrium is one in which no-one issues their own currency. A *laissez-faire* monetary equilibrium therefore does not exist in this model (Ritter, 1992, proposition 2; Williamson, 1992, 155).

One attempted solution, suggested by both Ritter and Williamson, is to introduce a monopoly currency issuer into the model. If some agent or group of agents can somehow get together to issue currency and simultaneously prevent others from issuing any competing currencies, then the monopoly issuer *may* be able to issue a currency that does not self-destruct in the way that competitive currencies would. Unlike a competitive issuer of indistinguishable inconvertible currency, a monopoly issuer might have some incentive to limit his issues to order to maintain the future demand for his currency and hence his future seignorage profits. If the monopoly issuer does not apply too high a rate of discount, his promises not to issue too much currency in the future might be credible, and in such circumstances he could issue a currency that retained at least some of its value over time. A monetary equilibrium would then exist.

But this 'solution' is hardly satisfactory. Even if we accept it at face value, it merely establishes that people would accept a new fiat currency, *provided* they have faith in it and believe that others will use it as well. However, it fails to provide *any* reasons for a member of the public to have that faith or to expect other members of the public to use it. Even if there is a fiat money equilibrium in the model, there is still the problem of how the economy gets to that equilibrium from an initial state of using commodity MOE. To do so, some individuals must start accepting intrinsically worthless pieces of paper for their goods even though other individuals are still wedded to commodity MOE. But why should an individual accept paper in exchange for his goods when he cannot count on trading partners accepting paper in return for their goods? People would only accept fiat currency if they felt that others would accept it as well, but no-one has any incentive to start the adoption process off by being the first to accept fiat currency whilst others are still refusing it. The upshot is that everyone waits for others to start accepting the fiat currency, and so no-one actually accepts it. A monetary equilibrium might exist, but the economy will never reach it – the fiat currency would be stuck at its 'launching pad' (Selgin, 1994b, 809–811).

At a deeper level, this 'solution' also sits very uneasily with the economic environment in which it is invoked. If we stay within the confines of a decentralised model where agents' actions are unco-ordinated, how does the monopoly ensure that its legal privileges are enforced? If no such means exist, then the monopoly is meaningless and we are stuck in a non-monetary equilibrium. There must therefore exist *some* means of enforcing the monopoly, but in that case there must be some way of coordinating agents' actions. Yet, if agents' actions *can* be coordinated, why do we need the monopoly? Why not simply use the co-ordination machinery to solve the underlying economic problem directly, without introducing a monopoly at all? To meet this point, Ritter and Williamson would have to specify the features of the underlying environment that made the monopoly feasible whilst also ruling out other means of coordinating agents' behaviour, but they fail to do so and instead invoke a *deus ex machina* that is tantamount to assuming the problem away. The Ritter–Williamson 'solution' is essentially another version of the discredited chartalist view espoused by Knapp (1905) and Keynes ([1930] 1971) that maintains that 'money is a creature of the state' because it relies on state power to give it value (see, e.g., Frankel, 1977).

The argument that a new fiat currency would not be accepted is also supported by Selgin's (1994b) assessment of the historical evidence on the launch of such currencies. Selgin reviews the experience of a variety of fiat currencies starting from John Law's fiat currency in the early eighteenth century, and he could not find a *single* case where a fiat currency had been successfully launched *de novo* without first tying it in to some *existing* currency or currency unit:

> The [new currency] units (or fractional counterparts) had in every case been in use to some extent in the marketplace prior to the reforms embodying them in new currencies. The units' definitions had, moreover, to be rendered operational through some kind of convertibility, typically involving one or more fixed or nearly fixed exchange rates to foreign monies. Legal tender and public receivability provisions were, on the other hand, either nonexistent or of obviously secondary importance. Experience therefore supports the conclusion ... that a new fiat money must be operationally linked to some established money if it is to achieve a positive value. (Selgin, 1994b, 823, emphasis added)

What actually happened, of course, was that commodity MOE gave way to *convertible* currencies, and fiat currencies only emerged when governments intervened later to suppress convertibility. It is curious that none of the studies that espouse the view that fiat currencies can somehow be launched out of nothing – the 'fiat money' theory, for want of a better label – even consider this possibility. The basic story was already set out in Chapter 1: starting from a position where they use a commodity such as gold as their medium of exchange, agents gradually resort to using goldsmiths' receipts circulate as exchange media, and a point comes where the goldsmiths have evolved into bankers and their receipts into a convertible paper currency that has substantially displaced gold as the dominant medium of exchange. The paper currency issued is very safe, and demands for redemption are relatively few and far between. The new currency is less costly to operate than gold was, but is not costless because notes are convertible and banks must maintain reserves of gold to meet redemption demands.

This story differs from the earlier fiat money story in a number of ways. Unlike the fiat story, it does not rely on a monopoly or any other way of enforced 'co-ordination' among the individuals concerned. The convertible currency system emerges spontaneously, driven only the pursuit of individual self-interest, and does not rely on any *deus ex machina*. The reason *laissez-faire* produces a convertible and not an inconvertible system is *precisely because* the public want some guarantee of the value of their currency, and a competitive fiat system does not give them that guarantee. The emergence of convertible currency under *laissez-faire* is consequently far from accidental: the currency is convertible because the public demand the reassurances that convertibility gives them. Unlike the case with the fiat currency theory just considered, the adoption of a convertible currency is not a bootstrap operation that relies on the blind 'trust' of the public to get off the ground; it takes off gradually, as the system slowly evolves and 'trust' in it grows. The convertible currency system does involve costs, but as discussed elsewhere, these costs will be low and there is no way that they can be significantly reduced (e.g., by abolishing reserves or convertibility) without undermining the system itself. 'Trust' in a currency is not some free good that can be produced at zero cost. The fiat system involves no convertibility costs, naturally, but neither does it provide the currency guarantees that the public want; if the public want those guarantees and are willing to pay the costs involved, then suppressing them by making the currency inconvertible must presumably make them worse off. The argument that a fiat currency is superior to a convertible one because it does not involve any reserve-holding costs is much like the argument, say, that sitting in the freezing cold is better than switching on the fire because it keeps down the heating bill. Sitting in the cold *does* keep down the heating bill, but people should not be compelled to freeze just to save the costs of heating – particularly when heating is cheap.

This convertible currency story also has the advantage of being more consistent with the historical evidence. The *fact* is that the basic prediction of the fiat currency story – that inconvertible currency would emerge directly from commodity currency – is flatly rejected by the evidence. Nowhere, apparently, did a system of commodity money jump directly to a system of fiat currency; and where commodity currency did give way to paper currency, it gave way, apparently in every case, to *convertible* paper currency. The currency then remained convertible for as long as competitive forces were allowed to operate to maintain convertibility, and fiat currencies only emerged when governments explicitly intervened to suppress convertibility by force and make the existing paper currency inconvertible. Only then did the currency genuinely become a fiat currency – a currency of a type made possible only by the *fiat* power of the state.[2] Any sensible story about the emergence of fiat currency must therefore come to terms with two basic facts, both of which are ignored by the fiat money theory – that fiat currency always arose out of previously convertible currency, and that fiat currency always arose because of state intervention to make the previously convertible currency inconvertible.[3]

The 'Legal Restrictions' Theory

Granted that agents will use paper currency as an MOE, there then arises the question of the so-called 'legal restrictions' theory of the demand for (non-interest-bearing) currency (see, e.g., Wallace, 1983; Cowen and Kroszner, 1987). This theory

> holds that non-interest-bearing debt is not an inherently superior transactions medium. Instead, it is argued that the use of non-interest-bearing notes – as opposed to interest-bearing government securities – in transactions is a consequence of artificial contrivance. If not for legal or institutional obstacles imposed by the government, adherents to this view claim, interest-bearing securities would circulate as money and non-interest-bearing notes would pass out of existence. (Makinen and Woodward, 1986, 261)

In his account of it, Wallace starts off noting the 'paradoxical pattern of returns among assets' between,

> on the one hand, US Federal Reserve Notes (US currency) and, on the other hand, interest-bearing securities that are default-free ... Examples of such securities are US savings bonds and Treasury bills. Our first task is to identify the features of these securities that prevent them from playing the same role in transactions as Federal Reserve notes. For if they could play that role, then it is hard to see why anyone would hold non-interest-bearing currency instead of the interest-bearing securities. (Wallace, 1983, 1)

What prevents arbitrage taking place, Wallace claims, is the existence of legal restrictions against the private issue of small-denomination bearer bonds combined with the Treasury refusal to issue such bonds themselves. In the absence of such restrictions, a private firm could buy up Treasury bills, say, for $10,000 each, and issue 10,000 $1 bear bonds against them to the general public. These small bearer bonds would be similar to the $1 bills issued by the Federal Reserve, but bear interest which Federal Reserve notes do not. If entry to this intermediation industry were free, Wallace argues that competitive forces would ensure that the marginal return from this intermediation activity would fall to a level where excess profits were eliminated. If Federal Reserve notes were to co-exist with these small-denomination interest-bearing securities, then the yield on the latter must be 'bounded above by the least costly way of operating such a financial intermediation business' (Wallace, 1983, 3). Given that many financial intermediaries operate at spreads of 1 percent or less, Wallace suggests that 'our hypothetical intermediary could operate with a discount that is close to zero and, hence, ... the upper bound on nominal interest rates on safe securities under *laissez-faire* would be close to zero' (Wallace, 1983, 4). It follows that the introduction of *laissez-faire* would have one of two results: either Federal Reserve notes would continue to circulate, in which case nominal interest rates would fall to something close to zero. Alternatively, nominal interest rates would not fall to a level close to zero, but then no-one would have any reason to use Federal Reserve notes when small-denomination interest-bearing securities were available. The demand for Federal Reserve notes (or more generally, the demand for non-interest-bearing currency) would then fall to zero and Federal Reserve notes would disappear from circulation.

However, this theory is open to both theoretical and empirical objections. One powerful objection – made in various forms by O'Driscoll (1985), L. H. White (1987) and Wärneryd (1989, 1990) – is that it ignores the peculiar role of the medium of exchange. If currency provides services that other assets do not (e.g., liquidity services), then it is possible for currency to survive even though it is non-interest-bearing. To quote O'Driscoll

> Money is not simply highly liquid, as are many other assets, but it is perfectly liquid. It trades in every market and need never be sold at a discount. (O'Driscoll, 1985, 11)

Currency may therefore be able to survive in competition with interest-bearing assets by virtue of its superior liquidity. Of course, we must then explain why currency has superior liquidity, but as Lawrence H. White says,

> An obvious and credible reason for the superior saleability [or liquidity] of non-interest-yielding currency is surely the simplicity of transacting with it. Transacting with an interest-yielding bank note (or small-denomination bearer bond) requires both parties to perform a cumbersome calculation or other routine for discovering its present value at the moment of transfer. If the date of original issue, initial value, and stipulated rate of appreciation were stated on the note, accumulated interest would have to be calculated. If a date of redeemability and terminal value were stated, the present discounted value would have to be calculated using an agreed-upon discount rate. (L. H. White, 1987, 452)

Alternative means can also be used to pay (at least implicit) interest, but the point is that none would be costless to operate.[4] It is therefore the costliness of these alternatives that gives non-interest-bearing currency its liquidity 'edge'.

White then makes this argument more concrete. The expected interest to be received must be large enough to compensate both parties to a transaction for the time and trouble they take to calculate it. These costs are more or less independent of the value of the note, but the interest they receive varies directly with the value of the note and so the value of the interest payment falls with the face value of the note. It follows that there must be some threshold denomination below which it is not worth while for any given individual to calculate the interest. Below that threshold, non-interest-bearing notes should be able to survive alongside interest-bearing ones, for the simple reason that no-one can be bothered with the interest. He then adds that

A thumbnail calculation indicates that this threshold value would in practice exceed historically common currency sizes, given historically common interest rates. On a note whose initial value equals two hours' wages, held one week while yielding interest at 5 percent per annum, accumulated interest would amount to less than 7 seconds' wages. If the note-holder's wage rate indicates the opportunity cost of his time, then he will not find it worthwhile to compute and collect interest if to do so twice (once at the receiving end and once at the spending end) takes 7 seconds or more, i.e., if it takes 3.5 seconds or more per note transfer. To give a specific example, a $20 note held one week at 5 percent interest would yield less than 2 cents. Notes held in cash registers by retailers generally turn over much more rapidly than once a week, of course, so that the threshold denomination may well be extremely high. (L. H. White, 1987, 453)

Wärneryd emphasises that the Wallace argument ignores the coordinating role of a medium of exchange. As he puts (1990, 118) it, a commonly accepted MOE

is an institutional solution to a co-ordination problem. The crucial feature of such problems is that no action is individually dominant independently of what other people do. Therefore, the interest yields on various instruments are in an important sense irrelevant for their ... potential

as a commonly accepted medium of exchange. Once we acknowledge that the selection of a commonly accepted MOE involves network factors – the medium chosen by an agent depends on the medium he thinks others will choose – it no longer follows that the medium that would be most efficient in the absence of network factors will be the one actually selected. A particular medium of exchange might remain as the dominant MOE simply because of agents' expectations that it will continue to be the dominant MOE.

At a deeper level, the Wallace argument also suffers from the drawback that Wallace has no real theory of exchange to back it up (Wärneryd, 1990, 121). Wallace assumes a standard, general equilibrium framework, but this framework assumes away the co-ordination and saleability issues that the use of a commonly accepted MOE is meant to help resolve:

The 'legal restrictions' theory of money seems to have its origin in the following problem: How can it be explained that anyone would want to hold ordinary currency in a typical, general-equilibrium-based macro-model world, unless they are forced to? In such a model, it is normally simply postulated that transactions must be carried out in a specific good which has no other uses. The Wallace argument serves the important purpose of focusing attention on the function of a medium of exchange.

In the real world, money is an important instrument for achieving what the auctioneer takes care of in general equilibrium models, i.e., the co-ordination of the differing economic plans of ... different individuals. While this may of course be assumed away in any given model, care must be taken when actually discussing what would happen in monetary anarchy, where no central coordinator is at hand. The 'legal restrictions' confusion consists in continuing to treat 'money' as one asset among others after restrictions on the means of transaction have been removed. From that point of view, it is hardly surprising that holding ordinary currency appears highly undesirable. (Wärneryd, 1989, 624)

Apart from suffering from these theoretical problems, the legal restrictions theory is also empirically falsified. To quote L. H. White again,

> An obvious place to look for possible falsification of the non-coexistence prediction is in historical cases of *laissez-faire* in money and banking. The clearest such case is the Scottish free banking system ... In examining Scottish experience, one finds that the non-coexistence prediction of the legal restrictions theory does appear to be falsified. Non-interest-yielding paper currency coexisted with interest-yielding assets, despite the absence of any legal impediments to entry into banking, to the issue of circulating liabilities (of £1 or larger), or, in particular, to the production of interest-yielding bearer bonds backed by interest-yielding assets. (L. H. White, 1987, 450)

Much the same conclusion can be found in the various other historical cases of relatively free banking (see, e.g., the readings in Dowd, 1992). In every case, non-interest-bearing currency circulated despite the existence of alternative interest-bearing assets and despite the absence of any particularly binding legal restrictions against the profitable arbitrage that the legal restrictions theory predicts. The legal restrictions theory is also falsified by a case history highlighted by Makinen and Woodward (1986). During and after the First World War, the French government issued small-denomination interest-bearing bonds which the legal restrictions theory would predict should have driven the existing non-interest-bearing currency out of circulation. Yet these bonds failed to catch on as a generally accepted MOE and most people continued to use the older non-interest-bearing currency.

Would the MOE be 'Separated' from the MOA?

We turn now to another controversial issue – the relationship between the MOE and the MOA. We have focused so far on exchange media and paid relatively little attention to the medium of account (MOA) or to the units in which the medium of account is denominated (i.e., the unit of account, UA). The functions of MOE and MOA/UA are conceptually very distinct, yet they are so often combined in the same commodity or asset that the association of the two functions can hardly be dismissed as accidental. Why therefore does one commodity or asset frequently function as *both* MOE *and* MOA? One answer, suggested by proponents of NME (e.g., Black, 1970; Fama, 1980; Hall, 1982; Cowen and Kroszner, 1988, 1994), is that there is in fact no reason for the two functions to be combined in the same commodity or asset, at least within a free market. The observation that the two functions are so often associated must be due to some other factor, presumably legal restrictions of some sort. If this view is correct, *laissez-faire* would lead the two functions to 'separate' – prices would be posted in terms of the unit of account, but exchange media would have no fixed or pre-determined nominal value in terms of the unit of account. As an example, Cowen and Kroszner (1988, 3) suggest that the dollar might remain as a non-traded or abstract unit of account, but media of exchange might be equity shares or interest-bearing assets whose dollar value was more or less constantly subject to fluctuation.

The weakness of this position is that it fails to acknowledge that there are good *economic* reasons why the two functions should be combined. As McCallum (1985, 17) puts it, 'it is important ... to recognize that in a monetary economy the benefits of having a common unit of account are incomplete unless the MOA is also the MOE' (see also Niehans, 1978, 121). The argument against separation was put most forcefully by L. H. White (1984b): it is in the self-interest of any seller to post prices in terms of units of the exchange media he is routinely prepared to accept. This practice economises on time spent negotiating over which commodities or assets would be acceptable in payment, but perhaps more importantly, it also reduces the information costs of carrying out the sale, since

> Posting prices in terms of a numeraire commodity [i.e., unit of account] not routinely accepted in payment ... would force buyer and seller to know and agree upon the numeraire price of the payment media due (L. H. White, 1984b, 704)

Under monetary separation, by definition, this price would be subject to fluctuation, so that up-to-date information on the current price would be necessary to complete the trade. Both parties would also have to pay potentially significant calculation costs. Any seller who posted prices in terms of units other than units of the exchange medium would therefore impose both information and calculation costs on potential trading partners – costs that can be avoided simply by posting prices in terms of units of the MOE. A seller who posted prices in terms of units of MOE would then have a competitive advantage over sellers who posted prices in units that fluctuated in value relative to units of the MOE. In White's words,

> a unit of account emerges wedded to a general medium of exchange. Prices are universally posted in the characteristic units of a medium or set of media that sellers are routinely prepared to accept in exchange. This process is self-reinforcing: a buyer or seller who communicated bid or ask offers in nonstandard units would impose calculation costs on potential trading partners. For this reason the unit of account remains wedded to the medium of exchange. (L. H. White, 1984b, 711)

The bottom line, then, is that 'unless provided with inducements to do otherwise, sellers will quote prices in terms of the medium of exchange; the MOA and MOE tend to coincide' (McCallum, 1985, 17)

The White–McCallum position against the monetary separation hypothesis is also supported by the evidence. Had there been economic forces pushing for separation we would have expected to see them operating in at least some of the various historical cases of relatively free banking, and yet these is no evidence of monetary separation taking place in any of these historical experiences. Going further back in time, Wicker (1987, 8–9) searched for evidence of monetary separation in the ancient Near East and Mediterranean, but found that MOE and MOA were identical in the countries he studied except where barter predominated. A third source of evidence relates to the way in which

> unit of account sticks with the medium of exchange even through the transition from commodity-based to fiat currency. A historical example is instructive here. In the suspension period of the Napoleonic Wars, 1797–1819 in Britain, Bank of England notes and deposits became the basic outside money. Gold coins ceased to circulate. The unit of account, the pound sterling, stuck with the actual medium of exchange rather than with the now-abstract gold definition. The pounds-sterling price of gold fluctuated rather than the pounds-sterling price of Bank of England notes. Commodity prices rose with the expansion of Bank of England notes and deposits, while the unit-of-account value of a banknote or deposit remained fixed. (L. H. White, 1984b, 711)

Much the same can be said of the many other cases where currencies have been made inconvertible. If ever there was a good time for separation to take place, it was presumably when the MOE became inconvertible and depreciated against its former value. Were there no forces keeping the MOE and MOA together, we would have expected the MOA to remain unchanged – we would have expected the pound sterling as MOA to continue to refer to the gold pound, for example – and separation should have occurred. The fact that separation did not occur in such cases is therefore strong evidence of economic forces working to keep the two functions together.

Nonetheless, there are two types of historical phenomenon that are sometimes cited as evidence of monetary separation. One of these is the phenomenon of 'ghost money' (see, e.g., Cipolla, 1956, chapter 4). A 'ghost money' is a unit of account that does not have a counterpart among existing exchange media. 'Ghost monies' were used in medieval and eighteenth century Italy, for example, and were used to facilitate economic calculation in an environment where there was a large number of different coins in circulation (see, e.g., Cippolla, 1956 and Einaudi, 1953, respectively). Yet ghost monies are *not* examples of monetary separation. For genuine monetary separation to take place, it is necessary that the MOA should *fluctuate in value against* the MOE, *not* that the MOA have no direct physical counterpart among existing MOE – and this condition was not satisfied by the historical ghost monies. The value of the ghost MOA was tied to the values of *existing* exchange media. Indeed, the ghost MOA *had* to be tied to existing MOE, since its purpose was to facilitate computation. The unit of account value of a given coin was a matter of its weight and fineness, and the information and calculation difficulties of genuine monetary separation did therefore not arise. As L. H. White (1984b, 705, n. 9) observes, a ghost money had a role something like that of the present Italian lira: it provided a unit of account that was tied to the value of existing exchange media, but (since there are no one-lira coins or notes) had no direct counterpart among them.

The other alleged example of monetary separation is the use of multiple units of account. Cowen and Kroszner (1990a) cite as examples the cases of medieval Italian city states and Swiss banks in the early nineteenth century which issued coins or notes denominated in foreign units of account as well as coins or notes denominated in their own units of account. But as with the ghost monies, these cases do not represent examples of genuine monetary separation because the multiple units of account could not be regarded at any given point in time as floating against each other (McCallum, 1990b, 285). The Swiss banks issued notes in different denominations of silver, but all bore a fixed relationship to each other and, hence, to current MOE. The case of the Italian cities was more complex because coins were used in three metals – gold, silver and copper – to facilitate trades of varying amounts, but even there, the function of the units of account was to provide calculation ratios to facilitate trading. At any given time, 'the unit of account would always refer to specified quantities of gold, silver, and copper' (1990, 284) and these systems did 'not leave the price of money – coins made of gold, silver, or copper – free to adjust' (McCallum, 1990b, 285). There was consequently no monetary separation. This conclusion is also consistent with those reached by Wicker (1987) and Lane and Mueller (1985) in their studies of historical multiple units of account. They found that multiple units of account arose because people were using different currency systems – one tied to gold, used primarily for foreign trade, for example, and one tied to silver, used primarily for domestic trade. The values of the gold and silver units did sometimes fluctuate against each other when there were fluctuations in the relative values of the different metals, but as in the case of the medieval Italian city states, the key point was that at any given time their relative values could be taken as given. Units of account were always fixed in value relative to coins made of the same metal, and could therefore be regarded as fixed in value relative to the coins made in other metals as well. Once again, there was no monetary separation.

PAYMENT SYSTEMS

The Evolution of Payment Systems

We come now to the second half of the chapter and consider payment systems. A payment system can be defined as 'the set of arrangements for the discharge of the obligations assumed by economic agents whenever they acquire real or financial resources' or, if one prefers, as 'the set of mechanisms for the transfer of money among agents' (Borio and Van den Bergh, 1993, 8). It therefore encompasses the institutions providing payment services, the various forms of money, the means of transferring them, including message instructions and communication channels, and the contractual relationships between the parties concerned (1993, 8).

The subject of payment systems is of obvious importance – payments systems of one form or another underlie modern economic activity and are essential if it is to continue. As Bauer points out,

> Today's advanced economies could not function without an efficient payments system that, from the viewpoint of the user, can handle transactions throughout the world almost as easily as across the street. Modern business organizations could not flourish with anything less. The production of everything from automobiles to the new financial derivative instruments requires coordinating people and capital across regions to ensure that all parties will be paid for their services in a timely manner. (Bauer, 1994, 1)

Yet payment systems have frequently been overlooked in the broader literature on monetary and financial economics, and, at least traditionally, were often covered properly only in their own specialist literature:

> While there is an enormous literature about [the] constituent parts [of the modern payment system], there is little unifying analysis. Monetary economists have long pursued deeper understanding of currency as the medium of exchange. But they have generally ignored the banking system and clearing-houses, even when focusing on monetary policy. Financial economists, on the other hand, have been keenly interested in banks as financial intermediaries and in government deposit insurance. But, by and large, they have ignored the payment system aspects of these institutions; and they have tended to treat medium of exchange and monetary policy issues only peripherally. (Good-friend, 1990, 247)

Perhaps the most convenient way to begin our discussion of payment systems is to set out a conjectural history of their development (see also, e.g., Selgin and White, 1987). This helps to introduce the subject and highlight some of the principal issues involved. We can regard this conjectural history as an elaboration of that set out earlier in Chapter 1, but with a specific focus here on payment system issues. As in Chapter 1, the driving force behind the evolutionary process is the pursuit of individual self-interest. At any given stage in this history, some individuals perceive certain gains from changing their behaviour in some way, and their efforts to reap these gains eventually lead the system itself to change; some agents then perceive further gains and the system changes again; and on. Particularly in the case of the payment system, reaping these efficiency also creates certain problems – usually monitoring problems of one sort or another – which need to be resolved if these gains are to be enjoyed and the way paved for further progress. The evolutionary process is therefore an interplay of the drive for efficiency gains, on the one hand, and the handling of the problems that arise from such gains, on the other.

Suppose we start at that point in the evolution of the economy where people are still using full-bodied coins as their MOE. Payments in this state are very straightforward: one agent simply hands over coins to another and the transaction is complete. However this payment system, while simple, is also very costly, and it is costly for two reasons: First, the principal MOE, gold coinage, is costly to store and handle. Coins require strongrooms to store them, gold is heavy to carry around and vulnerable to theft, and so forth. In addition, there is relatively little credit, and the comparative absence of credit limits agents' abilities to make payments, and hence their abilities to trade with each other. If no-one trusts IOUs, an agent must have gold coins or else he cannot make any payments at all, and if he cannot pay then he cannot trade.

Along come the goldsmiths, and people gradually switch over to using bank notes as media of payment. As discussed already, a banknote medium of exchange is cheaper to maintain than a full-bodied gold coinage (e.g., because notes are easier to handle and less costly to store). Society as a whole can then cut down its costly holdings of 'idle' gold stocks. The emergence of banks also means that agents can now pay on credit when they may not have been able to do so before. An agent who does not have ready gold coins can borrow notes from the bank and use them to make a payment. The person to whom he makes the payment does not need to 'trust' him personally, but will accept the payment medium if he 'trusts' the bank that issued it. 'Trust' in the bank becomes a partial substitute for the lack of 'trust' between separate individual agents, and the growth of this 'trust' widens the number of transactions – and hence trades – that individuals can make with each other. These benefits come at a price because resources must be expended to monitor the banks to ensure their notes are safe and that they themselves can be 'trusted'. The introduction of banks into the payments system increases its efficiency, but also introduces an element of vulnerability into the payments system that was not there before.

Banks would also issue deposit accounts as well as notes, and once they do so it makes sense for them to provide chequing services as well (i.e., facilities which allow agents to write claims against their deposit accounts which they can use as payment media). The public will value such services because cheques are more convenient than notes for certain types of payment (e.g., for large payments or for sending payments through the post), and banks can make a profit on them by reducing the interest they pay on chequable deposits or by charging explicit fees for chequing services. However, while someone who accepts a note will often keep the note to spend himself, and thereby keep it in general circulation, someone who accepts a cheque will normally deposit it in his own account and in so doing effectively ask his own bank to redeem the cheque at the bank on which it is drawn. (Why? Because cheques are harder to pass on, given (1) that parties who accept them need information about the state of the account on which they are drawn, as well as about the bank in which the account is kept, and (2) that cheques are usually written for amounts inconvenient for any other transactions that those for which they are initially intended.) Payments by note therefore typically involve only three parties – the two transacting agents, and the note-issuing bank – while payments by cheque typically involve four – the two transactors, the bank on which the cheque is drawn, and the bank to which the cheque is presented.

The banks can then reap a number of further gains once a system of cheque payments has been established. One such gain is the economisation of cheque-settlement costs:

> In general, checks send for collection from one bank to another tend to net out, so if payments were always made as checks were received, commodity money would simply be shipped back and forth with neither bank accumulating or disbursing any, on average. Banks could therefore economize on such shipping costs by simply holding credit balances on each other instead of requiring immediate settlement in commodity money. For example, instead of triggering immediate shipment of commodity money from bank A to bank B, checks sent for payment by bank B to bank A could result in bank A giving bank B a deposit. Bank B would then be said to have an interbank deposit at bank A. When the flow of collections reversed, bank A could acquire a deposit at bank B. To economize on commodity money shipping costs, banks agreed to make temporary loans to each other on demand as dictated by developments in the payment system. (Goodfriend, 1990, 254–255)

Banks can also reap additional gains from engaging in multilateral rather than bilateral cheque clearing. To quote Goodfriend again,

> Instead of making collections individually, each bank could take its checks to a central location for collection. Thus, centralized collection itself saved significantly on transport costs. Netting out provided an additional saving by greatly reducing the volume of currency and coin that was transported in the settlement process. Moreover, to further economize on shipments of currency and coin, clearing-house members kept the bulk of their reserves in the vaults of the clearing-house, receiving in return claims to their reserves known as clearing-house certificates ... Then, instead of shipping currency and coin to settle, member-banks could simply pass around clearing-house certificates. The keeping of reserves at the clearing-house, in turn, facilitated an interbank market that made possible a more efficient distribution of reserves among banks. These measures all contributed to reducing the efficient quantity of reserves that banks had to hold. By reducing checking fees, they also led to more intensive use of checks relative to currency on the part of the public. (Goodfriend, 1990, 259–260)

Up to this point, a bank would only release funds on a cheque once the bank on which it was drawn had honoured it; yet cheque-clearing takes time, and many customers would want access to their funds before their cheques had been cleared. In some cases, it might then make sense for banks to give immediate access to such funds even before they had been cleared; it might also make sense for banks to guarantee payment on certain cheques that are deposited with them (e.g., those that had been endorsed by other banks). In both cases, the bank in which the cheque is deposited runs some risk that the cheque will not be honoured, but it provides its customer with the service of immediate or guaranteed access for which it can presumably make some charge.

However, once banks start lending to each other – by guaranteeing payment on cheques drawn against each other, for example, or even by accepting each other's notes – then banks need to monitor each other to ensure that interbank loans are likely to be repaid. Each bank would have to watch its exposure to other banks in the system because of the danger that one of those banks might default on its obligations. A bank might try to protect itself by limiting the amount of credit it would grant to any other bank, and the banks as a whole might organise a club – a payment club, much like the banking club discussed in Chapter 8 – to monitor member-banks and perhaps impose 'regulations' on them (e.g., regarding their financial health or liquidity). This club would try to promote public confidence in the payment system by ensuring that participating banks came up to certain standards. A bank that failed to meet these standards could then be refused credit or expelled from the club to safeguard the interests of other club members. Members of the public would draw their own conclusions and be wary of channelling their payment business (or, indeed, any other business) through it. The public could then be reasonably confident that any banks that remained in good standing with the club would be safe to do business with.

This story also helps to explain why the payments system is normally operated by banks and not by other institutions. Unlike many other institutions, banks would already 'have in place much of the network, systems, and expertise to run a reliable and efficient payment system' (Goodfriend, 1990, 256). They would have many of the skills to run a payments system – the ability to evaluate and monitor credit, enforce agreements, and the like – from their other lines of business, and all they would then need to do is make their liabilities transactable by making notes payable to the bearer, offering cheque-writing facilities, and so on. Banks can therefore enter the payment business at relatively low cost, but for other firms the costs of entry would often be considerably higher.

The next stage is the development of more advanced payment systems such as credit-card systems, wire transfer systems, and the various forms of electronic funds transfer.[5] These systems are usually collectively described as forms of *electronic funds transfer* (EFT) even not all of them strictly use electronic means of transfer. All these have in common the point that payment is made without any medium of exchange as such. The payment essentially consists of a message to debit an account, with the transaction being either paid in advance or settled up afterwards. No physical medium of exchange actually changes hands, and payments are carried out on a purely accounting basis.

These EFT systems differ markedly between retail and wholesale markets, and it is therefore convenient to discuss retail and wholesale EFT separately. In the retail market, they made their initial impact in the form of credit-card systems, which make payment by debiting a customer's account and obliging the customer to settle up afterwards with the company that issued the card. The use of credit cards is now extremely widespread:

> The use of credit cards for cashless payments is most extensive in North America, and is increasing also in many European countries. In Canada, two-thirds of all adults carry at least one card. At the end of 1987 there were 25 million credit cards in Canada and 840 million in the US. About a quarter of the number of all cashless transactions in Canada in 1987 were made by credit cards, the corresponding figures for the US and the UK being 15 percent and 11 percent, respectively. (Zilberfarb, 1992, 97)

Credit-card systems were followed in the late 1970s and 1980s by the spread of *automatic teller machines* (ATMs). These are machines attached to bank branch offices which provide cash, accept deposits and offer various bill-payment services. In the USA, the number of such machines rose from less than 10,000 in 1978 to about 80,000 in 1990, and it is estimated that half of US households use them at least once a month (Zilberfarb, 1992, 97). The 1990s then saw the spread of *point-of-sale* (POS) payment systems involving terminals in retail outlets that read a code (e.g., a line on a cheque, or credit-card identification number) and relay a message via an *automatic clearing house* (ACH) for funds to be transferred from one account (e.g., the purchaser's) to another (e.g., a merchant's). POS systems are being followed by those based on the integrated circuit or *'smart card'* – a card with a silicon memory that can be used to store information which could refer for example to an individual's spending or credit limit. Where the appropriate reading machinery is installed, a smart card can be used to make a large variety of payments rapidly and at very low marginal cost. A transaction can be carried out simply by running a card over the appropriate reading machine – unlike credit cards, they do not need additional forms or signatures. Smart cards are therefore ideally suited for many types of transactions that otherwise normally require cash, such as paying a bus fare.

EFT started earlier and grew more rapidly in wholesale markets. Some indication of this growth is given by Humphrey (1986, 98) who reports that total wire transfers in the USA in 1950 were a little less than twice annual GNP; in 1960, they were almost 5 times annual GNP; in 1970, almost 13 times annual GNP; in 1980, almost 45 times; and in 1983, almost 62 times annual GNP. By 1990, they had grown even further to around 80 times GNP (Borio and Van den Bergh, 1993, 5). There are a number of wholesale wire transfer systems, of which the best known are probably FedWire and the Clearing House Interbank Payment System (CHIPS), which are operated on behalf of the Federal Reserve System and the New York Clearing House Association respectively (see, e.g., Humphrey, 1984, 1986;

Mengle, 1985, 15–17; and Clair, 1991). Others include BankWire, the Society for Worldwide Interbank Financial Telecommunications (SWIFT), GlobeSet, and in the UK, the Clearing House Automated Payments System (CHAPS). These systems transfer funds on an immense scale. In 1990, for example, FedWire and CHIPS alone between them averaged about $1.7 trillion daily in transfers (Solomon, 1992, 745). Wire payments accounted for no less than 82 percent of the total dollar value of all payments in 1986, while cheques by comparison accounted for only 16 percent of total payments, and all other media for the remaining 2 percent (Humphrey and Berger, 1990, 49). The amounts involved in EFT transfers thus dwarf the amounts transferred in all other payment systems.

These systems always involve a communication network by which one bank conveys a message to another bank to make a payment to one of the other bank's customers. In their simplest form, they might consist of nothing else:

> Wholesale wire transfer systems may simply take the form of communications networks that convey instructions to the receiving bank to debit the sending bank's correspondent account and to credit the receiver's account ... These networks ... have in common the characteristic that they do not themselves provide settlement services, that is, they do not include any mechanisms for consolidating or centralizing transactions between participating banks ... As a result, wire transfers on nonsettling networks are essentially bilateral exchanges. (Mengle, 1985, 14–15)

More sophisticated payment systems add settlement facilities to the basic communication network. The kind of settlement procedure varies. In its simplest form, it would consist of a *gross settlement* procedure that settles each transaction individually. However, where there are repeated transactions between a pair of banks, it often makes sense for the banks to consolidate their mutual transactions and settle the *net credit or debit* accumulated over any given period of time (e.g., a day). A net settlement system reduces the number of settlement transactions from one transaction per payment message to one transaction in the settlement period for each pair of participating banks, and therefore reduces overall transactions costs. The total amount handed over in settlement between the banks also falls from the total amount of funds actually transmitted to the difference between the amount transmitted in one direction and the amount transmitted in the other; net settlement therefore reduces the balances that banks need to maintain to be able to meet their settlement obligations. Once they realise the benefits of consolidation – such as lower transactions costs and the need for smaller amounts of the settlement medium – banks might consolidate further and arrange to have each bank pay or receive only what it owes or is owed by the other banks as a whole. The total number of transactions then falls even further – from one transaction per pair of banks, to one transaction per bank – with a consequent further fall in transactions costs; at the same time, the total amount handed over in settlement falls from the sum of the bilateral net credits (or debits) between each individual pair of banks to the sum of all banks' net credits (or debits) against the system as a whole. If a bank owed $10million to one bank and $5million to another, for example, then the amount it would handle in settlement transfers would fall from $10m + $5m or $15m to $10m-$5m or $5m, and the amounts handled by the other banks would fall in much the same way. Such a procedure is known as a *net net settlement* system and is used on payments systems such as CHIPS (Mengle, 1985, 15).

The Analytical Structure of Payment Systems

Having set the scene, as it were, we can now set out the formal structure of payments systems and discuss how they operate. A payment system can be considered as a network involving four types of agent. The first is the customer who originates the transfer (i.e., the *sender*). The second is the institution which sends the message on the sender's behalf. For reasons already explained, this institution will normally be a bank, so we shall refer to this agent for convenience as the *sending bank*. The counter-party to the sending bank is the *receiving bank*, which receives the message on behalf of the agent who is to be the ultimate recipient of the transfer (i.e., the *receiver*). (It will sometimes be the case that more than one of the different roles discussed here will be combined in one agent – for example, the receiver and the sender might both deal with the same bank – but there is no need to worry about such cases here.) The relationship between these agents is illustrated in Figure 10.1.

The sender directs his bank to make a payment to the receiving bank on behalf of the receiver. The sender's action sets in motion a chain of events – the sender pays his bank, the sending bank sends the message to the receiving bank, the receiving bank makes the payment to the receiver, the banks settle up between themselves, and the sender pays the sending bank. However, the order in which these events varies from one system to another, with the only constant feature being that the first move in the process is always the request from the sender to his own bank. The sender might pay his own bank before the message goes out or he might pay later, and the receiving bank may or may not wait for settlement before releasing funds to the receiver. Settlement between the two banks usually, but not always, takes place after the initial message has been sent out.

All payment systems require sets of finality rules that specify the legal rights and obligations of the parties involved during the various stages of the payments process. The most straightforward finality rule, and one that appears to be

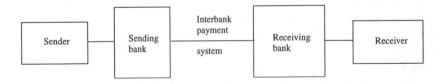

Figure 10.1   The formal structure of a payment system

universally adopted, is *sender finality*. This rule means that a sending bank cannot revoke a message once the message is sent. Should a message be sent by mistake, the sending bank must still settle up with the receiving bank, but would then aim to recover its funds by other means (e.g., by asking for them to be returned, or suing the receiving bank). This rule facilitates the operation of the payment system by ensuring that the amounts owed in settlement are unambiguous and clearly understood.

A second finality rule sometimes adopted is *cheque finality*, according to which the payment is considered final only when the receiver has access to 'good funds', much like the way in which the recipient of a cheque often gets his funds only when the cheque has been cleared (see, e.g., Mengle, 1990, 157). Under this rule, the receiving bank is only obliged to pay the receiver after the sending bank has settled up. If the sending bank fails to settle, the receiving bank is under no obligation to pay the receiver and, should it already have paid him, would have the right to ask for the funds to be returned. Cheque finality therefore protects the receiving bank against the risk that the sending bank does not settle.

An alternative to cheque finality is *receiver finality*, which specifies that a payment is considered final or legally binding when the receiving bank accepts the message from the sending bank (i.e., by receiving it). Under this rule, the receiver is legally entitled to payment by the receiving bank regardless of whether the sending bank subsequently settles up or not, and it is the responsibility of the receiving bank to make that the sending bank settles. Receiver finality therefore differs from cheque finality in that it allocates the risk that the sending bank will not settle *to the receiving bank*, while cheque finality allocates that risk *to the receiver*. If we regard receiver and cheque finality as polar alternatives to each other, we can also conceive of various intermediate finality rules – combinations of receiver and cheque finality – that assign the some liability for settlement risk to both the receiver and the receiving bank. We might then expect this risk to be traded on an explicit or implicit market, with the resulting risk allocation perhaps depending on factors such as the particular circumstances of the parties involved.

Payment systems can involve a number of distinct credit risks. The sender takes the risk that his bank might fail after he has paid for the message to be sent, but before the payment has gone through. For its part, if the sending bank transmits the message and settles before the sender has paid it, it takes the risk that the sender might default on his debt to it. However, these risks are essentially matters to be resolved by the parties concerned and there are no third-party effects peculiar to the payment system as such. We would therefore expect contracts between these parties to allocate these risks in the usual ways. On the other side of the transfer, the receiver runs the risk that the receiving bank might fail before it hands over the funds, as well as the risk, with cheque finality or some element of cheque finality, that he might have to repay at least some of the funds to his own bank if the other bank fails to settle. The receiving bank also runs the risk that, if it gives out funds before settlement, it may not be able to recover the funds from the receiver even under cheque finality, even though cheque finality in principle gives it the right to do so. These risks, too, are essentially matters to be resolved by contract between the parties concerned, and there are no effects on other parties qualitatively different from those that commonly arise in other business circumstances.

However, there are also risks between the two banks, and these risks *can* impinge on the payment system in a distinctive and important way. The principal risk here is that the sending bank will fail to settle. Where there is cheque finality in a pure form, all that would happen is that the receiving bank would bounce the cheque or do whatever was equivalent, or go looking for the receiver to recover what it had already given him, but there would be no major ramifications for the payments system *per se*. The receiving bank would suffer no loss at all, if it had not released the funds, or it would have the right to demand the funds back from the receiver, if it had already released them, and the latter situation would be much like that of any (other) borrower on the bank's books – an issue between the bank and its customer, rather than an issue of any particular concern for the payment system as such. However, the situation is potentially very different where there is any element of receiver finality. In such cases the receiving bank takes a risk by accepting a message from a bank that might subsequently fail to settle, because the act of accepting the message compels it to pay the receiver regardless of whether settlement occurs or not. This settlement risk is clearly a matter of concern for the two banks – the receiving bank for obvious reasons, and the sending bank because the risk could lead other banks to refuse to accept its messages – but it impinges directly on the payment system as well because it also concerns *other* banks: It concerns other banks because non-settlement by one bank could make it more difficult for the banks that are owed funds by the failing bank to settle themselves. The failure of one bank to settle can therefore lead to other settlement failures and possibly even threaten the system as a whole.

Payments System Risk

Systemic Risk and Payments 'Unwind'

This issue of systemic risk is potentially very serious. Not only can the failure of one bank to settle lead others to fail as well, but a bank might conceivably become illiquid, and hence fail to settle, because of some chance event unrelated to its general financial health:

> Liquidity problems usually result from sudden and unexpected events that are often completely unrelated to the financial soundness of the illiquid participant. For example, illiquidity can result from operational problems. A computer failure could prevent a participant from transferring or receiving funds. If the participant was in a large net debit position at the time and the computer problem prevented the participant from borrowing liquid assets, then the participant could be illiquid at settlement time. It is also possible that illiquidity could result from unexpected financial demands. If a customer directed the

bank late in the day to transfer a large-dollar volume of funds and if after sending the funds, the bank discovers it could not buy funds in the market to cover its position, then the bank would be illiquid. (Clair, 1991, 79)

These sorts of danger are by no means purely hypothetical. In 1985, the Bank of New York had a computer problem that prevented it sending outgoing payment messages. However, it continued to receive incoming messages and therefore accumulated a large daylight overdraft that required it to take an emergency loan from the New York Fed to settle (Mengle, 1992, 9). Banks can also face liquidity problems for other unexpected reasons. Bernanke (1990, 146–147) relates how declines in asset prices during the crash of October 1987 produced large demands for funds to meet margin requirements at the same time as creditors became cautious about advancing funds and the sheer volume of trade led to serious malfunctions of communication and payments problems and effectively jammed up the payment system. In these circumstances, even financially sound and prudent institutions could easily find themselves in serious difficulties, and there was a widely cited incident in which Kidder–Peabody and Goldman–Sachs collectively found themselves short by more than $1.5 billion after they advanced funds for margin calls for their customers and bank reimbursements to them were delayed.

The systemic risk problem is aggravated further by the size of the amounts involved. Banks frequently run up very large 'daylight overdrafts' – net debts against the rest of the system which they must settle at the end of the day – and even as far back as 1986, Humphrey (1986, 97) reported that these overdrafts were often more than $1 bn and frequently exceeded the individual banks' total capitalisation. If a bank with one of these overdrafts were to fail to settle, the other banks would have a very large settlement shortfall to cover and might well be unable to meet it.

Some idea of the consequences of a settlement failure on one of the major payment systems can perhaps be inferred from Humphrey's (1986) simulations carried out on CHIPS. Humphrey assumed that a large participant failed to settle on each of two randomly selected days in January 1983. If no other institution or group of institutions picked up the failed bank's settlement tab for that day's trading, then CHIPS Rule 13 provides that, as a last resort, the payments to and from that bank can be deleted from the day's transactions. The day's transactions are then recalculated, and settlement takes place provided the remaining institutions are able to settle. If one or more of *them* fails to settle, their transactions are also deleted, and another settlement is proposed; and this *unwinding* process continues, with non-settling banks being deleted, for as many times as is required for the banks that still remain to be able to settle. Humphrey then concluded:

One surprising fact that emerges in comparing the consequences of a failure of the same participant on two different days is the variability of other institutions affected. In view of the correspondent relationships among institutions, one might expect that those affected by a particular institution's failure would be fairly constant; in fact, there is a fair amount of variation ... These results suggest that the institutions most likely to be affected by a particular institution's failure cannot be readily identified beforehand. This day-to-day variation in systemic risk exposure means that an institution cannot limit its credit assessment to some small group of participants with which it most frequently deals. Rather, it must carefully monitor all participants in each network and its exposure across multiple networks. (Humphrey, 1986, 108)

More importantly, his results also suggested that a single bank initially failing to settle could have severe effects on the abilities of others to settle. His first simulation suggested that 49 institutions would subsequently fail before the remaining banks were able to settle, accounting for 30.8 percent of the total dollar value of all that day's transmissions; while his second simulation suggested that 33 institutions would fail, accounting for 22.6 percent of the total value of that day's transactions (Humphrey, 1986, 108–109).[6] These results led him to conclude that

the simulations do raise serious, if not fundamental, questions about whether settlement revision [i.e., unwinding] ... is feasible without also disrupting financial markets. More important, the simulations illustrate the dynamic interdependence of institutions that characterizes the payments system. Overall, the simulations indicate that close to half of the participants and one-third of the payment value could be subject to the CHIPS unwind provisions in the event of an unexpected settlement failure of a CHIPS participant. This demonstrates that systemic risk can be significant and that its possible effects on financial markets are substantial enough to constitute a serious problem. (Humphrey, 1986, 110)

Solutions to the Systemic Risk Problem

There are a number of possible remedies that could help to avoid this scenario and ensure that all participating banks can settle. One obvious point is that participating banks should maintain their financial health. A bank that is financially strong is less likely to fail to settle, if only because it is in a better position to get emergency loans if it needs them. Banks that are financially strong are also better placed to withstand the failure of another bank to settle and still be able to settle themselves. In the words of Corrigan (1990, 137), the capital adequacy of the participating members is the system's 'ultimate line of defense'. The banks as a whole may also have an interest in ensuring that individual participating banks offer collateral, as well as maintain high levels of liquidity and back-up credit. The argument then proceeds much along the lines of the banking club discussed in Chapter 8. If member-banks feel that individual banks might have insufficient private incentive to maintain their financial strength or liquidity, then they as a group will delegate powers to the institution (or club) operating the payments system to set minimum standards of financial strength, liquidity, operational soundness, management quality, and so on, and this institution will monitor banks to ensure those standards are met. A good example is to be found in the CHIPS system, whose members are subject to minimum standards and financial scrutiny by the New York Clearing House Association, and any bank that fails to meet these standards can be suspended from the system to protect others from the risks implied by its continuing participation.[7]

Banks could also be careful how much daylight credit they grant. A bank can do so by imposing bilateral caps on the amount of daylight credit it grants to any other bank, and the system can impose caps on the total net indebtedness of any one bank to the rest of the system. The lower these caps are, the smaller the amount that has to be covered for settlement to take place in the event that a bank fails. A potential problem is that bilateral caps would prevent messages being transmitted if the sending bank was up against a binding cap, but this problem can always be met by a queueing procedure (e.g., as CHIPS has). This procedure would automatically stop a message that would violate a cap and put the message in a queue to be sent when the cap would no longer be violated. Alternatively, a binding cap could be relaxed by some interim settlement procedure that would enable a bank to relax net credit constraints by paying off its debts. As a particular constraint threatened to become binding, an automatic trigger could be activated requiring the bank to settle up before the bank actually ran into the debit cap. The constraints could then be satisfied without the interruption to payments messages that queues might involve.

Net debit caps could also be complemented by charging interest on daylight overdrafts. A bank could be charged on its net debit positions to the system and paid interest on its net credit positions. The interest to be paid on net debit positions would encourage a bank to reduce its indebtedness to the system and thereby reduce the likely settlement shortfall in the event of its failure. The work of Humphrey (1984, 86–89) on the FedWire system in the US suggests that the introduction of charging for daylight overdrafts would result in a major reduction in overdrafts. Indeed, he went as far as to say that combined with other measures, in particular adequate collateralisation, charging would largely eliminate the problem of daylight overdrafts altogether (Humphrey, 1984, 89).

However, these measures should also be underpinned by appropriate rules to determine liability for settlement in the event that one or more banks fail to settle. If a bank fails, these *settlement finality rules* determine where liability lies to 'cover' the failed bank's settlement obligations and thereby ensure that settlement takes place without any further disruption or unwinding. If achieved, settlement finality would means that

> the clearing entity seeking to achieve final settlement has in place the financial resources and commitments – whether in the form of reserves, collateral, committed bank lines, guarantees, or some other arrangements – to ensure that, in the event of a problem or a default, settlement will still take place. (Corrigan, 1990, 137)

One such rule, which Mengle (1990, 160) describes as *ex ante settlement finality*, would have the sending bank guarantee its transmissions by posting bonds. It could offer collateral to the system and be obliged to keep its net indebtedness at a level low enough that its settlement obligations could always be met from its collateral. If the bank failed, its collateral could be seized by the system authority and used to ensure that settlement takes place. This rule would ensure, not only that settlement still takes place if a bank fails, but also that no other participant would be called upon to bear any settlement loss. The burden of settlement failure is effectively thrown onto the failing bank, and other banks would have little to worry about. The problem is that *ex ante* settlement finality requires banks to post 'adequate' collateral, and posting collateral is costly. If that amount of collateral is too costly, lower collateral requirements could be imposed but backed up by a further settlement rule designed to give receiving banks some incentive to limit their exposure. These *ex post* settlement rules would allocate liability for a failed bank's remaining settlement obligations – that is, any settlement 'shortfall' that remained after the seizure of the failed bank's collateral – to the remaining banks in accordance with some formula based on the amount of credit they had given the failed bank (see, e.g., Mengle, 1990, 160). A bank that granted a large daylight overdraft to a bank that subsequently failed to settle would then acquire a relatively large settlement liability, and the desire to avoid that such a liability would give it an incentive to be careful how much credit it grants. Each bank would therefore have an incentive to impose credit limits on each other bank in the payment system, as well as an incentive to push the system authority to implement net debit caps and other restrictions on participating banks. Overall settlement losses would be reduced, and such settlement losses as did occur would be allocated to banks that had, in effect, made prior decisions that they could bear them.[8]

It also goes for granted that banks – both individually and collectively – would normally respond to the danger of settlement losses by taking out lines of credit on which they could draw should the need arise. Should a bank or group of banks turn out to be short of settlement media because some other bank had failed to settle, they could then draw on their credit lines to obtain the credit or settlement media they need. Indeed, one of the advantages of having the *banks* being the principal participants of a payment system is that they are better placed than anyone else to ensure that such credit is available. Furthermore, should the payments system have a problem reaching settlement, it would normally be the banks or the banking club, if there was one, to which the system authority would go for additional credit or settlement media. However, if the major participants in the payments system are the banks themselves, then the system need look no further than its own members. The transactions, moral hazard, monitoring and related costs of arranging for such back-up are therefore lower for a payments system operated by the banks than for one operated by non-banks, and we have yet another reason why the banks should be the principal participants in such a system. It makes therefore makes sense for the payments system to be run by, or on behalf of, the bankers' club.

The various suggestions made above by no means exhaust the options for reducing or eliminating systemic risk.[9] One possibility would be to have more frequent settlement. Since an overdraft is represents the net debts accumulated since the last settlement, more frequent settlement would normally mean a lower overdraft at any given point in time. If a bank was accumulating an overdraft at the rate of $10 million an hour, for example, and settling were done every eight hours, then the bank's overdraft would reach $80 million before being settled. If settling were done every hour, however, the bank's overdraft would only reach $10 million before being settled. A payments system could therefore reduce overdrafts by settling two or more times a day instead of just once a day. In the limit, one could also have a system of continuous settling – much as GlobeSet does – which effectively requires a sending bank to transfer funds or equivalent assets simultaneously with its initial payment order (Stevens, 1993, 4). Such settlement has the drawback that it eliminates credit altogether and forces the banks to tie up resources in holdings of settlement assets – as in the mutual fund operated by the GlobeSet network – but it is technically feasible and would entirely eliminate the systemic risk problem. Finally, of course, we should not forget the most simple solution of all – to adopt cheque finality. The only real problem with cheque finality is that the receiving bank and the receiver might want trade to risk among themselves, and cheque finality might not be their preferred risk-sharing arrangement. Yet the option nonetheless exists, and if it is not adopted it is presumably because the parties involved are willing to accept payments system risk or to adopt some other solution for the problems it causes. The problem of systemic risk is therefore solvable, although not without some cost.

Is There a Case for Government Intervention in the Payments System?

The issue of payment system risk leads naturally to the question of whether government or central bank intervention in a payment system might improve upon the outcome that would be generated by *laissez-faire*. One obvious issue is whether central bank lender-of-last-resort or related forms of 'assistance' might be required to support the liquidity of a payment system. If a bank should be unable to settle for any reason, is there a case for a central bank to intervene, say, to provide liquidity to guarantee settlement? The answer is a fairly clear 'no'. In terms of our earlier discussion, the purpose of such intervention would be provide settlement media to prevent the day's payments unwinding. However, it should also be clear from that discussion that 'outside' (i.e., central bank) intervention is quite unnecessary. Banks under *laissez-faire* do not need such support because they are perfectly capable of providing suitable support for themselves. While individual settlement failures might be difficult or even impossible to predict, banks can predict the general circumstances in which such failures occur and in which liquidity support of some kind would be warranted. They can then design – and they have the appropriate incentives to design – the institutional mechanisms to handle such cases. If a failure subsequently occurred, those mechanisms simply come into play and the problem is dealt with. But the important point is that the banks themselves can solve the problem and provide the emergency loan, guarantee, or whatever, that is required. There is therefore no case for suppressing free banking in order to establish a central bank to provide payment system 'support'.

Nonetheless, the advocate of central bank support might perhaps argue that the central bank should intervene to provide such support *given* that the central bank already exists and that free banking has been suppressed. But even this argument is highly questionable, and not just because it is based on a dubious premise. The underlying problem that is used to justify 'support' for the payment system is the shortage of settlement media that might result from the failure of a settlement participant, and yet even then it *still* does not follow that the central bank should intervene to provide the missing settlement media even if the central bank has various legal privileges that restrict what other banks can do. Almost *regardless* of the restrictions under which they operate, the other banks can always 'solve' the settlement problem, if they wish to do so, by declaring some form of moratorium on settlement repayments. The banks, individually or as a group, can implicitly 'lend' the settlement media that they are owed, so that settlement can then take place as it otherwise would – without any support from the central bank. The banks could design the appropriate institutional machinery beforehand, so that the operation ran smoothly once it was started. There would of course be various follow-up problems – the 'lending' banks would have acquired debts against the 'borrowing' ones, and the like – but these problems ought to be resolvable and are not in any case that dissimilar to many problems that arise from borrowing, lending or bankruptcy under more normal conditions. The only situation in which this option would not be available to the commercial banks is that in which the central bank or the legal system actually prevented them from using it, but prohibiting something so that the central bank can provide it instead is hardly a strong argument for central bank provision.

There is also another problem with relying on the central bank to provide liquidity support to a payment system – central bank support in practice is subject to a serious time consistency problem. If central bank promises to support the payment system, then participants to the payment system will count on that support and alter their own behaviour accordingly. They will hold less liquidity themselves, they will let their financial strength degenerate, and they will change the rules of their payment club to make those rules less onerous. They might also not bother with other safety precautions they might otherwise have taken. In the absence of central bank support, they might institute more rigorous lending caps, better real-time monitoring systems, and settlement finality rules with a greater emphasis on cheque finality. But since each of these is costly, banks have no incentive to adopt them if they think the central bank will bail them out anyway. The banks would therefore respond to the central bank support mechanism by acting in ways that might not only make a settlement failure more likely to occur, but also ensure that the payment system is less able to handle a failure crisis than it would otherwise be. The central bank's most appropriate response would be to try to discourage such behaviour by limiting its prospective intervention, threatening to make liquidity support expensive and regulating the banks to limit moral hazard, but the central bank can only succeed in this strategy to the extent that its threats of limited or expensive support are credible. To the extent it lacks credibility, payment participants will call its bluff and in effect force it to support them on their terms. The central bank could presumably achieve credibility by binding itself sufficiently tightly to the mast, but doing so is tantamount to throwing away its future discretion to manage crises as it saw fit. That makes the central bank powerless to respond to a crisis in anything other than an automatic, rule-bound way – and also undermines one of the most common arguments put forward for central banking, namely, that a central bank is needed to 'manage' crises. If the central bank has room for discretion, private agents will expect it to use that discretion to support them in a crisis, and their very helplessness will force the central bank to support them. The very power of a central bank – its ability to make discretionary decisions, which is the basis of its ability to 'manage' a crisis – puts it at a disadvantage relative to a bankers' club whose discretionary power can be limited in advance in any way its members want.

There are also various 'market failure' arguments that have been put forward as possible justifications for government intervention. The alleged 'market failure' normally consists of the unappropriated benefits created by the existence of network externalities in (or between) payment systems. Network externalities could mean that people are 'locked-in' to an inferior payment system or inferior payment technology – everyone might want to switch, but no-one actually does because it is only individually rational to switch if one expects others to switch and there is no reason to expect them to. The superior system is then stuck at the launch pad. The argument could also be made that even if switching does occur, the existence of these externality problems could mean that switching takes place too slowly. A 'helping hand' from the authorities might therefore be required to speed up the adjustment process and ensure that the benefits of the superior system can be reaped earlier than they otherwise would.

Again, I do not find these arguments convincing. The mere existence of network externalities in payment systems does not in itself create a problem that requires 'outside' intervention to correct. There are many cases in which new products (e.g., the first telephones) or payment systems (e.g., new credit card systems) are adopted without government support despite the existence of network factors that some might regard as grounds for government intervention. The mere fact that network externalities exist is not in itself an argument for intervention. Suppose for example that a new payment technology becomes available, but there is some concern that network factors might discourage people switching over to it, or lead them to adopt it too slowly. The adoption of the new technology then presumably requires some concerted action, but there is nothing to stop the banks providing that action themselves. For example, if people were making excessive use of cheques (as suggested, e.g., by Humphrey and Berger, 1990, 57), and the objective was to get them to make more use of EFT, then the banks as a collective could presumably introduce the new technology and change their cheque-processing fees to encourage individuals to switch. In effect, they could try to break the reluctance of people to switch by adopting pricing policies that aim to counter that reluctance. Once the switch was made, the banks could if they wanted then reverse those pricing policies and go back to more normal prices. In short, even if the existence of network externalities implies collective action, which is often doubtful, collective action itself does not imply a need for government intervention.

Even if there is clear evidence of market 'failure' – the existence of possible benefits that the private sector is unable to reap – it *still* does not follow that we should then call in the central bank or the government to sort the problem out. The central bank or the government is not costless to operate, and it may be that those benefits cannot be appropriated at costs low enough to make doing so worthwhile. There is also the problem that the mere possibility, if it exists, that the government *could* do something to realise those benefits is not sufficient to justify calling the government in. The government has its own interests, its own favourite lobby groups, and so on and, once invoked, may well do something quite different from whatever it was that the advocate of government intervention had in mind. We must remember that the genie has a mind of its own before we let it out of the bottle. The fact that a government *could* do something does not establish that it *would*, or even that we could *reasonably expect it to*, and we need to be reasonably confident on these points before we really have any case at all for government intervention. The argument for government or central bank intervention in payment systems is still, at best, unproven.

Would Exchange Media Disappear?

There is one last payment system issue to be discussed. Is it likely that MOE as we know them might disappear? This rather general issue has been debated in various forms. It is sometimes asserted that currency or cash might disappear if the financial system were deregulated and/or developments in information technology were to continue to alter payments practices in the way that many people think they will. We already met a version of this argument when discussing the legal restrictions theory of the demand for currency, a theory that is normally interpreted as predicting that deregulation would lead to the disappearance of non-interest-bearing currency. Similar, but vaguer, claims are also found throughout the NME literature, where they are typically couched in terms of the disappearance of 'money' [sic] under *laissez-faire*. A good example is Fama (1980, 44) who argues that

> deposits are a means of payment only in the sense that all forms of wealth are a means of payment, and the banking system is best understood without the mischief introduced by the concept of money

but comparable claims are also to be found in the other NME writers (see, e.g., Black, 1970, 9).

Before considering these claims, we need to need to clarify a couple of points. The first concerns the meaning of the hopelessly ambiguous term 'money'. While none of these writers is explicit on the issue, the context in which they write suggests that they are talking about the disappearance of 'money' in its sense as a medium of exchange. Since the use of the term 'money' is at best ambiguous and at worst downright misleading, I shall it avoid using it wherever possible and use the more precise terms such as 'media of exchange'. There is no point adding unnecessary confusion, and the term 'money' has so many different meanings that academic economists should really have given up using it a long time ago, at least for scientific purposes. The second point regards the conditions that would have to be satisfied for the predictions about the disappearance of MOE to come true. The NME writers referred to earlier give the impression that they believe that MOE would disappear provided only that the financial system were deregulated. In other words, they suggest that deregulation would lead to the disappearance of MOE *under the current state of technology*. This is a very strong claim, and it is possible that one might reject it while still subscribing to the view that deregulation *could* lead to the disappearance of MOE *under some more advanced future state of technology*. Indeed, one might even argue that technology could lead to the future disappearance of MOE as we know them regardless of whether deregulation occurs or not. We must therefore be explicit about the conditions that are required for predictions about the disappearance of MOE to come true, and we must be particularly careful to distinguish between those predictions that *could occur now* if the financial system were deregulated and those that *might occur in the future* under certain future technological or regulatory conditions.

So are there any circumstances in which MOE are likely to disappear? The most plausible answer is that MOE are unlikely to disappear imminently, even if the financial system were fully deregulated; nor, indeed, are they likely to disappear in the future in the wake of further predictable technological progress. If MOE are to disappear, then all the individual forms of MOE must disappear as well; since those include currency, then currency must disappear too; and if currency is to disappear, it must be dominated in *all* its present uses by alternatives. Yet currency has certain advantages over its alternatives, and it is difficult to visualise it losing them. Currency is often more convenient for small transactions (e.g., using a vending machine or paying a bus fare), and even where alternatives exist their use often involves either higher transactions costs (e.g., using a credit card to buy a cup of coffee) or installation expenditures to make them operational (e.g., 'smart cards' could be used to pay a bus fare, but then the relevant machinery needs to be installed). Currency also has the advantage that its acceptance does not require normally information about the person from whom one accepts it, and,

> Moreover, every other means of transacting incurs costs not incurred when using cash. For instance, a check may be drawn fraudulently, or they may for other reasons be insufficient funds to pay the check upon presentment ... Further, any computer transfer involves potential loss through fraud or system failure. Cash alone avoids these costs. (O'Driscoll, 1985, 9)

Finally, as L. H. White (1984b, 710) points out, currency also has the advantage of anonymity – it leaves behind no records that might incriminate the parties to a transaction. The use of currency thus has a number of advantages, and it is difficult to see how deregulation could lead to the imminent disappearance of currency because it would have relatively little effect on the reasons why people demand it in the first place. Even in a deregulated world, currency would still be preferred for certain types of transactions because of its lower transactions costs, its lower information and information-related costs, and because people would still engage in some transactions where they desired anonymity. There is, in short, a strong theoretical argument against the NME view that deregulation would lead to the imminent disappearance of currency (and, *a fortiori*, of MOE generally). The fact that the vast majority of transactions are still carried out using currency – Bauer (1994, table 1) reports that over 83 percent of the total number of transactions in the USA in 1987 were carried out using currency – would also seem to suggest that the NME view is, to say the least, implausible.

But this conclusion still leaves open the possibility that future developments in transactions technology *might* render currency redundant by undermining the advantages it presently has. It is conceivable, perhaps, that future developments in 'smart-card' technology might make currency unnecessary for small transactions such as buying a coffee or using a bus. However, to the extent that we can predict the future, it is probably safest to say that all we can reasonably expect is for the demand for currency to fall, and it is one thing for such developments to *reduce* the demand for currency, but quite another for them to *eliminate it entirely*. There is therefore no particular reason to *expect* that future technological developments will lead to currency becoming completely redundant. We must also bear in mind that even if the transactions-costs reasons for using currency were to disappear, currency itself would only disappear if the other reasons for using currency (i.e., information-cost and anonymity reasons) were to disappear as well. A lot would therefore have to change to render currency redundant, and there is no particular reason to expect such changes to occur. As O'Driscoll (1985, 9) nicely puts it: 'The mere advance of technology does not fundamentally alter the benefit-cost calculus for using cash.'

These conclusions are supported by the available empirical evidence. We have already noted in a number of places that people demanded currency even under the relatively unregulated banking systems of the past, an observation that appears to falsify the NME prediction that deregulation would lead to the imminent disappearance of currency or MOE more generally. Other evidence also points to the same conclusion. For example, O'Driscoll (1985, 9) points out that the demand for precautionary holdings of currency has been 'even more invariant to institutional and technological change' than the transactions demand for currency has been. He then quotes work by Dale Osborne (1985, 13) that less than one third of the currency held in the USA in 1983 – $600 for every man, woman and child – seems to be for use as exchange media. The rest, presumably, is for precautionary use of one sort or another, and Osborne also estimated that precautionary hoards have remained 'almost constant' at 3 percent of annual GNP since 1890. O'Driscoll then says

Unless these fundamental determinants of the precautionary demand for currency change, it is highly unlikely that its role in our monetary system will change. Over the same period [i.e., since 1890], with all the technological and institutional changes taking place, currency in circulation has declined only one-third (as a percentage of GNP). (O'Driscoll, 1985, 9)

Even recent technological developments have had relatively little effect on the demand for currency. To quote O'Driscoll again,

> *with all the revolutions in the payments mechanism, there is no documented tendency for currency to be displaced.* New depository accounts (including nonbank accounts) seem to be substitutes for existing types of accounts, not for currency. Debit cards still have a very small share of the payments market. Moreover, debt cards thus far seem to be better substitutes for credit cards and checks than for currency. And electronic fund transfers, which typically involve very large amounts, are almost surely substitutes for transfers by check, not currency. (O'Driscoll, 1985, 9, my emphasis)

There is, in short, no reason to expect the demand for currency to disappear.

In any case, the NME position requires, not just that currency disappear, but that MOE in general should also disappear. This means, in particular, that chequable deposits and comparable exchange media would have to disappear along with currency itself, and yet it is very difficult to see why they should. Eisenmenger (1990, 1–2) points out, 'the check continues to be the preferred method of payment for 85 percent of all small-dollar payments other than cash payments', and it is difficult to argue that this preference is entirely a product of legal restrictions: Cheques have the advantages that they 'enable the writers to make payments at the time of their choosing, for variable amounts, at any location, and with paper record of payment' as well as the advantages of cheque float. There are also good reasons, as discussed in Chapters 2 and 3, for people to want debt-type financial instruments, and for reasons also discussed in earlier chapters, some types of debt instruments are very well suited to serving as media of exchange. It follows, then, that even if currency *did* disappear, there would *still* be no reason to expect all other MOE to disappear with it. People would continue to demand MOE and financial (and perhaps other) institutions would continue to provide them. We should remember that cash and cheques are still the overwhelmingly favoured transactions media – in 1987, they accounted for no less than 97 percent of the total number of transactions in the USA (Bauer, 1994, table 1) – and there is no reason to that suppose that this preference will change that much in the foreseeable future. The empirical evidence also suggests that people want MOE besides currency. The evidence from relatively unregulated historical systems clearly indicates such demand, but so too does the experience of many modern, albeit more regulated, financial systems. We cannot reasonably argue, for example, that the existence of chequable deposits in present-day Britain is entirely a product of legal restrictions.

Legal restrictions do exist, of course, but it is difficult to see how these deposits could be a product of legal restrictions alone, and would therefore disappear if the British banking system, say, were deregulated.

11 The Economics of the Unit of Account*

It is time now to examine the unit of account (UA) in more detail. We are concerned here with three principal issues. The first is the nature and uses of a unit of account. The UA is a unit of that commodity or asset – the *medium of account* (MOA) – in terms of whose units 'prices are quoted and accounts are kept' (Niehans, 1978, 118). The UA is that to which the numbers refer in price tags. The medium of account has a name – the dollar, the pound, or whatever – and refers to a specific commodity or asset, but prices are actually expressed in terms of dollar-units. The MOA is the dollar (or pound, or whatever), but the UA is the dollar-unit. This distinction is important because what matters is not so much the choice of unit *per se*, but the choice of whatever it is whose units are used to express prices. To illustrate, it is hard to believe that there would have been any significant economic effects if the USA had adopted the cent-unit as its unit of account instead of the dollar-unit. All nominal values would have been 100 times greater than they now are, but real values and economic outcomes would have been much the same. However, the monetary history of the USA would have been very different indeed had the USA adopted the pound sterling as it's MOA instead of the dollar – American inflation would have been determined by the policy of the Bank of England, and so on. It is the choice of MOA that matters, and not the choice of UA as such.

Our second main concern in this chapter is with the determinants of the area or network – the *unit-of-account area* or *unit-of-account network* – over which a particular unit (or medium) of account is used. (I shall use the term 'network' in preference to the more familiar term 'area' – it is more precise and avoids the unfortunate geographical associations of the latter.) The issues raised here are similar to those that arise in the traditional literature on '*optimal currency areas*' (OCA) pioneered by Mundell (1961), McKinnon (1963) and others, though we will be dealing primarily with the unit of account rather than with 'currency' as such. But perhaps the main problem with the models in the traditional OCA literature is that they pay insufficient attention to the *network effects*[1] of a UA or MOA (i.e., where the value of a particular UA to a user depends on how many others use it as well). I might think that the yen is the best UA in which to quote my prices, but whether I will use yen for that purpose will depend, in part, on my expectation of how many other people will also want to deal with yen-denominated prices, and I

---

*An earlier version of some of the material in this chapter appeared (under David Greenaway's name as well as mine) in the article 'Currency Competition, Network Externalities and Switching Costs: Towards an Alternative View of Optimal Currency Areas', *Economic Journal*, 103 (420) (September 1993), pp. 1180–1189.

may rationally decide not to use yen if I believe that others will continue to use the inferior current UA. Conversely, a Russian trader might think that the rouble is very unsatisfactory and prefer that everyone switch over to something else, but he might still continue to quote prices in roubles if the others do not switch. The point is that any individual must take account of the network of other users, and since there are non-trivial co-ordination problems getting everyone to switch together, all may end up using a particular unit of account which all nonetheless agree is inferior to some other. In addition to network factors, we must also take account of *switching costs* – the costs of changing our price lists, converting financial information into the new UA and generally getting familiar with it. Switching costs are important not only because they influence the decision whether to switch, but also because they imply that what is optimal now depends, in part, on the units of account that people already use.

Our final concern is with competition between units of account. If an existing currency has a network attached to it, anyone contemplating switching to a completely different unit of account would appreciate that they would (normally) lose the benefits of that network if they switch. As a result, they might be reluctant to switch, even if the new unit is 'better' than their current one (e.g., because it inflates at a lower rate). Individuals might therefore be 'locked-in' to an inferior unit of account because they lack the means to co-ordinate a simultaneous switch and no-one wants to switch themselves unless they can be confident – which they cannot be – that others will switch with them. This lock-in to an inferior unit of account might occur even though everyone might recognise its inferiority and prefer to switch if they could choose to do so simultaneously.

Does it follow, then, that competition between units of account necessarily 'fails'? The answer is 'no'. Competition only 'fails' if the new unit of account is *in*compatible with the old unit's network – if price tags have to be changed, and so on. If however a new unit is *compatible* with the old network – if it is another 'brand' of the same currency unit, as it were, rather than an unfamiliar new unit – then the new unit can access the existing network, and the existence of that network does not constitute an entry barrier against it. Compatibility eliminates the network entry barrier and the market 'failure' disappears. A 'good' unit can then drive out a 'bad' one with little difficulty – *provided* it is compatible with the 'bad' one's network.

THE UNIT (AND MEDIUM) OF ACCOUNT

An individual uses a MOA to reduce his accounting costs – the costs of the 'time and trouble to compare prices' and other nominal values (Niehans, 1978, 119). Accounting costs play a similar role for the medium of account that transactions costs play for the standard model of the transactions demand for money (see Niehans, 1978, 119). A MOA reduces these costs by decreasing the amount of information that an agent needs to assess relative prices, and also by reducing the calculational effort needed to process that information. Niehans gives a good illustration of these savings:

> If accounting costs are a penny for each price, an economy of 1,000 commodities, each traded at 999 trading posts, would impose on each household an accounting cost of slightly less than $5,000. Even seemingly trivial accounting costs can thus add up to substantial amounts. However, $(1/2)(q-1)(q-2)$ markets are, in fact, redundant. Without economic loss, the whole exchange program can be carried out at just $q-1$ trading posts by exchanging each of $q-1$ commodities against the qth commodity serving as the medium of account. In the above-given numerical illustration the aggregate accounting costs can thereby be reduced to about $10. (Niehans, 1978, 121)

The purpose of the medium (or unit) of account

> is to communicate information about value, and while it can not measure value in any absolute sense, it can summarize information about exchange ratios. Once a unit-of-account price is quoted for each good, a comparison of unit-of-account prices makes relative prices immediately apparent ... Further, once a unit-of-account price is quoted for each good, the value of a single 'unit' is a meaningful concept, and it is fixed relative to the values of all the different goods and services. (Woolsey, 1987, 16)[2]

The savings from the use of a UA are also illustrated by a number of historical examples. Kindleberger (1983, 384) points out that 'It took four months to test and count the 1,200,000 escudo random of the sons of Francis I in 1529 – 40,000 escudos more being demanded because of imperfect coin'. He also notes how banks in medieval Italy (and later, in the eastern Mediterranean) used to 'economize on weighing and assaying specie' by accumulating 'coin in purses marked with the amounts contained, and dealt in them without recounting', but had an incentive to make accurate statements because of heavy penalties for over-stating the amounts contained. Various writers have also discussed the phenomenon of 'bank money' which developed among the banks of Genoa, Venice, Amsterdam, Hamburg and other cities to counter the lack of any sufficiently precise MOA due to the mixed state of the coinage (see, e.g., Meulen, 1934, 67; Kindleberger, 1983, 384; Yeager, 1985b, 6). The banks would accept transferable deposits of coin from the public, but value them in terms of ideal units of specified weight and fineness such the Mark Banco of the Hamburg Bank. The saving in testing and counting costs is illustrated by Adam Smith's observation that bank money in Amsterdam traded at a premium of 4–5 percent above the equivalent coin (Smith, [1776] (1911), 293).

If the use of a UA/MOA reduces the accounting costs of the person who uses it, his use of it also confers benefits on other users. These external economies or network benefits are of two major types:

- They reduce the communication and transaction-related costs of trade. The more people use the same unit of account as I do, the easier it is for me to understand the prices they quote, the financial information they provide, and so on. The use of the same UA as my trading partners also ameliorates the signal-extraction problems that otherwise confuse my perceptions of relative prices: fluctuating relative prices between different UAs add noise to relative price signals, and this noise leads agents to make mistakes in their resource-allocation decisions which they would otherwise have avoided. An agent who uses a more widely-used UA can also count on lower expected transactions costs because there is a greater chance that any prospective trading will also use payment media denominated in the same unit of account, and the expected costs of converting payments media denominated in one UA to media denominated in another will therefore be lower.
- Using a more commonly-used UA also reduces 'exchange rate' risks. If agents use different units of account, the exchange rates between them might vary and agents would have to live with the relative price volatility and wealth redistributions which result. If rates of exchange can fluctuate,

> those engaged in [affected] transactions must either generate for themselves information about the likely course of such fluctuations, face the risks inherent in taking decisions in the light of incomplete information about them, or pay specialized agents to take such risks on their behalf. One way or another, real resources must be devoted to dealing with such problems, problems which would not ... [otherwise exist]. (Laidler, 1976, 2)

If an agent is part of a large group that uses the same UA, then many of his trades will involve no exchange rate risk, and the amount of exchange-rate risk he has to deal with will fall as the group gets bigger and encompasses a greater proportion of his trading partners.

Indeed, the very existence of network economies can often imply that welfare is maximised if *everyone* uses the *same* unit of account. The reason is very simple: If agents use two different units of account, some network benefits would be forgone that could be reaped by using a single UA, provided other things are reasonably equal. The existence of network externalities therefore means that there are *economies of standardisation* from the use of a single unit of account – economies much like those that arise from the use of common units of weight or measurement or a common language.

THE UA (OR MOA) NETWORK

The Optimal UA Network in the Absence of Switching Costs

We begin by examining the extent of the optimal UA network in more detail. Suppose there are N_i indistinguishable agents who use a particular unit of account i;

there are two units of account to choose from, so $i = 1, 2$. To make the analysis simple, let us also suppose that these agents live for ever and initially do not expect to change their unit of account. An agent who uses i from time T onwards derives the following utility from it:

$$u_i(T) = (a + bn_i) \int_T^\infty e^{-r(t-T)} dt = (a + bn_i)/r \qquad (11.1)$$

where a and b are fixed coefficients, r is the (given) discount rate which we can think of as an exogenous real rate of interest, and $n_i \equiv \ln N_i$.[3] (Note that N_i is the number of *other* agents using unit of account i, so the *total* number using it is $N_i. + 1$.) The parameter a captures the network-independent benefits of using the UA. If the value of the UA were fixed to that of gold, then a would be the value of gold if no-one had any use for it as a UA. However, if the UA were a unit of a fiat currency, we would normally expect the currency to be of no value to a user unless others were holding it as well, and so a would be zero. bn_i is the network-related benefit from the UA given that N_i other agents use it as well, and we assume $b > 0$ to indicate that utility rises with the number of other agents in the same network. We assume for the time being that a and b are the same for both units of account. $(a + bn_i)$ can then be interpreted as the instantaneous utility from using currency i, and $(a + bn_i)/r$ as the net present value of using it. Aggregating over the individuals in each UA network, and noting that there are $(N_i + 1)$ in each, we can see that total welfare is

$$(N_1 + 1)(a + bn_1)/r + (N_2 + 1)(a + bn_2)/r$$
$$= (N + 2)a/r + [n_1(N_1 + 1) + n_2(N_2 + 1)]b/r \qquad (11.2)$$

where $n \equiv N_1 + N_2$ and $n \equiv \ln N$. If all $(N + 2)$ agents use a single UA, by contrast, total welfare would be $(N + 2)a/r + (N + 2)b \ln(N + 1)/r$, and it is easy to show that this latter expression is higher.[4] Intuitively, if agents use two units of account, then some network benefits are necessarily lost that could have been appropriated by the use of a common UA; at the same time, there are no gains from agents using different units of account; hence, the social optimum requires that everyone use the same UA. The presence of network externalities implies that the *optimal UA network or area is the whole (i.e., world) economy,* other things being equal (see, also, e.g., Mundell, 1961, 662).

However, this conclusion *may* need to be modified if agents have different preferences for the services of each UA/MOA, and there are various resons why they might. For example, suppose that agents live in two different regions consuming differing baskets of goods and services, and agents in each region prefer a unit of account that stabilises their local CPI (i.e., the price of their particular basket). Even if purchasing power parity (ppp) means that the prices of 'traded' goods are the same in both regions, there is no reason to expect that the prices of 'non-traded' goods (e.g., housing) would also tend to be equalised. Differences in the prices of non-traded goods can therefore cause CPIs in the two regions to diverge, and there is considerable empirical evidence that they do diverge strongly in practice (see, e.g., Falvey and Gemmell, 1991). Divergent trends in CPIs in different regions might therefore lead agents who preferred price stability in their own region to prefer to use different units of account even though doing so reduces the network benefits they could enjoy. If so, there would then be a trade-off between satisfying differences in preferences for different UAs and exploiting network economies to the full.

'Preference' differences can also be motivated by other factors. Suppose we have the same two regions as before, and factor prices are costly to adjust. Imagine also that the costs of moving factors are low within a region but high between regions (or, more loosely, that factors are relatively mobile within regions but relatively immobile between them). The analysis now parallels the optimal-currency-area arguments of Mundell (1961) and Meade (1957). If there are differential real shocks to the two regions and only one UA, these shocks can only be accommodated by factor price adjustments or movements of the factors themselves, and both of these adjustment processes are costly. However, if the two regions use different UAs, it may be possible to bring about an equilibrating adjustment of real factor prices by means of an adjustment of the exchange rate between the two units of account. Such a change might also avoid the costs of co-ordinating the changes in factor prices that would otherwise be required. The size of the UA network is then determined by the *cost of adjusting factor prices, the cost of physically moving factors themselves, and the degree to which the regions face different (real) shocks*. The larger each of these factors is, provided all are present, the more likely it is that the optimum will require *more than one UA in the world economy*.

Alternatively, we could suppose that goods' prices are costly to change, but that the regional economy has a large volume of non-traded goods. If there is a shock to the relative prices of traded and non-traded goods – such as a shock to the demand for traded goods – then the costs of adjusting these relative prices might be lower if the exchange rate were allowed to change than if the exchange rate were fixed and other prices had to move instead. If the non-traded sector were very small, on the other hand, an exchange rate change would be of little use in changing relative prices, so agents may as well use the same UA to maximise their network benefits. We thus arrive at the McKinnon criterion (McKinnon, 1963): *The extent of the optimal UA area depends on the openness of the regional economies as proxied by the ratio of the values of traded to non-traded goods – the greater the openness of the world economy, the larger the optimal UA areas and the stronger the case for a single UA.*

A final criterion, that of Kenen (1969), emphasises the extent of a region's economic diversification. Other things being equal, if a regional economy is relatively diversified, its terms of trade will tend to be more stable because individual shocks will have a greater tendency to cancel out, and the more stable the terms of trade, the less the benefit from exchange rate changes even if factor or goods prices are costly to adjust. *The size of the optimal UA area rises with the degree of economic diversification between the two regions.*

The model can also be extended to deal with related issues such as the use of parallel units of account or parallel currencies. Parallel units of account are involved where agents use one UA for one type of transaction and a different one for another, and there are parallel currencies where the same agents use exchange media denominated in different units of account. This situation most obviously occurs where trade within regions is most efficiently carried out using one particular UA/currency, but trade between regions is best carried out using another. A good example is medieval trade. Domestic trade tended to require small-denomination exchange media (e.g., to pay for a loaf of bread) but international trade required exchange media of larger denominations (e.g., to pay for a shipload of cloth). The relative values of the different metals then implied that copper coins were best suited for small-denomination trades and gold coins were best suited for the larger ones. If agents used only copper, they would have to put up with the inconveniences of copper coins for international trade (e.g., the costs of transporting large amounts of copper); but if they used only gold coins, they would have to put up with the inconveniences it created for domestic purchases (e.g., the absence of small change). It therefore made sense to use both – to use copper-based currency for domestic trades and gold-based currency for international trades. Similar arguments also explain the use of other historical parallel currencies. In the Red Sea area in the nineteenth century, the Austrian Maria-Theresa dollar was widely used for 'long-distance' trade, but 'domestic' currencies were normally used for local trade, and the British sovereign was widely used as a parallel currency across the Middle East in the early part of the twentieth century. People used parallel currencies because they enabled them to bridge the conflicting demands of domestic and international trading networks.[5]

The Optimal Unit-of-account Network When Switching is Costly

Assume now that switching units of account is costly – it takes time and effort to get used to reckoning in a new UA, posted prices and records need to be altered, and the like. Let us also assume that switching costs are the same across all individuals, and each individual has to pay a fixed amount $s > 0$ when he changes his UA. We can think of s as the cost of psychologically adjusting to the new UA or the cost of changing records and price lists. When switching costs were zero and there were no preference differences between agents, we could safely say that the optimal UA area was the world economy not only because we would have picked a single UA if we could start the world off *de novo*, but also because total welfare would *still* be maximised by adopting a single UA even if two or more different ones were inherited from the past – assuming, of course, that we had an appropriate and sufficiently inexpensive way to co-ordinate agents' choices of units of account. However, once we bring switching costs into the picture, the fact that we would prefer to pick a single UA if we could start the world off again no longer suffices to establish that a single UA is optimal *given* the UA areas we inherit from the past – we must take account of switching costs.

To illustrate, assume as before that we have $(N_i + 1)$ agents using UA i. We know already that, other things being equal, we would prefer everyone to use the same UA if we could start the world *de novo*, but that option does not exist here and each agent who switches must pay s. The change in aggregate welfare from everyone switching from UA 2 to UA 1 is then

$$[(N + 2)\ln(N + 1) - n_1(N_1 + 1) - n_2(N_2 + 1)]b/r - (N_2 + 1)s \qquad (11.3)$$

and it is easy to see that this change can now be negative if N_2 or s is 'large' (i.e., if aggregate switching costs are 'large'). Even though there are always benefits from having a larger UA network in the absence of switching costs, the largest possible network – a single UA – is not optimal in this case because of the costs of switching over to it. The optimal number and sizes of the UA areas now depend on the technological or perhaps psychological factors behind s, and on the historical factors that determine the network sizes N_1 and N_2. Switching costs introduce an element of hysteresis into picture – what is optimal now depends, in part, on what happened before.

There is also the question of whether to replace UA 2 with UA 1, or vice versa. If we replace UA 1, we get an expression like (11.3), but with the last term being $(N_1 + 1)s$ instead of $(N_2 + 1)s$. It is therefore better to switch UA 2 for UA 1 if $N_2 < N_1$, and to replace UA 1 with UA 2 if $N_1 < N_2$. The explanation, of course, is obvious: to maximise the net benefits of switching, we need to minimise switching costs, and switching costs are minimised if the numerically smaller group of UA users makes the change. Observe too that it is *never* optimal in this model to introduce a common UA by making *everyone* switch to a new one. If everyone changes, total switching costs are $(N + 2)s$ which obviously exceed the switching costs of one group adopting the UA of the other. A new common UA is inefficient because it makes everyone bear switching costs, but adopting an existing UA as the common one saves at least one group – the original users – the costs of switching. Other things being equal, it is *never* optimal to introduce a new UA to replace existing ones.

UNIT-OF-ACCOUNT COMPETITION

Unit-of-account Switching

But what factors lead agents to decide whether to switch their UA or continue with the one they presently use? Suppose we have $N + 1$ agents who all use the same unit of account, UA 1. They all expect to use the same UA for ever, and each agent derives utility

$$u_1(T) = (a_1 + b_1 n)/r. \qquad (11.4)$$

Now assume that at time $T = T^*$ a new unit of account, UA 2, unexpectedly becomes available for agents to use. If $(N_2 + 1)$ agents use it, it provides each user with utility

$$u_2(T) = (a_2 + b_2 n_2)/r; T \geq T^* \qquad (11.5)$$

where the interpretation is much the same as before. To make the analysis interesting, we assume $a_2 \geq a_1$ and $b_2 \geq b_1$ to indicate that the new UA provides services at least as good as UA 1 for any given network size, and these greater benefits provide some reason for agents to switch over to it. Each agent now has to decide whether he wishes to switch or not, but if he chooses to switch he must pay a switching cost s.

We now need certain definitions. Let $u_1(T)_A \equiv$ utility of a user who stays with the old currency at T, given that all others adopt the new one at the same time; $u_1(T)_{NA} \equiv$ utility of a user who stays with the old currency at T, given that no others adopt the new one; $u_2(T)_A \equiv$ utility of a user who switches to the new currency at T, given that all others adopt it at the same time as well; and $u_2(T)_{NA} \equiv$ utility of a user who switches to the new currency at T, given that no others adopt it. It is then easy to show that

$$u_1(T)_A = a_1/r \qquad (11.6a)$$
$$u_1(T)_{NA} = (a_1 + b_1 n)/r \qquad (11.6b)$$
$$u_2(T)_{NA} = a_2/r - s \qquad (11.6c)$$
$$u_2(T)_A = (a_2 + b_2 n)/r - s. \qquad (11.6d)$$

These expressions all have appealing interpretations. The first tells us that an agent who does not switch when everyone else does forgoes all the benefits of being part of the currency network. He then derives only the net present value of the non-network benefits (i.e., a_1/r). The second states that if an agent does not switch and no-one else does either, he gets exactly the same benefit as he did before the new currency became available. The third indicates that an agent who switches when no-one else does also forgoes the benefits of the currency network and receives only the net present value of non-network benefits of the new currency *minus* the switching cost. The last indicates that an agent who switches along with all the others receives the full network benefit $(b_2 n/r)$ as well as the non-network benefit of the new currency, but he also has to pay the switching cost.

However, agents do not always know whether other agents will switch or not, and each clearly benefits the greater the number of others who make the same choice as he does. Nonetheless, an individual agent *will* switch *regardless* of what he expects others to do if it is his worth his while to switch even if the others do not, i.e., if

$$u_2(T)_{NA} > u_1(T)_{NA}. \qquad (11.7)$$

Since all agents are the same, each one will switch regardless, and the only possible outcome is a universal switching to the new currency. Using the expressions in (11.6a) and (11.6b), everyone will therefore switch if

$$(a_2 - a_1)/r > s + b_1 n/r \tag{11.8}$$

that is to say, everyone will switch if the present value of the non-network benefits are higher than the sum of the switching cost and the net present value to each agent of a jettisoned network. Conversely, no-one will switch if he reckons that the benefits of switching are less than the benefits of the old currency even if everyone else switches, i.e., if

$$u_2(T)_A < u_1(T)_A. \tag{11.9}$$

Hence no-one will switch if

$$(a_2 - a_1)/r + b_2 n/r < s. \tag{11.10}$$

At the same time, an agent *might* switch, depending on his expectations about what other agents will do, if

$$u_2(T)_A \geq u_1(T)_A \tag{11.11}$$

so at least some switching is possible if

$$(a_2 - a_1)/r + b_2 n/r \geq s. \tag{11.12}$$

There is, finally, the question of whether switching increases aggregate welfare or not. Assuming that everyone acts the same way, the net gain from everyone switching, G, is

$$G = (N + 1)[a_2 - a_1 + (b_2 - b_1)n]/r - (N + 1)s. \tag{11.13}$$

Hence $G > 0$ if and only if the net present value gain in benefits from switching exceeds the costs, i.e.,

$$[a_2 - a_1 + (b_2 - b_1)n]/r > s. \tag{11.14}$$

There are thus three basic classes of outcome:

- The first is where (11.8) holds and all agents switch to the new UA. The new UA has a non-network superiority so large that it makes switching worthwhile for each agent regardless of what he thinks the others might do and despite the fact that switching is costly – switching is a unique Nash equilibrium. Universal switching is also optimal because the *per capita* gains from everyone switching (i.e., $[a_2 - a_1 + (b_2 - b_1)n]/r$) exceed the *per capita* costs s. Incidentally, we might note in passing that (11.8) will only generally hold if we are dealing with convertible currencies. If we have a fiat currency, as mentioned earlier, then $a_1 = a_2 = 0$ and (11.8) cannot hold. This result supports the claim that it is more difficult to launch a new fiat currency than a new convertible one (see, e.g., Selgin, 1994b).
- The second is where no switching takes place, and not-switching is the unique best course of action for any agent. This outcome is also efficient since the net gain from everyone switching is negative.

- The third is the intermediate case where switching is possible by some agents, but there is no guarantee that all (or, indeed, any) agents will switch. Since $u_2(T)_A \geq u_1(T)_A$, a typical agent will switch if he expects others to switch as well, but there is no mechanism in the model to ensure that he has these expectations. On the other hand, since $u_2(T)_{NA} \leq u_1(T)_{NA}$, he will not switch if he thinks that others will not either. What he does depends crucially on what he thinks the others will do – expectations are critical. Switching may or may not be welfare-improving, and there can therefore be one of two types of undesirable outcome. The optimal outcome might have everyone switching, but universal switching may not actually occur – switching might only be partial or non-existent. To use the terminology from Farrell and Saloner (1986), *excess inertia* might occur – an undue reluctance to switch. Alternatively, some switching might occur even though the optimal outcome has no no-one switching – there may be *excess momentum*.

Unit-of-account Competition

The Reluctance to Switch Units of Account

It turns out, nonetheless, that excess inertia is much more likely than excess momentum. Everyone might appreciate that the currency is depreciating very rapidly and that non-inflationary alternatives are available, but what each will do will often depend on what he thinks the others will do. Most agents in this situation will reckon that if everyone else was using the old currency yesterday, it is probably reasonable to expect most of them to use it again today, and this expectation will encourage them to continue using it themselves – a kind of expectational inertia develops because there is no way to co-ordinate a switch to the alternative even though everyone might prefer that everyone switch.

If we go back to the original switching costs model, we know that agents will all switch regardless of their expectations about others if $u_2(T)_{NA} > u_1(T)_{NA}$, and we know that they will choose not to switch regardless of expectations if $u_2(T)_A < u_1(T)_A$. We also know that what happens if neither of these conditions holds will depend on agents' expectations of whether *other* agents will switch. Before he decides whether to switch, a typical agent has to anticipate whether others will switch. But whether other agents will switch will depend on what they individually expect others to do; hence, to anticipate what other agents will do, our first agent must anticipate their anticipations of everyone else. Yet their anticipations of everyone else will depend on their anticipations of what others will anticipate, and so on. The anticipation of x depends on the anticipation of the anticipation of x, which in turn depends on the anticipation of the anticipation of the anticipation of x, and so on. We end up trapped in an infinite loop of anticipations reminiscent of Keynes' famous beauty contest

in which the competitors have to pick out the six prettiest faces from a hundred photographs, the prize being awarded to the competitor whose choice most nearly corresponds to the average preferences of the competitors as a whole; so that each competitor has to pick, not those faces which he himself finds prettiest, but those which he thinks likeliest to catch the fancy of the other competitors, all of whom are looking at the problem from the same point of view. It is not a case of choosing those which, to the best of one's judgment, are really the prettiest, nor even those which average opinion genuinely thinks the prettiest. We have reached the third degree where we devote our intelligences to anticipating what average opinion expects the average opinion to be. (Keynes, [1936] (1977), 156)

We then try to anticipate what average opinion expects average opinion expects average opinion to be, and on it goes. What gives this infinite loop problem its edge is that there is no reliable way to break into the loop at, say, the nth level of anticipation, make some arbitrary assumption about those anticipations, and get a result that is robust to the assumption we made. If everyone anticipates that everyone anticipates that ... that everyone will switch, where there are n levels of anticipation, then the $(n - 1)$th level will also anticipate everyone switching, and therefore the level before that, and so forth, until everyone anticipates that everyone will switch, and everyone actually does switch. But if the nth level of anticipation involved no switching, the same sort of argument then establishes that no-one would switch. The outcome depends on the nth level of anticipation, however large n might be, and we can't solve for that because it depends on the next highest level of anticipation, which in turn depends on the one above that, and so on. There is no way to untie the Gordian knot.

There may however be a way to cut it. If he was in a position to do so, the entrant in Keynes' beauty competition could win by waiting to see what choices the other contestants made. He would wait till the other entries were all in, find out the most popular one, and choose that. An entrant in a newspaper competition would not normally have that option, of course, but the entrant in our switching competition does. All he needs to do is wait and see. To be more precise, he selects a threshold level of N_2 at which he judges it worth his while to switch regardless of whether any others switch after him. He then observes others switch, if they do, and switches himself when the number of previous switchers reaches his threshold level. The others adopt the same strategy, and the result is that everyone waits for others to switch first and no-one actually switches – the critical switching mass is never reached. Even though the existing UA performs very badly, we all stay with it because in the absence of any way to co-ordinate a mass-switchover we are trapped by the privately optimal strategy of wait-for-the-others-to-do-it-first. The existence of network factors and the absence of any way to co-ordinate a general switchover means that people are to a considerable *extent locked–into the old currency even though they might all realise they would be better off if they all abandoned it*. Network factors thus create an entry barrier against new currencies that are incompatible with the old currency's existing network.[6]

Competition Between Network-compatible Units of Account

We might be tempted to conclude that unit-of-account competition 'fails' because the banks issuing the old currency can use the network externality entry barrier to choose whatever anchor/inflation rate they like regardless of what the public want. However, such a conclusion would be unwarranted. If an existing currency has a network that functions as an entry barrier against a new currency unit incompatible with that network, then competition must come from a *new unit that is* compatible *with that network.*

What makes one currency unit compatible with the network of another? A new unit of account can be said to be compatible with the network of another when an unspecified price could easily refer to either unit. The new unit can therefore be said to be compatible if it has the same value when first introduced as the existing dollar and goes by a similar name. But if the new unit is worth, say, 1.67 existing dollars when first introduced, a price of 30 units of account would be quite different depending on what the relevant unit of account is taken to be, and most people would find it difficult to translate information about one into information about the other. The choice of name can also have some impact – if people are used to using units of account called 'dollars', then I would be advised to call my brand-name unit of account some kind of dollar as well – but the similar name will only have an impact if the first condition is satisfied and if information in the old unit of account is easily translatable into information in the new one. The new name needs to be close enough to the old one to minimise unfamiliarity on the part of the public, but it needs to be clearly distinguishable from the old one to compete successfully against it. The new brand-name unit of account thus has to be perceived by the public as *close enough* in characteristics space to be compatible with the existing network, but *better than* the existing one in order to win over its market share. The problem with a totally different unit of account, such as a foreign one, is that it is too far away in characteristics space to be able to access the network, and therefore falls foul of network externalities.

To see how this competition would work, imagine for the sake of argument that the banks for some reason issue currency that inflates at a secular rate of $\pi_1 > 0$ but for reasons to be explained in Chapter 15, the public prefer a unit of account in which prices remain stable. If banks thought they could act as a cartel, we might perhaps think of them attempting to select π_1 to maximise their seignorage revenues in the hope that members of the public would feel obliged to put up with the inflation they were generating. However, the cartel runs into a problem as soon as it is set up: while the banks might *collectively* agree that they would all be better off if they all stuck with the π_1 policy, this policy is not compatible with banks' *individual* interests. If the cartel generates an inflation rate of π_1, cartel members (or new entrants) would realise that they could increase their market share by offering the public MOE denominated in new units with anchors chosen to produce a lower inflation rate, π_2, *provided* the new units were compatible with the old one's network.

The rebel banks would still offer dollar-denominated MOE, but they would offer a slightly different 'brand-name' dollar unit of account which had the same value as the old dollar at the time when it was introduced. If the existing unit of account is the 'dollar', for example, they could offer MOE denominated in 'superior dollars', or whatever, which had their own legal identity. A new $1 dollar note might say 'I promise to pay the bearer five superior dollars' and the small print (or an accepted legal convention) might specify the commodity or commodity basket to which the value of the 'superior dollar' was tied. The new dollar would be similar to the old one in most respects, but otherwise be superior to it. For example, the issuers could promise that it would depreciate in value at a lower rate, by specifying that the commodity or commodity basket to which it was tied would shrink at a slower rate than the commodity or commodity basket behind the old dollar. When it is introduced, members of the public would recognise its superiority and therefore prefer to hold exchange media denominated in the new dollar.[7] If we imagine exchange media denominated in both dollars as circulating side-by-side, people would choose to retain those denominated in the new dollar, and spend those denominated in the old one.[8] The demand for exchange media denominated in the new dollar would rise, and demand for exchange media denominated in the old one would fall. Indeed, since the two dollars are otherwise close substitutes, there would be no reason to hold any exchange media denominated in the old dollar at all, and the demand for them should go to zero. Since their circulations are demand-determined, exchange media denominated in the old dollar would disappear from circulation and be entirely replaced by exchange media denominated in the new dollar.[9]

It might perhaps be helpful to put the argument a slightly different way. An individual agent has to decide whether to use MOE denominated in the new dollar in preference to MOE denominated in the old one. If he thinks that other agents will switch to it, then he has no reason whatever to choose to hold MOE denominated in the inferior dollar, and he has at least one good reason (i.e., a higher return) to choose the opposite. He will therefore choose MOE denominated in the superior dollar. But what if he thinks (for whatever reason) that other agents will continue to accept MOE denominated in the old dollar and interpret the phrase 'dollar' as referring to the old dollar? Even then he will *still* choose to hold MOE denominated in the superior dollar because he will reckon that other agents will accept such MOE even though they might quote prices in inferior ones. If I offer to sell a good at a price of, say, one inferior dollar, then I could be expected also to accept a $1 note denominated in superior dollars because the latter would be worth at least as much as the former – I can always accept it and redeem it to get at least my asking price in terms of inferior dollars. The strategy of holding MOE denominated in superior dollars therefore dominates the strategy of holding MOE denominated in inferior ones, regardless of whether our agent thinks the future 'dollar' will be the superior dollar or the inferior one. Everyone consequently holds MOE denominated in superior dollars, and the demand for instruments denominated in inferior dollars goes to zero.

Once exchange media denominated in the old dollar have disappeared, the phrase 'dollar' will be unambiguously interpreted as referring to the new, superior dollar, so the new dollar will displace the old one as unit of account as well. Given that people use MOE denominated in the new dollar, it is natural for them to interpret nominal values as being units of the exchange media they accept and hand over. To interpret them as being units of anything else increases transactions, calculation, bargaining and other costs, and is quite unnecessary. As explained in more detail in Chapter 10, the unit of account will be a unit of the exchange media that people use in routine trade. The everyday term 'dollar' thus subtly changes its meaning. Initially, it refers to units of the old dollar. When the new dollar is introduced, the term 'dollar' can refer to either old or new dollars, but when the new dollar displaces the old one, the term 'dollar' comes to refer to the new dollar only. A shop price tag of '$1' that would have meant 'one old dollar' before the reform would now mean one 'new dollar' after it, but there would be little outward change in the high street, and people would still refer to so many 'dollars' in their everyday activities. The only significant change would be a change in the precise unit of account which goes by that name.[10]

The competitive process of course does not stop with the π_2-brand dollar driving out the π_1-one. If π_2 is itself positive, the very process that led to the π_2-dollar displacing the relatively inferior π_1-dollar will lead to the displacement of the π_2-dollar by some π_3-dollar that had an even lower inflation rate. If π_3 is also positive, the π_3-dollar will be displaced in its turn, and the process of successive replacements will continue until we arrive at last at a dollar brand that does not inflate at all. The process of replacements then stops since (we have presumed that) the public have no demand for a dollar with a negative inflation rate. The process of competition ensures that the public get the unit of account with the characteristics – for example, inflation characteristics – they most desire. *If the public want a stable-valued unit of account, competition ensures that they get it.*[11] Even if the banks preferred some alternative characteristics (e.g., more inflation to exploit the seignorage from non-interest-bearing currency), competitive forces would undermine any attempts to rig the market and the final outcome would reflect their *customers' preferences rather than their own*. We have a classic case of Bertrand competition where a group of banks takes its rivals' 'prices' as given and steals their market share by undercutting them. The process of successive 'price-cutting' (or, in our context, inflation-cutting) continues until the 'price' has gone down far enough to satisfy the customers, and only then does it stop falling. Any preference the banks might have for some other inflation rate is undermined by competitive pressures that *force* them to satisfy the desires of the public.

Having set the basic story out, we should however also appreciate that there is no particular reason to suppose that the banks would in fact want to inflate the currency anyway, even if they could get away with doing so. The purpose of supposing that the banks *might* want to do so was merely to emphasise that the public's preferences would win out over the banks', if there was any conflict between the two, in order to highlight the forces making for consumer sovereignty under competitive conditions. Whether there *would* be any conflict of interest between the two is in fact highly doubtful. Even though the banks might be able to gain some seigniorage from inflation, inflation also increases their bookkeeping costs and, if it makes prices more volatile, destabilises the value of their portfolio and makes longer-term prices more difficult to predict. These additional costs ought not to be under-estimated, and own feeling is that the banks would want long-term price stability as much as everyone else. Nonetheless, it is important to establish that price stability would emerge anyway, even if the banks tried to undermine it.

Nor would we actually expect to see the 'live' competition just described in which a π_2-brand dollar drives out a π_1-dollar, only to be driven out by a π_3-dollar which is itself driven out by a π_4-dollar, and so on. Setting out the story in these terms is merely a hypothetical device that helps to highlight the underlying forces at work. In practice, the competitive process would not work out in the way described earlier because the banks involved would be able to anticipate the outcome and spare themselves the costs of a 'live' competition. If the unit of account appears to be veering away from delivering the price-level behaviour the public want, then the issuing banks would sense their vulnerability and 'correct' the fault to pre-empt the launch of an alternative brand-name dollar that might drive out the existing one. It is the *threat* a new brand, rather than its *actual launch*, that would keep the banks in order. The mere threat of competition would be enough to ensure that the fault was corrected and the public obtained the *price-level behaviour they desired*. Banks would always be free to offer alternative dollar brands, but we would only ever observe the launch of a new brand in the relatively unlikely event of them making a major misjudgement of what the public wanted. Barring such a misjudgement, we would only ever observe one dollar brand being used, and the process of 'live' competition between rival brands would be short-circuited.

12 The Mechanics of Convertibility*

Chapters 12–14 consider various mechanical issues relating to the operation of the monetary standard, and we begin in this chapter with the mechanics of a *convertible monetary system*.[1] We can talk of the convertibility of a monetary system in two different senses. In a weaker and less familiar sense, convertibility involves a commitment by one or more banks of issue to maintain continuously or every so often a pre-announced exchange rate between the MOE they issue and something else (i.e., they peg the latter's nominal price). For example, they might undertake to peg the nominal price of an ounce of gold throughout each trading day, or on the first day of every month or year. We can also talk about convertibility in a stronger and more familiar sense. *'Strong' convertibility* involves a similar price-pegging rule, but also includes a supplementary requirement that banks continuously offer an 'over the counter' (OTC) service to the general public by which they commit themselves to redeem and sell their liabilities for some medium (or media) of redemption (MOR) at an exchange rate determined by a preannounced formula.[2] There may be certain conditions attached to the banks' obligation to buy and sell their liabilities (e.g., members of the public might have to give advance notice to withdraw certain deposits), but in what follows it is easier to abstract from such conditions and implicitly presume that the banks agree to redeem and sell their liabilities on demand without notice. To give a well-known example, £1 notes issued by the Bank of England used to carry the legend 'I promise to pay the bearer on demand the sum of one pound' and this phrase constituted a legally binding obligation on the Bank's part to exchange each such note presented to it for a particular quantity of gold. Legally speaking, the note was only a *claim* to a pound, and the pound *per se* was the gold which the Bank was obliged to hand over in exchange for the note.

One difference between 'strong' and 'weak' convertibility is that the former allows a more rapid 'reflux' of unwanted exchange media than the latter. Should the demand for MOE fall, the excess MOE can be returned very quickly over the counter under strong convertibility, but the MOE can only be returned under weak convertibility when the next price-fixing date arrives. The typical member of the public will receive no 'over the counter' redeemability service, and even then MOE can only be retired at the banks' desk in the market where they were intervening, and anyone who redeemed in this way would have to accept in return for his MOE the commodity or asset traded in that market. A corollary is that the public can get rid of excess holdings of bank liabilities under weak convertibility only when the

*A large part of this chapter appeared as 'The Mechanics of Indirect Convertibility', *Journal of Money, Credit and Banking*, 27(1) (February 1995) pp.67–88.

intervention dates occur, but they can get rid of excess holdings of bank liabilities under strong convertibility at any time they choose. Strong convertibility thus imposes a stronger discipline on banks than weak convertibility. The continuous redemption provided for under strong convertibility may also be important if bank liabilities are to function as exchange media. As already discussed in Chapter 10, if the banks are to provide an efficient payments system, it is important that cheques and other credit instruments be cleared and, where necessary, redeemed, relatively quickly, and rapid redemption is exactly what strong convertibility provides. Our discussion shall accordingly focus on strong convertibility.

A convertible monetary system thus has certain important features: (1) It (typically) has a (single) unit of account (e.g., the dollar) in which nominal values are denominated. This property is one it shares, of course, with any well-defined monetary system. (2) Issuers of exchange media are obliged to exchange them when required to for specified amounts of redemption media, and the latter can be anything – a single commodity, a group of commodities, or one or more other assets – considered suitable for the purpose. (3) There exists some good, service or financial asset, or bundle of goods, services or assets, whose price is pegged by the relevant banks, and which we shall refer to as the *anchor commodity or asset*, or simply *anchor* for short. The unit of account, the dollar, will have a par value at any point in time in terms of units of the anchor. Market forces will then ensure that the market price of the anchor is consistent with this par value. We can then think of nominal values throughout the economy (e.g., all dollar prices) as 'anchored down' by the combination of the pegged nominal price of the anchor – hence its name – and the conditions determining the relative prices of the anchor against other goods and services. The choice of anchor helps to determine the kind of monetary system that results – the choice of a commodity or commodity bundle as anchor implies a *commodity-based monetary system*; the choice of a foreign currency implies a *fixed exchange rate* or *crawling peg exchange rate system*, and these latter two systems will take on the nature of the foreign monetary system whose currency is used as anchor (i.e., they will correspond to commodity-based systems if the foreign system is commodity-based, and so on); and the choice of certain other financial assets, such as Treasury bills, can imply that nominal values are indeterminate. We will discuss the implications of different anchors in later chapters, but in this one we take the anchor as given and focus on the operational mechanics of convertibility *per se*.

DIRECTLY CONVERTIBLE MONETARY SYSTEMS

The best-known type of convertibility is *direct convertibility* where banks of issue are obliged to redeem all or at least some of their liabilities with the very commodity or asset which also serves as the anchor. A directly convertible system is thus a strongly convertible one in which the MOR and the anchor are identical. Direct convertibility is familiar from both historical experience[3] and from the extensive discussion it has received in the theoretical literature. An obvious example is the traditional gold standard in which the dollar price of gold was pegged (i.e., gold was the anchor) and issuing banks were typically obliged to redeem their issues in gold (so gold was the MOR as well). There have also been directly convertible standards based on silver, and such standards have been proposed based on other commodities such as bricks (e.g., Buchanan, 1962). Directly convertible systems have also been proposed based on baskets of commodities instead of a particular individual commodity, and two well-known examples are Marshall's *symmetallic system* and the *commodity-reserve systems* proposed by Frank Graham (1942) and Benjamin Graham (1944). Many historical currency board and fixed-exchange rate systems also took the form of directly convertible systems, but with the difference that they were based on a foreign currency.

Directly convertible systems are relatively straightforward to understand. A good starting point is to consider how nominal prices are determined in this type of system, and what economic forces exist to return prices to equilibrium levels should the system be shocked away from them. Recall that the direct convertibility rule implies that the banks must buy or sell their currency for the anchor-MOR (e.g., gold) at a fixed nominal price. Suppose that we choose our units of the anchor such that the nominal 'par' price of one unit at the banks of issue is $1. The banks therefore buy and sell gold, say, at a fixed price of $1 per unit, and the zero-arbitrage condition will ensure that the market price of gold is $1 as well (or something very close). We can then think of the nominal prices of other goods and services as being tied down by the combination of this 'par' price of gold and the 'real' factors that determine the relative prices of these goods and services against gold. If the equilibrium exchange rate between the anchor commodity and some other commodity is 2 to 1, then the other commodity has an equilibrium nominal price of $2, and so on. Disturbances of these other prices from equilibrium can then be thought of as corrected by conventional market equilibrating forces. If the equilibrium price of a particular commodity is $2, but the market price rises, say, to $3, the commodity will be in excess supply and market forces will force it back down towards $2 until the system equilibrates again. Other nominal prices are therefore both determinate and stable. The quantities and types of exchange media are then determined by the demands to hold them. Agents have demands for real holdings of exchange media based on factors such as their incomes, interest rates, wage rates, and expectations. Given the nominal prices whose determinacy we have just discussed, we can then derive agents' nominal demands for exchange media, and these nominal demands determine the amounts in circulation since the convertibility rule obliges the issuers to buy or sell their exchange media on demand for a given price in terms of the MOR-anchor (i.e., the supplies of MOE are perfectly elastic at the margin). Should the issues in circulation be too much or not enough, agents would return the excess issues to the banks or go to them to demand more, and either way the supplies of exchange media in circulation would move into line with the amounts the public are willing to hold.

However, we cannot simply *assume* that private agents will act in such a way that the market price of the anchor commodity will always happen to be $1 – we have to explain what economic forces will tend to keep the market price at this 'par' level, and thereby make the convertibility system operationally meaningful. We therefore have to show how the market price of the anchor would tend to be restored to par if it should happen for some reason to deviate from it. Imagine then that the price of anchor rose above par. If one likes, one can think of the anchor as gold, as under a traditional gold standard. Private agents would then make arbitrage profits by buying gold from the banks and selling it on the market. If the price of gold was p_g on the market, redeeming a one-dollar liability at the issuing bank would generate an amount of gold worth $p_g > \$1$ on the gold market, and the arbitrager would make a profit of $p_g - \$1$. In the process the outstanding stock of notes would fall by \$1 and the smaller stock of notes would imply a slightly lower market price for the anchor. Profit opportunities of this kind would continue to be available for as long as p_g exceeded its par value, and each arbitrage operation would further reduce the stock of notes and, hence, the price of gold. Arbitrage operations would therefore continue and both the note stock and the price of gold would keep falling until the source of the arbitrage profits – the difference between the banks' price of gold and the market one – had been eliminated and the price of gold had fallen back to \$1. If the price of gold fell below \$1, on the other hand, there would be arbitrage profits to be made from selling gold to the banks in return for notes or deposits, and each such operation would increase the supply of exchange media and hence the market price of gold. Arbitrage operations would then continue until the note supply had increased sufficiently to raise the price of gold back to par. A deviation of the price of gold in either direction would thus set in motion arbitrage forces that would automatically alter the supply of exchange media to restore the price of gold to \$1.[4] The nominal price of gold is thus stable as well as determinate.

Yet despite their apparent familiarity, directly convertible systems suffer from two important drawbacks, both of which have received relatively little attention. The first is the inefficiency which results from having the one commodity or asset performing both MOR and anchor roles. To see the source of the inefficiency, imagine for a moment that we could pick the MOR and the anchor independently. We would then draw up criteria for the suitable choice of each and make our choices, but given that we would have different criteria in each case, it would only be by coincidence that we would pick the same commodity or asset for both roles, and the directly convertible system is inefficient precisely because it forces us to do so. To make the discussion more concrete, a 'good' MOR would 'be well-known, uniform in quality, easy to store [and to handle], have desirable risk-return properties ... and be traded in thick, liquid markets' (Cowen and Kroszner, 1990a, 6, n. 7). A 'good' anchor, on the other hand, would satisfy quite a different list of criteria, perhaps the most important of which would be that it generated desirable price-level behaviour. It would therefore be surprising if whatever best satisfied the first condition was also best at satisfying the second. The conflict between these two roles is likely to be particularly acute where – as is likely to be the case – the ideal anchor commodity is chosen to maximise price-level stability and some 'wide' basket of goods or services is chosen as anchor because movements in its composite price closely follow those of one's 'target' price index (e.g., the CPI). Stabilising the price of the former would then stabilise the latter and produce the desired degree of price-level stability, but the problem is that no such bundle would make a good MOR. The wider the basket, the greater the handling and probably the storage costs of dealing with the goods involved, and these difficulties are potentially much greater still if the basket also includes services as well. The bank would have to hand over half a box of matches, a tin of peas, some fraction of a specificy type of hair-cut, and goodness knows what else, every time someone presented a note for redemption. A 'wide' anchor consisting of a large bundle of goods and services would not sit well with the requirement that the MOR-anchor have reasonable handling costs, and the costs may be so high that they effectively rule out such a basket in a directly convertible system (see also Friedman, 1951). The conflict between the requirements of the anchor and those of the MOR could thus mean that whatever was chosen would be inappropriate in at least one, and possibly both, of its monetary uses.

The other problem with a directly convertible system is its potential to destabilise the financial system (Dowd, 1991c, 1992c; Greenfield and Yeager, 1989; Meulen, 1934; Yeager, 1983). Suppose that there is an unexpected increase in the demand for the MOR-anchor. To make the example more familiar, imagine that we had a traditional directly convertible gold standard and there was an increase in demand for gold. We would now expect there to be an excess demand for gold at its initial relative price against other goods and services. Given that the supply of gold is relatively inelastic, much then depends on how flexible the relative price of gold is, which is to say, given its fixed nominal price, much depends on how flexible *other* prices are in adjusting downwards to clear the gold market. These prices would presumably be reasonably flexible in the longer run, but in the short run we might expect some degree of price-level stickiness. What happens then? Were the system an indirectly convertible gold standard in which gold only performed the role of anchor, we would expect there to be longer-run deflationary consequences, but no particularly obvious short-run effects other than the standard ones resulting from the shock of the increased demand for gold and the deflation which is expected to follow it. Were the system an indirectly convertible gold standard, if one may call even it that, in which gold was the MOR but the anchor was something else, we would expect that the nominal price of gold would rise to reflect the higher demand for gold and the gold market should clear relatively easily without any significant deflation. (Recall that it is the price of the anchor which is fixed, and the price of the MOR would be allowed to rise.) The gold market would absorb the impact of the shock, at least in the first instance, and those who hold gold would make a windfall gain. Banks holding reserves of gold would experience both a capital gain and an increase in their liquidity resulting from the increased value of their reserves – an increased demand for gold therefore makes them better off on both counts.

The consequences would be very different if gold were *both* anchor *and* MOR. The gold market would exhibit excess demand, but the banks would be legally obliged to sell it at the old price by virtue of gold being the MOR as well.[5] If someone wanted gold, he could insist that an issuing bank sell it to him at that price by presenting the bank with liabilities for redemption, and a bank that failed to comply would default on the contract it had made. The increased demand for gold could then translate into a run on the banks, and the run might be particularly perilous in a 'mature' banking system in which the banks operated on low reserve ratios. The banks would therefore need a legal way to protect their solvency, and they would presumably do so by borrowing gold and in the process raising the interest rate on gold-denominated loans. The higher 'gold interest rate' would discourage hoarding of gold and release more of it onto the market, and that interest rate would rise to a point where the spot gold market finally equilibrated. *Since the spot price of gold would be fixed, gold would be in inelastic supply, and prices elsewhere would be (to some extent) sticky,* the gold market would have to be equilibrated by a rise in the gold interest rate. The banks might also respond with higher deposit interest rates to discourage demands to redeem deposits, and the combination of higher gold interest rates and higher deposit interest rates would put upward pressure on interest rates generally. Lending interest rates would rise with them, and we would get a credit squeeze (see, e.g., Dowd, 1991c, 723–725). The fact that gold functions as both anchor and MOR – that is, that the system is directly convertible – thus produces a degree of financial instability that does not occur when gold performs one or other but *not* both of these roles.[6]

INDIRECTLY CONVERTIBLE MONETARY SYSTEMS

We turn now to a second type of convertible system, indirect convertibility. Imagine again that we have banks which issue dollar-denominated convertible exchange media which we can think of as banknotes or chequable deposits. However these exchange media are now indirectly convertible,[7] that is, a bank is obliged to redeem each $1 exchange medium it issues with a redemption medium which is different from the anchor commodity (or whatever) which defines the dollar, but which has the same market value.[8] If we continue to choose our units of the anchor such that the legal value of one unit is $1, but that unit has a market price (which might be different, as will become clear) of p_A, and the market price of a unit of the MOR is p_{MOR}, an exchange medium denominated as $1 must be redeemed for an amount of the MOR of the same market value as p_A. The issuer must therefore hand over p_A/p_{MOR} units of the MOR for each $1 liability presented to him. The media of redemption can be any commodities or assets which are convenient to use for that purpose. MOR could be gold, as in Schnadt and Whittaker (1990) and Yeager and Woolsey (1991), or they could be specified financial instruments, such as Treasury bills as in Woolsey (1987, 1989a), and the choice of redemption media is presumably governed by factors such as portability and storage costs, and the costs of ascertaining their value. As already discussed, there is no particular reason for the MOR and the anchor commodity to be the same

– the list of characteristics that might make a commodity a good MOR has little bearing on whether that commodity would also be a good anchor. The choice of MOR is thus substantially independent of the choice of anchor commodity, and it would be something of a coincidence, theoretically speaking, if one particular commodity or asset turned out to be the one best suited for both roles.

It is important to emphasise that the price level in this system is quite determinate. The combination of commodity-definition of the dollar and the banks' indirect convertibility rule ensures that the nominal equilibrium price of the anchor commodity is $1. The nominal prices of other goods and services can then be thought of as determined by the 'real' factors that determine relative prices. If the equilibrium exchange rate between the anchor commodity and some other commodity is 2 to 1, the other commodity has an equilibrium nominal price of $2, etc., and disturbances away from equilibrium are corrected by conventional equilibrating forces in the market. The quantities and types of exchange media are then determined by the demand to hold them – agents have demands for real holdings of exchange media,[9] and these real demands translate into unique nominal demands given the price level which all agents take to be given – and a law of reflux operates to ensure that excess issues that no one wants to hold are returned to their issuers. In these respects the indirectly convertible system is much like a directly convertible system such as the traditional gold standard. In that system the dollar was equivalent in value to a fixed quantity of gold, and the combination of this commodity-equivalence and the convertibility rule ensured that the equilibrium price of this quantity of gold was $1. Other nominal prices were then tied down by real factors, and equilibrating forces ensured that deviations from equilibrium were reversed. Where the indirectly convertible system differs from the traditional gold standard is that banks under the latter undertook to convert their liabilities into fixed *amounts* of the redemption medium (i.e., gold), but banks under the former would redeem their liabilities into redemption media of a fixed *value*. These redemption media would however have a value that was fixed in terms of quantities of the anchor commodity, so the value of a $1 note, say, would still be tied to that of a specific quantity of real goods. It would therefore be a mistake to suppose that the rule by which exchange media are redeemed for a given value of redemption media implies that the system has no real anchor for nominal prices. The system of indirect convertibility described here is *not* a real-bills system in which banks redeem notes for a given value of gold, say, but where there is nothing to tie prices to physical quantities and the 'price level and the money supply are anchored to their own consequences and so are not anchored at all' (Yeager and Woolsey, 1991, 5). The fact that both indirectly convertible systems and real-bills systems involve banks redeeming their currency in terms of redemption media of given nominal value should not blind one to the fact that indirectly convertible systems provide a mechanism to tie nominal values down, but the latter do not. There is no nominal anchor under a real-bills system and it is the absence of an anchor that makes nominal prices indeterminate. The indirectly convertible system is thus very different from a real-bills one.

But, as with direct convertibility, we cannot simply assume that private agents will act in such a way that the market price of the anchor commodity will happen to be $1. We have to explain what economic forces will tend to keep the market price of the anchor at its par level of $1, and thereby make the par value of the anchor operationally meaningful (see also Woolsey, 1987, chapter 1 and Woolsey, 1989a, 5–7). To do so, we need to show how the market price of the anchor would be returned to par if it should for some reason deviate away from it. The equilibrating process is similar in some respects to that which occurs under direct convertibility. Suppose then that the price of the anchor commodity rises to p_A which is greater than the par value of $1. Since the indirect convertibility rule obliges banks to redeem their notes with enough MOR to buy the anchor commodity at its market price, a noteholder can again make arbitrage profits by selling notes to the issuing banks and then selling the MOR on the market for more notes. A one-dollar bill can be presented to the bank that issued it for p_A/p_{MOR} units of the MOR. The MOR obtained in this way can be sold on the market for $p_{MOR} p_A/p_{MOR} = p_A$ units of dollar bills. The arbitrager will have thus converted a one-dollar bill into notes with a face value of p_A and made a profit on the operation of $p_A - $1, and he can of course continue to make arbitrage profits for as long as p_A exceeds $1. As before, each of these operations reduces the stock of outstanding exchange media,[9] and each reduction in this stock will tend to push prices down, including the price of the anchor commodity. Provided that the latter is free to adjust, the arbitrage operations will keep reducing the price of the anchor commodity until it falls back to par and eliminates the scope for further profitable arbitrage. If the price of the anchor commodity falls below par, on the other hand, there are arbitrage opportunities, as before, from selling the MOR to the banks and then selling the notes obtained in this way for greater quantities of the MOR, and these operations increase the supply of exchange media and continue until the price of the anchor commodity has again reached par.[10]

The previous discussion of the forces tending to reverse deviations of the price of the anchor commodity from par is best interpreted as a conceptual experiment rather than a literal account of what would happen in practice. As Yeager and Woolsey put it, we would

> not expect that deviations would first begin, then grow [and, hence, persist], then reverse themselves, and subsequently repeat themselves, perhaps in the opposite direction. We see no reason to expect such cycles. Supposing that deviations do occur and then undergo reversal merely gives us an opportunity to describe processes and forces that would forestall such deviations in the first place. (Yeager and Woolsey, 1991, 8)

The reason we would not expect to see equilibrating forces working in the way described earlier is because of the influence of agents' expectations. To see why expectations matter, suppose that for some reason agents expect the price of the anchor commodity to alter from par at a definite time in the future. They would realise the arbitrage profits that could be made when the price discrepancy arose, and they would be ready to take those profits as soon as the price of the anchor began to move. The price of the anchor would then be corrected as soon as it began to move, and except for a possible momentary blip, there would be no significant price change at all. Anticipations of movements in the price of the anchor from par conflict with rational expectations equilibrium, and any changes in the price of the anchor that do occur must be unanticipated ones. Rational expectations would also ensure that the deviations from par that do occur would not persist for any significant length of time. An agent who waited before acting to exploit arbitrage opportunities would lose them – he could not count on the opportunity persisting, and if he did not exploit it immediately, he would have to presume that someone else would. Competition for arbitrage profits – from the banks themselves, as well as from the public – ought therefore to eliminate those profits very quickly. The elimination of arbitrage profits would also be assisted by speculative factors. Those who deal in the anchor would appreciate that even if its current price was different from par, it would soon return to it, and they would take into account the capital gains or losses that would result as the price of the anchor returns to par. If the price was above par, they would anticipate that it would fall, and so they would have an incentive to hurry up sales of it while the price was still temporarily high and postpone purchases until after the fall had taken place. Their speculative holdings of exchange media and other assets would therefore rise accordingly, and the combination of a 'speculative' increase in the supply of the anchor and a speculative increase in the demand for exchange media would itself tend to push the price of the anchor down and help restore equilibrium. If the price of the anchor fell below par, on the other hand, agents would anticipate it rising back again, and the resulting speculative changes in net demands would help the necessary price adjustment to take place. Speculative forces would thus reinforce the effect of arbitrage forces in rapidly eliminating any deviation in the price of the anchor. In short, rational expectations should ensure that the expected price of the anchor would be $1, and any deviations from that value that do occur should be unpredictable ones that would be quickly corrected.

The 'Paradox of Indirect Convertibility'

This analysis has been criticised by a number of writers who have claimed there is a serious problem with it – the 'paradox of indirect convertibility'. This problem was first[11] noted by Wicksell (1919) working with an indirectly convertible system where gold was the anchor commodity and silver the MOR. Suppose that the price of gold doubles from its initial par value of $1. Since an amount of gold previously worth $1 is now worth $2, the banks must give out twice as much silver as they previously did for each one-dollar bill presented to them, and an initial price ratio between gold and silver that was initially, say, 30 to 1, is now 60 to 1. A dollar bill at the banks therefore buys 60 units of silver, so the price of silver *at the banks* has fallen to $1/60, and the *market* price of silver subsequently falls to the lower price being charged for it by the banks. The price of gold remains at $2, however, so a one-dollar note is now redeemable against 2 times 60 units of silver. The banks' selling price of silver has thus halved again, to $1/120 per unit, and so the market price of silver also halves again. But the dollar price of gold is still $2, and so the banks find themselves redeeming dollar bills for 2 times 120 units of silver. The banks' selling price halves yet again, and the market price follows it. The process continues in this way and the price of silver keeps halving and goes in the limit to zero. We thus get the strange result that a rise in the price of gold (i.e., the anchor commodity) leads to a collapse in the price of silver (i.e., the MOR). We also get problems in the opposite case where there is a fall in the price of gold. Suppose the price of gold fell to half a dollar. The banks would redeem each dollar bill for 15 units of silver instead of the 30 units they used to give out. The price of silver at the banks would therefore double to $1/15. The market price would double with it, but since the market price of gold would still be only half a dollar, the banks would now be buying silver for a price of one-half of $1/15, or $1/7.5. The market price of silver would then double again, and the banks would be forced in turn to double it yet again. The market price of silver would then rise again to $1/3.75, then to $1/1.875, and so on; a fall in the price of gold consequently leads the price of silver to rise without limit. We thus arrive at the paradox result: a change in the relative price of gold, however small, leads the price of silver to spiral away towards either zero or infinity. As Yeager and Woolsey (1991, 11) put it,

> Wicksell's argument amounts to a claim that under readily imaginable circumstances, redemption and issue operations would kill off any free-market price of the redemption medium.

It is important to be clear about the process behind this result. Given the banks' redemption rule, a deviation of the price of the anchor commodity from its par value produces an automatic deviation between the (initially given) market price of silver and the price at which the banks stand ready to buy or sell it. If equilibrium is to be maintained in the silver market, the market price of silver has to adjust to the banks' price, but as it tries to do so, the movement of the market price itself pushes the banks' price even further away from its initial value, and the two prices drive each other towards either zero or infinity. The change in the banks' price forces the market price to adjust to try to restore silver market equilibrium, but the change in the market price of silver alters the banks' price since the latter itself must move *pari passu* with the currently prevailing market price. The process of silver market equilibration tries to push the two prices together, as it were, but the two prices *cannot* go together because the deviation of the price of the anchor commodity from par *requires* that the two prices be different. If the price of silver on the market is currently p_s a unit, the price at which the banks are required to buy and sell it is p_s/p_g, and these two prices will *necessarily* differ if p_g is different from par. The banks' price therefore moves further and further away from its initial level as quickly as the market price adjusts in its direction. It turns out, then, that once the market price of the anchor commodity deviates from par, *there is* no way to equilibrate the silver market and simultaneously operate an indirect-convertibility redemption rule – the former requires that the bank and market prices come together, but the latter prevents them from doing so.

Yet it turns out on closer examination that there are serious problems with the paradox argument itself. To see the issues involved, let us go back to the equilibrating mechanism under indirect convertibility and examine it again more closely. The equilibrating process has two essential elements. The first is a positive relationship between the quantity of exchange media in circulation and their exchange value against the anchor commodity. The greater the quantity of exchange media, the lower their relative value against goods in general, and against the anchor commodity in particular, and hence the greater their dollar prices. Should more exchange media be issued than were compatible with the par price of the anchor commodity, there would be arbitrage profits to be made from presenting excess exchange media for redemption to the issuing banks. If there were less exchange media in circulation than were compatible with the par price of the anchor commodity, there would be arbitrage profits to be made from selling the redemption medium to the banks and thereby increasing the supply of exchange media. The supply of exchange media falls if the price of the anchor commodity is too high, and rises if that price is too low (see also Yeager, 1987, 8, 16 and Coats, 1990, 16). The equilibrium characterised by (p_A*, MOR*) in Figure 12.1 is therefore a stable one.

The other element of the equilibrating process is that the price of the anchor commodity adjusts 'rapidly' in response to changes in the quantity of exchange media – the price of the anchor commodity should not 'stick' at a non-par value. Assuming that this condition holds, any deviation of the quantity of exchange media from its equilibrium level would produce arbitrage opportunities that would correct the deviation, and the price of the anchor commodity would return to par in the process.

We need to be clear why the paradox does not arise under this scenario. The deviation of the price of the anchor commodity from par does produce two prices

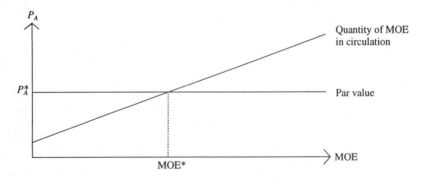

Figure 12.1   The equilibrium quantity of MOE

for the MOR, one on the market, the other at the banks, and this price differential rewards arbitragers who retire exchange media from circulation, if the quantity of them is excessive, or who put more into circulation, if the quantity already in circulation is too small. Both the paradox and anti-paradox arguments agree on this point, but the key issue is whether this price differential first arises and then persists. Assuming it does arise in the first place, the changing quantity of exchange media that results from the arbitrage operations just described presumably *must* return the price of the anchor to par provided that price is 'flexible'. Each arbitrage operation incrementally reduces the price of the anchor, and thereby reduces the profits to be made from the next such operation, and the returns from successive arbitrage operations continue to fall until the price of the anchor has returned to equilibrium and there are no further profits left. We thus get the two-way equilibrating process described in Figure 12.2, where arbitrage operations in the market for MOR restore the price of the anchor commodity to par.

The paradox argument effectively ignores the second arm of the equilibrating process – the effect of the changing quantity of exchange media on the price of the anchor commodity – by implicitly assuming that once it has moved away from par, supposing it does, the price of the anchor commodity remains stuck at a disequilibrium level, or at least persists in disequilibrium long enough to allow the paradox to come into play.[12]

If the price of the anchor is stuck at a non-par value, we also get a second result which is closely related to the paradox: there is no sensible limit to the quantity of redemptions or purchases of exchange media, and the stock of exchange media zooms off towards either zero or infinity. Since the price of the anchor commodity is effectively stuck as far as arbitragers are concerned, the optimal strategy from their point of view is to redeem all exchange media if the price of the anchor commodity is above par, and to increase the quantity of exchange media without limit if that price is below par. If the price of the anchor commodity were flexible,

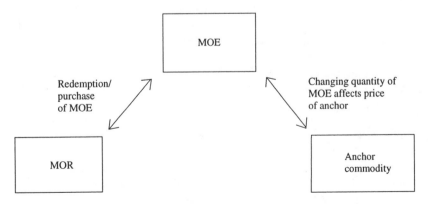

Figure 12.2   Equilibration Under Indirect Convertibility

however, marginal arbitrage profits would fall until they disappeared and the price of the anchor had returned to par. The flexibility of the price of the anchor commodity keeps down the banks' exposure to arbitrage losses and prevents excessive fluctuations in the quantities of exchange media, while an anchor commodity with a price which deviates from par and is sticky returning to it can greatly increase the banks' exposure to these losses and make the quantities of exchange media in circulation very volatile.

There is however no reason why the price of the anchor must necessarily deviate from par at all. It is possible to construct indirectly convertible systems in which the price of the anchor always remains at par, and we shall outline such a scheme in Chapter 14, once we have had a chance to discuss certain index issues that underlie it. The disequilibrium then never occurs and the paradox argument cannot apply. Since it keeps the price of the anchor always at par, such a scheme has the obvious attraction that it does not depend on the price of the anchor moving sufficiently quickly; it is therefore immune to disputes about whether or not the anchor price moves sufficiently rapidly to beat the paradox. By keeping the price of the anchor at par, it also has the attraction of ensuring that the banks are never exposed to the arbitrage losses they would suffer if the price of the anchor did deviate from par. We shall return to this scheme presently, but for present purposes it suffices merely to be aware of its possibility and note how it short-circuits the paradox mechanism.

The bottom line is that those who support the paradox argument require *both* that the price of the anchor moves away from par, *and* that it be 'sticky' returning to it. We can therefore 'beat' the paradox and make indirect convertibility feasible either by having an anchor whose price moves 'rapidly' back to par, if it should ever deviate from par, or by having one whose price never deviates from par in the first place.

Finally, it is useful to point out that the paradox and the associated problem of the demand for MOE becoming zero or infinite if the price of the anchor deviates from par are by no means unique to indirect convertibility. Paradox problems also arise under direct convertibility. Imagine that we had a directly convertible gold standard, and the market price of gold deviated from the par price maintained by the banks and was then stuck. (One might ask why it should, but we have allowed this type of conceptual experiment so far.) If the market price of gold exceeds the bank price, private operators would wish to keep selling gold to the banks to make arbitrage profits, and the demand for MOE would rise without bound. If the market price fell below the bank price, they would wish to buy gold from the banks, and the demand for MOE would fall towards zero. An outcome in which the demand for MOE goes to infinity or zero if the price of the anchor deviates from par and remains stuck at a non-par value can thus arise in a directly convertible system as well as an indirectly convertible one. The proximate cause is the same in both cases – a discrepancy between the price of the anchor in the market, and the price of the anchor at the banks – and it is this discrepancy that is at the heart of the paradox itself. The answer, in both cases, is also the same: if the system is to work either the price of the anchor must remain always at par, or it must return rapidly to it if it should move away. It would be a mistake to suppose that paradox-related problems only apply to indirectly convertible systems, or to suppose that other types of convertible systems are necessarily immune to them.[13]

CONCLUSIONS

We have two main choices if we wish to have a feasible system of convertibility. The first and most obvious is a directly convertible system. Such systems are very familiar – so much so, in fact, that we need to shake ourselves free of the danger of presuming that all convertible currencies must necessarily be directly convertible – but there is no presumption that the commodity or asset best suited to serve as anchor is also the one best suited to serving as the banks' redemption medium, and having the same commodity or asset perform both roles (usually) has the additional disadvantage of exposing the financial system to avoidable instability. The alternative is to adopt an indirectly convertible system in which the roles of MOR and anchor are separated. We found that this type of system is subject to potential paradox-related problems, but these problems can be avoided by selecting an anchor whose price returns quickly to par, or one whose price never deviates from par in the first place. But before we can explain more fully how such a scheme might work, we need to discuss certain other issues relating to the anchor itself. We therefore turn now to consider the simplest such systems, those in which the anchor is a single commodity.

Appendix: 'Real-Bills' Systems

THE ESSENCE OF THE 'REAL-BILLS' DOCTRINE AND ITS FALLACY

We now take a brief but important detour to clarify the relationship of the monetary systems discussed in the text to the *pons asinorum* of monetary economics – the notorious 'real-bills' doctrine. This doctrine

> is a rule purporting to gear money to production via the short-term commercial bill of exchange [i.e., via lending], thereby ensuring that output generates its own means of purchase and money adapts passively to the legitimate needs of trade. The doctrine states that money can never be excessive when issued against short-term commercial bills arising from real transactions in goods and services. More precisely, the doctrine contends that so long as banks lend only against sound, short-term commercial paper the money stock will be secured by and will automatically vary ... with real output such that the latter will be matched by *just enough money to purchase it at existing prices*. In other words, inflationary overissue is impossible provided money is issued on loans made to finance real transactions. (Humphrey, 1982, 3-4, my emphasis)

The attraction of the doctrine is that it purportedly allows bank lending and the supply of exchange media to vary with the 'legitimate needs of trade' and thereby ensures that sound projects are not passed over for want of finance.[14] However, the critical issue is the (false) claim made by its proponents that a real-bills policy guarantees that the price level would remain stable.

The basic argument and what is wrong with it can be illustrated by a simple example based on Humphrey (1982, 4, n.2). Suppose firms need inventories of working capital to produce current goods-in-process G. For simplicity, suppose also that the working capital needed by firms is a fixed proportion a of the value of the goods they have in process, and that firms have no working capital of their own. Each dollar's worth of G must therefore be financed by a bank loan worth a – it is traditional to think of this loan as the issue of a commercial bill to a bank, and to regard aG as representing the 'needs of trade' for loans – so the demand for bank loans, L_d, is equal to aG. These loan demands satisfy the real bills criterion (i.e., they are secured by claims to real goods, and are generated as an outcome of the 'real' production process). If banks follow the real-bills rule, they provide whatever loans are demanded:

$$L_s = L_d. \tag{12A.1}$$

Banks are assumed to supply their loans in the form of notes or demand deposits, the sum of which comprises the 'money' stock M_s. The stock of money is then equal to a times the value of the goods-in-process G:

$$M_s = L_s = aG. \tag{12A.2}$$

Recall now that G is the *nominal* value of goods-in-process, and can be decomposed into the product of the quantity of 'real' goods Q and their nominal (or dollar) price P. Hence:

$$M_s = aPQ. \tag{12A.3}$$

(12A.3) captures both the attraction of the real-bills system and its weakness. The money supply is ultimately secured by goods-in-process such that when those goods reach the market they will be matched by just enough money to purchase them at existing prices. (Humphrey, 1982, 4, n. 2)

Its attraction, consequently, is that it is *consistent* with banks issuing loans to satisfy the 'needs of trade' at existing prices, a point on which its proponents have often insisted. Its weakness, however, is fatal: the real-bills system provides *nothing* to tie prices down and is therefore consistent with *any* price level. The real-bills rule leaves *prices indeterminate, and the fact that it might be consistent with the existing price level is quite irrelevant.*
Proponents of the doctrine overlook the point that the demand for loans depends

not only upon the quantity of real transactions but also upon the level of prices at which those real transactions are effected. And rising prices would require an ever-growing volume of loans just to finance the same level of real transactions. Under the real bills criterion these loans would be granted and the stock of money would therefore expand. This monetary expansion would raise prices thereby requiring further monetary expansion leading to still higher prices and so on in a never-ending inflationary sequence. In this way, price inflation would induce the very monetary expansion necessary to perpetuate it and the real bills criterion would provide no effective limit to the quantity of money in existence. Here is the error of the real bills doctrine, namely the tendency to treat prices as given when in fact they vary directly with the monetary stock. Associated with this is the failure to perceive the two-way inflationary interaction between money and prices that results once money is allowed to be governed by the needs of trade. (Humphrey, 1982, 4)

A real-bills policy in practice is therefore likely to produce an unstable, never-ending process in which higher (lower) prices lead to higher (lower) monetary growth, and the monetary growth (contraction) contributes in turn to further inflation (deflation) with the result that prices shoot off in one direction or the other. To illustrate these dynamics, suppose that production remains constant over time but takes place with a one-period lag (i.e., production takes place one period to be sold the next). Firms' loan demand is therefore aQP_{t-1}, and the banks accommodate this demand along real bills lines:

$$M = M_s = aQP_{t-1}. \tag{12A.4}$$

We now complete the model by introducing a conventional equation of exchange to specify its demand side:

$$MV = P_t Q \tag{12A.5}$$

(see, e.g., Fisher, 1911), where V is the velocity of circulation of money which we can take for the moment as given. We rearrange this equation to put P on the left-hand side, substitute out M using (12A.4), and solve the resulting difference equation to obtain:

$$P_t = P_0(aV)^t \tag{12A.6}$$

where P_0 is the (given) initial price level. Far from maintaining a stable price level, as advocates have claimed, the real-bills policy will cause prices to rise without limit if $aV > 1$, or decline towards zero if $aV < 1$. Only in a very peculiar case – if $aV = 1$ – will the price level remain stable, but there is no reason to expect this particular case to hold since a and V are determined independently by different factors. a is determined by factors such as businessmen's desired inventory/output ratios, ... the proportion of working capital financed by bank loans, and ... the proportion of total bank loans made for working capital versus nonworking capital purposes. (Humphrey, 1982, 5, n. 3)

V, by contrast, is determined by real income, interest rates, wage rates and the various other factors which influence the demand for real balances. It would be an unlikely coincidence if their product happened to equal 1, but even if this coincidence did occur, we could not realistically expect a and V to remain constant and equal to each other indefinitely, and a time would come when the price level would move off in one direction or the other.

The advocates of the real-bills doctrine thus fail to realise that tying the quantity of money to the 'legitimate needs of trade' is insufficient[15] to tie down the price level because the needs of trade is itself a nominal variable which moves with the price level. Monetary expansion raises prices, and the rising prices increase needs of trade, and the higher needs of trade leads to further monetary expansion in a never-ending inflationary process (see also, e.g., Thornton, [1802] (1978); Mints, 1945). Monetary contraction, on the other hand, leads to a falling price level, falling needs of trade, and further never-ending deflation. To quote Humphrey again,

because it ties the money supply to a nominal magnitude that moves in step with prices, the real bills doctrine provides no effective constraint on money or prices, both of which can rise [or fall] without limit ... Here is the fallacy of using one uncontrolled nominal variable (the money value of real transactions) to regulate another nominal variable (the money stock). This is the fundamental fallacy of the real bills doctrine. (Humphrey, 1982, 5)

ADDITIONAL PROBLEMS WITH THE DOCTRINE

If the fundamental weakness of the doctrine is the error of supposing that one uncontrolled nominal variable can be used to control another, it is by no means the only error made by its proponents. Arguments for real bills policies also involve two other serious errors:

1. The volume of eligible bills, or the demand for loans, depends not only on the quantity of goods produced, as proponents of the doctrine have often maintained, but also on their turnover, and the maturity of the loans. Adam Smith[16] and Henry Thornton pointed out clearly that the same goods might be sold a number of times, with each sale giving rise to another real bill – which, incidentally, also makes it very difficult in practice for a bank to distinguish a genuine 'real' bill from a 'fictitious' one. Thornton also pointed out that the quantity of real bills might exceed the quantity of goods which provide the security for them because the period for which a bill is drawn might exceed the turnover period of the goods. To borrow an example from Thornton, suppose that A sells a dollar's worth of goods to B, and B pays by issuing a six-months bill. A month later, B sells the goods to C, and C issues him a six-months bill. A month later, C sells the goods to D, who issues another six-months bill, and so on. After six months there would be \$6 in eligible bills, but only \$1 in goods to secure them. If the maturity of the bills were 12 months instead of 6, then there would be \$12 in eligible bills after a year, and so forth. The maximum volume of eligible bills is therefore mGt, where m is their maturity, t the rate of goods turnover, and G, as before, the quantity of goods produced (Humphrey, 1982, 9). The volume of eligible bills thus depends on the turnover of goods and the maturity of bills as well as the volume of goods, and increasing the first two factors can lead to virtually any volume of bills on the basis of any given quantity of

real goods. It is thus a serious error to suppose that each real bill is secured by a separate bundle of real goods or, indeed, that a real-bills policy would limit issues of money to whatever one considers the legitimate needs of trade to be.

2. Advocates of the real-bills doctrine also overlook the point that the demand for loans is not given, but depends on factors such as the rate of interest on loans. In particular, they overlook the point that the demand for loans can become insatiable if the loan rate of interest is held below the expected rate of profit on new investment. Thornton ([1802] 1978) and Wicksell (1907) both explained how such a differential would create a cumulative process of rising money and prices which would only end once the differential itself was eliminated. Following Humphrey (1982, 10, n. 18), imagine that loan demand is a function of this differential

$$\Delta L_d = f(\pi - r) \tag{12A.7}$$

where π is the profit rate, r the loan rate, and $f'(\ ) > 0$. We can think of loan demand expanding because ΔL_d additional projects are profitable at the differential $\pi - r$. These additional loan demands translate into additional real bills which banks accommodate by issuing more money:

$$\Delta L_d = \Delta M_s. \tag{12A.8}$$

If prices P rise with the increased stock of money, it follows that:

$$\Delta P = f(\pi - r). \tag{12A.9}$$

The differential between the profit rate and the loan rate causes the price level to rise, and the price level *keeps rising* for as long as this differential persists. The differential thus causes a *continuous* and not just a *one-time* increase in the demand for loans, the money stock and the price level, and these variables only stop rising once profit and interest rates are brought back together again. In Wicksell's (1907) well-known analogy, the price level behaves like a cylinder on a flat surface: a discrepancy between π and r gives it a push, and it keeps moving for as long as the discrepancy persists. It stabilises once the discrepancy has gone, but shows no tendency to revert to any previous historical level.

THE REAL-BILLS DOCTRINE, CONVERTIBILITY, AND FREE BANKING

The failure of the real-bills doctrine to tie down the price level highlights the need for some other rule to achieve that purpose, and the most suitable type of rule is a convertibility rule with a real commodity anchor.[17] If the relative price of the anchor against goods and services is k, say, and its nominal price is \$1, the equilibrium price level is:

$$P = 1/k \tag{12A.10}$$

which the banks take as given. Convertibility with a commodity anchor thus produces a determinate price level. The equation of exchange then implies that the money stock is:

$$M = PQ/V = Q/(kV). \tag{12A.11}$$

The supply of money is determined by the demand to hold it (i.e., by V), and banks have no discretionary control over it. These conditions also constrain bank lending via the banks' balance sheet constraints, and therefore imply that banks can only satisfy the 'needs of trade' to a limited extent.[18]

If agents are averse to price-level instability, the foregoing implies that they would prefer a convertible system to any other one since convertibility would generate the price-level behaviour they most wanted. Provided they had the freedom to choose, they would patronise banks which offered the convertibility guarantees they desired, and banks that offered inferior guarantees, or none at all, would lose their market share. The competition for market share would therefore force banks to satisfy the public's demands for convertibility. *Free banking thus implies a commodity- based convertible system.* Given the public preference for price stability or, at least, predictability (see Chapter 15 in this volume), free banking therefore *could not* produce any inconvertible monetary system, including any real-bills one. *Free banking and the real-bills doctrine are mutually exclusive.*[19] It also follows that a *necessary* condition for the establishment of a real-bills system is the *suppression* of free banking to eliminate the convertibility guarantee that would otherwise rule out any kind of real-bills policy. It is consequently no accident that historical attempts to implement or justify real-bills policies – those of John Law,[20] the Bank of England directors during the Restriction,[21] the Federal Reserve in its early years,[22] the Reichsbank during the German hyperinflation of the early 1920s,[23] and more recent attempts to target interest or unemployment rates[24] – have all occurred in a context where free banking was suppressed and there was little or no convertibility discipline to restrain over- issue.

13 Monometallic, Bimetallic and Related Monetary Standards*

This chapter and Chapter 14 consider *commodity-based monetary standards*, i.e., monetary standards in which the value of the unit of account is tied by some rule to specific quantities of one or more 'real' commodities. However, before we can discuss such systems, we need first to clarify what the term monetary standard actually means. Too many writers launch off into detailed discussions of *particular* monetary standards without ever specifying what a monetary standard *as such* actually is. As Mason wrote in his *Clarification of the Monetary Standard* (1963), the concept of the monetary standard

> has been almost entirely neglected in modern literature. Dictionaries and encyclopedias completely ignore [it] ... Even writers who prefaced their treatment of monetary standards with a purported delineation of basic concepts typically ignore *the* basic concept. (Mason, 1963, 3–4, his emphasis)

The result is a bewildering variety of confusing and indistinguishable standards, a confusion further aggravated by the failure to distinguish standards proper from monetary policies and objectives. As a result, even 'experts often cannot even individually decide, much less collectively agree, as to what it is they are talking about' (1963, 6) and fundamental questions are 'left unanswered and unanswerable' (1963, 7):

> The inconclusiveness of the interminable arguments on these questions is too well known to need laboring. But the fundamental reason has apparently escaped detection. The difficulty, as usual, is in the premises, which are seldom explicit and often sunk in the subconscious. The monetary standard means different things to different people. These issues can never be resolved until it is realized that the genus monetary standard must be established before the species can be identified ...
>
> What the 'money muddle' cries out for is a concept of a monetary standard sufficiently precise, reasonable, and realistic to permit isolation of the phenomenon and identification of its species. Achievement of this objective would enable us to distinguish the issues of substance from those of terminology. (Mason, 1963, 7)

If the monetary standard can be defined as the set of rules governing the value of the

*Part of this chapter draws heavily from 'The Analytics of Bimetallism', forthcoming, *Manchester School*.

unit of account, we can define commodity-based monetary standards (or commodity monetary standards, for short) as that class of monetary standard in which the nominal price of one or more real commodities is fixed. To give an example, under the old British gold standard the price of an ounce of gold was fixed at £3 17s 10^1/$_2$d by the Bank of England which stood ready to buy and sell at that price on demand. More generally, the price of the anchor commodity could be allowed to vary, but it would have to vary in accordance with the relevant price-setting rule. A system in which the price of gold was fixed at time 0 and thereafter grew by 3 percent a year would consequently be as much a commodity standard as the traditional gold standard. Once the nominal price of the anchor commodity is given, the relative price of that commodity can vary if and only if the price level itself varies – for any given nominal price, the relative price of the anchor commodity can only rise if the price level falls, and vice versa – so the problem of determining the price-level and the problem of determining the relative price of the anchor commodity are the mirror images of one another. We can thus assess how the price-level changes by taking the nominal price of the anchor as given and then examining how its relative price changes in response to exogenous developments.

A commodity standard is to be distinguished from other standards variously described in the literature as *fiat, inconvertible, irredeemable* or *fiduciary standards* which do not as such involve any price-fixing (or, put another way, have no anchor). There are many treatments of these monetary standards, but most are unsatisfactory because they lack any adequate notion of a monetary standard to work with. To quote Mason again,

> Its (their) characteristics cannot be described – cannot even be listed – because the absence of a generic concept of a monetary standard means that there is practically no limit to the variety of attributes that this (these) monetary arrangement(s) – for lack of a better term ... – may display. Textbook writers – those courageous souls who must deal resolutely with unsolved problems – are forced to reverse their technique and treat this range of phenomena negatively. In short, they simply admit that a noncommodity standard does not possess the characteristics of commodity standards – a truism that sometimes takes several pages to demonstrate. The basic methodological defect that accounts for the prevailing confusion is the attempt to identify the species before the genus. (Mason, 1963, 5)

Non-commodity monetary standards – that is to say, anchorless monetary standards – were relatively rare until this century, and were usually associated with the 'fiscal exigencies' of war. For example, the UK operated on an inconvertible standard during the French Revolutionary and Napoleonic Wars from 1797 until 1821, and the USA from 1861 to 1879 as a response to the Civil War and its aftermath. However, they have become the norm following the collapse of the Bretton Woods system of fixed exchange rates in the early 1970s. Since they lack any anchor, there is no commodity (or commodity basket) whose price is fixed, and so, unlike the case under a commodity standard, the price level is not tied to the relative price of *any* commodity. This in turn means that we cannot analyse price-level movements under a non-commodity standard as changes in any relative commodity price; instead, the price level is best thought of as determined along quantity-theoretic lines as suggested, for example, by Friedman (1956). But we shall come back to these systems later.

The basic taxonomy of monetary standards discussed here is outlined in Figure 13.1. The genus (i.e., the monetary standard) is the set of rules governing the value of the unit of account. It divides into two classes – commodity and non-commodity standards – where a commodity standard is identified by the pegging of the price of one or more commodity (or service, or appropriate financial instrument), and a non- commodity standard is any other. Commodity standards can then be subdivided into those in which the price of *one* good is fixed at any point in time – these include those standards in which there is only one anchor (e.g., a gold standard), but also those in which there is more than one anchor (e.g., bimetallism) – and those in which the price of some *basket* of goods is fixed, but the prices of *individual* goods are still free to alter. We discuss the former in this chapter, and the latter in Chapter 14. Non-commodity standards can be subdivided in many ways, but the most important distinction is between those in which the price level is determinate, and those in which it is not (i.e., 'real-bills' systems). The former are discussed in Chapter 16, and the latter have already been discussed, in the appendix to Chapter 12.

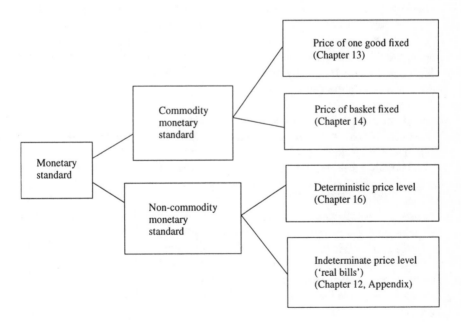

Figure 13.1   Taxonomy of monetary systems

The definition of a commodity standard in terms of a price-fixing rule differs somewhat from the traditional definition (e.g., Friedman, 1953, 205) of such a system as one where people use as exchange media either real commodities or paper liabilities issued by financial institutions that themselves use commodities as media of redemption – that is, they define a commodity system as one in which there is a positive 'monetary' demand for one or more real commodities.[1] While any definition is arbitrary, this traditional definition is less helpful because it excludes indirectly convertible standards which exhibit many of the same price-level properties as commodity systems with a positive monetary demand for the standard commodity. If the price of gold is fixed there is very little difference between a system where the monetary demand for gold is very small and one where it is zero – in particular, the price level is determined in an almost identical way – and yet the traditional definition would regard the former as a gold standard and the latter as something quite different. At the same time, the definition adopted here encompasses all historical systems traditionally referred to as commodity systems since it includes all non-trivial systems where there is a positive monetary demand for some commodity. What is required is a definition that encompasses the historical systems just referred to, but is also broad enough to cover the indirectly convertible systems that the traditional definition excludes.

There are many types of commodity standards to choose from. Apart from the gold standard which enjoyed worldwide hegemony for a generation or so in the later nineteenth and early twentieth centuries, there are also a number of instances of *silver standards* based on silver rather than gold anchors. There have also been standards based on other metals (e.g., copper), and there have been proposals for others which have not yet been tried (e.g., a *brick standard*). Besides systems based on only one commodity, there have also been *bimetallic standards* in which the price of gold *and* the price of silver were *both* fixed in unit-of-account terms, and debts could be discharged by means of payment valued in terms of whichever of these two metals the debtor chose. Though largely forgotten by now, bimetallic systems operated in the western world for centuries, and they are arguably more important historically than the gold standard that replaced them (see, e.g., Friedman, 1990a,1990b). The underlying principle of the bimetallic system can be extended to cover three or more metals, and it can be extended further to encompass commodities other than metals and systems where the creditor rather than the debtor has the right to choose the commodity used to value payments. The systems mentioned so far all have in common the property that there is at least one commodity whose nominal price is fixed at any given time, but one can also envision commodity systems where *individual* prices are all free to vary but a price *average* is fixed. However, these latter schemes – *basket-based* ones – give rise to very different analytical issues than do monometallic, bimetallic and related systems, so it makes sense to discuss them separately. The gold, bimetallic and similar systems are therefore discussed in this chapter, and the basket schemes in Chapter 14.

THE GOLD STANDARD

Despite a vast literature on the subject, our understanding of the gold standard (or any other monocommodity standard) is still relatively limited.[2] To explore it further, we need a formal model, and perhaps the easiest way to obtain one is to build a model of the gold market under the assumptions that the nominal price of gold is fixed and that the supply of gold grows at an exogenous rate. The fixed nominal price of gold characterises the model as one of a gold standard, and we can think of the price level under the gold standard as if it were determined by demand and supply in the gold market because the gold-standard price level moves inversely with the relative price of gold. We can then use the model to examine the effects on the price level of exogenous changes such as gold discoveries, technological progress in gold mining, increases in income, changes in the rate of secular economic growth, changes in the interest rate, and changes in monetary and non-monetary demands for gold. We can also analyse the impact of changes in the banking and exchange technologies that drive the monetary demand for gold. Among other things, it therefore allows us to examine the process by which secular progress causes the monetary demand for progress causes the monetary demand for gold to fall and eventually lead a directly convertible gold standard to give way to an indirectly convertible one. And, though it is initially couched in terms of the gold standard, the model can easily be adapted to analyse other monocommodity standards as well.

Of course, the model has its limitations. Ideally, we would like to endogenise the supply of gold and start from an optimisation exercise in which the gold mining problem is solved explicitly. However, such an exercise makes the analysis difficult and relatively little is lost in practice by taking the short cut of an exogenous gold supply. In any case, given that gold is durable, most of the currently existing stock was produced in previous periods, and this pre-existing stock is necessarily perfectly inelastic in supply. Since current gold output only amounts to a small fraction of the current gold stock – no more than about 2–4 percent – the overall supply elasticity of gold would still be very low even if current gold output were elastic, which is arguable anyway. We can therefore treat the supply of gold as being at least approximately exogenous.[3] A second limitation of the model is that it treats the non-gold sector and all prices other than the relative price (and rental) of gold as given. There is however no obvious need to endogenise the non-gold sector, and a partial equilibrium treatment makes the analysis considerably more tractable.

The Model

Suppose gold is demanded by identical households who are each sufficiently small to be considered price-takers. These households live for many periods, but their utility functions are separable such that each first chooses expenditures for each period, and then decides how to allocate that period's expenditures between different goods. We therefore treat the first stage as given and assume that a household has already chosen its total expenditures $Y(t)$ for each period t, where $t = T, T + 1, ...$ In each period, a household maximises a utility function:

$$U(t) = G_n(t)^a C(t)^b \; ; \; a, b > 0 \; ; \; a + b = 1 \qquad (13.1)$$

where $U(t)$ is its utility, $C(t)$ its consumption of goods other than gold, and $G_n(t)$ the household's non-monetary stock of gold, all in period t. (Strictly speaking, it is the flow of gold services rather than the stock of gold *per se* that enters into the utility function, but if we assume that the former varies directly with the latter we can write the utility function 'as if' it depended on the gold stock, as in (13.1).) The gold rental $r_g(t)$ over t is:

$$r_g(t) = p_g(t) - [1/(1 + R)]p_g(t + 1) > 0 \qquad (13.2)$$

where $p_g(t)$ is the relative price of gold against commodities in general over t and R is the real rate of interest which is assumed to be the same in all periods. Since the nominal price of gold is fixed, $p_g(t)$ moves inversely with the general price level $p(t)$ and all results about the relative price of gold can be translated directly (but with opposite signs) into statements about the general price level.

The household also faces a transactions technology that generates a monetary demand for gold. In particular, the household is assumed to spend a given proportion d of its income each period on monetary gold holdings:

$$r_g(t)G_m(t) / Y(t) = d \; ; \quad 0 \le d < 1. \qquad (13.3)$$

The parameter d enables us to examine the effects of the monetary demand for gold, with a positive value of d indicating a directly convertible gold standard, and a value of d equal to zero indicating an indirectly convertible one. The move towards an indirectly convertible gold standard can then be analysed by letting d fall towards zero. Our household now allocates its total expenditures each period $Y(t)$, selects its monetary holdings according to (13.3), and maximises utility (13.1) subject to the budget constraint:

$$(1 - d) Y(t) = r_g(t) G_n(t) + p_c(t) C_j(t). \qquad (13.4)$$

The non-monetary demand for gold is then:

$$G_n(t) = a(1 - d) Y(t) / r_g(t) \qquad (13.5)$$

and the total demand for gold is:

$$G(t) = G_n(t) + G_m(t) = [a(1 - d) + d] Y(t) / r_g(t). \qquad (13.6)$$

Using (13.6) and rearranging,

$$p_g(t) = [a(1 - d) + d]Y(t)/ G(t) + [1/(1 + R)]p_g(t + 1). \qquad (13.7)$$

We now substitute out $p_g(t + 1)$ by leading (13.7) one period and substituting the resulting expression into (13.7). We then get rid of $p_g(t + 2)$ by leading (13.7) two periods and substituting that expression into (13.7), and we carry on in this way for all future relative gold prices. Assuming that $Y(t)$ and $G(t)$ grow at constant rates, we can replace $Y(t+1)$ with $Y(t)(1+\Delta Y)$, $G(t+1)$ with $G(t)(1+\Delta G)$, etc., and end up with:

$$p_g(t) = [a(1-d) + d]\{1 + [(1+\Delta Y)(1+\Delta G)^{-1}(1+R)^{-1}]+$$
$$[(1+\Delta Y)(1+\Delta G)^{-1}(1+R)^{-1}]^2 + \ldots \}Y(t)/G(t). \qquad (13.8)$$

Providing $[(1+\Delta Y)(1+\Delta G)^{-1}(1+R)^{-1}] < 1$ – which is not unreasonable in any case – we then solve for the relative price of gold:

$$p_g(t) = [a(1-d) + d]\{[(1+R)(1+\Delta G)]/$$
$$[(1+R)(1+\Delta G) - (1+\Delta Y)]\}Y(t)/G(t). \qquad (13.9)$$

The elasticities of the relative price of gold with respect to the exogenous variables can now be derived by partial differentiation. If we now calculate these elasticities and invert their signs, we get the relevant price-level elasticities listed in Table 13.1, where $\eta(p(t), a)$ is the elasticity of $p(t)$ with respect to a, and so on.

The first condition, (a), states that the elasticity of the price level with respect to the non-monetary demand for gold, a, is negative but no less than -1. The price level thus falls with a. (b) states that the elasticity of $p(t)$ with respect to the monetary demand for gold, d, is negative, provided that d itself is positive; however, as d approaches zero, the elasticity also approaches zero. The elasticity of the price level with respect to d is therefore negative, but it approaches zero as d does. (c) states that the elasticity of the price level with respect to real income is -1, implying that an increase in real income reduces the price level *pari passu*. Since a, d and $Y(t)$ are each demand-side parameters, these first three conditions tell us that higher gold demand causes the price level to fall. This outcome makes sense because the stock of gold is given and the only way the market can accommodate an increase in the demand for gold is by means of an increase in its relative price, and, hence, a decrease in the price level.

Table 13.1 Elasticity Results for the Price Level Under the Gold Standard

	elasticity	value and bounds, if any
(a)	$\eta(p(t), a)$	$-1 \leq -a(1-d)/[a(1-d)+d] < 0$
(b)	$\eta(p(t), d)$	$-1 < -d(1-a)/[a(1-d)+d] \leq 0$
(c)	$\eta(p(t), Y(t))$	-1
(d)	$\eta(p(t), G(t))$	1
(e)	$\eta(p(t), 1+R)$	$(1+\Delta Y)/[(1+R)(1+\Delta G) - (1+\Delta Y)] > 0$
(f)	$\eta(p(t), 1+\Delta G)$	$(1+\Delta Y)/[(1+R)(1+\Delta G) - (1+\Delta Y)] > 0$
(g)	$\eta(p(t), 1+\Delta Y)$	$-(1+\Delta Y)/[(1+R)(1+\Delta G) - (1+\Delta Y)] < 0$

The fourth result, (d), tells us that the price level rises one-for-one with the gold stock. However, this one-for-one effect only arises because we have assumed the gold supply to be exogenous. Once we drop this 'helicopter assumption', the marginal cost of producing gold starts to play a major role and we would not expect this 'quantity theory' to hold in its strict form (see also Niehans, 1978, 147–148). Nonetheless, we still get the qualitative prediction that a discovery of gold ore leads to a rise in the price level (see, e.g., Dowd and Sampson, 1993a, 387–388). This prediction also makes intuitive sense: if the stock of gold rises, and demand remains the same, then the relative price of gold must fall, and it can only do so if the price level rises.

The fifth result, (e), states that the elasticity of the price level with respect to the real interest rate, R, is positive; there is a positive association between real interest and the price level (i.e., there is a *Gibson paradox*). This result arises because a higher real interest rate raises the rental cost of holding gold, and hence reduces the demand to hold it; since the stock of gold is given, the gold market can then only equilibrate if the relative price of gold falls and the price level rises.

(f) states that the price level rises as the rate of growth of the gold stock rises. Intuitively, a faster rate of growth of the gold stock implies that the relative price of gold is lower in the future than it would otherwise be. The rental cost of gold is therefore higher, and the higher rental causes a reduction in the demand to hold gold. The relative price of gold therefore falls, and the price level rises.

The last result, (g), indicates that economic growth decreases the price level. It thus supports the widely-held view (see, e.g., Barro, 1979 or Bordo and Ellson, 1985) that economic growth under the gold standard tends to produce secular deflation. Note however that it tells us that a rise in the economic growth rate reduces the price level quite apart from the effects of any once and for all changes in $Y(t)$ itself. This result arises because an increase in the rate of economic growth raises the rate of growth of the relative price of gold, and the latter in turn reduces the gold rental, increases the demand for gold, and therefore lowers the price level.

Perhaps the most significant conclusion overall is that there is no particular reason to expect a gold standard to produce price-level stability. What these results tell us is that the path of the price level over time under a gold standard is the outcome of a balance of forces operating in the gold market, and it could rise, fall or remain stable over any given period depending on the relative strengths of these competing forces. Any factors that increase the demand for gold, such as increases in a, d, $Y(t)$, or ΔY, will push the price level down, whereas discoveries of gold ore, improvements in the technology of gold mining, and increases in interest rates, will push the price level up.

Secular Change in the Monetary Demand for Gold and the Resource Costs of the Gold Standard

The model also sheds light on various other aspects of the gold standard. One such issue is the impact of secular change in the monetary/financial system on the price level. As the economy emerges from barter, people start demanding gold not for its own sake, but for the sake of the commodities they can obtain for it (i.e., they start to demand gold for monetary purposes), and the proportion of their income spent on monetary gold, d, gradually rises. At the same time, real income, $Y(t)$, is also rising, so both components of the overall monetary demand for gold, $dY(t)$, are rising. Later, people start experimenting with paper substitutes issued by reputable middlemen such as goldsmiths; and these paper substitutes make up an increasing proportion of the circulating medium as the financial system becomes more sophisticated. d then starts to fall. $Y(t)$ nonetheless continues to grow, and for a while the overall monetary demand continues to increase as the growth in $Y(t)$ outweighs the effect of the falling d. However, the increase in the overall monetary demand for gold slows down and a point comes where it stops altogether, and thereafter the effect on it of the decline in d more than outweighs the effect of the continued growth in $Y(t)$. The overall monetary demand for metals then continues to decline until the only monetary demand left is the bankers' demand for 'till money' with which to meet occasional demands for redemption. (Remember that public confidence in the banks is founded on their general capital position and not on their reserve ratios as such. The main reason for holding any gold at all is to reduce the transactions costs of having to obtain it at short notice.) We then arrive at a gold standard with an almost zero monetary demand for gold – a gold standard with near zero reserves, as Black (1987, 114) calls it – and even the little remaining monetary demand will disappear if the agents involved come to regard gold as an inefficient redemption medium and switch over to something else instead. The gold standard becomes indirectly convertible and the only 'monetary' function of gold is to provide an anchor for the unit of account. This story tells us that the monetary demand for gold will have profound effects on the price level over the course of the gold standard's evolution. The initial rise in d in the early years of the gold standard will drive down the price level, but the subsequent fall in d in the mature gold standard will push prices back up again: secular progress in the underlying monetary/financial system is first deflationary and then inflationary.

These secular developments have important implications for the so-called 'resource costs' of operating the gold standard – the opportunity cost of the monetary holdings of gold. In the model outlined earlier, these costs are given by the monetary holdings of gold. These costs therefore rise in the earlier stages of development, but they fall in later stages and in the limit become trivial. The old and still widely-accepted argument (e.g., by Fischer, 1986a, 21, 25–26 and others) that the gold standard involves significant resource costs is consequently mistaken, at least as it applies to a mature financial system, since it fallaciously presumes that a gold standard requires a 'significant' monetary demand for gold. Resources costs are more important in an immature financial system, but even in that case there is still no presumption that the resource costs incurred are necessarily inefficient. Given the state of technology and mutual trust, the agents involved choose to pay those resource costs for the sake of the reassurance they bring. At any point in time while the financial system is still maturing, it is always physically possible for agents to cut down on the resource costs they incur (e.g., by using more paper exchange media, or by banks cutting down on their metallic reserves), but cutting down on such expenditures is itself costly (e.g., agents find it difficult to get banknotes accepted in trade, and banks are insufficiently safe) and these other costs must also be taken into account. As discussed elsewhere (see, e.g., Chapter 8, and the last section of this chapter), there is no obvious way in which these resource costs can be dispensed with while still retaining the reassurance benefits they bring, and the fact that agents are willing to pay these costs even though they could choose not to suggests that the outcome cannot be improved upon given the current state of development of the financial system. There is therefore no presumption of inefficiency even where resource costs are still significant.

Implications of the Model for the Development of the Historical Gold Standard

The model also sheds light on the historical gold standard and can be used to give some indication of the outcome of certain counterfactual experiments, the most obvious being what would happened if the gold standard had not been abandoned. Since the model does *not* predict that prices should be stable under the gold standard, it suggests that whatever price-level stability it *did* achieve was the product of a balance between relatively even matched inflationary and deflationary forces. Making for inflation were periodic gold discoveries, technological progress in mining, and secular progress in the monetary and financial systems, each of which was helping to push the demand for gold down. On the other hand, economic growth, the increase in the demand for gold resulting from the switch from bimetallism to the gold standard in late 1860s and afterwards, and the growth of government-imposed gold reserve requirements were each making for deflation. The extent to which these forces apparently balanced each other over the long run was almost certainly an historical accident, and there is no particular reason to believe that they would have continued to produce long-run price stability had the pre-1914 gold standard been allowed to operate after that date without disruption. The apparent acceleration of economic growth and the growth of government and central bank stockpiles of gold after the First World War would presumably have strengthened the deflationary forces further, to be offset by the continued decline in private-sector monetary holdings of gold. The likely outcome would have been a prolonged deflation, and prices would probably have continued to be low, if not falling, until such time as the national monetary authorities realised the futility of stockpiling gold for 'monetary' purposes and decided to sell it. The relative price of gold would then have fallen to the point where the former monetary holdings of gold were absorbed in non-monetary uses – that is to say, the relative price of gold would have collapsed – and brought about a very sharp rise in the price level in the process. Far from offering further price-level stability, a continuation of the gold standard would probably have produced a long spell of deflation that eventually culminated in a sudden and severe inflation once monetary gold stocks were finally disposed of.

The Historical Experience of the Gold Standard

We now consider the actual historical experience of the gold standard. Perhaps the most clear-cut stylised fact about the historical gold standard is the very considerable degree of long-run price stability it exhibited. Hayek (1960, 329) observed that

> During the two hundred years preceding 1914, when Great Britain adhered to the gold standard, the price level, so far as it can be meaningfully measured over such a period, fluctuated around a constant level, ending up pretty well where it started.[4]

Bordo (1984, 211) finds that UK prices declined by an average of 0.4 percent a year from 1821 when Britain formally established the gold standard to 1914 when it left it on the outbreak of the First World War. He also finds that US prices declined by an average of 0.14 percent a year from the time when the USA switched to a *de facto* gold standard in 1834 to 1913 (1984, 214).[5] Similar figures are presented by Schwartz (1986, Table 2.1) and others. In short, there is very strong evidence for *long-run* price-level stability under the historical gold standard.

The evidence is less clear-cut on whether the price level was also stable in the short run. Bordo points out that

> periods of declining price levels alternated with periods of rising price levels ... Prices fell until the mid-1840s ... Following the California and Australian gold discoveries of the late 1840s and early 1850s, prices turned around and kept rising until the late 1860s. This was followed by a twenty-five year period of declining prices ... This deflation ended after technical advances in gold processing and major gold discoveries in the late 1880s and 1890s increased world gold supplies. (Bordo, 1984, 211)

Some indication of the short-run variability of prices can be gauged from comparing the standard deviations of price-level changes during and after the gold standard. The standard deviation of annual price change for the UK was 6.20 for 1821–1913 and 12.0 for the period 1919–1979, excluding 1939–1945. Comparable figures for the USA were 6.29 for the period 1834–1913, excluding 1838–1843 and 1861–1879, and 9.28 for the period 1919–1979, excluding 1941–1945 (Bordo, 1984, 218–219, n. 40). Additional evidence is also provided by Schwartz (1986, Table 2.1) who finds that the standard deviation of annual price change for the UK over the period 1870-1914 was 4.6, as compared with 6.2 for the period 1946–1979, with corresponding figures for the USA of 5.4 and 4.8 respectively. Overall, these figures suggest that the price level might have been less volatile during the gold standard than it was afterwards, but we cannot be sure, and even if it was, the difference in price volatility during and after the gold standard was far less than a straight comparison of average inflation rates might otherwise have led one to expect. There is also some evidence that prices during the gold standard might have been less predictable than they have been since (e.g., Meltzer, 1986, 141).

There is also some evidence in favour of a Gibson paradox. Economists have long suspected a correlation between interest rates and prices, and most formal studies that have examined the issue have found evidence in favour of a Gibson paradox under the gold standard (e.g., Lee and Petruzzi, 1986; Barsky and Summers, 1988; Mills, 1990; Dowd and Sampson, 1993b). The Gibson paradox appears therefore to be a fairly well-established feature of the historical gold standard.

OTHER MONOCOMMODITY STANDARDS

Monocommodity standards can of course also be based on other commodities. An obvious alternative is silver. Except for a couple of small differences (e.g., relating to the relative suitabilities of the two metals for high- and low-valued exchanges; see, e.g., Redish, 1990), a silver standard functions in many respects like a gold one.

Another possibility is a *brick standard*. For obvious reasons bricks are not particularly suitable as exchange media, but the originator of the brick standard, Charles Hardy, also suggested that people might overcome this problem by using warehouse claims to bricks instead (see, e.g., Friedman 1953, 212–213; Buchanan, 1962, 172–179; and Burstein, 1986, 48–49). The major advantage of the brick standard, according to Hardy, was that the supply of bricks is very elastic – a decline (rise) in the price level would stimulate a large increase (decrease) in the output of bricks that would reduce (increase) their relative price and bring the price level back up (down) – and Friedman (1953, 213) concluded that

> There is real merit in Hardy's contention that the chief defect of the brick standard is simply the impossibility of getting anyone to think seriously of bricks as money.

There are nonetheless two major defects with this proposal, one easily remedial and the other less so:

- The easily remedial one is that it envisions that even if there is a paper medium of exchange, bricks should be used as redemption media and the issuers of exchange media should observe a 100 percent reserve ratio. The Hardy brick standard is therefore open to the usual objections against any system based on a 100 percent reserve ratio – reserve costs would be very high, and the issuers of exchange media would have to charge fees to cover their storage costs. These problems could be ameliorated to some extent by dropping the 100 percent reserve requirement, but bricks would still be the redemption medium and it is doubtful, to say the least, that they are the most suitable commodities to use for that purpose. The obvious remedy would be to have an indirectly convertible brick standard and dispense altogether with the monetary demand for bricks.

- The other defect is that the Hardy elasticity argument confuses the supply of *newly-produced* bricks with the *total* supply of bricks. The supply of newly-produced bricks may be highly elastic, but as we have already discussed with reference to the gold standard, even highly elastic production does not necessarily produce an elastic total supply when the commodity in question is highly durable. If most of the current supply consists of bricks that were produced earlier, an elastic current output does not necessarily make the overall supply elastic. Furthermore, the durability of bricks – and indeed, the durability of gold or silver – also leads to a ratchet effect. Whatever elasticity the supply might have in an upward direction, durability imposes a constraint that severely reduces, to put it mildly, its downward elasticity of supply. For both these reasons – because bricks are durable, and because of this ratchet effect, which itself arises from bricks' durability – the supply of bricks would be much less elastic than the advocates of a brick standard have hitherto suggested. This defect should be kept in perspective, nonetheless, and it might well be that the supply of bricks is still more elastic overall than the supply of gold, and this conclusion would be reinforced if, as seems plausible, the proportion of the outstanding stock of bricks 'used up' in production is greater than the proportion of gold similarly 'used up'. It might also be an advantage, from a price-level stability perspective, that bricks are made from a non-exhaustible primary input (i.e., clay) rather than from an exhaustible input such as gold ore. In short, the brick standard has its problems, but it might still be preferable to a gold standard.

The anchor commodities considered so far have all been highly durable, and we have seen that durability creates a supply inelasticity that might be regarded as undermining the stability of the relative price of the commodity concerned. If we are concerned about price-level stability, we might therefore prefer a less durable anchor commodity. Two broad options then suggest themselves – agricultural commodities or raw materials. These commodities are relatively perishable in use – food and oil are consumed, for instance – but they have varying degrees of durability in storage – certain agricultural products deteriorate quickly, but others do not. There is however not much point picking a perishable anchor commodity (or one which is expensive to store) if one has a directly convertible monetary standard. The very fact that the anchor is perishable (or costly to store) makes it expensive (and perhaps unsuitable in other ways) for use as an MOR. If we are to pick a perishable anchor, we must therefore do so in the context of an indirectly convertible system. If we are to pick a more durable commodity, on the other hand, we must also wonder what advantage that commodity would have as an anchor over other durable commodities such as gold or bricks. We must also bear in mind that these other commodities have quirks of their own. Agricultural commodities exhibit pronounced seasonality, and their supply tends to be very dependent on fluctuations in external factors like the weather. Their relative prices are consequently very volatile, both over the year and from one year to the next. Raw materials are generally less prone to seasonal factors, but casual observation suggests that their demand and supply are also relatively volatile – both demand and supply are often very cyclical, for example – and neither are easy to predict in the longer run. It is therefore questionable how much price-level stability we could get from a monocommodity monetary standard based on any of these commodities.

THE BIMETALLIC STANDARD

We now leave monocommodity systems and consider bimetallism. A bimetallic monetary standard is one in which the unit of account has a fixed legal value in terms of either of two metals – gold and silver, say – and the debtor has the choice of which metal to use to value the payments media with which he settles his debts. Bimetallism was the dominant monetary system in the world for centuries until it was superseded by the gold standard in the late nineteenth century. There were fierce controversies over it at the time, but bimetallism was subsequently almost forgotten, and relatively little has been written about it for many years.[6] Few modern economists have thought much about it, and most seem to take for granted that it is demonstrably inferior to the gold standard that replaced it. The extent to which knowledge and understanding of bimetallism has been lost over the years is illustrated by Friedman, who notes that few textbooks

> even mention bimetallism ... typically taking it for granted that a gold standard is the only kind of commodity standard that needs to be mentioned. I have examined seven popular monetary and macroeconomics texts, dated from 1968 to 1986. Only two mention a bimetallic standard, and only the earliest has any reasoned discussion of its advantages and disadvantages and that in a footnote .... I have also examined seven texts on American economic history, dated from 1964 to 1987 ... [and] the most recent, and I understand also the most widely used, states flatly, 'Bimetallism is a poor metallic system to use because the two metals fluctuate constantly *against each other* in price with strange results' .. (Friedman, 1989, 28, n. 1, his emphasis)

Nonetheless, this conventional view does not stand up well to scrutiny. In Friedman's words, it is 'dubious, if not outright wrong' and, 'far from being a thoroughly discredited fallacy, bimetallism has much to recommend it on theoretical, practical, and historical grounds', at least as superior to monometallism (Friedman, 1990a, 87, 102).

This section examines these claims by extending the earlier gold-standard model to analyse bimetallism, and obtains results that provide considerable support for Friedman's claims about the superiority of bimetallism over monometallism. It also provides support for the older proponents of bimetallism who claimed that bimetallism provided a 'parachute' that cushioned the price level against fluctuations in the relative supplies of precious metals (see, e.g., Chevalier, 1859), but goes beyond their analysis in predicting there should also be parachute effects (or, if one prefers, a more stable price level) in the face of shocks to the relative demands for precious metals as well. In addition, the model illustrates the truth of the bimetallist claim that there is an economic mechanism at work under bimetallism by which the market price ratio between the two metals is pulled towards the legal ratio. Within limits, shocks to the relative supplies of precious metals are absorbed by changes in the relative amounts of the metals used for monetary purposes. If there was an unexpected discovery of gold, gold would drive an appropriate amount of silver from the monetary circulation and thereby help to keep the market and legal price ratios together. This mechanism explains the 'stylised fact' – which monometallists such as Giffen (1895) could not easily explain – that the market values of the two metals were sufficiently close to their legal ratio that people using bimetallic currencies were usually unaware of any major discrepancy (see, e.g., Fisher, 1911, 132), and this despite large fluctuations in their relative supplies. Bimetallism was therefore more than just a crude attempt to impose an untenable price ratio between gold and silver, as some of the monometallists maintained, and some of the key criticisms levelled against it were simply based on a failure to understand how it worked.

Before setting out the model, it might be useful to give an informal account of how the bimetallic system actually works. The defining feature of bimetallism is a law that stipulates that a debtor may discharge a debt of a given nominal amount by handing over x units of gold or y units of silver, or by handing over financial instruments (e.g., banknotes) of equivalent value. The ratio y/x is a relative price ratio between gold and silver, so bimetallism can also be thought of as specifying a legal price ratio between gold and silver. (In bimetallic France in the nineteenth century, for example, this ratio was 15.5/1.) The choice of which metal to use is the debtor's, but should there be any discrepancy between the values of x units of gold and y units of silver – or, put another way, should the market price ratio between gold and silver depart significantly from the given legal ratio – then it is in the debtor's interest to discharge his debt using whichever metal is over-valued by the bimetallic law. If x units of gold is worth less on the market than y units of silver, the law that specifies that a debt can be settled using x units of gold or y units of silver would over-value gold and encourage the debtor to hand over gold and keep any silver he holds. A version of Gresham's law then comes into operation by which the 'bad' (i.e., over-valued) metal drives out the 'good' (i.e., under-valued) one from the monetary circulation, and should the price discrepancy continue, the under-valued metal would disappear entirely from the monetary circulation. However, in the case where the market price ratio is more or less the same as the legal ratio, the debtor will be more or less indifferent to the choice of metal, and both metals would circulate side by side.

The bimetallic system thus gives rise to three qualitatively different kinds of outcome. The first is where there is so much gold relative to silver that the market price ratio falls below the legal ratio, gold becomes overvalued, and the overvalued gold drives all the monetary silver out of circulation. The fact that a debtor can use silver to discharge a debt is then irrelevant, because no debtor would choose to do so, and to all intents and purposes the bimetallic system functions as if it were a gold monometallism. For the sake of a convenient label, we describe this outcome as a '*gold bimetallism*'. There is also an opposite case (i.e., the '*silver bimetallism*') in which there is so much silver relative to gold that the market price ratio rises above the legal ratio, silver becomes overvalued, and the overvalued silver drives all the monetary gold out of circulation. The third type of outcome – the '*effective bimetallism*', for want of a better term – is the intermediate one in which the relative stocks of the precious metals are somewhere in between, the market price ratio is at (or at least close to) the legal ratio, and both metals circulate side-by-side. The effective bimetallism was also the case that was most important historically – France was on an effective bimetallism for most of the nineteenth century, for example – and the one that formed the focal point of the old controversies on bimetallism.

Not surprisingly, the response of the bimetallic system to various shocks generally depends on which particular kind of bimetallic case we are dealing with. A shock to the supply of silver would typically have no effect on the price level if there was a gold bimetallism, but it will affect the price level – though in different ways – if there is a silver or effective bimetallism. The responses in each case are generally different, but since the gold bimetallism and the silver bimetallism are mirror images of each other, there is no need to consider both explicitly. We shall therefore restrict ourselves to the effective and gold bimetallisms and the reader can easily infer what happens with the silver bimetallism. Furthermore, since the gold bimetallism functions as if it were a gold monometallism, provided the stock of gold remains high relative to the stock of silver, we can immediately infer how the gold bimetallism operates from our previous knowledge of the gold monometallism. It follows, then, that all we really need to do is work out how the effective bimetallism operates and compare that with the earlier gold monometallism reinterpreted as a gold bimetallism.

The Bimetallic Model

The model explains the price level on the basis of factors affecting the gold and silver markets in a world economy with a bimetallic legal regime. As before we assume that the supply of gold is exogenous. Since we ought to treat the metals symmetrically, we assume that the supply of silver is exogenous as well. We then assume that gold and silver are demanded by the same representative price-taking household we had earlier, but we break down its bundle of non-gold goods $C_j(t)$ into two components – goods other than precious metals (i.e., $C'(t)$) and non-monetary silver (i.e., $S_n(t)$). Letting $C(t)^b = [C'(t)^{b'} S_n(t)^c]$, the utility function becomes:

$$U_j(t) = G_{j,n}(t)^a C_j'(t)^{b'} S_{j,n}(t)^c \,,$$

$$0 < a, b', c < 1 \,;\ a + b' + c = 1 \tag{13.10}$$

where $C_j'(t)$ is again assumed for convenience to be non-durable. The gold and silver rentals $r_g(t)$ and $r_s(t)$ are:

$$r_g(t) = p_g(t) - [1/(1 + R(t))] p_g(t + 1)$$
$$r_s(t) = p_s(t) - [1/(1 + R(t))] p_s(t + 1) \tag{13.11}$$

and are presumed always to be positive. Similar to before, the household also faces a transactions technology which generates monetary demands for the precious metals of the form:

$$[r_g(t) G_m(t) + r_s(t)\ S_m(t)]/Y(t) = d \tag{13.12}$$

where $G_m(t)$ and $S_m(t)$ are the household's monetary holdings of gold and silver. The household allocates its total expenditures each period $Y(t)$, selects its monetary holdings according to (13.12), and maximises utility (13.10) subject to the budget constraint:

$$(1 - d)\,Y(t) = r_g(t)\,G_n(t) + r_s(t)\,S_n(t) + p_c(t)\,C(t). \tag{13.13}$$

The non-monetary demands for gold and silver are then:

$$G_n(t) = a\,(1 - d)\,Y(t)\,/\,r_g(t)$$
$$S_n(t) = c\,(1 - d)\,Y(t)\,/\,r_s(t). \tag{13.14}$$

The 'Gold', 'Silver' and 'Effective' Bimetallisms

The bimetallic system now generates one of three outcomes depending on the relative demands and supplies of the two precious metals. The first case – the gold bimetallism – occurs where the stock of gold is sufficiently high that the market price ratio $p_s(t)/p_g(t)$ rises above the legal ratio ρ and causes all the monetary silver to be replaced with gold. The bimetallic system then operates as if it were a gold standard since the monetary demand for silver is zero and the legal price ratio ρ is of no immediate operational significance. The opposite case – the 'silver bimetallism' – occurs where the stock of gold is sufficiently small that the market price ratio falls below ρ and causes all the monetary gold to be replaced with monetary silver. The system then behaves as if it were a silver standard since the monetary demand for gold is zero and ρ is of no immediate relevance. The intermediate case occurs where the relative stocks are such that the market price ratio is (more or less) at the legal ratio ρ, and both metals circulate side-by-side. This is the range of 'effective bimetallism' where the system operates as a recognisable bimetallism.

Our next task is to determine the switchover points between these outcomes. The switchover between the gold bimetallism and the effective bimetallism is given at the point where the market price ratio is (only just) equal to the legal ratio r, and where there is (only just) no monetary demand for silver, that is,

$$p_s(t)/p_g(t) = \rho , \quad S_m(t) = 0. \tag{13.15}$$

We can then show that the relative demands for the two metals are:

$$G(t) = [a(1-d) + d]\, Y(t)\, r_g(t)^{-1}, \quad S(t) = c(1-d)\, Y(t)\, r_s(t)^{-1}. \tag{13.16}$$

The relative stocks of the two metals at this point are therefore:

$$G(t)\, /\, S(t) = \rho_r\, [a(1-d)+d]\, /\, c(1-d) \tag{13.17}$$

where $\rho_r = r_s(t)/r_g(t)$. The other switchover point is found in the same way:

$$G(t)\, /\, S(t) = \rho_r\, a(1-d)\, /\, [c(1-d)+d]. \tag{13.18}$$

We therefore have the gold bimetallism if $G(t)/S(t) > \rho_r[a(1-d)+d]/[c(1-d)]$, the silver bimetallism if $G(t)/S(t) < \rho_r a(1-d)/[c(1-d)+d]$, and the effective bimetallism if $G(t)/S(t)$ falls in the intermediate range between $\rho_r a(1-d)/[c(1-d)+d]$ and $\rho_r[a(1-d)+d]/[c(1-d)]$. Note that the width of this range is:

$$\rho_r\, d\, [(a+c)(1-d)+d]\, \{\, c(1-d)\, [c(1-d)+d]\,\}^{-1} \tag{13.19}$$

which tells us that the range within which the bimetallism is effective varies directly with d. As d falls, the two switchover points move towards each other, and they converge to the common point $\rho_r a/c$ when d goes to zero. In other words, the 'effectiveness' of the bimetallic system hinges critically on the monetary demand for the precious metals, and the system becomes decreasingly effective as d falls. When the system becomes indirectly convertible and d falls to zero, the bimetallism is no longer effective for *any* relative stock ratio $G(t)/S(t)$ – it becomes a gold bimetallism if $p_s(t)/p_g(t) > \rho$, a silver bimetallism if $p_s(t)/p_g(t) < \rho$, and it is perched on a knife-edge between the two if $p_s(t)/p_g(t) = \rho$.

The Bimetallic Price Level

The price level under the effective bimetallism can be derived from the equilibrium condition for the precious metals, gold and silver:

$$[(a+c)(1-d)+d]\, Y(t)\, r_g(t)^{-1} = G(t) + \rho_r S(t). \tag{13.20}$$

Proceeding as before, we get:

$$p_g(t) = [(a+c)(1-d)+d]\, \{[(1+R)(1+\Delta Z)]/ \\ [(1+R)(1+\Delta Z) - (1+\Delta Y)]\}\, Y(t)/Z(t) \tag{13.21}$$

where $Z(t) \equiv G(t) + \rho_r S(t)$. The elasticity results for the effective bimetallism can then be derived easily. Since we are interested primarily in the parachute effect, we shall focus only on the effects of changes in the relative demands and supplies of the two precious metals, though a more complete treatment is to be found in Dowd (1994c). Proceeding as before, the elasticities of the bimetallic price level with respect to changes in a, c, $G(t)$ and $S(t)$ are, respectively:

$$-1 < -a(1-d)[(a+c)(1-d)+d] < 0$$
$$-1 < -b(1-d)/[(a+c)(1-d)+d] < 0$$
$$0 < G(t)/Z(t) < 1$$
$$0 < \rho_r S(t)/Z(t) < 1.$$

These conditions are directly analogous to comparable earlier conditions (i.e., those for a and $G(t)$) for the gold monometallism/bimetallism. The main difference is that the price level under the effective bimetallism is now vulnerable to silver shocks in much the same way as it is vulnerable to gold ones. Intuitively, the effective bimetallism treats gold and silver in the same qualitative way; if gold shocks affect the price level under the effective bimetallism, then silver shocks should affect it as well, and in much the same way.

Is the effectively bimetallic price level more or less stable than the price level under a gold monometallism? The answer depends on the shocks to which the system is subject. If we consider only silver shocks – shocks to c or $S(t)$ – then the price level is clearly more stable under a gold monometallism/bimetallism, for the simple reason that it is completely unaffected by such shocks, whereas the price level under an effective bimetallism *does* respond to them. But what happens in the face of gold shocks? To answer this question, we need only take the ratio of the relevant price-level elasticity under the effective bimetallism to the ratio of the relevant price-level elasticity under the gold monometallism. These ratios turn out to be

$$0 < [a(1-d)+d]/[(a+c)(1-d)+d] < 1 \qquad (13.22a)$$
$$0 < G(t)/Z(t) < 1 \qquad (13.22b)$$

for a and $G(t)$ respectively. These tell us that the price level under the effective bimetallism is *more* stable than the price level under a gold monometallism in the face of a shock to either gold variable. The second, in particular, is a formal representation of the parachute effect claimed by the nineteenth-century bimetallists (see, e.g., Chevalier, 1859; Jevons, [1875] 1907, 139),[7] while the first shows that we also get parachute effects in the face of changes in relative demands for the metals as well. Nonetheless, it is important to understand that the parachute effect only applies if the system is operating in its 'effective' range, which will only be the case if both precious metals are being used for monetary purposes. What lies behind the parachute is the ability of one metal to perform the monetary function of the other – the changing composition of the monetary circulation then absorbs part of the shock and dampens the effect on the price level

– regardless of whether the shock originates on the demand side or the supply side of the model. The parachute effect consequently applies to more shocks than just the gold discoveries on which the old bimetallists concentrated. To the extent that we are concerned about price-level stability, the case for bimetallism is even stronger than they realised.

The price level under an effective bimetallism is thus less stable than the gold standard price level in the face of silver shocks, but more stable in the face of gold ones. Yet, by the same token, the price level under an effective bimetallism is *more* stable than a silver standard price level in the face of silver shocks, but *less* stable than a silver standard price level in the face of gold shocks. If we knew that shocks would always be silver shocks, we would presumably prefer a gold standard to a bimetallism or silver standard; and if we knew that shocks would always be gold ones, we would presumably prefer a silver standard to any other. Adopting either monometallism provides *perfect* protection against shocks from the other metal, but provides *no* protection against shocks from whatever metal *is* chosen. Under an effective bimetallism, however, the price level is vulnerable to shocks from either metal, but the parachute effect to some extent cushions the effects on the price level of whatever shocks do occur. If gold and silver variables are equally volatile, or approximately so, the effectively bimetallic price level may indeed be more stable than the price level under either monometallism.

A bimetallic system can also generate a more stable price level than a monometallism even independently of parachute effects. Suppose we assume that d is zero to abstract from parachute effects. Under a gold monometallism, a discovery of gold ore will always have a positive impact on the price level, but its effect under bimetallism will depend on the ratio $G(t)/S(t)$. If the ratio exceeds $\rho_r a/c$ (i.e., if the bimetallism is in its gold bimetallism range), the shock will have the same effect as it would have under a gold standard; if the ratio is less than $\rho_r a/c$ (i.e., if the bimetallism is in its silver bimetallism range), the shock will have no effect at all on the price level, unless $G(t)/S(t)$ is close to the switchover point and the shock pushes the system from a silver bimetallism to a gold one. The gold shock will thus have an effect on the bimetallic price level that is no greater and quite possibly smaller than its effect on the gold standard price level. *Ex ante*, having a bimetallism instead of a monometallism still provides us with *some* insurance against price-level instability from shocks to the metal chosen under the monometallism – even if $d = 0$ and there is no range over which the bimetallism is effective. The cost, of course, is that the bimetallic price level is also vulnerable to shocks from the other metal, but we may still prefer to put our eggs into two baskets rather than one.

Implications for Historical Bimetallism

The model explains several important features of the historical experience of bimetallism. It explains why the market price ratio in bimetallic countries like France should have stayed so remarkably close to the legal ratio for the whole of the period for which France was on the bimetallic standard – a stylised fact that gold monometallists could not easily explain and one that must otherwise be dismissed as an historical 'accident'. The fact that the market price ratio remained so close to par for so long is strong evidence that the bimetallic system was able to absorb shocks to the demands and supplies of the precious metals and still maintain its effectiveness. The same stylised fact also lends credence to Irving Fisher's claim that, since the 'steadying power' of bimetallism 'depends on the breadths of the reservoirs' (i.e., the monetary demands for the two metals),

> it remains in full force, no matter what be the proportions of gold and silver money, and is as great when only one country is bimetallic as when the whole world adopts the system. (1894, 536)

This in turn suggests that the world monetary system until the 1870s is most appropriately seen as a bimetallic system in which effectively bimetallic countries 'kept the balance' between the two metals while gold standard countries such as Britain were necessarily peripheral. The key player in the international monetary system was therefore not Britain, as is often supposed, but France.

The model also helps to explain the deflation that hit the world economy from the 1870s until the 1890s. The model predicts that a widespread abandonment of silver in favour of gold would lead the price of silver to fall against gold and cause the relative price of gold to rise (and, hence, the price level to fall). These are exactly what occurred after the abandonment of silver in the 1870s: having been between 15 and 16/1 since the early nineteenth century, the ratio of the market price of gold to the market price of silver rose steadily after the early 1870s to somewhere over 30/1 in the 1890s; and this rise in the gold–silver price ratio was accompanied by a major fall in the general price level. The 'Great Depression' of the last quarter of the nineteenth century may have been a by-product of the general switch away from bimetallism to the gold standard.

If the model suggests that the bimetallic system performed better than its critics generally acknowledged, it also suggests that secular declines in the monetary demand for precious metals were gradually undermining its effectiveness. Even if silver had not been abandoned, a point would eventually have come where it would have become impossible to keep the market price ratio at the legal ratio. The effective bimetallism would then have 'switched' into a silver or gold bimetallism and the old bimetallic parachutes would have disappeared. Contemporary economists were aware of the possibility of the effective bimetallism 'collapsing' in this way, and Irving Fisher went so far as to concede that such a collapse would 'in all probability' happen (1894, 534); nonetheless, he concluded optimistically – perhaps over-optimistically – on the basis of a numerical example that

> we may be tolerably confident that, *if initially successful with the film near the middle position* [i.e., more or less equal monetary demands for gold and silver], bimetallism would continue successful [i.e., effective] for many generations [yet]. (1894, 535, his emphasis)

RELATED MONETARY STANDARDS

'Debtor' and 'Creditor' Bimetallisms

The basic principles underlying bimetallism also extend to a number of related systems. One alternative is to give the *creditor* rather than the *debtor* the choice of which precious metal to use to value debt payments – to have a '*creditor bimetallism*' instead of the traditional or 'debtor' bimetallism. The essential difference between the two is that the debtor will always choose the cheaper metal (i.e., the metal that is overvalued at the legal price ratio ρ) to value his debts, but the creditor will always choose to be paid with the more expensive one. A Gresham's law therefore operates under the debtor bimetallism in which exchange media valued in the cheaper (or overvalued) metal drive out those valued in the dearer (or undervalued) one, but an 'inverse Gresham's law' operates under the creditor system in which the undervalued metal drives out the overvalued one. The price level would therefore be higher under the debtor bimetallism than under the creditor bimetallism, except where the ratio of the market valuations of the two metals happened to be the same as the legal price ratio ρ. It also follows that the price level under the debtor bimetallism will never be *lower* than the price level under any monometallism or creditor bimetallism, and the price level under the creditor bimetallism will never be *higher* than under any monometallism or debtor bimetallism. The claim that bimetallism is typically associated with a higher price level than a monometallic system is consequently only valid for the debtor bimetallism.[8]

Trimetallism, Polymetallism and Polycommodity Standards

There is also no particular reason why we could not base a switching standard on three metals instead of two. We would then have a *trimetallism*. Debts might be discharged using valuations of gold, silver, or, say, platinum. We can then define a *debtor trimetallism* as a system where the debtor chooses the valuation metal, and a *creditor trimetallism* as one where this choice is made by the creditor. A trimetallism can be analysed in much the same way as a bimetallism. If shocks to the relative demands and supplies of gold, silver and platinum were not too unequal, we might argue that a trimetallism would be likely to produce a more stable price level than a bimetallism, for much the same reasons that we might argue that a bimetallism would produce a more stable price level than a monometallism. A trimetallism would put its eggs in three baskets instead of two. Although there is then a greater probability of dropping one of the baskets, we might still prefer three baskets if the expected loss from dropping any particular basket was lower. Similarly, since a debtor trimetallism would generate a price level that was no lower than the price level that would arise with any other type of standard, and a creditor bimetallism would generate a price level that was no higher than that which would arise under any other standard, the trimetallic price levels –

the price levels from debtor and creditor trimetallisms – would as it were enclose the price levels from all monometallic or bimetallic standards. In short, a trimetallism would generate a more extreme but perhaps more stable price level than a bimetallism.

The analysis of trimetallisms can be extended to polymetallisms where one of n metals is chosen to value debts, and we might expect the earlier results to carry over – polymetallisms with n metals might generate more extreme but perhaps more stable price levels, other things being equal, than those with $(n - 1)$ metals. Provided we were dealing with other commodities that could also be used as exchange or redemption media, or else we were dealing with an indirectly convertible system, we could also extend the analysis to encompass *polycommodity systems* instead of just polymetallic ones. With indirectly convertible systems, indeed, there is little limit to the number of commodities that could be included 'in' the system. There is however no *guarantee* that adding any additional commodity to the system would necessarily improve its expected price-level stability. In contrast to the familiar basket-type of commodity standard to be discussed in Chapter 14, there is no reason to suppose that the price level becomes perfectly or even approximately stable as the number of included commodities gets large. Adding a new commodity to the system always means adding a new potential source of price level instability. If the new commodity has a particularly volatile relative price, or just unfortunate covariance properties, it might add more instability than it took away. The bottom line, then, is clear: If we are seeking price-level stability, we cannot expect to achieve it by any of the monetary standards considered so far.

OBJECTIONS TO MONOMETALLIC, BIMETALLIC AND RELATED STANDARDS

Before ending our discussion of these standards, it might be useful to examine two of the main objections sometimes made against them. At the risk of a bit of repetition, these arguments are broadly as follows:

First, there is the argument that gold and bimetallic standards are inefficient because of their resource costs (e.g., Fischer, 1986a, 25). One counter-argument is that the resource costs *per se* are not what matter:

> So-called resource costs are an inadequate proxy for total costs or opportunity costs, unless the former term is defined in such a way as to make it synonymous with the latter two, in which case the modifier *resource* becomes redundant and misleading. The inadequacy is especially pronounced when the issue is the relative costs of alternative institutional arrangements. (Garrison, 1985, 67, his emphasis)

But even if we accept that the resource costs of a monetary standard *were* the relevant criterion, there are still reasons to dispute that these costs would be high, or at any rate higher than the resource costs of a fiat currency. The usual figures cited in this context are those provided by Friedman (1953, 1960) for a pure gold reserve standard. Friedman (1953, 210) estimated that for the first half of this century the resource costs of a pure commodity standard would have amounted to about 1.5 percent of national output, or about one-half to three-quarters its annual growth rate. Allowing for velocity then gave a figure of about 2 percent of output, or two-thirds its growth rate, and Friedman (1960, 5) later revised the estimate upwards to about 2.5 percent of national output. A somewhat lower estimate was offered more recently by Allan Meltzer (1983, 105) – 16 percent of the annual growth rate of output – but he still concluded that 'the resource cost of a full commodity standard remains high'. There are several problems with these estimates,[9] but perhaps the most important one is that they only refer to a 100 percent reserve commodity standard and there is no reason to believe that such a standard would survive in the long run under *laissez-faire* conditions. Precisely because of its resource costs, a pure standard would soon give way to one that was more economical to operate, and the process of economisation would reduce resource costs in the end to negligible levels. Resource costs would only be significant in the interim as the monetary system matured, and even then there is still no *prima facie* case that they are a social waste that could be eliminated without costly side-effects. As discussed already, the argument that we could simply dispense with the resource costs of a commodity standard fails to appreciate the 'reassurance' benefits they bring. The same logic in another context would suggest that we should abolish the police force to cut down on the costs of operating it. We would certainly save on police officers' salaries, but few would argue that that would necessarily constitute a net saving when allowance is made for the costs of the increased criminal activity, the increased need to invest in security measures, and so on, that it would plausibly entail. Yet an argument that would be laughed at in that context is still widely regarded as accepted wisdom when applied to commodity standards.

In any case, we must recognise that irredeemable currencies also involve 'resource costs' even though the issuers have no need to keep reserves. These resource costs include the costs incurred as agents use up resources trying to protect themselves against the instability associated with fiat currencies, but they also include the costs of the fiat-produced instability itself:

> The true costs of the paper standard would have to take into account (1) the costs imposed on society by different political factions in their attempts to gain control of the printing press, (2) the costs imposed by special-interest groups in their attempts to persuade the controller of the printing press to misuse its authority (print more money) for the benefit of the special interests, (3) the costs in the form of inflation-induced misallocations of resources that occur throughout the economy as a result of the monetary authority succumbing to the political pressures of the special interests, and (4) the costs incurred by businesses in their attempts to predict what the monetary authority will do in

the future and to hedge against likely, but uncertain, consequences of monetary irresponsibility. (Garrison, 1985, 68)

We shall examine some of these costs in Chapter 16, but it suffices for the moment merely to note that they are definitely far from small. The earlier view that commodity systems involve significant resource costs and fiat systems do not must therefore be reversed. In the words of Milton Friedman,

> In earlier discussions, other monetary economists and I took it for granted that the real resource cost of producing irredeemable paper money was negligible. Experience under a universal irredeemable paper money standard makes it crystal clear that such an assumption, while it may be correct with respect to the direct cost to the government of issuing fiat outside money, is false for society as a whole. (Friedman, 1986, 643)

A second argument sometimes made against commodity standards is that they have not 'met the test of survival' (Fischer, 1986a, 21), but we has to ask why the mere *fact* that fiat currency replaced commodity systems should constitute an *argument* against the latter. One has to look at the process by which the one gave way to the other and judge both the process itself and the factors behind it. Had commodity systems shown clear deficiencies and been replaced by the operation of a process that was itself reliable – suppose, for example, that they had been replaced by spontaneous market forces, and we had some reason to believe that the market iterated towards a 'good' outcome – then we might plausibly maintain that the act of replacement constituted *prima facie* evidence of the inferiority of the replaced system. But the historical record indicates that in apparently *every* case the commodity standard disappeared because of explicit government intervention to suppress it, and *not* because it failed some reliable (e.g., market) test. Commodity systems disappeared for essentially political reasons, and there can be *no* presumption that failing the political test demonstrates any inherent weakness on the part of the system that fails it, especially if we look closely at these cases and investigate the reasons that led governments to intervene as they did.

The survival argument is also premature even if we were predisposed to accept it at face value. At the very most, fiat systems have been the norm for well under a century, and much less if we place the break with the collapse of the Bretton Woods system in the early 1970s. By contrast, commodity systems have existed for millennia and were the norm historically. Dinosaurs might be extinct now, but they ruled the earth for over a hundred million years and Man who might become extinct tomorrow would be unwise to boast of his superior survivability. In any case, unlike the dinosaurs, commodity systems might make a comeback – they always have historically – and we would be ill- advised to assume that they have gone for good. To quote Niehans:

> from a practical point of view, commodity money is the only type of money that, at the present time, can be said to have passed the test of history in market

economies. Except for short interludes of war, revolution, and financial crisis, Western economies have been on commodity money systems from the dawn of their history almost up to the present time. More precisely, it is only since 1973 that the absence of any link to the commodity world is claimed to be a normal feature of the monetary system. (Niehans, 1978, 140–141)

14 Commodity-basket Monetary Standards*

We turn now to monetary systems in which the value of the unit of account is tied to a commodity basket rather than to any individual commodity. While bimetallism and the systems related to it might provide some protection for the price level in the face of 'excessive' fluctuations in the relative value of the anchor commodity, there is a strong argument that the price level would be more stable if it were tied to a basket of gold and silver rather than to fixed amounts of either metal because a basket would normally have a more stable relative price. We thus arrive at *symmetallism* – a system in which the price of a basket of gold and silver (i.e., a weighted average of the prices of gold and silver) is pegged, but the individual prices of gold and silver are left floating. The underlying idea is that shocks to the relative prices of each metal will cancel out to some extent in their impact on the relative price of the basket as a whole; the relative price of the basket will therefore be more stable, and so a system that pegs the nominal price of the basket should lead to a more stable price level than a monometallic or bimetallic system that pegs the nominal price of an individual metal. The same logic also suggests that a basket would normally generate more price-level stability if it included three metals instead of two, and that it would generate more still if it had *n* metals. We can thus go from a 'narrow' basket with a relatively small number of included commodities to a 'broader' one with many. Nor is there any decisive reason why we should restrict our choice of included commodities to metals alone: if we wish to stabilise the relative price of the basket as a means of stabilising the price level, the implication is that we should peg the price of a 'broad' basket that includes a large number of different goods, and perhaps services as well. The individual relative price risks should largely cancel out and produce a basket with a stable relative price. Pegging the price of this anchor should then produce a stable price level.

But the more goods are included in a basket, the more difficult it usually is to maintain the price of the basket by buying and selling the basket itself – as the number of included commodities (and services?) increases, storage and handling costs will normally rise – and there comes a point where trading in the basket itself is no longer feasible and we need to devise a way to maintain its nominal price by stabilising a price index instead.[1] All sorts of questions then arise – what sort of index to use? what are the mechanics of such a system? how would the system operate on a day-to-day basis? and how would it be protected against speculative attack? – and we need to organise our discussion so that we can come to grips with these issues in a straightforward way. Perhaps the best approach is to retrace the

---

* Part of this chapter appeared as 'A Proposal to End Inflation', *Economic Journal*, 104 (425) (July 1994), pp. 828–840.

history of thought behind the use of indices to stabilise the price level, and then to discuss each issue as it arises. The underlying idea goes back to the nineteenth century, but the most detailed and important treatment is to be found in the work of Irving Fisher on the 'compensated dollar' around the time of the First World War. It therefore makes sense to discuss Fisher's ideas in some detail not only because we need to see what is wrong with Fisher's work if we are to develop anything better, but also because we can use Fisher's scheme to provide a backdrop to discuss other issues that need to be addressed. Once the basic issues have been properly aired, we can then go back to first principles and construct a new system – a 'stable dollar' system – from scratch.

THE 'NARROW-BASKET' APPROACH

Symmetallism

Perhaps the best-known example of a 'narrow-basket' approach is symmetallism, which involves the pegging of the nominal price of a basket of specific quantities of gold and silver, and was initially proposed as an improvement on monometallic or bimetallic systems.[2] The

> monetary unit would no longer be based on *either* gold *or* silver, but on an alloy of gold *and* silver in which the two metals are represented in a legally fixed quantitative proportion. (Butenschön, 1936, 27, his emphasis).

The weighted average of the prices of gold and silver would be pegged – the weights being implied by the relative quantities of gold and silver in the basket – but the individual prices of gold and silver would be free to float subject to this constraint, and shocks to the relative price between gold and silver could be accommodated with no diffculty. We could visualise a symmetallic system operating with or without full-bodied coinage, and with or without the banks using the composite metal as MOR. As first set out by Marshall, the basic idea was that the basket should be adopted as anchor and MOR, but not as MOE[3]–

> currency should be exchangeable at the Mint or Issue Department [of the Bank of England] not for gold, but for gold and silver, at the rate not of £1 for 113 ounces of gold, but £1 for 56 $\frac{1}{2}$ grains of gold, together with, say, twenty times as many grains of silver. (Marshall, [1887b] 1966, 204)

Anyone who wanted one or other of the individual metals could obtain what they wanted on the relevant market by paying the market price.

It is easy to see why symmetallism can be expected to generate a more stable price level than monometallism. Suppose for the sake of argument that the shocks to the two metals have the same variance, σ^2. Let p_g be the relative price of gold and p_s the relative price of silver, and consider a symmetallic basket made up of x percent gold and $(1 - x)$ percent silver. This basket then has a relative price of $xp_g + (1 - x)p_s$, and the variance of this relative price is

$$x^2\sigma^2 + (1 - x)^2\sigma^2 + 2x(1 - x)\operatorname{cov}(p_g, p_s). \tag{14.1}$$

Unless p_g and p_s are perfectly correlated, the variance of the basket's relative price as given by (1) will be less than the variance of the relative prices of the two individual metals. This result is of course simply the standard diversification result that a portfolio – or, in this case, a basket – of two assets will normally have a lower risk than a portfolio consisting of one asset alone. A basket with two metals (i.e., symmetallism) would consequently have a more stable relative price – and generate a more stable price level – than a basket consisting of one metal alone (i.e., a monometallism).

Symmetallism also has certain advantages over bimetallism. One advantage stressed by Marshall ([1887b] 1966, 206) and Edgeworth (1895, 444) is that symmetallism is less prone to the switching outcomes – such as a switch from an effective to a gold bimetallism – that can occur under bimetallism when there is a change in the relative market price of the two metals. Should there be an abnormal increase in the supply of silver under symmetallism, the price of silver would fall relative to that of gold, and the nominal prices of each would adjust to ensure the appropriate weighted average remained at its pegged 'par' value. A 'large' silver shock would imply a 'big' relative price adjustment, but for as long as silver continued to be valuable, there would be no 'switching' away from silver. The symmetallic system would continue to operate in much the same way and be distinct from a gold monometallism (or gold bimetallism) for as long as silver had a positive price. As Edgeworth put it:

> The worst that can ensue is that the redundant silver will be unable to mate itself with [monetary] gold. A certain quantity of gold might be forthcoming from the arts in which the metal has not been fixed by manufacture, or from hoards and unsymmetallic currencies. But at worst the new silver would pine unmated. (Edgeworth, 1895, 445)

The more important issue is whether symmetallism generates a more stable price level than bimetallism. However, we know that a gold or silver bimetallism is equivalent (for present purposes) to a gold or silver monometallism, and we already know that symmetallism generates a more stable price level than monometallism. Hence, we can infer that it generates a more stable price level than a gold or silver bimetallism as well. The question, then, is whether symmetallism also generates a more stable price level than an effective bimetallism. The answer depends on the size of the monetary demand for the precious metals, the results being provided by Edgeworth (1895, 449–450). Assuming that shocks to gold and silver are independent, he proved that symmetallism would generate the more stable price level if the monetary demand for the metals was 'low' relative to the non-monetary demands, but the bimetallic price level would be more stable if the monetary demand was 'high' relative to the non-monetary demand.

To understand the first result, imagine that the monetary demand for metals was zero. As discussed previously, the bimetallism then functions as if it were a monometallism, and we already know that a symmetallic price level is more stable. Continuity arguments then indicate that the symmetallic price level would continue to be more stable provided the monetary demand for the metals was relatively 'small', which is Edgeworth's first result.

To understand his second result, consider the 'reservoir diagram' in Figure 14.1 borrowed from Fisher (1894, 531). The shaded areas G_m, G_n, S_m and S_n are the monetary and non-monetary stocks of gold and silver respectively. These stocks are contained in three reservoirs – the one on the left for the stock of non-monetary gold, the one on the right for the stock of non-monetary silver, and the one in the middle for the monetary stock of both precious metals, with the stocks of gold and silver in the latter being divided by the film ff. The left and right reservoirs have inflow pipes by which additional supplies of gold and silver can flow into the system, and each of these reservoirs is connected to the middle one as shown in Figure 14.1. The height of the 'liquid' in the middle reservoir gives a measure of the price level – the greater this height, the higher the price level. The film ff separating the monetary gold from the monetary silver then illustrates the differences between the bimetallic and symmetallic systems. Under bimetallism, this film moves around in the middle reservoir to ensure as far as it can that the levels of the 'liquids' in the three reservoirs are the same. Should there be an influx of silver, the level in the right reservoir would rise, silver would overflow into the middle reservoir, and gold would be displaced into the left reservoir until the levels of all three reservoirs were the same. (The bimetallism continues to be 'effective' for as long as the film can still move around in this way, but it ceases to be 'effective' when the film hits a side wall and one of the metals is driven out of monetary circulation.) Under symmetallism, the film ff is fixed reflecting the fixed relative composition of the monetary circulation in the middle reservoir. Should silver enter the right reservoir, some would overflow as before into the middle one, but instead of *displacing* gold as it did earlier, the extra silver would now *draw additional* gold into the middle reservoir from the one on the left-hand

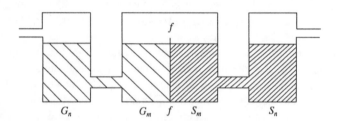

Figure 14.1   Symmetallic and bimetallic reservoirs

side – remember that the composition of this reservoir must remain the same – and the level in the latter would fall.

Imagine now that a shock to silver supplies pushes the non-monetary silver stock to a new higher equilibrium value. Under bimetallism, some of the additional silver displaces monetary gold, and the displaced monetary gold is used for non-monetary purposes. The stocks of non-monetary gold and of both monetary metals are then pushed up to the same equilibrium level as the stock of non-monetary silver. However, under symmetallism the additional monetary silver leads to some non-monetary gold being adopted for monetary purposes. The stock of monetary metals rises, but the stock of non-monetary gold falls – the level of the middle reservoir rises, and that of the left reservoir falls. Now imagine that we have the same change in the stock of monetary metals in both cases, so the price level change is the same for both systems. The change in the stock of non-monetary silver is still the same in both cases, but the stock of non-monetary gold *rises* under bimetallism and *falls* under symmetallism. The bimetallism therefore requires a *greater* change in the supply of precious metals than symmetallism to get the *same* price-level impact. It follows, then, that a *given* shock to the supply of either metal would have a *smaller* impact on the price level under bimetallism than under symmetallism. We have thus demonstrated Edgeworth's second claim.

Whether the price level under symmetallism is more or less stable than under bimetallism thus hinges on the relative size of the monetary demand for the metals. If the monetary demand is non-existent or 'small', the symmetallic price level is generally more stable for the same reason that a basket with two metals normally generates a more stable price level than a basket with one. But if the monetary demand is relatively 'large', the symmetallic diversification effect is dominated by the bimetallic parachute and the bimetallic price level would be more stable. If we believe that any 'modern' symmetallism would have little or no monetary demand (e.g., because it would be indirectly convertible), then the first result is the important one and we could expect the symmetallic price level to be more stable.

Commodity-reserve Currency

Once we accept that a symmetallic system is superior to monometallic or bimetallic ones, it is not obvious why we would wish to stop with a symmetallism based on a basket of gold and silver only. Marshall himself suggested that other commodities might be added to the symmetallic basket ([1887b] 1966, 206)[4] and Jevons ([1875] 1907, 327–328) had made much the same point even earlier,[5] but neither developed the idea any further. We thus arrive at the commodity-reserve currency (CRC) scheme under which the issuers 'would offer to buy and sell unlimited quantities of a specified bundle in terms of nominal currency units' (Friedman, [1951] 1953, 221).[6] The

total price of the commodity bundle would in this way be held within narrow limits, [but] the prices of individual items would be free to vary, and, with any large number of items in the bundle, to vary enormously. Any one item or group of items could rise or fall in price so long as other items fell or rose. (Friedman, 1953, 221)[7]

Friedman goes on to suggest that the necessity of dealing in specified quantities of different goods should

raise no special problem so long as the commodities were openly traded in fairly broadly based markets. Under such circumstances specialists would develop who would act as arbitragers, putting together bundles for sale to the monetary authorities [i.e., the issuers] when the total market value of the bundle fell below the official buying price and buying bundles from the monetary authority when the total market value of the bundle rose above the official selling price. (Friedman, 1953, 221)

A CRC system is thus a directly convertible one in which the banks adopt a particular basket of commodities as their anchor and redemption medium.

CRC schemes have two principal attractions. Since they peg the price of the basket, at least within certain limits, the price level varies with the relative price of the basket against goods and services generally, and we can achieve at least some degree of price-level stability by choosing a basket whose relative price is stable. The more commodities are included, other things being equal, the less vulnerable the relative price of the basket to shocks in the relative prices of the individual commodities included in it, and the more stable the price level. As Friedman explained,

In principle, the ultimate extension of the idea of symmetallism is to include in the standard [i.e., anchor] every commodity and service produced in the economy roughly in proportion to the amounts produced. (1953, 213)

If this could be done, which Friedman himself doubted,

the unit [i.e., anchor] would be a market basket of commodities and services representing in microcosm the total national basket and would provide an almost ideal commodity currency standard [i.e., basket, again]. Since the price of this same market basket would be the price index, stability of the price index would be immediately and perfectly attained ... Technological change could not, at least initially, affect the currency unit differently from aggregate output. The elasticity of supply of currency would, again at least initially, be essentially infinite. (Friedman, 1953, 213–214)

It is this ideal, Friedman adds a little later,

that animates the commodity-reserve scheme and gives it its real appeal. The commodity-reserve scheme is essentially an attempt to go as far in the direction of this ideal as the hard facts of life will permit. (Friedman, 1953, 214)

The other attraction of a CRC scheme is its potential to counteract cyclical instability. A CRC scheme would stabilise the economy in various ways. Like all commodity-based systems, it has the property that when the prices of other goods rise (or fall), the output of the anchor commodity (basket) falls (or rises) and the demand for them rises (falls), and these factors will help to restore its equilibrium relative price and put downward (upward) pressure on the prices of other goods (see Friedman, 1953, 207). These equilibrating factors will clearly be stronger, the greater the elasticities of supply and demand, and one would presume that these elasticities would get greater, other things being equal, the greater the number of commodities included in the basket.[8] A CRC system can also stabilise economic activity in a way that a system with a single-commodity anchor normally cannot. Suppose that we have a CRC system with a raw materials anchor, then as Hayek observed,

> As in the past gold mining used to be the only industry that regularly prospered during periods of depression, so the producers of raw commodities might under this plan enjoy in the same circumstances even a moderate increase in prosperity through being able to exchange their products at more favorable terms against manufactures. But while gold-mining is far too small an industry for its prosperity to have significant effects outside it, the secure income of the producers of raw commodities would also go far to stabilize the demand for manufactures and to prevent the depression from becoming serious. (Hayek, 1948, 215)[9]

An obvious question is what commodities should be included in the CRC basket. Friedman suggested that

> To qualify for inclusion ... commodities would have to admit of precise price quotation – which means that they must be capable of accurate specification and standardization. It would be highly desirable, if not essential, that they be traded in fairly broad markets, so that trading in the commodity bundles could be carried on readily and inexpensively. They should be supplied under reasonably competitive conditions ... They would obviously have to be storable in both a physical and an economic sense; that is, it would have to be possible to preserve relatively inexpensively not only their physical characteristics but also their economic value. (Friedman, 1953, 223–224)

He continued,

> These elementary criteria rule out all services except in so far as they are incorporated in the value of storable goods, practically all manufactured goods, many products of mining (coal, especially bituminous coal, deteriorates very rapidly outside the mine; petroleum and natural gas would be inordinately, if not prohibitively, expensive to store), and many agricultural products (e.g.,

perishable foods and livestock). There remain primarily storable agricultural products, such as corn, wheat, and cotton, metallic mineral products, and some highly standardized manufactured products such as standard cotton textiles, steel rails, newsprint, standard storable chemicals, and similar items. (Friedman, 1953, 224)

Yet even this list is probably too long, and Friedman suggested that most agricultural products should be excluded on other grounds. Their supply tends to be volatile and hard to control; the relative inelasticity of their supply makes their prices generally less stable and reduces the system's counter-cyclical effectiveness; and we might not want large stocks 'locked-up' for monetary purposes in the event of negative supply shocks such as famines. These considerations suggest that we should exclude foodstuffs and most other agricultural products, and we end up with little more than metallic mineral products and standardised manufactures. Friedman estimated that these probably represented only about 3–6 percent of national output, and he was very doubtful that such a 'narrow' anchor would have generated a more stable price level than the gold standard did (see Friedman, 1953, 223–228, 239).[10]

The Failure to Identify a Suitable 'Narrow Basket' Empirically

Before giving up on CRC schemes, however, we ought at least to see if we can find any potential CRC basket that *might* generate a stable price level. At first sight, finding an appropriate basket does not appear to be too difficult. Three possibilities were suggested by Benjamin Graham (1944, 145) – a food basket of 19 articles, a materials basket of 26, and Graham's own preferred basket of 15 commodities. He found that during 1921–1940 the average price of the food basket was 6 percent lower and that of the materials basket 4 percent higher than it had been sixty years earlier. His evidence also suggested that

> both subgroups showed very much the same relative price changes from year to year during the wide swings of 1921–1940. In these years the [price] index itself declined from 155 to 79 and recovered to 128. Yet the food index never fluctuated more than 9 percentage points from its average or normal position in relation to the total index, and the materials index stayed correspondingly close to its normal position in nearly every year. (Graham, 1944, 146)

Graham also claimed that fluctuations in the value of his preferred basket

> paralleled closely those in much more comprehensive indexes, especially if rubber is excluded from the unit value because of its particularly high 1913–1914 price,

but with deviations of 30 percent from par in 1920 and around 30 percent again in

1932, his own evidence does however indicate that the it is less close than he suggests (1944, 146).

An alternative is a basket of metals and metallic products considered by Friedman (1953), but this basket

> has shown a tendency to decline substantially in price over the last century and a half relative to other commodities. A commodity-reserve scheme with a similar currency bundle would have produced ... substantial inflation in other prices ... [Prices] would have risen by 75 percent from 1800 to 1870, fallen by over 10 percent in the next decade, more than doubled from then to 1920, and fallen by more than a sixth from 1920 to 1940. During the decade ending in 1949 prices would have first risen by almost a third and then have fallen by almost a seventh. Indeed, for the period as a whole, the range of price fluctuations would have been greater under the commodity-reserve scheme than it actually was .... [The scheme would have produced] no greater stability than the actual index even over short periods and considerably less secular stability. (Friedman, 1953, 230–231)

Another possibility is Robert Hall's (1982) ANCAP basket – a bundle of specified quantities of ammonium nitrate, copper, aluminum, and plywood.[11] While Hall's evidence suggested that this bundle had a relatively stable purchasing power in the USA over the period 1950–1980, the stable relationship between the ANCAP and the US price level seems to have broken down in the 1980s after Hall's data set ended, and we can have little confidence that the ANCAP would have generated much price stability had it been adopted outside Hall's data period.[12]

Other attempts to find a suitable basket have also failed. Brunner (1984) searched for an equilibrium relationship between raw materials prices and the price level, but could not find one. Garner (1985) looked for a stable relationship between the US GNP deflator and 15 raw materials prices over various periods spanning 1955–84, and concluded that

> Most of the correlations [between the latter and the former] are small, and only two of the 15 are statistically significant. The switch from positive to negative correlations between the 1955–70 and 1970–84 periods shows that this is a particularly unstable relationship on which to base policy decisions. (1985, 20)

Boughton and Branson (1989) also looked for but failed to find a stable relationship between commodity prices and the prices of other goods and services in the USA. So too did Baillie (1989). He examined whether there was a relationship between the CPI in each of France, Italy, Germany and the UK, on the one hand, and one of two commodity price indices, on the other, and found no evidence of cointegration (i.e., a long-run equilibrium relationship) between any of these pairs of series (Baillie, 1989, 214–216). Finally, I tried to find such a relationship myself in early 1990. I took the price series of 11 different traded commodities and tried to find a combination of these that closely followed the (Australian) CPI over the period 1960: 119–89: 4. Regressions of the CPI against these prices gave very poor firts with appalling residual diagnostics which I traced to the commodity price spikes of 1973–1974. Nothing could be done about these problems and there was clearly no basket to be found.

The picture that emerges is not encouraging for the 'narrow-basket' approach. If it is to be operationally feasible, we must be able to identify a suitable basket. A number of studies have looked for one, but to my knowledge only two have claimed success, and there is evidence that the relative price relationship underlying one of those (i.e., the ANCAP) broke down in the 1980s anyway. We are left then with the food and materials baskets suggested by Graham (1944). However, Graham's claims are questionable anyway, and we have no idea whether the relative prices of his baskets would have been stable in the post-war period. It is surely disturbing that none of the studies using post-war data has apparently been able to identify any suitable relationship, and we must wonder whether one exists at all. In short, we have yet to identify an appropriate 'narrow basket' with any confidence, or even to establish that one actually exists. The 'narrow-basket' approach is thus ultimately a dead-end. What we really need is an alternative way to take the symmetallic logic to its limit – a scheme that enables us to get the benefits of a 'broad-basket' but avoids the handling costs and other problems of CRC systems.

THE 'BROAD-BASKET' APPROACH

The Antecedents and History of the 'Broad-basket' Approach

We therefore turn now to the 'broad-basket' approach, and it is perhaps best to begin by putting it into its historical perspective. A good starting point is Simon Newcomb's (1879) suggestion that the paper currency be redeemable, not in gold dollars of fixed weight, but in such quantities of gold and silver bullion as should suffice to make the price level stable. It was also Newcomb who first clearly enunciated the important notion of indirect convertibility – that the paper notes were to be redeemable in amounts of a redemption medium of the same value as the market price of some anchor – where the anchor in his system was to be chosen to stabilise the price level.

A few years later, in 1885, Walras proposed a 'gold standard with a silver regulator' under which gold coins would be used as the basis of the currency, but would be supplemented by silver coins of 15.5 times the weight (and, therefore, at a market price ratio of 15.5 to 1, of approximately the same value). The silver coinage would then be manipulated to stable the value of the currency. If gold became scarce, silver coins would be added to the circulation to prevent the value of the currency rising, and silver coins would be withdrawn from circulation if gold became abundant. The Walras proposal has obvious drawbacks, but it did at least encourage Marshall to think about it, and he came up with two improved versions in a famous article in 1887. The first would require that an

> automatic Government Department would buy Consols for currency whenever £1 was worth more than a unit [of constant purchasing power], and would sell Consols for currency whenever £1 was worth less (the ordinary issue and withdrawal of Consols which takes place when the Government wants to borrow or to pay off its debt would be arranged independently, perhaps, by another Department which had no power to issue or cancel currency). Those who had to pay balances to foreign countries would buy gold or silver in the open market; they would be certain of getting in exchange for this money gold and silver that had a fixed purchasing power in England. (Marshall, [1887b] 1966, 206–207, n. 2)

The other plan would have the government redeem each £1 note for amounts of gold and silver as would have the same value as the unit of constant purchasing power. Marshall regarded the idea as 'able and ingenious' and saw no great practical diffculty with either version, but nonetheless felt unable to endorse either version because he thought they would require an international agreement which he believed could not in practice be obtained.

Soon afterwards, Aneurin Williams (1892) offered a more detailed proposal to change the gold content of the unit of account to keep its purchasing power constant. As he wrote,

> if we could by magic increase the weight of gold in a sovereign just in proportion as the purchasing power of a single grain of gold decreased, and decrease the weight just as the purchasing power of the grain increased, we should keep the total purchasing power of the sovereign constant. This in effect without any magic, but substituting 'pound sterling' for the word 'sovereign' I propose that we should do. (Williams, 1892, 280)

There would be only token coinage, and most of the currency would consist of paper notes issued by the Government. A price index would be frequently prepared – Williams suggested it be prepared daily and the mint price of gold would be raised (or lowered) in proportion to any rise (or fall) in prices above (or below) par. Were the change from par an isolated change, he suggested it would be rapidly corrected; were it part of a general upward or downward movement, the mint price of gold would be increased or decreased period after period until the price level was again restored to par; and were it a response to an increase, say, in the supply of gold, he suggested that the mint price of gold would fall and any rise in the price level would still be corrected. Williams also discussed the effects of his scheme upon the exchange rates *vis à vis* gold standard currencies, but felt that such fluctuations would be relatively limited (1892, 285–286).[13]

Irving Fisher's 'Compensated Dollar'

The idea of altering the content of the 'monetary unit' to stabilise the price level was by now fairly familiar, but proposals to implement it were still somewhat sketchy. Irving Fisher then tried to put the idea into more concrete operational form with his proposal for a 'compensated dollar' in *The Purchasing Power of Money*, first published in 1911. He subsequently presented papers on the subject to the meeting of the International Congress of Chambers of Commerce in Boston in September 1912, and three months later to the meeting of the American Economics Association that year in Minneapolis. Papers outlining the proposal subsequently came out in the *Economic Journal* in December 1912 and in the *Quarterly Journal of Economics* in February 1913. The *QJE* article was followed later that year with a technical appendix in the same journal, and the AEA seminar meanwhile came out in the *AEA Papers and Proceedings* in March 1913. Fisher's proposal[14] attracted a great deal of attention, and he replied to many of the criticisms in an article in the *AER* of December 1914. He continued to write about it during the First World War, and his 'definitive' version of the scheme finally appeared in *Stabilizing the Dollar* in 1920. The essence of his proposal is

> to make the purchasing power of the dollar constant. It would compensate for any loss of purchasing power of each grain of gold by increasing the number of grains which go to make a dollar. In other words it aims to standardize the dollar as a unit of purchasing power. We have standardized the yard, the pound, the kilowatt, and every other important commercial unit except the most important of all, the dollar, the unit of purchasing power. We now have a gold dollar of constant weight, but of varying purchasing power. We need a dollar of constant purchasing power and varying weight. (Fisher, 1913a, 214)

He gives a concrete illustration a little later:

> Today prices are nearly 50 percent above the level of 1896; that is, a dollar will now buy about two-thirds of what it would buy then. Yet the dollar has remained the same in weight – 25.8 grains. If the plan here proposed had been in operation since 1896, the weight of the dollar would virtually (but not literally) have increased until today it would have been heavy enough to possess 50 percent more purchasing power than it actually does possess ... The level of prices would then be the same today (in terms of this supposed heavier dollar of 38.7 grains) as it was in 1896 (in terms of the actual dollar of 25.8 grains). In order to have preserved this same level of prices throughout the period 1896–1912 it would only have been necessary, beginning in 1896, to have increased gradually the weight of the dollar. This gradual increase in the weight of the dollar would have taken the place of the increase in prices which has actually been experienced in the last fifteen years. (Fisher, 1913a, 217–218)[15]

An important question now arises – how would it be possible to know the proper adjustment to be made in the weight of the dollar without putting a dangerous discretionary power in the hands of government officials or anyone else? Fisher suggested that adjustments could be put on an automatic footing by the use of price indices. There are various price indices to choose from, of course,

> but they practically all agree remarkably well with each another. When once a system of index numbers is agreed upon, their numerical calculation becomes a purely clerical matter. A statistical bureau ... would compile and publish these statistics periodically and the actual prices on which they were based. If at any time the official index number showed that the price level had risen 1 percent above par, this would be the signal for an increase of 1 percent in the virtual dollar. (Fisher, 1913b, 23)

The plan, in brief, is therefore to

> mark up or down the weight of the dollar (that is, to mark down or up the price of gold bullion) *in exact proportion to the deviations above or below par of the index number of prices.* (1913b, 23, his emphasis)[16]

To indicate how his scheme might have worked, Fisher provided some illustrative simulations for the period that suggested there would have been a stable price level under any of three similar versions of his plan. 'It is clear', he wrote,

> that the proposed system, if not perfect, certainly tends strongly to bring the index number back toward par or to restrain its movements from par, and that if properly planned ... it could always maintain substantial constancy ... of the level of prices. (Fisher, 1913c, 394).

Complications From the Existence of a Gold Coinage

There are however some complications. One such issue arises from the existence of a gold coinage. Fisher's scheme is easiest understood in a world where exchange media are paper or token coins (i.e., ones whose intrinsic value is significantly less than their face value), but complications can arise if there is a full – bodied coinage. Imagine that the weight of the coin dollar is 25.8 grains, as it was when he wrote, but that the issuer is required to redeem these coins for an amount of gold with a purchasing power equal to that of the dollar at some base year. If that year was 1896, then under his scheme we would be dealing with a 1911 virtual dollar with a weight of about 35.8 grains, and the difference of 10 grains can be regarded as the issuer's seigniorage. Gold coins, as Fisher explained,

> would simply become what the silver dollar now is, token coins. Or, better, they would be, like the gold certificates, mere warehouse receipts, or, as it

were, 'brass checks' for gold bullion on deposit in the Treasury. Otherwise expressed, *gold coin would be merely gold certificates printed on gold instead of on paper.* (Fisher, 1913b, 24, his emphasis)

But if the weight of the virtual dollar should fall below 25.8 grains, the gold coinage would be worth more as bullion than as its face value in coin. It would then pay agents to melt down gold coins into bullion and make a profit at the Treasury's expense by presenting the bullion at the Treasury for gold coins. If the weight of the virtual dollar were 12.9 grains, for example, a gold coin weighing 25.8 grains could be melted into bullion and presented to the Treasury to be coined, and arbitragers would have converted one gold coin into two. They could then repeat the operation indefinitely and make arbitrarily large profits at the government's expense (see Fisher, 1913a, 226). Some means would therefore need to be found to prevent such an outcome, and Fisher suggested that the gold currency be re-coined at a lower weight, much as the Philippine peso had been re-coined when the gold-exchange system had been adopted there, or the gold coinage could be dispensed with altogether, as he actually preferred. However, as a practical matter, he also felt that this outcome would be unlikely anyway, since he expected gold to continue to depreciate, but some provision needed to be made in case the need arose (Fisher, 1913b, 25).

Problems Arising From Fixing the Price of the Redemption Medium

Much more serious difficulties for Fisher's scheme arise from the government issuer's fixing of the price of the MOR, gold. Fisher himself stumbled across the problem in a particular context, but never got to the bottom of it. He understood that the change in the weight of the gold dollar could itself affect the value of gold bullion (see Fisher, 1913c, appendix 3), and he acknowledged that some allowance had to be made for this effect in the government's price-fixing rule. If the weight of the dollar were increased – i.e., if its price were reduced – then domestic gold minting would be discouraged, more gold would be used up in the arts, and so on, and the relative price of gold would fall. If prices were to be stabilised, the gold weight of the dollar would have to increase *by more* than the percentage increase in the price index. The problem is to determine by how much more, and Fisher had no clear answer. He suggested that it might be by twice as much, and felt that any greater increase might be destabilising because it would '*over* correct the deviation so much as to produce a deviation greater than the original in the opposite direction' (Fisher, 1913c, 397, his emphasis), but this suggestion was little more than a guess and Fisher had nothing further to offer. The point is that the issuer really needs to know what the *relative* price of gold should be, and then adjust its *nominal* price appropriately. This problem is of course effectively intractable. The issuer cannot know the appropriate relative price, and any mistakes he makes will spill over and push the price level away from its par value. Fisher could not give the government the discretionary power to 'do its best' without throwing away the automaticity of his system which was one of its main attractions, and yet he could offer no rule that would give the government issuer any indication how to respond.

This problem is also more fundamental than Fisher realised. He came across it whilst exploring the extent to which a change in the nominal price of gold would affect mining, the demand by the arts, and so forth, but he appeared to overlook the point that the same basic problem arises whenever *any* factor changes to influence the relative price of gold. Under Fisher's system, the government has to adopt a rule to change the nominal price of gold whenever there is a change in the price level, but the effect of that nominal price change on the price level will depend on the factors that determine the relative price of gold, and the government's rule therefore needs to allow properly for what the latter would be. To see what can happen if the rule does not make such allowance, suppose the currency-issuer follows a Fisher-type rule that changes the nominal price of the medium of redemption, gold, by a times the deviation of the price level from its target p^*:

$$\Delta p_{g,t} = \alpha(p_{t-1} - p^*) \qquad (14.2)$$

where $p_{g,t}$ is the log of the price of gold over t, and p_{t-1} is the log of the price-level index over $t - 1$. (a is the parameter which Fisher usually took as -1 for illustrative purposes, but which he suggested might be -2 in his discussion in Fisher, 1913c, 397.) If we choose our units so that $p^* = 0$, then

$$\Delta p_{g,t} = \alpha p_{t-1}. \qquad (14.3)$$

Assuming for convenience that the market for gold clears at all times, we can write out an inverse demand function for gold of the form:

$$p_{g,t} - p_t = \beta_t \qquad (14.4)$$

where β_t can be interpreted as the equilibrium relative price of gold in period t. If we now substitute out the price of gold and rearrange, we derive a first-order difference equation in the (log of) the price level:

$$p_t - (1 + \alpha)p_{t-1} = -\Delta\beta_t \qquad (14.5)$$

which can easily be solved in textbook manner. (14.5) implies that the price level has a 'long-run equilibrium' value given by

$$p_t = -\Delta\beta_t[1 - (1 + \alpha)L]^{-1} \qquad (14.6)$$

where L is the lag operator, and this 'long-run equilibrium' value is to be interpreted as the value around which the actual price level p_t oscillates, or from which it diverges, or towards which it converges, depending on the dynamics of (14.5). Given $\Delta\beta_t$, the stability or otherwise of the price level depends on the root λ of the auxiliary equation corresponding to (14.5). A necessary and sufficient condition for p_t to be stable is that

$$-1 < \lambda < 1 \qquad (14.7)$$

(see, e.g., Goldberg, 1958). To solve for this root, we rearrange the homogeneous counterpart of (14.5), $p_t - (1 + \alpha)p_{t-1} = 0$, to get $p_t = (1 + \alpha)p_{t-1}$, and then solve backwards to get $p_t = (1 + \alpha)^t p_0$, where p_0 is an assumed initial starting value. The root, λ, is therefore equal to $1+\alpha$.

The behaviour of the price level over time thus depends on α, and stability requires that $-2 < \alpha < 0$. The value of a also determines whether p_t oscillates around its 'equilibrium' value or stays on one side of it. If $\alpha < -1$, the root α is negative, and p_t oscillates around its equilibrium value; and if $\alpha > -1$, the root λ is positive and p_t stays on one side or other of its equilibrium value.

We get four principal outcomes, depending on the value of α: (1) If $\alpha < -2$, then $\lambda < -1$, and p_t would oscillate with ever greater oscillations around its equilibrium value. The price level would then be highly unstable. (2) If $-2 < \alpha < -1$, p_t would oscillate around its long-run equilibrium because the root is still negative, but the oscillations would dampen over time. Shocks to the price level would gradually be corrected. (3) If $-1 < \alpha < 0$, the root becomes positive so the price level would stay on one side of its equilibrium value, but would converge towards that value over time. (4) Finally, if $\alpha > 0$, the price level would move further away from its equilibrium value over time, and would therefore be highly unstable.

In addition to these four cases, we also get three 'knife-edge' cases where α equals -2, -1 or 0. The first case (i.e., $\alpha = -2$) was the one that Fisher actually preferred. The root λ is then equal to -1, and the price level would fluctuate around its equilibrium value with no tendency ever to settle down. The basic stability requirement that shocks to the price level be corrected would not be satisfied.[17] Fisher's attempt to allow for a changing relative price of gold by choosing $\alpha = 2$ would have therefore proven to be highly counterproductive. The second case is the one Fisher usually quoted for illustrative purposes. The root of the difference equation becomes zero, and (14.5) generates the price-level equation:

$$p_t = -\Delta\beta_t. \tag{14.8}$$

The price level now moves inversely with the *rate of change* of the relative price of gold. The third case is simply the gold standard in which the price of gold is fixed. (14.4) then implies that the price level is

$$p_t = p_{g,t} - \beta_t = k - \beta_t, \quad k \text{ constant} \tag{14.9}$$

indicating that the price level moves inversely with the relative price of gold. If our objective is to stabilise the price level, the choice between a compensated dollar with $\alpha = -1$ and a gold standard (i.e., $\alpha = 0$) depends on whether we think the level of the relative price of gold would be more or less stable than its rate of change.

In short, any value of α less than -1 would produce oscillations around the equilibrium value of the price level, and any value less than -2 would produce growing oscillations. A value of α greater than -1 but less than 0 would produce gradual convergence towards the equilibrium value, and any value greater than 0

would produce gradual divergence away from it. A value equal to -1 would make the price level move with the *rate of change* of the relative price of gold, and an α-value equal to 0 would make the price level move with the *level* of the relative price of gold.

However, there is no reason to suppose that the long-run equilibrium value of p_t would remain stable. As (14.6) indicates, any change in the *relative* price term $\Delta\beta_t$ would alter the long-run value of p_t. Ironically, the long-run equilibrium price level under the compensated dollar would be as *vulnerable to a change in the relative price of gold as it would have been under the gold standard itself*. Even if the price level was (somehow) always maintained at its long-run equilibrium value, the failure of the Fisher rule to allow for changes in the relative price of gold would still prevent it from delivering price-level stability. Fisher was therefore right to worry about changes in the equilibrium relative price of gold, but his attempted solution merely ensured that a fluctuation in the price level away from its target value would never be properly corrected.

The difficulty of Fisher's position now becomes clear: he needed a rule that would produce stable price-level dynamics around the long-run equilibrium price level *and* ensure that the long-run equilibrium value itself is not vulnerable to changes in the factors that determine the relative price of gold. At the same time, he needed to find such a rule *ex ante* and ensure it was not tampered with *ex post* if the system was to retain the automaticity that was one of its key attractions. Fisher's problem is for all practical purposes intractable.

Yet, curiously, it is also very avoidable. The problem arises from Fisher's insistence on pegging (and re-pegging) the price of the redemption medium, gold. Having set up a system in which the government periodically pegs the price of the MOR, the government must know how the relative price of the MOR will change if it to be able to formulate a rule that will allow for this change and thereby hit the price-level target, and *any failures to anticipate the appropriate relative price of the MOR will inevitably destabilise the price level*. If the government-issuer cannot make this allowance, it has no alternative but to abandon any attempt to peg the price of the MOR if it wishes to stabilise the price level. Yet the odd thing is that it is never clear in Fisher's work why he wanted to peg the price of the MOR in the first place. Had he simply gone for an indirectly convertible system, he would not have had to peg the price of the MOR, but would have pegged the price of some anchor instead. The nominal price of the MOR would have been free to fluctuate, and changes in its relative price could have been easily accommodated without the damaging consequences that arise when the nominal price of the MOR itself is fixed. If the demand for MOR increased, the nominal and relative prices of the MOR would rise without any particularly significant implications for the price level. If there were pressures to decrease its relative price, on the other hand, the nominal price would fall and that would more or less be the end of it as far as the price level was concerned. Changes in the relative price of the MOR are of no particular significance under indirect convertibility, but cause very serious problems for Fisher's scheme and others like it.

The Issuer's Vulnerability to Speculative Attack

A third complication in Fisher's proposal was his insistence that the Treasury operate a spread between the price at which it would buy bullion and that at which it would sell it, and impose certain restrictions on the rates at which these prices could change. He regarded this spread as an 'essential detail' (1913a, 220) and suggested a figure of perhaps 1 percent. The Mint (or purchase) price would be the lower of the two, and the margin between the two prices he suggested be considered as a 'brassage' charge for minting. The purpose of this spread was not to cover minting charges as such, but to 'avoid speculation in gold [potentially] disastrous to the government' (1913b, 2526). Suppose that agents expected the price of gold to rise from $18 to $18.10 an ounce. Speculators would then buy gold from the government in order to sell it back to it after its price had risen. They would make a profit at the government's expense of 10¢ an ounce, and in theory could make arbitrarily large profits by demanding arbitrarily large amounts of gold before its price rose. If the price of gold was expected to fall, say, from $18.10 to $18 an ounce, speculators would sell all the gold they could to the government for the present higher price, and then buy it back again after its price had fallen, and once again make arbitrarily large profits at the government's expense (see also Fisher, 1913a, 227; 1913b, 26).

To rule out this sort of speculation, Fisher suggested that the brassage differential be accompanied by a proviso that any change in the government pair of prices not exceed this differential. The profits from speculative purchases or sales of gold within any period would then be outweighed by the brassage charge, and there would be no net profit at the government's expense. Suppose that the government's buy price was $12.28 and its sell price $12.41, representing a brassage charge of 1 percent, and that the price changes were restricted to under 1 percent as Fisher suggested. If an agent receives interim information that the prices next period will rise, the new government buy price would still be less than the present government sell price, and there would be no profit to be made by speculating on that information. The government should therefore be immune to that sort of attack (Fisher, 1913b, 26). The only avenue of speculative attack then left is where an agent speculates on future prices two or more periods away, when the future government buy price might be more than the current sell price. To rule this sort of attack out, Fisher suggested that it might be 'possible and perhaps advisable' to require that the proportionate rise in the prices of gold should be less than an appropriate rate of interest on short-term investments (1913a, 227, n. 3; 1913c, 386387).

However, there restrictions still leave the issuer exposed to damaging speculative attack if the government's gold prices are expected to fall. Let the government's bid – ask spread be x percent, the rate of interest over each period y percent, and the expected percentage price change (in absolute terms) be z percent. Fisher's claim that the government is always protected against speculative attack provided $z \leq x$ is wrong. Imagine that an agent at the beginning of a period (correctly) expects that the government's gold prices will fall at the start of the next period, so he sells gold, invests in an interest-bearing asset with the proceeds, and then liquidates the investment and buys gold again when it has fallen. He could obtain a net profit of up to $z + y - x$ from each such operation, and the fact that this profit can clearly be positive even if $z \leq z$ proves that the government is not adequately protected.[18] This example illustrates, indeed, that the government is even more vulnerable to speculative attack when its gold prices are expected to fall than when they are expected to rise. When the prices are expected to fall, arbitragers will sell gold now and invest the proceeds in the interim period before prices fall, and the interest from that investment is therefore to be considered as an additional element in the *profit* from the arbitrage operation. When gold prices are expected to rise, on the other hand, arbitragers will buy gold and hold it in the interim, and the interest they would have received constitutes a *cost* of the operation. The arbitrage profit in the one case is $z + y - x$, but in the other is $z - y - x$, which is less. Fisher's restrictions are still not enough to protect the system against speculative attack.[19]

Recent Relatives of the 'Compensated Dollar'

Interest in the 'compensated dollar' seemed to wane after the 1920s, and there were few further developments until a number of variants on the compensated dollar theme began to appear in the 1980s. Principal amongst these were Black (1987), Hall (1982, 1983, 1984b), Woolsey (1987), and Schnadt and Whittaker (1990, 1993). Black's proposal envisaged a government-issuer which pegs the price of gold and periodically alters that price to stabilise a target price index. Like Fisher (1920), the issuer is also constrained to observe a reserve ratio, but unlike Fisher, Black emphasises that the government can operate the system on virtually no reserves. Hall makes a number of proposals. Hall (1982, 1984b) suggests that a government issuer aim to hit a price level target, but suggests quite different means to achieve it. Hall (1982, 119) suggests that the dollar price of an ANCAP MOR be decreased (increased) each month by one-twelfth of a percentage point for every such point by which the CPI exceeds (falls short of) its target, and Hall (1984b, 313) suggests that the Fed raise (lower) its bill rate by one-tenth of a point above its previous rate for every percentage point by which the CPI exceeds (falls short of) its target.[20] All these schemes – and those of Woolsey and Schnadt–Whittaker as well – have in common with the 'compensated dollar' the basic idea that the government decrease (increase) the price of some asset or commodity by some arbitrary rule in the face of a given increase (decrease) of the target price index from par. Suppose that the price index deviates above par. Intuitively, the higher price index reflects an excessive quantity of exchange media in circulation, and the quantity outstanding needs to fall if the price index is to be pushed back down. Since the index is now above par, the rule obliges the banks to decrease the price of the dollar against MOR, or as Fisher had it, to increase the gold content of the dollar. The relative price of gold, already lowered because of the increase in the price index, is now lowered further by this fall in its nominal price. Since 'real' fundamentals appear to be unchanged, a typical agent would expect that the relative price of gold would eventually rise back again, and the most rational course of action (at least in the medium term) is to buy gold in anticipation of making gains as its price rises. Agents would then buy gold by redeeming exchange media, and the quantities of outstanding exchange media would fall. The fall in the amounts of exchange media in circulation in turn pushes down prices generally, in the longer run at least, and the target price index should eventually return to par. If we like, we can think of the rule as encouraging the necessary fall in the quantities of exchange media in circulation by making gold artificially cheap and encouraging agents to buy it by redeeming exchange media. If the price index falls below par, the banks raise the dollar price, and in the process push the nominal price of gold further above its longer-run value and encourage agents to sell it by demanding additional exchange media from them. The quantity of exchange media in circulation then rises and should help to restore the price index to par. The scheme thus creates incentives to demand redemption and reduce the stock of exchange media if the price index is above par, and increases the stock of exchange media and puts upward pressure on the price index if it is below par.[21]

Generic Weaknesses of 'Compensated Dollar' Schemes

It might be useful to wrap up our discussion of the compensated dollar by summarising the weaknesses common to all versions of the compensated dollar type of system. Two particular weaknesses stand out. The first is that decreasing the price of the MOR when the target price index exceeds par, and increasing it when the target price index falls short of par, is by no means sufficient to ensure that we get a stable price level. As our earlier analysis of Fisher's system indicated, these types of scheme generally lead the price level to follow a difference equation, and it is doubtful that any such scheme could be guaranteed to produce a difference equation that yielded a sufficiently stable price level around its 'long-run equilibrium' level. It is also very doubtful whether the 'long-run equilibrium' price level would itself be stable. In Fisher's scheme, for instance, the 'long-run price level' would only be as stable as the relative price of gold. The short-run price level would fluctuate around – or perhaps move away from – a 'long-run equilibrium' level that would itself be fairly volatile. It is therefore likely that a 'compensated dollar' in practice would have delivered even less price-level stability than the gold standard Fisher intended it to replace.

This pessimistic conclusion is reinforced by a variety of other considerations. For example, the optimal control literature tells us that we cannot select an 'optimal' feedback rule without knowing the 'structure' of the economy, and the fact is that we do not know enough about this 'structure' to say what the 'optimal' rule should be. The leads, lags, and other relevant factors we would need to know are unknown, and probably unknowable, and subject to frequent change anyway. These difficulties are compounded by the Lucas critique (Lucas, 1976) which suggests that we ought not to take past behavioural rules as given in the face of experiments that seek to alter the regime under which agents live. If the regime itself changes (e.g., when the new rule is adopted), agents' expectations will alter with it, and what was previously identified as the 'structure' of the economy will change as well. Conventional estimates of what was previously considered to be the economic 'structure' would then be of questionable value, and what we need instead is an estimate of the 'true' underlying structure (i.e., that based on taste and technology parameters) that is invariant to the policy experiment taking place. Yet reliable estimation of such 'deep structure' is virtually impossible, and likely to remain so.

The second basic problem is that the anticipation of future changes in the price at which the banks are prepared to buy and sell the MOR will destabilise both prices and interest rates, expose the banks themselves to speculative attack, and generally destabilise the economy. The compensated dollar requires that the price of the MOR should return to its expected long-run level by a series of discrete and predictable changes, and since they are predictable, rational agents would speculate on them. As the time approaches for the next change to be made, they would act to avoid capital losses on securities and commodities whose prices were expected to fall, and to reap capital gains on those whose prices were expected to rise. Prices and interest rates would then have to adjust to eliminate expected arbitrage opportunities and ensure that there were no expected profits to be made when the price of the MOR actually changed. Let us consider the price changes first, and leave the interest rate changes aside for the moment:

Unless the prices of other goods and services were sufficiently flexible, speculative forces would ensure that by the time the price change was due to be implemented by the banks, the market price of the MOR would have already reached the post-change level it was expected to take in order to eliminate expected gains or losses. The market price of the MOR would thus gradually change in anticipation of the change in the MOR price that the banks were expected to implement, but this changing market price would not be consistent with the fixed price which the banks would be committed to maintain in the interim – the anticipation of the future change in the banks' price would cause the present market price to alter and drive a wedge between it and the presently fixed price operated by the banks. This price differential would give us a situation reminiscent of the earlier 'paradox' (see Chapter 12) – banks would be exposed to potentially large arbitrage profits, and quantities of exchange media could fluctuate in a very volatile manner – and perhaps the most likely outcome of this particular paradox would be the breakdown of the compensated dollar rule the banks were trying to follow. Still leaving aside the interest rate changes to be discussed shortly, the only way to avoid this outcome is for the prices of *other* goods and services to adjust in such a way that the *relative* price of the MOR against goods and services generally is expected to remain constant at the time its *nominal* price changes (see also Stockman, 1990, 23). If the nominal price of the MOR is expected to fall, the real demand for bank liabilities would tend to rise in anticipation, and then fall back afterwards. To maintain equilibrium and eliminate expected arbitrage profits across the time when the nominal price of the MOR is to change, prices elsewhere would have to be expected to fall until that price change occurred, and then immediately jump back up to a level consistent with the relative price of the MOR against goods and services remaining constant throughout. If the nominal price of the MOR is expected to rise, on the other hand, the same line of reasoning suggests we should expect to see the price level rise in anticipation, and then jump back down again when the (MOR) price change occurs, and the price level would of course have to jump by an amount sufficient to keep the relative price of the MOR constant. Unless we believe that prices elsewhere have the upward and downward flexibility required to behave in this way – which, presumably, we don't – we are forced to the conclusion that price changes alone cannot equilibrate the system in the face of the predicted changes in the prices of redemption media that this rule implies.

Interest rate changes are therefore essential if the system is to equilibrate. Imagine then that the price of the MOR is expected to decline. The

> nominal rate of interest on [the MOR] must [then] be higher than the nominal interest rate on Bankclaims [and the anchor] by the amount of the expected depreciation, adjusting for costs of arbitrage. A high 'nominal interest rate' on [MOR] loans is expressed through futures or forward market prices [which would be] ... low compared to the spot price ... Similarly, the nominal rate of interest on Bankclaims should fall because the real value of Bankclaims with respect to [the MOR] is expected to increase. (Cowen and Kroszner, 1991, 29–30)

The appropriate term interest rate on MOR must rise to offset the expected capital loss from holding MOR when the banks devalue it, and the corresponding shorter-term interest rates would then have to rise to be consistent with that rate. The initial change in these shorter-term rates will still be relatively small, but as the date approaches for the price change to occur, those rates would have to rise to reflect the expectation of the capital loss occurring that much sooner. Short-term rates on MOR-denominated loans would thus keep rising, and they would have risen to very high levels indeed by the time the change was imminent. In the opposite case of an expected rise in the price of the MOR, the MOR-denominated interest rate would fall and nominal (i.e., dollar-denominated) interest rates would rise, and the same logic as before suggests that short-term dollar-denominated rates would rise to very high levels just before the change occurred. Whether the price of the MOR is expected to rise or fall, the fact that the price change is predictable creates considerable volatility in interest rates. Associated market prices – such as those for futures or equity – are also affected since they must be consistent with prevailing interest rates. The changes in interest rates combine with arbitrage in asset markets throughout the economy to disrupt asset prices generally. All things considered, it is hard to avoid the conclusion that compensated dollar systems are practically unworkable.

A 'STABLE DOLLAR' SYSTEM

The Problem Defined

It is time now to take stock of our position. Our primary objective is to design a system that will generate the desired time path for our chosen price index. To anticipate the conclusions of Chapter 15, we shall assume we want to stabilise the value of our chosen price index over time around some particular level, but we are concerned at the moment primarily with the issue of *how to achieve* a particular target rather than with what the target *should be*. To keep the discussion as straightforward as possible, we shall also defer any technical issues relating to the construction of the index to an appendix. We therefore assume that we have our index, and want to stabilise its value over time.

We have five principal constraints to satisfy: (1) It is reasonably clear that any system based on a single-commodity anchor or any 'narrow' anchor will be unsatisfactory because unpredictable movements in the relative price of the anchor will destabilise the value of our price index. We must therefore choose a system based on a 'broad–basket', which means we have to come to grips with the problem of how to stabilise the price of a broad basket without the banks actually handling the basket itself. (2) Our discussion of the 'compensated dollar' suggested that schemes of this type (i.e., schemes that peg and periodically re-peg the price of the MOR) are not feasible, so we need a 'broad-basket' approach that is not just another version of the 'compensated dollar'. Going back to Chapter 12, we then have a choice between directly and indirectly convertible systems. (3) Directly convertible systems are generally inferior, so we would presumably prefer an indirectly convertible system. (4) If we adopt some version of indirect convertibility, we need to ensure that we can avoid any paradox problems. Again referring to Chapter 12, we must pick an anchor whose price the banks can keep pegged at its par value, at least on 'intervention days' when the banks are 'in' the market to peg its price, or else we must pick an anchor whose price moves quickly back to par should it be disturbed from it. The former is preferable, if we have a choice, because it has the attraction that the banks would never be exposed to arbitrage losses from the price of the anchor being away from par, so we might look for an anchor whose price the banks can keep pegged at par on their intervention days. (5) Referring back to the first constraint, we have to ensure that pegging the price of this anchor will stabilise the price of the 'broad' basket, and thus stabilise our target price index.

A 'Stable Dollar' Standard

Suppose our target price index takes the value p_t at time t, p_{t+1} at $t + 1$, and so on. The idea is that the banks of issue create a new kind of financial instrument and indefinitely commit themselves to buy and sell this instrument every so often at a fixed price. This new financial instrument is related to a price-index futures

Table 14.1 Equilibration under the 'stable dollar' rule

Disequilibrium state	Interpretation	Arbitrage process	Consequences
$E_t\$p_{t+1} > p^c_{t+1}$	Excessive expected MOE supply	Arbitragers buy QFCs	MOE supply falls, expected future prices fall
$E_t\$p_{t+1} < p^c_{t+1}$	Insufficient expected MOE supply	Arbitragers sell QFCs	MOE supply rises, expected future prices rise

contract, so I shall refer to it for convenience as a quasi-futures contract (QFC).[22] The QFC is a contract between a purchaser, A, and a seller, B, in which A makes a payment to B at the time t when the contract is made, and B promises in return to make a payment to A the next period that is the product of two terms: a payment indexed to the value of the price index at $t+1$ (i.e., p_{t+1}), and a compounding factor that compensates A for the interest he loses by paying B at t instead of at $t+1$.[23] The reasons for these payment features will become apparent as we proceed. The payment A makes at time t is the price of the contract, and it is this price the banks would peg.

The Equilibrium Condition and Equilibrating Forces

The principles underlying the proposal are relatively straightforward. Let r_t be some 'representative' market interest rate prevailing between t and $t+1$. If we interpret each period as a quarter, r_t might be the 3-month LIBOR rate or something similar. A QFC made at time t might call for B to make an index-linked payment of $\$(1 + r_t)p_{t+1}$ at time $t+1$. (Note that p_t is an index number, but $\$(1 + r_t)p_{t+1}$ is a monetary payment and is therefore denominated in dollars. Hence all monetary payments have a '$\$$' prefix, but index-number terms such as p_t on its own do not.) $\$p_{t+1}$ is the index-contingent payment mentioned earlier, and $(1 + r_t)$ is the compounding factor. In return for the promised future payment, A makes B an immediate payment of $\$p^c_t$ (i.e., he pays the contract price) and the banks undertake to buy or sell contracts as required to keep $\$p^c_t$ at a preannounced level. The present value of the expected profit from buying a contract will consequently be:

$$E_t\$(1 + r_t)p_{t+1}/(1 + r^*_t) - \$p^c_t. \qquad (14.10)$$

E_t is the expectations operator taken on information available at t and r^*_t is an appropriate discount rate which we can think of as a 'representative' money market interest rate (e.g., the LIBOR itself, or some closely related interest rate). We can therefore presume that $[(1 + r_t)/(1 + r^*_t)]$ is equal to unity, or approximately so.[24] The (perhaps approximate) expected profit from buying a contract will then be:

$$E_t \$p_{t+1} - \$p_t^c. \qquad (14.11)$$

Ignoring risk premia for simplicity, equilibrium requires that the expected profit from buying or selling contracts is approximately zero. Hence:

$$E_t \$p_{t+1} \approx \$p_t^c. \qquad (14.12)$$

(14.12) gives us an expression for the equilibrium value of the expected future price index. The pegging of $\$p_t^c$ by the banks should then suffice to stabilise the equilibrium value of the expected price index.

As an aside, it should now be apparent from (14.12) why the contingent payment made by B is compounded to compensate A for his foregone interest. Without that compounding, (14.12) would be replaced by $E_t \$p_{t+1} \approx \$p_t^c (1 + r_t^*)$ and the value of $E_t \$p_{t+1}$ would depend on the nominal discount (or interest) rate r_t^* without the offset from r_t that is implicit in (14.12). The problem then is that the expected price level would no longer be 'tied down': suppose for example that prices were initially stable, but private sector agents for some reason expected prices to rise by 5 percent in the next period. Then r_t^* would (under plausible circumstances) jump 5 percent, and $E_t \$p_{t+1}$ would jump by the same amount, and there would be no mechanism to penalise those agents who bet on inflation despite the fact that the central bank was holding $\$p_t^c$ constant. Inflationary expectations could become self-fulfilling, and the system could no longer be relied upon to deliver price stability. To achieve price stability, we need an equilibrium condition in which $E_t \$p_{t+1}$ depends on $\$p_t^c$ alone, and not on r_t^*. The point of having B pay compensatory interest is therefore to ensure that we get such a condition (i.e., (14.12)) because the interest and discount terms effectively cancel out and leave $E_t \$p_{t+1}$ depending only on $\$p_t^c$. In short, the contract with compensatory interest stabilises the expected future price level, but a contract without compensatory interest does not.

To assess the stability of the equilibrium under the proposed rule, suppose that (14.12) did not hold and $E_t \$p_{t+1}$ significantly exceeded $\$p_t^c$. Intuitively, the expected future price level is now too high because agents expect an excessive money supply in the future, and the restoration of equilibrium requires that the money supply should fall. Speculators now perceive that QFCs are underpriced relative to the high future payout they expect from them. A speculator who buys a contract pays $\$p_t^c$ but expects to earn a present-value return of about $E_t \$p_{t+1}$: he would therefore expect to make an approximate present-value profit of $E_t \$p_{t+1} - \$p_t^c$. Speculators would then purchase more contracts to reap these profits, and the banks would have to create the additional contracts they demanded if they were to keep their price constant. However, in order to purchase the additional contracts, speculators would have to hand over MOE at the time they make their purchases, and the supply of MOE in circulation would fall. The increased speculative demand for contracts would thus translate into a fall in the supply of MOE, which would help push expected future prices down.[25] $E_t p_{t+1}$ would therefore fall towards p_t^c. These expected arbitrage profits would continue, and with them the speculative operations and the falling money supply, until $E_t p_{t+1}$

had fallen to about p_t^c and equilibrium been restored. The equilibrating process is illustrated in Table 14.1.

If $E_t\$p_{t+1}$ fell significantly short of $\$p_t^c$, on the other hand, the expected future price level would now be too low. A speculator would perceive the contracts as over-priced relative to the low expected future payout, and he could make an expected present-value profit of about $\$p_t^c - E_t\$p_{t+1}$ from selling a contract. Speculators would therefore sell contracts to the banks, and each such sale would raise the supply of MOE. Expectations of future prices would rise, and equilibrium would be restored. In short, if (14.12) did not hold for some reason, arbitrage operations would take place that would tend to restore it.

We may wonder whether this equilibration story would undermined by delays in the effects of changing MOE on prices, or by the effects of 'price stickiness' more generally. These factors complicate, but do not undermine, the story. If all prices took two periods to adjust, for example, we would have to tell the equilibration story two periods ahead: (14.12) would become $E_t\$p_{t+1} \approx \$p_t$, and so forth, but the underlying story would remain much the same. If we believe that price stickiness is a serious issue, we might prefer a longer contract term to a shorter one, but the contract length of one year suggested later on should still be adequate. We should also bear in mind that even though some prices are sticky, the price index itself will still be flexible provided that a significant number of the included goods and services have flexible prices. In any case, what is relevant here is the stickiness of the *expected* rather than of the *actual* price index, and arguments about the stickiness of the latter are not sufficient to establish the stickiness of the former.

In practice, we might also expect these equilibrating forces to be reinforced by other agents acting on the anticipation that equilibrium would be restored. If the value of the expected price index is too high, a representative supplier will anticipate that the relative price of the commodity he supplies will be high that period. He will plan to increase his supply, and his action and that of others like him will lead expected future prices to fall. High expected future prices will also lead purchasers to reduce their expected future purchases, and these actions will further reinforce the equilibrating process. Similarly, if expected future prices were too low, expected supplies would fall and expected demands would rise, and reinforce the equilibrating process in the other direction.

Though arbitrage forces would push the system towards equilibrium, if it should depart from it, we also need some reassurance that arbitrage forces do not over-compensate – that is, transform a deviation from equilibrium in one direction into a greater deviation from equilibrium in the other – and produce an unstable system in which deviations from equilibrium were magnified over time rather than reduced. However there is a second arbitrage argument that suggests that this kind of instability should not occur: the equilibrium condition (14.12) tells us roughly what the price index expected next period should be; by extension, there are longer-term analogues of (14.12) that tell us roughly what expected prices should be in periods after that; if the kind of instability being discussed here *did* occur, the price level expected for at least *some* future times would then be well away from its equilibrium level, and (14.12) and/or some of its longer-term analogues would be violated; hence, the equilibration arguments that give us (14.12) and its longer-term analogues would appear to rule out the kind of instability being discussed here. We thus have some reason to believe that arbitrage forces would not only push the system towards equilibrium, but also produce a reasonably stable price level as well.

The Stability of the (Actual) Price Index Under the Proposed Rule

However, the critical question is how far the proposed rule would stabilise the *actual* (as opposed to *expected*) price level. Assume for the time being that the rule is credible, so that private agents expect zero inflation over the relevant future. Given rational expectations, we can decompose the realised price index at $t + 1$ into its rational expectation at t plus a shock ε_{t+1} that is orthogonal to information available at t:

$$p_{t+1} = E_t p_{t+1} + \varepsilon_{t+1} , \ E_t \varepsilon_{t+1} = 0. \tag{14.13}$$

If we now normalise by dividing throughout by p_t^c, (14.13) becomes

$$p_{t+1} / p^c{}_t = E_t \, p_{t+1} / p^c{}_t + \varepsilon_{t+1} / p^c{}_t \approx 1 + u_{t+1} \tag{14.14}$$

where $u_{t+1} \equiv \varepsilon_{t+1}/p_t^c$ and the approximation comes from (14.12). (14.14) tells us that the actual (normalised) price index is (approximately) the sum of an expected component, i.e., unity, and an unexpected price-index forecast error u_{t+1}.

Given that the banks would peg p_t^c under the QFC regime, (14.14) tells us that the standard deviation of the actual price-index under the QFC regime would be approximately equal to the standard deviation of price-level forecast errors under that regime. While we cannot directly predict the latter standard deviation, we can estimate the standard deviation of price-level forecast errors for historical regimes and there are good reasons to believe that the historical standard deviation of price-level forecast errors would be higher than the comparable standard deviation under the QFC regime. An estimate of the standard deviation of price-level forecast errors can therefore be regarded as providing an upper bound for such errors under the QFC regime. Perhaps the best estimates for past regimes are those derived from ARCH models, and Engel's (1982) estimates for the UK over the period 1957: II to 1977: II suggest that (quarterly) price-level forecast errors had standard errors varying from 0.5 percent in the 1960s to a maximum of 2.2 percent in the 1970s. These figures are likely to over-state price-level unpredictability under the QFC regime because the price level under previous regimes was subject to various shocks that would not arise under the QFC regime. Under the gold standard, the price level would rise in response to discoveries of gold ore or refinements in the gold extraction process. Under the fiat system, the price level is vulnerable to shifts in government or central bank monetary policy, and there is good reason to believe that at least part of the relatively high price-level forecast errors that Engel estimates for the 1970s were due to the volatile monetary policies of that period. Under the QFC rule, however, discoveries of gold would have no particular influence on the general price level because there would be no link with gold, and there would be little scope for shifts in monetary policy to affect the price level because a credibly implemented QFC rule would replace monetary policy as it is currently understood.

The Need to Avoid the 'Interest-free Loan Problem'

We now consider a number of further issues. Once a contract has been sold by the banks, there is no reason to prevent agents trading it among themselves before it matures, but it would be unwise for the banks to maintain the same price for a particular contract throughout the period until it matures. A particular contract might start off with (say) 90 days to mature, and would trade for a particular price when it was first issued, but 85 days later the same contract would have only a few days to run, and this changing maturity must be acknowledged in the contract price if the banks are not to expose themselves to profitable speculative attack. If the banks tried to trade contracts of both maturities for the same price, arbitragers could make a riskless profit by selling contracts with a relatively long time to maturity to the banks, obtaining base money in exchange, investing the base money to earn some interest on it, and then buying the contracts back when they were close to maturity. They would receive the same price for the contracts as they had paid earlier themselves, and they would keep the interest they had earned by investing the money in the interim. Their profit – and the banks' loss – would then be the interest on the proceeds. The banks would have effectively committed themselves to providing intra-quarter loans at a zero rate of interest. The optimal strategy for arbitragers is then to sell as many contracts as they can when the banks open to trade 'new' contracts, invest the proceeds, and buy the contracts back just before they mature. (In other words, the optimal strategy is to maximise the number of interest-free loans they take out and invest the proceeds.) Private agents could presumably increase their profits to arbitrarily high levels, and the banks' ability to maintain their pricing policy would be very doubtful.

Perhaps the easiest way to avoid this interest-free loan problem and its consequences would be for the banks every so often to peg the price of contracts with a specified period to maturity (e.g., 90 days). The banks would peg the price of contracts with 90 days to mature by offering to buy and sell them on demand at a particular price, and the prices of contracts with less than 90 days to run would be left to the market to determine. Market agents would price contracts with less than 90 days to run as they wished, but they would do so anticipating the banks' periodic 'interventions' into the QFC market to peg the prices of contracts with exactly 90 days to run. Rational-expectations arbitrage would then ensure that the prices of contracts with other than 90 days to run were consistent with the periodically pegged prices of 90-day contracts, and the banks would no longer be vulnerable to unlimited demands for interest-free loans.

As an aside, it is worth emphasising that the monetary standard suggested here is also immune against the better-known form of speculative attack that arises when a central bank or group of banks periodically change an asset price, but agents can anticipate the direction and timing of the asset price changes. The usual example is where a central bank tries to operate a policy of crawling-peg exchange rates, but private sector agents anticipate the exchange rate changes and speculate against them; we also saw much the same problem with the 'compensated dollar' when agents can predict future changes in the price of the MOR. However banks operating such rules are vulnerable to attack only because they *change* an asset price in a *predictable* way, and banks that could credibly commit themselves to maintaining an asset price indefinitely would clearly have no such problem. We shall discuss credibility issues shortly, but assuming for the moment it was credibly implemented, the monetary standard proposed here would be protected against this form of speculative attack because there would be no anticipated price changes against which to speculate.

The Market for Quasi-futures Contracts

At the moment there does not exist any market in QFC contracts or even 'regular' Retail-Price-Index (RPI) futures contracts. A market for Consumer Price Index (CPI) futures contracts did exist for a short while in the USA, operated by the Coffee, Cocoa, and Sugar Exchange in New York (see Horrigan, 1987), but trading was so thin that the Exchange eventually closed it down. The question therefore arises: would there be a market for QFC contracts if the rule proposed here were implemented?[26] The answer appears to be that there would be a market, if one were needed. Imagine that the banks initially offered such contracts but there were no takers. The banks would nonetheless be committed to buy and sell such contracts at a specified price, and (14.12) tells us what $E_t\$p_{t+1}$ must (approximately) be to equilibrate the market. If there were still no takers for the contract, a time would presumably come when $E_t\$p_{t+1}$ would deviate from this equilibrium level. (One would have thought it most unlikely that $E_t\$p_{t+1}$ *never* drifted away from its equilibrium value by a sufficient amount to provoke arbitrage activity in the QFC market, but even in this unlikely event the key point would be that (14.12) would always be satisfied and we would get the price-level outcome we desired. What really matters is not that trading *actually* takes place, but that the trading necessary to restore equilibrium (i.e., (14.12)) would take place if (14.12) *were* disturbed.) When that time comes, private agents could expect to make arbitrage profits by buying or selling QFC contracts, and the market would start to come alive. The amount of MOE in circulation would alter, expectations of future prices would change, and equilibrium would be restored. In short, the argument is that *given* the banks' offer to buy or sell contracts at a specified price, private agents would have an incentive to trade if their expectations of future prices were not consistent with equilibrium. We can rely on private arbitrage activity to ensure that enough trading takes place to restore equilibrium, should equilibrium ever be disturbed.

Enhancing the Credibility of the Monetary Standard

An important advantage of the QFC rule is that it provides a basis from which the banks, if they need to, can enhance the credibility of their commitment to the QFC rule in the longer term. It is important for the banks to have some means of enhancing the credibility of this commitment: If the banks' commitment were seen as lacking credibility, private agents would attach some significant probability to the rule being altered or abandoned. Their expectations would be altered accordingly (e.g., they might expect inflation in the long term) and these altered expectations might have 'undesirable' consequences such as higher long-term interest rates. Private agents might also speculate against the rule and conceivably, perhaps, even force the banks to abandon it. Should the banks adopt the rule, it is therefore important that they do so credibly.

There is a simple and (literally) profitable way for them to establish their credibility. If they adopted the rule but did so lacking credibility, their lack of credibility would be reflected by private-sector expectations of positive rather than (approximately) zero inflation in the long term. If the banks wished to solve their credibility problem, they must therefore persuade the private sector to expect zero long-term inflation, and they can do so by staking their own wealth on the achievement of zero long-term inflation by offering to bet on it. Suppose the banks were 'genuinely' committed to indefinite zero inflation, but the private sector doubted their commitment and expected the price level in 5 years to have risen by, say, 25 percent. The banks could then offer to sell instruments promising a payoff in 5 years contingent on the realised value of the retail price index in 5 years' time and private agents would be willing to buy them because they would expect to make a profit from the rising RPI.[27] Since this long-term betting contract provides for bank payments to be contingent on the RPI in 5 years' time, it provides for an automatic financial penalty if the banks create long-term inflation. The private sector would recognise this financial incentive and consequently revise their own expectations of future inflation downwards. The more of these contracts the banks sell, the greater that incentive will be and the closer private-sector inflation expectations will be to the banks' own expectations. If the banks wish to bring private-sector expectations of long-run inflation down (e.g., to somewhere 'close' to zero), they can therefore do so by selling enough of these long-term price-level 'bets'.[28]

Selling bets would offer the banks an ideal way to enhance their credibility if the private sector doubted their commitment to long-term price stability. If they were sincere about their commitment to long-run price stability, the banks could issue bets to the public fully expecting to win them when the period of the bets expired. Private agents who bet against the banks would lose and the banks would profit at their expense. In a manner reminiscent of the judo expert who uses his opponent's weight to beat him, the banks would have turned the weight of private-sector doubt about their commitment into profit for themselves. The only cost to the banks would be that by issuing bets the banks would be making it more costly for themselves to 'renege' on their commitment, but it is precisely because there would be a penalty for 'reneging' that the issue of bets would enhance the banks' credibility. In any case, 'sincere' banks would not want to renege on that commitment and would have no problem exposing themselves to potential financial penalty. 'Sincere' banks could both enhance their credibility and make a profit, and the only cost of doing so would be to foreclose an option they did not want to exercise anyway.

We may wonder why the banks should bother with QFCs at all when they could always issue price-level bets. Why not have the banks issue bets of various maturities and forget about the complications arising from QFCs? The answer is simple: A bet (e.g., a 'pure' futures contract) only gives the banks an *incentive* to *deliver* a particular price level, but does not *actually* deliver it (or tell the banks how to achieve it). If the banks dispensed with QFCs and merely issued bets, they would still have to solve the difficult problem of managing monetary policy to ensure that they won their bets, and they would therefore be taking bets without being sure they could win them. The *point* about the QFC rule is that it would automatically tie down the price level, give or take a 'small' random error, and thus solve the banks' 'delivery' problem for them. If the banks adopted the QFC rule and issued price-level bets, they could *then* be reasonably confident that they would win them. Far from being an *alternative* to the banks' issuing bets, the QFC rule in fact provides the *foundation* from which they can safely issue them.

The QFC System as Indirectly Convertible

The last remaining task is to explain how the QFC rule can be incorporated into a system of day-to-day indirect convertibility. Recall that a system of indirect convertibility requires that a bank redeem its currency with MOR of the same market value as the anchor whose nominal price is pegged. The anchor in this system is the basket of future goods and services, and the banks peg the price of this basket by pegging the price of QFCs. Banks can then refer to the price of QFCs to determine the amount of MOR they must hand over whenever they are faced with demands for redemption. There is, however, a complication. Banks might be legally obliged to redeem their currency at any time on demand, but there may be no current trading in QFCs that tells them what a QFC is currently worth; indeed, even if there is current trading in QFCs, their prevailing market price might conceivably depart from par and thereby expose the system to possible paradox problems. The solution is simply to take the relevant market value of QFCs to be their value as determined on the banks' last 'intervention day' (i.e., par). Whenever someone presents a note for redemption, a bank would then merely check the current market price of MOR and hand over MOR of the same value as the anchor valued at par. If the par price of a QFC is $1, for example, the bank would hand over MOR worth $1. If the price of a unit of the MOR is $2, the bank would hand over half a unit of the MOR; if the price of the MOR is $3, it would hand over one third of a unit of MOR, and so on. The banks face the discipline of convertibility on a continuous day-to-day basis, even though the QFC (or anchor) might not itself be continuously traded. The QFC rule is thus compatible with a fully operational system of indirect convertibility.

CONCLUSIONS

It might perhaps be useful now to draw the discussion together. Our main purpose is to achieve a 'stable dollar' – a dollar of reasonably stable purchasing power – by stabilising the price of some basket. We started by examining symmetallism and the various systems related to it (e.g., commodity-reserve currency) which try to achieve price stability by pegging the price of a 'narrow' basket. However, we found that the narrow-basket approach has serious disadvantages that effectively rule it out. In particular, we need a basket that has a stable relative price, and no-one has established that one exists. The only baskets whose relative prices can be counted on to be stable are then 'broad' baskets consisting, perhaps, of thousands of goods (and services), and whose prices are reflected in the standard price indices. But their very breadth makes trading in such baskets effectively impossible. We therefore need to find some way to *make use of index numbers as a substitute for trading in the basket itself*. The traditional solution to this problem is to adopt some version of the 'compensated dollar'. We therefore examined the 'compensated dollar' in detail, but found that the scheme is pretty much unworkable. We also found that it is unworkable for reasons that make more modern versions of it unworkable as well. If we reject the 'compensated dollar', we are then presumably looking for an indirectly convertible system that makes use of a price index. We know that at least one such system does exist – the QFC scheme just described – and there may be others as well (e.g., those of Thompson, 1986; Glasner, 1989a, 230–236;[29] Hall, 1983[30] or Hetzel and Friedman, see Friedman, 1992, 227–229). The technical means therefore exist to stabilise the price level or achieve whatever other price-level target we may set. Our next task is now to determine what the most appropriate price target might be.

Appendix 1: The Construction of the Price Index

This appendix examines some of the main technical issues involved in the construction of a price index. As indicated in Chapter 14, the purpose of such an index would be to measure the price of a basket of goods and services, so that the index can be used to assess movements in the price 'level' over time. Formally speaking, our basic problem is as follows: Given data on the prices and quantities of n goods in period t – denoted by the $n{\times}1$ vectors p_t and q_t respectively – we wish to find numbers, P_t and Q_t such that $P_t Q_t \equiv p_t' q_t$. P_t can be regarded as the price index for period t, q_t as the basket of which P_t represents the price, and Q_t as the corresponding quantity index (Diewert, 1987, 767). Given that we have data on p_t and q_t, we can immediately infer their product $P_t Q_t$. Our problem is therefore to break down $P_t Q_t$ into its component parts P_t and Q_t. If we can work out P_t we can deduce what Q_t must be, and vice versa. Solving the price index problem (i.e., working out P_t) is the mirror image of solving the quantity index problem (i.e., working out Q_t). Once we have solved one, we can easily solve the other.

Focusing now on the price-index problem and translating it into plain English, our problem is to find some index P_t that can be regarded as 'representative' in some sense of the vector of prices p_t. The first point to realise is that a theoretically 'perfect' index number is quite unobtainable. As Fisher pointed out, 'none' of the 'innumerable methods' available

> is perfectly satisfactory from a theoretical standpoint. [For example, the] effect of a changed volume of currency or changed velocity of circulation on the whole series of prices is complex, and cannot, even in theory, be compressed into one figure representing all price changes. (Fisher, 1911, 199)

The most we can hope for is therefore an index that gives at least a reasonable indication of the 'central tendency' of the prices in p_t.

What properties should a 'good' index satisfy? Diewert (1987, 768–769) lists 11 such properties,[31] but the problem is that the standard index numbers all fail one or more of these tests and we have to decide which of these properties we can live without. Our choice of index number is then determined by the particular properties we are prepared to drop, and there is of course no easy way to decide which must go. Fortunately, the choice between different indices does not appear to make a great deal of difference in practice. The key result in the literature is that any 'ideal' index (i.e., one which satisfies the properties we would want to impose) must normally lie between the *Laspeyres* and *Paasche indices* (see, e.g., Diewert, 1987, 770).[32] The critical factor is then how close the bounds might be, and experience indicates that these two indices will typically differ by less than one-half of one percent in most time-series contexts (Diewert, 1987, 773). Either of these two indices will therefore give an approximation to the 'true' index that is (usually) accurate to within one-half of one percent, and any index in between – for example, Fisher's '*ideal index*', the geometric mean of the Laspeyres and Paasche indices – will normally produce a more accurate approximation still. The accuracy of the approximation can be increased further by picking a *superlative index*.[33] While the Laspeyres and Paasche indices can be considered as *first-order* approximations to each other, and hence, to anything in between, Diewert (1978) showed that all known superlative indices are *second-order* approximations to each other, and hence to any 'true' index, and experience indicates that they are typically accurate to within 0.2 percent of each other in time-series contexts (Diewert, 1987, 773). The exact choice of index thus makes relatively little difference in practice, at least as regards time-series, especially if we choose a superlative one.

MULTILATERAL INDICES

There are also a number of other issues. One problem is that when we go beyond *bilateral* comparisons involving two sets of prices to *multilateral* ones involving three or more, none of our superlative indices will obey the circularity condition that our indices be intransitive to the choice of base (Diewert, 1987, 773). The choice of base therefore 'matters' even though we would prefer it did not. Perhaps the best approach to this problem is to adopt the chain principle suggested by Marshall ([1887b] 1966) and Fisher (1911). This approach 'makes use of the natural order provided by the march of time' in an intuitively plausible way (Diewert, 1987, 773). We first set the price level in period 1 equal to unity. To obtain this index we then compute the bilateral index for period 2 using period 1 as the base. Denoting this index by $P(p^1, p^2)$, we then compute the period 3 index as $P(p^2, p^3).P(p^1, p^2)$, the period 4 index as $P(p^3, p^4).P(p^2, p^3).P(p^1, p^2)$, and so on. The period i price level is thus obtained, not by comparing period i prices with those in some arbitrary base year, but as the product of period-by-period relative price indices. The chain approach has a number of advantages: It treats all periods in a comparable way, and does not single out any one period as an arbitrary base; previous price levels do not need to be altered as new observations become available; and the various indices will approximate each other reasonably closely if the chain principle is used because changes in prices and quantities for adjacent periods will be relatively small. The main drawback of the chain approach, as with the alternatives, is that the bilateral formulas involved still fail the circularity test, but experience suggests that deviations from circularity for superlative indices are small in time-series applications, and that indices will often satisfy circularity to a first approximation (Fisher, 1922; Diewert, 1987, 774). The non-circularity problem is consequently not too severe in practice.

NEW GOODS, OLD GOODS AND QUALITY CHANGES

Other problems are caused by changes in the composition of the basket of commodities whose price the index is meant to represent. These changes occur all the time, and real-world indices typically rely on periodic quantity surveys to detect them. However, three sources of such change are particularly troublesome – those caused by the introduction of new goods, the disappearance of old ones, and quality adjustments in traded goods. Consider first the new goods question. Indices normally require that all included goods have defined prices over all included periods, but a new good introduced at T obviously has no price in earlier periods. Yet if we ignore new goods the index can become increasingly unrepresentative over time – as time goes by, an increasingly large proportion of goods would not have been available when the index first started, and the omission of these goods can make our index increasingly diverge from the index that we would have used if we could start again now. For example, an index begun in 1700 would exclude the bulk of goods available today. The failure to include new goods can also make bias our estimated price index in another way. A new good will typically follow a product cycle, with high prices initially and lower prices later on, so ignoring new goods whose prices are generally falling means that our index will tend to overstate the 'true' price level. The extent of the bias will vary, but back-of-the-envelope simulations presented by Diewert suggest that 'ignoring new goods could lead to a substantial overestimation of price inflation' (Diewert, 1987, 779).

One solution, suggested by Hicks (1940), is to set the price of a new good in earlier periods at that level such that the demand for that good would have been just equal to zero, but this approach presupposes that we could simulate what the demand would have been. A better approach is to include that good as soon as possible in the basket. Since its initial sales would be low, introducing the new good rapidly into the basket would have relatively little impact on the price level at first, and thus cause relatively few practical problems, but it would have a growing effect over time as the demand for the new good grew. It would therefore ensure that the price index remained reasonably 'representative' as new goods were gradually added to the basket whose price the index is meant to reflect. Adding new goods to the basket in this way would also help mitigate the changing-quality problems that are discussed a little further below.

Problems can also arise if 'old' goods disappear. Once they have disappeared, goods would no longer have a market price and a fixed-quantity basket (i.e., one that presumed that the good was still being produced) would, strictly speaking, be no longer computable. There are also potential bias problems comparable to those that arise with the appearance of new goods. One way to handle these problems is to impute a price for those goods in later periods along the lines suggested by Hicks, but this option is still open to the objection that we do not know what demand would have been. An alternative is to drop the disappeared good from our complete data set, but that would require that we recompute all our historical indices each time a good disappears. Our estimate of a price index value for 1700 would have to be recalculated each time a good 300 years later disappeared. Dropping the old good altogether also has the disadvantage that it makes a 'final' value of the price index for any period impossible, which would in turn undermine agents' ability to write contracts contingent on realised values of the relevant price index.[34] A more satisfactory approach would be to drop the old good from the basket as it disappears. Presumably, its sales would fall to negligible levels in the period before it disappears, so the 'change' in the basket would make little difference at the time it occurred. As with the appearance of new goods, the basket would then remain reasonably representative over time, but it would also avoid the problems that arise from Hicks' solution of simulating what demand would otherwise have been.

There is also the related issue of what to do about changes in 'quality' over time. There is a danger that an index that ignores quality changes might produce a biased estimate of the inflation rate. If the quality of goods was generally improving, an index that ignored quality would tend to over-state price increases over time, relative to a 'true' index that took account of such changes. If the measured price index remained the same, but the quality of the goods improved, then a consumer buying the basket would pay the same amount in both periods, but he would be getting more in the second period and it might be more reasonable to suppose that the 'true' index of prices had actually fallen. However, it is not clear just how serious a problem this quality-change bias actually is.[35] The actual bias is not just a function of whether goods are generally improving or deteriorating in quality over time, but also depends on the type of index, how far the prices of quality-changed products move in line with the prices of quality-unchanged ones, and other issues. The extent of the quality bias is thus an empirical matter, and it is not necessarily the case that improving quality always leads to an overstatement of the price index (Triplett, 1983, 381).

Nor is it clear what should be done about this bias, even granted that it is a problem. The procedure usually used with the US Consumer Price Index (CPI) is to classify quality changes as major or minor, ignore the minor ones, and use an arbitrary rule to deal with the major ones. It works, but it is not clear how good a solution it is. An alternative is to use hedonic indicators to make appropriate adjustments. This approach uses a cross-section regression to 'price' the different quality attributes of a good, and then uses these attributes to make appropriate allowances to changes in the price of the good over time. A third option, less subtle, but simpler to implement, is to use an expert assessment of the quality-change bias to make adjustments to the reported price index. If the unadjusted or 'measured' index is estimated to be subject to a quality-change bias of 1 percent a year, say, then the 'reported' inflation rate would equal the 'measured' inflation rate minus 1 percent. Presumably, there would no great changes in the bias from year to year, so an expert view of the average bias could simply be built into the price-index generation process as an automatic adjustment. Every now and then, the expert assessment of the bias could re-evaluated, and the adjustment altered accordingly until the next reassessment.

DURABLE GOODS AND ASSETS

Then there is the question of what to do about durable goods and assets. The source of the issue is that agents use up utility or production services, rather than the goods themselves. If all goods (or services, in the normal sense of the term) were non-durable, then there would be no problem, since the utility or input services flows they use up can be directly related to the goods or services they purchase over any given period. However, when goods are durable, purchases of goods in any period no longer give us a clear indication of the service flows they receive from those goods in any given period. Ideally, we would want those service flows to go into our basket, and we would want to price those service flows accordingly, but how do we infer those services – not to mention put prices on them – when agents obtain them by buying durable goods?

There is no ideal solution to this problem. One solution sometimes adopted is to use rental equivalences. If we were concerned about housing services, for example, we would use ignore house purchases as such and use data on house rentals, even if the individuals involved owned their homes rather than rented them. However, rental data do not always exist, and the data that do exist might be of poor quality for the purposes for which we would want them. Houses are extremely heterogeneous, and there may be little or no rental market in a particular kind of house. The same solution, to the extent it works, can also be used for certain other types of durable good (e.g., cars), but there are also many other types of durable goods where no such data are available, and estimating implicit rentals in these cases might be little more than educated guesswork.

A different aspect to this problem is the role of asset prices. Theoretically, there is a good case that asset prices should be included as well other prices (Alchian and Klein, 1973), and serious biases can result if asset prices are excluded but behave differently from the prices of the goods or services that are included in the basket. Alchian and Klein provide a good illustration:

> The sharp decrease in the growth rate of money during 1969 provides a classic example of the bias involved in measuring inflation by considering only, for example, movements in the CPI ... The CPI, which rose at a 5.8 percent annual rate during the second half of 1969 shows no sign of decelerating and rose at a 6.0 percent annual rate during the first half of 1970 ... But there is some evidence that asset prices responded almost immediately and quite dramatically to the change in policy ...
>
> This evidence suggests that asset prices declined relative to flow prices over the period and that movements in the CPI severely underestimated the deflationary effects of the tight money policy. (Alchian and Klein, 1973, 180–181)

CONCLUSIONS

While it is impossible to attain theoretical perfection in the construction of a price-index number, it is possible to produce price-index numbers that satisfy many of the properties we would wish them to have. The exact type of index number is still a problem, but the most promising index would be one of the superlative ones and the empirical evidence suggests, fortunately, that the differences that do exist between the various indices we might choose from are relatively small in practice anyway. Once we have chosen a superlative index, we would then want the index to be multilateral rather than bilateral. The only theoretical drawback of a multilateral index is that it violates the circularity condition, but an incidental advantage of a superlative index is that the non-circularity is negligible, at least to a first approximation. The more difficult problems relate to the appearance of new goods, the disappearance of old ones, quality changes, and the handling of durable goods and asset prices. Perhaps the best solution to the first two problems is to let the composition of the basket vary – using expenditure shares as weights, for example – so that new goods could be introduced immediately into the basket and disappeared goods could be dropped from it. Letting the basket change in this way would also go some way towards handling the third problem – how to deal with quality changes – but if further measures were required, we could resort to the use of hedonic indicators or adjust the 'reported' value of the price index to take account of the perceived quality-change bias. A fourth problem – how to handle durable goods – is perhaps more difficult, but it is not clear that too much can be done about it. In practice, if we followed these guidelines, we would probably end up with an index not too dissimilar from the CPI/RPI that is already widely used. For practical purposes, then, we may as well use the CPI/RPI.

Appendix 2: 'Tabular Standards'

THE HISTORY OF THE TABULAR STANDARD IDEA

If the idea behind 'stable dollar' schemes is to protect agents against the adverse effects of price-level changes by minimising the extent to which such changes occur, the idea behind the *'tabular standard'* – sometimes referred to as indexing, index-linking, or monetary correction – is to protect agents by adjusting the number of monetary units to be paid out to settle contracts. Instead of specifying that a debt is to be discharged by a payment of so-many dollars at time t, a tabular standard would specify that the debt is to be discharged by a payment of so-many dollars multiplied by some index of the price level at time t. The 'stable dollar' puts the correction into the *monetary unit itself*, while the tabular standard puts the correction into the *number of monetary units* to be paid out. Tabular standards can be applied to almost any case where payment is deferred beyond some minimum period, and can be applied in individual, isolated cases or across much (though not all) of the economy.

Tabular standards were discussed by a number of writers in the early nineteenth century and then developed further by Jevons ([1875] 1907) and Marshall ([1886] 1926, 1013; [1887b] 1966, 197–199). Under Marshall's version, a government Department, 'having ascertained the prices of all important commodities, would publish from time to time the amount of money required to give the same general purchasing power as, say, £1 had at the beginning of 1887' ([1887b], 1966, 197).

> If, for instance, it declared in 1890 that 18s. [i.e., 90p] had this purchasing power, then a contract to pay a unit [of constant purchasing power] would be discharged by paying 18s. If it declared in 1892 that 23s. [i.e., £1.15p] had only the same purchasing power as £1 had in 1887 ... then any contract to pay a unit in 1892 would require for its settlement the delivery of 23s. ([1887b] 1966, 197)

When loans are made, those concerned would choose whether to contract in terms of standard monetary units or price-level-adjusted ones, but the latter would protect both sides to any contract against the losses of unexpected adverse changes in the price level. Marshall also suggested that wages, rents, mortgages and government debt might be specified in terms of his units, and that law courts should enforce contracts made in terms of them. Marshall made no claims for the scheme's 'theoretic perfection', but felt that it would be a 'great improvement on our present methods, and obtained with little trouble' and that the public would soon get used to the tabular standard and make widespread use of it ([1886] 1926, 10). Since Marshall, the tabular standard has been endorsed by many other economists, including, among many others, Bach and Musgrave (1941), Goode (1951), Friedman (1974), and Hall (1981).

ADVANTAGES OF TABULAR STANDARDS

The main purpose of a tabular standard is to protect agents against the risk associated with price-level changes: tabular standards eliminate, or at least reduce, the redistributions that arise from unanticipated inflation. An argument for tabular standards can also derived from standard portfolio theory. If a perfect hedge against price-level risk does not already exist, or is relatively costly to construct, then the availability of indexed bonds adds a new instrument to agents' portfolios – one, furthermore, that has little or no price-level risk – and a risk-averse borrower or lender would be willing to pay something for that protection. Borrowers would therefore prefer to issue indexed bonds, and lenders would prefer to buy them, and non-indexed bonds should be replaced by indexed ones (see, e.g., Sarnat, 1973; Fischer, 1977; Levhari and Liviatan, 1977; and Niehans, 1978, 134). The result that agents would normally prefer indexed bonds to non-indexed ones is a very strong one, and the problem, if anything, is how to explain the continued existence of non-indexed bonds when agents can use indexed ones instead.[36]

Indexation also makes agents better of by reducing or eliminating their need reduce contract maturities to protect themselves against inflation. The choice of contract length reflects a variety of 'real' factors – such as the costs of periodic renegotiation, and borrowers' (or workers') desires to be secure against imminent contract renegotiation – and one of the costs of inflation is that it encourages them to reduce contract maturities 'excessively' to protect themselves against inflation risk. Giersch observes that

> In the absence of escalator provisions, the uncertainty that accompanies an inflation produces short-term agreements, quite contrary to the basic interest of the market participants who ... need security for longer-range planning and thus ... need contracts that will remain binding over longer periods. In capital transactions, contract terms are shortened because interest rates depend on the rate of inflation and are therefore unpredictable over longer periods. (Giersch, 1974, 10)

By contrast, with a tabular standard agents need only agree on the real return or real wage to be paid and then protect it by inserting a suitable standard clause into their contract. Contract lengths can then remain (approximately) unaffected by inflation, and agents can avoid the various costs and inconveniences that 'excessively' short contract lengths would bring.

Tabular standards can also protect deferred payments in another way: they can counter the 'tilt' problem on scheduled debt repayments. Tilt is the extent to which inflation brings forward real payments. A higher inflation rate means that any given schedule of nominal debt payments is paid back more rapidly in real terms, and this more rapid repayment can pose a problem because it reduces the borrower's liquidity. Even if nominal interest rises in anticipation of higher inflation to leave the real rate unchanged, the degree of tilt rises because of the compounding effect of inflation, and a borrower would still have to repay his real indebtedness faster than before (Howitt, 1986, 184185). Should inflation be unexpectedly low, the borrower would have more liquidity than he expected, and the lender would be short of it. Tabular standards can prevent this problem by stipulating the schedule of real repayments in advance. There would be no unexpected tilt, and both parties would be as liquid as they expected to be.

LIMITATIONS AND COSTS OF TABULAR STANDARDS

Limitations

It is generally agreed that while tabular standards might mitigate some of the adverse effects of inflation, they are at most a second-best alternative to eliminating the inflation itself (e.g., Friedman, 1974, 25–26, 35; Niehans, 1978, 138). Part of the explanation is that two factors the dependence of tabular standards on price indices that are published only at discrete intervals, and the impossibility of maintaining price determinacy in the face of universal indexation imply that universal indexation must be ruled out. Since they link payments to published price indices, tabular standard contracts can normally only apply to contracts that are deferred over a date when a price index 'announcement' is made. For practical purposes, tabular standards can therefore only be applied to contracts calling for payments that are deferred by at least some minimum period, but not very short-term payments.

But we would still have to rule out universal indexation even if the discreteness of published price indices posed no problem. If all payments were covered by a tabular standard, then every payment would be tied to the price index, and there would be nothing to tie down the value of the dollar or the price index itself (see also Niehans, 1978, 132–133). The value of the dollar – and the value of the price index – would be indeterminate. The tabular standard effectively piggybacks on the existing unit of account, the dollar, and we need something to tie the dollar itself down. The obvious solution is to specify the dollar value of a particular bank liability (e.g., a banknote), and issuing rules adopted by the banks of issue would determine the value of one-dollar notes in terms of goods and services. Nominal values in the monetary system would then be tied down and agents could write tabular standard clauses into contracts *other than* banknote contracts. The latter would *have* to remain unindexed, and banknote holders would be deprived of the protection that tabular standards could offer. The bottom line, then, is that price determinacy requires that the price of *something* remain unindexed – universal indexation is impossible.

Costs

However, tabular standards also impose a number of costs. For reasons just explained, an agent who uses tabular standards must normally operate with two separate units of account – an original, unindexed unit of account, and a tabular standard. Operating with two units of account is not only inconvenient (e.g., because prices need to be converted one from unit into another), but also makes it more difficult for agents to monitor their financial position over time (Niehans, 1978, 138). The use of two units of account can also reduce the network benefits that agents obtain by using a single unit of account. An agent can no longer assume that a prospective trading partner will post prices or accept or offer payment in terms of instruments denominated in one particular unit of account, and must be ready instead to deal in either. Since the exchange rate between the two units of account can vary, the use of two units of account also introduces exchange rate risks that are absent with a single unit of account (see, e.g., Fisher, 1911, 336–337). Fisher noted that

> A business man's profits constitute a narrow margin between receipts and expenses. If receipts and expenses could *both* be reckoned in the tabular standard, his profits would be more stable than if both were reckoned in money. But if he should pay some of his expenses, such as interest and wages, on a tabular basis, while his receipts remained on the gold basis, his profits would fluctuate far more than if both sides, or all items of the accounts, were in gold. ... [He] would prefer to have the same standard on both sides of the account, even if this standard fluctuated, rather than have two standards, only one of which fluctuated; for his profits depend more on the parallelism between the two sides of his account than on the stability of either. (Fisher, 1911, 336–337, his emphasis)

Finally, there are negotiation and contracting costs, and agents would have to agree on such issues as the type of index to be used and the precise clause to be written into the contract.

EFFECTS OF TABULAR STANDARDS ON MACROECONOMIC STABILITY[37]

Then there is the question of the impact of tabular standards on macroeconomic stability. There are a number of arguments here. Jevons ([1875], 1907, 333) and Fisher (1911, 335) stressed the point that tabular standards stabilise the economy by taking out the element of price-level speculation from everyday transactions, which in turn reduces the severity of speculative cycles. When prices fall unexpectedly, firms would find that their liabilities fall as well, and would therefore have a smaller burden than if their liabilities had been unindexed. The firms' smaller debt burden would then help counteract the recessionary effect of the fall in prices, and the recession should be less severe than it would otherwise be. More recently, Friedman (1974) and Giersch (1974) have argued that tabular standards stabilise real output. They argued that a nominal shock would feed through more quickly and therefore have a smaller (or at least, more transitory) effect on output in an indexed economy than an unindexed one. Both writers also claimed, for example, that disinflationary policies in the USA in 1974 would have had a smaller impact on output had wages been indexed. On the other hand, Bernstein (1974) argued that wage indexation exacerbates macroeconomic instability by making real wages excessively sticky in the face of real shocks that require them to alter, and he pointed to a number of instances where indexation had apparently had that effect.

More recent theoretical work by Gray (1976) suggests that the arguments of Friedman and Giersch, on the one hand, and Bernstein on the other, are each correct on their own terms. Their basic result is that real output tends to be more stable in an indexed economy than in an unindexed one in the presence of *nominal* shocks, but less stable in the presence of *real* shocks. When a nominal shock hits the economy, indexing causes nominal wages to adjust to maintain the level of real wages, and hence the level of real output, but if there were no indexation then real wages and output would be shocked away from their initial levels. Indexing thus stabilises output against nominal (i.e., monetary) shocks. If there were a real shock, however, then equilibrium real wages would adjust, but indexing would interfere with that adjustment; hence, indexation would now destabilise real wages and output (e.g., Fischer, 1986b). However, these results depend on the assumption that prices are flexible, and it is not altogether clear what happens when we relax that assumption.

THE HISTORICAL EXPERIENCE OF TABULAR STANDARDS

Precedents for tabular standards can be found in the age-old practice of tying monetary payments to the prices of individual commodities, a number of instances of which were reported by Irving Fisher (1911, 333–334; 1920, 279–280), but the first tabular standards proper were apparently adopted in Massachusetts in 1747 and 1780 – interestingly, *before* there had been any substantial of indexation by monetary economists – both against a background of inflation created by the over-issue of government paper currency. Many tabular standards were later adopted to cope with the effects of the inflation of the First World War. In the USA, a number of different ones were adopted to cover various labour contracts, with contracts indexed to government or private indices, while in Britain textile workers' pay was tied in 1918 to an index compiled by the Board of Trade, and similar devices were adopted in Australia (Fisher, 1920, 282–284)). Escalator clauses were adopted for wage and salary payments in countries such as Belgium and Denmark in the 1920s, and adopted by a much larger number of countries and extended to loans, rents and other payments from the late 1940s onwards (see, e.g., Giersch, 1974, 16–23). By the mid-1970s, Friedman could report that

> over 5 million US workers are covered by union contracts with automatic escalator clauses, and there must be many nonunion workers who have similar implicit or explicit agreements with their employers. Many contracts for future delivery of products contain provisions for adjustment of the final selling price either for specific changes in costs or for general price changes. Many rental contracts for business premises are expressed as a

percentage of gross or net receipts, which means that they have an implicit escalator clause ... Some insurance companies issue fire insurance policies the face value of which is automatically adjusted for inflation. No doubt there are many more examples of which I am ignorant. (Friedman, 1974, 38–39)

In Chile, a tabular standard was widely used in the early 1980s to quote mortgage payments, apartment rentals, and a number of other deferred payments (Hall, 1981, 18), and a system of general, though not universal, indexation was used in Brazil in the 1960s and 1970s to combat the effects of that country's rapid inflation. The Brazilian system was perhaps the most widely adopted indexation system to date, and covered wage and salary payments, pensions, bank deposits, tax liabilities, and many forms of loans, life insurance, equity, mortgages and rents (Kafka, 1974, 87–93).

The qualitative nature of this evidence makes it difficult to judge how extensively tabular standards have been used, but Howitt (1986) provides more precise evidence for Canada. His data suggest that perhaps one-third to one-half of Canadian workers were covered by explicit index clauses, though there is evidence that these clauses provided less than complete protection (Wilton, 1980). Howitt (1986, 178) also cites evidence that the extent of wage indexation is positively associated with both the inflation rate and the uncertainty surrounding it. Howitt reports that 'there has been virtually no debt indexation in Canada' and the most that has occurred to protect borrowers and lenders against inflation has been a reduction in the duration of debt contracts (1986, 184). Finally, there was some indexation of pensions in Canada, but in 1980 only 4.9 percent of employees were covered by indexed pensions, and even in those cases the indexation was restricted (1986, 190).

The historical experience thus indicates that agents do (sometimes) resort to tabular standards when inflation makes existing units of account unsatisfactory, but it also poses a major puzzle. Even when inflation poses very severe problems – when the inflation rate is high and/or there is considerable inflation uncertainty – agents actually make far less use of tabular standards than the earlier theoretical considerations might have led us to expect. Indexation in Canada was relatively limited even during the 1970s when Canadian inflation rates were well into their teens and inflation was by all accounts a major problem. Many Canadian wage settlements still remained unindexed, and there was virtually no indexing of debt payments. Nor is there any reason to believe that the Canadian experience is unusual. Even in the Brazilian case where tabular standards were more widely adopted than anywhere else, the use of index clauses was by no means universal, and in any case probably owed something to government measures to promote it. In no case do we observe the widespread indexation some of the arguments for indexation might have led us to expect.

RESOLVING THE NON-INDEXATION PUZZLE

So why have agents been so reluctant to adopt tabular standards? A number of factors appear to have some bearing on this issue, but by no means fully explain it. Among these are accounting and contracting costs, the risk of subsequent legislation to abrogate indexing clauses (e.g., Niehans, 1978, 135), the imperfections of existing index numbers (e.g., Alchian and Klein, 1973, 185), legal or regulatory restrictions,[38] lags in the collection and dissemination of the data from which price indices are compiled,[39] and the unfamiliarity of index clauses.[40]

More promising, perhaps, are co-ordination problems of one kind of another (see also Eden, 1983). A key factor would appear to be how assets and liabilities fit into an agent's portfolio. What usually matters is not whether a particular asset or liability is risky in itself, but how it contributes to the holder's overall portfolio risk. If an agent wishes to reduce the risk on his asset portfolio, he would choose assets whose returns are negatively correlated so that the risks to some extent cancel out. If he holds liabilities as well as assets, he would also reduce his overall portfolio risk by acquiring assets and liabilities whose returns are negatively correlated. This sort of consideration suggests that any particular decision whether to index is influenced, at least in part, by other indexation decisions. A firm might prefer to index all its assets and liabilities against price-level risk, but doing so might not be feasible (e.g., because of co-ordination problems), and in practice might have to make indexation decisions sequentially. In that case, it might be quite rational for the firm to decide against indexation each time the decision is made, because to index on a partial basis introduces additional price-level risk to his portfolio (see, e.g., Fisher, 1911, 335–337). Suppose a firm has a single asset A and a single liability L, and is averse to price-level risk (e.g., because a more volatile price-level increases the risk of bankruptcy). Suppose too that if they remain unindexed, A and L are each subject to a price level shock e with a variance σ^2. Since it is averse to price-level risk, the firm would clearly prefer to index both A and L together – the variance of its net worth would then be zero – but suppose that L, say, must remain unindexed for some reason (e.g., because it would be difficult to arrange indexing with the liability-holder). The firm now has to decide whether or not to index A alone. But it would then choose not to index at all, since the variance of its net worth would be $A^2\sigma^2$ if it indexed its asset and $(A - L)^2\sigma^2$ if it chose not to. Even if he preferred 'full' indexation, an agent might prefer no indexation at all to a partial indexation that left it even more exposed to price-level risk.

This sort of hedging argument can apply to the non-indexation issue in various ways. It helps to explain why banks might prefer to index their mortgages or loans, other things being equal, but were reluctant to do so because they believed that deposits would need indexing as well, and they may have felt that that would not be feasible (e.g., because they were afraid of losing depositors).[41] Hedging arguments might also help to explain firms' failure to issue indexed bonds. Since most firms have real profits that are negatively correlated with inflation, we might expect them to prefer to hedge themselves with unindexed bonds. But this explanation is only partial because we might have expected that in some instances at least investors would be willing to pay firms to bear the price-level risk and issue indexed bonds instead. In any case, not all firms have real profits that are negatively correlated with inflation – utilities' returns appear not to, for example (Howitt, 1986, 208) – and the hedging argument fails to explain why firms do not index to industry-specific prices or why intermediaries do not arise to bridge the gap and issue indexed assets *and* indexed liabilities. Hedging arguments might also help to explain the non-indexation of pensions, but again only partially. If a worker's main asset is his house, the real return on which is positively affected by inflation, he may prefer to hedge against price-level risk by holding pensions whose real returns are negatively associated with inflation (Howitt, 1986, 208). The failure to hedge pensions might also be partially explained by the hedging difficulties that underwriters would face. They would presumably need short-term money market instruments with which to hedge their liabilities, but the empirical estimates provided by Pesando (1983) suggest that such instruments would yield a very low return of 1 percent or less per annum. However, this explanation is also partial, because it fails to explain why more attractive hedging instruments do not *already* exist for underwriters to use.

Each of these hedging arguments factors might have something to contribute, but it is also clear that they too do not suffice to explain the non-indexation puzzle. The main problem with all of them is their potential circularity. It might be correct to say that a firm does not index its assets because its liabilities are unindexed, but such an explanation is at most a partial one because it fails to explain why the liabilities are unindexed to start with. Why does the firm not decide to index its liabilities first, or index its assets and liabilities simultaneously? The answer, presumably, is that the firm cannot index its liabilities, or its liabilities and assets simultaneously, because doing so would only be worthwhile if other agents also chose to index. Other agents are in a similar position, of course, so they all choose, in effect, to wait for others to index first. Even if everyone preferred relatively widespread indexation, and therefore preferred some co-ordinated adoption of indexation if one were on offer, the fact is that such a 'collective' adoption might not be on offer and few bother to index on their own. No single agent or group of agents might be in a position, or have the incentive, to initiate a collective adoption of a tabular standard, and the net result would be that most agents would individually decide that indexation is not worth their while (see also Fischer, 1986b, 154; Howitt, 1986, 210). The situation would be analogous to that which arises when individual agents are locked in to an unsatisfactory unit of account. Everyone might wish to switch units of account provided everyone else switches with them, but it might still be privately optimal for each individual to remain with the existing unsatisfactory unit of account. No explanation of the non-indexation puzzle is convincing without some reference to the network or co-ordination problems that keep agents locked in to what must otherwise appear an irrational outcome.

15 Price-level Optimality*

This chapter addresses price level optimality, but our focus of interest is with price-level *changes* over time rather than with the absolute *level* of prices as such. The absolute level of prices is of little or no interest in itself, but price-level changes can have profound and complex consequences. Most economists believe that a continually rising price level (i.e., inflation) damages the economy and, indeed, the social order more generally, but there is much controversy over how it does so and how damaging it is. This chapter tries to address these issues and come to a judgement on what the optimal price-level path might be.

Since these issues are extremely complex, the strategy is to start with the simplest possible framework and then gradually extend it by adding further complications to build up a cumulative picture of the effects of a changing price level. The first section of the chapter therefore deals with the relatively straightforward case of fully anticipated inflation, starting with a very simple model of the effects of anticipated inflation on economic growth and welfare. We then examine the literature that seeks to assess the cost of (anticipated) inflation by means of its effect on the demand for real balances. This literature yields quantitative estimates of the cost of inflation which are, I believe, higher than is commonly realised. We also assess the potential 'monetary saturation' benefits of 'optimal deflation', as suggested by Friedman (1969), and find that the benefits forgone by having price stability instead of optimal deflation are smaller than they are sometimes portrayed to be. As an aside, we also examine – and reject – Samuelson's (1969) well-known argument that real balances under *laissez-faire* are suboptimal. We then finish our discussion of the effects of anticipated inflation by examining the various effects of anticipated inflation on relative prices.

The second section of the chapter looks at sporadic inflation. We begin with some general observations of the effects of sporadic inflation on the operation of markets, and then consider some of the more formal literature, focusing particularly on how inflation can create confusion over current relative prices and over the extent to which recent price changes are transitory or permanent. The section ends with a look at the effects of sporadic inflation in redistributing income and wealth.

The third section examines the empirical evidence on the effects of inflation. The empirical literature is very complex and covers a wide range of issues. These include the relationships between inflation variables and relative prices; the relationships between the inflation rate, the volatility of the inflation rate, and inflation unpredictability; the various relationships between inflation variables and real economic activity, and what they indicate about the magnitude of the cost of inflation; and the evidence on the redistributions created by inflation.

* Part of this chapter is forthcoming as 'The Costs of Inflation and Disinflation', *Cato Journal.*

The fourth section then examines the 'deeper' effects of inflation on the broader social order. These are effects that the standard economic literature has difficulty handling, and often ignores. Amongst these are the impact of inflation on the exchange process; the 'broader' information problems created by inflation, particularly the virtual impossibility of predicting the long-run price level; the distortion of economic activity created by inflation, including the thinning out of long-term investments, the promotion of speculative booms and busts in (allegedly) 'inflation-proof' assets, and the artificial growth of the financial services sector at the expense of the rest of the economy; the impact of inflation in undermining the integrity of the legal system; and the more general destructive effects of inflation on the social order.

After all this, the last section tries to pull some of the earlier material together to assess what the optimum price-level path actually is, and comes down firmly in favour of price stability. An appendix at the end of the chapter then reviews arguments for the productivity norm – according to which prices should fall with productivity growth – but concludes that the productivity norm is to be rejected in favour of price stability.

ANTICIPATED INFLATION, CAPITAL ACCUMULATION AND GROWTH

Money and Growth

Superneutrality in a Simple Sidrauski Economy

Suppose we have a single representative family which lives for ever. This family maximises the intertemporal utility function:

$$U = \int_0^\infty u(c_t, m_t)e^{-\delta t}dt \qquad (15.1)$$

where c_t is its flow of real consumption services and m_t its stock of real balances at t, and δ is its (constant) rate of time preference.[1] Real balances are assumed for convenience to be costless to produce, but bear no explicit interest – we can think of real balances as consisting only of non-interest-bearing currency – and the household's income (or output) is a linearly homogenous function $f( )$ of its capital stock k. The household has to decide at each point in time how to allocate its real non-human wealth a_t between holdings of capital and money. Dropping the subscripts for convenience, it faces a stock constraint:

$$a = k + m. \qquad (15.2)$$

The household also faces a flow constraint governing the rate of accumulation of real assets:

$$\dot{a} = f(k) + x - c - na - \pi m \qquad (15.3)$$

where x is the profit made by the issuer(s) of real balances, consolidated within the private sector, c is household consumption, n the rate of population growth, and p the rate of inflation. $a, f(k), k, x$ and c are all in *per capita* terms. (15.3) tells us that the rate of *per capita* capital accumulation equals current *per capita* real output plus *per capita* profits from the issue of real balances minus the sum of *per capita* consumption, the capital growth required to maintain the *per capita* capital stock, and the capital loss on real balances due to inflation. We then set up the present value Hamiltonian:

$$H = u(c,m) + q[f(k) + x - c - na - \pi m] + \lambda [a - k - m] \qquad (15.4)$$

where q is the costate variable associated with (15.3) and λ is the Lagrange multiplier associated with (15.2) (see, e.g., Sidrauski, 1967, 536–537; Orphanides and Solow, 1990, 237). It is easy to show from the first-order conditions that the steady-state real rate of interest is the sum of the discount rate and the rate of population growth:

$$f_k = \delta + n. \qquad (15.5)$$

The real rate of interest in the steady state is thus tied down by 'real' factors and is independent of the rates of inflation or monetary growth (i.e., the 'Fisher effect' holds). The real rate of interest then ties down the steady-state capital stock, and the latter ties down steady-state output. If money is costless to create, x equals π in the steady state, and consumption is also unaffected by inflation and monetary growth. All real variables other than real balances are unaffected in the steady state by the rates of change of the nominal variables. The latter can therefore be said to be *superneutral* (see, e.g., McCallum, 1990a, 972). However, real balances *are* affected, and since real balances enter the utility function, welfare is affected as well. The higher the inflation rate, the greater the opportunity cost of holding real balances, the lower the stock of real balances the household will hold, and the lower its utility. In short, in this model *the real interest rate, the capital stock, and consumption are all independent of nominal variables in the steady state, but a higher inflation rate means lower real balances and lower welfare.* Even though nominal variables are superneutral, the perfectly anticipated inflation of a steady-state is still bad because it increases the wedge between the private opportunity cost of holding real balances, which increases with the inflation rate, and the social cost of holding them, which is zero.[2]

Departures from Superneutrality

This simple Sidrauski economy provides a useful benchmark, but the super-neutrality result is restrictive and far from robust. One limitation is that it breaks down outside of steady states, and both Sidrauski (1967, 541–544) and Fischer (1979b) showed that nominal variables are not superneutral in the transition to the steady state even when they were superneutral in the steady state itself. Even when it does hold in the steady state, the superneutrality result depends on the assumed production function and the implied role of real balances (see Dornbusch and

Frankel, 1973, 150–152). Suppose that we think of real balances as facilitating production and so put them 'in' the production function. Output now becomes a function of real balances as well as *per capita* capital stock:

$$y = f(k, m); \quad f_k, f_m > 0. \tag{15.6}$$

We can then show that the capital stock *is* affected by the inflation rate even though the real rate of interest (i.e., the marginal product of capital, (15.5)) might *not* be (see, e.g., Orphanides and Solow, 1990, 239–240). Superneutrality also breaks down if we make labour or leisure a choice variable. If we put leisure into the utility function, the *per capita* capital stock is no longer the same as the marginal product of capital normalised by labour inputs, so even if real interest is unaffected by inflation, *per capita* capital will be affected because of its impact on labour supply (see Brock, 1974; Orphanides and Solow, 1990, 240). In both these cases nominal variables are no longer superneutral even though they do not affect the real rate of interest, but the signs of the impacts are ambiguous and there is no easy way to resolve the ambiguities (Orphanides and Solow, 1990, 241).

   Non-superneutralities can also arise in other ways.[3] One possibility widely discussed in the literature is the *Tobin effect* (Tobin, 1965) which is a portfolio allocation effect driven by real balances and capital being substitutes in agents' portfolios. The argument is that a higher rate of anticipated inflation increases the opportunity cost of holding real balances and induces agents to reallocate their portfolios away from real balances towards capital, and this reallocation leads to an increased stock of capital and a higher level of real output. Tobin effects can also be derived from other models (e.g., Fischer, 1972, 1979a; Orphanides and Solow, 1990, 242–245), but the factor driving them is always the assumed substitutability of real balances and capital in agents' portfolios. Indeed, in many of these models real balances have no useful role at all; inflation is then 'good' because it leads agents to shift out of useless holdings of real balances into productive holdings of real capital; social welfare is then maximised by hyperinflating the currency to minimise real balances and maximise holdings of real capital!

   However, once we give real balances a meaningful role to play, we can no longer treat them as a mere portfolio substitute for capital and we often find that inflation tends to *lower* the capital stock instead of raise it. Levhari and Patinkin (1968) find that the impact of anticipated inflation on the capital stock becomes ambiguous if we treat real balances as if it were a production good, for example, and Stockman (1981) finds that anticipated inflation has an unambiguously negative impact on the long-run stock of capital if real balances are needed to purchase consumption and investment goods. The McKinnon–Stockman thesis is that, because real balances are needed for purchases, then higher inflation indirectly taxes both consumption and investment; it thereby induces less of each, and both output and the capital stock fall. A rise in the anticipated inflation rate puts the economy on a path with lower output and a lower capital stock, and the growth of output and capital accumulation both fall in the interim as the economy approaches that path. Put another way, real balances in these models are a complement to capital, and inflation reduces the capital stock (and, in the interim, the rate of capital accumulation) because it taxes the factor that is complementary to capital.

Tentative Conclusions from the Money and Growth Literature

It might be useful to come to some preliminary conclusions before proceeding further. One point that comes across clearly is the impact of inflation in raising the private opportunity cost of (non-interest-bearing) real balances. Unless the costs of issuing real balances are particularly large, inflation drives a wedge between the social and private opportunity costs of holding real balances – provided, of course, that the latter do not bear a 'market' rate of interest – and this wedge will tend to reduce welfare in any model where real balances have a remotely well-defined role. This welfare effect is the only such effect in economies where nominal variables are superneutral, but additional effects arise when superneutrality is absent. The key issue is the impact of anticipated inflation on the capital stock and the level of output. (These two effects tend to go together – if the capital stock rises, so does output, and vice versa.) If the capital stock falls with inflation – and there are a number of plausible models to suggest it does – the impact of anticipated inflation on the capital stock represents a second welfare loss *in addition* to the loss that results from the earlier real-balance 'wedge' effect. This *anti-Tobin effect* is more plausible than its opposite, and appears to be confirmed by the empirical evidence reviewed below.

Anticipated Inflation and the Demand for Real Balances

Traditional Theoretical Considerations

It was apparently Bailey (1956) who first suggested modelling the costs of anticipated inflation by the welfare loss that results from the lower real balances

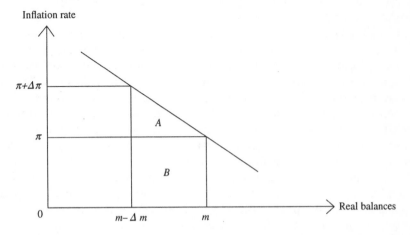

Figure 15.1   The welfare loss from the effect of inflation on the demand for real balances

agents hold when inflation rises. An optimising agent will demand real balances until the marginal benefit they yield is just equal to their marginal cost. If real balances bear no interest, the opportunity cost of holding them is proportional to the nominal rate of interest. Higher inflation then leads to higher interest, and hence lower real balances, and this reduction in real balances involves a welfare loss because the social cost of producing real balances has remained substantially unaffected. If we think of the benefits that real balances provide as given by the area under the demand curve for them, the current-period loss L_0 of an increase in anticipated inflation is (arguably[4]) equal to the inflation-induced fall in the area under the demand curve for real balances (see, e.g., Driffil *et al.*, 1990, 1016).[5] If inflation rises from π to $\pi + \Delta\pi$, and real balances fall as a result from m to $m - \Delta m$, the current-period welfare loss is given by the area $A + B$ in Figure 15.1.

The current-period loss is therefore:

$$L_0 = \Delta m \, \Delta\pi/2 + \pi\Delta m. \tag{15.7}$$

Rearranging, we get:

$$L_0 = -m \, \varepsilon_{mi}[\Delta\pi/2 + \pi] \, \Delta i/i \tag{15.8}$$

where ε_{mi} is the interest elasticity of the demand for real balances and i is the nominal rate of interest. We can then estimate the welfare loss resulting from any given change in the inflation rate using a measure of the monetary aggregate (m), an estimate of the interest elasticity of the demand for real balances (ε_{mi}), and assumptions about the relevant inflation and nominal interest rates.

Estimates of the Welfare Cost

There are a number of available estimates of this type of loss, and it is perhaps most convenient if we standardise our estimates by focusing on the cost of each percentage inflation point (i.e., by putting $\Delta p = 1$ percent in (15.8)) for a given benchmark inflation rate. To give the reader some feel for the size of this cost, it makes sense to express the cost as a percentage of national income, and I shall refer to the ratio of this cost to national income as the inflation cost ratio. To illustrate what the cost ratio might be, let us therefore take the benchmark inflation rate to be, say, 5 percent, and assume for the sake of argument that the interest elasticity ε_{mi} is -0.2 and the nominal interest rate i is $\pi + 4$ percent, or 9 percent. Taking m as M1, and taking GDP as national income, then (15.8) gives us a current-period cost ratio of 0.021 percent, or \$1.37 billion,[6] for the USA in the last quarter of 1993.[7]

It might help to compare this figure with those implied by other studies. Most quote figures for the cost of all inflation above zero percent, rather than a cost ratio for each percentage inflation point, but the different estimates can be made comparable by going back to (15.8) and re-estimating the cost of some given inflation rate relative to zero inflation. For example, Foster (1972, 7) and Garfinkel (1989, 5) provided estimates of the cost of a fully anticipated 4 percent inflation rate, which Foster estimated to be less than one-twentieth of 1 percent of GNP and

Garfinkel to be about 0.3 percent of national income. To estimate a comparable figure using (15.8), we simply substitute $\Delta\pi = 0.04$ and $p = 0.05$ for the previous assumptions of $\Delta\pi = 0.01$ and $\pi = 0$, and the cost of a fully anticipated inflation rate comes out to about 0.069 percent. My estimate is therefore higher than Foster's, but much lower than Garfinkel's. Similarly, Fischer (1986b, 46), McCallum (1989, 127), and Lucas (1981, 43–44) estimated the cost of a fully anticipated 10 percent inflation rate, the first two putting it at 0.3 percent of national income and Lucas putting it at 0.9 percent. To estimate this cost ourselves, we set $\Delta\pi = 0.1$ and $\pi = 0$ using (15.8), and the cost of a 10 percent inflation rate comes out as about 0.12 percent of national income – a considerably lower estimate than those reported by Fischer, McCallum or Lucas. In short, my approach and Foster's tend to give relatively low estimates, Garfinkel's, Fischer's, and McCallum's give middling ones, and Lucas' estimate is relatively high. There is no way to tell which of these figures, if any, is the 'right' one, so all of these estimates are probably best regarded as illustrative.

Not surprisingly, given (15.8), estimated welfare losses rise as inflation becomes more rapid. For example, Barro (1972, 994) estimates that the welfare loss from inflation was something under the range 3–7 percent of national income for inflation rates between 2 percent and 5 percent a month, but the welfare loss 'advances rapidly' when the rate of inflation rises over the latter figure. When inflation reaches the 'typical' hyperinflationary rate of 25–30 percent a month, his welfare losses approach the range 11–22 percent of national income, and climbs to 22–38 percent of national income for inflation rates between 100 and 150 percent a month.

But whichever of these estimates we might take, they all refer to losses borne in the current period and ignore comparable losses in the future, and an estimate of the 'full cost' of inflation must also take these future losses into account. We therefore need to estimate the present value of the current and discounted future losses. If we switch to continuous-time for convenience and let L_0 be the instantaneous welfare loss, the present value of the permanent loss from inflation is:

$$L = \int_0^\infty L_0 e^{-rs} ds = L_0 \, / \, r \qquad (15.9)$$

for the discount rate r and an assumed infinite horizon. The present value loss is thus equal to the instantaneous loss L_0 – which we can take as estimated by the procedures just discussed – multiplied by $1/r$. If we take r as 5 percent for the sake of illustration, then my earlier current-period cost ratio of 0.021 percent of GNP would translate into a present-value cost ratio of 0.42 percent of GNP (or $27.3 billion), and so on.

However, all these estimates involve the 'fundamental error' that they ignore the impact of the expected future growth in real balances, and allowing for such growth can drastically increase our estimates of the losses involved (Feldstein, 1979, 754; see also Tatom, 1976, 16–17). If future real balances grow at a rate g, it is easy to show that the discount rate in the exercise above needs to be replaced with the 'net' discount $(g - r)$. *The present value of our instantaneous loss then becomes*

$L_0/(g-r)$ and the resulting estimates can be very much higher. For example, if we take g as 2.5 percent, the net discount rate becomes 5 percent minus 2.5 percent, or 2.5 percent, and the earlier present-value cost ratios would be doubled. The earlier estimate of L_0 as equal to about 0.021 percent of GNP for each percentage inflation point now translates into a present-value cost ratio of 0.84 percent of GNP (or $54.7 billion) instead of the 0.42 percent it was before. Indeed, as g approaches r, the numerator term $(g-r)$ approaches zero and the (present-value) cost ratio approaches infinity. *Ignoring future growth in real balances can lead, to put it mildly, to a drastic understatement of the 'true' costs of inflation.*

Recent Extensions to Traditional Approaches

There are also other reasons to believe that loss estimates like these are understatements. Traditional approaches such as Barro (1970, 1972) were usually based on an underlying transactions theory of the demand for real balances, but the more recently developed consumption-smoothing approach of İmrohoroğlu (1992) suggests that this approach ignores certain important welfare losses. In her model, individual agents cannot always find work, and they cannot insure themselves completely against the loss of income because work opportunities are idiosyncratic. They therefore carry real balances to allow them to consume when they cannot work. Inflation then forces them to economise on real balances and in so doing undermines their ability to smooth consumption over time – an effect on welfare not picked up by the earlier approaches. İmrohoroğlu finds that inflation rates of 5 percent and 10 percent produce steady-state welfare losses equal to 0.57 percent and 1.07 percent of national income respectively (1992, 88–89) – figures clearly well above those typically obtained in traditional exercises that ignore consumption smoothing. The difference between the traditional and consumption-smoothing loss estimates arises because the earlier estimates presuppose that marginal rates of substitution are the same across agents – and therefore that the only loss from inflation is that given by the reduction in the area under the demand curve for real balances. However, under consumption-smoothing, inflation also distorts these marginal rates of substitution *across* agents – agents face 'liquidity' constraints whose shadow values will vary from one agent to another, depending on whether they have work or not – and this distortion creates *further* losses that must be *added to* the standard losses on which the traditional approach focused. The traditional approach can thus seriously under-state the 'true' losses in circumstances where consumption-smoothing is an important motive for holding real balances.

Nor are these the only reasons to believe that traditional approaches understate 'true' losses. (1) Many treatments assume that agents have either a costless alternative to holding cash or no alternative at all, but if agents face a costly alternative, Gillman (1992) shows that *inflation will also involve costs arising from the greater use of this costly alternative.* Taking account of this additional cost, he estimates losses that are nearly four times greater than the losses that arise from traditional approaches that do not allow for costly credit (Gillman, 1992, 189). (2)

Leach (1983) makes the point that if inflation is a tax on real balances, then it functions in some ways like a general commodity tax which has the effect of reducing the supply of labour and, hence, total output. The costs of this distortion to the labour market must be added to the earlier real balance 'triangle' loss. (3) Eckstein and Leiderman (1992) and Den Haan (1990) show that many earlier estimates of the welfare loss depend in an important way on the maintained assumption of a Cagan-style semi-log specification of the demand for real balances. Both studies develop alternative approaches based on a Sidrauski model, and Eckstein and Leiderman use theirs to estimate the (steady-state) welfare loss on Israeli data. Their results suggest that an inflation rate of 10 percent produces a current-period welfare loss of about 1 percent of national income (Eckstein and Leiderman, 1992, 406–407), and confidence in them is reinforced by the fact that the Eckstein–Leiderman specification produces seigniorage/national income ratios much closer to observed experience than the traditional Cagan specification does (Eckstein and Leiderman, 1992, 403–405). Den Haan (1990, 402) estimates that the current-period welfare loss of a 5 percent inflation relative to zero inflation is about 3.12 percent of output, a figure that is also much bigger than figures from traditional exercises. Clearly, Sidrauski models generate considerably bigger losses than traditional Cagan (1956) models of the demand for real balances. (4) While studies of money and growth typically take the monetary sector to be exogenous, there are reasons to regard the monetary sector as evolving along with the general economy, and taking account of this evolution can substantially increase our estimates of the welfare cost of inflation (Ireland, 1994). Intuitively, as the economy grows, people make more use of money substitutes; the effect of inflation on money holdings then falls as the economy develops, but the effects on the payments system do not. Ignoring the effect of inflation on the payments system thus biases downwards our estimate of the welfare cost of inflation, and Ireland's simulations suggest that this bias can be very considerable (Ireland, 1994, 62).

But arguably the most important problem with traditional treatments of the welfare cost of inflation is that they *ignore the impact of inflation on the capital stock*, and there is evidence that these effects are not only quantitatively important, but perhaps *much more* important than the losses just examined. The theory is set out by Cooley and Hansen (1989, 1991) and Benabou (1991). In the basic model (Cooley and Hansen, 1989) agents decide how much to work, consume, and invest, and the real balances to hold, in a cash-in-advance framework that requires them to pay for their purchases of consumption goods each period with prior holdings of currency. Inflation functions as a tax on real balances, and agents respond to this tax by reducing the activities that expose them to it. The higher the steady-state inflation rate, the lower agents' real balances, and, given the cash-in-advance constraint, the lower their consumption. Since inflation indirectly taxes the return on investment, higher inflation also leads agents to reduce their investment, and the capital stock falls. The falls in consumption and investment imply that agents work less, and the combination of a lower supply of labour and a lower capital stock means that output is lower as well. Cooley and Hansen (1991) and Benabou (1991) then proceed to modify the earlier Cooley–Hansen model by allowing for agents using credit goods along Lucas–Stokey (1983) lines, and the key result that emerges is that the *'true' welfare losses from inflation dwarf traditional estimates,* the former being a *first-order* function of the inflation rate, and the latter being a *second-order* one (Benabou, 1991, 509–510). Benabou's simulations suggest that the traditional estimates are less than a tenth of the 'true' welfare loss for a steady-state inflation rate of 10 percent. The traditional estimates improve as inflation rises, but even with an inflation rate of 100 percent they are still well under half the 'true' cost (Benabou, 1991, 509). The difference between the two arises primarily because the traditional estimate ignores the consequences of the decline in the capital stock, and Benabou's results clearly indicate that the capital stock effect on welfare is much more important than the money-holding losses emphasised by traditional studies. If we accept his results, the traditional estimates of the welfare loss from moderate inflations need to be adjusted upwards by a factor of 10 or more for 'moderate' inflations, and our earlier illustrative present-value cost ratio of 0.84 percent would become something upwards of 8.4 percent. The costs of inflation are starting to look very big indeed.

The 'Optimum Quantity of Money'

The discussion of the welfare cost of anticipated inflation leads naturally to the question of the welfare-*maximising* rate of inflation. Most economists agree that a necessary condition for an optimum is that the social and private opportunity costs of holding real balances holdings should be equal. The costs generally relate to the forgone returns from holdings of alternative assets, and the benefits to savings in shoeleather costs, and factors such as the convenience of being able to satisfy sudden impulses to buy. Rational agents will always hold just enough quantities of MOE to ensure that the private costs and private benefits of holding them are equal, but a social optimum will only occur if these private costs and benefits are also equal to the social ones. Imagine then that it costs a bank k each year to put out and maintain a marginal issue of $1 worth of real balances. We can think of the real balances as exchange media, and of k as reflecting the operating costs, reserve and capital costs from the additional issue. If there is no significant cost to paying interest on MOE – if the MOE are deposit accounts, for example, and there exists a negligible-cost technology to pay interest on them – then market forces should lead banks to pay a competitive interest on their issues of MOE and our necessary condition for an optimum would be satisfied for *any* anticipated price-level path. In that case, the present analytical framework would give us no reason to prefer one particular price-level path to any other. If there is an optimal price-level path, it would be determined by other factors such as agents' preferences for price-level stability, the costs of changing prices, and so on.

But this conclusion no longer holds if it is costly to pay interest on holdings of MOE. Suppose that MOE include hand-to-hand currency on which it is not feasible to pay interest. (We only need to assume that *some* MOE are subject to this constraint, and we have no reason to be concerned here about those that are not.) Since the social opportunity cost of holding currency is k percent, and the private opportunity cost r percent, our condition for a social optimum requires that:

$$k = r + \pi^* \tag{15.10}$$

where π is the optimal percentage inflation rate. The nominal interest rate $(r + \pi)$ is equal to the percentage operating cost k. It follows that the optimal inflation rate is:

$$\pi^* = k - r < 0, \tag{15.11}$$

i.e., the price level *declines* annually at the rate $(r - k)$ (see, e.g., Friedman, 1969). The socially costly constraint against paying interest on holdings of MOE now makes the optimal price-level path determinate. Deflation is superior to inflation or stable prices because it relaxes the constraint more, and this so-called 'optimum quantity of money' result indicates that a deflation rate of $(k - r)$ is optimal because it relaxes the constraint entirely (Friedman, 1969).[8] Put another way, if real balances are produced at a social (and private) cost of k percent a year, and holders pay a private opportunity cost equal to the nominal rate of interest, optimality requires that the private and social costs be equalised by bringing the nominal interest rate down to k. With the real interest rate given by r, we therefore require a deflation rate of $(r - k)$.[9] Holders of real balances then pay the social opportunity cost of holding them, and we get essentially the same outcome as that which would have occurred had there been no constraint at all against the payment of interest on real balances.

An important and much discussed special case occurs where $k = 0$ and (15.11) collapses to the famous 'Chicago rule' that the price level should fall at the same rate as the real rate of interest.[10] If real balances can be produced at zero cost, optimality requires that the private and social holding costs be equalised by making the nominal interest rate zero, and holders of real balances can be satiated with as many real balances as they want. Some peculiar consequences can then follow. If debt is costly to issue, but currency can be obtained at zero cost, it is arguable that no agent would issue debt when he can obtain currency costlessly. Currency would therefore drive out debt, and credit markets would be eliminated (Niehans, 1978, 97). We also get the disturbing result that the price level would be indeterminate if we had a fiat currency and additional holdings of real balances beyond the satiation point produce no disutility. If some price level p_0 is an equilibrium, any lower price level $p_1 > 0$ must also be an equilibrium, and in the absence of some 'outside' convertibility rule there is nothing to determine what value the price level should take. Apart from being indeterminate, the price level is also very prone to collapse. A small shock (e.g., a fall in the marginal product of capital) that made real balances a more attractive asset to hold than capital would cause the demand for real balances to rise and, barring a sufficient increase in the nominal supply of monetary balances, this increased demand would push down the price level. However, rational agents would anticipate the price fall and take speculative positions accordingly; but this increased 'speculative' demand for real balances would be effectively unlimited, and the price level would have collapse to accommodate it (see, e.g., Brock, 1975; Niehans, 1978, 96).

These peculiar outcomes do however depend on the assumptions that the currency is a fiat one and that k is zero, and neither of these is really appropriate here. As discussed already, market forces under *laissez-faire* would force banks to issue a convertible currency, and if the currency is convertible, we can treat the price level as if it were tied down for present purposes. The price level can then no longer be indeterminate or vulnerable to collapse. A convertible currency also undermines the assumption that $k = 0$. If the currency is convertible, the costs of issue must include the costs of keeping currency in circulation and redeeming it when required to, and these latter costs are typically much greater than the mere costs of printing currency and putting it into circulation. So even if the latter were negligible, k must be considered significantly above zero if only because of maintenance and redemption costs. There is also another reason why k should be considered positive. The justification, such as it is, for treating k as negligible is based on k being the cost of issuing *nominal* balances, and yet k is actually the cost of issuing *real* balances. These costs are very different. The cost of issuing additional real balances is *not* the cost of putting another note into circulation and keeping it there, but the cost of increasing the supply of monetary balances *at a faster rate than any induced rate of inflation*. There is a strong presumption that the latter is greater than the former, but the key point is that the two are conceptually very different and we cannot justify a particular value for one on the basis of an assumption about the other. But once we accept that k is positive, we no longer get the Chicago result that agents are satiated with real balances – agents are not satiated because real balances now have a positive opportunity cost – and if agents are not satiated we no longer get the odd consequence that costless currency destroys the credit market. We are back in a relatively 'normal' world again.

Estimating the Welfare Loss from the Absence of 'Optimal Deflation'

The size of the welfare loss from the non-payment of interest on currency can be estimated using much the same procedure as that used earlier to estimate the welfare loss from inflation. If the actual inflation rate differs from the optimal one by an amount $\pi - \pi*$, or $\pi + r$, the (current-period) welfare loss arising from agents' holding suboptimal real balances is given by the triangular area A in Figure 15.2.

Bearing in mind that $\Delta i \approx i$, the current-period loss becomes:

$$L_0 \approx \Delta m \, (\pi + r)/2 \approx -m \, \varepsilon_{mi}(\pi + r)/2. \tag{15.12}$$

Since we are interested here in the cost difference between zero inflation and 'optimal' deflation, we can set our benchmark inflation, π, equal to zero, and (15.12) becomes:

$$L_0 \approx -m \, \varepsilon_{mi} \, r \, / \, 2. \tag{15.13}$$

Assuming away for the moment any future growth in real balances, the present-value loss is then:

$$L / r \approx -m\varepsilon_{mi}/2. \tag{15.14}$$

The interest rate term comes out in the wash. We can therefore estimate of the cost of zero inflation relative to 'optimal' deflation without needing to know what the latter actually is.

We can now estimate the cost of zero inflation by selecting a proxy for m and making some assumption about ε_{mi}. In his study, Friedman used the stock of high-powered money as a proxy for m, and his figures gave a ratio of the stock of high-powered money to national income in the USA in early 1968 of about 0.12. As regards the interest elasticity, Friedman acknowledged that most empirical studies indicated that the demand for money was not interest elastic – a point that more recent work confirms (see, e.g., Laidler, 1985) – but argued that these studies might have under-estimated the relevant elasticity on the odd grounds that 'a change in market interest rates is partly offset by a change in the rate of interest paid on money' (1969, 42). He then suggested a figure of –10, and inserting these figures into (15.14) gives us a present-value cost equal to 60 percent of annual national income.[11]

It is however arguably better to use non-interest-bearing M1 as a proxy for m, and the figures we used earlier give a ratio of M1 to national income in the USA of about 17 percent. Using M1 would then increase Friedman's cost estimates by nearly a half. I would also argue that Friedman's justification for imposing a very elastic interest elasticity is not convincing, and we are better off sticking with the estimates provided by the empirical 'demand for money' literature. Since conventional estimates usually put the interest elasticity in a range, say, between –0.05 and –0.25, the net effect is to slash Friedman's cost estimates drastically. If we take an m/y ratio of 0.17, these figures would give us cost estimates varying from just over 0.4 percent to a maximum of little more than 2 percent; if we take

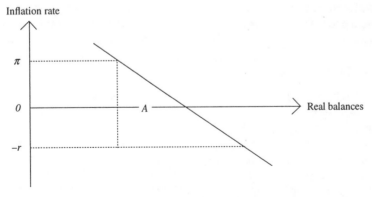

Figure 15.2   The welfare difference between price stability and 'optimal' deflation

Friedman's own m/y ratio of 0.12, on the other hand, they give us even lower cost ratios varying from 0.3 percent to 1.5 percent. If we accept these figures at face value, the (present value) cost of having price stability instead of 'optimal' deflation is probably under 2 percent of national income, and possibly much less.[12]

However, readers will recall that we assumed away any future growth in real balances, and our discussion of the welfare cost of inflation indicated that such growth could have important implications. Not surprisingly, it turns out that they have important implications here as well. If we now let real balances grow at a rate g, but discount future losses at a rate r, the present-value loss becomes:

$$-m\,\varepsilon_{mi}\,r\,/\,[2(r-g)] \qquad (15.15)$$

provided $g \leq r$. (15.15) can then be rearranged as

$$-(1-g/r)^{-1}\,m\,\varepsilon_{mi}/2 \qquad (15.16)$$

and we are back to the old problem of the relative sizes of g and r. As g gets small relative to r we approach the special case given in (15.14) where g is zero and the welfare loss is independent of r. However, for positive values of g, (15.16) indicates that the welfare loss will exceed the 'static' welfare loss given by (15.14). As with the cost of inflation, (15.16) also indicates that the welfare loss grows without bound as g approaches r. The various present-value loss estimates reported earlier must therefore be regarded as lower bounds associated with an implied real growth rate of zero, and how much the 'true' figures exceed those lower bounds depends on g/r. If g/r is 0.5, for example, the 'true' loss given by (15.16) is twice that given by (15.14), and our earlier welfare loss of something under 2 percent of national is doubled to something under 4 percent. Readers can provide their own favourite estimates of g/r, but my own feeling, for what it is worth, is that it would be fairly difficult to mount a compelling case for the welfare loss to be much more than 4 percent, and a more plausible estimate is probably considerably lower.

The 'money demand triangle' loss from having price stability instead of 'optimal' deflation is therefore unlikely to be large enough to justify abandoning the former for the latter, particularly bearing in mind the problems of implementing 'optimal' deflation and the menu, calculation and other costs entailed by deflation which this sort of exercise ignores. The case for 'optimal' deflation remains, at best, unproven.

Are Real Balances Non-optimal under Laissez-Faire?

Closely related to the OQM issue is an important argument that purports to establish that holdings of real balances under *laissez-faire* are not optimal. Arguments to this effect have been made in a number of places (e.g., Johnson, 1967), but perhaps the clearest argument was that spelt out by Samuelson (1968, 1969). Imagine we have a representative transactor in a stationary state who has to choose his consumption and real balance holdings subject to his long-run budget constraint and the opportunity cost that holding real balances entails. As before, we can think of real balances as non-interest- bearing currency, and the holding cost is the foregone return from holding other assets. As Samuelson explained,

> Each man thinks of his cash balance as costing him foregone interest and as buying himself convenience. But for the community as a whole, the total [stock of currency] is there and is quite costless to use. Forgetting gold mining and the historical expenditure of resources for the creating of [the currency] stock, the existing [stock] is, so to speak, a free good from society's viewpoint. Moreover, its *effective* amount can, from the community's viewpoint, be indefinitely augmented by the simple device of having a lower absolute level of *all* money prices. (Samuelson, 1968, 9, his emphasis)

In other words, his claim is that the social cost of increasing the supply of real balances is zero or something very close to it. He then continued,

> Evidently we have here an instance of a lack of optimality of *laissez-faire*: there is a kind of fictitious internal diseconomy from holding more cash balances, as things look to the individual. Yet if all were made to hold larger cash balances, which they turned over more slowly, the resulting lowering of absolute price would end up making everyone better off. Better off in what sense? Better off in the sense of ... having to make fewer trips to the bank, fewer trips to the brokers, smaller printing and other costs of transactions whose only purpose is to provide cash when you may have been holding too little cash. (Samuelson, 1968, 10)

The optimum thus occurs when agents are 'satiated with cash', and since this optimum cannot occur under *laissez-faire*, Samuelson concluded that real balances under *laissez-faire* must be suboptimal.

There are some serious problems with this argument. That there is something wrong with it may be seen intuitively by noting that it implies that *any* equilibrium with positive prices is inefficient because real balances can always be increased further by reducing prices still more. If Samuelson's argument is correct, the *only* efficient outcome is one where nominal prices are zero. In any case, as Clower asked,

> can anyone seriously believe that there exists some "simple device" by which all money prices can be *permanently* reduced without either changing the nominal quantity of money ... or altering prevailing technological possibilities? (Clower, [1969] 1984, 125)[13]

Clower then continued,

> To make the analysis meaningful in an operational sense, it is necessary *explicitly* to introduce into the system certain data in the form of parameters which, in changing, cause the values of unknown variables to change. ([1969] 1984, 125, his emphasis)

and Samuelson fails this test:

> Does Samuelson's model contain any explicit parameter, other than the nominal quantity of money, the value of which could be assumed to be variable at no cost to society? The answer is in the negative. Equilibrium real balances are a *constant* in Samuelson's system ... The logical musculature of the model, as distinct from its verbal fat, does not permit us to discuss changes in equilibrium holdings of real cash balances except in terms of changes in *unspecified* parameters that implicitly underlie the definition of individual utility and production functions. This being so, Samuelson's assertions about people being 'better off' for making 'few trips to the brokers' when they are 'made to hold larger cash balances,' are analytically vacuous and operationally meaningless. (Clower, 1984, 125–126, his emphasis)

Samuelson's argument is thus an illusion. Yes, it is true that agents would have greater real balances if we could (somehow) reduce prices and prevent them responding by buying more goods, rearranging their portfolios, changing their trips to the bank, and so on. But there is nothing in the model to indicate how that would benefit them since none of the exogenous factors on which their welfare depends has altered. The increase in real balances in those circumstances *is of no use to them*, and the fact that increases in real balances under less bizarre circumstances might be associated with higher welfare – if income rose, say, and real balances were a normal good – is irrelevant. We can only say they would be better off in the presence of greater real balances if one of these exogenous factors changes favourably, but it would then be the change in that factor that was the cause of their greater welfare and the change in real balances would only be an endogenous response.[14] If we wish to change an endogenous variable, we have to change one of the exogenous variables on which it depends, and the conceptual experiment of changing an endogenous variable as if it were exogenous is not logically permissible. As Clower later continued,

> From society's viewpoint, the effective amount of real cash balances can be altered only by devices that increase the technological efficiency of monetary institutions or by changes in existing parameters of production technology and personal taste.
>
> Evidently we have here a classic instance of the optimality of *laissez-faire*. Each individual thinks of himself as choosing his own cash balances on the basis of selfish maximizing motives. Yet no matter how large or small may be the nominal quantity of money objects possessed by the community, the real amount of cash is determined ultimately by productivity and thrift. (Clower, 1984, 127)

We can also look at the Samuelson argument another way. What drives the argument is the (already disputed) claim that the social cost of increasing the supply of real balances is zero. But the fact that we can *hypothesise* a general fall in prices in the way Samuelson describes does not tell us *how* such a fall can be brought about – crying down prices is not an operational policy as such – and he fails to explain what is to be done to bring the price fall about. Nor does Samuelson explain what the price fall would cost. We cannot tell what the cost would be without knowing how the price fall was to be brought about and what else would be involved, and we cannot assume that cost to be trivial simply because it appears to be in Samuelson's hypothetical experiment. To make matters still more difficult, Samuelson requires not only that prices *fall*, but that they *stay* at their new level after they have fallen. He therefore has to explain how prices are to be kept down once they have been cut, *and* his argument also requires that the cost of keeping prices down is negligible. The problem, of course, is that agents would individually have more real balances than they wanted to hold, and their efforts to get rid of surplus balances would push prices back up. How Samuelson would prevent prices rising back again – and, moreover, do so at zero cost – is not altogether clear. Wage and price controls have a very poor record at containing 'inflationary' pressure, and are hardly costless, and the only other way to keep prices down – to reduce the money supply to a level consistent with our target price level – will hardly do if our objective is to increase the supply of real balances. Even if we could *put* our agents in Samuelson's hypothetical 'optimum' at zero cost – and there is of course no reason to believe we could – they would not stay there because they would have more real balances than they were willing to hold, and their attempts to cut down on their real balances would return them to the point where they started. In short, it is almost certainly not possible to reach Samuelson's 'optimum', and agents would not stay there even if they somehow found themselves in it. Samuelson's 'optimum' is simply not feasible.[15]

Anticipated Inflation and Relative Prices

Anticipated inflation can also have 'real' effects on the economy through its impact on relative prices. Perhaps the most widely studied source of such effects relates to the cost of changing a price. This type of cost might be the cost of changing an offer price in a shop window, the cost of changing a coin machine, or the cost of having a new price list produced and distributed – costs usually known collectively as 'menu costs' – but it might also cover the cost of renegotiating a contract or the cost of the information or goodwill lost when a price is changed (see, e.g., Mussa, 1977, 277). When it considers whether to change a price, a firm must weigh the cost of changing the price against the cost of leaving it as its current, presumably undesirable, level. The firm will therefore change the price only at discrete intervals – price-changing costs thus lead to prices becoming 'sticky'. One way these costs lead inflation to influence relative prices is illustrated by Mussa (1977, 278–279; 1981).[16] Let p_t^i be the (log) price of commodity i at time t, p_t^{i*} be its equilibrium value, and

$$b[p_t^i - p_t^{i*}]^2 \qquad (15.17)$$

be the flow loss from having a price that differs from its equilibrium value, where b is a positive constant. If equilibrium values never changed, the firm would set actual prices equal to their equilibrium values, and the term in (15.17) would always be zero. Suppose however that equilibrium prices are subject to aggregate and relative demand pressures, and the equilibrium price changes at the rate π_t^{i*}. Integrating (15.17) over the interval between price changes, T_i, the loss becomes

$$b \int_0^{T_i} [p_t^i - p_t^{i*} + \pi_t^{j*}]^2 dt \qquad (15.18)$$

and the pricing rule that minimises this loss is

$$p_t^i = p_t^{i*} + [T_i/2]\pi^{i*}. \qquad (15.19)$$

The new price is set at a level that not only corrects for the existing disequilibrium, but also anticipates approximately half the change in the equilibrium relative price that will occur over the interval for which the price is fixed. (15.19) implies a loss from disequilibrium prices per unit time of $(b/12)[\pi^{i*}]^2/[f_i]^3$, where f_i is the frequency of adjustment. An increase in the frequency of price adjustment reduces this loss, and hence reduces the average difference between actual and 'equilibrium' prices, but each adjustment is assumed for convenience to cost a fixed amount a. We can then derive the optimal value of f_i, i.e.,

$$f_i = [(1/6)(b/a)(\pi^{*i})^2]^{1/3} \qquad (15.20)$$

from the total cost function. (15.20) tells us, as we might have expected, that higher inflation leads prices to be adjusted more frequently.[17] Given that $f_i = 1/T_i$ and the average π^{i*} is the same as the inflation rate, we can easily show from equations (15.19) and (15.20) that the price of a typical good i will become more volatile relative to the price level as the inflation rises (see also Sheshinski and Weiss, 1977; Danziger, 1984; and Caplin and Spulber, 1987). Following Danziger (1987a, 286), we can therefore say that *inflation increases the inter-temporal variability of the relative price* of the good concerned.

The average welfare loss l_i created per unit time by this relative price variability is now:

$$l_i = [(9/16)a^2 b(\pi^{*i})^2]^{1/3} \qquad (15.21)$$

and we can derive the total welfare loss over all goods by integrating this expression with respect to i (Mussa, 1977, 279). Provided that relative demand pressures are symmetrically distributed around zero, the *optimum inflation rate is then zero* (see also Gillman, 1995). Inflation is costly because it necessitates more (costly) price changes than would be needed if the price level were stable. Deflation is also costly for the same reason.

Higher inflation might also influence other relative prices. Unless all prices were changed simultaneously, price adjustments would be staggered across different firms, and relative prices *between different goods* would change over time depending on the timing of the individual price changes. If the price of good 1 was changed before that of good 2, the relative price of good 1 against good 2 would rise when the price of good 1 was increased, and subsequently fall again when the price of good 2 was increased (see, e.g., Sheshinski and Weiss, 1977, 301). As Laidler observes,

> It is thus perfectly possible that the overall value of an economy's general price index can change at a continuous and perfectly foreseen rate while the pattern of relative prices underlying it fluctuates as different firms and industries change their output prices at different moments. Such inflation induced fluctuation in the pattern of relative prices would both reduce the amount of information about relative prices to be generated from any particular sampling of money prices, and it would also open up incentives for the devotion of resources to speculative activity that would not exist in the absence of inflation. (Laidler, 1977, 325)

Relative prices might also be affected by inflation if prices exhibit different degrees of stickiness. Some prices are more or less continually flexible, but others are set in 'customer' markets (to use the terminology from Okun, 1975) and therefore exhibit some degree of stickiness (see Okun, 1975; Bordo, 1980; Carlton, 1982, 141–142). Anticipated inflation might also produce changes in the relative market price of a good *compared to the price that would otherwise have prevailed*, and Danziger found that a relative price thus defined would tend to fall behind inflation under reasonably plausible conditions (see, e.g., Danziger, 1987a, 294). Anticipated inflation might also influence the *dispersion of the price of a given good within a particular market* through its impact on search behaviour. If search is a costly activity, it is never optimal for agents to carry out complete searches, and equilibrium prices within a market will show some degree of dispersion (Stigler, 1961). If inflation rises, prices will change more rapidly, and it is arguable that the information obtained by search will obsolesce more rapidly. Alternatively, as in Paroush (1986, 334–335), higher inflation raises the cost of search by raising the tax on the real balances agents carry about them on their searches. Either way, the return to search will fall, less search activity will take place, and the equilibrium dispersion of prices within any market will rise (see also Stigler and Kindahl, 1970). In each of these cases, we would presumably expect, as in the Mussa story, that the losses associated with the relevant form of relative price instability are minimised by a zero rate of inflation.[18]

THE COSTS OF SPORADIC INFLATION

General Considerations

The assumption of fully anticipated inflation is a useful starting point that helps illustrate certain basic issues – most particularly, the real-balance 'triangle' costs of inflation, the effects of anticipated inflation on the capital stock, the effects of anticipated inflation on relative prices – but there comes a point where we need to drop this assumption if we are to make further progress. We then arrive at *sporadic inflation* – inflation that varies from one period to the next, and in ways that the agents affected usually did not anticipate. A key implication of sporadic inflation is that since agents often get their inflation forecasts wrong, it no longer makes no sense (as it might have done before) to assume that they hold their expectations of inflation as if with certainty. Agents will still form expectations of future inflation rates, but their point estimates will now be associated with a positive variance or some other indication of the subjective uncertainty with which those expectations are held. *Sporadic inflation thus raises the general issue of inflation risk or uncertainty,* which complicates matters enormously, to put it mildly. Sporadic inflation also forces us to draw a distinction between the *ex ante* and *ex post* costs of inflation. The *ex ante* costs occur 'whenever inflation is expected and individuals are affected or change their behaviour on this account' (Jaffee and Kleiman, 1977, 288). We have dealt with some of these costs already, albeit in a somewhat restrictive framework in which agents hold their expectations of future inflation rates as if with certainty. By contrast, the *ex post* costs are those that arise because the realised inflation *differs* from the anticipated rate, an example being the redistribution of wealth resulting from an unexpected change in the price level. These costs are a new type of cost that was ruled out earlier by our assumption that the realised and anticipated inflation rates were always equal.

If we are to get to grips with the issues raised by sporadic inflation, we first need to take a close look at the system upon which the inflation impinges. A good starting point is to

> dispense with the notion that individual economic activities are coordinated by a fictitious 'auctioneer' or – what comes to much the same thing – by vaguely specified 'forces of supply and demand'. In real life, economic plans are formulated and carried out within the framework of a complicated structure of market institutions that have evolved gradually out of an interplay of political, social and technological factors with everyday economic forces. (Clower, 1984, 244)

This economy differs from the mythical Walrasian economy in that much of 'the day-to-day coordination of economic activities is carried out by highly visible exchange intermediaries – economic agents who act in a specialized capacity as brokers and auction agents or as outright dealers in various commodities that are produced and consumed in any considerable volume within the community' (Clower, 1984). These intermediaries help to overcome the transactions and related costs involved if consumers were to deal directly with producers without any middlemen, but they also reduce the information problems that agents face when they trade in 'real world' economies without the help of an auctioneer. A potential customer has the problem of deciding which supplier to patronise, and in many markets it is costly for him to search around. His best strategy is therefore to find a supplier who appears to be offering him a good deal, and then stay with that supplier until something happens to make him think he should search around again. A supplier responds by trying to keep his existing customers, and he does so by offering them stable prices that

> encourage customers to return to buy, or at least to sample, using yesterday's experience as a guide to today's offerings. A kind of intertemporal comparison shopping develops in which yesterday's offer influences today's demand, as a result of an implied commitment of the seller to maintain his offer. (Okun, 1975, 361)

The intermediary/supplier therefore holds buffer stocks so that he can absorb 'small' fluctuations in market demand and supply and provide customers with readily available quantities at reasonably stable prices, and he only changes prices at discrete, often irregular, intervals, when it has become reasonably clear that his current prices are now out of line with market conditions and must be changed if he is to retain control of his stocks.[19] We find these 'customer relationships' not only in retail sales markets, but also in labour markets and within firms themselves, and they play a critical role throughout much of the economy. As Okun continued, these relationships

> are valuable institutions to society, because information costs are really high. In comparison with a dominantly auction economy, they cut the cost of shopping, and reduce the resources devoted to trading in spot and futures transactions and to the negotiation of formal contracts. They lower job turnover and create reasonably predictable career income profiles; they encourage firms to invest in workers and to build career ladders for them. They economize on resources devoted to point-estimate forecasting of the future. They promote reliance on custom and habit. They allow accounting systems and hence orders, capital budgeting, and financing to be guided by reliable historical costs rather than conjectural future costs. They make money and, more generally, fixed-dollar assets valuable and reasonably reliable claims over a wide range of consumer goods and services that may be desired many years in the future. (Okun, 1975, 382–283)

Whether individual markets are customised or not, resource allocation is ultimately driven by market prices which provide signals of relative scarcity and inducements to allocate resources efficiently. As Hayek (1945), Horwitz (1991) and others have argued, one of the main functions of market prices is to promote economic efficiency by communicating information about relative scarcities to guide economic decision-making. Market prices can provide agents with information in three different ways:

> First, prices play an *ex ante* communicative role by providing information about the current state of relative scarcity ... Prices also play an *ex post*

communicative role by informing us after the fact whether our actions improved our economic well-being. To the entrepreneur, profit and loss statements provide information about how effective past action actually was. Finally, prices play a role in discovering opportunities and information that might otherwise be passed over. Israel Kirzner's (1973) view of the entrepreneur as an arbitrageur between differing prices for the same resources is the best example of this function of prices. (Horwitz, 1991, 3)

An economy is critically dependent on its price system, and all sorts of 'wrong' decisions will be made if the price system starts to malfunction and send out 'misleading' signals.

The first impact of an inflationary monetary stimulus will typically be felt by the intermediaries who will find that sales will rise and their stocks of goods will fall. They will initially respond by increasing their orders, their suppliers will then step up production and increase their orders of materials, and so on, and the increased stock of money will gradually but unevenly percolate throughout the system. Increased demands will eventually produce rising prices, but price rises will also be uneven. Relative prices will then become distorted and cause all sorts of problems. To quote Horwitz again,

> inflation affects resource allocation through the *ex ante* role of prices by encouraging producers to readjust their production toward those goods with inflated relative prices. It also affects allocation through the *ex post* function by making the past production of the inflated-price goods appear more profitable due to the rise in price of the final product. Inflation also affects the discovery role of prices in that entrepreneurs will be more likely to discover future profit opportunities in the inflated- price goods as the spread between the apparent final price of the product and the costs of its inputs may widen due to the inflation. What is crucial here is that the inflation plays havoc with the knowledge-conveying ability of the price system. (Horwitz, 1991, 4)

Even if the inflationary impulse is a one-off one and the economy eventually settles down to a new 'equilibrium', the adjustment process will still be a turbulent, drawn-out and, presumably, costly affair. If the stimulus is part of a sustained inflationary policy, however, the turmoil and the problems that go with it will carry on indefinitely:

Actual inflations – even sustained and rapid ones – always proceed by fits and starts. Because of this the operations of intermediaries as coordinators of economic activity are thrown into a more or less constant state of turmoil. Inventories of goods are always either too low or too high. Price increases are introduced at some times in anticipation of increased demands that do not materialize, while at other times price increases are delayed and sudden shortages then occur because demands suddenly increase. No outside observer can make sense of price movements. Depending on prevailing levels of inventories in relation to desired holdings, prices can rise even when stocks are increasing ... and remain constant or decline even when stocks are declining ... The velocity of money undergoes odd and erratic movements ... Search activity increases ... Resources are unemployed because owners do not wish to commit them too quickly in one direction lest commitment in another direction should shortly turn out to be more desirable. In short, economic 'laws' appear to break down. In fact, what breaks down is the capacity of intermediaries effectively to coordinate economic activities. It is one thing to operate in the face of mere ignorance – this is the usual situation of any intermediary. Plain ignorance can be dealt with in normal circumstances by operating on the assumption that tomorrow will be something like the average of experience over the past week or month or year. But when ignorance is compounded with Knightian uncertainty and the past becomes an essentially worthless guide to the future, intermediaries cannot follow conventional rules and still stay in business. ... [And] their ability to serve effectively as coordinators of economic activity is diminished accordingly. (Clower, 1984, 251–252)

Okun's assessment is very similar:

Prolonged and intense inflation upsets many habits of economic life, confronting customers with price increases and price dispersions that send them shopping; making them doubt their ability to maintain their living standards; ... and forcing them to compile more information and to try to predict the future – costly and risky activities that they are poorly qualified to execute and bound to view with anxiety. (Okun, 1975, 383)

Furthermore, since

Customer markets depend heavily on – and in turn enhance – the usefulness of money as a yardstick and as a store of value [this] usefulness is impaired in a world of inflation, as are many aspects of buyer–seller relationships that are 'efficient' in a complex world. Thus the welfare costs usually attributed to inflation ... should be viewed in a broader context as disturbances to a set of institutions that economize on information, prediction, and transaction costs through continuing buyer–seller relationships. Inflation does fool people ... . But it does so ... by depriving them of a way of economic life in which they need not depend heavily on the formulation of costly and uncertain point-estimate expectations. (Okun, 1975, 359)

Relative Price and Price-level Misperceptions

There are thus a number of plausible arguments to suggest that sporadic inflation can be very damaging, but these arguments are mainly heuristic and formal economic theory has so far made only limited progress getting to grips with them. However, considerable progress has been made in the analysis of how monetary instability can affect the 'real' economy by influencing agents' *perceptions* of relative prices. The Lucas (1972, 1973) model postulates that household-suppliers live in decentralised markets where they observe the price prevailing in 'their' market, but not prices in other markets. They are ignorant of the prevailing price level, and therefore of the relative prices of their own goods, and make the best forecasts they can on the basis of the information they have. Monetary factors can then impinge on those forecasts, distort their relative price perceptions, and lead them to make production 'errors' they would otherwise have avoided. *The price system malfunctions because monetary 'noise' produces misleading relative-price signals which lead to resource misallocation.*

The basic model is as follows:[20] The (log) quantity supplied to each market i is the product of a normal or secular component $y_{ct}(i)$ and a cyclical component $y_{ct}(i)$. The former follows an exogenous trend and the latter increases with its perceived relative price,

$$y_{ct}(i) = \gamma[p_t(i) - Ep_t/I_t(i)], \quad \gamma > 0 \tag{15.22}$$

where $p_t(i)$ is the log of the price in market i at time t, and $Ep_t/I_t(i)$ is what suppliers in market i believe the general price level p_t to be on the basis of the information set $I_t(i)$ available to them in their market. This set includes the current price in that market, and lagged values of all other prices, so agents are ignorant only of current prices in other markets. (We can think of the information contained in past prices being already published in the form of price indices, but indices take time to publish, and so agents do not know the prevailing price level. More generally, Karni, 1981 shows that aggregate-relative price confusion still arises provided the number of unobserved aggregate shocks exceeds the number of centralised asset markets that can provide indicators of the state of the aggregate economy.) Nominal demand is given by

$$y_t(i) + p_t(i) = x_t + w(i) \tag{15.23}$$

where x_t is an exogenous random shift variable common to all markets, and $w(i)$ is a market specific random shock whose distribution is known to all agents. Assuming that the shocks are distributed normally and independently,

$$\Delta x_t \sim N(\delta, \sigma^2_x), w \sim N(0, \sigma^2_w). \tag{15.24}$$

Total nominal income is found by summing (15.23), and Cukierman and Wachtel (1979, Appendix B) show that Δx reflects the rate of change in nominal income when the number of markets is large. σ^2_x can therefore be interpreted as the rate of change in nominal income. The general price level p_t is a weighted average of market prices and is independent of individual market prices because the price of each individual good enters the average with a small weight, but agents still do not know the contemporary price level because they do not know x_t.

If agents form expectations rationally, we can show that the equilibrium price in market i can be decomposed into an economy-wide price level, p_t, and a market-specific deviation from that price level, $z(i)$, which we can interpret as the relative price of the good in market i. We can also show that

$$\text{var } (p_t) = \sigma^2 = \sigma^2_x/(1 + \theta\gamma)^2, \text{var } z(i) = \tau^2 = \sigma^2_w/(1 + \theta\gamma)^2 \qquad (15.25)$$

where $\theta \equiv \sigma^2_w/(\sigma^2_x + \sigma^2_w)$ (see, e.g., Cukierman and Wachtel, 1979, 597–599). (15.25) tells us that the variance of the price level and the variability of individual relative prices both depend on the exogenous variables σ^2_x and σ^2_w. The effects of changes in these variables on σ^2 and τ^2 can then be found by partial differentiation. In particular,

$$\partial\sigma^2 / \partial\sigma^2_x > 0, \partial\tau^2 / \partial\sigma^2_x > 0. \qquad (15.26)$$

An increase in the variance of the economy-wide nominal shock will lead to a larger price-level variance and more volatile relative prices. This result rationalises the claim of Vining and Elwertowski (1976) and others that a more volatile price level tends to be associated with more volatile relative prices. However, causality runs, *not* from the inflation variability, σ^2, to relative price variability, τ^2, but from the variability of nominal demand, σ^2_x, *and* the variability of market specific shocks, σ^2_w, to *both* the former.

Misperceptions also influence cyclical output. It is easy to show that agent i's optimal forecast rule for the price level is a weighted average of the current price in market i and his forecast of the price level on the basis of all his past information, with weights equal to $(1 - \theta)$ and θ respectively (see, e.g., Cukierman and Wachtel, 1979, 599). Agents' expectations of the current price level are influenced by the price they observe in 'their' market, but the weight this price receives in their forecasting rule falls as σ^2_x rises relative to σ^2_w. (Recall that $q\sigma^2_w/(\sigma^2_x + \sigma^2_w)$, so $(1 - \theta)$ rises with σ^2_x/σ^2_w. Intuitively, the greater σ^2_x/σ^2_w, the more any change in the market price is likely to reflect a general increase in prices, and the greater the weight attached to the current market price in forecasting the current price level.) The optimal price-level forecasting rule and the output equation (15.22) then imply

$$y_{ct}(i) = \gamma\theta[p_t(i) - \mu_t] \qquad (15.27)$$

and

$$y_{ct} = [\gamma\theta/ (1 + \gamma\theta)](\Delta x_t - \delta) = [\gamma\sigma^2_w/ (\sigma^2_x + (1 + \gamma)\sigma^2_w](\Delta x_t - \delta) \qquad (15.28)$$

(see, e.g., Cukierman, 1984, 46–47) which tells us that output rises with unanticipated monetary growth $(\Delta x_t - d)$, but with a factor of proportionality (i.e., supply elasticity) that is itself a decreasing function of the variance of monetary growth. Any monetary shock will stimulate output by an amount that depends on the relative noisiness ratio σ^2_x/σ^2_w. For any given value of σ^2_w, a more noisy aggregate demand implies a lower effect on output, because each individual producer is more inclined to view the rise in his own market price as reflecting an aggregate demand expansion rather than a rise in his own relative price (see also

Lucas, 1973). Any given aggregate demand shock consequently has a smaller impact on output. As σ_x^2 / σ_w^2 gets large, aggregate demand noise drowns out relative price signals, agents interpret all market price rises as reflecting aggregate demand shocks, and the output response goes to zero.

A number of other results also follow. The optimal price-level forecasting rule implies that as σ_x^2 rises, agents will attach more weight to their individual market prices in forecasting the price level. The distribution of price level forecasts will therefore rise with σ_x^2 for any given distribution of market prices, but the market price distribution itself will also spread because the rise in σ_x^2 will also lead to an increase in t^2 (Cukierman and Wachtel, 1979, 600). *Greater aggregate 'noise' thus increases the divergence of views about the current price level and makes agents more inclined to misperceive true relative prices.* We can also show that greater monetary noise also produces welfare losses by increasing the dispersion of *inflationary* expectations and thereby impairing the efficiency of capital allocation.[21] Following Cukierman (1984, Chapter 5), suppose that borrowers and lenders have inflationary expectations $\pi^e(B)$ and $\pi^e(L)$, and let

$$D_B = a_B - [R - \pi^e(B)]/b_B$$
$$S_L = -a_L + [R - \pi^e(L)]/b_L \qquad (15.29)$$

respectively be the borrower's demand curve for investment funds and the lender's supply curve of them, where R is the nominal interest rate and all the parameters are positive. Agent i's demand for or supply of funds depends on his perception of the real interest rate $[R - \pi^e(i)]$, and the latter depends on his expectation of inflation. Differences in inflation expectations then imply differences in expected real interest rates, and these differences violate the optimality conditions that the (expected) marginal returns be equalised at the margin for all borrowers and lenders of comparable risk classes. Differences among real interest rates therefore cause capital to be misallocated, and the welfare losses involved can be captured by the areas under the appropriate curves. If the actual inflation rate is π, an agent who expects an inflation rate $\pi^e(i)$ suffers a welfare loss equal to $[\pi^e(i) - \pi]^2/2b_i$. His expected welfare loss is therefore $E[\pi^e(i) - \pi]^2/2b_i$ and the total expected welfare loss is again found by summing over i (see Cukierman, 1984, 74). Since $E[\pi^e(i) - \pi]^2$ is a natural measure of the uncertainty attached to an individual's inflationary expectations, this result provides a formal demonstration that *inflation uncertainty undermines the efficiency of capital markets.* More volatile aggregate demand leads to greater inflation uncertainty, and the greater inflation uncertainty leads to more capital misallocation.[22]

Misperceptions over Transitory and Permanent Prices

Agents might also face price inference problems of a different sort. Even if they perceive current prices correctly, they may still have difficulty assessing how 'permanent' current prices might be. Suppose that an agent wishes to sell an asset, but the market price of the asset has just fallen. If he believes that the fall in price is only temporary, it might make sense for him to wait for the price to rise again before selling. If he believed that the price fall was permanent, however, there would be no particular gain from waiting, and he might as well sell straight away. His perception of the length of time the current price will last has a critical bearing on the decision he has to make, and the same goes for many other economic decisions. Inflation affects these temporary–permanent perceptions in much the same way as it influences agents' perceptions of relative prices and the price level, but with the important difference that while the earlier type of confusion should normally disappear quickly as new information (e.g., a price index) becomes available, this second type of confusion might be much longer-lasting. Published prices do not reveal how much of a given price change is likely to stay and how much of it is merely temporary.

To focus on the temporary–permanent issue, let us assume that all agents have the same information. Following a slightly modified version of Cukierman (1984, Chapter 10), suppose that production takes place with a one-period lag – so producers must decide this period how much to produce for the next – and that the (logged) supply and demand functions for good i at time t are

$$y_t^s(i) = \gamma[E_{t-1}p_t(i) - E_{t-1}p_t], \gamma > 0;$$
$$y_t^d(i) = \varphi[x_t(i) + m_t + \varepsilon_t(i) - p_t(i)], \varphi > 0 \quad (15.30)$$

where $x_i(t)$ is a random taste parameter, m_t is the (logged) money supply, and $e_i(t)$ is a term which captures the (transitory) differential impact of a monetary shock on different markets. This latter term captures the idea that monetary shocks have different (temporary) impact effects on different markets, and it would seem reasonable to suppose that a more volatile money supply would lead to a greater differential effect. These variables are assumed to obey

$$x_t(i) = x_{tp}(i) + x_{tT}(i); \Delta x_{tp}(i) \sim N(0, \sigma_{xP}^2); \Delta x_{tT}(i) \sim N(0, \sigma_{xT}^2);$$
$$\Delta m_t \sim N(\delta, \sigma_m^2); \varepsilon_t(i) \sim N(0, \sigma_\varepsilon^2) \quad (15.31)$$

where P and T refer to the permanent and transitory components of $x_i(t)$, so called because innovations to the former have a permanent effect while innovations to the latter have a temporary effect on $x_t(i)$. The distributions of the other random variables are self-explanatory, and we assume for reasons stated just above that σ_m^2 and σ_ε^2 are positively correlated.

Everyone is assumed to observe all current market prices and know the stochastic and deterministic structure of the economy. Since it must decide this period what next period's output should be, a firm will want to predict next period's relative price and produce accordingly, but to predict that price it needs to assess how much of the current relative price is permanent, and to do that it must estimate how much the current relative price is influenced by an unobserved transitory changes in taste $x_{tT}(i)$ or the monetary impact variable $\varepsilon_t(i)$. It turns out that the optimal forecast of next period's relative price is

$$E_t[p_{t+1}(i) - p_{t+1}] =$$
$$\theta[\varphi/(\gamma + \varphi)][p_t(i) - p_t] + [1 - \theta\varphi/(\gamma + \varphi)][E_{t-1}p_t(i) - E_{t-1}p_t],$$
$$\theta = [(\sigma_{xP}^2 / \sigma_T^2) + (\sigma_{xP}^2 / \sigma_T^2)^2 / 4]^{1/2} - (\sigma_{xP}^2 / \sigma_T^2)/2 \qquad (15.32)$$

where $\sigma_T^2 \equiv \sigma_{xT}^2 + \sigma_\epsilon^2$ (Cukierman, 1984, 150–153). (15.32) indicates that relative prices are best forecast using an error-learning rule with a learning coefficient θ that depends (as in the previous model) on the noisiness of the underlying stochastic variables. The optimal forecast of next period's price is thus a weighted average of last period's forecast of this period's 'permanent' price and this period's actual relative price. The weights sum to one, and the weight given to this period's relative price increases with θ and the elasticity of demand relative to the elasticity of supply of good i. Intuitively, if the variance of permanent shocks is large relative to the variance of temporary ones, then it makes sense to attach more weight to innovations in the current relative price when forecasting the price next period, and we get a high value of q. But if the variance of permanent shocks is relatively low, it makes sense to attach more weight to our previous perception of the permanent price, and θ is low.

Since the optimal forecast rule is a weighted average of current and past information, an agent who uses it will interpret any change that takes place as partially permanent and partially temporary. He will therefore under-estimate the effects of permanent changes and over-estimate the effects of temporary ones. Production decisions will consequently under-react to permanent changes and over-react to temporary ones. When the next time period comes round, he will use his new price information to revise his forecast of the permanent price and reduce his perception error. If the price change was permanent, he will revise upwards the proportion of it that he regards as permanent. The period after that, he will reduce that amount even further, and so on, and his perception error will fall towards zero as new price data gradually persuade him that the change was fully permanent after all. If the price change was temporary, the price would fall back to its initial level and stay there, and the agent would gradually learn that the change had been a temporary one. In either case, the initial effect on output would gradually die away as the agent rectified his mistake and adjusted output towards its 'correct' level. Mistaken perceptions thus take time to correct, and they produce a trail of distorted output (and unemployment) in their wake that only corrects itself as they themselves are corrected.

To examine the further effects of these misperceptions, we need to compare the 'full-information' (FI) benchmark case where such misperceptions are absent with the 'normal' (NFI) case where they are not. After deriving the variances of relative prices under each case, we can show after a certain amount of manipulation that

$$\text{var}_{FI}[p_t(i) - p_t] - \text{var}_{NFI}[p_t(i) - p_t] \approx$$
$$[\theta^2\sigma_T^2 + (1 - \theta)^2\sigma_{xP}^2]/[\theta(2 - \theta)] > 0 \qquad (15.33)$$

if each agent is 'small' relative to the market (Cukierman, 1984, 168–169). Confusion between temporary and permanent prices thus produces additional relative-price variability beyond that which would already exist in its absence. Given that the right-hand side of (15.33) rises with both σ_T^2 and σ_{xP}^2, it is clear that an increase in the variance of temporary or permanent excess demand shocks increases the relative-price variance that arises from agents' confusion between temporary and permanent prices. Since $\sigma_T^2 \equiv \sigma_{xT}^2 + \sigma_\varepsilon^2$, this result also tells us that the variance of output rises with the variance of the monetary impact differential (i.e., σ_ε^2), and given that σ_ε^2 is positively correlated with σ_m^2, it follows that the variance of relative prices also rises with the volatility of monetary policy. Since the variance of the inflation rate is approximately the same as the variance of the money supply growth rate under the same assumptions (see Cukierman, 1984, 170), this result gives us another reason why the variance of relative prices and the variance of inflation might be positively correlated.

The effect of temporary–permanent price confusion on output is found in much the same way. If the 'full-information' output level is $y_t^{FI}(i)$. the variance of output around that level is

$$E[y_t(i) - y_t^{FI}(i)]^2 \approx [\theta^2 \sigma_T^2 + (1 - \theta)^2 \sigma_{xP}^2]/[\theta(2 - \theta)] \qquad (15.34)$$

provided again that each agent is 'small' relative to the market (see Cukierman, 1984, 155, 163–164). We can therefore regard (15.35) as a quantitative measure of the output distortion that the misperceptions create. Since this measure rises with $\sigma_{T\varepsilon}^2$ and $\sigma_{xP\varepsilon}^2$, and the former rises with σ_ε^2 which in turn rises with $\sigma_{m\varepsilon}^2$, it follows that the variance of output around its full-information level rises with the volatility of monetary policy. If we wish to minimise this output distortion, we therefore need to minimise the monetary variance σ_m^2. We thus get yet another version of the familiar result that volatile monetary policy leads markets to misallocate resources.

Income Redistributions Through Unanticipated Inflation

Economists have long recognised the importance of the income and wealth redistributions that inflation can produce. Imagine that two agents have the same inflationary expectations and enter into an agreement whereby one lends to the other an amount I at a nominal rate of interest r. If the expected inflation rate is π^e, there is an implied (expected) real interest rate of $R - \pi^e$, and one could reasonably say that there was an inflation-induced redistribution from one to the other if the *ex post* inflation rate and, hence, the *ex post* real interest rate, turned out to be different from expected. If $\pi > \pi^e$, the borrower pays less than he expected to pay in real terms, and the lender makes an involuntary transfer to him; but if $\pi < \pi^e$, the borrower pays more than he expected in real terms and makes an involuntary transfer to the lender. Similar transfers can occur if inflation causes agents to have more diverse inflationary expectations (as in Cukierman, 1984, 79–80), and they enter into contracts whose *ex post* returns turn out to be different from expected, or if agents find themselves already locked-into contracts promising particular nominal returns, and cannot adjust those returns in the light of new information about the inflation rate. In each case, one agent – and, in the middle case, perhaps both agents – might feel that reasonable expectations about the *ex post* return or payment had been disappointed by the price level turning out to be different from what they had expected it to be. *Unexpected price-level movements redistribute income and wealth in arbitrary ways that bear no relation to any accepted notions of fairness.* The more unpredictable the inflation rate, the greater the likely amounts involved in these redistributions, and the more 'unfair' the inflationary process will be perceived to be.

But it is not just that inflation redistributes *ex post* in ways that the agents involved did not (or could not) allow for. There is also an *ex ante* cost as the agents who might be affected by inflation-induced redistributions take into account the *prospect* that such redistributions *might* occur. One way to think about these costs is to view the inflationary process as a lottery, and the *ex ante* costs as the (normally negative) value of a ticket to the inflation lottery. Most agents would presumably want to avoid the lottery if they were 'inherently' risk-averse or if they faced nominally-denominated constraints that made them act as if they were risk-averse. An owner-manager might for example face credit constraints or covenant restrictions denominated in nominal rather than real terms, and these constraints would make him act as though he were risk-averse even if he were 'inherently' risk-neutral. We can therefore presume that the existence of the inflation lottery imposes a positive social cost.

There are two components to this social cost – the redistribution risk itself, and agents' attitude (i.e., usually aversion) towards it. To illustrate some of the issues involved, suppose we go back to the loan demand and supply schedules (15.29). If we (heroically) assume that the inflation process is statistically 'well-behaved', we can consider the variance of the inflation forecast error as a measure of the redistribution risk, and we can derive an expression for the *ex ante* cost to each agent if we are prepared to make assumptions about his (perhaps constrained) preferences. Following Cukierman (1984, 79–80), a borrower who borrowed I_B at a fixed nominal interest rate on the expectation of an inflation rate $\pi^e(B)$ would make a loss *ex post* of $(\pi^e(B) - \pi)I_B$. Similarly, a lender L who lends I_L on the expectation of an inflation rate $\pi^e(L)$ makes an *ex post* loss of $-(\pi^e(L) - \pi)I_L$. Assuming each agent is 'small' relative to the market, Cukierman (1984, 80, 83) showed that the expected loss to agent i is

$$(1/b_i)(1 - \rho) \text{ var } (\pi^e) \tag{15.35}$$

where ρ is the coefficient of correlation between the expectations of different traders, and var(π^e) again refers to the overall variance of inflationary expectations. It follows that inflation will impose positive expected losses on each trader as long as this variance is positive and there is some degree of difference among agents' expectations. More importantly, *the expected cost rises with* var(π^e), *which in turn rises with the amount of monetary instability.* If increasing monetary instability also raises the degree of dispersion of agents' inflationary expectations, as earlier theory suggests it might, then greater monetary instability will also reduce ρ, and the reduction in ρ will add further to the expected cost of inflation. If agents are risk-averse, or face constraints that make them act as if they were, the *ex ante* cost of inflation to them is not just the expected loss (15.35), but also includes the *premium they would need to induce them to choose the inflationary gamble*. The more risk-averse they are, or the more binding the constraints they face, the greater that premium must be (see also Jaffee and Kleiman, 1977, 290).

EMPIRICAL EVIDENCE

We now focus on the empirical evidence on these various issues. This literature is extremely complex, not to mention tedious in places, and readers might want to skip this section and go directly to the next one on the broader effects of inflation. For those who are interested, the main potential relationships on which empirical work has concentrated are summarised in the table:

Evidence on Price Instability, the Inflation Rate and Relative Price Variability

There is much relatively casual evidence to suggest that a higher rate of inflation is associated with greater relative price variability. Frederick Mills in 1927 noted such a relationship in his study of the US economy (Mills, 1927), and Frank Graham observed a similar relationship three years later in his study of the German hyperinflation (Graham, 1930, 175–177). Vining and Elwertowski (1976, Figures 1 and 2), Parks (1978, 83–85) and Fischer (1981a) observed a comparable relationship for the USA, and Parks also observed one for the Netherlands as well. Nonetheless, there is some dispute over how robust the relationship might be and

Table 15.1   The principal empirical relationships between inflationary and other variables

---

Type of empirical relationship
- Relationships between the inflation rate and relative prices
- Relationships between inflationary/monetary shocks and relative prices
- Relationships between the inflation rate and inflation variability
- Relationships between the inflation rate and inflation unpredictability/uncertainty
- Relationships between the inflation rate and output/unemployment/output growth
- Relationships between inflationary/monetary shocks and
- output/unemployment/output growth
- Relationships between inflation variability/uncertainty and output/unemployment/output growth
- Redistributive effects of inflation

---

over how it should be interpreted, with Glejser (1965), Parks (1978), Fischer (1981a), Blejer (1981, 1983) and others reporting positive relationships, and Blejer and Leiderman (1982), Hesselman (1983), Leser (1983), Mizon, Stafford and Thomas (1983), and Jaffee and Kleiman (1977, 303) reporting that the relationship was insignificant. However, it is noteworthy that more recent empirical studies by Danziger (1987b), Stockton (1988) and Domberger (1987, 560) each suggest that the relationship between relative price variability and inflation may be significant after all. Domberger also looked at *intra*-market as well as *inter*-market relative price variability, and found that both were 'strongly related' to the rate of inflation.[23]

Unfortunately, there are also problems with much of this evidence. (1) To begin with, there is evidence that some of these results are far from robust. Driffil *et al.* (1990, 1050–1051, 1057–1061) showed that the Vining–Elwertowski results were extremely sensitive, while Parks' (1978, 85–86) and Fischer's (1981a, 388–389) estimates show evidence of instability from one period to another. (2) Most studies use data that are too highly aggregated, and excessively aggregated data leads one to 'miss' distortions that arise between the relative prices of different goods lumped together in one aggregate (Danziger, 1987a, 287; Domberger, 1987). The greater the level of aggregation, the more goods are lumped together, and the greater the problem becomes. Greater weight should therefore be given to the findings of studies such as Domberger that use more disaggregated data, and Domberger's finding (1987, 561) that intra-market volatility was at least as important as inter-market volatility raises the possibility that other studies might have overlooked the more important relative price effects of inflation. (3) If the length of the period between price changes is not independent of the inflation rate – and the evidence suggests it is not – the standard measures of relative price distortion can depend on when the price readings are taken, and Danziger (1987a, 287; 1987b, 704, 706) shows that we can then easily find that our *measure* of relative price variability *falls* with inflation even if 'true' relative price variability actually *rises* with it. Danziger's finding (1987b, 711–712) that a 'correct' measure of relative price variability has a statistically significant relationship with inflation is then presumably more important than the findings of earlier studies which investigated such a relationship using inappropriate measures. (4) It might in practice be very difficult to distinguish the relationship of interest here (i.e., a relationship between inflation and relative price variability) from alternative relationships such as those between inflation shocks and relative price variability or between the change in inflation and relative price variability. Inflation, its unanticipated component and the change in inflation often appear to be highly correlated and when the underlying 'true' relationships are so weak anyway it can be extremely difficult to disentangle them. The difficulty is illustrated by a simple stochastic model developed by Hartman (1991). His model does not depend on costs of price adjustment, misperceptions, or any of the usual features that one finds in the relevant literature and yet it makes much the same predictions as they do. It follows that the sorts of regression results usually reported may have little power to discriminate amongst the different theories and we ought perhaps not to rely too much on any of them. (5) A last problem relates to the existence of trended time series. The basic procedure is to regress some measure of relative price variability on one or more regressors, with inflation or price-level variance included among these, and to interpret the significance or otherwise of the relation by a conventional *t*-test of the estimated inflation parameter based on the assumption that the ratio of this parameter estimate to its estimated standard error is distributed as a Student *t*-statistic. However when series are trended, as these often are, conventional interpretations of these ratios as *t*-statistics lead us to over-state their true significance and find relationships that do not exist (see, e.g., Granger and Newbold, 1974). It is therefore difficult to judge how much of the time-series evidence survives the critique of conventional time series econometric practice posed by recent developments in cointegration. We cannot really tell how strong the evidence of a relationship between inflation and relative prices actually is.[24]

Evidence on Unanticipated Inflation, Monetary Shocks and Relative Prices

Then there is the question of how relative prices are affected by *unanticipated inflation or unanticipated monetary growth*. The usual procedure used in studies of this issue, due to Parks (1978), is to regress some measure of the variance of relative price change on some unanticipated inflation variable and evaluate the significance of the relationship by a conventional *t*-test on the relevant parameter, with a supplementary equation being used to predict inflation and thereby extract values for unanticipated inflation. A number of studies then found that the unanticipated inflation parameter was significantly positive, with or without the presence of an anticipated inflation term (e.g., Parks, 1978; Blejer, 1981, 1983). *If* we take these results at face value – and the discussion of the previous subsection suggests reasons why we might not wish to do so – these results appear to suggest that unanticipated inflation has a significant positive effect on the variability of relative price changes. An alternative approach used by Hercowitz (1981, 1982) and Cukierman and Leiderman (1984) is to modify the Lucas (1973) model to obtain a reduced-form equation in which a measure of relative-price-change variability depends on monetary shocks, and test the significance of the monetary shock parameter. Results from these studies are generally mixed, but if we accept them, they appear to suggest that monetary shocks have significant effects on relative price variability under rapid inflation, but not under moderate inflation.

Evidence on Inflation, Inflation Variability and Inflation Uncertainty

Are higher rates of inflation associated with more volatile inflation or greater inflation uncertainty? These are both important issues. If higher average inflation is also more volatile, we cannot analyse the optimum rate of inflation without also taking account of the consequences of the changing variance that accompanies it. If the mean and variance rise together, the costs of higher inflation not only include the greater shoeleather, menu and real balance costs of an anticipated inflation, but also the extra costs implied by the greater variability or uncertainty of the inflation rate – we can no longer divorce the 'mean' and 'variance' costs of inflation.[25]

Evidence on Inflation and Inflation Variability

Perhaps the most straightforward way to examine the first issue – the possibility of a relationship between the inflation rate and inflation variance – is to regress the variance of inflation against its mean, and studies that have done so have by and large found a positive correlation between the two or between similar variables (e.g., Okun, 1971; Logue and Willett, 1976; Foster, 1978; Jaffee and Kleiman, 1977; Fischer, 1981b; and Taylor, 1981). Katsimbris and Miller (1982) and Katsimbris (1985) disputed these results and claimed that they were products of aggregation bias, but a more recent (and technically more sophisticated) study by Baillie, Chung, and Tieslau (1992) found strong evidence of a positive link between the mean and variability of inflation, at least for high inflation countries.

Evidence on Inflation and Inflation Unpredictability

However, we are often more interested in the *unpredictability* of inflation than in its *variability per se*. Variability and unpredictability are by no means the same and the difference between them is important. A variable can change considerably, but still be predictable. If inflation is merely variable, but predictable, then agents need only suffer the shoeleather and related costs of anticipated inflation, and they can avoid losses from unanticipated inflation such as those arising from confusion over relative prices and unanticipated wealth redistributions. But if inflation is unpredictable, agents will suffer all these losses *as well as* the losses from anticipated inflation. From a welfare point of view, it is the unpredictability rather than the variability of inflation that really matters. But what factors determine inflation unpredictability?

A large number of studies have examined this issue using a variety of different approaches,[26] and most of them found a positive relationship between some measure of inflation unpredictability and the mean inflation rate (e.g., Taylor, 1981; Frohman *et al.*, 1981; Holland, 1984; Cukierman and Wachtel, 1982b; Engle, 1982; Pagan, Hall and Trivedi, 1983; Froyen and Waud, 1987; Brunner and Hess, 1990; and Schmidt, 1991). Two contrary results were reported for the postwar USA by Engle (1983) and Cosimano and Jansen (1988), but the reliability of this conclusion was challenged by Brunner and Hess (1990), Evans (1991) and Ball and Cecchetti (1990). The latter two papers are particularly important in that they examined both short-term and long-term inflation unpredictability. Like Engle, Evans found that short-term inflation unpredictability shows little relation to the inflation rate, but he also found that long-term inflation uncertainty moved 'very strongly' with it (1991, 182). Ball and Cecchetti (1990) found that both short-term and long-term inflation uncertainty rise with the inflation rate, and that the effect of inflation on long-term inflation uncertainty is especially strong (1990, 234, 244). In short, there is strong evidence that a *higher inflation rate is also a more uncertain one, especially, perhaps, in the longer term.*

An alternative notion of inflation uncertainty is the dispersion of inflationary expectations across individuals, and there is evidence that measures of this dispersion are also systematically related to certain other inflation variables. For example, Cukierman (1984), Cukierman and Wachtel (1979, table 2), Frohman *et al.* (1981) and Holland (1984) found that such measures were correlated with the *mean inflation rate*, Cukierman and Wachtel (1982b, Table 2), and Engle (1982) found that they were correlated with measures of *inflation variability and/or uncertainty*, and Mitchell (1981), Jaffee and Kleiman (1977) and Zarnowitz and Lambros (1987) found that they were correlated with the *expected inflation rate.* Finally, Cukierman and Wachtel (1982a) found that the Livingston and University of Michigan measures of the dispersion of inflationary expectations were positively and significantly correlated with the Vining–Elwertowski (1976) and Parks (1978) measures of *relative price variability.* By and large, measures of the dispersion of inflationary expectations thus appear to be *positively correlated with the mean inflation rate, the variance of the inflation rate, the variance of unanticipated inflation, and the variability of relative price changes.* A considerable amount of the empirical work can therefore be summarised by the simple statement that each of these five variables – the variance of inflation, the variance of relative price changes, the variance of inflationary expectations, the dispersion of inflationary expectations, and inflation uncertainty – appears to be positively correlated with each of the others.

Evidence on the Effects of Inflationary Factors on Economic Activity

There is also considerable empirical literature on how inflationary factors might affect real economic activity. A good place to begin is with the evidence on the *relationship between inflation and economic growth.* Most studies found that inflation had a negative effect on growth (e.g., Kormendi and Meguire, 1985; de Gregorio, 1992; Cozier and Selody, 1992; Roubini and Sala-i-Martin, 1991; and Grimes, 1992), although others reported mixed results (e.g., Grier and Tullock, 1989) or found no relationship at all (e.g., Logue and Sweeney, 1981). Note that there is no evidence of inflation having a positive effect on economic growth. However, Levine and Renelt (1992) cast some doubt on these results by conducting an extensive analysis of the sensitivity of many of the results from the growth literature and concluding that results pertaining to the effects of inflationary factors on growth were generally fragile to relatively small specification changes. That said, however, there is also indirect evidence that inflation reduces output growth provided by Clark (1982), Selody (1990b) and Smyth (1994) for the USA and Jarrett and Selody (1982), Selody (1990b) and Novin (1991) for Canada, each of which examined the relationship between inflation and productivity growth and found evidence that the former significantly reduced the latter.[27]

The quantitative implications of reported negative effects of inflation on economic or productivity growth are very considerable. Grimes (1992, 641) reported that the coefficient of inflation in his growth equation had a fairly precisely defined value of -0.11, and a crude present-value formula with a discount rate r implies that the present value of the output loss from a 1 percent rise in inflation is $0.11(1 + r)^2/r^2$ of current income.[28] Taking r as 5 percent, the (present-value) cost ratio is therefore $0.11(1.05)^2/0.05^2 = 48.5$ percent. Smyth (1994, 265) reported a comparable coefficient of -0.193, which would give us a (present-value) cost ratio of 85 percent, Jarrett and Selody (1982) and Novin (1991) obtained even higher figures (in absolute terms). Lastly, Selody's (1990b, 11) four variable analysis of the relationship between inflation, productivity growth, hours worked, and labour hoarding suggested that a permanent 1 percent fall in inflation raises productivity growth by 0.23 percent for Canada and 0.11 percent for the USA, figures which (on the continuing assumption that $r = 5$ percent) imply cost ratios of just over 101 percent and 48.5 percent respectively. Even if the higher estimates are dismissed as implausibly high, it is nonetheless striking how the 'double discounting' of lost output growth translates into very large output losses even for low estimates of the effect of inflation on productivity growth. Even if we accept the lowest figure among those reported above – Selody's estimate that inflation reduces US productivity growth by 0.11 percentage points – *a rise in inflation of 1 percent would still have an effect on productivity growth equivalent in value to a fall in current output of nearly 50 percent.* The costs of inflation would of course be even larger if we accept some of the other estimates of the effect of inflation on productivity growth.

Then there are the predictions of Lucas-type models about the dependence of the elasticity of output on the variance of nominal aggregate demand (or inflation). (15.27) implies that an estimate of

$$y_{ct} = \alpha \left(\Delta x_t - \delta \right) \qquad (15.36)$$

over a cross-section of different countries should produce estimates of α that are negatively correlated with the variance of nominal demand in each country. This prediction was broadly supported by the empirical evidence of Lucas (1973) and Alberro (1981); the related prediction, that the output elasticity should decline with the variance of inflation, was supported by the evidence of Froyen and Waud (1984) and Cukierman (1984), but disputed by Katsimbris (1985). With the exception of the latter, empirical studies thus largely support the predictions that greater nominal demand or inflation volatility are associated with a steeper aggregate supply curve.

There are also the predictions concerning the effects of anticipated and unanticipated inflation (or monetary growth) on output or related variables like unemployment. The evidence here is far less clear. The basic procedure, pioneered by Barro (1977), is to estimate an equation in which output depends on anticipated and unanticipated money, and on other variables, and then test the predictions that output is *not* affected by anticipated money, but *is* positively affected by unanticipated money. Barro claimed that his own results (e.g., those of Barro, 1977) supported these predictions, but some features of his work were heavily criticised by other studies which cast serious doubt on his conclusions (see, e.g., by Small, 1979). Barro's work gave rise to a huge and well-known literature which applied different versions of the Barro approach to a large variety of periods and countries, but it is extremely difficult to draw any firm conclusions from it. In any case, since most of this work predates the development of cointegration and fails to take any real account of trends in the time-series used, there is reason to believe that many of the test statistics reported would be unreliable anyway.

Finally, there is the question of the impact of inflation variability or uncertainty on output or unemployment. In his Nobel lecture, Friedman (1977) implied that inflation variability has a detrimental effect on economic activity by making agents less willing to enter into long-term relationships and by reducing the effectiveness of market price signals as indicators of relative scarcity. To the extent that agents have not adjusted to it, higher inflation variability should then lead to a temporary though perhaps long-lasting reduction of output and employment (see also Azariadis, 1975). However, the Friedman–Azariadis logic applies more naturally to inflation *uncertainty* than to inflation *variability* as such, and applied in this way, suggests that greater inflation uncertainty should lead to lower output and employment, and higher unemployment. To distinguish these two effects, let us therefore call this second effect the 'Friedman II' hypothesis, as distinct from the earlier 'Friedman I' hypothesis of inflation variability on output or unemployment. We can also apply this same thinking to the effects of inflation variability and inflation uncertainty on output growth. Let us call these the 'Friedman III' and 'Friedman IV' hypotheses respectively.

There have been a number of attempts to examine these arguments empirically. The work of Froyen and Waud (1984) and Cozier and Selody (1992) supported the 'Friedman I' hypothesis that inflation variability significantly reduces output. Support for the 'Friedman II' hypothesis of the effects of inflation uncertainty on output and/or unemployment is provided by Levi and Makin (1980), Mullineaux (1980), Ahimud (1981), Evans (1983), Hafer (1986), Holland (1986), Kantor (1986) and Froyen and Waud (1987). The effects reported in these studies appear to be robust, and they are often quite large. For example, Evans presented estimates of the output gains that the USA would have enjoyed had inflation been eliminated there in the last quarter of 1980. Using a 5 percent discount rate, his estimates suggest that the present value of the output gains from eliminating inflation would have been equal to 29.4 percent of national output had the private sector taken two years to adjust to the change, and 23.8 percent of national output had they taken five years to adjust (1983, Table 1). The 'Friedman I' and 'Friedman II' hypotheses thus receive *considerable empirical support, and simulations suggest that a substantial amount is lost through inflation in this way.*

There are also studies that have examined the impact of inflation variability or uncertainty on output growth. Logue and Sweeney (1981) found little evidence in favour of the 'Friedman III' hypothesis relating to the effect of inflation variability on growth, but Grier and Tullock's more comprehensive 1989 study *did* find such evidence. (In any case, it is arguable that Logue and Sweeney would not have been able to find such an effect because most of the countries in their sample were on the Bretton Woods system and therefore had fairly similar inflation rates.) The 'Friedman IV' hypothesis relating to the effect of inflation uncertainty on growth is supported by the evidence of Makin (1982), Kantor (1986), Holland (1986), and Zarnowitz and Lambros (1987). As far as I know, only Jansen (1989) failed to find that inflation uncertainty had any impact on output growth, but even he was doubtful about the power of his test because he suspected his measure of inflation uncertainty had been too stable over his sample period. There is thus some evidence in favour of the 'Friedman III' and 'Friedman IV' hypotheses, and it is at least arguable that studies that failed to find such effects did so because they used inappropriate data sets.

Evidence on Inflation-induced Redistribution

We turn finally to the evidence on the redistributive effects of inflation. A major problem with empirical work on this issue is that much of it pays little attention to the important distinction between anticipated and unanticipated inflation. The redistribution created by inflation depends, not on the inflation rate *per se*, but on the difference between the *actual* and *anticipated* inflation rates. How then do we gauge the redistribution that took place without knowing what agents' expectations were? One possibility is to perform back-of-the-envelope simulations such as those carried out by Fischer and Modigliani (1978, 825–827). Their data indicated that the total value of nominally-denominated assets held in the USA at the end of December 1975 was about $4.7 trillion, in 1975 dollars. An unanticipated rise of 1 percent in the price level would therefore have reduced the real value of these assets by about $47 billion – almost 3 percent of annual GNP – and produced an unanticipated transfer of the same amount to those who had issued these assets. *The transfers involved can thus be very large even for relatively small unanticipated changes in the price level.* Since many agents would have held both assets and liabilities denominated in nominal terms, these transfers would sometimes offset each other, but the gross amounts are still important because they give us some idea of the size of the wealth reshuffling the price-level shock creates. In any case, the amounts involved are still large even if we consider net positions instead of gross ones. To give an illustration, Fischer and Modigliani also pointed out that the household sector at that date had a net holding of about $1 trillion in nominally-denominated assets, so a 1 percent unanticipated rise in the price level would still produce a *net* loss to that sector of about $10 billion, in 1975 dollars, a loss between one half and one percent of national income that year. *The transfers involved can still be considerable even if we just look at net rather than gross figures.*

Moreover, figures like these – and, indeed, most of the estimates in the literature – are likely to be *under-statements* because they look only at redistribution between *groups*. If we are interested in redistribution *per se*, we really need data on redistributions among *individuals*, and any study that looks at redistributions between groups will overlook any redistributions that occur between individuals *within* any group. We would also presumably expect the size of this 'aggregation bias' to rise with the sizes of the groups. It is therefore significant that one of the few empirical studies to examine the impact of inflation in redistributing individual (as opposed to group) incomes came to the conclusion that, for every 1 percent reduction in income inequality (as measured by the coefficient of variation across incomes) caused by inflation, inflation also caused individual incomes to alter by between 3 and 10 percent (Nordhaus, 1973, 394). Much the same point also emerged from the earlier study by Bach and Ando (1957). In Nordhaus' words, inflation caused 'a considerable amount of unsystematic reshuffling of individual fortunes' much of which is overlooked if we only examine redistributions between groups.

The empirical literature on inflation-induced redistribution of wealth has concentrated on two main areas where redistributions might occur. The first concerns redistributions from those with assets denominated in nominal terms ('creditors') to those with liabilities denominated in such terms ('debtors'). Perhaps the clearest result to emerge from this literature seems to be that agents form rational expectations of inflation which preclude *systematic* wealth transfers (see, e.g., the surveys by Rozeff, 1977 and Singleton, 1984), but there is little clear evidence on the size of the *unsystematic* transfers. Some studies do however suggest that gains or losses might depend on agents' net nominally-denominated positions. For example, Bach and Stephenson (1974) found that middle-income households are generally less affected by inflation because they have more balanced portfolios than households at either extreme, thus producing a greater tendency for gains and losses to cancel out (see also Rozeff, 1977). Similarly, a number of studies indicate that non-financial corporations are the greatest private-sector gainers from inflation, presumably because of the extent of their net debt position. However, one has to keep in mind that the evidence of these matters is overwhelmingly based on US data and it is not clear to what extent we can generalise from it.[29]

The second focus of empirical research concerns possible redistributions between groups of differing incomes or wealth. While it is relatively clear that the household sector as a whole is the main loser from inflation (see, e.g., Laidler and Parkin, 1975, 789), the evidence on the incidence of the inflation tax within that sector is very mixed. But, whatever other results they find, studies nonetheless agree that the transfers that do occur seem to be relatively small (see, e.g., Budd and Seiders, 1971, 134; Nordhaus, 1973). In fact, Budd and Seiders (1971, 134, 138) commented that the smallness of the transfers was the most striking and robust feature of their results. However, this evidence is also almost wholly based on postwar US data, and it is not clear how far we may generalise from it to other economies or other periods; in any case, as just noted, evidence of small transfers between *groups* does not necessarily mean that transfers between *individuals* were also small.[30]

The empirical work thus gives a rather unsatisfactory picture of the redistributive consequences of inflation. In any case, such evidence as we have still does not give us much idea of the *ex ante* welfare costs of (expected) inflationary redistributions. Even if we were confident we had it, knowledge of what inflation did *after* the event does not tell us what expected inflationary redistributions mean for the individuals who *anticipate* that they might occur. From the viewpoint of *ex ante* social welfare, the relevant question is not the size of *ex post* redistributions, but what the agents who expect to be affected would be willing to pay *ex ante* to avoid them. These *ex ante* costs are virtually impossible to estimate, and it is easy to imagine situations where the *ex ante* costs can be high even if the *ex post* redistributions turn out to be relatively small. For a firm that faces severely binding constraints such as tight credit limits, the prospect of an inflationary gamble could be very damaging because the gamble could significantly increase its perceived danger of being driven into default. The same might be said for a mortgage-holder looking at the gamble implied by the gyrating interest rates that often accompany inflation. Part of our difficulty is that we do not observe the prices that agents would pay to avoid inflationary lotteries, but a much deeper problem is that we do not even have an adequate conceptual apparatus to model the issues involved. The inflationary lottery is not a simple, unidimensional lottery, but a package of interrelated lotteries that cover many different outcomes occurring at many different times, and we have little idea how to model such lotteries even if we had a complete characterisation of agents' expectations. In any case, the nature of the inflation process is such that it would be extremely difficult to model agents' expectations anyway. The process of assessing the probability that inflation might be x percent at some time in the future is quite different from the process of assessing the likely colour of a ball to be pulled out of an urn. As Leijonhufvud (1981, 264, n. 52) points out, the type of uncertainty involved is better illustrated by a game of chess than a game of dice. We cannot exhaustively specify all relevant possible outcomes, and therefore cannot apply the normal actuarial calculus. To make matters worse, the outcomes of real-world business decisions depend crucially on monetary policy decisions that are very difficult to predict because they are not themselves the outcomes of any 'well-behaved' stochastic processes. The appropriate metaphor, as Leijonhufvud continues, is that of

> playing 'chess' in the presence of an official who has and uses the power arbitrarily to change the rules – i.e., a man who may interrupt at move 14 with the announcement: 'From now on bishops will move like rooks and vice versa ... and I'll be back with more later'. (1981, 264, n. 52)

THE BROADER EFFECTS OF INFLATION

Worrying about the unpredictability of the future price level under inflationary conditions leads naturally to the difficult and largely unresolved issues that arise when we consider the broader effects of inflation. It is also at this point, when the going gets difficult, that economic theory really starts to let us down. Economic theory is necessarily predicated on *ceteris paribus* assumptions of one sort or another that *presume* the existence of an underlying economic structure that remains reasonably stable in the face of the changes being considered.[31] But the longer inflation lasts, or the higher or more volatile it is, the less tenable it becomes to continue to assume that other things are still roughly equal. The underlying 'structure' of the economy starts to change – generally for the worse – and models that treat that structure as given become increasingly inappropriate:

> Out of the totality of interactions among individuals in society, we [economists] abstract (by none-too-clearly articulated rules) the 'economic', the 'political', and the 'social'. The workings of the 'economy' are then analyzed as if interactions with the 'polity' and 'society' can be ignored. The political and social settings of economic problems are among the *ceteris paribus* assumptions.
>
> Now it is fortunately true that many useful things can be said about asset prices, for example, while abstracting from the mating rituals of yuppie stockbrokers. Financial theory is no doubt further advanced today for having made that abstraction. The same conclusion applies to economic theory in general – it has progressed as far as it has in large measure by ignoring complications that could not have been rigorously handled in any case. Like physics in the natural sciences, economics made the most rapid progress by being first to pick the easy problems (and especially the easily quantifiable problems) and leaving the intractable ones to others.
>
> The price for these advances of disciplinary specialization, however, turns out to be a *certain trained incapacity on the part of most economists to think straight about problems that involve interactions between the economic and the political or social spheres.* (Leijonhufvud, 1988, xvi, my emphasis)

Economic theory is like the street lamp in the proverbial anecdote about the drunk who drops his key – it is very helpful if he dropped the key near the lamp, where *ceteris paribus* assumptions hold, but apt to be misleading otherwise.

Yet there are also reasons to believe that much of the damage done by inflation arises *precisely because* it undermines certain features of the environment – features, moreover, on whose integrity the economic order, and more broadly the social order, depends if it is to function well. We can no longer assume that people's attitudes, exchange processes, contract forms, the legal system, or other social institutions remain substantially unaffected by inflation. Indeed, the very distinction between 'economic' and 'social' or other spheres on which we traditionally rely now breaks down, and we can no longer take the latter for granted while we play around with the former. We are no longer dealing with narrowly defined economic effects, but with much broader social repercussions of staggering complexity. These broader effects are perhaps the most important consequences of all, and we should not ignore them simply because we do not know how to model them.

Inflation, Real Balances and Exchange

A good place to start is with the effects of rapid inflation on real balances and the exchange process. While conventional treatments such as Barro (1970, 1972) suggest that agents respond to rapid inflation by economising on their holdings of real balances and increasing payment frequency, and the empirical evidence strongly supports these predictions, historical accounts also suggest that the effects of rapid inflation go much deeper. A paradox of rapid inflations is that as the economy becomes flooded with hyperinflating currency it often becomes very difficult to satisfy the demand for *real* balances. One English observer of the German hyperinflation in the early 1920s reported that,

> There were always long queues at the banks. Sometimes before I reached the counter the window was shut. The supply of notes, which we were all waiting for and for which we had brought cases to carry them away, had run out. (Guttman and Meehan, 1975, 55)

The effect of hyperinflating exchange media on the exchange process is one of the few of these 'deeper' effects of inflation for which formal models have been developed. In Casella and Feinstein (1990), would-be buyers set out each period with holdings of hyperinflating currency to search out potential sellers and negotiate trades with them. Since the hyperinflation erodes the real value of their currency, potential buyers are under pressure to make trades quickly before prices rise much further and they no longer have enough currency to buy anything. The pressure to buy quickly is intensified further by the entry of later buyers who arrive with larger holdings of currency and threaten to price existing shoppers out of the market. However, potential sellers face no such pressure to trade quickly because they hold stocks of goods whose real value is not substantially affected by the inflation. Hyperinflation thus distorts the bargaining process between buyers and sellers, to the advantage of the latter and the detriment of the former. This distortion makes prices even higher than they would otherwise be, and clearly makes buyers worse off. The effect of the hyperinflation on sellers is mixed. Sellers *qua* sellers initially benefit because hyperinflation gives them an improved bargaining position *vis à vis* purchasers, but if the hyperinflation continues to escalate, even they lose out because shoppers are eliminated so quickly from the market that the sellers have great difficulty making any sales at all. In the end, it becomes impossible to make sales and economic activity grinds to a halt.

The historical evidence broadly supports this picture. It strongly suggests that inflation undermines established trading relationships, increases search and other transactions-related costs, and generally disrupts trading patterns to the point where in extreme cases trading virtually ceases. Another observer of the German inflation reported that

> At eleven o'clock in the morning a siren sounded and everybody gathered in the factory forecourt where a five-ton lorry was drawn up loaded brimful with

paper money. The chief cashier and his assistants climbed up on top. They read out names and just threw out bundles of notes. As soon as you had caught one you made a dash for the nearest shop and bought just anything that was going. At noon every day the new value of the mark was announced and if by that time you hadn't converted your money into some *Sachwerte* [i.e., real good] you stood to lose a large proportion of your salary. (Quoted in Guttman and Meehan, 1975, 57–58)

This sort of experience was no means unusual. Producers and retailers also suffered: by the time they obtained the revenue from their sales, prices had risen so much that their revenue was often worth little in real terms. As a consequence,

Shopkeepers were never sure of covering the cost of replenishing their stocks, irrespective of the prices at which they sold the goods; many goods had completely disappeared. Factories were no longer interested in selling to the home market against money, the value of which was rapidly vanishing. Foreign goods were scarcely obtainable ... Shopkeepers treated their customers almost as enemies – they deprived them of stock which could not be replaced. Buying, like kissing, went by favor. (Ringer, 1969, 100)

In the end,

food virtually disappeared from the shops. Farmers simply would not sell for paper money. Any supplies that did get through had to run the gauntlet of desperate people. (Guttman and Meehan, 1975, 185)

Historical accounts indicate that people were increasingly malnourished, children were underweight, and there were noticeable increases in illnesses and mortality resulting from poor diet and lack of necessities such as fuel. And yet there would be times when goods would remain unsold because people did not have the currency to buy them. There would be occasions, for instance, when thousands of tons of desperately needed milk remained unsold in Berlin because no-one could afford to buy it (Guttman and Meehan, 1975, 185).

Information Problems

Rapid and erratic inflation also makes it more difficult and costly to keep informed. It

becomes a bother to keep up with it all ... Most households will not try to maintain their stock of price-information at the 'quality' they normally desire – even as they spend more effort at it. If beef prices go up in every odd-numbered week and potatoes every even week, sensible beef-and-potato eaters will resign themselves to a constant proportions diet that is non-optimal every week. (Leijonhufvud, 1981, 258–259)

These problems go beyond those addressed in the theoretical literature discussed earlier:

> *Transactors will not be able to sort out the relevant 'real' price signals from the relative price changes due to these inflationary leads and lags.* How could they? Messages of changes in 'real scarcities' come in through a cacophony of noises signifying nothing ... and 'sound' no different. To assume that agents generally possess the independent information required to filter the significant messages from the noise would, I think, amount to assuming knowledge so comprehensive that reliance on market prices for information should have been unnecessary in the first place ...
>
> Transactors will gradually loose all firm conception of where the equilibrium neighbourhood for relative prices lies. Setting prices ... becomes a more difficult problem – and also a problem that no longer 'makes sense' in the way it used to ... With prices 'popping all around' and in irregular sequence ... [the old approach no longer makes sense and] the pot in which all its *ceteris paribus* presumptions have been thrown together is boiling furiously and cannot be ignored. (Leijonhufvud, 1981, 259–260, his emphasis)

There are many other information problems too. A publisher does not know what price to put on his newspapers or magazines, and retailers do not know what markups to charge. Accounting costs rise massively. One bank clerk in the German inflation reported that

> Writing all those noughts made work much slower and I lost any feeling of relationship to the money I was handling so much of. It had no reality at all. (Guttman and Meehan, 1975, 46)

An entry to a ledger that in normal times might have run to three or four digits ran to ten or twelve at the height of the inflation, and the Reichsbank's balance sheet for 1923 culminated in a number with no less than 24 digits (Guttman and Meehan, 1975, 191). Accountancy in these circumstances became 'maddening' (1975, 191), symbolised by the 'grotesque spectacle' towards the end of the inflation of the Reichsbank

> recording, with a sort of lunatic solemnity, the sum of 79 pfennigs in a balance sheet that went into thousands of trillions of marks. The cost of the printing ink used for the purpose was many times the value of the pfennigs themselves. (Guttman and Meehan, 1975, 198)

Inflation also causes serious problems for accounting even when it is moderate. Accounting conventions presuppose that prices are relatively stable, and they deliver unsatisfactory results even when inflation is moderate and predictable. For example, inflation creates problems for the valuation of fixed assets. Are such assets to be valued at their current replacement value, in which case they have to be revalued all the time and accounting costs would be very high, or are they to be valued at their historic cost, in which case the accounting numbers become increasingly meaningless? Inflation can play havoc with the valuations of fixed assets even when it is fully anticipated, and sporadic inflation causes even more problems by making future planning of investment decisions more difficult and injecting noise into attempts to estimate the 'real' returns to investments. Inflation also interferes in much the same way with the valuations of inventories. Are inventories to be revalued each time their prices rise, or do firms leave inventories valued at a meaningless historic cost? These problems in turn create difficulties for the valuations of profits, tax liabilities and the like. Inflation usually leads profits to be over-stated, and firms find themselves forced to pay out higher taxes and perhaps higher dividends on illusory 'paper' profits. Their 'real' capital falls as a result, and their ability to absorb losses, renegotiate credit on advantageous terms, and so on, is correspondingly diminished. These problems often create further accounting costs as the organisations concerned respond to them as best they can in ad hoc ways, which often means that they must operate on multiple systems of accounts in an effort to form even a remotely balanced overall picture. The inability of accountants to develop 'inflation-proof' accounting systems is surely ample testimony of how serious these problems are.

Then of course there is the sheer unpredictability of the future price level. In Leijonhufvud's words,

> Future inflation rates are not to be drawn from one of Nature's Urns. Decision-makers can hardly assume that current observations are drawn from some 'normal distribution'. What the rate will be five or ten years down the road is 'uncertain', but it is not uncertainty in that domain of their 'natural' expertise where transactors have learned to make (implicit) probability judgements. Farmers cope with uncertain harvest outcomes ... To have learned to manage rationally despite the vagaries of weather, however, will not leave much experience applicable to coping with the consequences compounded from the vagaries of voters in future elections, of legislatures and governments, and of Central Bank responses to the contingencies that the polity produces. (Leijonhufvud, 1981, 263)

This kind of uncertainty places the agents who must deal with it in an almost impossible position. As Leijonhufvud wrote elsewhere,

> There is no 'scientific' way to forecast future price levels in this system ... [E]ven short-term expectations are likely to be somewhat *incoherent*. The uncertainty attaching to any individual forecast of the price level will grow exponentially with distance from the present. The price level 10 years into the future is a subject for joking, not for rational discussion. Yet, of course, in an economy such as ours *people are forced to bet on it all the time*. (Leijonhufvud, 1983, 134, his emphasis)

The Distortion of Economic Activity

This chronic inability to forecast the future price level has all sorts of further effects on real economic activity beyond those we have already discussed. Being good at the production and distribution of 'real' goods and services becomes less important, and it becomes more important to be able to forecast inflation and find ways of living with it. The rewards for these types of activities change accordingly, and with them the structure of economic activity.[32] To quote Leijonhufvud again,

> The product designer who can come up with a marginally improved or more attractive product, the production manager who in a good year is capable of increasing the product per man hour by a percent or two, the vice president of sales who might reduce the real cost of distribution by a similar amount, etc., have all become less important to the stable functioning and/or survival of the organisations to which they belong. Other functions requiring different talents have increased in importance: the vice president of finance with a talent for so adjusting the balance sheet as to minimise the real incidence of an unpredictable inflation rate is an example. But the 'wise guy' who can do a good job at second-guessing the monetary authorities some moves ahead is the one who really counts. Smart assessment of the risks generated by the political game comes to outweigh sound judgement of 'ordinary' business risks. ...
>
> In short, being good at 'real' productive activities – being competitive in the ordinary sense – no longer has the same priority. Playing the inflation right is vital. (Leijonhufvud, 1981, 247–248)

The financial services industry then experiences an artificial boom, and rising salaries there draw in much of the best young talent. Howitt put this point very well:

> It is no accident that finance was among the sectors with the most noticeable innovations during the 1970s and 1980s. The need to protect against inflation uncertainty, and the opportunity to take advantage of other's inability to do so, diverted a lot of innovative thinking away from creating new goods and processes and into the invention of new financial contracts, new banking techniques, and new corporate financial strategies. Young people on Wall Street were paid huge salaries, but the cost of those salaries was paid by the rest of us, who were deprived of the medical services, scientific research, and so on that the financial whizz kids could have been producing. (Howitt, 1990a, 93–94)

Similarly, workers perceive that old-fashioned effort is no longer enough to ensure that they get a modest increase in real income each year, or even enough to prevent their real incomes falling. Morale falls, the climate of industrial relations deteriorates, and the typical worker is more inclined to turn to a union for protection, and more inclined to take industrial action.

Inflation-induced uncertainty about the future price level also reduces any willingness to enter into long-term commitments and make long-term investments. There is considerable evidence that inflationary factors have played a large part in reducing the maturity structure of corporate debt. Klein (1975b, 478) notes how

> One hundred year railroad bonds were ... issued around the turn of the century, while it is now quite uncommon to find a maturity of a new corporate issue that is greater than 30 years.

The decline in maturity structure is well attested (see e.g., Klein, 1975a, 146–147 or Fischer, 1982, 177), and Klein's empirical work (1975b, 478) relates it to the increased ratio of long-term to short-term price-level variability. The empirical work of Bordo (1980) suggests that inflation also reduces contract length and that of Klein (1975b, 481–482) suggests that inflation led to the increased use of escalator clauses in labour contracts in the USA. Many writers have also noted how inflation appears to have led to increased debt-equity ratios among US firms (see, e.g., Fischer, 1982, 177). Similar effects have been observed elsewhere. Howitt (1986, 184–187), for instance, documents how the maturity structures of corporate debt and household mortgages in Canada declined over the previous two decades, effects which he also ascribed to increased price-level uncertainty. A related consequence is a decline in the economy's liquidity. Even if nominal interest rates rise *pari passu* with inflation, inflation still has the effect of 'tilting' real repayments forward and reducing a debtor's liquidity. As Howitt observes,

> By 1983, the Canadian corporate sector was characterised by historically high debt-service ratios, debt equity ratios, and dependency upon short-term finance. The liquidity problems faced by home-owners and small business firms when interest rates rose in 1981 and 1982 were a major source of political unrest in Canada ... *While not all of these liquidity problems can be attributed to inflation, there is little doubt that it was the most important contributing factor* (Howitt, 1986, 188, emphasis added).

To the extent that people look to investments as inflation hedges, inflation also diverts investment into other areas like real estate, and works of art and thus contributes to speculative booms and busts in those areas. The loss and uncertainty of nominal value encourage people to seek alternative assets, so they seek 'real' assets – *Sachwerte* – which they believe will have a more stable real value in face of the inflation. This 'flight into physical values' has been observed in many inflations, and helps to explain why inflations are so often associated with temporary booms in 'real' assets that might be considered as inflation hedges. Such booms were observed in a number of the major developed countries in the 1970s and 1980s even though inflation was mostly in single digits or teens. They were also observed in hyperinflations where they appear to have been more pronounced.

In the German hyperinflation, there was a huge demand for anything physical, 'real' goods became increasingly difficult to find, and there was the

> widespread hoarding of exotic perfumes or soaps, hairpins, telescopes, *bric-à-brac* and a thousand other articles of no practical use whatsoever to the owner. On a higher scale there was the acquisition of what could be termed 'investments' – country houses, antiques, *objets d'art*, jewellery, luxury goods of all descriptions. (Guttman and Meehan, 1975, 179)

This indiscriminate buying in turn 'produced a lowering of tastes and standards of quality; if they could not get objects of the highest quality, second- or third-rate articles would do' (1975, 180). But almost inevitably, the market at some point corrects itself, and many of those who thought they had bought safe assets when the market was booming end up losing much of their investment – their assets might be 'real', but they are not safe.

Inflation also distorts investment by distorting interest rates and credit availability. Inflations appear to be associated with much more volatile yield curves, and yield curve volatility will distort the intertemporal profile of investment, sometimes leading to short-term investments that 'should' have been longer-term ones, and sometimes the opposite. A further distortion often arises from the central bank's discount policy. The inflationary process is fed by additional base money which is generally introduced into the system by the central bank holding down short-term interest rates. As inflation rises, we might expect agents in commercial debt markets to incorporate inflationary premiums as best they can into the prevailing market interest rates, but even as they try to do so, the central bank's discount rate will *not* incorporate such a premium, or only incorporate an inadequate one. As inflation rises, the central bank keeps its discount rate at a low level and injects base money into the system at an ever faster rate, and it is the failure to revise its discount rate appropriately that actually produces the slide into hyperinflation. Those who can get access to credit at interest rates related to the central bank discount rate effectively get loans at negative real interest rates, and these rates become even more negative as the inflation increases. Anyone who can get such credit then has an incentive to get as much of it as possible and buy virtually anything, and repay later with depreciated currency. Virtually any investment then looks like a good deal because the purchaser acquires some real asset at very little cost to him, and the resulting demand for investment assets further feeds the flight into *Sachwerte*. In hyperinflationary Germany, 'the demand for these magic credits rose by leaps and bounds, and [though] private interest rates scaled astonishing heights' as inflation premiums rose, these premiums still lagged way behind the actual inflation due to the Reichsbank's policy of holding its discount rate down (Ringer, 1969, 82). It had a 5 percent discount rate up to July 1922, increased it to 30 percent in August 1923, and then finally raised it to 90 percent in September 1923 and kept it at that rate for the duration of the inflation. With an inflation rate running into thousands and then subsequently millions of percent a year, and still rising, the loans were effectively give-aways, and such credits in paper marks became 'an abundant and riskless source of profits and led to the accumulation of huge new fortunes' for those who had the right connections and knowledge to get them (Ringer, 1969, 82).

The Undermining of the Legal System

One of the more insidious consequences of inflation is to undermine the integrity of the legal system. The law tries to ensure that agents receive and make the payments specified in their contracts, but if the legal system is to 'work' properly and deliver satisfactory outcomes – that is, outcomes similar in real terms to those the parties involved could reasonably have expected – the payments made *ex post* must bear some 'close' relationship, in real terms, with the payments expected *ex ante*. A major problem is that what agents expect to get or to pay is never observable, and cannot credibly be verified after the event, so the legal system cannot adjudicate on agents' inflation expectations. Nor is it simply a matter of the law courts being unable to verify expectations because the parties involved would have incentives to lie about them. Part of the reason for the importance of the law is that expectations are far more complex than talk of *the* expected rate of inflation might suggest:

> The recorded terms of a contract will *never* reveal the original expectations of the parties 'in their entirety' ...; nor will they ever anticipate all relevant contingencies and specify outcomes preagreed upon for each. ... [Agents'] expectations will in general not be completely structured; innumerable contingencies will be unanticipated, and not in the sense of being assigned a low or zero probability, but in the sense of not envisaging the situation that would arise, if and when they materialise, in the specifics of its behavioral structure ...
>
> The contingencies capable of significantly affecting the outcome to contracting parties will never be exhaustively enumerated. Again, one may explain this by reference to the 'cost' of letting the fine print go on indefinitely. And this would be a true statement ... But, beyond that, the conditions of human understanding will not allow for the anticipation of every relevant contingency. (Leijonhufvud, 1981, 240, his emphasis)

In practice, there is often little alternative but for the court to enforce the nominal payments specified in contracts more or less regardless of what inflation might have been expected and regardless of what it turned out to be. The legal system must operate on the 'as if' assumption that inflation is predictable, but it only delivers satisfactory outcomes and ensures that agents get roughly the returns they could reasonably have expected if that assumption *actually* holds. In short, the legal system needs price stability, and cannot function properly without it.

Inflation also undermines the legal system by undermining the original intent of many laws. It does so by eroding the real values of many prices, fines, and pecuniary clauses, and these changes in turn have various other consequences. A good example is given by Klein (1976, 189, n. 7) who notes how inflation had unbalanced penalties like the traditional choice between 30 days in jail or a fine of $250. Because of inflation, the real value of the fine had fallen to a fraction of its former value, and the imbalance between the two penalties had eventually become so pronounced that the US Supreme Court finally ruled that defendants too poor to pay the fine were being treated unequally under the law by being 'forced' to go to jail. Another example is given by Lucas (1989, 85) relating to the effect of inflation on the Saskatchewan matrimonial law providing for the disposal of property in divorce cases. These clauses stipulate that half the nominal accumulation of property during the marriage is to be awarded to each party, the presumption being that each partner contributed equally to it. If there is no inflation, each party gets half of the real property accumulated during the marriage and the property is divided along the lines originally intended. But if there is inflation, the property rises in nominal value even if there is no accumulation in real terms, and the party that brings less into the marriage benefits at the expense of the other. Inflation can thus generate severe redistributions that were never intended when the law was enacted. These redistributions then produce unpleasant side effects, such as aggravating the bitterness accompanying a divorce or influencing people's willingness to marry in the first place. Examples like these are important precisely because they are so down to earth and there are so many millions of others like them.[33] In every case, inflation *changes the real impact of the relevant law, and changes it without any rational discussion over whether it should be changed in this way* – which, presumably, is not a sensible or desirable way to change the law. It also changes it in ways that few people if any ever foresaw or could justify *ex ante* even if they did foresee it.

These inflation-induced changes in the law produce a vast array of further consequences, like increased crime because of the falling real value of a $250 fine or an increased unwillingness of Saskatchewan farmers to marry in case they lost their farms. 'Correcting' these changes is no simple matter, not only because there are so many of them, but also because the process of 'correcting' the law is itself fairly random, and because once the changes have taken place those who benefit from them will fight to retain them. In Klein's example, the original framers presumably intended to give those convicted a reasonably balanced choice between jail or a monetary fine, but the real value of the fine fell with inflation and the response of the Supreme Court was not to raise the fine back again, which would have been consistent with the law's original intent, but instead to alter the stipulation about going to jail. The inflation not only undermined the original intent by unbalancing the choice of penalty, but eventually led to a very different penalty structure when the Supreme Court finally reacted to it. In the Saskatchewan case, attempts to restore the original intent of the law by indexing the appropriate provision were successfully opposed by women's groups. In short, inflation changes the law in 'real' terms in an almost *infinite variety of arbitrary, incalculable and often irreversible ways*. Any idea that the legal system somehow remains unaffected by inflation is laughable.

The Undermining of the Social Order

Inflation also undermines the social order in other ways. Even if a particular individual feels that he is coming out approximately even in purely monetary terms – if the gains from the reduced real value of his mortgage payments roughly offset the losses he suffers on his life insurance, for example – it would still be a mistake to suppose that he would normally be indifferent to the inflationary process:

> You may happen to come out even, as the dice fall, but the game is not inherently fair. At no point in time do its rules make sense. Besides, 'the House' will switch them on you without warning (Leijonhufvud, 1981, 247)

and take a cut for itself. The social order thus starts to lose its legitimacy as it delivers increasingly erratic and unpredictable outcomes. Even if they continue to 'come out even' materially – and many of course do not – individuals feel increasingly insecure and lose much of their sense of having any control over their own destiny.

We can form an idea of how threatened people can feel by looking at some of the sweeping redistributive effects of rapid inflation. Before the First World War, German farmers had mortgages worth some 15 billion gold marks, and they used to pay about 600 million marks a year in interest. In 1913, the payment of interest was the equivalent of about 4 million tons of rye a year; by 1921, it had dwindled to the equivalent of 200,000 tons of rye (Guttman and Meehan, 1975, 110) – and it became negligible by the end of the inflation. The hyperinflation effectively wiped out the bulk of the debt on German agriculture. Of course, other groups lost as dramatically as the agriculturists gained. A section of the middle class, of outstanding financial wealth before the War and even before the inflation took off, was 'utterly ruined' by the inflation (Guttman and Meehan, 1975, 123). These people included pensioners and the owners of capital whose return was fixed in nominal terms, including the holders of life insurance, State and municipal bonds, and other assets such as war loans. As these claims were denominated in nominal terms, they were repaid in virtually worthless marks and their real income fell to about 3–4 percent of what it had been before the War (Guttman and Meehan, 1975, 124).

The German experience is littered with many tragic stories of how individuals were robbed of their wealth by inflation. A typical one is the story of how a man died leaving life insurance to provide for his family and the education of his daughter, but the proceeds of the insurance turned out to be just sufficient to buy a loaf of bread (1975, 129). Many middle-class people suffered from malnutrition – and not a few of them starved to death. Again,

> for the very old, particularly for the women, there was no hope anywhere. Particularly sad was the plight of those daughters for whom a prudent and loving father had made comfortable provision against the time when his own

protection would be removed by death. Unmarried and unskilled in any profession, they became the flotsam of the Inflation, kept alive in the end by the kindness of strangers. (1975, 138)

The German inflation also had devastating effects on academics. Much research done in Germany had been done by well-to-do people who devoted much of their wealth and years of their lives to their research. This species

> was killed by the Inflation. The income from his, or his father's, investments had gone the way of all paper marks; there was no money for books or learned journals – the tools of his trade – not even enough money to keep body and soul together. (Guttman and Meehan, 1975, 128)

Many academics were forced to sell their books and other possessions in order to have enough to eat – and some still died from malnutrition – and those who could often worked as manual workers because they could no longer survive on their academic salaries.

Not surprisingly, the fear and resentment produced by inflation often translate into demands for 'action' – organised action by labour unions or various forms of political action – to correct perceived wrongs. A typical individual will identify certain groups and organisations as the source of his sufferings, profiting at his expense, and he will side with those who want reform to curtail their benefits. As inflation rises, these pressures for reforms increase, and

> When inflation gets into double digits by a good margin, one ... has to expect that virtually all the institutions providing the framework of economic order will in this way come under attack. To some extent, of course, they always are – there will always be critics with some following among dissatisfied groups. But normally most such 'movements' will be ineffective ... Great inflations, however, are capable of letting loose a social epidemic of effective but uncontrolled and incoherent pressures for institutional change. (Leijonhufvud, 1981, 253)

Most people will be too busy attacking particular parts of the *status quo* to defend the rest of it, and in any case, few people will be willing to defend a *status quo* widely regarded as having lost its legitimacy.

The *status quo* also comes under attack from the state itself as the various demands for the redress of particular grievances translate into political action to establish or extend privileges, control prices, and regulate certain markets. As Leijonhufvud and others have stressed, the polity reacts to inflation-induced grievances in a biased way. Most people fail to make the connection between inflation and monetary policy, and even for those who do, there is no easy way to translate their dissatisfaction with inflation into pressure on those responsible for monetary policy to stop inflating. Instead, the problems created by inflation produce a great variety of demands to resolve *particular* grievances – demands to tackle specific symptoms of the inflationary problem rather than a single clear-cut demand to tackle the *root* cause (i.e., inflationary monetary policy). Instead of leading to the correction of inflationary policy, the problems created by that monetary policy translate into many *additional* policies to deal with an almost infinite variety of *specific* problems which the inflation has aggravated or created.

The situation can then slide from bad to worse. As dissatisfaction with the arbitrariness of inflation leads to demands for redress through the political process, the frequent consequence is to add a new element of political arbitrariness to the inflation arbitrariness that already exists, and they create the cause for more dissatisfaction and even more demands for government action. Society becomes more polarised and politicised, and the rule of law gives gradually gives way to the rule of men. The increasing chaos and disorder can also make policy – monetary policy included – more volatile and more difficult to predict, so agents find themselves operating in an environment that is increasingly unpredictable as well as increasingly arbitrary. There is then a growing danger that factors such as these will feed on each other and destroy much of what is left of the social order. If life is to be tolerable, and in some cases, if it is even to go on at all,

> Some measure of basic continuity must be ... maintained. One cannot treat *all* the laws and political compacts as perpetually 'fresh' issues, up for renegotiation or open to fundamental reform in every season. This is not so much because 'change' will thwart particular individuals or groups ... It is rather because some continuity is necessary for any individual to 'make sense' of his social setting, to be able simply to *set* goals for himself and his family and to formulate plans to work towards them. The rights, immunities, and obligations with which one goes to bed at night must be there in the morning and not found unpredictably reshuffled or a meaningful social existence becomes impossible. (Leijonhufvud, 1981, 252–253, his emphasis)

The great inflations illustrate these dangers all too well. Old habits of thrift and prudence become a serious liability, and inflation encourages people to stop saving and spend as quickly as possible. It becomes quite impossible to make any serious plans for the future. Economic life becomes a scramble for day-to-day survival, and many writers have noted the deteriorating moral standards that accompanied especially rapid inflations. What Guttman and Meehan wrote of the German experience could be said of many others:

> With devaluation of the currency had come devaluation of most of the old virtues: the respect for law and order, for morality, for one's fellow man, the simple and contemplative life, thrift, even good taste and the appreciation of the truly good things in life. (Guttman and Meehan, 1975, 189–90)

More sinister still is the tendency for people to assume that other people must be profiting at their expense and seek scapegoats. People become embittered and less tolerant, and they can become easy prey to demagogues with simple 'solutions'. Thus during the Assignat inflation in France,

> The washerwomen of Paris, finding soap so dear that they could hardly purchase it, insisted that all the merchants who were endeavoring to save something of their little property by refusing to sell their goods for the wretched currency with which France was flooded, should be punished with death ... Marat declared loudly that the people, by hanging shopkeepers and plundering stores, could easily remove the trouble. (White, 1980, 32–33)

Much the same happened in Germany. The people became bitter and resentful, and

> The bitterness and resentment ... turned against those who were blamed for the state of affairs: against the government, and the former enemies of Germany; against the Allies for exacting, and against the government for agreeing to pay, reparations; against the people who did well out of the Inflation ... All this meant an upsurge of hatred against the democratic regime of the Weimar Republic, resulting in right-wing radicalism, reaction, nationalism, xenophobia, and anti-semitism. People had lost their faith ... and in despair they turned to extremism. (Guttman and Meehan, 1975, 140)

THE OPTIMAL PRICE-LEVEL PATH

So what should the optimal price-level path be? Perhaps the least contentious conclusion from the preceding discussion ought to be that the optimal price-level path should *minimise price-level uncertainty*. Price-level uncertainty harms agents in a variety of ways, and there are few if any benefits to set against this damage. The optimal price-level path should therefore minimise such uncertainty and make the price level as predictable as possible. Buchanan drew a nice analogy with the weather:

> Predictability in weather is a widely accepted criterion for meteorologists, and we all know what is meant by improved weather prediction. I have seen no claim or argument to the effect that improvement in weather forecasting, in predictability, will not also 'improve' over-all efficiency in resource usage. The correspondence between improvements in predictability here and improvements in economic performance generally is, in fact, taken for granted and rarely mentioned explicitly at all. Improved weather forecasting is acknowledged to be one of the 'desirable' results to be expected from greater investment in scientific research. (Buchanan, 1962, 158)

This view accords well with common-sense. If agents can predict the weather more accurately, they will make fewer mistakes, they will be able to protect themselves more effectively against the vagaries of the weather, and so forth. The agreement that weather predictability is good is also quite independent

> of the trend in the weather over time. The winters in the northern hemisphere may gradually be getting 'worse' or 'better' by certain commonly accepted standards ... But the direction of change in the weather, described in this way, is irrelevant to the conclusion that improved predictability can lead to greater economic efficiency. (1962, 158)

The more difficult issue is what *trend* our predictable price level should take. Should the price level rise over time, fall over time, or remain stable? There are, I believe, very strong reasons against preferring a price level that rises over time. Even if it is fully anticipated (and therefore satisfies the predictability criterion), inflation produces welfare losses arising from excessive economisation of real balances, lower capital stock – recall that anti-Tobin effects are more plausible than Tobin effects – excessive price-changing costs, and the various undesirable broader effects discussed in the last section. So even if inflation were perfectly anticipated, these considerations suggest we should prefer a stable price level to one that rose over time. The main counter-argument is that we might prefer inflation to 'exploit' a Phillips curve 'trade-off' between inflation and output or employment, but there is little evidence that such a trade-off actually exists, at least in the long run, especially one between *predictable* inflation and output or employment.[34] Another counter-argument sometimes is that a low inflation rate might be 'good' because conventional price indices tend to understate quality adjustments. If this bias leads the 'true' inflation rate to be 1–2 percent less than the 'measured' one, as sometimes suggested, a price index that remained stable would imply a 'real' price level that was actually falling by 1–2 percent a year. Proponents of this line of argument therefore conclude that measured price indices should be allowed to rise by that amount each year to keep 'real' (i.e., quality-adjusted) prices stable. However, given the various costs of a changing price level, it would seem more natural instead to build some adjustment into our chosen 'measure' of the price level, and then stabilise the adjusted index. The quality-bias argument is thus fundamentally an argument with the way conventional indices are constructed, and not an argument for inflation *per se*. We should also bear in mind that real-world inflation is never perfectly anticipated, and the fact that it is not lends further support to arguments against it. The notion of perfectly anticipated inflation is a mirage, as Okun (1971) observes, and real-world inflations always create additional uncertainty that hypothetical anticipated inflations assume away. Sporadic inflation undermines market efficiency, confuses price signals, and so on, and generally causes resources to be misallocated. It also causes mindless redistributions between individuals, erodes private property, undermines the efficiency of the legal system, and undermines the efficiency of social institutions more generally. In any case, if we take the earlier predictability criterion seriously, and a rising price level does or cannot not satisfy this criterion in practice, then we have no alternative but to dismiss inflation on our predictability criterion, more or less regardless of other considerations anyway. In short, the choice between a rising price level and a stable one comes down firmly in favour of the latter.

What about the choice between between price stability and 'optimal' deflation? Again, I would argue in favour of price stability. The attraction of 'optimal' deflation over price-level stability is the extra surplus appropriated by equalising the private and social costs of holding real balances in a world where there is some constraint against the payment of 'market' rates of interest on currency holdings. It is not easy to assess the quantitative size of these benefits, but our earlier illustrative example put them at perhaps as much as 4 percent of national income. We cannot therefore easily dismiss them as negligible.

Nonetheless, there are some serious problems with the 'optimal deflation' norm. First of all, there are the various costs of a changing price level, even if price-level changes are fully anticipated. A changing price level creates menu costs, disrupts relative prices, and so forth, and also has other consequences such as undermining the legal system. Defendants would start preferring to go to jail than paying monetary fines, for example, and women's groups would complain that deflation was biasing divorce settlements against them. Secondly, the derivation of the OQM result typically presupposes that the *real interest rate is both known and perfectly predictable, and there are good reasons to believe that neither condition is met in practice*. The notion of 'the' real interest rate is itself ambiguous, and there are non-trivial data problems to be resolved even if we had a precise theoretical concept of the real interest rate to work with. The real interest rate is almost certain to be estimated or forecast with error. The theoretical result that in a world without uncertainty the price level should fall in line with an unambiguous and usually fixed real interest rate therefore cannot translate easily to a more plausible world where agents have to operate under conditions of uncertainty. Thirdly, and following on from the last point, if real interest rates are uncertain in practice, an 'optimal' deflation norm would not satisfy our predictability criterion. If real interest cannot be predicted, any 'optimal' deflation rule that ties the change in the price level to the real interest rate must also make the price level itself unpredictable. If we believe that prices should be predictable, we cannot also support an objective of 'optimal' deflation. If we accept the predictability criterion, we must reject 'optimal' deflation.[35] Fourthly, we have to keep in mind that the costs of 'excessive' deflation are qualitatively different from the costs of 'insufficient' deflation. The costs of errors are not symmetrical, and the fact that they are not gives us another reason why, when the real interest rate r has to be estimated, we cannot simply plug an estimate of r into the deterministic, full-information 'optimal' deflation rule and then carry on as if that rule were still optimal under these new conditions. Some allowance must be made for the asymmetric consequences of insufficient and excessive deflation in the derivation of the price-level rule, which in turn means that the rule itself needs to be derived again with appropriate allowance for the possibility that the price level may deflate too little or too much. In short, while the 'optimal' deflation objective might appear attractive in a perfect foresight world where the real interest for all time is known with certainty – and even in that case there are serious drawbacks – there are strong reasons to doubt that the basic result carries over to less restrictive environments. 'Optimal' deflation is effectively a non-starter.

We are left with price stability.[36] As we have seen, there are various arguments for price stability even in a world where the price level is fully anticipated, but the arguments for price stability become even stronger when we acknowledge that price-level changes in practice are often unanticipated. Many agents deal with the uncertainty of economic life and the cost and difficulty of economic calculation by adopting certain rules of thumb, and perhaps the most important rule of thumb they adopt is to treat nominal values as if they were stable in real terms. This presumption underlies many accounting conventions, not to mention legal clauses, tax rules, and the like. Much, perhaps most, of the damage from inflation arises because this presumption only 'works' and delivers satisfactory outcomes to the extent that prices actually *are* stable. The difficulties that so many individuals and institutions have had adjusting to inflation seem to underline the importance and pervasiveness of this presumption, and are very suggestive of the extent of the damage that occurs when that presumption is falsified.

Appendix: Productivity Growth and the Price Level

An important option not considered in Chapter 15 is the 'productivity norm' according to which the price level should fall as productivity increases, and rise as productivity falls. Were it put into practice, the productivity norm would deliver stable prices

> only under conditions of stationary output *per capita*; in times of intensive growth in productivity prices would fall. If the past is any guide, a secular decline in prices of between one and three percent per year could be expected in 'normal' times. Exceptions would be periods of extraordinary progress, when prices would fall more rapidly than usual, and periods of increased scarcity and reduced output *per capita*, such as during wars, harvest failures, and other 'supply shocks', when prices would rise, perhaps sharply. (Selgin, 1988b, 62)

The productivity norm has a long history and was supported by many prominent economists of the past. Perhaps its earliest advocate was Samuel Bailey (1837), but it has also been endorsed by later economists such as Marshall, Robertson, Lindahl, Myrdal, Machlup, and Mints (Selgin, 1990, 270–271). By the early 1930s, the productivity norm had become a widely debated alternative to price stability, but it was eclipsed along with price stability by the Keynesian revolution and its de-emphasis of price-level objectives in favour of unemployment ones. The productivity norm had been largely forgotten by the time Keynesianism became discredited and price-level issues resumed their former importance. It was then rediscovered and endorsed by George Selgin (1988b, 1990, 1991, 1992c), David Glasner (1989a, 236–240) and Larry Sechrest (1993, 68–71). They claim that it would distribute the gains from productivity improvements more equitably than they would be distributed under price stability, and would also involve lower price-adjustment costs and generate greater macroeconomic stability than price stability. If advocates of the productivity norm are right, then arguments for price stability are seriously flawed and most present-day 'hard money' economists have been pursing a false ideal. The productivity norm therefore deserves to be examined closely. However, it turns out to be ultimately unconvincing, and the majority view among hard money economists is right after all.

In theory, the productivity norm amounts to the stabilisation of an index of factor prices, but one does not need to have such an index to be able to implement the productivity norm in practice. Selgin points out that it

> can be implemented, or approximately implemented, by directly stabilizing some readily available measure of the flow of money payments or income such as nominal GNP or domestic final demand. (1990, 282)

Since we are interested in factor prices and not factor incomes *per se*, we would presumably want to adjust any measure of factor incomes to allow for growth in the

The material in this appendix previously appeared in 'Deflating the Productivity Norm', *Journal of Macroeconomics,* 17(4) (Fall 1995), pp 717–732.

quantities of the factors involved, but it ought not to be too difficult to provide plausible estimates of the factor growth. If factors grew on average by k percent a year, we would let our target measure of factor income grow by the same rate to keep factor prices constant, and he argues that we could implement this rule in approximate form by holding nominal *per capita* income constant. The productivity norm would thus be relatively easy to implement, at least in approximate form, and the estimate of *per capita* nominal income it requires should not be much more difficult to obtain than the price index required to stabilise the price level.[37]

THE 'EQUITY ARGUMENT' FOR THE PRODUCTIVITY NORM

Proponents of the productivity norm have offered three main arguments in support of their claims for its superiority. The first of these is the argument that the productivity norm is a superior means of promoting 'equity' between those who have contracted to make future payments of fixed nominal values (i.e., 'debtors') and those who have contracted to accept such payments (i.e., 'creditors') (e.g., Glasner, 1989a, 237). The argument hinges on who should benefit (or lose) from unexpected productivity changes. The issue was first raised by defenders of price stability, who argued that any unexpected changes in the price level imply 'unjust' redistributions from creditors to debtors, or the other way round, and the only way to avoid these unjust redistributions is to make the price level stable (or at least predictable). Considerations of debtor–creditor 'justice' thus implied a case for price-level stability. However, the proponents of the productivity norm responded that if price changes were associated with changes in real income – due in particular to productivity shocks – then it was no longer obvious that any 'unjust' redistribution was actually taking place. To quote Selgin:

> if the price level is kept constant in the face of unexpected improvements in productivity, readily adjusted money incomes – including profits, dividends, and some wage payments – will increase; their recipients will benefit exclusively from the improvements in real output. Creditors, on the other hand, will not be allowed to reap any gains from the same improvements. Although a constant price level may fulfil their price-level expectations, creditors may still regret their involvement in fixed-money contracts, for they may rightly sense that, had they anticipated the widespread improvements in other persons' real (and, in this case, money) earnings, they could have successfully negotiated better terms. On the other hand, if the price level is allowed unexpectedly to fall to reflect improvements in productivity, creditors will automatically enjoy a share of the gain, while debtors will have no reason to complain: Although the real value of their obligations rises (along with everyone else's), so does their real income. (Selgin, 1990, 273–4)

The 'ethical' argument is that windfall gains in productivity should be shared by all, not just the 'entrepreneurs', and the productivity norm ensures that they are. Price stability by contrast awards all the gains to the 'entrepreneurs' alone. Similarly, if productivity fell, the argument is that the losses should also be borne by all, and not just by the 'entrepreneurs'.

One problem with this argument is that it is not clear why the possibility that creditors under price stability may 'regret' their involvement in fixed money contracts in the event of a positive productivity shock should be regarded as a consideration in favour of the productivity norm. One might argue with equal validity that we should have price stability because creditors would regret fixed money contracts under the productivity norm if there was a negative productivity shock instead of a positive one. But focusing on the fact that one particular group 'loses' under one norm when a certain type of shock occurs gets us nowhere.

The point, of course, is that since we are talking of productivity *shocks*, and shocks are by definition unpredictable, there will *always* be *some* people under *either* norm who 'regret' their previous decisions when shocks occur. The relevant question is *not* that this or that group will 'regret' decisions they have previously made – there will always be such people – but *how the relevant (ex ante) risk is allocated*. We shall come back to this issue shortly.

Another problem is that, contrary to what Selgin says, debtors *will* have some reason to complain if prices fall unexpectedly due to a positive productivity shock, and the fact that their real incomes might have gone up is beside the point. Even if debtors benefit from positive productivity shocks because such shocks raise their real incomes – and that cannot always be taken for granted – debtors will still lose under the productivity norm *because their debts will be higher in real terms than they would otherwise have been*. If a price-level fall means that an individual debtor has to pay more in real terms, we cannot say that the price-level fall does not matter to him just because his real income was rising anyway. In any case, we cannot take for granted that any particular individual debtor will actually benefit from a positive productivity shock. Whether he benefits or not depends on what assets he has, among other factors, and we can easily imagine the existence of debtors who would get nothing from a positive productivity shock, but would still lose under the productivity norm because such a shock would lead to an increase in their real indebtedness.

More fundamentally, there are also problems with the 'ethical' position underlying the productivity norm that it is better to share out 'windfall' productivity gains or losses than it is to concentrate them. What is the 'ethical' premise underlying this position, and what is attractive about it? We could perhaps try to argue this issue out, but it seems to me that we miss the point if we dwell too much on it. Rather than trying to resolve the relative merits of the 'ethical' position that everyone should bear the productivity risk against the competing 'ethical' position that only entrepreneurs should bear it, it would be better to take the analysis one step back and allow agents to interact in a market where they can choose how much productivity risk they want to bear and on what terms they will bear it. Instead of making people bear risk when they would prefer to pay others to bear it, or preventing them bearing risk when they would prefer to accept payment to bear it, we should allow them to interact in a market that prices and allocates that risk appropriately. The productivity shocks then occur, and the agents *ex post* get the returns provided for in the contracts they made *ex ante*. There is no longer any 'equity' issue of how the gains or losses from productivity shocks should be divided other than that they be divided in accordance with the contracts the agents made before the shocks occurred. As Yeager points out, people who gain when prices fall under the productivity norm

> are in a position like that of stockpilers of oil who reap a 'windfall profit' if an energy crunch occurs. In either case, do economists really recommend redistributing the gains or losses resulting from good and bad foresight and luck? (These are gains or losses judged relative to the distribution that would have emerged from a different course of events.) Do economists really recommend operating a monetary system to second-guess the parties to voluntary contracts? (Yeager, 1992, 60)

To analyse the issue further, suppose for the moment that our agents take the price-level norm as given and then decide how to share out productivity risk between them. The allocation of risk between different individuals will depend on factors such as differences in their attitudes to risk, the composition of their portfolios, and the costs and relative efficiency of different risk-sharing arrangements. We can then think of agents making decisions along the lines of conventional portfolio analysis, with those more averse to risk choosing safer portfolios and those less averse to it choosing riskier ones. Agents are of course concerned with 'real' risks, and do not suffer from 'money illusion'. Consider now the position of an agent who is sufficiently risk-averse that he wants a contract that guarantees him a fixed real return. The contract form that guarantees him such a return would then depend on the particular price-level norm under which he operated. Under a stable-prices norm, his real return would be guaranteed merely by holding an asset of a fixed nominal value, but under the productivity norm he would have to hold an asset whose nominal return made some allowance for the possibility of a changing price level (e.g., by indexing the return to the price level). Agents would thus take the operative norm into account when making their contracts, and nominal payment terms would differ across the two norms *precisely because* agents would be concerned about real and not nominal risks and returns. The implication is very clear: we cannot take the contract form as given, and then compare how that fixed contract form performs across two different price-level norms. *The choice of contract depends on the norm itself.*

Given the conditionality of contracts on the regime, the critical question is then whether there is any reason for agents to prefer one regime to the other. One way to approach this question is to imagine that agents found themselves in a Rawlsian state of ignorance where they had to choose the price-level norm not knowing anything about their own particular individual circumstances. Which norm would they choose? Leaving aside the menu costs of price-changing which are discussed in the next section, I believe there are various reasons why they would choose price stability. Perhaps the most important reason is that the productivity norm would make the price level less predictable, and price-level uncertainty is highly undesirable. Under the productivity norm, any shock to productivity would influence the price level, and since productivity shocks by definition cannot be predicted, the price level cannot be predicted either (or at least not without errors arising from productivity shocks). The price level next period would depend on next period's productivity shock, and, since the price level T periods ahead would depend on all the productivity shocks that would occur over the next T periods, price-level uncertainty would increase the further ahead one tried to predict the price level. The productivity norm would thus make the price level uncertain, and this uncertainty is highly undesirable for reasons already explained in Chapter 15. Price stability, by contrast, avoids these costs completely.

Tying the real value of nominal returns to productivity growth also creates other problems. If agents are concerned about real returns, they can fix real returns under the price-stability norm simply by fixing nominal payments. Under the productivity norm, however, they can only fix real returns by indexing nominal returns to the price level, and such indexation is not costless. Contracting costs are therefore higher under the productivity norm, because agents would have to 'unravel' the effects of price-level changes. Nor is it clear why we would want contractual real payments between two typical parties to be made dependent on factors such as economy-wide productivity growth that usually have little or nothing to do with either party. Why should real payments be made dependent on factors that are exogenous to the parties involved, especially when both parties will typically be risk-averse and actually prefer that real payments be predictable? And if real payments are to be dependent on any exogenous factor, why pick economy-wide productivity growth and not something else? There is also the ethical issue of why those who don't contribute to productivity growth should get an automatic share of the gains from such growth at the expense of those who do contribute to it. What is 'special' about productivity growth that everyone should have an automatic right to the benefits it provides?

There is also the important point that the productivity norm can discourage productivity improvements from occurring in the first place. Under the productivity norm, the benefits of improvements in productivity are dispersed to all who hold assets whose nominal values are fixed, whereas under price stability they accrue (in the first instance at least) to those who own the factors whose productivity rises. This difference might not matter so much, perhaps, if productivity improvements were exogenous (as, incidentally, the productivity norm literature tends to assume), but it certainly *does* matter if productivity improvements depend on what the entrepreneurs do (as is surely the case). If realised productivity improvements depend on factors such as the entrepreneurs' incentives to innovate, and the productivity norm weakens those incentives by sharing out productivity gains among a wider group, then the productivity norm would lead to fewer productivity improvements and lower economic growth.

For all these reasons, I believe that the agents involved would prefer the stable-prices norm to the productivity one. They would then make contracts whose risk and return features were optimal given that norm, and the only substantial 'equity' issue left would be to ensure that the contracts freely made *ex ante* were honoured *ex post*. Agents would be exposed to whatever risks – including productivity risks – that they had contracted for or not insured themselves against. Depending on the realisations of the random variables involved, some agents would suffer unexpected losses and 'regret' the contracts they made, and others would make unexpected gains. But these gains or losses would already have been allowed for (at least implicitly) in the contracts they made, and however much an outside observer might disapprove of any particular outcome (e.g., the gain or loss accruing to some particular party), there would be no way to 'correct' that outcome without interfering with (i.e., violating) the contracts agents had made. The only 'equity' issue left is to ensure that agents get the gains or losses to which their contracts entitle them.

PRICE-CHANGING COSTS AND THE PRODUCTIVITY NORM

Proponents of the productivity norm have also defended it against price stability on the grounds that the productivity norm would involve lower price-adjustment costs. The premise of their argument is that productivity shocks necessitate changes in relative prices, which in turn necessitate changes in at least some nominal prices. They then argue that the overall cost of nominal price changes is lower if the price level is allowed to change in response to the productivity shocks, than if the price level is held stable. Selgin offers an illustration. Suppose there are 1000 goods being produced and a

> technological improvement causes the output per period of good *x*, which formerly had a price (included in the price index) of one dollar, to double. Assuming (1) a constant money supply and velocity of circulation of money; (2) that *x* has a unitary price elasticity of demand; and (3) that demand for goods other than *x* is independent of real purchases of *x*, holding nominal income unchanged (thus abstracting from the need for any 'secondary' relative price adjustments), the price of *x* will fall to 50 cents. This implies a slight decline in the price index. Prices of all other goods, including the three factors of production, remain unchanged. [Under the productivity norm the] new equilibrium price structure requires one price adjustment only. (Selgin, 1990, 275)

Under a regime with a stable price level, on the other hand, there must be a

> uniform, though very slight, increase in the prices of 999 goods and of the three factors of production. The sole exception is good *x*, the price of which must (as in the previous case) still be allowed to fall, only [now] less than in proportion with the improvement in its rate of output. This approach alone serves to keep the price index stable while also allowing needed adjustments in *relative* prices. (Selgin, 1990, 275, his emphasis)

He readily acknowledges that 'arguments such as [these] ... are distressingly dependent upon artificial assumptions', but claims that

> insofar as *any* case can be made (by appropriately stringent assumptions) for a particular price-level policy using the price-adjustment criterion, it is one that favors the productivity norm rather than a stable price level. (1990, 276, his emphasis)

The point of Selgin's example is that if one good experiences a productivity shock, but others do not, then price-changing costs would be lower if the price of that one good were reduced rather than the prices of all other 999 goods. However, Selgin picks an odd example on which to base his argument and it does not follow that one can generalise from *this particular case* to conclude (as he does) that price-changing costs are *generally* lower under the productivity norm (see also Yeager, 1992, 63). One problem with Selgin's example is his strange scenario in which a single *idiosyncratic* productivity shock affects the price of one commodity only, with everything else remaining the same,[38] and it is perhaps more natural to deal with *common* productivity shocks that affect the prices of large numbers of commodities.[39] An increase in the productivity of labour, for example, will generally affect the production of a large number of different commodities, and not just the production of one commodity only. But once one allows for common productivity shocks, the earlier presumption in favour of the productivity norm is reversed. To illustrate, imagine that there was a common productivity shock that affected the production of *all* 1000 commodities in Selgin's example. All goods then become cheaper to produce, but relative goods prices remain the same. Under the price stability norm, there would be no need to change *any* nominal goods prices, and so all such prices would remain the same and there would be no price-changing costs. Under the productivity norm, on the other hand, *all* goods prices would have to be reduced, and price-changing costs would be very high. Once we replace the assumption of a single idiosyncratic productivity shock with the more reasonable assumption of a common productivity shock, price-changing costs are much lower under price stability than they are under the productivity norm.

There is also another and in some ways more straightforward argument in favour of price stability. If we adopt the productivity norm, we would fix (average) factor prices and let commodity (and service) prices adjust; if we adopt the stable-prices norm we would fix (average) commodity (and service) prices and let factor prices adjust. Assume that there is some change in the average price of goods and services relative to average factor prices, but other things remain roughly equal. In the former case, we would have to pay the costs of adjusting the prices of goods and services; in the latter case, we would have to pay the costs of adjusting factor prices. Now assume that there are n goods and m factors, and that changing any nominal price costs a fixed amount a. (We can think of a as the cost of changing the prices advertised in a shop window or sales catalogue, and so on.) If we adopt the productivity norm, we would therefore lose na in goods-price-changing costs; but if we adopt the price-stability norm, we would lose ma in factor-price-changing costs. Price-changing costs would therefore be lower under the price-stability norm if and only if the number of factors (i.e., m) is less than the number of goods (i.e., n). Since the number of factors *is* presumably smaller than the number of goods, we must conclude that price-changing costs *are* indeed lower under price stability than under the productivity norm.

THE STABILISING PROPERTIES OF THE PRODUCTIVITY NORM

Lastly, proponents of the productivity norm have claimed that it has superior macroeconomic stabilising properties to price stability. The argument is as follows: (1) The productivity norm stabilises real income because it makes prices move to offset changes in productivity. (2) The price level obviously cannot move under the stable prices norm, so there is nothing under it to prevent productivity shocks 'spilling over' to affect real output. (3) The productivity norm therefore generates more real output stability than the stable-prices norm. The argument can be illustrated formally by means of a simple model borrowed from Bean (1983). Imagine an economy in which deviations in output from their 'natural' (or, if one prefers 'full-information') levels depend on both price-level and productivity shocks:

$$y_t - y_t^* = \beta[(p_t - E_{t-1}p_t) + (u_t - E_{t-1}u_t)] \qquad (A15.1)$$

where y_t is the log of real income, y_t^* the log of natural or 'full-information' real income, p_t the log of the price level, and u_t the log of a productivity variable, all in period t, and E_{t-1} represents the expectation of the relevant variable given information publicly available the previous period. If one likes, one can think of wage bargains for period t as being struck in the previous period, so the contract governing wages is already given when t starts. $(y_t - y_t^*)$ is the deviation of output from trend, and $(p_t - E_{t-1}p_t)$ and $(u_t - E_{t-1}u_t)$ are the price-level and productivity shocks in period t. If our objective is to minimise the deviation of output from its natural level, its proponents argue that the productivity norm is a natural means to achieve this objective because a positive productivity shock would produce a negative price shock, and vice versa, and thus offset each other to stabilise real income: the change in the price level cushions real income against the productivity shock. But if prices were stable, the price-level shock $(p_t - E_{t-1}p_t)$ would be zero, and there would be nothing to cushion real income against the productivity shock $(u_t - E_{t-1}u_t)$. The advocates of the productivity norm then conclude that their norm would generate a more stable level of output.

However, this argument rests on the highly questionable premise that we can compare the two norms while taking nominal wages as given. As discussed already, agents are interested in real payments rather than nominal ones *per se*. If they have any reason to want wage payments to be fixed over the contract period, it is real wages they would want to fix, and not nominal wages as such. Assume then that they do want to fix real wages. If they operated under a stable-prices norm, they would do so by fixing their nominal wages, but under the productivity norm they could only fix their real wages by making their nominal wages *contingent* on the price level. The objective of fixing real wages thus leads agents to fix their nominal wages under the stable-prices regime, but to *avoid* fixing them under the productivity norm. The problem with the argument of the last section is now clear: if agents are concerned about real payments, a contract that might optimally fix nominal payments under one norm *cannot* be optimal under the other. The earlier argument implicitly assumes that agents are not optimising under at least one of the two norms.

We therefore need to modify equation (15A.1) to accommodate the effects of the different wage bargains that would occur under the two norms. Perhaps the easiest way to do so is to replace (A15.1) with:

$$y_t - y_t^* = \beta[(p_t - E_{t-1}p_t) + (u_t - E_{t-1}u_t) - (w_t - E_{t-1}w_t)] \qquad (A15.2)$$

which indicates that output rises with increases in prices and productivity and falls with increases in the wage rate. It is then easy to show that the real outcome will now reflect whatever preferences agents have been output fluctuations and real wage rigidity, *regardless of the price-level norm*. Suppose agents are only concerned about output fluctuations, and not at all about fixing their real wages. If they lived under the stable-prices norm, they would then prefer flexi-wage contracts in which the nominal wage was contingent on productivity. Any shock to productivity would be matched by an offsetting change to (real and nominal) wages, and so leave output unaffected. If they lived under the productivity norm, on the other hand, then wages would be fixed instead of prices, and prices instead of wages would adjust to offset productivity shocks. Regardless of the regime, real wages adjust to the productivity shocks to ensure that output remains unaffected. Alternatively, we could suppose that agents are not concerned about output fluctuations but are very concerned about fluctuations in real wages. Real wages would then be fixed under either norm, and output would adjust in response to any productivity shocks. We could also imagine intermediate cases in which agents were concerned both about output fluctuations and about real wage flexibility, in which case they would trade off these 'bads' against each other in accordance with their relative distaste for each. The bottom line, in short, is that the behaviour of output and real wages would reflect agents' preferences over how much they wanted each to vary, regardless of the price-level norm. The norm is neutral because agents will structure their contracts 'around' it to achieve the real outcome they desire.

Nonetheless, the argument that the productivity norm would generate more macroeconomic stability than price stability also takes another form, one which one of the most prominent advocates of price stability, Leland Yeager, regards as 'the most embarrassing case' for the price-stability school (Yeager, 1992, 64). This is where there is a large negative shock – such as a supply shock worse than the oil shock of 1973–1974, or a war. If we think in terms of the equation of exchange, we can think of there being a sharp fall in T, which under price stability translates into a proportional fall in nominal income MV. Under the productivity norm, by contrast, MV would be held constant and the fall in T would lead to a proportionate rise in P. The argument is then that macroeconomic stability is better served by keeping MV constant, as under the productivity norm, than forcing it to fall, as price stability would do.

I do not find this argument convincing. Granted that the shock is exogenous, the economy has to absorb the loss regardless of the price-level norm under which it operates. If we grant that unexpected price changes are bad, then the advocate of the productivity norm is in effect arguing that we should respond to this loss (which the economy has to accept anyway) by a response (i.e., allowing prices to rise) that damages the economy even further. The advocate of price stability argues instead that we should absorb the loss and avoid compounding it by further, self-inflicted, damage. The best solution is to ensure that market prices respond appropriately, and, in Yeager's words,

a firm and credible commitment to a stable price level ... would encourage price-setters and wage negotiators to yield to market pressures for market-clearing adjustments [and hold down the unemployment costs of a major macroeconomic shock]. (Yeager, 1992, 66)

By contrast, under the productivity norm, agents would not know what the price level was likely to be in the aftermath of a major shock. They would therefore have difficulty setting prices and wages, and the relative price adjustments that must take place would be confused by unnecessary monetary noise. The real adjustment costs are therefore likely to be that much greater.

16 Financial and Monetary Reform

We have so far focused on hypothetical *laissez-faire* systems, but what about modern real-world systems with their ubiquitous state intervention? What bearing does *laissez-faire* have on the real world? The answer is that it provides an ideal benchmark – not only a benchmark, but also an ideal to be aimed for – against which we can measure real-world systems. As we saw repeatedly in earlier chapters, and despite many claims to the contrary, there are no convincing reasons to suppose that *laissez-faire* 'fails' in any reasonable sense – most particularly, *laissez-faire* provides a safe, stable and efficient financial system, and ensures that the currency has a guaranteed stable value. *Laissez-faire* is highly efficient, but it is efficient not only in the narrow sense most familiar to economists, but also in a broader institutional sense – the institutions that arise under *laissez-faire* serve socially useful roles, they are regarded as legitimate, and so forth. The key to its efficiency is very simple: *laissez-faire* harmonises the disparate interests of different individuals, interests which we cannot assume to be naturally harmonious, and which, under alternative arrangements, could easily produce all sorts of undesirable outcomes. In the words of Adam Smith, a man will be more likely to obtain what he needs from others

> if he can interest their self-love in his favour, and show them that it is for their own advantage to do for him what he requires of them ... Give me that which I want, and you shall have this which you want, is the meaning of every such offer; and it is in this manner that we obtain from one another the far greater part of those good offices which we stand in need of. It is not from the benevolence of the butcher, the brewer, or the baker that we expect our dinner, but from their regard to their own interest. (Smith, [1776] 1911, 13)

Under *laissez-faire*, all mutually beneficial trades therefore take place and all appropriable externalities are appropriated; and there are no ways in which the *laissez-faire* outcome can obviously, feasibly be improved upon.

If there is reason to regard *laissez-faire* as ideal, there is also reason to suppose that departures from *laissez-faire* are not. Even if we could confidently identify cases in which *laissez-faire* 'fails' by some standard, we cannot simply invoke state intervention as a *deus ex machina* and assume that the problem has been solved. State agents – politicians, civil servants, and regulatory officials – have their own private interests just like anyone else, and we cannot assume that their interests coincide with the general social interest; nor, alternatively, can we assume that they are willing to forgo their own private interests for the broader social good. These

446

agents differ from 'ordinary' private agents in one respect only – their roles in the state apparatus give them unique powers of coercion, or access to such powers, that no ordinary agent ever has. They can then use these unique powers to do many things that ordinary private agents cannot do, and which no-one could do under our *laissez-faire* anarchy: they can change the laws within which everyone operates; they can restrict the activities in which individuals and firms can engage; they can legally seize the resources of other agents (i.e., they can tax them); they can establish central banks and systems of deposit insurance; they can regulate the financial system; and they can monopolise the currency, make it inconvertible, and debauch it. In practice, they have done these things, and the social order that has resulted from these interventions is very different from *laissez faire*.

This chapter consequently has two objectives. The first is to spell out the main effects of each principal type of intervention – to examine the effects of establishing a central bank and a system of deposit insurance, the effects of regulating the financial system, and so on. In doing so, we shall focus on the precise ways in which these interventions depart from *laissez-faire* and produce outcomes that are patently inferior, by any reasonable criterion, to the outcomes that would occur under *laissez-faire* itself. In other words, we shall highlight government failure and try to identify the factors underlying it. The conclusion that governments generally 'fail' is reinforced by the histories of specific interventions which reveal that the motives behind them were seldom, if ever, any selfless desire to improve economic outcomes; instead, they were the results of political deals in which, more often that not, politicians and powerful lobby groups would collude to exchange favours at the broader public expense. Most of our present-day financial and monetary problems can then be seen to arise, not because of any inherent weaknesses within the private sector itself, but because of specific government interventions into the financial system and, moreover, interventions whose motivations were often highly questionable. Ironically, while its advocates often portray public policy as a means of solving problems and making the world a better place, the truth of the matter is that public policy is more often than not the *cause* of our problems, an undesirable intrusion that we would be better off without.

The second objective of the chapter is a corollary to the first. If intervention is undesirable, then what should be done about removing it? Our second task is therefore to outline a programme of reforms to roll back these interventions, and establish the safe and efficient financial system, as well as the sound currency, that we all presumably want. However, reform must be carefully thought through. It is one thing to prescribe medicine to a healthy patient, but it is another to prescribe medicine to one who is already sick. *Laissez-faire* might be the best way to *maintain* the health of the financial system, but it does not follow that we should establish *laissez-faire* as quickly as possible *starting from where we now are*, and not worry too much about *how* we go about establishing it. Those affected by reforms need to be given enough time to prepare themselves – for example, banks would need time to build up their financial strength to cope with the abolition of deposit insurance and a lender of last resort – and reforms would also need to be appropriately sequenced. Lastly, and certainly not least, we need to ensure that the new system, once established, is adequately protected against any attempts by future government to interfere with it.

INTERVENTION IN THE FINANCIAL SYSTEM

Restrictions on Banks

Restrictions on Bank Size

We begin with government intervention into the financial system, and in particular, with restrictions on permissible bank activities. These restrictions can be divided into three main types – restrictions on bank size, restrictions on bank assets, and restrictions on bank liabilities – and all three types of restriction have been historically important. A good example of the first type of restriction is the six-partner rule, applied to English banks until 1826, which restricted all English and Welsh banks other than the Bank of England to be partnerships with no more than six partners. This rule was introduced and then maintained as part of a series of deals between the Bank of England and the government, in which the Bank provided funds to the government in return for various privileges (see, e.g., Smith, 1936, 10–11). The six-partner rule gave the Bank very considerable monopoly power over the English banking system by ensuring that the Bank's rivals remained small and weak. The amount of capital that six partners could put into a bank was fairly limited, and, given the nature of partnership, also of uncertain duration. Yet the Bank faced no such limits and also enjoyed the (not inconsiderable) benefits of a joint-stock company. In an industry characterised by extensive economies of scale, the six-partner rule left English banks severely undercapitalised and very vulnerable to shocks. When shocks did occur, the banks easily lost the confidence of the public and failed in large numbers (see, e.g., Meulen, 1934, 95–96; L. H. White, 1984a, 40–42).

Other examples of such restrictions are the laws against banking amalgamation in the USA. In states where they existed, these laws typically restricted banks to operate in the state or sometimes only the county specified in their charters. Such restrictions date from the earliest years of US banking and were motivated by the desire of small bankers – the unit bankers – to prohibit branching so that they could maintain local monopolies. Apart from restricting local competition, which was their purpose, these laws had the effect of limiting banks' freedom to exploit benefits of economies of scale; they also severely restricted banks' abilities to diversify on both asset and liability sides of their balance sheets (see, e.g., Wells and Scruggs, 1986; L. H. White, 1986). The limitation on economies of scale is obvious. The limitation on asset diversification arises because allowing banks to operate in a single small community makes their financial health disproportionately dependent on the community in which they operate, while larger banks could have diversified away most local community risk by holding assets from a range of different parts of the country. On the liability side, these laws made banks more vulnerable to withdrawal demands in their particular community, since it was generally more difficult for a unit bank to borrow than for one branch to obtain funds from another branch of the same bank. To add to the problems of the banking system, the growth of an interbank market for funds that would have helped banks obtain funds was also crippled for most of this century by restrictions preventing the payment of interest (see, e.g., O'Driscoll, 1988, 174). These restrictions also hindered the development of clearing systems that would have improved the market discipline under which banks operated and strengthened the forces keeping the value of bank currency at par.

Apart from weakening and reducing the efficiency of the US banking system, branch-banking restrictions also created a powerful lobby group with a vested interest, not only in maintaining branch-banking restrictions, but in promoting protectionist measures to keep the unit banks in existence. As Calomiris says

> Historians have long stressed the destabilizing influence of unit banking, and linked its peculiar prevalence in the United States to the unique vulnerability of US banking historically. Indeed, studies of the political economy of deposit insurance legislation show that it was the desire to preserve unit banking, and the political influence of unit bankers, that gave rise to the perceived need for deposit insurance ... It was understood early on ... that branching – with its benefits both of greater diversification and coordination – provided an alternative stabilizer to liability insurance. But unit banks and their supporters successfully directed the movement for banking reform toward creating government insurance funds. (Calomiris, 1989, 4–5)

These protectionist measures in turn had further, highly undesirable, effects on the banking system, which we shall consider presently.

Restrictions on Bank Assets

Governments have intervened in various ways to restrict banks' choice of assets. The usual purpose of such restrictions is fiscal – to force banks to buy government debt at higher than market prices, or to force commercial banks to hold central bank debt at lower than market interest rates. Again, there are many real-world examples. Some very common ones are reserve requirements on the commercial banks. Such rules oblige banks to hold minimum holdings of central-bank debt proportional to some subset of their liabilities, such as the chequable deposits they issue. The interest income the banks lose on such holdings can then be regarded as a forced loan to the central bank. Though one occasionally meets arguments in the older literature that reserve requirements help or might even be necessary for the central bank to achieve its monetary or financial targets, most modern monetary economists (rightly) tend to dismiss such claims and regard reserve requirements as essentially no more than a device to extract seigniorage revenues from the financial system.

Other examples of this general type of restriction are the 'bond collateral requirements' common in the USA from the 1830s onwards. These were requirements that note-issuing banks hold specified proportions – usually, at least 100 percent – of designated collateral assets against their note issues. Such measures were characteristic of the so-called 'free banking laws' of the *antebellum* USA, first introduced in Michigan in 1837, and New York and Georgia in 1838, and widely copied in subsequent years. These laws allowed free banking only in the sense that they allowed free entry – in so doing, marking a major departure from the traditional US requirement that banks obtain operating charters from their local legislatures – but these laws also stipulated various restrictions, of which the bond collateral requirement was perhaps the most onerous (see, e.g., Rockoff, 1975; Rolnick and Weber, 1984; L. H. White, 1986; Dowd, 1992a). The eligible assets required by these laws were typically bonds from the legislating state, and sometimes federal bonds or bonds from certain other states as well, and the main purpose of the bond collateral requirements was to promote the demand for state debt. These restrictions made the banks subject to them particularly vulnerable to movements in the prices of state debt. On a number of occasions – principally, in the early 1840s, and on the outbreak of the Civil War – some states either defaulted on their debts, or were expected to, and the holders of their debt experienced very heavy losses. These losses were sometimes enough to wipe out the net worth of otherwise solvent banks, and were a major cause of 'free bank' failures. States thus undermined 'free banks', first by requiring them to buy up their debt, and then, having made them vulnerable, by (occasionally) engaging in irresponsible fiscal policies that inflicted large losses on them (see, e.g., Rolnick and Weber, 1983, 1984, 1985 or Dowd, 1992a).

After the Civil War, the federal government adopted the bond collateral principle at the national level. The new 'national banks' were required to secure their note issues with holdings of federal government debt; at the same time, the federal government taxed the state 'free banks' out of existence, and in so doing drove the states out of a lucrative tax field which they had hitherto had for their own. However, the new bond collateral system had the defect that it made the supply of currency dependent on the supply, and on the price, of government debt. In subsequent years, the federal government ran persistent budget surpluses and retired the greater part of its debt; and the price of its debt rose to very high levels and undermined much of what remained of the profitability of issuing notes. The result was that many banks retired their note issues and the currency supply contracted sharply in the 1880s (Cagan, 1963, 22–23). The bond collateral system thus produced a falling supply of currency despite the fact that the economy was generally growing and the demand for currency growing with it. The system also made the supply of currency inelastic. This problem was particularly acute in the autumn when there was a seasonal increase in the demand for currency for crop moving; the system had great difficulty accommodating these increases, and the result was considerable interest rate volatility, and, on occasion, serious financial crisis (see, e.g., Sprague, 1910; Smith, 1936, 133).

A final and important instance of restrictions on banks' asset-holdings is the enforced separation of 'investment' and 'commercial' banking in the US under the Glass–Steagall Act of 1933. This measure prohibited deposit-issuing banks from dealing in investment securities, and consequently led to an artificial separation of the banking system into commercial banks that issued deposits but did not deal in securities, and investment banks that dealt in securities but did not issue deposits. The Act was justified on the basis of a variety of claims about how the holding of securities affiliates weakened commercial banks and made them more vulnerable to failure, but more recent research by Eugene White (1986) suggests that none of these claims has any real substance. His work suggests, on the contrary, that banks that combined commercial and investment banking functions were able to benefit from various complementarities (e.g., greater diversification) that were closed to other banks, and he finds that banks with affiliates were less likely to fail than those without (E. N. White, 1986, 40). The Act itself is then best explained in public-choice terms – it served the interests of the banks and securities firms, by protecting each against the competition of the other, and they were able to get the measures enacted by exploiting the alarm prevailing in the early 1930s about dealing in securities. As Shughart (1988, 98) aptly puts it, the Act was a

> government-sponsored market-sharing agreement for the financial services industry .... [and] a classic example ... of collusion through which the members of a cartel can maximize their joint profits.

Restrictions on Bank Liabilities

Finally, there are interventions to restrict banks' liabilities. A classic and now near-universal intervention is to restrict the issue of banknotes, usually to give one bank a monopoly. Such restrictions usually limit banks' profits and harm the public by denying them the currency they would want to hold, and by denying them banking services whose profitability depends on the note issue, such as branch banks in out of the way areas. These restrictions also make the banking system artificially dependent on the bank with the note monopoly. Should the demand for currency rise for some reason, then the failure of that bank to issue the additional currency demanded by the public can bring on or aggravate a crisis. This problem is particularly acute where the monopoly bank itself faces restrictions on its note issue, a good example being the 1844 Bank Charter Act which gave the Bank of England an effective monopoly over the issue of banknotes in England and Wales, but imposed on the Bank itself a 100 percent marginal reserve requirement against the note issue. The note issue was therefore tied rigidly to gold, and the system had no easy was to accommodate an increase in the public's desired currency/deposit ratio (see, e.g., Dowd, 1988b). Apart from leaving the Bank unable to create additional currency without corresponding deposits of gold, it also created a danger of self-fulfilling crises in which members of the public, apprehensive of a possible currency shortage, would demand additional currency to be on the safe side, and the resulting speculative increase in the demand for currency could bring about the very crisis everyone feared. This happened on three occasions – in 1847, 1857 and 1866 – and in each case, the resulting crisis was only stopped when the government indicated that it would not prosecute the Bank for issuing additional notes beyond those it was allowed to issue under the 1844 Act. The knowledge that additional notes would be forthcoming then settled the public, and the panic subsided. This problem of self-fulfilling crises was very similar to that which plagued the USA during the national banking system era, when restrictions on bank assets made the currency supply inelastic and crises could occur when there were increases in the demand for currency.

Another common example is usury regulation – ceilings, perhaps set at zero, on deposit interest rates. These have been used many times over the centuries. The payment of interest on M1 deposits was prohibited for much of this century, for example, and usury restrictions have been very prominent in the developing world in the postwar era. Though sometimes defended as providing the authorities with an additional monetary 'tool', or helping to increase investment by keeping interest rates down, usury restrictions produce relatively little good and their main effect is to distort the financial system. They discourage saving on the part of the general public, and thereby reduce the pool of funds available for investment; the reduced pool of funds then pushes loan interest rates up, and if the authorities respond by controlling loan interest as well, they merely push the allocation of credit out of explicit markets which can allocate it properly and create considerable scope for rent-seeking, corruption, and so on; and usury ceilings also undermine incentives for banks to lend to each other, and therefore cripple the inter-bank loan market.

The Establishment of Central Banking

But perhaps the most important form of state intervention was the establishment of central banking. The ways in which central banks were established varied from one country to another. In Britain, for example, central banking was not established as such, but evolved in an environment that was itself heavily influenced by government intervention. The Bank of England was founded in 1694, not as a central bank, but as a bank to provide loans to a government that sought funds to finance a continental war, and which could not otherwise borrow the funds because of previous defaults. The government therefore paid for the loan by granting the Bank legal privileges, and over succeeding years the Bank provided further loans in return for more privileges. The Bank's privileged status then gave it easy hegemony over the English banking system (see, e.g., Smith, 1936; Dowd, 1989, Chapter 5). With English banks rendered artificially weak by the Bank's privileges, and in particular by the six-partner rule, they also became artificially dependent on the Bank for support. Only the Bank could effectively meet any substantial increase in the public demand for liquidity, and the Bank was eventually forced, reluctantly, to accept the role of guardian to the banking system. But if it was going to 'protect' the banking system, the Bank also wanted some influence over it, if only to prevent banks taking undue advantage of its support and taking excessive risks at its expense. Having become its guardian, the Bank naturally acquired the role of supervisor of the banking system as well. At the same time, the Bank's currency was becoming the standard redemption medium of the commercial banking system, and gold largely disappeared from circulation. Eventually, the government intervened to suspend the convertibility of Bank currency from gold, and in so doing put the country on an inconvertible standard. The Bank of England had thus started off as an institution to provide loans to the government, but evolved over time into a fully-fledged central bank with responsibilities both to support and regulate the financial system, and to manage a fiat currency.

In many other countries, the central bank was explicitly established as a central bank. In some countries, the main motivation was fiscal, to set up a bank to lend to the government; in others, central banks were established to imitate 'model' countries such as the UK or USA (as in many Commonwealth countries or Latin American countries (see, e.g., Schuler, 1992b; Meisel, 1992); and in others, central banks were established with the (alleged) intention of stabilising the existing banking system (see, e.g., Schuler, 1992b). To take the USA again, the Federal Reserve was set up as a central bank in 1914 to correct the perceived deficiencies of the earlier national banking system. This system, it will be recalled, involved legal restrictions that made the supply of currency highly inelastic and rendered the system as a whole vulnerable to crisis. The system itself had responded by creating its own emergency currency – the clearinghouse loan certificates – which helped to meet crisis demands for additional currency, and, while the issue of these certificates worked well, their legal status was unclear and the fact that they had to be issued in the first place was clearly unsatisfactory (see, e.g., Timberlake, 1984, 1993). Yet rather than abolish the relevant restrictions in the national banking legislation and allow an elastic supply of currency, Congress instead decided to establish a central bank to put the issue of emergency currency on an 'official' basis. A proven, quasi-automatic system was replaced by a 'managed' one that depended for its success on the 'right' use of its managers' discretionary powers, and yet this system gave those managers relatively weak incentives to use their powers 'properly'. As Timberlake (1984, 15) nicely put it, the integrity of the banking system was divorced from the self-interest of those who were responsible for protecting it. The new system also created a pressure group – the officials of the Federal Reserve itself – that not only had its own interests (i.e., power and prestige), but was also uniquely placed to lobby Congress to further those interests. The performed very badly in the 1930s when the Fed failed to provide the emergency loans needed to contain the banking collapses (see, e.g., Friedman and Schwartz, 1963), but even then the Fed was able to turn its failures to its own advantage by diverting the blame and using the opportunity created by the emergency to increase its own powers (Timberlake, 1986). In that case, and in others, the Fed was able to use its own intellectual superiority over Congress to divert legislative reforms for its own ends, and even to use the consequences of its mistakes as justifications to promote its own interests. Over time, the initially relatively limited and decentralised Federal Reserve System transformed into a powerful centralised central bank with vast influence over the financial and monetary system. The Fed changed

> from a system in which the Federal Reserve Banks were autonomous and Federal Reserve Board a refereeing committee, to a System in which the Board in Washington is all powerful and the Federal Reserve Banks not much more than administrative units; from an occasional discounter of real bills at the initiative of member banks, to a constant and heavy monetizer of government securities ... ; from an institution specifically subordinated to the gold standard, to one that has a monopoly on the initial creation of money, with no vestige of a gold standard remaining; from a lender of last resort for banks, to a perpetual motion machine of money creation; from an institution with an avowed interest in providing liquidity in support of sound banks, to one whose every act is to enhance the power and prestige of itself and the government. Unless one can argue that what is good for the government is good for the general public, one cannot defend either the mutation of the Fed as it has occurred, or the Fed's continued existence as an all-powerful central bank. Its 70-year history as a bureaucratic institution confirms the inability of Congress to bring it to heel. Whenever its own powers are at stake, the Fed exercises an intellectual ascendancy over Congress that consistently results in an extension of Fed authority. This pattern reflects the dominance of bureaucratic expertise for which there is no solution as long as the specialized agency continues to exist. (Timberlake, 1986, 759)

The Lender of Last Resort and Deposit Insurance

Often associated with the establishment of central banking is the establishment of a lender of last resort and a system of deposit insurance. As discussed earlier, central banks have often been established as lenders of last resort, as in countries such as the USA; alternatively, a pre-existing institution has sometimes accepted a lender of last resort function in the process of its evolution into a fully-fledged central bank, as in the UK. However, deposit insurance systems have typically been established apart from any existing central bank. The classical model is that of the USA, where an institutionally separate deposit insurance agency would be established to manage the deposit insurance system. Both a lender of last resort and deposit insurance essentially provide guarantees that undermine a bank management's incentives to maintain their bank's financial health. In the first case, a bank's management can rely on the central bank to provide it with emergency loans – loans it presumably could not obtain elsewhere in the market, or could only obtain at greater cost. The availability of such loans reduces the penalty to the bank for allowing its credit-worthiness to deteriorate, and thereby implicitly encourages the bank to act in ways that promote such deterioration. In the second case, a bank's depositors are guaranteed against loss, and therefore lose any incentive to monitor the management of the banks with which they keep their funds. The management need no longer worry about maintaining depositor confidence, and so they take more risks, run down the bank's capital, and generally undermine the bank's financial health. Either way, the existence of the relevant guarantee undermines banks' health by reducing their incentives to look after themselves.

A particularly important manifestation of this effect is on bank capital. The main purpose of a bank maintaining its capital strength under *laissez-faire* conditions is be to safeguard customers' confidence and give depositors no reason to run. But if deposits are insured, for example, then depositors have no reason to run more or less regardless of the bank's capital position, and there is no point maintaining capital strength, which, in any case, is expensive. (We can of course tell a similar story about the lender of last resort.) The rational response of a bank to deposit insurance is therefore to reduce its capital and in so doing undermine its own financial health (Peltzman, 1970). We see this effect very clearly with the introduction of federal deposit insurance in the USA. In the first ten years of the federal deposit insurance regime, bank capital ratios more than halved, from 14.1 percent in 1934 to 6.2 percent in 1945 (Salsman, 1990, 56). Bank capital continued to deteriorate in later years and, though regulators tried to stem the deterioration by various means, there is little evidence that their efforts had much success (Peltzman, 1970; see also Kaufman, 1992).

The other major consequence of deposit insurance or a lender of last resort is to encourage banks to take more lending risks. This effect is related to the bondholder expropriation hypothesis considered in Chapter 2, according to which a manager might be tempted to engage in excessive risk-taking to maximise his expected return at the expense of his creditors. In the deposit insurance context, a bank manager will reckon that if he takes additional risks and they pay off, then he keeps the additional profits; but if he takes the risks and they fail, he can pass some of the expected losses to the deposit insurance agency which has to pay his depositors in the event that he fails to do so. The *existence* of deposit insurance thus provides a marginal inducement to take more risks than he would otherwise do and, more to the point, to take more risks than would be socially optimal (see also L.J. White, 1989). This effect is apparently also verified by empirical evidence (see, e.g., Grossman, 1992).

To make matters worse, this inducement to take additional risks also increases as the bank's capital position deteriorates. The lower a bank's capital, the greater the expected losses transferred to the deposit insurance agency in the event that lending risks fail and, hence, the bigger the incentive on the bank management's part to take additional risks. As the bank's capital goes to zero in the limit, virtually all the expected losses from failure are passed on to the deposit insurance agency, but the bank always keeps the profits if the risks succeed. A bank might then have little incentive to avoid risks, however wild those risks might be. The two effects of deposit insurance on bank behaviour consequently interact in a potentially lethal way: when deposit insurance is introduced an initially healthy bank responds by lowering its capital standards and taking marginally more risks, but it gradually takes more risks as its financial health deteriorates, and a point can eventually come where it has become a zombie institution that has no capital left and very little incentive to restrict its risk-taking.

Deposit insurance also reinforces these destructive tendencies by undermining any 'good' banks that try to uphold higher standards. Whereas a bank that reduced its capital under *laissez-faire* conditions would risk going to the wall, a bank that now does so manages to cut its costs – it no longer has so many dividends to pay – and establishes a competitive advantage over its more conservative rivals. A strong capital position – which, from a social point of view, is still highly desirable – is now a competitive liability. Deposit insurance also forces the good banks to pay more for their deposits and accept less on their loans, and undermines the discipline of bankruptcy that would otherwise put the weaker institutions out of business. However large the losses it has made, a bad bank can always obtain the funds to meet its current bills merely by raising its deposit interest rates. Since their deposits are guaranteed, depositors have no reason to be concerned about what the bank might do with their funds; a bad bank can therefore always remain solvent if it is prepared to offer a higher rate than other banks. (This phenomenon was observed, for example, in Texas in the late 1980s where the large number of weak institutions bidding for funds forced the solvent ones to pay a substantial premium on their deposit rates (see, e.g., Thomson, 1993, 3).) Deposit insurance consequently undermines the only reliable mechanism there is (i.e., the process of bankruptcy) to put unsound banks out of business, and it does so in a way that imposes additional costs (e.g., the need to pay higher deposit rates) on the 'good' banks that try to resist the process of deterioration. Banking becomes a legalised Ponzi game in which participating institutions can keep on meeting their losses by issuing yet more debt, gambling almost indefinitely at the expense of the deposit insurance agency that must ultimately foot the bill.

Given that the normal market mechanism for closing down weak institutions has been suppressed, it is then essential that the regulatory authorities either stop institutions becoming zombies in the first place, or else have some means of intervening to close down problem institutions before their losses get out of hand. Yet there is little evidence that the attempts of US banking authorities to impose capital standard had that much effect (e.g., Peltzman, 1970; Salsman, 1990, Chapter 3); nor did they mount the energetic failure resolution policy that would have been needed to keep their losses under control. They were overwhelmed by the scale of their problems, and the best that can be said was they did not have the resources (e.g., the qualified manpower) to mount the failure resolution policy that was needed. However, there were also additional, more fundamental, reasons for the regulatory failure, perhaps the main one being that regulatory officials wanted to cover themselves. If the problem gets out of hand, the best option from their point of view is to hide it, divert the blame (e.g., by blaming incompetent or dishonest bank management), or make up excuses.

Since they will be under political pressure to leave problems unsolved and face the danger of being blamed for the failures that occur on their watch, regulators' best hopes may be to make 'clean getaways' by delaying the recognition of failure costs until after their terms of office have expired and they have landed more lucrative jobs in the private sector. (Miller, 1991, 30)

The regulators therefore responded to the growing problems in their sector by failing to enforce existing standards, by watering standards down to make the health of the banking system look better than it actually was, and by providing elaborate 'theories' of regulatory 'forbearance' that were little more than excuses for doing nothing.

Some idea of the extent to which US banking regulators failed to apply their own standards can be inferred from the observation that, as of 30 June 1990, 35 banks reported no equity capital and another 148 reported equity capital below 3 percent of assets, but both groups still remained in operation controlling some $30 billion in assets (Miller, 1991, 31). The costs of forbearance were extremely high – an FDIC study estimated that the present value of delaying closure of a sample of 952 failed institutions that closed between January 1981 and July 1992 was more than twice the projected costs of resolving them back in 1979 (Thomson, 1993, 3) – and few such institutions survived anyway. The regulatory policy of excessive forbearance went hand-in-hand with attempts to disguise problems by relaxing standards. In 1976, the accounting definition of capital was broadened to allow goodwill and loan loss provisions to count as capital (Salsman, 1990, 64–65), and in the early 1980s, the relatively lax Generally Accepted Accounting Practices (GAAP) were replaced for regulatory purposes by the even laxer Regulatory Accounting Practices (RAP). The RAP differed from the GAAP in that they allow subordinated debentures, pledged deposits, unamortised deferred gains, and even unrecognised losses, losses and gains on future transactions, and accounting forbearances to count as capital as well. Not surprisingly, the RAP have been condemned as a 'fraud and an unprincipled cover-up for the insolvent' (Salsman, 1990, 115). Where regulators had to find solutions to problem cases, they tended to opt for short-term measures that protected their own funds, even though such measures were extremely expensive in the long run. They therefore preferred to avoid foreclosures – which would have depleted their own resources – and often paid handsomely (e.g., by offering loan guarantees, tax breaks, or knock-down prices for problem assets) to get relatively sound banks to take problem institutions off their books. Arrangements like these minimised the strain on the insurance agencies' reserves, but also passed many of the costs to others (e.g., the Internal Revenue Service) or into the future (which didn't matter, since the agencies were going bust anyway). As regulatory guarantees often gave new owners little or no incentive to sort out problem loans, these mergers did nothing to resolve underlying problems and their main effect was to buy time for the regulators at enormous expense to taxpayers. In the end, the deposit insurance agencies had effectively become zombie institutions themselves and were playing much the same game with Congress that their own problem institutions were playing with them – disguising their problems, making excuses, and opting for short-run 'solutions' that were disastrous in the longer term.

These problems were aggravated further by the actions of politicians, who had even less incentive to face up to problems than the regulators. Politicians tend to have relatively short-term horizons, if only because they have to face re-election, and they tend to be excessively preoccupied with the appearance of policies rather than their substance, with their main concern often being plausible deniability. The sheer complexity of financial issues also puts them at a disadvantage relative to regulators, who can often use that complexity to outmanoeuvre them. Any tendency there might be to act responsibly is often further undermined by games of political chicken (e.g., between Congress and the Administration or between different political parties) and by politicians' vulnerability to pressure from well-organised interest groups, particularly since the gains from lobbying for protection in the financial services industry are often very large and concentrated relative to their costs. Lobbying for protection against the regulators was a particular problem for the thrift industry:

> Large political contributions were made by the thrift industry to Congress to postpone legislative action that would increase the cost to the industry through higher deposit insurance premiums ... reduce its independence [or] bring about the removal of managers/owners of insolvent or near insolvent institutions. Because the dollar amounts were so massive, contributions were extraordinarily large even by Washington, DC, standards ... Many Congressmen ... acted ... to delay potentially corrective legislative and regulatory actions. (Kaufman, 1989, 11)

It was perhaps no wonder that the regulatory agencies fared as badly as they did.

MONETARY POLICY

The Creation of a Fiat Currency

Governments also interfered with the monetary standard as well as the financial system, and perhaps the most important such interference was the establishment of fiat currencies. The process usually began when the government intervened, generally for fiscal reasons, to grant one particular bank monopoly privileges, and we have already discussed the important case of the Bank of England. The Bank bought privileges from an impecunious government, and these privileges led to a pyramid system in which other banks usually redeemed their liabilities with those of the Bank of England, while the Bank itself continued to redeem its liabilities against gold. Eventually, the government would intervene to break the link between the liabilities of the privileged bank and the anchor commodity. In the

British case, the government's excessive demands for credit from the Bank of England left the latter unable to maintain specie payments, and the government intervened in 1797 to legalise the Bank's insolvency and order it to suspend such payments. The currency became inconvertible, and remained so until 1821. Convertibility was restored again, but suppressed again in 1914. Increased political interference rendered later attempts to restore convertibility even less successful, and any formal link with gold was finally abandoned with the collapse of the Bretton Woods system in the early 1970s.

The same process of political pressure eroding the link with gold is also evident in US history. In the nineteenth century, US governments intervened a number of times to suppress convertibility and then subsequently restore it. The most notable case occurred with the outbreak of the Civil War in 1861, when the federal government's demands for bank credit forced the principal commercial banks to abandon convertibility. The US remained on the inconvertible greenback standard until 1879, and then stayed on the gold standard without interruption till 1933. When the Federal Reserve was founded in 1913, it was intended that the Fed should operate within the confines of that standard, yet the international gold standard collapsed within a year and the Federal Reserve was soon the only major central bank that remained tied to gold. The Fed therefore found itself with much more discretion than central banks on the gold standard used to have, and it had no clear idea what it should do. It still had considerable discretion even after the ill-fated attempt to restore the international gold standard in the 1920s, and again after the Second World War, when the international gold standard was re-established in the modified form of the Bretton Woods system. After the war, encouraged by the government itself, the Fed embarked on monetary policies that were more expansionist than the system would allow in the long run. The Fed's gold stocks therefore gradually ran down, and as its gold reserve requirements threatened to become binding, it lobbied Congress to have them abolished. Congress did so, and what remained of the discipline of the gold exchange standard was eroded further. However, the increased freedom of the Fed from the constraints of the gold exchange standard also reduced its ability to resist political influence, and the Fed came under increasing pressure to 'accommodate' the heavy spending of the Johnson administration. The Fed offered only weak resistance to this pressure and the gold outflows continued; the inevitable result was that the Fed could no longer maintain the dollar price of gold and the gold exchange standard was finally abandoned in the early 1970s. By then, for the first time in history, the major countries were now on fiat standards in peacetime, with no serious intention of ever restoring convertibility.

The establishment of fiat currencies implied a fundamental change in the nature of the monetary standard. Previously, the monetary standard had always tied the value of the currency to the value of one or more precious metals, and the need to preserve this link severely restricted the ability of a government or central bank to pursue its own monetary policy (or at least do so while maintaining the commodity link). A central bank like the Bank of England might be able to manipulate interest rates at the margin, but this influence, such as it was, was limited by the need to maintain convertibility. The system was largely, though not entirely, automatic, and the principal problem facing participating central banks was to ensure that they continued to maintain convertibility. But once convertibility is abolished, the central bank no longer has to meet any external constraint, and is free to do more or less as it wishes. This new-found freedom corresponds with the change in the monetary standard. Previously, the price level had been tied down by the combination of the convertibility rules under which currency was issued, on the one hand, and demand and supply in the market for the 'anchor' commodity, on the other. But now the price level is determined by demand and supply in the market for the central bank's 'base money', pure and simple, and the link between the price level and the value of any individual commodity is gone. For any given demand for base money, the price level is determined by the amount of base money the central bank chooses to create, and the central bank can issue as much base money as it wishes to. The price level is therefore determined by central bank *policy*, and we have to consider what determines that policy, and what effects it has.

Political Factors in Monetary Policy

Some of the most obvious factors determining policy are political ones. To the extent that they can influence or control central bank policy, elected politicians might obviously want to use central bank policy for electoral purposes (see, e.g., Nordhaus, 1975). If the electorate make their voting decisions on the basis of the state of the economy, and central bank policy influences that state, politicians might want to use monetary policy to produce that particular state on election day that would maximise their chances of re-election. The most plausible scenario would have the government intend to produce an artificial sense of prosperity – perhaps an unsustainable combination of low inflation and low unemployment – in the run-up to an election, whilst aiming to get any unpopular measures (e.g., tax rises, or higher interest rates) over with while the election is still some way off. The result is a cycle, with governments promoting popular policies in the periods before elections and unpopular ones in the periods after them. In terms of monetary policy, governments would therefore want expansionary (i.e., inflationary) policies in the run-up to elections, and disinflationary ones when the elections were over. There are a number of unresolved issues with these models (see, e.g., Blackburn and Christensen, 1989), but the basic point that governments have an incentive to try to use monetary policy for electoral purposes is surely correct. Since the resulting political business cycle would make interest rates, inflation rates and other economic variables less stable and probably also less predictable than they would otherwise be, we can only conclude that the cycle is harmful as far as the economy itself is concerned: the political business cycle is a game that elected politicians play at the expense of society as a whole.

Another such game is where politicians use monetary policy (or, indeed, any policy instruments they can lay their hands on) to distribute favours to special-interest groups that are powerful enough to lobby successfully for them. It is often possible for small but well-organised or otherwise powerful interest groups to obtain special favours at the expense of a less well-organised or otherwise less powerful majority. A good example is provided by Willett and Banaian:

> even apart from the effects of campaign contributions in influencing votes, we can see how minority interest groups could have a substantial impact on a president's, and even more on a farm district legislator's, chance of reelection. Suppose that farmers constitute only 5 percent of voters, but that for them the farm bill is an extremely important determinant of their vote. Thus voting against a general farm bill would substantially affect the vote calculus of farmers. The other 95 percent of the voters may have gained, so that in a narrow, self-interest-based referendum vote the cut in spending would pass overwhelmingly. But in a presidential vote, for how many voters would opposition to the farm bill be decisive in influencing their vote? Probably only a handful. Thus even in a strict one person-one vote model we can see how such special interest bills can be politically attractive. The addition of lobbying and campaign contribution considerations of course only serves to reinforce this conclusion. (Willett and Banaian, 1988, 110–111)

In terms of monetary policy, we often see how groups favouring low interest rates (e.g., mortgage owners, or industry) are able to lobby successfully for policies that produce temporarily lower interest rates, while those who want higher interest rates (e.g., savers) seldom have much influence on monetary policy. The result is a tendency for monetary policy to be excessively expansionary. Yet, ironically, such policies are often self-defeating as they involve higher rates of monetary growth that in the end produce higher inflation and higher rather than lower interest rates.

Monetary policy can also be heavily influenced by conflict between various groups *within* the policy establishment. The most commonly cited conflict is that between central bankers and politicians, although there can also be conflict among the politicians themselves (e.g., between the executive and legislative branches of government). A point often made in the literature is that politicians tend to have relatively short horizons, if only because their tenure in office is generally short and often uncertain. From a social point of view, politicians therefore tend to discount the future relatively heavily, and they have difficulty taking the 'long view' that the general social good may require. (Politicians might also be tempted into socially detrimental policies such as inflation because they want more tax revenues and alternative forms of taxation are politically more costly, but we shall come back to this issue shortly.) However, central bankers enjoy more secure tenures and can afford to take the longer view. They might also take the longer view because they normally have a better understanding of financial and monetary issues than politicians, and are not always sympathetic to the politicians' concerns about the next election or the political problems of raising revenue. Conflicts like these between politicians and central bankers can be socially harmful because the resulting policy is often an inappropriate compromise (e.g., when central bankers bow to politicians' concerns about the next election, and thus allow necessary but unpopular measures to be watered down). They are also harmful because of the uncertainty they produce. Policy conflicts are seldom definitively resolved, and outcomes generally reflect some compromise depending on the relative bargaining powers of the parties involved. Since the factors behind this balance of power change all the time, the resulting policies tend to vacillate and be difficult to predict. Thus

> the objectives of monetary policy are often likely to be in a state of some flux, reflecting a constant struggle between different groups in the centralized policy-making process to impose their views on economic management. In particular, monetary policy decisions are to be seen in terms of a compromise between advocates of anti-inflation and economic stimulation, whose relative importance ... may shift repeatedly. (Blackburn and Christensen, 1989, 32)

Nonetheless, conflict between central bankers and politicians does not necessarily prevent them colluding to play games at the expense of the public. Politicians want to influence monetary policy, and yet at the same time want to avoid blame for unpopular monetary policies. Since the central bankers do not have to face the electorate, the politicians can therefore use the central bank as a scapegoat that allows them to disown responsibility for unpopular policies; and they can bribe the central bankers to co-operate and take the abuse thrown at them by granting them the various privileges, higher salaries, and the like, that central bankers enjoy. What is significant about this game is how the politicians *could* supervise the central bank closely and limit its discretion, but they *choose not to* because the central bank must have discretionary powers if it is to be a credible scapegoat:

> It is no accident that, through the Fed's seventy years of existence, Congress and the president have remained content *not* to force the Fed to submit openly to their wills. By leaving the Fed's high command a substantial amount of *ex ante* discretion, elected politicians leave themselves room to blame the Fed *ex post* for whatever aspects of its policies happen to go wrong. (Kane, 1988, 483, his emphasis)

The Fed consequently retains a high degree of discretion, *not* because anyone seriously thinks that such discretion serves a socially useful purpose – indeed, most informed observers think that such discretion is harmful, if only because of the uncertainty it creates – but because it enables the politicians and the Fed to collude to mislead the public. To quote Kane again,

> If US politicians' only goal was to give our country better macroeconomic performance ... they would long ago have made themselves and Federal Reserve officials more directly accountable for short-run central bank behavior ... [But] Putting the Fed under more *explicit* short-run political

pressure would greatly lessen politicians' ability to disclaim responsibility for past policy decisions. (Kane, 1988, 487, his emphasis)

That of course would never do because it would make it more difficult for politicians to try to manipulate the macroeconomy for their own ends.

Monetary Policy as Taxation

Monetary policy can of course also be motivated by fiscal reasons (i.e., the government's desire to extract resources from the private sector). The use of inflation by the government to raise revenue from the private sector is the most recurrent theme in monetary history, and virtually all governments have eventually succumbed to the temptation to do it. From 'the time of the ancient Greeks', Timberlake (1993, xx-xxi) observes, 'wherever and whenever money has appeared, state intervention, regulation, and monopoly privilege for state-sponsored institutions have not been far behind'. Politically, raising revenue in this way is often attractive because the costs of this tax are disguised, and most of those who pay it are not aware of how much it really costs them, nor even that it is a tax that they are paying. Governments can therefore levy the inflation tax without incurring the political flak of more visible alternative taxes, and even where inflation visibly hurts, can often manage to shift the blame for inflation onto others (e.g., unions, big business, or foreign oil producers). Whether it involves tampering with coins or printing notes, levying this tax is also very easy:

> A Government can live for a long time ... by printing paper money. ... The method is condemned, but its efficacy, up to a point, must be admitted. A Government can live by this means when it can live by no other. It is the form of taxation which the public find hardest to evade and even the weakest government can enforce ... (Keynes, [1923] 1971, 37)

There are three different channels through which a central bank can use monetary policy to raise revenue. The first is where the central bank issues additional quantities of high-powered money which it uses to acquire real resources from the private sector. The resources obtained in this way can be regarded as a form of hidden taxation because they are obtained in return for irredeemable pieces of paper, and the amounts involved for moderate rates of inflation are probably under 1 percent of national income for the USA and UK, though perhaps higher for some continental European countries. The second channel is where inflation leads people to pay greater real income taxes because it pushes them into higher income tax brackets – the inflation creates 'fiscal drag' which leads taxpayers in a progressive income tax system to pay a greater proportion of their income in tax. The amount that can be obtained in this way depends on factors such as the progressivity of the income tax system, the degree to which the tax system is indexed against inflation and the inflation rate itself, and is therefore hard to quantify in general terms. The third and most important case is where inflation leads to the erosion of the real value of nominally denominated liabilities issued by the public sector, at interest rates that did not anticipate the inflation. The amounts to be obtained in this way are potentially very large. As an illustration, Friedman and Schwartz note that

> At the end of World War II, the funded (US) federal debt amounted to 6 percent more than a year's national income. By 1967 it was down to about 32 percent of national income despite repeated 'deficits' in the official federal budget. Since then it has risen as deficits have continued and increased, but even so only to about 36 percent currently. (Friedman and Schwartz, 1986, 57)

So can the use of the inflation tax be justified? The standard argument for it, due to Phelps (1973), is that governments in the real world have no access to theoretically ideal lump-sum taxes, so they need to rely on taxes that distort economic activity to finance their expenditures. Income taxes distort labour supply decisions, taxes on rates of return distort investment decisions, and so forth. If a government has to rely on such taxes, then it ought to do so by minimising the inefficiencies they create, and it does so when it follows the so-called Ramsey rule and ensures that the marginal efficiency losses from each form of taxation are equal. The 'optimal' taxation package would therefore include *some* use of the inflation tax, as well as some use of other distorting taxes, and so the 'optimal' inflation rate in such a world would almost certainly be positive.

There are some serious problems with this argument. Even if we accept the basic logic, there is considerable evidence that the efficiency losses from inflation are so high that they render inflation an inefficient form of taxation *even* in a world where other taxes are also costly to raise. To give an illustration of the costs involved, Tatom (1976, 19) estimated that the average collection cost of the (relatively small) revenue from a 5 percent inflation rate in 1975 would have been between 80 percent and 120 percent of the amount collected. The average collection costs of the income tax, by contrast, were about 3 percent of the amount collected. The higher *average* collection cost of the inflation tax is also matched by a higher *marginal* cost, and Tatom (1976, 20) estimates that the marginal cost per dollar of the inflation tax is 44 percent of the revenue collected. This estimate is sensitive to the maintained assumption that the interest elasticity of the demand for money was -0.15, and some might regard this elasticity figure as too close to zero, but if we make the demand for money more elastic and change the elasticity to -0.25, the marginal collection cost then rises even further to almost 84 percent (Garfinkel, 1989, 10, n. 27). The marginal collection cost is therefore upwards of 44 percent of the revenues obtained, and quite possibly double that figure. The marginal collection costs of other taxes are much lower, with Browning (1987) estimating that the welfare cost of labour taxes varies from 7.5 percent to 28.5 percent of the revenues raised. Even the top figure in his range is therefore still appreciably lower than the bottom figure in our range for the marginal collection costs of the inflation tax. Fischer (1981b) also found that the excess burden of inflation was several times that of labour taxes. Since these studies suggest that the marginal collection cost of inflation exceeds the marginal collection costs of alternative sources of revenue for all positive inflation rates, it follows that inflation is *never* an optimal tax to collect. As Tatom (1976, 22) concludes, having gone through various simulations to try to discover circumstances in which the inflation tax might be justified, *'efficient taxation [still] warrants price stability' even 'under the most extreme assumptions used ... to support inflationary finance'*.

There are also other reasons to question the Phelps argument. (1) Garfinkel (1989, 10) and Selody (1990a, 18) have pointed out that the Phelps view of inflation as a tax tends to overlook the impact of inflation on the tax collection machinery as a whole. The tax collection system was not designed to operate in an inflationary world, and functions very badly in the presence of inflation. As a result, inflation significantly raises the marginal collection costs of *other* taxes, and the true marginal collection cost of inflation is consequently considerably higher than the estimates discussed in the last paragraph might suggest. Lowering inflation would not only reduce the 'direct' welfare losses from the use of the inflation tax *per se*, but would also reduce the welfare losses from other forms of taxation as well. It is consequently bizarre, to say the least, to defend inflation on fiscal grounds. (2) The Phelps result comes from a model in which real balances are simply 'put' into the utility function and therefore treated as if they were a good like any other final good. However real balances are not desired for their own sake but for the sake of the convenience and other services they bring, and should therefore be considered as intermediate goods used up in the production of the 'final' goods and services the consumption of which is the final end of economic activity. Whether we treat 'money' as a final or an intermediate good often does not matter, but it matters in this case because the work of Diamond and Mirrlees (1971a, 1971b) suggests that intermediate goods should not be taxed even in a world where non-distorting taxes are not available. The Ramsey rule consequently applies only to final and not to intermediate goods. Applying the Diamond–Mirrlees result to inflation then tells us that inflation is an inefficient form of taxation quite regardless of any of the other problems already discussed (see also Kimbrough, 1986; Faig, 1988).

A final argument is that reliance on the inflation tax can also prove to be highly dangerous, and has often led to disaster. Apart from the obvious temptation to increase the inflation rate to eke out more resources from the private sector, there is a very real danger that a government that resorts to inflation can inadvertently wreck the rest of its tax collection machinery and find itself forced to inflate at an ever faster rate. Once it gets trapped on this treadmill, the almost inevitable result is hyperinflation and monetary collapse. What Keynes wrote of the German hyperinflation of the early 1920s also applies to many others,

Reliance on inflationary taxation, whilst extremely productive to the exchequer in its earliest stages ... gradually broke down the mark as a serviceable unit of account, one of the effects of which was to render unproductive the greater part of the rest of the revenue-collecting machinery – most taxes being necessarily assessed at some interval of time before they are collected. The failure of the rest of the revenue rendered the Treasury more and more dependent on inflation, until finally the use of legal-tender money had been so far abandoned by the public that even the inflationary tax ceased to be productive and the government was threatened by literal bankruptcy. (Keynes, [1923] 1971, 23)

Reliance on the inflation tax is thus not only very costly from a social point of view, but also dangerous and sometimes catastrophic.

The Time Inconsistency of Monetary Policy

Another important source of the suboptimality of central bank monetary policy relates to the limited inability of the central bank to pre-commit itself (see, e.g., Kydland and Prescott, 1977; Barro and Gordon, 1983a, 1983b). Suppose the monetary authorities face an objective function with inflation as one 'bad' and the deviation of unemployment above its natural rate as the other. They wish to optimise this objective function over time, but face an expectations-augmented Phillips curve, the expectations in which are formed rationally. We then get the situation described in Figure 16.1.

The *social optimum* is for the central bank to engineer a permanent zero rate of inflation that also keeps unemployment at its natural rate (i.e., point *A* in Figure 16.1), but *A* is not a *privately optimal* outcome for the central bank because

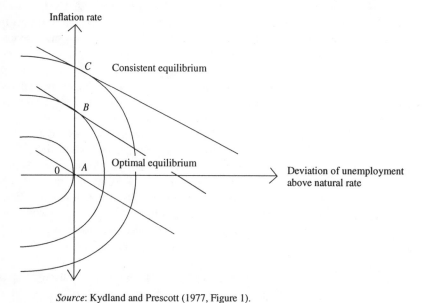

Source: Kydland and Prescott (1977, Figure 1).

Figure 16.1   The time inconsistency of discretionary monetary policy

it does not equalise the central bank's marginal costs and benefits of inflation. If the economy were at *A*, the central bank would want to move up the indifference curve running through *A* by generating a 'surprise' inflation. However, the public, being rational, would expect the central bank to do just that, and so *A* cannot be a consistent (i.e., long-run) equilibrium. Indeed, given the freedom of the central bank to do as it wishes, the only consistent equilibrium is that at which the marginal costs and benefits of inflation to the central bank are equal (i.e., point *C*). The central bank therefore delivers an outcome *C* that involves excessive inflation relative to the socially optimal outcome *A*.

The source of the failure of the central bank to deliver the optimal outcome is the central bank's own discretion. Imagine that the central bank promised to deliver the socially optimal outcome *A*, and the public believed it. The public would then expect zero inflation, but the central bank would no have no incentive to deliver it. It would therefore inflate, and the public's expectations would not be fulfilled. A rational public would therefore disbelieve the central bank's promise to deliver zero inflation, or, indeed, any promise to deliver an inflation rate between 0 and that given by point *C* in Figure 16.1. The central bank's problem is that it cannot pre-commit itself with the credibility needed to bring rational private-sector expectations of inflation down. Its ability to change its future policy – that is, its discretion – undermines its credibility, and in the absence of credibility it cannot deliver the socially optimal outcome.

A partial answer is for the central bank to try to build up a reputation for good behaviour. If a central bank promises low inflation and actually delivers it, it may become rational for the public to start believing it when it promises future low inflation. The central bank then acquires credibility, and inflationary expectations fall. Conversely, if the central bank misbehaves, it loses credibility and inflationary expectations rise again. The central bank thus builds up a reputation, which it values because it gives it credibility, and it offers this reputation as a hostage for its future good behaviour. We now get an intermediate outcome, *B*, which lies between the socially optimal outcome *A* and the earlier, fully discretionary, outcome *C*. The stronger the central bank's reputation, the greater its credibility, and the lower the public's inflationary expectations – a better reputation therefore pushes *B* towards the socially optimal outcome and away from the fully discretionary (or zero reputation) one. While a good reputation can push the outcome towards the socially optimal one, it cannot actually deliver that outcome because there will always be *some* chance that the central bank would decide to cash in on its reputation and 'cheat'. Building up a reputation for good behaviour is therefore a partial, but not a complete, response to the time-inconsistency problem.

Since reputations typically evolve slowly over time, the reputational equilibrium will also give rise to a cycle. Imagine that the economy starts off in a position where the central bank has a good reputation for delivering low inflation (i.e., *B* in Figure 16.1 is relatively close to *A*). Since low inflation is credible, people buy government debt at relatively low interest rates, they bargain for relatively low pay rises, and so on. They therefore act in ways that expose themselves to inflation and so give the central bank considerable temptation to engineer a surprise inflation to catch them out. At some point, the central bank gives way to this temptation and inflation rises. The central bank's good reputation depreciates, inflationary expectations rise, and B drifts up towards the zero-reputation outcome C. The central bank then finds itself in a high inflation equilibrium, but a time comes when it decides to get serious about inflation again and disinflate. Of course, by this time it has a poor reputation and few people believe it, but it persists and over time gradually acquires a renewed reputation for monetary toughness. Inflationary expectations therefore fall, and the central bank rebuilds its reputation. Eventually, its reputation is more or less fully restored, and the economy returns to the point where it started. The temptation to inflate slowly rises again, and at some point the central bank gives in to the temptation to inflate and the process starts again. We get a cycle, in which a central bank starts off with a good reputation, squanders it by going off on a monetary binge, then does its penance, gets inflation down again and restores its reputation, and then starts all over again. Interest rates, unemployment and other macroeconomic variables also cycle along with the inflation rate. Since the cycle is driven by the combination of the central bank's credibility problems and the central bank's unobservable concern (or lack of it) for its own reputation, private agents cannot easily predict the movements of these variables. The cycle is therefore damaging, not just because these variables move, but also, and more particularly, because they move in unpredictable and often erratic ways.

The historical evidence of monetary policy is certainly consistent with these predictions. Monetary policy is most countries has been a series of monetary binges followed by 'mornings after' in which a short-lived attempt would be made to bring inflation back down. As Timberlake summarised US monetary policy,

> money stocks and price level fluctuations behaved similarly to a remorseful but irresolute alcoholic and his bottle. A period of monetary drunkenness would be followed by a weeping and wailing and gnashing of teeth and a return to monetary austerity. Then rationalizations would appear: 'High interest rates are hurting the fragile economic recovery.' ... 'We need monetary relief from ____.' (Here, the reader can furnish his favorite scapegoat policy, such as 'monetarism'.) With a happy gasp, the bottle would appear again. (Timberlake, 1986, 753)

Unfortunately, nothing has yet been done to give us any reason to believe that the cycle has come to an end.

FINANCIAL AND MONETARY REFORM

The earlier chapters suggested that *laissez-faire* ought to work well by any reasonable standard if put into practice. Indeed, they also suggested that it *has* worked well whenever it has been tried in the past. Introduce an interventionist government into the picture, however, and things start to go badly wrong – the banking system becomes weaker and inefficient, and the currency becomes debauched. The banking system becomes weak because the government preys on it, or because it sets up a system of deposit insurance or lender of last resort that undermines the banks' own incentives to maintain their financial health; inflation arises because the government severs the link between the currency unit and gold, and then pressures the central bank to reduce interest rates or finance its own fiscal deficits. Many problems also arise because special interest groups use the power of the state to acquire or extend their privileges at the expense of society as a whole, and because the government or its agents insist on taking on responsibilities that they cannot discharge properly, if only because they lack the necessary knowledge and understanding of how the market economy operates. They place themselves in situations where they try to assess the 'right' level (and structure) of interest rates, the 'right' capital adequacy requirements to impose on the commercial banks, and the like. But *none* of us can properly answer such questions, and one of the most compelling attractions of *laissez-faire* is precisely that it relieves us of the need to do so. The interventionists have suppressed or interfered with the only means we have – the spontaneous market process – that could deliver the 'right' outcomes for us, and replaced it with a discretionary system that imposes on them a responsibility that they cannot possibly be expected to discharge.

Financial Reform

Protection of the Financial System From Government Predation

What is to be done? If markets work, and governments fail, we presumably want a package of reforms to roll back the government intervention and establish *laissez-faire*. Such a package would have two components – a programme of financial reform and a programme of monetary reform – and we need to consider each of these in turn. We shall therefore consider financial reform in this section, and monetary reform in the next. I would suggest that financial reform be guided by three main principles. The first of these would be the prohibition of government predation on the financial system. The reason for such a prohibition is fairly obvious – government predation has been one of the major causes of historical banking system weakness and, indeed, has often been an underlying cause of inflation as well. This principle implies the abolition and subsequent prohibition of all 'special' or discriminatory taxes on the financial system. Among other things, it implies the prohibition of official reserve requirements; the prohibition of requirements that financial institutions buy specified quantities of government debt, or pay over the odds for any government debt they buy; the prohibition of any taxation rules that subsidise or otherwise 'artificially' encourage the market for government debt; and the prohibition of foreign exchange restrictions.

Financial Liberalisation

The second plank would be a programme of thorough-going financial liberalisation. The more liberal the legal framework is, the greater the number of mutually beneficial trades that can take place, and the better off people will generally be. The essential principle should be that trade in financial services operate under a liberal (i.e., permissive) general commercial law, and not be subject to any restrictions designed to bring about specific results (e.g., redistributions from one group to another) in the financial services area. The role of the law should be a purely enabling one – to enable trades to take place by enforcing all contracts, provided only that the parties involved are deemed to be competent and to have entered into them of their own free will – and there should be no attempt to mandate or prescribe what particular contracts people should make. A package of financial liberalisation measures would include:

- The repeal of discriminatory legal tender laws to allow courts to enforce contracts made in any medium or unit of account the parties involved freely choose. The law should not be used to make people use a particular unit of account (e.g., to promote the demand for the 'national' currency), or to abrogate contracts for political reasons (e.g., as happened with the notorious 'legal tender' cases in the US).

- The amendment of existing laws to eliminate, or at least reduce, discrimination between different liability arrangements. The purpose of the law should be to enable, not to mandate, and the liability arrangement that might be suitable in one situation could be quite unsuitable in another (see Chapter 2 above). The law should therefore make it easier for parties to contracts to choose the liability arrangement that most suits them.

- The abolition of restrictions on the liabilities that financial institutions can issue and the assets they can hold. Existing restrictions against the issue of private bank notes would be abolished, and financial institutions would be allowed to issue whatever forms of deposits they can persuade the public to hold. Existing restrictions on asset-holdings would also be abolished. Such restrictions would include restrictions that limit banks' real estate lending, as well as restrictions that limit the involvement of thrifts in the USA and building societies in the UK in 'regular' bank lending activities. They would also include market-sharing restrictions, of which the most obvious are Glass–Steagall-type restrictions that artificially divide banking into 'investment' and 'commercial' sectors and then prohibit banks in one sector from entering the other. The principle of not restricting institutions' liability and asset-holding decisions also implies the abolition of amalgamation restrictions such as those in the USA against branch-banking, as well as the abolition of the restrictions that still exist in many countries against the entry of foreign banks into domestic banking markets.

- The abolition of all 'official' regulations on financial institutions. Such measures would include, among others, the abolition of reserve requirements, capital adequacy requirements, and interest rate ceilings. Banks would learn from experience the reserve and capital ratios to observe, the interest rates to pay and charge, and so on.

The Abolition of Deposit Insurance and the Lender of Last Resort

The third plank in the financial reform package would be to get rid of the artificially distorted incentives created by compulsory deposit insurance and the existence of a central bank lender of last resort function. However, it is vital that this third plank in the reform package be carried out carefully. Once they have been abolished, bank creditors would become much more demanding of their banks because they would appreciate that their funds would be at risk. They would therefore demand that banks maintain higher capital standards and take fewer risks, but banks cannot provide higher safety standards overnight. If deposit insurance were abolished with inadequate warning, there is therefore a danger that banks might lose depositors' confidence and face runs they did not have the resources to withstand. The abolition of deposit insurance therefore needs to be pre-announced, to give banks time to prepare themselves for the post-deposit insurance world. The position of the reformer is comparable to that of a circus manager who decides that his circus is no longer drawing crowds because working with a safety net has caused his acrobats to lose their skill. He decides that they must dispense with the safety net and gives them a firm date in the future when it will be withdrawn. The net will remain in the meantime, and the acrobats have to decide what to do. Those who wish can leave, and those who stay had better get some practice in. If he has any sense, the manager will give his acrobats sufficient notice to ensure that they will have the skill to survive when the day comes to remove the net, but if he fails to give them that warning he invites disaster in the form of the acrobats walking out on him or someone having an accident for which he must take responsibility. The moral is that it is not enough to get the long-run incentives right; we must get the adjustment process right as well. The same to some extent also goes for the abolition of the lender of last resort. If banks cannot count on last resort loans from a central bank, they had better build up their credit-worthiness to be able to obtain any loans they need on the market, and building up credit-worthiness will take some time. The best policy is to announce that the support will be withdrawn, but give banks enough time to prepare themselves to stand on their own.

Setting dates for these reforms would concentrate minds in the financial services industry and set in motion a sequence of events that would restore the industry to health. Those involved would have to anticipate what conditions would be like once deposit insurance had been eliminated, and then decide whether or not they wished to operate under those conditions. The healthier banks would decide to make a go of it, and set about building up their capital, reappraising lending policies, and so on. However, if a bank was in sufficiently bad shape, its managers would decide that it would not be worthwhile to invest in the measures that would be required to make it competitive when the guarantee is lifted. The managers of such a bank would therefore make no effort to restore confidence, and their lack of any effort to restore their bank's financial health would soon become obvious. Depositors would realise that they stand to lose their deposits if they do not withdraw them by the time the guarantee is lifted, so they would demand redemption while their deposits are still guaranteed. Similarly, the bank's loan customers would realise that they had better find alternative sources of funds. The upshot is that the weaker banks would already be out of business by the time the guarantee was lifted. The announcement of the reform package would thus lead the banks to divide themselves into two groups – the strong banks that would build themselves up, and the no-hopers that would go into terminal decline. The difference between the two would become increasingly stark – the strong banks getting stronger, and the weaker ones getting even weaker – and when the date finally arrives for the guarantee to be lifted, the no-hopers would already be out of business and the strong banks ought to be fit enough to survive on their own.

Reforming the Monetary Standard

Freezing the Monetary Base?

We turn next to the issue of the monetary standard. We need a monetary standard that would maximise price-level stability, but also be compatible with free banking. One suggested option would be to freeze the monetary base (e.g., Selgin, 1988a, 1994a). Responsibility for maintaining the supply of base money could be transferred to some body – presumably, some residual body to be left after the abolition of the central bank – and commercial banks would be allowed to issue whatever liabilities they wanted convertible into units of 'base money'. However, a serious problem with this option is that it would almost certainly lead to inflation, and possibly very high inflation. Given that the supply of base money would be fixed, its value (and, hence, the price level) would be determined by the demand for base money, but that demand is almost certain to fall and lead to a rising price level. The demand for base money consists of the demand for cash for small-valued transactions, on the one hand, and the demand for reserves by financial institutions, on the other. For reasons explained already in Chapter 10, the public demand for cash is likely to fall as technology advances, and for reasons explained elsewhere, banks under *laissez-faire* would have relatively little reason to demand base money except for purposes of maintaining till money, and even that demand is likely to fall over time. The overall demand for base money is therefore likely to fall, and in the process push up the price level. Freezing the monetary base is not a good way to try to establish price stability.

To make matters worse, the price level would also be very uncertain. Since the supply of base money would fixed, the price level would only be as certain as the future demand for base money, and that demand would be extremely difficult to predict. The demand for base money appears to be less well understood than the demand for other monetary aggregates – it has been less well- researched, and monetary economists have less of a 'feel' for the appropriate elasticities. The demand for base money in the past has also been particularly vulnerable to regulatory and technological changes, and such changes make it difficult to estimate an 'underlying' stable demand function, even assuming one exists. Trying to predict the demand for base money after significant changes in the regulatory/technological environment would be even more difficult. Freezing the monetary base would therefore produce a highly unstable price level, and also one that would become even more uncertain the further ahead we tried to predict it.

Reconverting the Currency

The alternative would be to make the currency convertible again. The reader will recall from Chapters 13 and 14 that there are a number of convertible monetary standards to choose from, but given that we wish to make the value of the currency as stable as possible, the most attractive option would appear to be a broad-basket approach such as the quasi-futures contract (QFC) scheme suggested in Chapter 14. Initially, the scheme could be set up by the central bank, which could then be abolished once it was up and running. To recapitulate briefly, the basic idea would be for the central bank to issue a new kind of financial instrument – the QFC – and be legally committed to pegging the price of this instrument at periodic intervals. This new instrument would be similar though not identical to a price-index futures contract, and would promise the holder a payment on maturity that was contingent on the 'announced' value of a price index on that date. The expected price level would then be determined by a market equilibrium condition, and arbitrage operations would correct deviations of the expected price level from its equilibrium value. The expected value of the price level should therefore be stable, and there should be relatively little 'slippage' between expected prices and the subsequently realised actual price level. The QFC scheme could therefore deliver a reasonably stable price level without any need for the central bank to exercise any 'discretion'.[1]

Since the QFC scheme relies so much on the chosen price index, it is also important to establish adequate safeguards to prevent 'tampering' with the index. Once the scheme is operational, the reported values of the price index would become more important than they are now because people trading in QFCs would effectively be betting on the values the price index would take. Those who had bought QFCs would have bet on the relevant price index announcement taking a relatively high value, and those who have sold them would have bet on it taking a relatively low value. There is therefore a danger they might want to interfere in the process by which the index is produced to influence the outcome in their favour. Perhaps the best way to protect the integrity of the price-index process, at least in the early years, would be for legislation to specify the broad criteria that the index should meet. The responsibility for compiling the index could then be handed over to a commission which would adopt the legislated criteria as their terms of reference and take operational responsibility for the process by which the index is produced. The legislation should also specify membership criteria and ensure that the rights to nominate members are suitably dispersed. Members might be appointed, for example, by relevant professional associations. But the key safeguard is to make the commission's terms of reference sufficiently clearcut that outsiders could assess whether the commission had been faithful to them. Professional pride and the desire to pre-empt or win any legal challenge should then ensure that the commission remains true to its mandate.

Legislation to Abolish the Central Bank

Once the new monetary system is up and running, the issue of currency could be transferred entirely to commercial financial institutions and the central bank could be abolished. It cannot be stressed too strongly that the new system would be an automatic one with no need to rely on – and, indeed, no place for – central bank discretion. Perhaps the easiest transition arrangement might be to have the large commercial banks start to issue both currency and QFCs side by side with the central bank. The commercial banks could thereby acquire some experience of issuing currency and operating the new monetary standard while the central bank was still fulfilling those roles as well. The central bank's currency could then be gradually withdrawn from circulation and its issues of QFCs allowed to mature without replacement. Finally, the management of the national debt and the provision of financial and monetary statistics could be privatised, or at least contracted out to the private sector, the government could close its account with the central bank, the latter's remaining assets could be sold off and the proceeds distributed to its shareholders (i.e., the government in the UK, and Federal Reserve member-banks in the USA), and the central bank itself could be abolished.

The Need to Erect Barriers Against Future Government Intervention

The last remaining task – but a vitally important one – would be to protect financial and monetary institutions against future government attempts to interfere with them. There is of course no way we can design a system that is guaranteed to be interference-proof for ever, but we can at least try to make future intervention as difficult as possible for the would-be interventionist. In doing so, perhaps the most important point to keep in mind is that government intervention has an innate tendency to grow. As we have seen, the government usually starts off with some recognised but limited function; a problem arises, and the 'solution' is to extend the government's function to sort the problem out; this process repeats itself again and again, and the eventual result is a much larger role for the government than anyone initially intended. The lesson to draw is that we must not concede the thin end of the wedge – the separation of the financial/monetary system from the state must be absolute, and the government must be permitted no justification whatever for interfering in that system. Here again American history is instructive. The only monetary powers the constitution gave the federal government were the power to specify the precious metal content of the dollar and the power to authorise coinage. Yet since then the federal government has chartered its own banks, regulated the banking system, issued its own inconvertible currency, levied forced loans from the banks, rewritten legal tender laws, expropriated private holdings of gold and demonetised both the precious metals. The federal government has taken the very limited monetary power granted it by the constitution and turned it into a monetary despotism. The solution, therefore, is to eliminate altogether the limited monetary powers that the constitution grants the federal government. What is required is a constitutional amendment that provides for total separation between government and the financial/monetary system.

The defenders of the *status quo* will of course deride such a suggestion as politically unrealistic. But so what? If our research leads us to the conclusion that financial *laissez-faire* is superior to any alternative, as I believe it does, then those of us who accept that conclusion are compelled to recommend it regardless of whether it is politically fashionable or not. We should not tailor the conclusions of our analysis to suit those who want answers acceptable to some transient conventional 'wisdom' that is going to change anyway. Economists should not accept the role of courtiers, only willing to tell those in power what they want to hear. If we as economists have anything to offer those who would try to reform our existing institutions, it is to tell them which options are justifiable and, perhaps more importantly, which options are *not* justifiable, as far as is possible within the constraints of our subject. It is up to them whether they listen or not, but we should not change our answers just because they don't like them. We should also try to reach the broader public and, at the very least, deprive the politicians of convenient excuses, until such time, if ever, as they show any willingness to listen. The alternative – to pander to politicians by trying to make our advice 'convenient' to them – is to negate our own comparative advantage (i.e., economics) and ultimately to lower ourselves to the level of political propagandists and, indeed, to the level of the politicians themselves.

Notes

1 INTRODUCTION

1. There is already a considerable literature on free banking, with books on the subject by Hayek (1978), L. H. White (1984a, 1989), Selgin (1988), Dowd (1988a, 1989, 1993a), Glasner (1989a), Salsman (1990), Horwitz (1992), and Sechrest (1993). There are also many books that discuss free banking (e.g., Timberlake, 1991, 1993; Cowen and Kroszner, 1994) as well as numerous recent journal articles on it. In addition, there is also a very large earlier literature on the subject (e.g., Wesslau, 1887; Hake and Wesslau, 1890; Meulen, 1934; Smith, 1936; and many others).

2. The use of conjectural history to examine financial and monetary issues has a long pedigree. Menger (1892) made effective use of it, and so did Karl Marx before him. A conjectural history was also used by Meulen (1934), and they have been used more recently by Selgin and White (1987), Selgin (1988a), Dowd (1988b, 1989), Glasner (1989a), Horwitz (1992), Sechrest (1993) and various others.

3. There are many other examples one could choose. Amongst these are medieval Celtic Ireland (Peden, 1977), Viking Iceland (Miller, 1990), and the nineteenth-century American West (Anderson and Hill, 1979). The reader might also look at Rothbard's (1978) insightful overview of some of these and other historical anarchies.

4. The theory of private legal systems is discussed, among other places, in D. Friedman (1978), Rothbard (1978), the Tannehills (1970) and Wooldridge (1970). As is well-known, Nozick (1974) attacked the viability of free-market law and order by claiming that the anarchy would collapse into an ultra-minimal state, but Nozick's position has itself come under devastating attack from libertarian anarchists whose work suggests that anarchy is indeed stable (e.g., Childs, 1977). I find their arguments very persuasive, but all that matters for my purpose here is that the state keeps 'out of the way'. Readers who have difficulty with libertarian anarchism can therefore assume there is a state if they wish, but only one that adopts a strictly *laissez-faire* approach towards the financial system.

5. There are of course many specialised financial institutions, as well as 'regular' banks and mutual funds, and some of these specialised institutions (e.g., pension funds and insurance companies) play important roles in the financial system. However, I cannot discuss these institutions here, and can only suggest that readers interested in these institutions look at the relevant specialist literature.

2 BILATERAL FINANCIAL CONTRACTS

1. To the extent that this earlier literature *did* attempt to explain why particular contract forms are used, it argued that debt was used because of its tax advantages over equity, but there had to be some scope for equity because exclusive reliance on debt would involve excessively high expected bankruptcy costs. However this sort of explanation is very limited: it does not explain why debt was used before it received its modern tax advantages, and debt was issued hundreds of years before income and corporation taxes; it does not explain why debt and equity have the

particular features they have; it not explain why there should be bankruptcy costs in the first place; and recent work suggests that it might not be empirically valid anyway (e.g., MacKie-Mason, 1990). We should therefore begin by explaining contract structure in the absence of taxation, and we can always consider taxation at a later stage if we wished to examine its effects (e.g., as in Gertler and Hubbard, 1993).

2. If the constraint that verification is costly is to 'bite', there must be some limit to A's exposure to pecuniary or non-pecuniary penalties, as well as to P's wealth. If A can expose himself to unlimited penalties, verification costs can be reduced to an arbitrarily low level by making verification stochastic, with a low probability of verification being matched by ferocious penalties if A is found out to be lying. If the penalties and verification costs are suitably chosen, A can be 'trusted' to be telling the truth when he claims that output is low because he has no incentive to lie. The higher the penalty, the lower the required probability of verification, and the lower are verification costs. In the limit verification costs go to zero and the costliness of verification is irrelevant. However, if A's liability is limited, a comparable outcome can also be achieved if P's wealth is unlimited. Instead of imposing ferocious penalties on A if he is verified and found to be lying, P offers him fabulous rewards if he is verified and found to be telling the truth. As the reward rises, the probability of verification required to induce him to tell the truth falls, so verification costs can be reduced to a level arbitrarily close to zero provided that P has sufficient wealth to make his promised rewards credible (see also Guesnerie, 1992, 306–307).

3. These CSV models should not be confused with the superficially similar 'plunder' models of Border and Sobel (1987) and Mookherjee and Png (1989) which arrive at the conclusion that certain forms of non-debt contracts are optimal. These models analyse a fundamentally different problem – the problem faced by brigands and tax collectors in the process of extracting wealth from their unwilling victims – while we are concerned here with situations where people deal with each other by mutual choice.

4. Moral hazard refers to the tendency of insurance to encourage behaviour on the agent's part that produces the event(s) against which the agent is insured. For example, if an agent has fire insurance, he might behave in a way that makes a fire more likely. In this literature, our main focus is the agent's *choice of effort*, but there can also arise moral hazard over the agent's *choice of project*, where the latter (or strictly speaking, some important feature of it) might be unobservable. This latter type of moral hazard is formally similar to adverse selection, so we shall discuss it in the context of adverse selection in the next sub-section.

5. It is sometimes claimed in the literature that credit rationing can also occur in adverse selection cases where investment projects differ in their degrees of riskiness in ways that the lender cannot observe (e.g., Jaffee and Russell, 1976; Keeton, 1979; Stiglitz and Weiss, 1981). The argument is that higher interest makes marginal profits unworthwhile and, since the borrower's expected profit rises with the riskiness of the project, leads the low-risk projects to be displaced from the pool of investment projects the lender faces. The lender might therefore prefer to keep interest low and ration credit to prevent the expected losses he would face if he raised interest and let the investment pool deteriorate. However, the problem with this line of reasoning is that the optimal contract in these circumstances is actually equity, not debt (see, e.g., Hart, 1986; de Meza and Webb, 1987). The issue of credit rationing does not arise because a loan is a form of debt and there are no loans to ration.

6. The basic idea behind Myers under-investment can be seen through a simple example. Taking all figures to be in net-present-value terms for simplicity, suppose

a firm has previously issued debt with a face value of $20 to fund an investment project, and it is now apparent that the project will succeed with probability one-half and yield a return of $20 that enables the firm (just) to pay its debt, and that it will fail with probability one-half and yield a return of nothing. (Note, therefore, that the value of the firm to its shareholders is zero.) If the firm has no assets, the expected value of the firm's debt is $10 and the creditors have suffered an expected loss of $10 also. Now suppose that an additional investment opportunity becomes available that requires an input of $10 from the shareholders but yields a return of $15. The new investment is clearly socially worthwhile because it converts $10 into $15, but shareholders will still refuse to fund it because too many of the gains go to existing creditors. If they proceed with it, the total expected shareholder return will consist of $15 (i.e., the return on the new project) plus one-half times $20 (i.e., the expected return on the old project) minus $20 (i.e., the full repayment of the old $10 debt, plus the additional $10 required from the shareholders), or $5. The shareholders therefore expect to *lose* $5 on the additional investment. The creditors however get repaid their full $20, instead of their currently expected payment of $10, and make an expected gain of $10. The shareholders thus pass up a socially worthwhile investment opportunity, because too many of the expected gains go to debtholders.

7.   The legal system therefore has a relatively straightforward task: to ensure that contracts are honoured, period. By contrast, contemporary bankruptcy law often forces courts have to make all sorts of 'judgmental' [sic] decisions: judges have to assess what course of action would be in the best interests of the different parties, how much to 'trust' management that claims it can reorganise a firm successfully, and so on. The need to make such decisions imposes severe burdens on those who have to make them, creates incentives for interested parties to invest resources trying to influence those 'judgmental' decisions, and the process involved can be very time-consuming (especially, for example, if a dissatisfied party appeals a decision). The legal procedure suggested here is far more efficient: the court merely needs to establish facts and then pass a more or less automatic (and presumably reasonably rapid) judgement.

8.   The optimal liability regime can also depend other factors such as the extent of information asymmetry between the parties involved. Where such asymmetries are severe, extended liability might be preferable where the shareholders find it more profitable to bear the majority of the monitoring costs themselves than to attempt to provide the information necessary for others to monitor for them and compensate them for doing so (Evans and Quigley, 1992, 1–2; see also Winton, 1993). However, should changes in available information and monitoring technologies reduce information costs, then limited liability might replace extended liability as the most appropriate liability arrangement. The optimal liability arrangement may therefore vary from one case to another, and may also vary over time in any given case.

9.   A number of models assume that both A and P are risk-averse, but making P risk-averse complicates the optimisation problem and means that the optimal contract between the two parties cannot be analysed independently of the other contracts in which P may be involved. P's risk-aversion therefore severely erodes the tractability of the analysis, and, if P has a diversified portfolio, it will often be the case that we can treat P as if he were approximately risk-averse anyway. An alternative is to assume that P is risk-averse and A is risk- neutral, but this approach is open to the objections just noted that making P risk-averse is analytically difficult and (often) of limited usefulness; in addition, if one or other is to be risk-averse, it usually makes more sense to assume that the agent is risk-averse rather than the principal, if only because the argument that diversification leads to 'as if' risk-neutrality is more plausibly applied to the lender than the borrower.

3 CAPITAL STRUCTURE AND CORPORATE FINANCIAL POLICY

1. There are of course huge literatures on both corporate governance and the market for corporate control, and I cannot possibly do justice to them here. The text therefore restricts itself to providing an outline of some of the main issues, and the reader who wishes to pursue them in more detail can do so elsewhere. Apart from pursing the studies cited in the text, the reader interested in following up some of these issues more extensively might look at Campbell (1990) and the *Accounting and Business Research* special issue on corporate governance published in January 1993.

2. Whether it *actually* does promote corporate efficiency is controversial, however, and a number of economists, not to mention others, have argued that there is a tendency for too many mergers to take place. For example, Ravenscraft and Scherer (1987) conclude from their empirical work that too many mergers take place because of managerial empire-building. On the other hand, Jensen nonetheless feels able to state, quite categorically, that "the evidence from dozens of studies by financial economists is almost universal in its endorsement of the value-creating nature of control transactions and their associated organizational innovations" (Jensen, 1992, 664).

3. In theory, some anti-takeover devices can increase shareholder wealth if they force the bidding firm to pay more for the firm's shares without unduly discouraging it from making the bid in the first place (see, e.g., Linn and McConnell, 1983). This argument could apply, say, to poison pill devices but clearly not to golden handshakes (or to super-majority provisions, as indicated by the Harris and Raviv (1989) model discussed later in the text). However the evidence on poison pill defences actually suggests that a firm's share value typically falls when it adopts poison pill provisions, and typically rises when plans to adopt such provisions are dropped (see Malatesta and Walkling, 1988; Ryngaert, 1988). This evidence therefore suggests that these devices are normally used to entrench management rather than promote the interests of the target shareholders.

4. The prediction that widely-held firms should have one-share, one-vote does not appear to be empirically rejected. Of the many thousands of firms traded on the American Stock Exchange examined by DeAngelo and DeAngelo (1985, 39), only 78 had multiple classes of votes, and even these firms were typically ones in which the management had a controlling interest. There was therefore no danger of takeover and market-for-corporate-control considerations were largely inoperative.

5. This result is however sensitive to the rival's private control benefits. If the rival has greater private control benefits than the incumbent, the rival might be able to oust a superior incumbent if the latter has no votes. The latter might therefore wish to retain some votes to protect himself against such an outcome. There is consequently a trade-off between the desire to have the incumbent maximise his vulnerability to a superior rival, which implies he should hold no votes, and the desire to protect him against an inferior rival who has greater private control benefits, which implies that he should hold some votes. See Harris and Raviv (1989, 267–272).

6. Dann and DeAngelo (1988, 87) indicate that these defensive restructurings are typically quite large, and involve either the consolidation of voting power in hands friendly to the incumbent or the creation of specific barriers to the rival taking over. Their evidence indicates that shareholder wealth fell on average by a statistically significant 2–3 percent on the announcement of such plans. The fact that shareholders were harmed rather than benefited by such plans suggests that their primary purpose is to entrench incumbent management rather than extract higher

prices from the would-be acquirer, and this interpretation of the evidence is supported by Dann and DeAngelo's observation that management normally avoid putting defensive restructuring plans to a shareholder vote.

7.   Most of these studies start by dividing firms into two samples, those believed on *a priori* grounds to be seriously cash constrained, and believed not to be. These classifications are made using a variety of different criteria (e.g., access to bond markets (Whited, 1992); whether firms have large (and therefore unrecoverable) sunk costs (Worthington, 1992); whether firms are paying dividends, on the assumption that cash-constrained firms would not; or whether they belong to a large industrial group or not (in Hoshi, Kashyap and Scharfstein's, 1990, 1991) Japanese studies). They then estimate investment equations – either Euler equations or Q equations – which enable one to assess 'unconstrained' investment demand and test whether the addition of a cash flow variable significantly adds to explanatory power. A positive and significant result is then interpreted as evidence that cash flow is a serious constraint, and one would expect that constraint to be binding for firms in the first group but not necessarily those in the second group. They find that smaller firms are significantly cash-constrained and larger firms are generally not. Two potential problems with this approach are that cash flow might only appear to be a constraint because the investment demand variable is inappropriately proxied (so the cash flow variable picks up some investment demand) or because cash flow and investment opportunities might correlated, but some papers (e.g., Gilchrist 1990; Devereux and Schiantarelli (1990) deal with these problems quite convincingly and still conclude that cash flow constraints are binding for smaller firms. The finding that smaller firms are significantly cash-constrained is thus very robust.

8.   The idea that financial conditions matter and can cause (or aggravate) fluctuations in real economic activity is an old one. It was already widely accepted in the early twentieth century and was prominent in the work of such economists as Ralph Hawtrey and particularly Irving Fisher (Fisher, 1933) before being overshadowed by the Keynesian revolution. As Gertler (1988, 562–563) points out, the Keynesian theory of liquidity preference encouraged the subsequent literature to ignore the link between the financial system and the real economy, and focused instead on the link between bank debt – usually identified as 'money' – and the economy. The emphasis on 'money' was challenged by Gurley and Shaw (1960) who stressed the importance of bank lending and the economy's financial capacity. The Gurley-Shaw ideas were picked up in some literature (e.g., Patinkin, 1961; Tobin and Brainard, 1963)), but were subsequently submerged by the renewed emphasis on 'money' that came from the historical work of Friedman and Schwartz and the later empirical literature (e.g., Sims (1972), Barro (1977, 1979), and many other studies) on the real effects of monetary variables (see, e.g., Gertler, 1988, 565–566).

9.   Bernanke and Gertler (1990, 106–9) suggest that an outside agency with redistributive powers can improve on the anarchic outcome if it can redistribute wealth from 'non-entrepreneurs' to 'entrepreneurs'. The idea is that redistribution lowers agency costs by increasing entrepreneurs' net worth, and they claim that the "transfer policy is likely to be beneficial for a wide variety of specifications of the agency problem [because] the proposition that increased borrower net worth reduces agency costs, although not true in literally every case, is quite general" (1990, 106). They then cite cases where they claim such policies have worked (e.g., Roosevelt's financial rehabilitation policies during the New Deal, and more recent bailouts). One might counter that strictly speaking the model deals with *ex ante* redistributions to those who can reliably be classified as 'entrepreneurs', and it says nothing about *ex post* bailouts to businesses that have failed, or are about to. If the government starts to subsidise 'entrepreneurs', however, it will also encourage

other agents to pose as 'entrepreneurs' to get the subsidy and avoid being taxed, and I do not seriously believe that the types can be reliably distinguished in practice. But even if they could, and Bernanke and Gertler reworked their results so that agents took the redistribution regime into account when solving their optimisation problems, the Bernanke-Gertler case for redistribution is still very weak. Redistribution is not Pareto-superior in their model, and their argument for redistribution really boils down to an assertion that 'society' would be better off if some measure of aggregate agency costs were be lowered, even though lowering these costs would make some agents worse off and may not even be feasible anyway. One might just as well argue in favour of any (not necessarily feasible) redistributive policy that reduces total measured deadweight losses, regardless of its impact on individuals' welfare. As for the historical examples they cited, one could plausibly argue that these policies did more harm than good because of the moral hazard created by agents' anticipation of them (i.e., the Roosevelt financial policies), or because of the effect they had in creating moral hazard problems later on (e.g., the Penn Square and Continental Illinois bailouts).

10. Shocks give rise to multiplier effects in this type of model because of information-related externalities operating through equity levels and collateral constraints (Greenwald and Stiglitz, 1988a, 151). If a producer faces an unexpected decrease in demand, he reduces his demands for inputs and increases the probability of bankruptcy of his suppliers. Those who have extended credit to his suppliers then face a greater expected probability of bankruptcy themselves. Everyone reduces their own demands and other producers make fewer sales, and so on.

11. This result is all the more significant in that the obvious alternative model of the cycle, the real business cycle (or stochastic growth) model, implies that investment demand should be less rather than more sensitive than the demand for consumer goods. The reason is that if firms are risk-neutral and have rational expectations, then even firms facing constraints should undertake some counter-cyclical investment because installation costs would be lower and future output rises require long lead times. The difficulty for these models is aggravated by the fact that the investment responses seem greatest in sectors where prices are more flexible (e.g., construction), so it is hard to bail out the real-business-cycle model by attributing observed cyclical investment behaviour to sticky prices. See also Greenwald and Stiglitz (1993, 103–104).

12. Of course, the question arises why workers don't accept interim jobs elsewhere, but Greenwald and Stiglitz suggest a variety of factors that might explain this behaviour. If

> layoffs are recognizably temporary, then training considerations may militate against temporary employment [elsewhere] ... since alternative employers may not be able to recoup hiring and training costs in the time available. At the same time, employment in similar jobs to those from which workers have been laid off may not be available since 'shocks' which deplete the equity stock of one firm in an industry are likely to affect other firms in a similar way. Finally, informational imperfections in the labor market may make it costly for workers to accept temporary jobs. First, acceptance of an alternative job ... may be taken as evidence that the worker himself has doubts about his abilities and future prospects with his original employer. ... Second, if temporary employers observe a worker's ability and are willing to 'allow' him to return to his original employers when recalled from being laid off, this may in itself constitute a negative signal about the worker's ability. And, if at some future time, the worker seeks to leave his original employer, this negative signal may reduce the value of the alternative jobs available. (Greenwald and Stiglitz, 1987, 450)

13. Finally, this approach can also explain the 'stylised fact' that banks in a recession typically find themselves awash with loanable funds which they cannot easily lend (Greenwald and Stiglitz, 1988a, 124). It is not so much that banks are turning away borrowers away, but that individuals and firms cannot (or will not) borrow on the term offered by banks. The problem is that potential borrowers face more severe collateral constraints in a recession, and therefore find it harder to qualify for loans even if banks' collateral demands remained the same. The problem is aggravated further if the banks raise their collateral demands, as they might do, in response to greater risk or uncertainty.

4   WHY FINANCIAL INTERMEDIARIES EXIST

1. These implied verification costs derive from an underlying adverse selection problem where a prospective purchaser cannot easily distinguish between 'good' and 'bad' assets, and resources then have to be expended to reassure him that the asset is 'good'. Analytically, verification costs are similar in some respects to search costs, but they differ in terms of the transferability of the information obtained (Chant, 1987, 20). The results of a search can be easily and credibly transferred, while the results of a verification (usually) cannot. Verification costs differ from monitoring costs, on the other hand, in that verification costs are borne after output has taken place while monitoring takes place before and during the production process. They also differ in that verification involves checking output, while monitoring involves checking actions. The role of verification costs in motivating financial intermediation is discussed by Leland and Pyle (1977), Campbell and Kracaw (1980), Boyd and Prescott (1986), Williamson (1986), Chant (1987) and Lacker and Weinberg (1989).

6   MUTUAL-FUND INTERMEDIARIES

1. Whether they actually do perform better is unclear. Jensen (1968) suggested that the earnings of actively managed mutual funds, net of expenses, were dominated by a strategy of buying and holding an appropriate indexed security. Similarly, Davidson (1992, 731) reported that only 2 out of 102 'general' unit trusts in the UK were able to outperform the FT100 index in the year from 15 February 1990, while the average performance was substantially less. However, some other studies have come to different conclusions. For example, Mains (1977) challenged the Jensen study on the grounds that it underestimated rates of return and overestimated risk, and when he corrected for these factors, found that 80 percent of the funds in the sample were able to beat the market well enough to cover their expenses. See also Copeland and Weston (1989, 383–390).

2. In practice, of course, if there are fixed costs to buying and selling assets, the fund might keep a buffer fund of ready cash or some other appropriate redemption medium, and add or subtract from that fund as members of the public demanded or sold shares. When the size of the buffer reached critical values, the fund would then go to capital markets and buy or sell shares as the changing demand required. The process described in the text is therefore not a strictly accurate representation of what the fund actually does, but it does illustrate the principles involved.

3. At first sight, UK building societies would appear to be an exception. A building society issues only the one kind of liability (and is therefore a form of mutual fund as defined here), but one might argue that their shares are similar to the deposits

held at regular banks (and therefore classify as debt, or at least as debt-like). How can building societies issue liabilities similar to debt and yet also hold assets whose values are subject to considerable fluctuation? A partial answer is that building societies maintain large internal reserves that serve a similar cushioning function as the equity of a bank, but the value of these reserves is not reflected in the price of building society shares. Any losses are absorbed by these reserves, and the intermediary can continue to buy and sell its liabilities at a stable price. The building society therefore has a positive net worth and operates as if it were a bank. But this explanation is only partial because we do not know why the prices of building society shares fail to rise to a level corresponding to the value of *all* assets. Why more outsiders haven't bought up controlling interests in building societies to get their hands on these unpriced reserves is an interesting issue that deserves further study.

4. A somewhat different stability issue is how open-end funds would provide protection for risk-averse investors. Enthusiasts of mutual funds argue that fund managers can choose from among a wide variety of assets (including various forms of hedging) to provide investors with their desired mix of risk and expected return. Investors who were more risk-averse could settle for less risk and a lower expected return, and those who were less averse to risk could go for higher expected returns at more risk. Mutual funds therefore enable investors to diversify their risks, and to select from among investments with a wide variety of characteristics. Yet I would still insist that the ability of open-end funds to satisfy investors is seriously limited: (1) An open-end fund cannot accommodate investors who wish to hold investments with predetermined values (i.e., debt), and who are willing to pay others to bear risks to enable them to do so, whereas banks can (and do) accommodate these investors. (2) Since such a fund will have to avoid imperfectly marketable assets, its range of portfolios is restricted, and it may not be able to offer a portfolio that a bank could offer. For example, if the expected return on imperfectly marketable assets is very high and the expected returns on marketable assets very low, then a mutual fund could only offer portfolios with low expected returns, whereas a bank could offer portfolios with much higher ones.

5. The historical evidence also strongly supports the claim that people prefer debt-based financial instruments, and therefore prefer banks to mutual funds. The early history of deposit-banking in Mediterranean Europe reveals that the liabilities of these intermediaries were considered as fixed-value debts (see, e.g., Usher, 1943, 11) and not as mutual fund shares. Even though some banks issued deposits that were treated as equity claims, this practice appears to have been a device to overcome Church and state restrictions against the payment of interest on debt (see also Wicker, 1988, 4–7). English history also suggests that the liabilities of early banks were considered as fixed in value, and while it is arguable that this practice reflects a legal restriction that insisted that goldsmiths' liabilities be considered as debt, it is perhaps more plausible to argue that the legal convention merely reflected the practice of the early goldsmiths. It is often the case that the law – especially common law – simply reflects commercial practice.

6. Cowen and Kroszner (1988, 10–11) suggest that the reason why mutual fund exchange media have not been more widely adopted is because of legal restrictions. Discussing this issue in the US context, they suggest that one such restriction is Federal Reserve reluctance to grant mutual funds access to the bank clearing system and the Fed's own payments system. This Fed policy puts the mutual funds at a disadvantage relative to the banks, and forces the mutual funds to clear through accounts at commercial banks. At the same time, the threat of a predatory response by the Fed prevents the funds from setting up their own clearing system. Cowen and Kroszner also suggest that mutual funds have not been

more successful because of the existence of capital gains taxation – the higher taxation of capital gains than interest income puts the mutual funds at an artificial disadvantage. I would not dismiss these explanations entirely, but I do not believe they are fully convincing explanations for the failure of mutual funds to displace banks. They fail to explain why funds were not more successful in earlier periods or in other countries, and one must also bear in mind that for a very long time US regulatory policy gave mutual funds a major artificial *advantage* in the form of the ceilings imposed on the interest that banks could pay their depositors. Mutual funds were exempt from these ceilings, and when inflation started to rise in the early 1970s the constraint on the banks began to bind increasingly severely. Mutual funds grew rapidly during precisely this period – an article in *The Economist* of January 12th 1991 reported that money market mutual funds assets had grown form \$10 billion in 1978 to nearly \$250 billion only four years later – and their growth only flagged when the interest ceilings were removed from the banks. The timing of mutual fund growth is therefore consistent with the hypothesis that such growth was driven by the combination of interest rates ceilings and inflation.

7   BANK INTERMEDIARIES

1. Curiously, it is very difficult to pin down the term 'bank' (or any reasonable synonym) in the literature. Most writers avoid explicit definitions and seem to assume that the reader already knows what a bank is. For example, Niehans (1978, chapter 9), Baltensperger (1980), Fama (1980), Santomero (1984), Goodhart (1989, 124–128) and Lewis (1990) all talk of 'banks' or 'banking firms' but avoid defining them, and Fama seems to be referring to mutual funds anyway. Lewis and Davis (1987, chapter 7) give a broad-ranging discussion of bank characteristics, but don't actually define a bank either. Other writers focus on particular tasks that banks perform, such as lending out deposits made with them or creating 'money', but stating what a typical bank *does* is not the same as defining what a bank *is* and is of limited use in separating out banks from non-banks.

2. The literature there is that touches on this issue can be divided into the following groups: (1) There is the (so-called) 'perfect markets' approach which assumes away any information asymmetries or market 'frictions', but in the process rules out any convincing reasons why intermediaries should exist in the first place. Its ability to address the debt–equity issue is therefore limited, and to the extent that it does address it, the ruling out of any substantial differences between debt and equity forces it to the Modigliani–Miller conclusion that the optimal debt–equity mix is indeterminate. (2) There is the capital asset pricing (CAPM) framework, but this approach provides a restricted means of handling the debt–equity issue because it does not explain why there should be any debt–equity distinction to begin with. It also leads to the odd conclusion that a shock that increases the riskiness of a bank's capital would lead (risk-averse) investors to hold less capital, whereas an acknowledgement of the role of capital would lead one to expect the bank to issue more equity and share-holders to choose to hold it (Chant, 1987, 32). (3) There is literature that seeks to analyse bank capital decisions on lines analogous to the 'standard' precautionary-demand model that has often been used to model banks' choice of reserves. However, this approach involves an awkward inconsistency. If bankruptcy is costly and more likely to occur with a higher debt–equity ratio, as one would presume, then one would expect the opportunity cost of equity funds to rise to take these greater expected bankruptcy costs into account. Instead, the model takes the cost of funds as given, and the model breaks

down when one tries to make this cost endogenous. (4) Finally, there is literature that supposes that capital is chosen to determine an 'acceptable' probability of bankruptcy, but this literature is limited because it fails to explain what determines the acceptable probability of bankruptcy in the first place (Santomero, 1984, 594).

3.   The claim that paper exchange media take the form of transactable debt is also largely consistent with the evidence. Most paper exchange media do take the form of transactable debt, and historical exceptions to this rule – the post-dated bills of exchange and post-dated bank notes used as transactable instruments in the US in the early nineteenth century, for example, and the bills of exchange used as large-scale exchange media in early nineteenth century Lancashire – can be plausibly explained as the results of legal restrictions of one sort or another against the issue of the demandable debt that the public would have preferred to use.

4.   A modern analogy that illustrates the potential usefulness of the option clause is the standard clause in airline booking contracts that gives the airline the right to overbook seats. Since there are often passengers who pay for seats but do not turn up to travel in them, it makes sense for airlines to overbook seats in the expectation that not all passengers will turn up. If overbooking were not allowed, then some seats would have to remain empty that would otherwise be filled, and the airlines' revenues (and therefore profits) would be lower. If an airline can overbook, it can reduce the number of unoccupied seats and pass some of the gains onto to passengers by reducing fares. Both airlines and passengers can therefore gain. The option clause can therefore reduce a bank's reserve-holding costs in a manner reminiscent of the way in which overbooking reduces the cost of the airline's excess seats.

5.   Arguably, the scenario portrayed in the text – where liquidity costs are high relative to agency ones – helps to explain the rare cases where option clauses have actually been used. The best documented case is their use in Scotland in the period 1730–1765 (see, e.g., Meulen, 1934; Dowd, 1988d, 1991a; and Gherrity, 1992. Option clauses were first introduced by the Bank of Scotland in 1730 to protect itself from the attempts of its rival, the Royal Bank of Scotland, to drive it out of business by collecting its notes and presenting them unexpectedly for redemption. The option gave it the right to defer redemption for 6 months provided it paid compensation of one shilling in the pound (i.e., interest of five percent over the six month period). The Bank announced the reason for the clause, and though the Royal Bank for a long time refused to follow suit and advertised the fact that its notes were redeemable on demand, its attempts to win over the Bank's market share proved futile, and the notes of the two banks circulated side-by-side at par. In the subsequent years other banks were set up in Scotland, and the pressure of high interest rates in London and the resulting drain of specie southwards apparently led all Scottish note-issuing banks to adopt the option clause by mid-1762. The Bank of Scotland and the Royal Bank both exercised the option clause at least once in that period, in March 1764, and the use of the option clause by note-issuing banks was sometimes threatened on other occasions. Nonetheless, the option clause was controversial and, for reasons that are still not entirely clear, the Westminster Parliament prohibited it in 1765.

6.   There are many aspects of the large literature on credit rationing which I have glossed over, but the interested reader can pursue them elsewhere (see, e.g., Baltensperger and Devinney, 1985; Hillier and Ibrahimo, 1993). My own feeling is that the amount of literature on this topic is out of all proportion to its real importance, and no-one has yet established that the issues this literature examines are of any major quantitative importance. As a recent empirical study of credit rationing by Berger and Udell concluded

> While commercial loan rates are 'sticky', consistent with rationing, this
> stickiness varies with loan contract terms in ways not predicted by equilibrium
> credit rationing theory. In addition, the proportion of new loans issued under
> commitment does not increase significantly when credit markets are tight,
> despite the fact that borrowers without precommitments can be rationed
> whereas commitment borrowers are contractually insulated from rationing.
> Overall, the data suggest that equilibrium rationing is not a significant
> macroeconomic phenomenon. (Berger and Udell, 1990b, 1047)

Those who 'believe' in credit rationing seem to do so either on *a priori* grounds or
on the basis of relatively casual evidence (e.g., like observation of the way banks
appear to operate). That said, there *is* formal evidence of credit rationing – see, e.g.,
Zeldes (1989, 305) or Japelli (1990, 220) – but the kind of credit rationing
'uncovered' in these empirical studies is of a somewhat different kind. Even if one
accepts these results at face value, they therefore provide tenuous evidence for the
kinds of credit rationing with which the theoretical literature discussed here is
concerned.

One other comment might also be made about this literature. A number of
writers have drawn the conclusion that intervention by an outside agency (i.e., the
state) would produce an outcome Pareto-superior to the *laissez-faire* credit-
rationing equilibrium (e.g., Keeton (1979, ix), and Stiglitz and Weiss (1981); see
also Rothschild and Stiglitz (1976, 638)). This conclusion is highly dubious. Even
if we ignore the operating costs of state intervention and assume that it will do
exactly what the interventionists want – both heroic assumptions – we ought first to
explain why the private sector is unable to achieve a Pareto-optimal outcome on its
own. The obvious explanation is the existence of a hidden technological constraint,
but if such a constraint exists the state would have to operate under it as well, and
the *laissez-faire* outcome would presumably turn out after all to be optimal when
this constraint is accounted for. If there is no such constraint, on the other hand, the
advocates of state intervention would need to explain why people in the private
sector fail to harvest the surplus. They also need to explain why the act of putting a
private agent in charge of a government department enables him to do what he
could not or would not have done earlier in a purely private capacity. In any case,
even if one rejects these arguments, the fact is that we do not understand credit
rationing well enough to know what the interventionist policy should be. As the
last note makes clear, we don't know with any degree of confidence whether the
credit rationing these models talk about even *exists*, let alone what should be done
about it if it does.

7.   Fama himself also suggested an additional source of evidence in favour of his
hypothesis. He noted that CDs tend to bear a similar return to commercial paper
(CP), but are subject to a reserve requirement which CP is not, and one can hardly
argue that the reserve requirement tax on CDs is offset by CDs providing, say,
superior transactions services to commercial paper. The viability of the CD reserve
requirement must therefore mean that the costs to banks of handling inside loans
are lower than the comparable costs to other intermediaries by at least the cost of
the CD reserve requirement, *and* that the incidence of the CD tax is borne by bank
borrowers (Fama, 1985). The viability of CDs would therefore imply that bank
loans are different from other forms of credit in the way that Fama hypothesised.
However, Fama's claim about the incidence of the CD tax found mixed support in
later studies. James (1987, 218) looked at the extent to which the behaviour of CD
rates changed around the various times when CD reserve requirements were
altered, and his results were consistent with the Fama hypothesis without being
open to the objection, as Fama's evidence was, that CD rates were similar to CP

rates merely because the implicit federal deposit insurance subsidy happened to offset the reserve ratio tax. On the other hand, the more recent work of Osborne and Zaher (1992) reported results inconsistent with the implicit prediction of Fama's hypothesis that the *entire* cost of CD reserve requirements should be borne by bank borrowers.

8. Some further insight into bank monitoring is provided by Lummer and McConnell (1989). There are two views of how banks gain their 'private' information about borrowers. One view maintains that banks have an advantage evaluating new borrowers (e.g., because they can exploit specialist economies in doing so) while the other view (and the one to which Fama himself subscribed) maintains that banks gain their information by working with borrowers by gradually getting to know them better. These views are not mutually exclusive, but can be distinguished empirically since the first predicts that a firm's stock price should rise when a firm first initiates a relationship with a bank, while the second predicts that the firm's stock price should rise when it announces that a loan has been renewed or, strictly speaking, renewed on more favourable terms than expected. Lummer and McConnell (1989, 109) found that announcements of improved terms for the borrower, such as relaxed covenant restrictions and lower interest, were associated with a significantly positive stock price effect; and announcements of less favourable contracts or termination were associated with significantly negative stock price effects. This evidence strongly supports Fama's view that banks learn about their borrowers through their *ongoing relationship* with them. Their results also suggest that the stock price effect for new loans was insignificantly different from zero, so there is no substantial evidence to support the first view that the signal comes from the *initiation* of a borrower's relationship with a bank.

9. A good example of the successful use of this kind of strategy is given by the history of City Bank – a predecessor of Citicorp – in the nineteenth century. City Bank was conservatively run and maintained large holdings of spare cash, and was probably the strongest bank in New York City in the second half of the nineteenth century. This conservative policy consistently helped it in times of financial distress: City Bank was safe and strong, and with each panic its market share grew as it won over depositors from weaker banks (Cleveland and Huertas, 1985, 28). Over the long run, City Bank grew very rapidly – it grew at a real rate of 5.6 percent a year – and this policy did not compromise its profitability (Cleveland and Huertas, 1985, 29–30). The history of City Bank thus illustrates that a bank can win market share by being conservative – *and* grow rapidly *and* make decent profits as well.

10. Another banking stability issue is that of bank lending manias – the possibility that banks might engage in mania-lending binges and thereby get themselves into difficulties. A number of writers (e.g., Goodhart, 1988) have argued that unregulated banks would engage in such maniacal activity, and draw the conclusion that some banking authority is required to control it, or to bail banks out when they get themselves into difficulties. We have more to say on this issue in the next chapter, but two points should be noted about the mania argument here. First, it is simply not in a bank's own interest to engage in this kind of activity, since it undermines its longer-term financial health. Furthermore, even if some banks *did* engage in it, the other banks have an incentive to distance themselves from them and position themselves to capture their market share, as discussed in the text. Second, there is little *evidence* of maniacal activity under relatively *laissez-faire* conditions, and the most obvious instances of lending manias (e.g., lending to Third World and Communist countries in the 1970s) can be plausibly ascribed to specific interventions such as deposit insurance or expectations of central bank bailouts. For more on the bank lending mania issue, see also Selgin, 1992a).

11. The claim that there was little or no contagion has however been challenged by Hasan and Dwyer (1988, 1989) on the basis of some circumstantial evidence and the results of some logit analysis. In their model the probability of failure depends on the value of the bank's bonds relative to its capital, the remoteness of the bank's location and a dummy variable that takes the value 1 if another bank failed in the same county and the value 0 otherwise. They find that the coefficient on the dummy variable is positive and statistically significant, and interpret this finding as evidence of contagion. However, the problem is that this interpretation is not the only reasonable one. While the dummy *could* be picking up contagion, if it was there, it could *also* be picking up *any other* factor that the first two variables proxy inadequately, but which is also linked to the failure of a neighbouring bank – the obvious one being local economic conditions. These alternative interpretations need to be ruled out before one can say that Hasan and Dwyer's results are convincing evidence of contagion. A later version of their paper (Hasan and Dwyer, 1994, 284) merely concludes that the "evidence is consistent with the existence of contagious bank runs", but the point at issue is not whether the evidence is *consistent* with contagion, but whether the evidence is so compelling that it *forces us* to *accept* there was contagion. The evidence may be consistent with contagion, but we cannot say that there is evidence *of* contagion unless it makes the no-contagion position untenable.

12. There is of course the argument that the banking collapses of the 1930s indicate that widespread bank failures *can* be very damaging, as illustrated by the empirical work of Bernanke (1983), Haubrich (1990), and others. The counter-argument is that widespread banking collapses of this sort have *never* occurred under free banking, not even during the Australian crisis of the early 1890s (Dowd, 1992b), and the fact that the US banking system collapsed as it did in the early 1930s is a graphic illustration of the failure of *central* banking. The failure of the US central banking in this period also comes out from a comparison of the US experience with that of Canada. Since thousands of banks failed in the US, but not a single bank failed in Canada, a comparison of the two experiences enables us to separate out the influence of the bank failures, and the work of Haubrich, 1990) suggest that Canada's superior banking system – and in particular, the absence of bank failures – saved Canada from the much more severe depression that hit the US. As he puts it, the experience of Canada in the 1930s indicates that "The mere contraction of a financial system has little feedback upon the economy. It takes a crisis of the sort experienced in the US – waves of failures culminating in the government's complete shutdown of banking activity – to affect output on an aggregate level" (Haubrich, 1990, 250–251). Largescale bank failures of the sort experienced in the US in the 1930s therefore appear to have significant impacts on economic activity, but such failures are largely due to government intervention and (botched) central bank policy.

8 THE STRUCTURE OF THE BANKING INDUSTRY

1. It must be said, nonetheless, that the *threat* of entry exercises a useful discipline against a natural monopolist that tries to use its position to exploit its customers or allow itself to be run inefficiently. The natural monopolist must always reckon with the possibility that another firm will invade its market and an invasion will be costly to it regardless of whether it successfully fights off the invader or not. Excessive pricing and other abuses will encourage other firms to believe they can make easy profits by invading its market and the monopolist will have to limit

these abuses to safeguard its position. The fact there is only one firm operating in a market therefore does not imply that the market is incontestable – or that it poses some 'problem' that can only be resolved by government intervention.

2. The argument in the text is reinforced if there are factors that produce *diseconomies* of scale in banking. A plausible example of such a factor is the greater difficulty of monitoring a larger bank, as suggested by Krasa and Villamil (1992). To the extent such factors are present, the optimal scale of the bank would be lower than suggested in the text, other things being equal, but this only strengthens the argument against banking being a natural monopoly.

3. There are also other versions of this argument which I discuss elsewhere. One version maintains that a problem exists because an individual bank will take insufficient measures to promote public confidence in it, but this claim runs up against the arguments made in the previous chapter that individual banks under competitive conditions actually have very strong incentives to maintain confidence. A bank that loses public confidence also loses its business; a bank must therefore maintain public confidence if it is to survive at all. This version of the argument can therefore be dismissed fairly easily. A second version maintains that there is some systemic confidence problem that might give rise to concerted action by the banks such as that of a banking club, but it is better to leave this version till we come to banking clubs a little later below.

4. Melvin also makes related claims in a more recent paper (Melvin,1988). However, as L. H. White (1989, 103) points out, the fixed confidence costs on which his natural monopoly argument hinges are not in fact fixed at all and he therefore has no basis for a natural monopoly even by his own argument. Melvin also claims that the costs of individually contracting for high-quality 'money' are prohibitive and concludes that money-holders therefore need to pay 'protection money' to the issuer to discourage him from hyperinflating. The initial premise is theoretically questionable and empirically refuted, as noted elsewhere, but even if it is granted,

> the comparative cheapness of government production does not follow unless it can be shown that an equally large protection premium does not have to be paid to a government producer to assure quality. If the government has an uncertain tenure and therefore ... a higher discount rate than a private firm, as Klein has noted to be the case, then the quality-assuring premium necessary for stability with government production of money would be even higher than the premium necessary with private production. (L. H. White, 1989, 104)

5. A number of other studies were not included in these surveys. These include Nelson (1985), Goldberg and Hanweck (1988), Hunter and Timme (1986) and Hardwick (1989). All these studies bar Goldberg and Hanweck found that economies of scale were relatively limited and Hardwick actually found some evidence of diseconomies of scale.

6. *If* scalar economies are quite limited, it has been suggested (e.g., by Nelson (1985) that lifting restrictions on branch-banking in the US (as advocated, *inter alia*, by Horwitz and Selgin (1987), England (1988) and many others) might have relatively little impact because branch-banking restrictions are mostly non-binding. However, Gilbert (1984, 637, n. 17) and Peltzman (1984, 651) both suggest the appearance of such limited economies might arise from a failure to account for additional (non-measurable) services that larger banks can provide. In any case, the conclusion that economies of scale are trivial beyond a small size' does not sit well with the stylised fact that where branching is unrestricted, it becomes the dominant mode of bank organization' (Peltzman (1984, 651).

7. If the bankers are to delegate powers to a bankers' club, it might make sense for them to delegate those powers to a clearinghouse if one exists. A good reason for making

the clearinghouse into a banking club is that the clearing process creates a by-product – information on banks' clearing gains and losses over time, which often provides advance warning of future difficulties – that helps to assess their credit-worthiness. A clearinghouse could therefore monitor (member) banks at less cost than an alternative banking club that would not have access to clearinghouse accounts.

8. A somewhat different reserve-externality argument is made by Cothren (1987). In his model, a bank's reserve and investment policies cannot be made part of the bank-depositor contract because these factors cannot be observed by the depositors. As a result, the bank holds too few reserves and takes too many risks relative to an optimum which can be achieved by a central banking authority imposing suitable reserve requirements. However, if the central authority has the technology to monitor bank policies, then the banks can presumably make use of that technology themselves by establishing their own organisation to impose reserve requirements along the lines discussed in the text. There is no need for 'outside' intervention to appropriate the benefits of reserve requirements.

9. There would be costs to entering the market for clearinghouse services, but there is little reason to suppose that they would be so high as to make the market effectively incontestable. A good historical example of banks 'voting with their feet' even when the market could only support one clearinghouse is provided by the demise of the Suffolk system. The Suffolk system was a club managed by the Suffolk Bank of Boston, but some members found the club rules too constraining and there were complaints about the Suffolk's high-handed attitude towards members. Discontent led to the founding of a rival, the Bank for Mutual Redemption (BMR) and when the latter opened in 1858 many of the Suffolk's clients defected to it. A brief 'war' followed, but in the end the Suffolk abandoned the market to its rival. See, e.g., Trivoli (1979), Mullineaux (1987), Selgin and White (1988) and the text below.

10. The Suffolk experience also provides a useful example of how club competition can provide information about banks' preferences for club services. The Suffolk provided a relatively 'hierarchical' product mix that included loans and monitoring services as well as just note-clearing, but the BMR restricted itself primarily to clearing services and its victory over the Suffolk suggests that banks preferred its more limited bundle to the Suffolk's.

11. The reserve externality argument also suffers from another drawback, at least in so far as it is used to defend the imposition by banking clubs or central banks of reserve ratios on commercial banks. Reserve ratios can be self-defeating in a crisis because the obligation to hold them freezes reserves and prevents them being used just when they are most needed (as happened, e.g., in US banking crises during the National Banking era). The logic of the reserve externality argument would appear to suggest that reserve holdings should be *subsidised* and it is not at all clear how it can be used to defend reserve requirements that are effectively *taxes* on the banks.

12. Most major banking crises exhibited 'flights to quality' rather than indiscriminate runs on all banks. Even in the Australian banking crisis of 1893 – arguably the most severe crisis in any historical free banking system – the two biggest banks in Melbourne experienced deposit inflows so large they were embarrassing (Butlin, 1961, 305; Dowd, 1992b, 62). The banking crisis that most closely resembles the run-at-everything model is the English crisis of December 1825, but even so the run-at-everything interpretation does not fit easily with the fact that the crisis hardly touched the Scottish free banking system. In any case, one could argue that this episode was largely due to Bank of England policy and the law that restricted other English banks to partnerships of no more than six partners (see, e.g., Dowd, 1991b).

13. Of course, even under conditions of relatively 'free' banking, 'big' banks occasionally made 'last resort' loans to smaller banks and their managers

sometimes regarded themselves as guardians of the system (see, e.g., Goodhart, 1988; Dow and Smithin, 1992, 385–388). The Royal Bank of Scotland made such loans to the Scottish provincial banks, for example and Bank of Scotland's Alexander Blair was the Scottish system's self-appointed 'policeman' (Munn, 1985, 341). I would argue, however, that it is natural for smaller banks to enter into a client relationship with a larger one in much the same way that a firm would enter into such a relationship with a bank and to label distress loans as 'last resort lending is to exaggerate the similarity between these loans and the 'last-resort lending' of a genuine central bank. Be this as it may, the lending and supervisory functions of 'big' banks under free banking were still constrained by the primary objective of maximising profits and the banks in question had few if any privileges, were heavily exposed to competition and had no 'official' regulatory status.

14. Nor is there any strong evidence, populist views about 'banking power' notwithstanding, that banks were able to cartelise the market successfully. In a variety of countries, the uniform interest rates that would-be cartels 'set for their members gave way to rate wars as soon as any bank ... spotted a competitive opportunity and action to punish renegades was futile' (Schuler, 1992b, 18). That cartels were unsustainable is also suggested by the evidence that free-banking systems were highly competitive even when there was only a small number of big banks, as in Australia (Dowd, 1992b, 58) or Scotland (L. H. White, 1984a, chapter 2).

15. A related analysis is that of Sheila Dow and John Smithin, who argue that the requirements of a credit-based economy under *laissez-faire* would produce a degree of centralisation of power that is effectively the same as central banking (e.g., Dow and Smithin, 1994). When a crisis occurs under free banking, there is a scramble for safe assets which focuses on the banking system's ultimate settlement asset. *The* issuer of this asset then has great power over the system and effectively becomes a central bank (see, e.g., Dow and Smithin, 1994, 14–15). To give this argument empirical support, Dow and Smithin point to the role of the three big banks in making emergency loans and disciplining minor banks in Scottish free banking (Dow and Smithin, 1992, 385–388; Dow, 1995, 17–18). This argument is open to various objections: (1) We would expect a scramble for safe assets to take the form of a flight to quality and the evidence confirms that it generally does. It does *not* usually take the form of a scramble for any ultimate settlement asset. (2) Even if there *was* a scramble for 'ultimate' settlement assets, it does not follow that such assets are issued by *one* institution only. To *assume* that there is only one such institution consequently begs a key point at issue. The experience of historical free banking also indicates that there is always more than one 'big' bank and no bank ever spontaneously established its supremacy over all the others. (3) Even if we accept their logic, Dow and Smithin establish the existence of the wrong animal. As discussed in the text already, a private bankers' 'club' is one thing, but full-blown central banking is quite another.

16. A similar argument has been made more recently by Dow (1995, 8). Her argument is distinctive in that it rests on an underlying post-Keynesian view of the uncertainty attached to valuing bank assets and not just on a herd theory of bankers following each other over the cliff. However, despite its distinctiveness, it is still open to the objections made in the text against the excessive cycling theory: it ignores the point that individual free banks *do* have incentives to go against the market trend and thereby counteract it, because doing so enables them to increase their long-run market shares; and it empirically falsified, because there is little evidence of such cycles under historical free banking. Dow's post-Keynesian version of the cycling argument also has its own distinctive problems. If assets are so difficult to value, then it is difficult to see how central bankers can be expected to know where the private

bankers are going off the rails; and if they don't know, it is difficult to see what central banks can do to prevent them going off the rails anyway.

17. The evidence in favour is circumstantial and consists of occasional episodes like the victimisation of the Knickerbocker Trust in 1907 referred to by Goodhart. The evidence against is stronger. The historical experience of free banking broadly suggests that clubs treated comparable banks, including late entrants, in not-too-unequal ways. Since banking clubs under approximate *laissez-faire* typically had few powers, there seems to have been little to gain by rigging rules anyway and it is significant that the Knickerbocker case occurred in the US when banks were subject to branch-banking laws and the legal restrictions of the National Banking System.

9   RECENT MODELS OF BANKING INSTABILITY

1. To anticipate the later discussion, the text assumes that these costs must also be paid when the intermediary redeems 'deposits' in $T = 1$, an assumption which then implies that runs have 'real' production costs. The alternative assumption is that the intermediary can hand over the maturing investment without 'killing' it in the process, but this assumption would expose the intermediary to losses from arbitrage – to anticipate the later discussion again, type 2 depositors would always wish to withdraw for $c_{1,1}^*$ and then hold the investment until it matures in $T = 2$ and yields them a return of $c_{1,1}^* R$. The investors would then have no reason to invest in the intermediary, since they would know that it would be unable to redeem all its deposits.

2. There are various ways these costs could be modelled. The text assumes that the cost is merely the opportunity cost of the foregone return in $T = 2$ which means that the investment process is fully reversible in $T = 1$, but one might instead suppose that the investment process has some degree of irreversibility and yields only B units in $T = 1$ for each unit invested in $T = 0$, where $0 \leq B < 1$. I shall indicate where appropriate how results might be sensitive to the assumed degree of irreversibility, but one should note that irreversibility does not 'bind' the optimal outcome provided that there exists a costless storage technology and there is no aggregate uncertainty. To anticipate the later analysis, any optimum that exists when there is no irreversibility can then be attained when there is irreversibility by using the storage technology to provide for $T = 1$ withdrawals, and there is no inefficiency (relative to the no-irreversibility case) because the amount of storage required is perfectly predictable.

3. The corner preference assumption is a convenient way to motivate differences in agents' desired consumption patterns, but it can be relaxed. One could then assume that agents' preferences are 'smooth' over consumption in both periods, but that type 1 agents (unobservably) desire more consumption in period 1 (i.e., are more impatient, as in Anderlini (1986b) or Waldo, 1985). Alternatively, one could assume that all agents have the same preferences, but face differing (unobservable) endowments in $T = 1$ (e.g., as in Haubrich and King, 1984, 1989). Results sometimes hinge on which of these specifications is chosen, but any major differences will be flagged as we go along.

4. While the text emphasises the role of an intermediary in sharing risk, the intermediary might also help agents overcome the constraints imposed by the costs of liquidating assets before they mature. In contrast to an agent with his own portfolio, an intermediary need never liquidate capital prematurely or hold low-return storage asset for two periods because it can predict with certainty the proportions of type 1 and type 2 agents. Even risk-neutral agents would then prefer an intermediary contract provided there was some degree of investment

irreversibility.

5. Agents' self-selection also means that the 'full-information' optimum is achieved even though their types are not observable, but this result hinges on the assumption that agents have corner preferences. If we had smooth preferences or preferences that are identical but associated with varying $T = 1$ endowments, then individual agents in the 'full-information' optimum would not self- select because everyone would claim to be type 1 and it would be impossible to identify the false claims. The 'full-information' insurance arrangement is therefore unfeasible, and the optimal feasible contract is constrained by the private information about agents' endowments (see respectively Anderlini, 1986c, 160–1; and Haubrich and King, 1984, 1989).

6. An additional difficulty with the DD model is that depositors do not take the possibility of runs into account when deciding whether to invest in an intermediary or not. The problem is that if depositors have utility functions that are unbounded below, and a run entails a positive probability of zero consumption, they may never make any deposits in the first place (Anderlini, 1986b, 1–2; 1986c, 158); see also Postlewaite and Vives, 1987, 485). If depositors have to decide whether to invest all or nothing in a bank, they might only invest in the bank if there was some mechanism in place to guarantee that a run could not take place. If we allow them to invest only part of their endowment in a bank, then DD, 1983, 409–10) suggest, and Anderlini, 1986b) proves, that they would still make some investment in the intermediary provided that they had a low enough expected probability of a run. (See also Waldo, 1985, 276).) Depositors would then willing to take the risk of a run because the part of their endowment they keep under the mattress provides them with insurance against a run and enables them to avoid the possibility of having nothing to consume.

7. If the extraneous variables ('sunspots') governing expectations were publicly observable and had a known influence on expectations, it would also be possible to write contracts in which payments were made contingent on these variables (e.g., as in Freeman, 1988, 52–4) and Bental, Eckstein and Peled, 1990, 3–4). Panics could then be avoided by ensuring that sunspot-contingent returns to $T = 1$ withdrawals were low enough (relative to later returns) to eliminate any incentive for type 2 agents to withdraw early. However, this contract delivers a lower expected utility than the contract in the text precisely because it lowers returns to type 1 agents when sunspot counts are 'bad'. Unlike the DD contract, it eliminates runs but the possibility of runs is costly even though runs might never occur. The assumption that the extraneous variables are publicly observable is also questionable since the point of bringing sunspots into the picture in the first place is to proxy the unobservable factors that influence agents' expectations, but which one cannot model explicitly.

8. The criticism that alternative arrangements can also produce the social optimum does not however apply when the DD preference structure is replaced by identical preferences and random endowments in $T = 1$. An optimal arrangement under these circumstances provides insurance against illiquidity and insurance against a low endowment. (This distinction between types of insurance does not arise with the other preference specifications.) A DD contract then provides an optimal tradeoff between liquidity insurance and income insurance, but an equity contract is inferior because it provides no income insurance at all (Haubrich and King, 1984, 8–14). The Haubrich-King specification is also immune to the criticism in the next paragraph as well.

9. Wallace, 1989, 4–8, 15–16) provides a nice analogy that illustrates the significance of the isolation assumption in motivating financial intermediation. He suggests we consider the problem faced by a group of people on the last night of a camping trip.

Each individual has to decide whether to take his last meal in the form of a late-night snack or breakfast the next morning. 'All the campers know in the evening that they will each awaken sometime during the night and either will be hungry and will prefer to eat then (and skip breakfast) or will not be hungry and will prefer to wait until breakfast to eat' (1989, 5). Each individual will have some idea of the probability that he will wake up hungry, and the proportion of individuals who wake up hungry can be predicted. Food is assumed to grow while it is stored, but any food taken out of storage during the night must be consumed or wasted. Since the proportion of late-night snackers is predictable, risk-averse campers can presumably come to a co-operative arrangement that is better than pure autarky. Wallace then suggests that we consider individuals as 'isolated' during the night in the sense that they cannot meet after lights out – think of each waking up at a random time – so any feasible arrangement must be consistent with this 'isolation'. He then suggests that they set up a food-dispensing machine that works something like a cash-dispenser, and this machine is analogous to a financial intermediary. If that individuals were not isolated, of course – if they all woke up at the same time, for example – the obvious solution would be to arrange a late-night meeting which is analogous to a $T = 1$ credit market. 'Isolation' is therefore critical to the existence of the financial intermediary.

10. The suspension arrangement is explored further by Wallace (1990) and Selgin (1993). Wallace presents an example of a DD-type economy in which the payouts to depositors who withdraw in $T = 1$ depend in part on their place in the queue. Those who arrive late are paid less than those who arrive earlier, and this feature of the contract discourages premature withdrawals by type 2 depositors. Wallace interprets it as a 'partial' suspension of payments, in contrast to the 'full' suspension where all payments cease, and casual observation of US banking history suggests that this distinction is an important one. Selgin motivates a similar distinction by linking the DD saving-investment scenario to a means-of-exchange technology.

11. Diamond and Dybvig's own description of their 'deposit insurance' scheme is difficult to follow because it fails to make an adequate distinction between expected and realised t. This distinction is critical. If payments to depositors are made on the basis of expected t, the DD contract achieves optimality *ex ante* (provided there is some means to eliminate runs), but it only achieves optimality *ex post* if the two t values are the same. If it makes contracts based on actual t, on the other hand, the intermediary can expect to achieve both *ex ante* and *ex post* optimality, but some topping up (or retrieval) is required *ex post* unless the two t values accidentally coincide because the intermediary cannot know until the last withdrawal what the realised value of t actually was.

12. The government's tax-subsidy policy is complicated by an additional factor. If those who withdraw in $T = 1$ are paid too little when they first go to the bank, there is no problem liquidating further investments to make 'top-up' payments to them to bring their returns up to promised levels. If they are paid too much, on the other hand, there is a social loss because too many investments have already been liquidated, and the 'excess interruptions' to the production process cannot be undone. The only way in which these excess interruptions can be eliminated is to make initial payments conditional on the minimum possible level of t (i.e., to pay 1 for every deposit withdrawn in $T = 1$). Top-up payments could then be made if the realised value of t exceeded this minimum, but there would never be any need to retrieve over-payments (see McCulloch and Yu, 1989, 7–8).

13. These are very questionable claims, but even if one accepts them at face value, the optimality of these policy interventions is still extremely delicate. The optimality of the Anderlini policy hinges on the rate of return R on physical capital being deterministic, and there is no presumption of optimality when R is made stochastic

instead (Anderlini, 1986b, 31). Similarly, the optimality of the Freeman policy is contingent on extreme assumptions about the government and the information at its disposal. In particular, the government 'must itself calculate the bank's optimal portfolio and liabilities in the absence of moral hazard, then impose them on the bank. ... the bank must be made to behave as if its expected tax depends on the risk of liquidation implied by its own behavior' (Freeman, 1988, 63).

10   MEDIA OF EXCHANGE AND PAYMENTS SYSTEMS

1.   As Selgin (1994b, 814–816) points out, the existence of this bootstrap problem highlights one of the major weakness of conventional Walrasian monetary theory. This theory provides an unexplained niche for 'money', and then *presumes* that the bits of paper the government provides for the purpose will *actually be accepted* as money. As should be clear from the text, such a government 'policy' is neither necessary for the acceptance of currency, nor sufficient to guarantee that a particular currency will be adopted by the public. It also begs other important issues, such as what is it about the government's *imprimatur* that should lead people to accept as currency pieces of paper issued by the government in preference to those issued by anyone else.

2.   It is astonishing, for example, that McCallum, 1985, 29) should appear to subscribe to the view that inconvertible currency somehow spontaneously emerged from previously convertible currency, as suggested by his comment that 'since it is costly for banks to maintain the requisite commodity reserves and since the convertibility option is very rarely exercised, banks might eventually do away with this guarantee' as if it served no particular purpose and the banks could simply disregard the preferences of their customers. He goes on to suggest that the abolition of convertibility by the Bank of England in 1797 might be an example of such a process. However, if one examines this episode at all closely, it is very clear that it does not bear out McCallum's interpretation. Far from being the outcome of some kind of spontaneous free market process, the suspension of 1797 is classic example of the government intervention mentioned in the text. For years the government had been leaning on the Bank for forced loans; these loans severely weakened the Bank, and made it increasingly difficult for it to maintain specie payments. A point then came when a relatively minor shock set off a run that the Bank did not have the resources to meet. The government then intervened to legalise the Bank's bankruptcy – a bankruptcy caused by the government's own profligate spending – by passing an Order in Council to prohibit it making any further specie payments (see, e.g., Dowd, 1991b, 162–163). It is difficult to see how the role of the government in this suspension could be any more clear-cut.

3.   One may of course ask why fiat currencies persist if the public prefer convertible ones. Part of the answer may be due to the impact of legal restrictions against competing currencies, the threat of pre-emptive attacks by the authorities against those who might try to promote such currencies, and so on, but a large part has to do with the existence of network externalities that leave private agents locked-in to currencies that they might otherwise easily repudiate. In the absence of network factors and legal restrictions, any inconvertible currency should be driven out of circulation by convertible alternatives. The real demand for the inconvertible currency would fall to zero, and the inconvertible currency would hyperinflate away. In the process, it would lose its 'market share' to competitors, and the resulting equilibrium would involve the restoration of convertible currency. However, once we introduce network factors, individual agents might each

continue to use the inconvertible currency, even though they all acknowledge its inferiority, simply because each one expects others to continue to use it – and this expectation makes it rational for each individual to continue using it. Everyone is then locked into the inferior currency, and there is obvious way of coordinating a simultaneous abandonment of it. Inconvertible fiat currencies can therefore persist even in the absence of legal restrictions and even when everyone involved would prefer a convertible alternative.

4.   There are alternatives such as the 'smart card' (which is discussed further below), but machines would be needed to read such cards, and 'smart card' systems would not be costless to operate anyway once machines had been installed. Another suggestion is that of McCulloch, 1986b), who suggested that banks might pay random returns via a lottery. But even a lottery imposes costs – individuals must check note numbers, and so on – and it might also create a potential for surges in demand for notes as lottery dates approach. These drawbacks notwithstanding, banks under *laissez-faire* might still use lotteries to increase the demand for their notes by making them more attractive to hold, but the important point here is that a lottery should not be regarded as a costless way to pay implicit interest on notes.

5.   One might also note the development of giro systems, which essentially involve credit rather than debit transfers. Giro systems involve many of the same issues as, say, credit card systems, the only major difference being that the sender has already made his payment when the transfer goes off. Giro systems are extensively used in continental European countries, in some of which they account for over 50 percent of non-cash payments; in the USA, by contrast, they account for less than 1 percent of payments (Humphrey, 1984, 9).

6.   While Humphrey's results clearly depend on the specific assumptions he made, it is difficult to tell (and expert opinion is divided) whether his assumptions lead him to over- or under-state the 'true' impact. Humphrey himself felt that his results were on the conservative side (Humphrey, 1986, 110). Schoenmaker (1993, 12) agrees with him, but Clair (1991, 73–74) reckons that his results are more like worst-case scenarios. But even if Clair is right, the worst-case scenario is still pretty bad.

7.   The fact that banks that participate as members of the payment system must satisfy these requirements does not of course mean that other, non-member, institutions are deprived of access to the system. They can still access the system as customers of one of the participating bank, and pay accordingly, but that bank implicitly takes responsibility for its customers as far as the system itself is concerned. The point is to protect the integrity of the system by requiring certain standards of those with *direct* access to it.

8.   This view nonetheless has its critics. Mengle (1990, 160) argues that since this rule concentrates liability on the banks that extended credit to the failed bank, it has the drawback that it does not involve much risk spreading. But it is not clear to me why this is a drawback. Spreading risks is not an advantage independently of other factors. If a bank cannot absorb a large clearing loss from the failure of one of its counterparties, then it ought not to lend too much to them, and the strength of this rule is that it concentrates the incentive to restrict lending on the one party (i.e., the receiver/lender) that is able to respond to this incentive. Any alternative rule would relax the link between a bank's settlement liability and its lending to the failed bank, and therefore indirectly encourage excessive lending to banks that might subsequently fail. Settlement losses would be greater, and banks individually would have less control of their own settlement liability. On the other hand, Schoenmaker (1993, 2) argues against this rule on the grounds that banks do not really have any choice in the credit they extend to each other. As he puts it, while 'Credit exposures in the interbank market [for example] are voluntarily taken on by banks on the basis of choice and assessment of counterparties. In contrast, banks

may have no choice over their counterparties in payment systems and credit exposures in payment systems can therefore be the result of some coincidental pattern of payment traffic.' In response, I would simply say that banks can *always* limit their exposure by imposing caps. If they choose not to do so, then they effectively choose to accept the risks involved.

9. One other option not discussed in the text is that of taking out insurance against the settlement problems that might arise from systemic risk. However, taking out insurance with an 'outside' party (e.g., an insurance company) involves moral hazard that is perhaps best dealt with by having the banks themselves provide the insurance (i.e., it is best dealt with by internalising it). There is also the problem that what is to be insured against here is not so much the risk of loss *per se*, as the danger of settlement embarrassment. The fact that an insurance company might later pay out on some insurance claim does not in itself provide the immediate settlement funds that are needed. At most, the future insurance payout only provides collateral that might be used to obtain immediate liquidity, and so insurance would need to be complemented by some credit facility with the banks. It is much easier for the payment system to integrate with the banking system and arrange for its own liquidity to be provided if it is needed. There is also the problem that the event to be insured against – settlement failure – is difficult to assess actuarially because it has rarely if ever occurred. Getting someone to provide the insurance could therefore be difficult. Finally, even if someone did provide it, the existence of moral hazard and/or adverse selection could make it expensive. One estimate – provided by Humphrey on the basis of the difference between the rates on 90-day commercial paper and 3 month T-bills – suggested that such insurance might cost about 1.5 percent of the value of the insured funds each year (Humphrey, 1984, 100–101). At that price one doubts that many payments participants would want to buy settlement insurance even if it was available.

11   THE ECONOMICS OF THE UNIT OF ACCOUNT

1. Network economies are demand-side economies of scale in which the benefit of a particular good or service to one user depends on how many others use it as well. Farrell and Saloner (1986, 940) point out three different types of situation where network economies arise: (1) where complementary parts are interchangeable (e.g., computer software, VCR tapes); (2) where networks ease communication (e.g., the use of a common language, or, as in the text, the use of a common unit of account); and (3) where cost savings can arise in the production of standardised products (e.g., through the interchangeability of parts). There is by now a sizeable literature on network economics (see, e.g., Arthur, 1990; and Katz and Shapiro, 1986; Liebowitz and Margolis, 1994; among many others). Amongst the various applications to monetary issues are Wärneryd (1989, 1990) who uses networks to study the adoption of commodity media of exchange, and Dowd and Greenaway (1993), which is based on an earlier version of the text.

2. These unit-of-account prices are not to be confused with the 'accounting prices' often found in the literature. As Woolsey goes on to note,
   > Unit-of-account prices are different from what are sometimes called 'accounting prices' (Patinkin, 1965, p. 16). Accounting prices are usually treated as an extra set of purely abstract prices that are calculated from the money prices actually quoted on the market. Unit-of-account prices are the prices actually quoted on the market. (Woolsey, 1987, 16–17))

3. Having n_i rather than N_i appear in the utility function implies that the marginal

value to an existing network user of a new network user is always positive, but falls with the size of the network. This assumption would seem reasonable – if we are more likely to trade with people 'close' to us, as suggested by 'gravity models' of international trade (see, e.g., Bergstrand, 1985), we would expect the benefit to us of our neighbour's joining our network to be larger than the benefit to us of someone on the other side of the world joining the same network.

4. Total welfare from a single UA is $(N + 2)a/r + (N + 2)b \ln(N + 1)r$. Subtracting (11.2), the difference between welfare with one UA and welfare with 2 is

$$(N + 2)b \ln(N + 1)/r - [(N_1 + 1) \ln(N_1) + (N_2 + 1) \ln(N_2)]b/r$$
$$= (N_1 + 1)[\ln(N_1 + N_2 + 1) - \ln(N_1)] + (N_2 + 1)[\ln(N_1 + N_2 + 1)$$
$$- \ln(N_2)]b/r > 0. \qquad\qquad \text{QED.}$$

5. The model can also distinguish between the benefits of using the same UA and the benefits of having a fixed relative price (or fixed exchange rate) between two different units of account. Having a single unit of account enables agents to enjoy *all* the network-related benefits discussed earlier, but *some* – though not all – of these benefits can also be obtained by fixing exchange rates between two technically distinct units of account. Principal amongst these is the reduction in exchange rate risk. Even if agents in different regions have difficulty processing information in 'foreign' units of account, and have to incur costs to convert the denominations of payments media used in interregional trade, they can still reap some interregional network benefits from the reduction of foreign exchange risk in a fixed-exchange rate system. The network effects of a fixed rate system thus lie somewhere between those of floating rates, which we earlier took to be zero, and the network benefits of a single UA.

6. The model therefore explains the frequently observed reluctance of agents to switch units of account even though they might be performing very badly. Such behaviour is puzzling if we only look at traditional factors such as differences in inflation rates – why should agents hold assets whose real value depreciates rapidly when relatively stable-valued alternatives are usually available? – but can be readily explained once we take account of network factors.

7. As an aside, it is important to note that the claim that agents will choose the best currency unit (i.e., the one that yields the highest expected return, *ceteris paribus*) if the units are close substitutes is a standard and relatively uncontroversial one in the literature on currency substitution (see, e.g., Girton and Roper, 1981). One might object, perhaps, that agents would have to bear the costs of telling the two apart, and so on, but I would reply that the problem of discriminating between 'good' and 'bad' media of exchange is one that they already face – they have to discriminate between 'good' and 'bad' cheques, for instance – and it is much easier to discriminate among good and bad currencies than it is to discriminate between good and bad cheques – the latter requires that we have information about both the bank and about the person on whose bank account the cheque is drawn, but the former only requires information about the bank of issue. The fact that the public already manage reasonably well to discriminate between different cheques is thus *prima facie* evidence that they could do the same between different brand-name dollars. In any case, there is also much evidence to indicate that people *do in fact* discriminate between 'inferior' and 'superior' exchange media and pass on the inferior ones. When coins were used as exchange media, people would keep the good coins and pass on the bad (i.e., worn) ones. Under bimetallism, they would keep coins denominated in the good (i.e., undervalued) metal and pass on coins denominated in the bad (i.e., overvalued) one, and so on. Even today, people tend to keep notes that are in better condition and pass on the scruffier ones. The claim that the public

would accept the bankers' currency is also supported by the willingness of the public – well-documented by Timberlake (1984, 1987) – to use privately issued currency as a substitute for inadequate 'official' currency. Indeed, the very fact that this 'scrip money' was never officially encouraged – and, moreover, was often illegal – indicates that its use could *only* be due to its superiority over inadequate 'official' currencies. There is therefore good reason to expect that the public would switch to the better units in the way I have just claimed.

8. We could imagine, for example, that an agent who preferred MOE denominated in the 'superior' dollar could sort the two out at very low cost (e.g., when going through the day's takings) and get rid of his holdings of MOE (e.g., banknotes) denominated in the 'inferior' dollar. He would pass them on, or return them to his bank and let it return them to the issuers at the clearing house. All he would need to do is make a point of keeping only 'superior' MOE in his transactions portfolio and getting rid of the rest.

9. The story in the text of course abstracts from certain complications, but these do not alter its basic validity. In particular, since contracts are often made for a considerable time in advance, the banks could not unilaterally change the meaning of the term 'dollar' in loan contracts, say, and expect their debtors to acquiesce. Where such contracts exist, the banks would either have to recalculate the old contracts in terms of units of the new dollar, or else continue to use the old dollar for the purposes of fulfilling the terms of those contracts. Either option is costly – the first, since it involves switching costs, the latter because it would involve the banks using both units of account simultaneously for some period. However, the banks can reduce these costs by preannouncing the change a long way ahead. The longer the period between the announcement and the introduction of the new dollar, the fewer the number of existing contracts that need to be re-negotiated or carried forward under the old unit of account, and the less vulnerable the innovating banks are to lawsuits from customers who might lose by the innovation. The banks would therefore 'preannounce' any changes a long way off, and the basic story in the text would continue to hold.

10. The process would be similar to that which occurred when convertible currency units became inconvertible. The unit, the dollar, was originally defined as a particular weight of gold, and the dollar note was a claim to a dollar rather than a dollar as such. When the link with gold was broken, the dollar was legally defined as a dollar note. The dollar subtly changed its meaning, but the man in the street barely noticed the change and continued to use the same old dollar notes that he had used before.

11. The important point is that the competitive process forces banks to provide the price-level behaviour the public want, as reflected in their demand for exchange media, and *not* that it forces the banks to provide price stability as such. For example, if the public wanted 'optimal quantity-of-money'-style deflation – a possibility we discuss in Chapter 15 – the undercutting process would continue through the zero-inflation barrier, and successive 'brands' of the unit of account would keep on displacing each other and only stop when the rate of inflation fell to minus the rate of interest. *Whatever rate of inflation the public want – zero inflation, 'optimal deflation', or whatever – competition ensures that they will get it.*

12   THE MECHANICS OF CONVERTIBILITY

1. While this chapter focuses on two types of convertibility – direct and indirect convertibility – there also exists a third type of convertibility scheme that involves

the pegging and periodic re-pegging of the price of some commodity or asset in order to stabilise the price of a 'broad' basket of goods and services, as represented by a price index. An example is the 'compensated dollar' scheme of Irving Fisher (1911). It is more convenient to put off discussing these systems until chapter 14 when we come to grips with the issues raised by commodity baskets and price indices, but it should be pointed out that these schemes are subject to serious flaws that rule them out as operationally feasible. If we wish to have convertibility, we must choose between the two systems discussed here.

2. If it is to avoid being vacuous, the MOR must be something other than the type of liability which is supposedly redeemed – one cannot redeem a pound note with another, identical one – and there must be at least some liabilities redeemable in something other than the liabilities of the issuer. A bank might make its deposits redeemable in notes, say, but if its issues are to be convertible in any substantive sense, the notes themselves must be redeemable in something other than the bank's own debt.

3. The vast majority of historical systems were of this type, and exceptions are rare. The most likely explanation for the historical prevalence of directly convertible systems is the combination of relatively underdeveloped financial systems and legal restrictions, i.e., either the financial services sector had not yet evolved to the point where it could easily separate these functions, or else it was not allowed to. It is unlikely to be an accident that it was the relatively advanced systems, such as that of free-banking Scotland, which evolved (or, at least, were evolving) from direct to indirect convertibility.

4. One could of course fill out the description of the equilibrating process by elaborating on possible changes in interest rates, expenditures, and the price level, and by explaining how the banks themselves might try to pre-empt arbitrage by others by carrying out arbitrage operations themselves, but these issues are essentially peripheral to the primary equilibrating process explained in the text. One could also add in how speculative factors would reinforce the tendency of the price of gold to return to par. If the price of gold differed from par, rational agents would normally expect it to return to par, and they would hurry up sales or delay purchases (or vice versa) to profit from the temporary deviation in the gold price, and such behaviour would itself help to correct that deviation.

5. The source of the problem is not so much that the anchor and the MOR happen to be the same, but that their relative price is fixed by virtue of their being the same. As Greenfield and Yeager observe in an insightful discussion of this point,

> An economist would be quick to diagnose the ... problem, were it cast in non-monetary terms. If, when the demand for something supplied in a fixed quantity ... strengthened, the total quantity supplied proved inadequate, then the price adjustment needed to equilibrate supply and demand must somehow have been jammed, perhaps through a price ceiling. (Greenfield and Yeager, 1989, 4)

They then note that under the traditional directly convertible gold standard,

> discoveries of new gold fields or improved methods of gold extraction would put downward pressure on the market price of gold. Miners would then be able to sell gold to the Federal Reserve for a higher price than they otherwise could have obtained on the market. The stock of monetary gold would increase ... producing inflationary pressures. (Greenfield and Yeager, 1989, 6–7)

Were something else to replace gold as anchor, however,

> a straightforward price adjustment would keep gold discoveries from unduly enlarging the money supply. A discovery of gold would reduce the market price of gold, and, as a result, each dollar [note] would be redeemable in a larger physical quantity of gold. The Federal Reserve ... would merely reduce the price at which it bought and sold gold. (Greenfield and Yeager, 1989, 7)

They conclude that the flexibly-priced redemption medium 'would take pressure off the general *level* of wages and prices and focus it upon one particular price, the price of the redemption medium' (1989, 9, their emphasis).

6. It is therefore arguable that much of the observed instability of the nineteenth century gold standard was due, not so much to it being a gold standard as such, but to it being a directly convertible one, and presumably, therefore, to the legal restrictions that forced required banks to use gold as the MOR:

    > Earlier studies of gold standard financial instability have tended to concentrate on the restrictions imposed by the 1844 Bank Charter Act, but the effects of the monetary legislation of 1765, 1819 and 1925 in enforcing a directly convertible gold standard have been largely overlooked ... excessive interest rate volatility or more general financial instability are not inherent either to fractional reserve banking or to the gold standard *per se*, but to the particular *kind* of gold standard that was enforced. The 'defenders' of the gold standard .... were all mistaken in supposing that the only feasible gold standard was a directly convertible one, and some of these writers were also mistaken in accepting that short-term financial instability was the price to be paid for the 'automaticity' of the gold standard and the protection it offered against over-issue. (Dowd, 1991c, 725)

7. The term 'indirect convertibility' was first suggested by James Buchanan (Yeager, 1987, 5) but the underlying idea goes back to John Rooke (1828) and Simon Newcomb (1879). Newcomb proposed that 'the legal tender dollar' be 'defined as the quantity of something, no matter what, sufficient to purchase on the public markets, at average wholesale prices, a definite collection of commodities' (1879, 235). An indirectly convertible system was also put forward by Anderson, (1917, 150–151) and criticised by Wicksell (1919). The first 'modern' proposal embodying indirect convertibility to my knowledge is Bilson (1981), and the various proposals by Greenfield, Yeager, and others followed in the 1980s. For more on the history of indirect convertibility, see especially Woolsey (1987, 21–22, 33–38) and Yeager and Woolsey (1991).

8. This definition differs slightly from other definitions (e.g., those of Woolsey, 1987, chapter 3; Woolsey (1989a,1), Schnadt and Whittaker (1990, 5) or Yeager and Woolsey, 1991, 2,4) in that it specifically excludes the case of 'direct convertibility' in which the anchor commodity and the MOR are identical. To keep the exposition simple, we shall continue to assume that currency is redeemable on demand and that banks undertake not only to redeem their issues, but also to sell them, at the same price.

9. Banks individually or collectively can do little to prevent to fall in the stock of exchange media. It is demand that determines the amount of exchange media that can remain in circulation, and the banks can do little to prevent the stock of exchange media falling if the demand for them falls. Furthermore, a bank only makes its situation worse if it issues more notes when the price of the anchor commodity is above par. Each such note exposes it to arbitrage losses, and issuing additional notes under those circumstances is tantamount to giving money away to those who conducted arbitrage operations against it. The optimal strategy for each bank, in fact, is for it to try to buy up notes itself – its own, and others' – so that it can obtain the arbitrage profits instead of letting them go to others.

10. The arbitrage process does not strictly depend on negligible transactions costs on the part of the public. Even if the general public face 'high' transactions costs, there will be some agents (e.g., financial institutions) who would face relatively small transaction costs, and they have much the same incentive as the general public to strive for the arbitrage profits for themselves. As Yeager (1985b, 16) and Yeager

and Woolsey (1991, 8) point out, implicit arbitrage can also take place, as when purchasers have an incentive to buy commodities quickly because their prices are temporarily low, or when 'industrial' users of the MOR decide to buy it from the banks because it is cheaper to buy it there than on the market.

11.   The paradox was apparently forgotten after Wicksell's work and economists only began to pay attention to it after Woolsey (1987) re-discovered and christened it, and set out the first modern paradox argument in Woolsey (1987, Chapter 4). Paradox arguments were subsequently put forward by Schnadt and Whittaker (1990, 1993), and Cowen and Kroszner (1991, 32–34), but Woolsey himself later retracted his earlier 'pro-paradox' position (Woolsey (1989b). For more on the anti-paradox position, see also Yeager (1987) and Yeager and Woolsey (1991).

12.   The argument here requires only that the price of the anchor adjust sufficiently quickly; it does *not* require that the prices of goods and services *generally* move back to equilibrium at the same rate. Many prices might be sticky for one reason or another, and price stickiness obviously has implications for the way the economy as a whole adjusts. The text is an exercise in partial (rather than general) equilibrium analysis concerned primarily with the particular equilibrating process by which certain arbitrage opportunities are eliminated, and the argument that the process described in the text equilibrates the anchor and MOR markets is in no way undermined by the (valid) claim that prices in other markets might take longer to equilibrate.

13.   Paradox issues also cause particularly acute difficulties for the 'compensated dollar' schemes discussed in Chapter 14. These problems arise when private agents anticipate that the banks will change the price they are currently pegging. They will buy or sell accordingly and the price peg will come under speculative attack. This speculative attack is essentially a form of paradox. There also exists the same paradox-type incentive to retire all outstanding MOE if the price is expected to move one way, and to demand an arbitrarily high amount of MOE if it is expected to go the other way. There is no apparent solution to these problems, and they make these schemes effectively unworkable. These paradox-related problems are consequently much more serious than those arising under direct or indirect convertibility.

14.   The real bills doctrine was originated by John Law (1705) who advocated a currency secured by the value of real property which would also respond to what would later be described as the legitimate needs of trade. He believed such a currency would result in price stability because the land collateral would prevent any inflationary over-issue. But as the text goes on to explain, he failed to see that the nominal value of the land collateral itself rises with the price level. The doctrine is also to be found in the arguments of the Bank of England directors during the Bullionist controversy in the first decade of the nineteenth century and in scattered references throughout the rest of that century. It was later written into the original Federal Reserve Act (1913) and appears in early Federal Reserve policy statements. In recent times, it has reappeared again in the form of proposals to target interest and unemployment rates. The standard references on the real bills fallacy are Thornton ([1802] 1978) and Mints (1945), but the reader might also look at Humphrey (1982), Selgin (1989), Glasner (1992), and Timberlake (1993).

15.   The term "sufficient" must be emphasised here. The fallacy is to believe that accommodating the needs of trade is *sufficient* (i.e., nothing else is necessary) to tie down prices. The real-bills fallacy is thus to be distinguished from 'legitimate' needs-of-trade theories which assert that banks should attempt to meet the needs of trade, but do not assert that doing so is sufficient to tie the price level down. Any 'legitimate' needs of trade doctrine is therefore always associated with some other rule (e.g., convertibility) to determine the price level. Even 'legitimate' needs of trade theories have their problems – see no. 5 – but they should be confused with the real bills system or dismissed as versions of it.

16. Adam Smith is often wrongly identified as one of the authors of the real bills doctrine. Mints (1945, 288) regarded him as "the first thoroughgoing exponent of the real bills doctrine" in its modern form with commercial bills rather than land as the security for the note issue, and most other writers broadly agree with him (e.g., Laidler (1981)). However, this interpretation of Smith is hard to reconcile with what he actually wrote. While he was not always clear and consistent, Smith saw the importance of convertibility onto a specie standard, and appreciated that the law of reflux that operated in such a system provided an effective check against over- issue (e.g., ([1776] 1911, 265)). He also clearly understood that bankers could not in practice distinguish 'real' bills from 'fictitious' ones, and he appreciated that the real bills doctrine therefore could not provide banks with an operational rule to follow ([1776] 1911, 277-278)). In addition, he strongly criticised the true author of the doctrine, John Law, for falsely imagining that the problems he sought to cure could be solved merely by creating more money ([1776] 1911, 282-283)). These passages demonstrate that, far from being one of the earliest supporters of the real bills fallacy, Smith was actually one of its most penetrating critics. His famous 'real bills' passage - where he talks of a bank discounting a "real bill of exchange drawn by a real creditor upon a real debtor" ([1776] 1911, 269) – is often interpreted as his statement of support for the real bills doctrine, but if the passage is read in context, it becomes reasonably clear that the policy rule he is recommending is for banks to protect their reserves, *not* to try to tell which bills are real and which are not, and then discount only the real ones. See also, e.g., Dowd (1984).

17. The alternative is a monetary rule (e.g., a k percent monetary growth rule) which determines the money supply. The price level is then given by

$$P = (V/Q)M$$

and is thus also determinate. However monetary growth rules are inferior to commodity-based convertibility systems because, among other reasons, they usually involve inefficient restrictions on commercial banks' activities, because they generally necessitate central control on the issue of base money, because 'slippage' (i.e., imperfect correlation) between M and P creates price-level instability, and because monetary targets are in practice extremely difficult to meet. They are discussed further in chapter 14.

18. In particular, banks can only increase their lending to the extent that they can issue more equity capital, run down other assets (e.g., reserves), or increase the demand to hold their liabilities. Since each of these has its costs, any increased supply of loans would normally require a higher loan rate of interest to make it worthwhile. The correct 'needs of trade' doctrine is therefore that competitive banks will normally meet an increased demand for loans by expanding their supply *and* raising the loan rate of interest, and the higher loan rate will choke off some of the increased demand. We would *not* expect an increased demand for loans to be matched *pari passu* with an increased supply at a constant rate of interest. Note also that the supply of money responds not so much to the demand for *loans*, as many versions of the 'needs of trade' doctrine imply, but to the demand for *money*, and any reaction of the money supply to the loan demand must take place through the banks' balance sheet constraints.

19. It is a sad irony that many writers have believed the two go together. In the nineteenth century British monetary controversies, the supporters of the currency school were quick to accuse their opponents in the free-banking and banking schools of adherence to it, but the basis of these criticisms was often the currency school's own failure to understand reflux mechanisms and the (partially correct) needs of trade doctrines on which the strongest of their opponents relied (see, e.g.,

Laidler (1975)) A more recent example is Sargent and Wallace (1982) who actually *identify* the real bills doctrine with free banking. (The 'real bills doctrine' they define as 'unfettered private intermediation or central bank operations designed to produce the effects of such intermediation' (1982, 1212).) They then announce 'something of a rehabilitation of the real-bills doctrine' (1982, 1214), but the doctrine they rehabilitate is *not* the real bills fallacy at all, but free banking. This identification of two very different positions does serious damage, not only tarnishing free banking with the brush of a discredited position with which it is actually inconsistent, but also lending a spurious credibility to an exploded fallacy which sound monetary economists have long recognised to be beyond rehabilitation. The Sargent–Wallace identification of the two positions was later destroyed by Laidler (1984) who pointed out that 'it was of the very essence of the real-bills doctrine that, far from bank lending being unrestricted, it should be confined to loans made on the security of' real bills, and who also pointed out that the real bills doctrine 'did *not* ... involve a defense of *laissez-faire* in the banking industry' (1984, 153, my emphasis).

20. Law's Bank opened in 1716 and initially issued convertible notes with great success. However, convertibility was dropped in 1719, and in early 1720 Law made the mistake of pegging the price of the stock of his Compagnie des Indes, and in so doing established a real- bills system. His attempts to maintain that price forced him to inflate the currency rapidly, but it soon became apparent that the experiment was unsustainable and despite attempts to salvage it, the system collapsed by the end of the year. Law then fled to Belgium, and it was a very long time before the French people could be induced to deal with banks again.

21. The anti-bullionists (who included the Bank directors) 'adhered to the doctrine in its crudest, most uncompromising form' (Humphrey (1982, 8)) and argued that even an inconvertible currency could not be overissued provided it was advanced against short-term commercial bills. They maintained that any excess issues would return to the issuer since firms would return what they did not need to keep their borrowing costs down. This position implies the very dangerous doctrine that the supply of money is constrained by the demand for it even under conditions of inconvertibility and is 'the origin of the notion that central banks cannot cause inflation since they merely supply money passively in response to a prior real demand for it' (Humphrey (1982, 9)). The fallacy of their position was laid out clearly by Thornton ([1802] 1978) and by the authors of the Bullion Report (1810). 'Respectable' monetary opinion in later years would – quite rightly – have nothing to do with it.

22. Unique among the cases mentioned here, the real bills policy of the Federal Reserve operated in the context of a convertible currency and did not immediately produce the inflation experienced in the other cases. Nonetheless, the Fed's adherence to the real bills fallacy would have weakened its commitment to maintain convertibility, and probably helped to pave the way for its subsequent acceptance of later versions of the real bills doctrine according to which it should target interest rates or unemployment.

23. The German hyperinflation is perhaps the most notorious example of inflationary policy stemming from the belief that central banks cannot cause inflation because they merely create money to accommodate the public's demand for it. Reichsbank President Rudolf Havenstein maintained this position throughout the hyperinflation and denied point-blank that his policy of accommodating the demand for commercial paper could be inflationary. Yet the Reichsbank's discount rate was never more than 90 percent a year at any time during the inflation, and with an inflation rate of many thousands of percent a year and rising, this discount policy created a massive and rising incentive to borrow. The more the Reichsbank accommodated the public demand for discounts, the worse the inflation became,

and the greater the demand for discounts. The Reichsbank became trapped in an inflationary treadmill which its own policy caused to accelerate out of control. Havenstein was right when he claimed he was accommodating the public demand, but he failed to see that the extent of that demand depends on the discount rate, and that it was his own discount policy which was the driving force behind the inflation process.

24. Tying the stock of money to any real variable - be it the real interest rate (or the nominal interest, with inflationary expectations assumed given), unemployment or output produces the same prices-money-prices feedback mechanism as one gets under older versions of the real bills proposal. Unless the target variable is pegged at its 'natural' level - in which case the policy is redundant anyway - the central bank gets caught in a trap in which it has to expand money supply at a faster rate to keep to its target, but in the process it creates more inflationary pressure which requires even faster monetary expansion the next period to keep the target variable in line. The attempt to keep real variables at inappropriate levels thus leads to a dynamically unstable process in which the inflation rate rises [or, indeed, falls] without limit (as explained, e.g., in Friedman, 1968). Consequently, the 'interest targeting proposal [and others like it] may be viewed as merely the latest reincarnation of the discredited real bills fallacy' (Humphrey (1982, 12)).

13 MONOMETALLIC, BIMETALLIC AND RELATED MONETARY STANDARDS

1. My notion of a commodity standard also encompasses but does not require the 'strict' or 100 percent reserve standard in which all exchange media are either commodities or warehouse claims to commodities. The 'strict' commodity standard has many adherents, but suffers from the drawback that it imposes relatively large 'resource costs'. These costs might be bearable if the benefits of a strict commodity standard could not otherwise be achieved, but not if (as is in fact the case) commodity standards can be maintained with few if any resource costs.

2. By and large, modern theoretical work has advanced certain areas of knowledge at the price of overlooking insights provided by older work, and it is arguable that economists a century ago had a better intuitive grasp of commodity systems than contemporary economists. To quote Niehans,

> The analysis of commodity money has made hardly any progress in the last fifty years. Actually, more knowledge was forgotten than was newly acquired. Economists seemed to feel that the books contained whatever there was to know in this field and tended to become bored whenever the subject was mentioned [and, he adds in a footnote, non-economists were bored even more] ... some of the leading economists around the turn of the century might have been better equipped to cope with [certain modern monetary] problems than many present-day experts, raised on models in which currency is printed costlessly and handed out for nothing. (Niehans, 1978, 141)

Another factor, which Niehans also notes (1978, 140), is the tendency for discussions of commodity monetary systems to ignore substantive issues and be dominated by Keynes' diatribes against the gold standard. We shall return to these issues later.

3. Where the assumption of an exogenous gold supply *does* make a difference, I shall flag the difference as we go along, but many results are much the same whether we endogenise the gold supply or not. However, one important difference should be noted upfront. Since supply is exogenous, the model cannot handle cases where

supply responds to a change in the relative price of gold. Given that gold is durable, this means that the model fails to pick up certain asymmetries that arise where supply is endogenised. Imagine that demand rises and supply rises in response. If demand then falls again, the greater output that occurred when demand rose cannot be 'undone', and the price has to fall to a lower level than it was before output first rose. If demand had fallen and then rose, on the other hand, supply would not have responded, and the relative price would return to its initial value. For more on these effects, see Dowd and Sampson, 1993a, 383, 389-390).

4.   Strictly speaking, Britain was on a bimetallic standard until 1797, but the legal gold-silver price ratio left gold overvalued. Gold consequently displaced silver, and the country was *de facto* on a gold standard. The convertibility of the currency was suspended in 1797 and restored in 1821 when silver was also demonetised and Britain established a formal (i.e., *de jure*) gold standard.

5.   The US had been formally on a bimetallic standard since 1792, but the revision of the legal price ratio in 1834 left gold overvalued and put the country on a *de facto* gold standard. Convertibility was suspended over part of the period 1838–1843, and then again from 1861 to 1879. The gold standard was then restored on a *de jure* basis, as with Britain in 1821, and remained formally unchanged for the rest of the period.

6.   The most detailed theoretical treatment of bimetallism in recent years is Chen (1972), but his model does not go beyond 'effective bimetallism' or have any detailed analysis of parachute effects. He does, however, have a detailed treatment of the effect of imperfect substitutability between the two metals in their monetary uses, while my model assumes they are (more or less) perfect monetary substitutes. Niehans (1978, 153–158), Bordo (1987, 243–245), Friedman (1990a, b) and Timberlake (1993) discuss bimetallism in some detail, and Dowd (1994c) provides a more detailed treatment of the model in the text. Briefer discussions of bimetallism are to be found in Burstein (1986, 54–7) and Barro (1979), though the latter simply echoes the traditional monometallist view that there is nothing under bimetallism to keep the market price ratio in line with the legal ratio.

7.   The parachute effect did however have its critics. For example, Giffen (1895) argued that there was very little interchangeability between gold and silver even for monetary purposes. Giffen thus denied the basis of the compensatory action, though he (inconsistently) acknowledged that some compensation did nonetheless take place. The correct position, as far as I can see, is that some compensation takes place provided there is some substitutability between the two metals in their monetary uses – and the closer substitutes they are, the more takes place. A modern critic is Chen (1972) who attempted to use his model to verify the parachute and found that he could obtain no clear results when he tried to allow for the differences in the gold-silver exchange ratio and in the demand for silver between the two regimes. He concluded by dismissing it – 'Enchanted perhaps by the elegance of the reservoir simile [they used], the bimetallists seem to have overlooked the significant implications of the structural differences involved' (1972, 107). I would suggest that Chen's failure to find a parachute effect merely reflects the weakness of his model – a weakness illustrated by the fact that his model is also unable to predict relatively 'straightforward' effects on prices such as the effect of a rise in the stock of silver, or of changes in the monetary or non-monetary demands for the precious metals (1972, 106). The old bimetallists were largely correct.

8.   One other difference between the two systems should also be noted, but one that applies only to directly convertible systems. Rothwell (1897, 94–95) pointed out in that under the traditional debtor bimetallism, a fall in the value of one metal will lead to an increase in its monetary demand – if gold falls in value, debtors will

demand more gold to settle their debts – and this increased demand helps to restore the value of the cheaper metal back to par. However, with a creditor bimetallism, there will be an increase in the monetary demand for the more expensive metal, and this increased demand will tend to push the values of the two metals even further apart, and 'might soon destroy the ratio' (Rothwell, 1897, 95).

9. As Garrison (1985, 66) points out, apart from assuming a pure commodity standard, these estimates also make the dubious assumption that the supply of gold is perfectly elastic, and the 'fact that the supply of gold is actually *inelastic* is simply brushed aside'. The more elastic supply is assumed to be, the bigger the resulting estimate of the resource costs involved, so it is perhaps not too surprising that the estimates are as big as they are. Had they assumed a perfectly inelastic supply, on the other hand, then the price level would adjust to clear the gold market with no output response, and the resource costs would (according to this procedure) be *zero*. An additional problem, also noted by Garrison (1985, 77, n. 13), is that estimating these costs by multiplying them by the growth rate of the economy gives rise to a curious paradox: 'If mismanaged paper money causes so much economic discoordination that the growth rate drops to zero, the estimated resource costs of maintaining a gold standard would also drop to zero; but if the adoption of the now-inexpensive gold standard creates economic stability and fosters new growth, maintaining the gold standard would once again become too costly'.

14   COMMODITY-BASKET MONETARY STANDARDS

1. The price-index schemes referred to in this chapter are not to be confused with the 'tabular standard' of Jevons ([1875] 1907) and others. The schemes considered here use indices to *stabilise the monetary unit itself* (e.g., the dollar), while the tabular standard uses an index to determine *the number of monetary units to be paid over*. The former are examined in this chapter, and the latter in appendix 2.

2. A symmetallic system was first proposed by Marshall ([1887b] 1966), though he called it a 'stable bimetallism' and objected that the conventional bimetallic system 'has no strict title to [the bimetallic] name' ([1887] 1966, 188). Marshall's terminology did not catch on, however, and the term bimetallism continued to be used to refer to the old switching system. The term symmetallism was first suggested by Edgeworth (1895, 442-443).

3. The use of full-bodied (as opposed to token) symmetallic coins has a number of disadvantages apart from the obvious ones of the wear and tear on coins and the wearing out of pockets. Unlike gold or silver, there is no obvious use for the alloy as such, so the use of full-bodied coins imposes the costs of fusing and splitting the metals which could otherwise be avoided (Butenschön, 1936, 27). Butenschon also points out that including silver might make them unsuitable for large-denomination transactions, but too high a gold content would make the coins unsuitable for small transactions, and it is also difficult to test the composition of such coins.

4. Marshall wrote that, 'If there should ever exist any other commodities besides gold and silver, which, like them, are imperishable, which have great value in small bulk, and are in universal demand, and which are thus suitable for paying the balances of foreign trade, then they could be added to gold and silver as the basis of the currency' ([1887b] 1966, 206). However, Marshall restricted his choice of commodities to those which might be suitable redemption or exchange media in an international trade system that still uses commodities for exchange purposes. As argued elsewhere, there is no reason to restrict the choice of redemption media, and the claim that international trade relies on commodity media of exchange was to

some extent anachronistic even in Marshall's day.

5.   Jevons ([1875] 1907, 327 – 328) suggested that a £100 note might 'give the owners a right to demand one quarter of good wheat, one ton of ordinary merchant bar iron, one hundred pounds weight of middling cotton, twenty five pounds of sugar, five pounds of tea, and other articles sufficient to make up the value', but then rejected the scheme on the grounds that, 'In practice, such a legal tender currency would obviously be most inconvenient, since no one would wish to have a miscellaneous assortment of goods forced into his possession.' Like Marshall, Jevons rejected schemes with a basket anchor because he *assumed* that they would require the issuer to use the basket itself as a regular MOR.

6.   The CRC idea was suggested by Goudriaan (1932), Benjamin Graham (1937, 1944) and Frank Graham (1942), and produced considerable discussion in the 1940s. CRC schemes have been proposed not only to stabilise the price level, but also to afford relief for certain industries by including their products in the basket in order to promote the demand for them. For more on these schemes, see also Friedman (1951) and Hart (1987).

7.   The limits themselves would be determined in part by any bid – ask spreads the issuers might operate. Most versions of the scheme call for such a spread, and some for spreads of 5 percent or more (see Hart, 1987, 498). A spread is convenient to the issuers, but the larger it is, the more the market price of the bundle itself can fluctuate, and less stable the price level would presumably be. One advantage of the price-level stabilisation scheme proposed later in this chapter over those considered here is that it would dispense with bid – ask spreads without inconveniencing the banks.

8.   In practice, this counter-cyclical effect might be limited by the relatively small number of goods that could be included in a CRC basket. For reasons to be explained shortly, Friedman (1953, 234) believed that no more than 4–8 percent of national output could be included. Assuming the basket has a supply elasticity of 2.5, then changes in the output of the basket would offset 10–20 percent of any change in aggregate nominal income, and Friedman felt that this figure was probably an overestimate anyway (Friedman, 1953, 235).

9.   The monetary demand for the basket might also lead a CRC system to stabilise the economy in other ways. If private agents wished to 'hoard' exchange media, their increased demand for the latter would increase the demand for the basket itself – 'The hoarding of money, instead of causing resources to run to waste, would act as if it were an order to keep raw commodities for the hoarder's account' (Hayek, 1948, 213) – and the production of basket-commodities would rise and help restore economic activity. Shifts between monetary and non-monetary uses of the basket-commodities might also stabilise the economy (see, e.g., Friedman, 1953, 211, 232–233), but Friedman concluded in the end that the possible changes in the supply of money arising from shifts between [these] stocks would still be 'extremely limited' (1953, 233).

10. These reserve-holding costs are especially high for those versions of the CRC system (e.g., Graham, 1944) that propose that issuers of exchange media should hold 100 percent reserves. Some indication of the costs imposed by 100 percent reserve systems is given by Friedman (1953, 210). He notes that it would have required about a 3 percent annual increase in the quantity of the circulating medium over the previous fifty years or so to have kept prices stable had velocity remained constant. Allowing for a decline in velocity of 1 percent a year, the quantity of circulating medium would have had to increase by a little over 4 percent a year. Given that this quantity was about 50 percent of national income, about 2 percent of national income would then have been required annually just to add to the circulating medium had velocity continued to decline, and 1.5 percent had velocity

stabilised. The resource costs of a 100 percent reserve requirement version of a CRC system are clearly very high indeed.

11. The ANCAP is a bundle consisting of '33 cents worth of ammonium nitrate, 12 cents worth of copper, 36 cents worth of aluminum, and 19 cents worth of plywood (all in 1967 prices)' and Hall claims that it had a 'market price very close to the cost of living throughout the postwar era' (Hall, 1982, 115). However, he then points out that in 1955 the price of the bundle rose 9 percent relative to the CPI, and in 1974 by 10 percent, while in 1970 it fell relatively by almost 9 percent, though the comovement was closer in other years. I would not share Hall's assessment that figures like these constitute a particularly good fit, but readers can judge for themselves.

12. Unpublished empirical work to assess how the ANCAP would have performed in the 1980s was carried out by Fernando Alvarez of Fairleigh Dickinson University who concluded that the relationship on which Hall had relied had subsequently broken down. I thank Lawrence H. White for this information.

13. There was of course also the work of Wicksell (e.g., Wicksell, 1898). He also suggested that price-level stabilisation should take precedence over fixed-exchange rates, but unlike the writers discussed in the text, suggested that the price level should be stabilised by manipulating the discount rate. Wicksell's work thus took a somewhat different direction from the literature considered here. For more on the Wicksell approach and its adherents, see, e.g., Humphrey (1990).

14. The potential for confusion over Fisher's scheme is not helped by his claim (which, in any case, is overly modest) that the earlier plans of Newcomb and Williams 'are so nearly identical with mine as to leave nothing vital which I can still claim as original and unanticipated' except his provisos against gold speculation (Fisher, 1914, 819, n. 1). The differences between these plans are actually quite significant. In particular, Fisher's scheme differed from Newcomb's in not involving indirect convertibility, and it differed from Williams' in that it involved a much greater level of operational detail. As the text makes clear later, these 'operational details' are very important. The reader interested in Fisher's 'compensated dollar' might also look at Humphrey (1990, 1992), Sumner (1990, 111, 115–116) and Patinkin (1993).

15. If we prefer, we can translate all statements about the weight of the gold dollar into statements about the price of gold. If each gold dollar consisted of 25.8 grains of gold 9/10 fine and there are 480 grains in the Troy ounce, it required 480 divided by 25.8–or 18.60 – dollars to weigh one ounce. The price of gold would therefore be $18.60 an ounce. If the weight of the gold dollar rises 50 percent to 38.7 grains, the price of gold therefore falls by two thirds (i.e., 25.8/38.7) to $12.40. The greater the weight of the gold dollar, the lower the dollar-price of gold. See also Fisher (1913a, 219–220, 223–224).

16. Two important qualifications should be noted here. The assumption that the weight of gold in the dollar must change by *exactly* the same proportion as the increase in the price level is made only for simplicity of exposition, and Fisher did not strictly hold to it. He was well aware that the change in the weight of the gold dollar could itself affect the value of gold bullion in much the same way that prying up a stone infinitesimally moves the earth, and he discussed this problem at length in Fisher (1913c, appendix 3). This issue raises the difficult question of how the central bank is to know what the *relative* price of gold should be, so that it can allow for it and still hit its price-level target, and what happens if the central bank should miss. We shall discuss this issue shortly. The other qualification is that the Fisher plan requires 'an increase of 1 percent in the weight of the dollar for every 1 percent excess of the index number *above par* then outstanding' (his emphasis), and does *not* require an increase of 1 percent in the weight of gold for every 1 percent

increase in the index number since the last adjustment (Fisher, 1914, 829); see also Fisher (1913d, 50–51). The difference is in the extent to which the price (or weight) of gold is to alter in the face of a persistent alteration of the price index from par. Imagine the index rose and then stayed at a certain level for several periods. Under the latter, incorrect interpretation of his system, the price of gold would rise to a particular level *and stay there* until after the index had started to fall again, but under the former, correct interpretation, it would *keep rising* until after the index had started to fall. The latter system thus provides a stronger cumulative push to the price index to steer it in the right direction, but there is a danger, which Fisher underrated, that it could push the price level too much and destabilise it. Again, we shall come back to this issue later.

17.   There was some contemporary discussion of whether the compensated dollar gave the appropriate degree of 'correction' to movements of the price index from par, but no contemporary writers got to the heart of the problem. Typical of the level of contemporary debate was Taussig's (1913) not-too-convincing assertion that the Fisher rule operated too slowly to correct the price level, and Fisher's lame response that the correction would begin as soon as the price level was altered, but would still take time. Exactly how long it would take 'we have no exact means of knowing', but he suggested that the recent evidence that Canadian and US price levels under the gold standard 'correspond with each other year by year with extreme precision' gives us some indication of the answer (Fisher, 1914, 821). This response does not of course address Taussig's criticism properly, but the criticism itself is not well substantiated.

18.   To make the argument more concrete, suppose y, the rate of interest, is 5 percent per period, z, the expected fall in the price of gold, is 10 percent, and x, the government's bid – ask spread, is 10 percent. Clearly, $z \leq x$, which satisfies Fisher's condition. Now suppose our agent forms his expectation of the fall in the price of gold at the start of the period, and acts immediately. He therefore sells gold, and invests the proceeds to obtain the full-period interest return of 5 percent. He then sells the gold back again to the government when the price has changed, making a capital gain of 10 percent (z) minus 10 percent (x), or nothing. He therefore finds himself with the gold he started with, but has made 5 percent interest in the meantime. He has effectively obtained an interest-free loan at the government's expense.

19.   Fisher appears to have overlooked this problem. After discussing why an additional restriction was needed against upward changes in price, he then dismissed the danger of speculative attack when prices were expected to fall:

> No similar precaution need be taken against the opposite form of speculation – for a fall in the price of bullion. Such speculation would not injure the Government reserve, but rather strengthen it by the temporary addition of stocks of bullion which dealers can spare for a time and so sell to the Government at present high prices ... . Moreover it could be shown that such speculation, besides being harmless, would be unimportant, for the reason that the stock of gold bullion outside the Government vaults available for such operations is never likely to be large. (1913c, 387)

This argument is uncharacteristically weak. It is true, but irrelevant, that the government's stocks temporarily rise, and the illustration in the text proves wrong Fisher's claim that such speculation would be harmless. Fisher is then left with the argument that the amount of gold available for such operations is limited, but limited as they are, private stocks of gold were (and are) still large in absolute terms. The government could therefore still face very large losses.

20.   These schemes are not to be confused with some of Hall's other proposals. Hall

(1984a) suggests targeting nominal GNP instead of the price level, with the monetary authority left to itself to decide how to achieve its objective, and Hall (1986) suggests that the monetary authority stabilise a weighted average of price and unemployment volatility by manipulating an interest differential. Hall (1983) suggests several schemes by which the government creates special 'reserve certificates' and stabilises the price level by indexing their return to the price level. (We shall come back to Hall, 1983, in note 30 below.) Hall (1981), by contrast, suggests that the government can achieve price-level stability by simply *defining* a stable-valued unit of account for private agents to use.

21. While compensated dollar rules involve feedback from the deviation of the target price index from par to the *price* of some MOR, we can also visualise 'quantity' rules in which the deviation of the price index from par feeds back to affect the *quantity* of some monetary aggregate and return prices to par. A good example is McCulloch (1991). The McCulloch rule is robust to some at least of the generic drawbacks of the compensated dollar that are explained in the next section, but the choice of parameter values is still arbitrary and it is unclear how much price-level stability it would generate. 'Quantity' rules also have the drawback that they appear to presuppose an issuer who can control the target monetary aggregate, which in turn presupposes some degree of government intervention and the evils that come with it.

22. Miles (1984, Chapter 10) and Sumner (1989, 1991, 1995) has also suggested using futures contracts (or similar contracts) to stabilise nominal variables, and the ideas involved in such schemes have also been examined by Woolsey in a variety of places (e.g., Woolsey, 1992a, 1992b, 1992c). Woolsey (1992c) is particularly good on these issues. The scheme set out in the text was first published in the *EJ* in July 1994, but was couched there as a rule for the Bank of England to follow (Dowd, 1994a). Nonetheless, the rule itself is essentially the same regardless of whether it is adopted by a group of free banks or by a central bank.

23. The difference between this contract and a 'pure' price- index futures contract is in the timing of A's payment: Agent A pays when the contract *matures* in the 'pure' futures contract, but pays when the contract is *agreed* in the quasi-futures contract. This difference is important and its significance will be explained presently. To complicate matters somewhat, 'real world' futures contracts typically incorporate a margin requirement that obliges the purchaser to make some part of his payment up-front, and futures contracts with margin requirements can be regarded as combinations of quasi-futures contracts and 'pure' futures contracts. We shall ignore this complication and discuss only quasi- and 'pure' futures contracts, but the interested reader might look at Woolsey (1992c).

24. We do not have to make this assumption, but if we do not make it, we have to carry the term $[(1 + r_t)/(1 + r_t^*)]$ through much of the rest of the discussion. Dropping the term clarifies the argument without loss of generality. In any case, the marginal financial operator on whom our basic equilibration story depends will choose some representative market interest rate as his discount rate, so the assumption that $[(1 + r_t)/(1 + r_t^*)]$ is approximately unity is not unreasonable.

25. The reader will now appreciate why it is important that the contract is paid for at the time it is made (i.e., we have a quasi-futures contract), and not on the maturity date (as in a futures contract *per se*): If no payment is made when the contract is agreed, the purchase of a contract would make no difference to the supply of MOE. If the supply of MOE does not fall, the equilibrating process described in the text would be short-circuited, and there is no obvious alternative equilibrating process that could take its place. The point of making purchase payments at the time the contract is made is to ensure appropriate changes in the supply of MOE.

26. Asking whether there would be a market for QFCs under the proposed monetary rule is *not* the same as asking whether QFCs would attract traders if some private

institution decided to make a market in them (as happened in the United States). There are good reasons to believe that any new attempt to launch a CPI-futures contract would meet much the same fate (see Horrigan, 1987), but the text nonetheless argues that the adoption of the proposed rule would still give rise to whatever trading was required *despite* the failure of the CPI-futures market in the United States. What matters is not that the issuing banks offer to trade contracts, as such, but that they offer to trade them at a *fixed price*. Horrigan considers the former, but it is the latter that matters here.

27.   The simplest suitable instrument is a 'pure' RPI-futures contract which we can consider as a simple bet on the future RPI (see Horrigan, 1987). In its essentials, this contract offers to make an RPI-contingent payment in 5 years' time, at a price agreed now but paid after 5 years. Suppose the current RPI has a value of 1 and each contract offers to pay $1 times the realised value of the future RPI. Since the banks would expect the future RPI to be the same as it is now, the banks would expect to pay out $1 on each contract they sold, and would therefore expect to make a profit by selling contracts at any price above $1. Since private agents would expect the RPI to be 1.25, they would expect to receive $1.25 for each contract they bought. They would therefore expect to make a profit from buying contracts at any price less than $1.25. Both the banks and private agents would consequently expect to make a profit for any contract price between $1 and $1.25. Their different expectations of the future price level thus create scope for a market in RPI-futures.

28.   The private sector would of course also want some reassurance that the banks would not then pursue a policy of deflation to maximise the real value of their winnings against private sector agents. All the banks need to do to provide this reassurance is to insert into their betting contracts a clause that implies that the banks will effectively lose the bet if prices fall, or fall too much. This clause might specify that if prices fall, the rate of deflation would be considered as if it were an inflation rate for the purposes of settling the bet. A deflation rate of 1 percent might be regarded as 'equivalent' for betting purposes to an inflation rate of 1 percent, a deflation rate of 2 percent as equivalent to an inflation rate of 2 percent, etc. The banks would then have the same incentive to avoid deflation as to avoid inflation.

29.   Under the Thompson–Glasner plan, banks undertake to redeem their currency on demand for gold valued at its current market price, but if the price level rises above target, they pay compensation to those who had bought gold from them, and demand compensation from those who had sold gold to them; if the price level falls below target, the banks demand compensation from those who bought gold from them, and pay compensation to those to whom they sold gold. Arbitrage operations then ensure that the supply of currency is adjusted in the right direction if the expected price level should deviate from its target. Apart from having a more complex settlement procedure once the value of the price index is announced, this plan differs from mine in relying on a formal feedback process whose stability properties still need to be demonstrated. It also omits operational details that need to be spelt out if it is to be properly evaluated. It *may* be the case, for example, that it is vulnerable to an 'interest-free loan problem' or other problems that are not immediately apparent.

30.   Hall (1983) actually suggests several schemes, but in his final one suggests that the government create two types of debt which are otherwise similar except for one being indexed to the price level and the other not. The central bank then engages in open-market operations to keep the relative price of the two types of debt at par, and he argues that arbitrage operations should stabilise the expected price level (Hall, 1983, 44). However, it is unclear whether this scheme could be modified to apply to a *laissez-faire* financial system, implying that it might rely on some implicit legal restriction or other government intervention. But even if we

accept it on its own terms, the scheme in practice comes down to maintaining parity between the prices of indexed and (otherwise similar) unindexed debt, and, while such parity might be *necessary* to achieve price-level stability, it is not obviously *sufficient* to achieve it. However, it may be that a modified version of the scheme might be adequate.

31. These are (1) the identity test (i.e., equal prices and quantities in two periods should imply that the index is one, where the index is the ratio of two price 'levels'); (2) the proportionality test (i.e., multiplying all prices in period 2 by α leads to an index that is α-times greater); (3) the invariance-to-changes-in-scale test, (4) the invariance-to-changes-in-units test, (5) the time-reversal test (i.e., if we interchange the role of periods 1 and 2 in our index, then new index should be the reciprocal of the old); (6) the commodity-reversal test (i.e., all commodities should be treated in an even-handed manner); (7) the monotonicity test (i.e., if any later period prices rise, the index cannot fall); (8) the mean value test (i.e., the index should lie between the small and largest price ratio over all included commodities); (9) the circularity test (i.e., a test of transitivity); (10) the factor-reversal test (i.e., the multiple of the appropriate price and quantity indices should equal an expenditure index); and (11) the 'irrelevance of tiny commodities' test (i.e., commodities demanded in very small amounts should have a very small effect on the overall price index). An extensive discussion of most of these tests is found in Fisher (1911, 385-429).

32. A problem with the Laspeyres index, and others that also use fixed-weight baskets of goods, is that they suffer from substitution bias in the face of relative price changes. Since the basket is fixed, they implicitly presume that agents carry on buying exactly the same quantities of goods even if their prices rise. In general, however, we would expect them to buy less of those goods whose price rose, and more of those goods whose price fell. The actual basket will then change, and the costs of maintaining, say, a given standard of living, would be less than a fixed-basket index would indicate. The fixed-basket index would thus overstate the true cost of living, and we may need to take this substitution bias into account. However, the empirical evidence indicates that this bias is relatively small in practice and makes a difference of 0.1–0.2 percent a year to the price index (Triplett, 1983, 378).

33. A superlative index is one that gives an exact price for a unit cost function with a flexible functional form, and a function is said to be flexible if it gives a second-order approximation to an arbitrary function which is twice-continuously differentiable (Diewert, 1987, 773). The advantage of a superlative index, as the text implies, is that it gives a more accurate approximation to the unknown 'ideal' index than traditional indices normally do.

34. It is important that index values be regarded as 'final' when they are published, and not be subject to *ex-post* revision. If announced values are later altered, those who lost out because the index took the value it did rather than the later revised value would have an incentive to seek compensation through the courts, with the consequence that those who sign contracts involving index-contingent payments would never know for sure what they owe or are owed.

35. Deaton and Muellbauer (1980, 254) quote a report of the Prices Statistics Review Committee of the US Congress in 1961 which stated that most economists then seemed to feel that the most important defect of price indices was their failure to take account of quality changes, but, as noted a little later in the text, Triplett (1983, 381) found that official indices were by no means automatically biased by this failure. It is therefore not clear how important the quality-change bias actually is, if indeed it exists at all.

36. Similar results apply to labour contracts. The studies of Baily, 1974, Azariadis,

1975 and others strongly suggest that wage contracts should be indexed because workers are primarily concerned with real and not nominal income.

37.   There is also the impact of tabular standards on the price level. The impact of any indexation is presumably negligible in a commodity monetary system, but it might be significant in a fiat system if it influenced the policies pursued by the central bank. Friedman, 1974, Bernstein (1974, 83–86) and Fischer (1986b, 154) suggested that indexation would lead to lower inflation by reducing the central bank's incentive to inflate (e.g., by reducing the costs of disinflation by making the Phillips curve steeper), and this argument receives support from the empirical evidence of Fischer (1986b, 193) that countries with indexation experienced lower rates of monetary growth than countries without it following the oil price shock of 1974. On the other hand, indexation might lead to higher inflation if the central bank responded to the loss in inflation revenue by increasing the rate of monetary growth (e.g., Fellner, 1974, 63; Fischer, 1986b, 152).

38.   Legal restrictions do not appear to be a major factor behind the failure to adopt indexation. In the first place, there are often relatively few obvious legal restrictions to contend with (see, e.g., Friedman, 1974, 38), and the fact that the legal (and tax) status of escalator clauses is still so uncertain in many countries also indicates that there has been relatively little demand for them. Had the demand been there, we would have expected test cases to clarify their status. The potential impact of legal restrictions in Canada was also investigated by the Canadian Lortie Committee which concluded that the obstacles they posed were 'fairly minor; probably no more severe than those encountered by issuers of variable-rate mortgages' (Howitt, 1986, 206).

39.   Fischer (1986b) discusses this issue in some detail and suggests that, while these lags might explain the absence of short-term bonds, they cannot explain the absence of long-term ones. The longer the term on a bond, the proportionately better approximation to maintaining its real value does indexing to the most recent price level provide. Fischer's estimates of these errors led him to conclude that 'The error from out of date price information is small relative to the uncertainty about the real return on a three-year nominal bond; for ten- or twenty-year bonds the price information lag is of almost no significance relative to price-level uncertainty over the lifetime of the bond. Thus price data collection delays cannot account for the absence of long-term indexed bonds.' (Fischer, 1986b, 266).

40.   The argument that agents are unfamiliar with the principles of indexation does not stand up well to scrutiny. As Howitt writes in his Canadian study,
      it is doubtful that Canadians would find indexed debt any more mysterious or complicated than they found variable- rate debt before it was introduced. Indexation of public sector pensions, the Canada Pension Plan and tax-brackets have been the subject of public debate for many years. Financial intermediaries are [also] now familiar with the detailed mechanics of indexed debt .... (1986, 206)

41.   The reluctance to index might also be due to there being so few assets or liabilities to choose from, thus making an indexed portfolio difficult to manage. As Howitt (1986, 207) notes, 'Intermediaries would be less reluctant to enter the indexed market if there were, for example, indexed assets other than mortgages to invest in when there is an unforeseen reduction in the supply of credit-worthy borrowers in the mortgage market, or an unforeseen increase in the demand for indexed deposits. At the least, it seems that some wholesale market in which intermediaries could trade indexed debt would be necessary to encourage them to enter the market'. Like the text, this explanation might have something to it, but it begs the question of why there isn't more indexation to start with. We shall come back to this issue shortly.

15 PRICE-LEVEL OPTIMALITY

1. We can think of real balances being put 'into' the utility function to capture the transactions and other services that money performs, but which we do not wish to address explicitly at present. We need to be wary how we interpret the implicit transactions technology – see e.g. McCallum (1990a, 968–969) – but the 'money-in-the-utility-function' approach suffices for our purpose here.

2. It is worth emphasising that it is the constraint that real balances are non-interest-bearing that enables inflation to be socially costly in this framework. If a market-determined interest rate could be paid on real balances, there would no longer be any reason for inflation to drive a wedge between the social and private opportunity costs of holding real balances, and inflation would have no welfare effects at all.

3. While the models just discussed presume that real interest is invariant to (anticipated) inflation, there is a great deal of evidence that inflation actually *reduces* real interest (see, e.g., Fried and Howitt, 1983, 968). Why it might do so is not well understood, but possible explanations are provided by Fried and Howitt (1983, 969) and Howitt (1990a, 76). The former suggest that, since inflation reduces the return to non-interest-bearing real balances, it presumably reduces the return to substitutes such as bonds; the latter suggests that if real balances are a complementary factor of production to capital, then inflation will reduce the marginal product of capital and hence the real interest rate. Of course, if inflation does reduce real interest rates, we might also expect it to reduce the return on investment, and hence reduce the capital stock. This particular effect of inflation is not considered in the text, but should not be overlooked.

4. There are however some awkward problems lurking beneath the surface. (1) To interpret the area under an individual's demand curve as an indicator of his welfare requires strenuous assumptions, foremost amongst which are that the marginal utility of the good in question (i.e., real balances) should be independent of the demands for other goods (see, e.g., Laidler, 1990, 44). When the good in question is real balances, this assumption would appear to require that real balances are superneutral, and if these conditions are not met, we are presumably dealing with shifts of the demand curve for real balances as well as movements along it. (2) We have to make the jump from our theoretical notions of *individual* consumer surplus to the area under the *market* demand curve we think we measure. (3) Even if we ignore the previous difficulties and are willing to accept the area under the demand curve for real balances as a reasonable indicator of the sum of individual surpluses, it is still arguable that welfare losses based on such a demand curve would understate the appropriate welfare loss from anticipated inflation. If real balances reduce transactions costs, and inflation causes agents to economise on holdings of real balances, then transactions costs will rise with the anticipated inflation rate and we should allow for these additional costs (see, e.g., Howitt, 1990a, 75). Howitt also suggested that the traditional measures of welfare loss might be large understatements because the theories on which they are based ignore the intermediate output sector and understate total transactions costs. We have little choice in practice but to sweep these issues under the carpet, but the reader should be aware that our estimates might be biased on the downward side.

5. Strictly speaking, the welfare loss is the area under the demand curve with the nominal interest rate on the vertical axis. With inflation on the vertical axis, the relevant area is the area under the demand curve plus a rectangle below it which is bounded below by a horizontal line emanating from the point on the vertical axis where the inflation rate equals the negative of the real rate of interest (see, e.g., Tower, 1971, 851–852; and Tatom, 1976). The true welfare loss is therefore

greater than indicated in the text, and Gillman's (1990) estimates suggest that the difference is actually quite large – he puts it somewhere in the range of 38 to 51 percent of the amount in the text, which in effect means that the text understates the true cost by a factor of half or close to half. The cost estimates that follow are therefore subject to a considerable *downward* bias – on top of the possible downward bias suggested in the last footnote.

6. For the sake of comparison, we get a cost ratio of 0.0043 percent of national income if we take a benchmark inflation rate of 0 percent, one of 0.026 percent if we take a benchmark inflation rate of 10 percent, and one of 0.029 percent if we assume a benchmark inflation rate of 20 percent. The cost ratio thus rises with the inflation rate.

7. M1 in November 1993 was $1122.4 bns (*Money Stock Revisions*, February 1994, table 1). Annualised GNP in the last quarter of 1993 was $6510.8 bns (*International Financial Statistics*, March 1994, 571). Both series are seasonally adjusted.

8. Clower (1969, 1984) nonetheless argues that OQM considerations do not apply when we take explicit account of the transactions role that MOE play. He argued that agents choose their inventories of goods and cash balances taking account of the holding costs of each. The amount invested in holding stocks of real commodities, making trips to the bank, etc., will therefore depend on the opportunity cost of holding currency (e.g., Clower, 1984, 132). It follows that equilibrium holdings of real balances will be 'inextricably linked with equilibrium holdings of commodity inventories, and *vice versa*' (Clower, 1984, 134–135), and Clower concluded that 'real marketing costs depend in an essential way on turnover rates of commodity inventories and cannot be inferred directly from information about individual or aggregate holdings of real money balances' (1984, 135). This argument was challenged by Harry Johnson (1972), but, as Howitt (1992, 82) observes, 'On the whole ... subsequent theoretical work has tended to confirm the optimum-quantity argument' (see, e.g., Feige and Parkin, 1971; Clower and Howitt, 1978; and Grandmont and Younès, 1973).

9. An important asymmetry should be noted here. Even if we accept that the area under the demand curve for real balances does give a good measure of the cost of a deflation rate *below* the social optimum, it does not follow that it also gives a good proxy for the costs of a deflation rate that *exceeds* the optimal rate. If the deflation rate should exceed the optimum, real balances would appear to dominate real capital as an investment asset, and we would expect agents to shift out the latter into the former. The demand for real balances would rise, and it is quite possible, depending on the monetary regime, that prices would collapse towards zero. (This last effect is discussed further a little later in the text.) It is therefore not surprising that many models find that an equilibrium does not exist if there is an 'excessive' deflation rate (see, e.g., Benhabib and Bull, 1983, 110). The fact that a deflation rate that is too high has qualitatively different consequences from a deflation rate that is too low has serious implications for any attempt to implement 'optimal deflation' in practice. *Unless the path of the optimal deflation rate for all time is known with certainty* – and, of course, we would not expect it to be – errors in hitting our price-level target will imply quite different costs depending on whether the actual price level was above or below target, and the 'optimal' price-level rule would presumably need to be modified to take this asymmetry into account. Implementing the 'optimal deflation' rule is considerably more difficult than the full-information, perfect-certainty approach used in the text (and in most of the literature) would suggest.

10. The basic result is found in many places in the literature (e.g., Friedman, 1969; Grandmont and Younès, 1973; Townsend, 1980; Kimbrough, 1986; Woodford, 1990). It is very similar to the well-known results that optimality requires that

nominal interest should be driven down to zero (e.g., Woodford, 1990, 1070–1071) or that interest should be paid on currency if it is possible to do so at a low enough cost (e.g., Tolley, 1957, 477; Johnson, 1972, 141).

11. This estimate appears to be compatible with Friedman's own (1969, 44) estimates: he reported present-value costs of anywhere between 8 percent and 111 percent of national income, depending on the capitalisation procedure used, but these estimates also referred to the cost of a 2 percent rather than zero percent inflation rate. The implied costs of a zero inflation rate would therefore be somewhat lower.

12. Do the figures that come from these exercises represent 'big' losses or not? Johnson (1972, 142) was inclined to ignore these costs on the ground that they 'would probably be a negligible fraction of national income', but he did not spell out how small the loss had to be to become 'negligible'. Friedman himself was ambivalent on the implications of his results. He maintained that 'the gain from shifting [from current inflationary policies to price-level stability] would, I believe, dwarf the further gain from going for the [optimum deflation] rule' (1969, 48), but still suggested that the gain from optimal deflation 'may well be substantial enough to be worth pursuing'. Yet even his own results did not persuade him that it was worthwhile to abandon the goal of price stability for the further benefits of 'optimal' deflation.

13. Samuelson replied to this point, but his reply is not convincing. He continued to assert that 'No something-for-nothing elixir is involved' (1969, 306), but his attempt to justify that claim misses the point. He began by suggesting that

We put a subsidy, s on holding[s] of cash balances big enough to counterbalance interest costs ... .

Now we have a parameter s. And when we differentiate the final level of utility achieved by identical men with respect to this subsidy, we find that [utility] rises as the subsidy rises positively from its zero *laissez-faire* level. (Samuelson, 1969, 307)

He then suggested that

An even better way ... is to replace my plateau of M [i.e., nominal 'money' supply] with an exponential trend e^{mt}, where m is a negative parameter in the case of deflation and positive in the case of inflation ... [Utility] grows as m declines and pushes the system away from its constant-price-level steady-state of *laissez-faire*. (Samuelson, 1969, 307)

This new argument is essentially an OQM argument that suggests we engineer a *rate of price-level change* to equalise the private and social costs of holding real balances. But the point at issue here is quite different. Samuelson's earlier claim – the claim that Clower attacked, and Samuelson purported to defend – was that agents would be better off if the *price level* was reduced, and Samuelson's reply has no bearing on this issue. Clower's objection still stands.

14. Once again, Samuelson gave an unconvincing response. 'To illustrate dramatically the falseness of Clower's assertion that *laissez-faire* is optimal', he (1969, 307) set out an example in which changes in the rate of time preference cause changes in real balances and welfare even though production and consumption are assumed to be unaffected. He then interpreted the fact that production and consumption were unchanged as proving his point that if the first equilibrium were a *laissez-faire* one, the second could not be, and yet was superior to it. The counter-argument is of course that *both* are *laissez-faire* equilibria, and they differ *precisely because* the rate of time preference has changed. Samuelson's example still provides no support to his earlier claim that 'real' factors can remain the same but agents can be made better off by somehow inducing them (e.g., by reducing prices, somehow) to

increase their holdings of real balances.

15.   Some related arguments should also to be noted. (1) One argument maintains that an individual who decides to increase his real balances must forego consumption, and given the nominal quantity of exchange media, this decision reduces prices marginally and thereby enables others to consume more than they otherwise would. There is thus an externality in the holding of exchange media, and *laissez-faire* is allegedly suboptimal because it provides no mechanism to appropriate this externality. But the counter argument is that what makes the price level change in this way is the fixity in the supply of exchange media, and the latter can presumably be fixed only if there is a fiat currency. Under a convertible monetary system, by contrast, the nominal supply of MOE would alter, the price level would remain as it was, and there would be no externality (see Girton and Roper, 1981, 24–25, n. 18). The externality is consequently a product of an artificial monetary regime in which *laissez-faire* has already been suppressed, and is absent under *laissez-faire* itself. (2) There is an argument than an agent's holdings of precautionary balances generate externalities on others (see, e.g., Laidler, 1977, 322). The greater the real balances one agent holds, the smaller the chance he will default on a payment and impose default-related costs on his creditors, and the like. Individual agents fail to take account of these externalities, and so they are not appropriated under *laissez-faire*. (3) Finally, there is the argument that there is an element of illusion in the benefits provided by precautionary balances if the contingencies against which they hold those balances are correlated across individuals (see, e.g., Hahn, 1971, 70). When those contingencies occur, individuals find that the services they had counted on from their precautionary balances do not materialise. Individuals therefore misperceive the 'true' *ex ante* benefits provided by their precautionary balances, and end up holding suboptimal amounts. There seems to be little to dispute in these arguments, but neither of them do any more than establish that externalities might exist. They do not establish that externalities are empirically important, and they do not establish that there is some superior, feasible alternative to *laissez-faire*.

16.   A popular alternative to the Mussa model is that of Sheshinski and Weiss (1977). They postulate a monopolistic firm operating under conditions of certainty which uses an (s, S) rule to change the price of its product (i.e., when the real price falls to s, the firm changes it to S). The assumption that inflation is perfectly anticipated was subsequently relaxed in different ways by Sheshinski and Weiss (1983), Danziger (1984) and Caplin and Spulber (1987), but they each retained the feature that firms followed (s, S) pricing policies. The main differences in the predictions of these models will be flagged as we go along.

17.   Cecchetti (1985, 938) gets the same result, but Sheshinski and Weiss (1977, 299–300) and Danziger (1984) find the effect of inflation on the frequency of price changes to be ambiguous. However, the empirical evidence strongly supports the common-sense Mussa-Cecchetti prediction that high inflation leads to more frequent price adjustment (see Mussa, 1981, 278; Cecchetti, 1986, 255).

18.   Anticipated inflation can also have real effects on relative prices through 'tilting' a stream of real interest payments over time. Suppose that a household contemplates a 30-year, $30,000 mortgage:

> With no inflation and a real [interest] rate of say 3 percent, annual payments necessary for full amortization would amount to $1,517. If a 2 percent inflation were anticipated, the contract payment would jump to $1,931, nearly a 25 percent increase. A 6 percent inflation would result in a 9 percent contract rate and payment of $2,895, nearly double the no-inflation payment. (Kearl, 1979, 1115)

The inflation increases the real burden of its initial repayments, and consequently has real effects even if the real interest rate and the household's real income are both constant. We might therefore expect higher inflation to lower the demand for housing and reduce its relative price, and there is empirical evidence to support this conjecture (Kearl, 1978, 613). We might also expect the lower relative price of housing to be associated with a smaller housing stock, and Kearl's simulations suggest that it is. His results indicated that anticipated inflation in the US had reduced the stock of single-family housing by an amount equivalent to at least a year's construction activity, and the total stock of housing by something less (Kearl, 1979, 1136). For more on the 'tilt' effect, see also appendix 2 to Chapter 14.

19. There is an additional reason for intermediaries to hold prices reasonably stable. Price changes have something of a zero-sum character and there is always the risk that the customer will feel that the supplier is taking advantage of him. This risk makes the customer suspicious and the firm responds by relying more on quantity changes which are not prone to the same problem. When it does change prices, the firm tries to do so in response to verifiable exogenous developments, so as to claim that the change is 'justified' and avoid customer suspicions. See Wachter and Williamson (1978).

20. There are many similar models to be found in the literature (e.g., Cukierman, 1979 and Hercowitz, 1981, 1982; among many others). What they all have in common is that agents trade in decentralised markets and know the price prevailing in their market but only learn about prices elsewhere with a lag. They therefore have to estimate the prevailing price level from the information they have and are apt to make mistakes doing so.

21. Cukierman addressed the dispersion of inflationary expectations across different individuals, but assumed each individual to have a point expectation of inflation with a subjective variance of zero. If we allows individuals to have some degree of uncertainty about inflation (e.g., as Jaffee and Kleiman, 1977, 293–294 do), we might expect each individual to become more uncertain (i.e., to attach an increased variance to his point forecast of inflation) as inflation and inflation variability rise. Taking account of each individual's increased subjective uncertainty would then of course add yet another element to the overall cost of inflation.

22. There may of course be additional costs. (1) If agents do not have uniformly changing expectations of inflation, the results of Cukierman (1984, 77) imply that the volume of capital traded will also vary with changes in the exogenous parameters. Any factor that increases the overall variance of inflation will also increase the variance of the amount of capital traded and, therefore, create additional welfare losses that should be added to those in the text. (2) Alternatively, the stochastic neoclassical model of Gertler and Grinols (1982) suggests that an increase in the variance of the inflation rate lowers investment and the costs of this reduced investment need to be taken into account. (3) Monetary instability might also distort agents' perceptions of the intertemporal price level profile, and thereby distort the yield curve and lead capital that should have been invested in short-term projects to be invested in long-term ones, and *vice versa*.

23. There is also some evidence that the inflation rate (or, perhaps, its rate of change) might influence relative prices by skewing them. Mills (1927, 284), Graham (1930, 175–177) and Blejer (1983, 473) found evidence that increases in the absolute rate of price-level change tend to increase the skewness of the distribution of relative price changes, a finding that suggests that a rate of inflation of x percent leads most prices to rise by a rate less of less than x percent, but a few prices to rise by much more.

24. There is also considerable dispute over how the evidence in favour of a relationship, such as it is, should be interpreted. While many authors suggest that a

relationship would reflect causality from inflation to relative prices, or causality from monetary factors to both inflation and relative prices, other interpretations cannot always be ruled out. Thus Fischer (1981a) argued that the relationship was essentially fortuitous, and due primarily to the coincidence of the food and energy shocks with the inflationary policies of the 1970s, and Blinder (1982), Cukierman (1983) and Stockton (1988) presented some evidence of causality going from relative prices to inflation. The most plausible explanation for this 'reverse causation' would be a monetary policy that 'accommodated' a relative price (e.g., oil) shock with a monetary expansion, and 'reverse causation' of this sort might also help to explain the apparent 'coincidence' of relative price shocks and inflation in the 1970s.

25.   There is some *a priori* reason to expect the mean and variability of inflation to be positively related. As Okun (1971), Holland (1984), Ball (1992) and others have pointed out, as the rate of inflation rises under a fiat system, the government/central bank will come under increasing pressures of various kinds and we might then expect – and casual observation seems to confirm – that monetary policy will become more volatile. In Ball's model, for example, the central bank is normally content to keep inflation low if it is low already, but it faces a dilemma if it should try to reduce high inflation because disinflation would cause a recession. Its policy is therefore harder to predict when inflation is high, and so high inflation will be associated with greater inflation uncertainty.

26.   Benjamin Klein (1975b, 1976, 1978) *identified* inflation unpredictability with various measures of inflation variability and then examined the latter's historical behaviour. This identification is correct only if agents have a constant expectation of inflation from one period to the next. If expectations are rational this condition normally requires that the stochastic process generating inflation should be a constant plus a stationary disturbance. Klein's empirical work in his 1975b paper suggested that the inflation process might satisfy this condition in the earlier 'gold standard' period before about 1955, but does not satisfy it afterwards. (In any case, more recent work on trend and difference stationarity by Nelson and Plosser, 1981 and other suggests that we should treat these earlier results with a great deal of caution.) Klein's own results therefore imply that we ought not to identify the post-1955 price-level variance with price-level unpredictability. To the extent agents correctly perceive the changing inflation rate, the variance of unanticipated inflation would be less than the variance of actual inflation and Klein's estimates would lead one to overstate inflation unpredictability. This sort of problem aside, Klein's empirical work made an important point that almost certainly carries over to other measures of inflation variability or uncertainty (see, e.g., Evans, 1991). Klein's work indicated that since the mid-1950s the long-term variance of the inflation rate increased very significantly relative to the short-term variance (1975b, 471), a result that appears to reflect the substitution of the anchorless fiat monetary standard for the older gold standard.

27.   There is also the question of whether the inflation rate has any impact on the volatility of output or output growth. Logue and Sweeney (1981) reported a strong positive relationship between the inflation rate and the variability of economic growth, but their analysis was at a relatively highly aggregated level, and Katsimbris (1985) found that the effect tended to disappear when he disaggregated his sample on a country-by-country basis. We do not therefore yet have any strong evidence that the inflation rate *per se* (as distinct from its variability) influences the volatility of output.

28.   Let l_i be the present value output loss from the decrease in growth in the ith period, where $i = 1, 2, 3, \quad \ldots$ Then $l_1 = 0.11[1 + 1/(1+r) + 1/(1+r)^2 + \ldots] = 0.11(1+r)/r, l_2 = l_1/(1+r), l_3 = l_2/(1+r)$, etc. The present value loss from a

rise in inflation that decreases output growth by 0.11 in all periods is therefore approximately $l_1 + l_2 + l_3 + \ldots = 0.11(1 + r)^2/r^2$.

29. In discussing redistributions between borrowers and lenders, we might also note here the effects of inflation on *ex ante* real interest rates. There is much evidence that higher anticipated rates of inflation lead to higher nominal interest rates (see, e.g., Yohe and Karnowsky, 1969; Feldstein and Chamberlain, 1973), but the evidence also suggests that nominal interest rates do *not* rise *pari passu* with expected inflation (see, e.g., Pearce, 1979; Summers, 1983). We could therefore interpret the reductions in real interest rates produced by inflation as implying another form of redistribution, but there is little clear evidence to indicate how important such redistribution might be.

30. A third focus of empirical research on inflation-induced redistributions might also be mentioned – the extent to which inflation redistributes income between workers and firms. The centre of attention here is the wage-lag hypothesis that asserts that real wages fall during inflation because price rises tend to run ahead of rises in nominal wages. If the wage lag exists, and is caused by inflation, we can then say that inflation redistributes income from workers to firms. However, the wage-lag hypothesis has a weak theoretical underpinning and no generally safe conclusions can be drawn from the empirical work. In the words of Laidler and Parkin (1975, 788), 'the only safe conclusion about the wage lag hypothesis must be that it postulates a phenomenon which is certainly not universal, but which may from time to time have happened'.

31. There have been some attempts, but not many, to model how inflation alters institutional structure. One is Wachter and Williamson (1978) which examines how existing institutions might tolerate relatively low-level inflation, but alter in the face of more rapid or permanent inflation. Contract forms might start to change (e.g., contracts might be negotiated for shorter periods), firms might alter their own structure, agents might move towards more liquid markets with standardised products and so on (see also Carlton, 1982). The effects of inflation on firm structure are examined further by Boudreaux and Shughart (1989) who discuss how price-level instability might produce greater vertical integration by leading firms to internalise activities that would previously have been traded directly on a market.

32. Inflation can also distort *measures* of real economic activity, so real 'genuine' output can fall even though measured real output appears to hold its own. Imagine that inflation leads to the employment of more financial consultants to help firms live with inflation. Real output might appear much the same as conventionally measured, but the resources used up on financial consulting are a waste if those services had not been needed under price stability. A good example is provided by Kleiman (1989): the rise in Israeli inflation in the late 1970s and early 1980s led to a massive growth in the number of people employed in the banking industry, and Kleiman estimated that this induced growth in banking employment amounted to the equivalent of 3–4 percent of total domestic product in 1982. The induced growth in the financial services sector as a whole would have been even larger. Nor should we forget that if inflation means that more time has to be spent lining up at the bank to get money to spend that day, if it means that it takes longer to do one's sums, and so on, then any sensible measure of welfare (as opposed to just output) would have to put some value on these time and calculation costs as well.

33. Many of these relate to the effects of inflation on the tax system, on which there is a huge literature to which I cannot possibly do justice here. To give but one example taken from Howitt (1990a, 86), the real after-tax return r on an investment is $r = R(1 - t) - \pi$, where R is the pre-tax nominal return, t is the marginal income tax rate, and p is the inflation rate. If we take t as 0.3, and assume that r rises *pari*

passu with π, then a rise in inflation of one percentage point reduces the real after tax return by 0.3 percent. Even moderate inflations can then have dramatic effects. If π is zero, and the nominal return R is 5 percent, then the real after-tax return is 3.5 percent. However, if p rises to 10 percent, and R rises to 15 percent, then r falls to 0.5 percent. Even single digit inflation can thus wipe out most of the after-tax return. For more on these and other effects of inflation on the tax system, see, e.g., Feldstein and Slemrod (1978), Feldstein, Poterba and Dicks-Mireaux (1981), Feldstein (1982, 1983) or Howitt (1990a).

34. Related to this argument is one that claims that disinflation might be too costly to be worthwhile (e.g., because of hysteresis). There is considerable literature on this issue (e.g., McCallum, 1988; Rose, 1988; Fortin, 1990; Scarth, 1990; Cozier and Wilkinson, 1991; and many others), but most studies find the costs of disinflation to be fairly low, and certainly lower than the costs of inflation itself. Dowd (1994b) provides an assessment of some of this work.

35. There may also be other reasons to reject 'optimal' deflation rules in a stochastic setting. Even leaving aside price-level predictability issues, introducing stochastic elements can also mean that 'monetary saturation' no longer means that the optimal rate of price change is negative, even in a 'monetary saturation' world (see, e.g., Bewley, 1983; Den Haan, 1990).

36. Price stability implies zero inflation, but is not just zero inflation. Under price-level stability, any unexpected shocks to the price level are to corrected in subsequent periods, so the price level returns to par. To the extent that interim price-level shocks are corrected, an agent trying to forecast the price level T periods away has relatively little reason to worry about them. Under zero inflation, by contrast, there is no attempt to correct any unexpected shock to the price level, and the objective is merely to prevent any *further* price-level shocks. An agent trying to forecast T periods ahead must then worry about *all* interim price-level shocks. The uncertainty attached to the future price level is thus greater under zero inflation, and the uncertainty rises with the forecast horizon. See, e.g., Gavin and Stockman (1991) or Balke and Emery (1994, 80–81).

37. There is nonetheless a major problem. Most of the arguments usually put forward for the productivity norm deal with *un*anticipated productivity changes, rather than productivity changes *per se*. If we interpret these arguments literally, we would want prices to move with only the unanticipated components of productivity changes. This distinction between productivity change and unanticipated productivity change is important, and proponents of the productivity norm usually overlook it. Either they stick with the traditional productivity norm – i.e., that prices should change with productivity – in which case they have to abandon the equity and macroeconomic stability arguments made for it (which are discussed below in the text), or they must modify the productivity norm to allow prices to respond only to unanticipated movements in productivity. However, in the latter case, they have to face the serious problem of having to derive an operational means of distinguishing between anticipated and unanticipated productivity changes, in which case Selgin's claim that the productivity norm would be easy to implement in practice is no longer valid.

38. There is also the point that unless the good experiencing the productivity shock had a large weight in the relevant price index, no single idiosyncratic productivity shock would have much effect on the price level anyway, regardless of the price-level norm. If we assume for the sake of argument that all goods have much the same weight, then the good experiencing the productivity shock in Selgin's example would have a weight of 0.1 percent. If other prices remained the same, the overall price index would fall by 0.5 times 0.1 percent, or 0.05 percent. The overall price index would therefore not move much anyway, even if the other 999 prices

remained the same.

39. One should also bear in mind that it is common productivity shocks, and not idiosyncratic ones, that the earlier advocates of the productivity norm had in mind. Indeed, even Selgin himself seems to be thinking in terms of common rather than idiosyncratic productivity shocks – see for example the earlier Selgin quote – and he only departs from common shocks in the numerical example just quoted. The assumption of common productivity shocks is thus more faithful to productivity norm controversy – and reverses Selgin's presumption that price-changing costs are lower under the productivity norm.

16 FINANCIAL AND MONETARY REFORM

1. A few operational details would of course still need to be sorted out: (1) We would need to select a QFC price that would not unduly disturb the price level as the new system was being established. We should therefore choose a QFC price that is roughly consistent with the price index at the time the first contracts are sold. For example, suppose the first contract is sold at time t and calls for the seller to pay the purchaser $\$p_{t+1}(1 + r_t)$ at $t + 1$, where p_{t+1} and r_t are our specified price index and interest rate. If we want zero inflation from t to $t + 1$, then the price of the first QFC at t should be roughly $\$p_t$. (2) We need to select the contract's term to maturity. The longer the term to maturity, the greater 'slippage' between the expected price index and the actual value the index turns out to take. Since the price-forecast error u_{t+1} picks up influences on the spot price index that arise between t and $t + 1$, but were not predictable at t itself, a longer period between t and $t + 1$ would increase the standard deviation of u_{t+1} if only because it would leave less scope for these interim shocks to occur. If we wish u_{t+1} to have a low standard deviation, we should choose a relatively short term to maturity (e.g., a quarter or two, or perhaps a year). (3) We need to select the contract's frequency. The contract cannot be any more frequent than the frequency with which price index 'announcements' are made, but otherwise we can pick whatever frequency we wish.

Bibliography

Aghion, P. and P. Bolton (1990) 'An "incomplete contract" approach to financial contracting', Paris: DELTA, mimeo.

Ahimud, Y. (1981) 'Price-level uncertainty, indexation and employment', *Southern Economic Journal* 47: 776–787.

Akerlof, G. (1970) 'The market for "lemons": Quality uncertainty and the market mechanism', *Quarterly Journal of Economics* 84: 488–500.

Alberro, J. (1981) 'The Lucas hypothesis on the Phillips curve', *Journal of Monetary Economics* 7: 239–250.

Alchian, A. A. and B. Klein (1973) 'On a correct measure of inflation', *Journal of Money, Credit and Banking* 5: 173–191.

Allen, F. (1990) 'The market for information and the origin of financial intermediation', *Journal of Financial Intermediation* 1: 3–30.

Allen, F. and D. Gale (1992) 'Measurement distortion and missing contingencies in optimal contracts', *Economic Theory* 2: 1–26.

Altman, E. I. (1984) 'A further investigation of the bankruptcy cost question', *Journal of Finance* 39: 1067–1089.

Anderlini, L. (1986a) 'Correctly anticipated bank runs', ESRC Research Project on Risk, Information and Quantity Signals in Economics, Economic Theory, *Discussion Paper* 95 (June).

Anderlini, L. (1986b) 'Central banks and moral hazard', ESRC Research Project on Risk, Information and Quantity Signals in Economics, Economic Theory, *Discussion Paper* 103 (November).

Anderlini, L. (1986c) 'Competitive banking in a simple model', in J. Edwards *et al.* (eds), *Recent Advances in Corporate Finance, Investment and Taxation*, Cambridge: Cambridge University Press, 144–177.

Anderlini, L. and L. Felli (1994) 'Incomplete written contracts: Indescribable states of nature', *Quarterly Journal of Economics* 99: 1085–1124.

Anderson, T. L. and P. J. Hill (1979) 'An American experiment in anarcho-capitalism: The *not* so wild, wild west', *Journal of Libertarian Studies* 3: 9–29.

Anderson, B. M. (1917) *The Value of Money*, New York: Macmillan.

Ang, J. S., J. H. Chua and J. J. McConnell (1982) 'The administrative costs of corporate bankruptcy: A note', *Journal of Finance* 37: 219–226.

Antle, R. (1984) 'Auditor independence', *Journal of Accounting Research* 22: 1–20.

Arthur, W. B. (1990) 'Competing technologies, increasing returns and lock-in by historical events', *Economic Journal* 99: 116–131.

Azariadis, C. (1975) 'Implicit contracts and underemployment equilibria', *Journal of Political Economy* 83: 1183–1202.

Azariadis, C. (1981) 'Self-fulfilling prophecies', *Journal of Economic Theory* 25: 380–396.

Bach, G. L. and A. Ando (1957) 'The redistributional effects of inflation', *Review of Economics and Statistics* 39: 1–13.

Bach, G. L. and R. A. Musgrave (1941) 'A stable purchasing power bond', *American Economic Review* 31: 823–825.

Bach, G. L. and J. B. Stephenson (1974) 'Inflation and the redistribution of wealth', *Review of Economics and Statistics* 56: 1–13.

Bailey M. J. (1956) 'The welfare cost of inflationary finance', *Journal of Political Economy* 64: 93–110.

Bailey, S. (1837) *Money and its Vicissitudes in Value; As They Affect National Industry and Pecuniary Contracts: With a postscript on joint-stock banks*, London: Effingham Wilson.

Baillie, R. T. (1989) 'Commodity prices and aggregate inflation: Would a commodity price rule be worthwhile?', *Carnegie–Rochester Conference Series on Public Policy* 31: 185–240.

Baillie, R. T., C.-F. Chung and M. A. Tieslau (1992) 'The long memory and variability of inflation: A reappraisal of the Friedman hypothesis', Michigan State University, *Econometrics and Economic Theory Paper* 9102.

Baily, M. N. (1974) 'Wages and employment under uncertain demand', *Review of Economic Studies* 41: 37–50.

Balke, N. S. and K. M. Emery (1994) 'The algebra of price stability', *Journal of Macroeconomics* 16: 77–97.

Ball, L. (1992) 'Why does high inflation raise inflation uncertainty?', *Journal of Monetary Economics* 29: 371–388.

Ball, L. and S. Cecchetti (1990) 'Inflation and uncertainty at short and long horizons', *Brookings Papers on Economic Activity* 1: 215–245.

Ball, R. (1989) 'The firm as a specialist contracting intermediary: Application to accounting and auditing', William E. Simon Graduate School of Business Administration, University of Rochester, mimeo.

Baltensperger, E. (1980) 'Alternative approaches to the theory of the banking firm', *Journal of Monetary Economics* 6: 1–37.

Baltensperger, E. and T. M. Devinney (1985) 'Credit rationing theory: A survey and synthesis', *Journal of Institutional and Theoretical Economics* 141: 475–502.

Baron, D. P. (1982) 'A model of the demand for investment banking advising and distribution services for new issues', *Journal of Finance* 37: 955–976.

Barro, R. J. (1970) 'Inflation, the payments period and the demand for money', *Journal of Political Economy* 78: 1128–1263.

Barro, R. J. (1972) 'Inflationary finance and the welfare cost of inflation', *Journal of Political Economy* 80: 978–1001.

Barro, R. J. (1977) 'Unemployment and anticipated money growth in the US', *American Economic Review* 67: 105–115.

Barro, R. J. (1979) 'Money and the price level under the gold standard', *Economic Journal* 89: 13–33.

Barro, R. J. and D. B. Gordon (1983a) 'Rules, discretion and reputation in a model of monetary policy', *Journal of Monetary Economics* 12: 101–121.

Barro, R. J. and D. B. Gordon (1983b) 'A positive theory of monetary policy in a natural rate model', *Journal of Political Economy* 91: 589–610.

Barsky, R. B. and L. H. Summers (1988) 'Gibson's paradox and the gold standard', *Journal of Political Economy* 96: 528–550.

Bauer, P. W. (1994) 'A beginner's guide to the US payments system', Federal Reserve Bank of Cleveland, *Economic Commentary*, (July 1).

Bean, C. (1983) 'Targetting nominal income: An appraisal', *Economic Journal* 93: 806–819.

Beatty, R. P. and J. R. Ritter (1986) 'Investment banking, reputation and the underpricing of initial public offerings', *Journal of Financial Economics* 15: 213–232.

Benabou, R. (1991) '"Comment" on "The welfare cost of moderate inflations"', *Journal of Money, Credit and Banking* 23: 504–513.

Benhabib, J. and C. Bull (1983) 'The optimal quantity of money: A formal treatment', *International Economic Review* 24: 101–111.

Benjamin, D. K. (1978) 'The use of collateral to enforce debt contracts', *Economic Inquiry* 16: 333–359.

Benston, G. J., R. A. Eisenbeis, P. M. Horvitz, E. J. Kane and G. G. Kaufman (1986) *Perspectives on Safe and Sound Banking: Past, present and future*, Cambridge, MA: MIT Press.

Benston, G. J. and G. G. Kaufman (1988) *Risk and Solvency Regulation of Depository Institutions: Past policies and current options*, New York: Salomon Brothers Center, Graduate School of Business. New York University, *Monograph* 1988–1.

Benston, G. J. and C. W. Smith (1976) 'A transactions cost approach to the theory of financial intermediaries', *Journal of Finance* 31: 215–231.

Bental, B., Z. Eckstein and D. Peled (1990) 'Competitive banking with confidence crisis and international borrowing', Foerder Institute for Economic Research, *Working Paper* 89, Tel-Aviv University.

Benveniste, L. M. (1992) 'Standby letters of credit', in P. Newman, M. Milgate and J. Eatwell (eds), *The New Palgrave Dictionary of Money and Finance*, vol. 3, London: Macmillan: 529–530.

Berger, A. N. and G. F. Udell (1990a) 'Collateral, loan quality and bank risk', *Journal of Monetary Economics* 25: 21–42.

Berger, A. N. and G. F. Udell (1990b) 'Some evidence on the empirical significance of credit rationing', *Journal of Political Economy* 100: 1047–1081.

Berglöf, E. and E.-L. von Thadden (1994) 'Short-term versus long-term interests: Capital structure with multiple investors', *Quarterly Journal of Economics* 99: 1055–1084.

Bergstrand, J. (1985) 'The gravity equation in international trade: Some micro-economic foundations and empirical evidence', *Review of Economics and Statistics* 67: 474–487.

Berle, A. A., Jr. and G. C. Means (1932) *The Modern Corporation and Private Property*, New York: Macmillan.

Berlin, M. (1992) 'Securitization', in P. Newman, M. Milgate and J. Eatwell (eds), *The New Palgrave Dictionary of Money and Finance*, vol. 3, London: Macmillan: 433–435.

Berlin, M. and L. J. Mester (1990) 'Debt covenants and renegotiation', Salomon Brothers Center for the Study of Financial Institutions, *Working Paper* S-90-23, Leonard N. Stern School of Business, New York University.

Berlin, M. and J. Loeys (1988) 'Bond covenants and delegated monitoring', *Journal of Finance* 43: 397–412.

Bernanke, B. S. (1983) 'Nonmonetary effects of the financial crisis in the propagation of the Great Depression', *American Economic Review* 73: 257–276.

Bernanke, B. S. (1990) 'Clearing and settlement during the crash', *Review of Financial Studies* 3: 133–151.

Bernanke, B. S. and M. Gertler (1985) 'Banking in general equilibrium', National Bureau of Economic Research, *Working Paper* 1647.

Bernanke, B. S. and M. Gertler (1987) 'Banking and macroeconomic equilibrium', in W. A. Barnett and K. J. Singleton (eds), *New Approaches to Monetary Economics*, Cambridge: Cambridge University Press: 89–111.

Bernanke, B. S. and M. Gertler (1989) 'Agency costs, net worth and business fluctuations', *American Economic Review* 79: 14–31.

Bernanke, B. S. and M. Gertler (1990) 'Financial fragility and economic performance', *Quarterly Journal of Economics* 105: 87–114.

Bernstein, E. M. (1974) 'Indexing money payments in a large and prolonged inflation', in H. Giersch, M. Friedman, W. Fellner, E. M. Bernstein and A. Kafka, *Essays on Inflation and Indexation*, Washington, DC: American Enterprise Instititute for Public Policy Research: 71–86.

Besanko, D. and A. V. Thakor (1987) 'Collateral and rationing: Sorting equilibria in monopolistic and competitive credit markets', *International Economic Review* 28: 671–690.

Bester, H. (1985) 'Screening vs. rationing in credit markets with imperfect information', *American Economic Review* 75: 850–855.

Bester, H. (1987) 'The role of colateral in credit markets with imperfect information', *European Economic Review* 31: 887–899.

Bester, H. (1990) 'The role of collateral in a model of debt renegotiation', Tillburg University, mimeo.

Bester, H. and M. Hellwig (1989) 'Moral hazard and equilibrium credit rationing: An overview of the issues', in G. Bamberg and K. Spremann (eds), *Agency Theory, Information and Incentives*, Berlin and Heidelberg: Springer Verlag: 135–166.

Bewley, T. (1983) 'A difficulty with the optimum quantity of money', *Econometrica* 51: 1485–1504.

Bhattacharya, S. (1979) 'Imperfect information, dividend policy and the "bird in the hand" fallacy', *Bell Journal of Economics* 10: 259–270.

Bhattacharya, S. and D. Gale (1987) 'Preference shocks, liquidity and central bank policy', in W. A. Barnett and K. J. Singleton (eds), *New Approaches to Monetary Economics*, Cambridge: Cambridge University Press: 69–88.

Bilson, J. F. O. (1981) 'A proposal for monetary reform', University of Chicago, mimeo.

Birch, D. E., A. A. Rabin and L. B. Yeager (1982) 'Inflation, output and employment: Some clarifications', *Economic Inquiry* 20: 209–221.

Black, F. (1970) 'Banking and interest rates in a world without money: The effects of uncontrolled banking', *Journal of Bank Research* 1: 9–20.

Black, F. (1987) 'A gold standard with double feedback and near zero reserves', in F. Black, *Business Cycles and Equilibrium*, Oxford: Basil Blackwell: 115–120.

Blackburn, K. and M. Christensen (1989) 'Monetary policy and policy credibility: Theories and evidence', *Journal of Economic Literature* 27: 1–45.

Blejer, M. I. (1981) 'The dispersion of relative commodity prices under very rapid inflation', *Journal of Development Economics* 9: 347–356.

Blejer, M. I. (1983) 'On the anatomy of inflation', *Journal of Money, Credit and Banking* 15: 469–482.

Blejer, M. I. and L. Leiderman (1982) 'Relative-price variability in the open economy', *European Economic Review* 18: 387–402.

Blinder, A. S. (1982) 'The anatomy of double-digit inflation in the 1970s', in R. E. Hall (ed.), *Inflation: Causes and Effects*, Chicago and London: Chicago University Press: 261–282.

Blitzer, D. M. (1992) 'Credit rating agencies', in P. Newman, M. Milgate and J. Eatwell (eds), *The New Palgrave Dictionary of Money and Finance*, vol. 1, London: Macmillan: 537–539.

Bolton, P. and D. S. Scharfstein (1990) 'A theory of predation based on agency problems in financial contracting', *American Economic Review* 80: 93–106.

Bolton, P. and D. S. Scharfstein (1992) 'Debt renegotiation', in P. Newman, M. Milgate and J. Eatwell (eds), *The New Palgrave Dictionary of Money and Finance*, vol. 1, London: Macmillan: 589–592.

Bolton, P. and D. S. Scharfstein (1993) 'Optimal debt structure with multiple creditors', London School of Economics Financial Markets Group, *Discussion Paper* 161 (June).

Bond, E. W. and K. J. Crocker (1993) 'Bank capitalization, deposit insurance and risk categorization', *Journal of Risk and Insurance* 60: 547–569.

Boot, A., A. V. Thakor and G. F. Udell (1987) 'Competition, risk neutrality and loan commitments', *Journal of Banking and Finance* 11: 449–471.

Boot, A., A. V. Thakor and G. F. Udell (1991) 'Credible commitments, contract enforcement problems and banks: Intermediation as credibility insurance', *Journal of Banking and Finance* 15: 605–632.

Booth, J. R. and R. L. Smith (1986) 'Capital raising, underwriting and the certification hypothesis', *Journal of Financial Economics* 15: 261–281.

Border, K. C. and J. Sobel (1987) 'Samurai accountant: A theory of auditing and plunder', *Review of Economic Studies* 54: 525–540.

Bordo, M. D. (1980) 'The effects of monetary change on relative commodity prices and the role of long-term contracts', *Journal of Political Economy* 88: 1088–1109.

Bordo, M. D. (1984) 'The gold standard: Myths and realities', in B. N. Siegel (ed.), *Money in Crisis: The Federal Reserve, the economy and monetary reform*, San Francisco: Pacific Institute for Public Policy Research: 197–237.

Bordo, M. D. (1987) 'Bimetallism', in *The New Palgrave, a Dictionary of Economics*, vol. 1, New York: Stockton Press: 243–245.

Bordo, M. D. and R. W. Ellson (1985) 'A model of the classical gold standard with depletion', *Journal of Monetary Economics* 16: 109–20.

Borio, C. E. V. and P. Van den Bergh (1993) 'The nature and management of payment system risks: An international perspective', Bank for International Settlements, *Economic Papers* 36, Basle: Bank for International Settlements.

Boudreaux, D. J. and W. F. Shughart, Jr. (1989) 'The effects of monetary instability on the extent of vertical integration', *Atlantic Economic Journal* 17: 1–10.

Bougheas, S. (1994) 'Widespread bank panics', Staffordshire University Business School, mimeo.

Boughton, J. M. and W. H. Branson (1989) 'Commodity prices as a leading indicator of inflation', in K. Lahiri and G. H. Moore (eds), *Leading Economic Indicators: New approaches and forecasting records*, Cambridge and New York: Cambridge University Press: 305–338.

Boyd, J. H. and E. C. Prescott (1986) 'Financial intermediary coalitions', *Journal of Economic Theory* 38: 211–232.

Brauer, G. A. (1992) 'Closed-end mutual funds', in P. Newman, M. Milgate and J. Eatwell (eds), *The New Palgrave Dictionary of Money and Finance*, vol. 1, London: Macmillan: 375–376.

Brennan, M. J. and A. Kraus (1987) 'Efficient financing under asymmetric information', *Journal of Finance* 42: 1225–1243.

Brennan, M. J. and E. S. Schwartz (1982) 'The case for convertibles', *Chase Financial Quarterly* 1: 27–46.

Brennan, M. J. and E. S. Schwartz (1992) 'Convertible securities', in P. Newman, M. Milgate and J. Eatwell (eds), *The New Palgrave Dctionary of Money and Finance*, vol. 1, London: Macmillan: 453–455.

Brickley, J. A. and J. J. McConnell (1992) 'Dividend policy', in P. Newman, M. Milgate and J. Eatwell (eds), *The New Palgrave Dictionary of Money and Finance*, vol. 1, London: Macmillan: 691–695.

Brock, W. A. (1974) 'Money and growth: The case of long run perfect foresight', *International Economic Review* 15: 750–777.

Brock, W. A. (1975) 'A simple perfect foresight monetary model', *Journal of Monetary Economics* 1: 133–150.

Brown, B. (1992) 'Swap markets', in P. Newman, M. Milgate and J. Eatwell (eds), *The New Palgrave Dictionary of Money and Finance*, vol. 3, London: Macmillan: 618–622.

Browning, E. (1987) 'On the marginal welfare cost of inflation', *American Economic Review* 77: 11- 23.

Brunner, K. (1984) 'From the "upper tail theory of inflation" to the "lower tail theory of deflation"', Shadow Open Market Committee, New York, mimeo.

Brunner, A. D. and G. D. Hess (1990) 'Are higher levels of inflation less predictable? A state-dependent conditional approach', Federal Reserve Board Finance and Economics, *Discussion Papers* 141, Washington, DC: Federal Reserve Board.

Bryant, J. (1980) 'A model of reserves, bank runs and deposit insurance', *Journal of Banking and Finance* 4: 335–344.

Buchanan, J. M. (1962) 'Predictability: The criterion of monetary constitutions', in L. B. Yeager (ed.), *In Search of a Monetary Constitution*, Cambridge, MA: Harvard University Press: 155–183.

Budd, E. C. and D. F. Seiders (1971) 'The impact of inflation on the distribution of income and wealth', *American Economic Review (Papers and Proceedings)* 61: 128–138.

Burstein, M. L. (1986) *Modern Monetary Theory*, London: Macmillan.

Butenschön, B. A. (1936) *Symmetallism: An alternative to orthodox bimetallism*, London: George Allen Unwin.

Butlin, S. J. (1961) *Australia and New Zealand Bank: The Bank of Australasia and the Union Bank of Australia Ltd, 1828–1951*, London: Longman.

Cagan, P. (1956) 'The monetary dynamics of hyperinflation', in M. Friedman (ed.), *Studies in the Quantity Theory of Money*, Chicago: Chicago University Press: 25–91.

Cagan, P. (1963) 'The first fifty years of the national banking system – An historical appraisal', in D. Carson (ed.), *Banking and Monetary Studies*, Homewood, IL: Richard D. Irwin: 15–42.

Calomiris, C. W. (1989) 'Is deposit insurance necessary? A historical perspective', Northwestern University, mimeo.

Calomiris, C. W. and R. G. Hubbard (1990) 'Firm heterogeneity, internal finance and "credit rationing"', *Economic Journal* 100: 90–104.

Calomiris, C. W. and C. M. Kahn (1991) 'The role of demandable debt in structuring optimal banking arrangements', *American Economic Review* 81: 497–513.

Cameron, R. (1967) 'Scotland, 1750–1845', in R. Cameron *et al.*, *Banking in the Early Stages of Industrialization: A study in comparative economic history*, New York: Oxford University Press: 60–99.

Campbell, D. (1990) 'Adam Smith, Farrar on company law and the economics of the corporation', *Anglo–American Law Review* 19: 185–208.

Campbell, T. S. and W. A. Kracaw (1980) 'Information production, market signalling and the theory of financial intermediation', *Journal of Finance* 35: 863–882.

Campbell, T. S. and W. A. Kracaw (1991) 'Intermediation and the market for interest rate swaps', *Journal of Financial Intermediation* 1: 362–384.

Cantor, R. and F. Packer (1994) 'The credit rating industry', Federal Reserve Bank of New York, *Quarterly Review* 19 (Summer–Fall): 1–26.

Caplin, A. S. and D. F. Spulber (1987) 'Menu costs and the neutrality of money', *Quarterly Journal of Economics* 102: 701–725.

Carlton, D. W. (1982) 'The disruptive effect of inflation on the organization of markets', in R. E. Hall (ed.), *Inflation: Causes and Effects*, Chicago and London: Chicago University Press: 139–152.

Carr, J. L. and G. F. Matthewson (1988) 'Unlimited liability as a barrier to entry', *Journal of Political Economy* 96: 766–786.

Carter, R. and S. Manaster (1990) 'Initial public offerings and underwriter reputation', *Journal of Finance* 45: 1045–1067.

Casella, A. and J. S. Feinstein (1990) 'Economic exchange during hyperinflation', *Journal of Political Economy* 98: 1–27.

Cecchetti, S. G. (1985) 'Staggered contracts and the frequency of price adjustment', *Quarterly Journal of Economics* 100: 935–959.

Cecchetti, S. G. (1986) 'The frequency of price adjustment: A study of the newsstand price of magazines', *Journal of Econometrics* 31: 255–274.

Chan, Y.-S. (1983) 'On the positive role financial intermediation in allocation of venture capital in a market with imperfect information', *Journal of Finance* 38: 1543–1568.

Chan, Y.-S. and G. Kanatas (1985) 'Asymmetric valuations and the role of collateral in loan agreements', *Journal of Money, Credit and Banking* 17: 84–95.

Chang, C. (1990) 'The dynamic structure of optimal debt contracts', *Journal of Economic Theory* 52: 68–86.

Chant, J. (1987) *Regulation of Financial Institutions – A functional analysis*, Bank of Canada, *Technical Report* 45.

Chant, J. (1992) 'The new theory of financial intermediation', in K. Dowd and M. K. Lewis (eds), *Current Issues in Financial and Monetary Economics*, London: Macmillan: 42–65.

Chari, V. V. (1989) 'Banking without deposit insurance or bank panics: Lessons from a model of the US National Banking System', Federal Reserve Bank of Minneapolis, *Quarterly Review*, 13 (Summer): 3–19.

Chari, V. V. and R. Jagannathan (1988) 'Banking panics, information and rational expectations equilibrium', *Journal of Finance* 43: 749–763.

Chemmanur, T. J. and P. Fulghieri (1994) 'Investment bank reputation, information production and financial intermediation', *Journal of Finance* 49: 57–79.

Chen, C.-N. (1972) 'Bimetallism: Theory and controversy in perspective', *History of Political Economy* 4: 89–112.

Chevalier, M. (1859) *On the Probable Fall in the Value of Gold* (trans Richard Cobden), London: W. H. Smith and Co.

Childs, R. A., Jr. (1977) 'The invisible hand strikes back', *Journal of Libertarian Studies* 1: 23–33.

Chirinko, R. S. (1989) 'Bank loans and information accumulation', University of Chicago, mimeo.

Cipolla, C. M. (1956) *Money, Prices and Civilization in the Mediterranean World: Fifth to seventeenth century*, Princeton: Princeton University Press.

Clair, R. T. (1991) 'The US clearing house interbank payment system', *Research in Financial Services: Private and Public Policy* 3: 63–94.

Clark, P. K. (1982) 'Inflation and the productivity decline', *American Economic Review* 72: 149–154.

Clark, J. A. (1988) 'Economies of scale and scope at depository financial institutions: A review of the literature', Federal Reserve Bank of Kansas City, *Economic Review* (September–October), 16–33.

Cleveland, H. B. and T. F. Huertas (1985) *Citibank, 1812–1970*, Cambridge, MA: Harvard University Press.

Clower, R. W. (1969) 'What traditional monetary theory really wasn't', *Canadian Journal of Economics* 2: 299–302.

Clower, R. W. (1984) *Money and Markets: Essays by Robert W. Clower* (ed. D. A. Walker), Cambridge: Cambridge University Press.

Clower, R. W. and P. W. Howitt (1978) 'The transactions theory of the demand for money: A reconsideration', *Journal of Political Economy* 86: 449–466.

Coase, R. H. (1937) 'The nature of the firm', *Economica* 4: 386–405.

Coats, W. (1990) 'In search of a stable monetary anchor: A "new" monetary standard', International Monetary Fund Treasurer's Department., mimeo.

Constantinides G. M. and B. D. Grundy (1989) 'Optimal investment with stock repurchase and financing as signals', *Review of Financial Studies* 2: 445–466.

Cooley, T. F. and G. D. Hansen (1989) 'The inflation tax in a real business cycle model', *American Economic Review* 79: 733–748.

Cooley, T. F. and G. D. Hansen (1991) 'The welfare costs of moderate inflations', *Journal of Money, Credit and Banking* 23: 483–503.

Copeland, T. E. and J. F. Weston (1989) *Financial Theory and Corporate Policy*. 3rd edn, Reading, MA: Addison-Wesley.

Corrigan, E. G. (1990) 'Perspectives on payment system risk reduction', in D. B. Humphrey (ed.), *The US Payment System: Efficiency, risk and the role of the Federal Reserve; Proceedings of a symposium on the US payment system sponsored by the Federal Reserve Bank of Richmond*, Boston/Dordrecht/London: Kluwer Academic: 129–139.

Cosimano, T. F. and D. W. Jansen (1988) 'Estimates of the variance of U.S. inflation based upon the ARCH model', *Journal of Money, Credit and Banking* 20: 409–421.

Cothren, R. (1987) 'Asymmetric information and optimal bank reserves', *Journal of Money, Credit and Banking* 19: 68–77.

Cowen, T. and R. Kroszner (1987) 'The development of the new monetary economics', *Journal of Political Economy* 95: 567–590.

Cowen, T. and R. Kroszner (1988) 'The evolution of an unregulated payments system', University of California, Irvine and Harvard University, mimeo.

Cowen, T. and R. Kroszner (1989) 'Mutual fund banking: A market approach', *Cato Journal* 10: 223–237.

Cowen, T. and R. Kroszner (1990a) 'Should the unit of account be stabilized in terms of a commodity bundle?', George Mason University and University of Chicago Graduate School of Business, mimeo.

Cowen, T. and R. Kroszner (1990b) 'Empirical predictions of the new monetary economics: Perspectives on velocity', *Journal of Policy Modelling* 12: 265–279.

Cowen, T. and R. Kroszner (1991) 'Commodity bundle media of account: "Black–Fama–Hall" reform proposals', George Mason University and University of Chicago Graduate School of Business, mimeo.

Cowen, T. and R. Kroszner (1994) *Explorations in the New Monetary Economics*, Oxford: Blackwell.

Cozier, B. and J. Selody (1992) 'Inflation and macroeconomic performance: Some cross-country evidence', Bank of Canada, mimeo.

Cozier, B. and G. Wilkinson (1991) 'Some evidence on hysteresis and the costs of disinflation in Canada', Bank of Canada, *Technical Report* 55, Ottawa: Bank of Canada.

Cukierman, A. (1979) 'Rational expectations and the role of monetary policy–A generalization', *Journal of Monetary Economics* 5: 213–229.

Cukierman, A. (1983) 'Relative price variability and inflation: A survey and further results', *Carnegie–Rochester Conference Series on Public Policy* 19: 103–158.

Cukierman, A. (1984) *Inflation, Stagflation, Relative Prices and Imperfect Information*, Cambridge: Cambridge University Press.

Cukierman, A. and L. Leiderman (1984) 'Price controls and the variability of relative prices', *Journal of Money, Credit and Banking* 16: 271–284.

Cukierman, A. and P. Wachtel (1979) 'Differential inflationary expectations and the variability of the rate of inflation: Theory and evidence', *American Economic Review* 69: 595–609.

Cukierman, A. and P. Wachtel (1982a) 'Relative price variability and nonuniform inflationary expectations', *Journal of Political Economy* 90: 146–157.

Cukierman, A. and P. Wachtel (1982b) 'Inflationary expectations: Reply and further thoughts on inflation uncertainty', *American Economic Review* 72: 508–512.

Dann, L. Y. and H. DeAngelo (1988) 'Corporate financial policy and corporate control: A study of defensive adjustments in asset and ownership structure', *Journal of Financial Economics* 20: 88–127.

Danziger, L. (1984) 'Stochastic inflation and the optimal policy of price adjustment', *Economic Inquiry* 22: 98–108.

Danziger, L. (1987a) 'On inflation and relative price variability', *Economic Inquiry* 25: 285–298.

Danziger, L. (1987b) 'Inflation, fixed costs of price adjustment and measurement of relative-price variability: Theory and evidence', *American Economic Review* 77: 704–713.

Davidson, I. R. (1992) 'Unit trusts', in P. Newman, M. Milgate and J. Eatwell (eds), *The New Palgrave Dictionary of Money and Finance*, vol. 3, London: Macmillan: 730–732.

de Bondt, W. F. M. (1992) 'Security analysts', in P. Newman, M. Milgate and J. Eatwell (eds), *The New Palgrave Dictionary of Money and Finance*, vol. 3, London: Macmillan: 435–438.

de Gregorio, J. (1992) 'The effects of inflation on economic growth: Lessons from Latin America', *European Economic Review* 36: 417–425.

de Meza, D. and D. C. Webb (1987) 'Too much investment: A problem of asymmetric information', *Quarterly Journal of Economics* 102: 281–292.

DeAngelo, H. and L. DeAngelo (1985) 'Managerial ownership of voting rights: A study of public corporations with dual classes of voting stock', *Journal of Financial Economics* 14: 33–69.

Deaton, A. and J. Muellbauer (1980) *Economics and Consumer Behavior*. Cambridge: Cambridge University Press.

Den Haan, W. J. (1990) 'The optimal inflation path in a Sidrauski-type model with uncertainty', *Journal of Monetary Economics* 25: 389–409.

Devereaux, M. and F. Schiantarelli (1990) 'Investment, financial factors and cash flow: Evidence from U.K. panel data', in R. G. Hubbard (ed.), *Asymmetric information, corporate finance and investment*, Chicago and London: Chicago University Press: 279–306.

Diamond, D. W. (1984) 'Financial intermediation and delegated monitoring', *Review of Economic Studies* 51: 393–414.

Diamond, D. W. (1989) 'Reputation acquisition in debt markets', *Journal of Political Economy* 97: 828–862.

Diamond, D. W. (1990) 'Seniority and maturity structure of bank loans and publicly traded debt', University of Chicago, mimeo.

Diamond, D. W. (1991) 'Debt maturity structure and liquidity risk', *Quarterly Journal of Economics* 106: 709–737.

Diamond, D. W. and P. H. Dybvig (1983) 'Bank runs, deposit insurance and liquidity', *Journal of Political Economy* 91: 401–419.

Diamond, P. A. and J. A. Mirrlees (1971a) 'Optimal taxation and public production, I: Production Efficiency', *American Economic Review* 61: 8–27.

Diamond, P. A. and J. A. Mirrlees (1971b) 'Optimal taxation and public production, II: Tax Rules', *American Economic Review* 61: 261–278.

Diewert, W. E. (1978) 'Superlative index numbers and consistency in aggregation', *Econometrica* 46: 883–900.

Diewert, W. E. (1987) 'Index numbers', in *The New Palgrave, a Dictionary of Economics*, vol. 1, New York: Stockton Press: 767–780.

Domberger, S. (1987) 'Relative price variability and inflation: A disaggregated analysis', *Journal of Political Economy* 95: 547–566.

Donaldson, R. G. (1988) 'Panic, liquidity and the lender of last resort: A strategic analysis', Board of Governors of the Federal Reserve System *International Finance Discussion Papers* 332.

Dornbusch, R. and J. A. Frankel (1973) 'Inflation and growth: Alternative approaches', *Journal of Money, Credit and Banking* 5: 141–156.

Dow, S. C. (1995) 'Why the financial system should be regulated', University of Stirling, mimeo.

Dow, S. C. and J. Smithin (1992) 'Free banking in Scotland 1695–1845', *Scottish Journal of Political Economy* 39: 374–390.

Dow, S. C. and J. Smithin (1994) 'Change in financial markets and the "first principles" of monetary economics', University of Stirling and York University, Ontario, mimeo.

Dowd, K. (1984) 'Adam Smith and the real bills doctrine', Ontario Economic Council, Toronto, mimeo.

Dowd, K. (1988a) *Private Money: The path to monetary stability*. London: Institute of Economic Affairs.

Dowd, K. (1988b) 'Automatic stabilizing mechanisms under free banking', *Cato Journal* 7: 643–659.

Dowd, K. (1988c) 'Is government deposit insurance necessary?', University of Nottingham, Mimeo.

Dowd, K. (1988d) 'Option clauses and the stability of a laisser faire monetary system', *Journal of Financial Services Research* 1: 319–333.

Dowd, K. (1989) *The State and the Monetary System*, Hemel Hampstead: Philip Allan and New York: St. Martin's Press.

Dowd, K. (1991a) 'Option clauses and banknote suspension', *Cato Journal* 10: 761–773.

Dowd, K. (1991b) 'The evolution of central banking in England, 1821–90', in F. Capie and G. E. Wood (eds), *Unregulated Banking: Chaos or order?*, London: Macmillan, 159–195.

Dowd, K. (1991c) 'Financial instability in a "directly convertible" gold standard', *Southern Economic Journal* 57: 719–726.

Dowd, K. (1992a) 'US banking in the "free banking" period', in K. Dowd (ed.), *The Experience of Free Banking*, London: Routledge, 206–240.

Dowd, K. (1992b) 'Free banking in Australia', in K. Dowd (ed.), *The experience of free banking*, London: Routledge, 48–78.

Dowd, K. (1992c) 'The monetary economies of Henry Meulen', *Journal of Money, Credit and Banking* 24: 173–183.

Dowd, K. (1993a) *Laissez-faire Banking*, London: Routledge.

Dowd, K. (1993b) 'Re-examining the case for government deposit insurance', *Southern Economic Journal* 59: 363–370.

Dowd, K. (1994a) 'A proposal to eliminate inflation', *Economic Journal* 104: 828–840.

Dowd, K. (1994b) 'The costs of inflation and disinflation', mimeo, Sheffield Hallam University. Forthcoming, *Cato Journal*.

Dowd, K. (1994c) 'The analytics of bimetallism', mimeo, Sheffield Hallam University. Forthcoming, *The Manchester School.*

Dowd, K. (ed.) (1992) *The Experience of Free Banking*, London: Routledge.

Dowd, K. and D. Greenaway (1993) 'Currency competition, network externalities and switching costs: Towards an alternative view of optimal currency areas', *Economic Journal* 103: 1180–1189.

Dowd, K. and A. A. Sampson (1993a) 'A new model of the gold standard', *Canadian Journal of Economics* 26: 380–391.

Dowd, K. and A. A. Sampson (1993b) 'The gold standard, Gibson's paradox and the gold stock', *Journal of Macroeconomics* 15: 653–659.

Driffil, J., G. E. Mizon and A. Ulph (1990) 'Costs of inflation', in B. F. Friedman and F. H. Hahn (eds), *Handbook of Monetary Economics*, vol. 2, Amsterdam: North Holland: 1013–1066.

Eckstein, Z. and L. Leiderman (1992) 'Seigniorage and the welfare cost of inflation: evidence from an intertemporal model of money and consumption', *Journal of Monetary Economics* 29: 389–410.

Economopoulos, A. J. (1988) 'Illinois free banking experience', *Journal of Money, Credit and Banking* 20: 249–264.

Eden, B. (1983) 'Competitive price setting, price flexibility and linkage to the money supply', *Carnegie–Rochester Conference Series on Public Policy* 19: 253–300.

Edgeworth, F. Y. (1888) 'The mathematical theory of banking', *Journal of the Royal Statistical Society* 51: 113–127.

Edgeworth, F. Y. (1895) 'Thoughts on monetary reform', *Economic Journal* 5: 434–451.

Eichberger, J. and F. Milne (1989) 'Bank runs and capital adequacy', University of Melbourne and Australian National University, mimeo.

Einaudi, L. (1953) 'The theory of imaginary money from Charlemagne to the French revolution', in F. C. Lane and J. C. Riemersma (eds), *Enterprise and Secular Change*, London: George Allen Unwin: 229–261.

Eisenmenger, R. W. (1990) 'Progress in bringing about a more efficient and safer payment system', in D. B. Humphrey (ed.), *The US Payment System: Efficiency, risk and the role of the Federal Reserve; Proceedings of a symposium on the US payment system sponsored by the Federal Reserve Bank of Richmond*, Boston/Dordrecht/London: Kluwer Academic: 1–7.

Engineer, M. (1989) 'Bank runs and the suspension of deposit convertibility', *Journal of Monetary Economics* 24: 443–454.

England, C. (1988) 'Agency costs and unregulated banks: Could depositors protect themselves?', in C. England and T. Huertas (eds), *The Financial Services Revolution:*

Policy directions for the future, Washington, DC: Cato Institute and Boston: Kluwer Academic Press: 317–343.

Engle, R. F. (1982). 'Autoregressive conditional heteroskedasticity with estimates of the variance of United Kingdom inflation', *Econometrica* 50: 987–1007.

Engle, R. F. (1983) 'Estimates of the variance of U.S. inflation based upon the ARCH model', *Journal of Money, Credit and Banking* 15: 286–301.

Evans, L. T. and N. C. Quigley (1992) 'Shareholder liability regimes, principal-agent relationships and banking industry performance', Victoria University of Wellington and University of Western Ontario, mimeo.

Evans, P. (1983) 'Price-level instability and output in the US', *Economic Inquiry* 21: 172–187.

Evans, M. (1991) 'Discovering the link between inflation rates and inflation uncertainty', *Journal of Money, Credit and Banking* 23: 169–184.

Faig, M. (1988) 'Characterization of the optimal tax on money when it functions as a medium of exchange', *Journal of Monetary Economics* 22: 137–148.

Falvey, R. F. and N. Gemmell (1991) 'Explaining price-service differences in international comparisons', *American Economic Review* 81: 1295–1309.

Fama, E. F. (1980) 'Banking in the theory of finance', *Journal of Monetary Economics* 6: 39–57.

Fama, E. F. (1983) 'Financial intermediation and price level control', *Journal of Monetary Economics* 12: 7–28.

Fama, E. F. (1985) 'What's different about banks?" *Journal of Monetary Economics* 15: 29–39.

Fama, E. F. and M. C. Jensen (1983) 'Separation of ownership and control', *Journal of Law and Economics* 26: 301–325.

Farrell, J. and G. Saloner (1986) 'Installed base and compatibility: Innovation, product preannouncements and predation', *American Economic Review* 76: 940–955.

Fazzari, S. M., R. G. Hubbard and B. Petersen (1988) 'Financing constraints and corporate investment', *Brookings Papers on Economic Activity* 1: 141–195.

Fazzari, S. M. and B. Petersen (1993) 'Working capital and fixed investment: New evidence on financing constraints', *Rand Journal of Economics* 24: 328–342.

Feige, E. L. and J. M. Parkin (1971) 'The optimal quantity of money, bonds, commodity inventories and capital', *American Economic Review* 61: 335–349.

Feldstein, M. S. (1979) 'The welfare cost of permanent inflation and optimal short-run economic policy', *Journal of Political Economy* 87: 749–768.

Feldstein, M. S. (1982) 'Inflation, tax rules and investment: some econometric evidence', *Econometrica* 50: 825–862.

Feldstein, M. S. (1983) *Inflation, Tax Rules and Capital Formation*. Chicago and London: University of Chicago Press.

Feldstein, M. S. and G. Chamberlain (1973) 'Multimarket expectations and the rate of interest', *Journal of Money, Credit and Banking* 5: 873–902.

Feldstein, M. S., J. Poterba and L. Dicks-Mireaux (1981) 'The effective tax rate and the pretax rate of return', NBER *Working Paper* 740 (August).

Feldstein, M. S. and J. Slemrod (1978) 'Inflation and the excess taxation of capital gains on corporate stock', *National Tax Journal* 31: 107–118.

Fellner, W. (1974) 'The controversial issue of comprehensive indexation', in H. Giersch, M. Friedman, W. Fellner, E. M. Bernstein and A. Kafka, *Essays on Inflation and Indexation*, Washington, DC: American Enterprise Institite for Public Policy Research: 63–69.

Fischer, S. (1972) 'Money, income, wealth and welfare', *Journal of Economic Theory* 4: 289–311.

Fischer, S. (1977) 'On the non-existence of privately issued index bonds in the United States capital market', in E. Lundberg (ed.), *Inflation Theory and Anti-inflation Policy*, London: Macmillan: 502–518.

Fischer, S. (1979a) 'Anticipations and the nonneutrality of money', *Journal of Political Economy* 87: 225–252.

Fischer, S. (1979b) 'Capital accumulation on the transition path in a monetary optimizing model', *Econometrica* 47: 1433–1439.

Fischer, S. (1981a) 'Relative shocks, relative price variability and inflation', *Brookings Papers in Economic Activity* 2: 381–431.

Fischer, S. (1981b) 'Toward an understanding of the costs of inflation: II', in K. Brunner and A. H. Meltzer (eds), *The Costs and Consequences of Inflation. Carnegie–Rochester Conference Series on Public Policy* 15, Amsterdam: North-Holland: 5–42.

Fischer, S. (1982) 'Adapting to inflation in the United States economy', in R. E. Hall (ed.), *Inflation: Causes and effects*, Chicago and London: Chicago University Press: 169–188.

Fischer, S. (1986a) 'Monetary rules and commodity money schemes under uncertainty', *Journal of Monetary Economics* 17: 21–35.

Fischer, S. (1986b) *Indexing, Inflation and Economic Policy*, Cambridge, MA and London: MIT Press, 1986.

Fischer, S. and F. Modigliani (1978) 'Towards an understanding of the real effects and costs of inflation', *Weltwirtschaftliches Archiv* 114: 810–833.

Fisher, I. (1894) 'The mechanics of bimetallism', *Economic Journal* 4: 527–537.

Fisher, I. (1911) *The Purchasing Power of Money: Its determination and relation to credit, interest and crises*, New York: Macmillan.

Fisher, I. (1913a) 'A compensated dollar', *Quarterly Journal of Economics* 27: 213–235.

Fisher, I. (1913b) 'A remedy for the rising cost of living: Standardizing the dollar', *American Economics Association Papers and Proceedings* 3–4: 20–28.

Fisher, I. (1913c) 'A compensated dollar: Appendix', *Quarterly Journal of Economics* 27: 385–397.

Fisher, I. (1913d) 'Reply [to objections]', *American Economics Association Papers and Proceedings* 3–4: 46–51.

Fisher, I. (1914) 'Objections to a compensated dollar answered', *American Economic Review* 4: 818–839.

Fisher, I. (1920) *Stabilizing the Dollar*, New York: Macmillan

Fisher, I. (1922) *The Making of Index Numbers*, Boston: Houghton Mifflin.

Fisher, I. (1933) 'The debt-deflation theory of great depressions', *Econometrica* 1: 337–357.

Flannery, M. J. (1989) 'Capital regulation and insured banks' choice of individual loan default rates', *Journal of Monetary Economics* 24: 235–258.

Fletcher, G. (1992) 'Discount houses', in *The New Palgrave Dictionary of Money and Finance*, vol. 1, edited by P. Newman, M. Milgate and J. Eatwell, London: Macmillan, 673–674.

Fortin, P. (1990) 'Can the costs of an anti-inflation policy be reduced?', in R. C. York (ed.), *Taking Aim: The debate on zero inflation*, Toronto: C. D. Howe Institute: 135–172.

Foster, E. (1972) 'Cost and benefits of inflation', *Federal Reserve Bank of Minneapolis Studies in Monetary Economics* 1, Minneapolis: Federal Reserve Bank of Minneapolis.

Foster, E. (1978) 'The variability of inflation', *Review of Economics and Statistics* 60: 346–350.

Frankel, A. B. and J. D. Montgomery (1992) 'Financial structure: An international perspective', *Brookings Papers on Economic Activity* 1: 257–310.

Frankel, S. H. (1977) *Money: Two Philosophies: The conflict of trust and authority*, Basil Blackwell: Oxford.

Freeman, S. (1988) 'Banking as the provision of liquidity', *Journal of Business* 61: 45–64.

Fried, J. and P. Howitt (1983) 'The effects of inflation on real interest rates', *American Economic Review* 73: 968–980.

Friedman, D. (1978) *The Machinery of Freedom: Guide to a radical capitalism*, New Rochelle, NY: Arlington House.

Friedman, M. (1951) 'Commodity-reserve currency', *Journal of Political Economy* 59: 203–232.

Friedman, M. (1953) *Essays in Positive Economics*, Chicago: University of Chicago Press.

Friedman, M. (1956) 'The quantity theory of money – A restatement', in M. Friedman *Studes in the Quantity Theory of Money*, Chicago: University of Chicago Press: 3–24.

Friedman, M. (1960) *A Program for Monetary Stability*, New York: Fordham University Press.

Friedman, M. (1968) 'The role of monetary policy', *American Economic Review* 58: 1–17.

Friedman, M. (1969) 'The optimum quantity of money', in M. Friedman *The Optimum Quantity of Money and Other Essays*, Chicago: Aldine: 1–50.

Friedman, M. (1974) 'Monetary correction', in H. Giersch, M. Friedman, W. Fellner, E. M. Bernstein and A. Kafka, *Essays on Inflation and Indexation*, Washington, DC: American Enterprise Institute for Public Policy Research: 25–61.

Friedman, M. (1977) 'Nobel lecture: inflation and unemployment', *Journal of Political Economy* 85: 451–472.

Friedman, M. (1986) 'The resource cost of irredeemable paper money', *Journal of Political Economy* 94: 642–647.

Friedman, M. (1989) 'Bimetallism revisited', Hoover Institution Domestic Studies Program *Working Papers in Economics* E-89-24.

Friedman, M. (1990a) 'Bimetallism revisited', *Journal of Economic Perspectives* 4: 85–104.

Friedman, M. (1990b) 'The crime of 1873', *Journal of Political Economy* 98: 1159–1194.

Friedman, M. (1992) *Money Mischief*, New York, San Diego and London: Harcourt Brace Jovanovich.

Friedman, M. and A. J. Schwartz (1963) *A Monetary History of the United States, 1867–1960*, Princeton, NJ: Princeton University Press.

Friedman, M. and A. J. Schwartz (1986) 'Has government any role in money?',*Journal of Monetary Economics* 17: 37–62.

Frohman, D. A., L. O. Laney and T. D. Willett (1981) 'Uncertainty costs of high inflation', *Voice* of the Federal Reserve Bank of Dallas July, 1–9.

Froyen, R. T. and R. N. Waud (1984) 'The changing relationship between aggregate price and output: The British experience', *Economica* 51: 53–67.

Froyen, R. T. and R. N. Waud (1987) 'An examination of aggregate price uncertainty in four countries and some implications for real output', *International Economic Review* 28: 353–73.

Gale, D. (1991) 'Optimal risk sharing through renegotiation of simple contracts', *Journal of Financial Intermediation* 1: 283–306.

Gale, D. (1992a) 'Standard securities', *Review of Economic Studies* 59: 731–755.

Gale, D. (1992b) 'Informational capacity and financial collapse', London School of Economics Financial Markets Group *Discussion Paper* 147.

Gale, D. and M. Hellwig (1985) 'Incentive-compatible debt contracts: The one-period problem', *Review of Economic Studies* 52: 647–663.

Gardener, E. P. M. (1989) 'The capital adequacy problem in modern banking', University College of Wales Institute of European Finance *Research Papers in Banking and Finance* 89/2.

Garfinkel, M. (1989) 'What is an "acceptable" rate of inflation? – A review of the issues', Federal Reserve Bank of St. Louis *Review*, July–August 1989, 3–15.

Garner, C. A. (1985) 'Commodity prices and monetary policy reform', Federal Reserve Bank of Kansas City *Economic Review* 70. February, 7–21.

Garrison, R. W. (1985) 'The cost of a gold standard', in L. H. Rockwell, Jr. (ed.), *The Gold Standard: An Austrian perspective*, Lexington, MA: D. C. Heath: 61–79.

Gavin, W. T. and A. C. Stockman (1991) 'Why a rule for stable prices may dominate a rule for zero inflation', Federal Reserve Bank of Cleveland *Economic Review* 27: 2–8.

Gendreau, B. C. and S. P. Prince (1986) 'The private costs of bank failures: Some historical evidence', Federal Reserve Bank of Philadelphia *Business Review* March-April, 3–14.

Gertler, M. (1988) 'Financial structure and aggregate economic activity: An overview', *Journal of Money, Credit and Banking* 20: 559–588.

Gertler, M. (1990) 'Financial capacity and output fluctuations in an economy with multiperiod financial relationships', New York University, mimeo.

Gertler, M. and E. Grinols (1982) 'Monetary randomness and investment', *Journal of Monetary Economics* 10: 239–258.

Gertler, M. and R. G. Hubbard (1993) 'Corporate financial policy, taxation and macroeconomic risk', *Rand Journal of Economics* 24: 286–303.

Gherrity, J. A. (1992) 'The option clause in Scottish banking, 1730–65: A Re-Appraisal', Department of Economics Northern Illinois University, mimeo.

Giersch, H. (1974) 'Index clauses and the fight against inflation', in H. Giersch, M. Friedman, W. Fellner, E. M. Bernstein and A. Kafka, *Essays on Inflation and Indexation*, Washington, DC: American Enterprise Instititute for Public Policy Research: 1–23.

Giffen, R. (1895) *The Case Against Bimetallism*, 3rd edn, London and New York: George Bell and Sons.

Gilbert, R. A. (1984) 'Bank market structure and competition: A survey', *Journal of Money, Credit and Banking* 16: 617–645.

Gilbert, R. A. and L. A. Kochin (1987) 'Local economic effects of bank failures', *Proceedings of a Conference on Bank Structure and Competition: Merging commercial and investment banking: Risks, benefits, challenges*, Chicago: Federal Reserve Bank of Chicago: 340–356.

Gilbert, R. A. and L. A. Kochin (1989) 'Local economic effects of bank failures', *Journal of Financial Services Research* 3: 333–345.

Gilchrist, S. (1990) 'An empirical analysis of corporate investment and financing hierarchies using firm level panel data', University of Wisconsin-Madison, mimeo.

Gillman, M. (1990) 'Standardizing estimates of the welfare costs of inflation', Emory University, mimeo.

Gillman, M. (1992) 'The welfare cost of inflation in a cash-in-advance economy with costly credit', University of Otago, mimeo.

Gillman, M. (1995) 'A zero optimal rate of inflation: Costly price and wage adjustment in general equilibrium', University of Otago, mimeo.

Girton, L. and D. Roper (1981) 'Theory and implications of currency substitution', *Journal of Money, Credit and Banking* 13: 12–30.

Glasner, D. (1987) 'Competitive banking: Safety without deposit insurance', *Cato Policy Report* 9, March–April, 1, 10–12.

Glasner, D. (1989a) *Free Banking and Monetary Reform*, Cambridge: Cambridge University Press.

Glasner, D. (1989b) 'How natural is the government's monopoly over money?', Paper presented to the Cato Institute Monetary Conference *Alternatives to Government Fiat Money*, Washington, DC.

Glasner, D. (1992) 'The real-bills doctrine in the light of the law of reflux', *History of Political Economy* 24: 867–894.

Glejser, J. (1965) 'Inflation, productivity and relative prices – A statistical study', *Review of Economics and Statistics* 47: 76–80.

Goacher, D. J., P. J. Curwen, R. Apps, J. G. Boocock, P. F. Cowdell and L. Drake (1987) *British Non-bank Financial Intermediaries*. London: Allen and Unwin.

Goacher, D. J. (1993) *The Monetary and Financial System*, 2nd edn, London: Bankers Books Limited.

Goldberg, S. (1958) *Introduction to Difference Equations*, New York: John Wiley and Sons.

Goldberg, L. G. and G. A. Hanweck (1988) 'What we can expect from interstate banking', *Journal of Banking and Finance* 12: 51–67.

Goode, R. (1951) 'A constant purchasing-power savings bond', *National Tax Journal* 4: 332–340.

Goodfriend, M. (1990) 'Money, credit, banking and payment system policy', in D. B. Humphrey (ed.), *The US Payment System: Efficiency, risk and the role of the Federal Reserve: Proceedings of a symposium on the US payment system sponsored by the Federal Reserve Bank of Richmond*, Boston/Dordrecht/London: Kluwer Academic: 247–277.

Goodhart, C. A. E. (1987) 'Why do banks need a central bank?', *Oxford Economic Papers* 39: 75–89.

Goodhart, C. A. E. (1988) *The evolution of central banks*. Cambridge, MA: MIT Press.

Goodhart, C. A. E. (1989) *Money, Information and Uncertainty*, 2nd edn, London: Macmillan.

Gorton, G. (1985) 'Bank suspension of convertibility', *Journal of Monetary Economics* 15: 177–193.

Gorton, G. (1986) 'Banking panics and business cycles', Federal Reserve Bank of Philadelphia, *Working Paper* 86–9.

Gorton, G. and J. G. Haubrich (1987) 'Bank deregulation, credit markets and the control of capital', *Carnegie–Rochester Conference Series on Public Policy* 26: 289–334.

Gorton, G. and D. J. Mullineaux (1987) 'The joint production of confidence: Endogenous regulation and nineteenth-century commercial bank clearinghouses', *Journal of Money, Credit and Banking* 19: 457–468.

Gorton, G. and G. Pennacchi (1989) 'Are loan sales really off-balance sheet?', *Journal of Accounting, Auditing and Finance* 4: 125–145.

Gorton, G. and G. Pennacchi (1990) 'Banks and loan sales: Marketing non-marketable assets', National Bureau of Economic Research, *Working Paper* 3551.

Gorton, G. and G. Pennacchi (1992) 'The opening of new markets for bank assets', in R. A. Gilbert (ed.), *The Changing Market in Financial Services: Proceedings of the fifteenth annual economic policy conference of the Federal Reserve Bank of St. Louis*, Boston: Kluwer Academic Press: 3–33.

Goudriaan, B. (1932) *How to Stop Deflation*, London: The Search Publishing Company.

Graham, B. (1937) *Storage and Stability*, New York: McGraw Hill.

Graham, B. (1944) *World Commodities and World Currency*, New York and London: McGraw-Hill.

Graham, F. D. (1930) *Exchange, Prices and Production in Hyper-inflation: Germany 1920–1923*, Princeton, NJ: Princeton University Press.

Graham, F. D. (1942) *Social Goals and Economic Institutions*, Princeton: Princeton University Press.

Grandmont, J. M. and Y. Younès (1973) 'On the efficiency of a monetary equilibrium', *Review of Economic Studies* 40: 149–165.

Granger, C. W. J. and P. Newbold (1974) 'Spurious regressions in econometrics', *Journal of Econometrics* 2: 111–120.

Gray, J. A. (1976) 'Wage indexation: A macroeconomic approach', *Journal of Monetary Economics* 2: 221–235.

Green, R. C. (1984) 'Investment incentives, debt and warrants', *Journal of Financial Economics* 13: 115–136.

Greenfield, R. L. and L. B. Yeager (1983) 'A laissez-faire approach to monetary stability', *Journal of Money, Credit and Banking* 15: 302–315.

Greenfield, R. L. and L. B. Yeager (1989) 'A real-GNP dollar', Fairleigh Dickinson University and Auburn University, mimeo.

Greenwald, B. C. and J. E. Stiglitz (1987) 'Imperfect information, credit markets and unemployment', *European Economic Review* 31: 444–456.

Greenwald, B. C. and J. E. Stiglitz (1988a) 'Imperfect information, finance constraints and business fluctuations', in M. Kohn and S.-C. Tsiang (eds), *Finance Constraints, Expectations and Macroeconomics*, Oxford: Clarendon Press: 103–165.

Greenwald, B. C. and J. E. Stiglitz (1988b) 'Financial market imperfections and business cycles', National Bureau of Economic Research, *Working Paper* 2494.

Greenwald, B. C. and J. E. Stiglitz (1993) 'Financial market imperfections and business cycles', *Quarterly Journal of Economics* 108: 77–114.

Grier, K. B. and G. Tullock (1989) 'An empirical analysis of cross-national economic growth', *Journal of Monetary Economics* 24: 259–276.

Grimes, A. (1992) 'The effects of inflation on growth: Some international evidence', *Weltwirtschaftliches Archiv* 127: 631–644.

Grossman, R. S. (1989) 'The macroeconomic consequences of bank failures under the National Banking System', United States Department of State Bureau of Economic and Business Affairs Planning and Economic Analysis Staff, *Working Paper* 89/14.

Grossman, R. S. (1992) 'Deposit insurance, regulation and moral hazard in the thrift industry: Evidence from the 1930's', *American Economic Review* 82: 800–821.

Grossman, S. J. and O. D. Hart (1988) 'One share-one vote and the market for corporate control', *Journal of Financial Economics* 20: 175–202.

Guesnerie, R. (1992) 'Hidden actions, moral hazard and contract theory', in *The New Palgrave Dictionary of Money and Finance*, vol. 2, edited by P. Newman, M. Milgate and J. Eatwell, London: Macmillan: 304–309.

Guffey, D. M. and W. T. Moore (1991) 'Direct bankruptcy costs: Evidence from the trucking industry', *The Financial Review* 26: 223–235.

Gurley, J. G. and E. S. Shaw (1960) *Money in a Theory of Finance*, Washington, DC: Brookings Institute.

Guttentag, J. M. and R. J. Herring (1983) 'The lender-of-last-resort function in an international context', Princeton University, *Essays in International Finance* 151.

Guttman, W. and P. Meehan (1975) *The Great Inflation, Germany 1919–23*. Farnborough: Saxon House.

Hafer, R. W. (1986) 'Inflation uncertainty and a test of the Friedman hypothesis', *Journal of Macroeconomics* 8: 365–372.

Hahn, F. H. (1971) 'Professor Friedman's views on money', *Economica* 38: 61–80

Hake, A. E. and O. E. Wesslau (1890) *Free Trade in Capital, or Free Competition in the Supply of Capital to Labour and its Bearings on the Political and Social Questions of the Day*, London: Remington and Co.

Hall, R. E. (1981) 'The government and the monetary unit', Hoover Institution and National Bureau of Economic Research, mimeo.

Hall, R. E. (1982) 'Explorations in the gold standard and related policies for stabilizing the dollar', in R. E. Hall (ed.), *Inflation: Causes and effects*, London and Chicago: Chicago University Press: 111–122.

Hall, R. E. (1983) 'Optimal fiduciary monetary systems', *Journal of Monetary Economics* 12: 33–50.

Hall, R. E. (1984a) 'Money policy for noninflationary growth', in J. H. Moore (ed.), *To Promote Prosperity: U.S. domestic policy in the mid-1980s*, Stanford, CA: Hoover Institution Press: 60–71.

Hall, R. E. (1984b) 'A free-market policy to stabilize the purchasing power of the dollar', in B. N. Siegel (ed.), *Money in Crisis: The Federal Reserve, the economy and monetary reform*, San Francisco: Pacific Institute for Public Policy Research: 303–321.

Hall, R. E. (1986) 'Optimal monetary institutions and policy', in C. D. Campbell and W. R. Dougan (eds), *Alternative Monetary Regimes*, Baltimore and London: The Johns Hopkins University Press: 224–239.

Hardwick, P. (1989) 'Economies of scale in building societies', *Applied Economics* 21: 1291–1304.

Harris, M. and A. Raviv (1979) 'Optimal incentive contracts with imperfect information', *Journal of Economic Theory* 21: 231–259.

Harris, M. and A. Raviv (1988a) 'Corporate control contests and capital structure', *Journal of Financial Economics* 20: 55–86.

Harris, M. and A. Raviv (1988b) 'Corporate governance: Voting rights and majority rules', *Journal of Financial Economics* 20: 203–235.

Harris, M. and A. Raviv (1989) 'The design of securities', *Journal of Financial Economics* 24: 255–287.

Harris, M. and A. Raviv (1990) 'Capital structure and the informational role of debt', *Journal of Finance* 45: 321–349.

Harris, M. and A. Raviv (1991) 'The theory of capital structure', *Journal of Finance* 46: 297–355.

Hart, A. G. (1987) 'Commodity reserve currency', in *The New Palgrave, a Dictionary of Economics*, vol. 2, New York: Stockton Press: 498–499.

Hart, O. D. (1986) 'Comment [on "Credit rationing and collateral" by J. Stiglitz and A. Weiss]', in J. Edwards et al. (eds), *Recent Advances in Corporate Finance, Investment and Taxation*, Cambridge: Cambridge University Press: 136–143.

Hart, O. and B. Holmström (1987) 'The theory of contracts', in T. F. Bewley (ed.), *Advances in Economic Theory: Fifth world congress*, Cambridge: Cambridge University Press: 71–155.

Hart, O. and J. Moore (1988) 'Incomplete contracts and renegotiation', *Econometrica* 56: 755–786.

Hart, O. and J. Moore (1989) 'Default and renegotiation: A dynamic model of debt', Massachusetts Institute of Technology and London School of Economics, mimeo.

Hart, O. and J. Moore (1990) 'A theory of corporate financial structure based on the seniority of claims', Massachusetts Institute of Technology Department of Economics, *Working Paper* 560.

Hart, O. and J. Moore (1993) 'Debt and seniority: An analysis of the role of hard claims in constraining management', London School of Economics Financial Markets Group, *Discussion Paper* 168.

Hart, O. and J. Moore (1994) 'A theory of debt based on the inalienability of human capital', *Quarterly Journal of Economics* 99: 841–879.

Hartman, R. (1991) 'Relative price variability and inflation', *Journal of Money, Credit and Banking* 23: 185–205.

Hasan, I. and G. P. Dywer, Jr. (1988) 'Contagion effects and banks closed in the free banking period', in *The Financial Services Industry in the Year 2000: Risk and efficiency: Proceedings of a conference on bank structure and competition*, Chicago: Federal Reserve Bank of Chicago: 153–177.

Hasan, I. and G. P. Dywer, Jr. (1989) 'Contagious bank runs in the free banking period', Federal Home Loan Bank of Atlanta and Federal Reserve Bank of St. Louis, mimeo.

Hasan, I. and G. P. Dywer, Jr. (1994) 'Bank runs in the free banking period', *Journal of Money, Credit and Banking* 26: 271–288.

Haubrich, J. G. (1989) 'Financial intermediation: Delegated monitoring and long-term relationships', *Journal of Banking and Finance* 13: 9–20.

Haubrich, J. G. (1990) 'Nonmonetary effects of financial crises: Lessons from the Great Depression in Canada', *Journal of Monetary Economics* 25: 223–252.

Haubrich, J. G. and R. G. King (1984) 'Banking and insurance', National Bureau of Economic Research, *Working Paper* 1312

Haubrich, J. G. and R. G. King (1989) 'Banking and insurance', *Journal of Monetary Economics* 26: 361–386.

Haubrich, J. G. and J. B. Thomson (1993) 'The evolving savings and loan market', Federal Reserve Bank of Cleveland, *Economic Commentary*, July 15.

Hayek, F. A. (1943) 'A commodity reserve currency', *Economic Journal* 53: 176–184.

Hayek, F. A. (1945) 'The use of knowledge in society', *American Economic Review* 35: 519–530.

Hayek, F. A. (1948) *Individualism and Economic Order*, Reprinted 1980. Chicago: Chicago University Press.

Hayek, F. A. (1960) *The Constitution of Liberty*, 1978 edn, Chicago: Chicago University Press.

Hayek, F. A. (1978) *Denationalisation of Money*, 2nd edn, London: Institute of Economic Affairs.

Heinkel, R. (1982) 'A theory of capital structure relevance under imperfect information', *Journal of Finance* 37: 1141–1150.

Helsey, R. W. and W. C. Strange (1991) 'Exclusion and the theory of clubs', *Canadian Journal of Economics* 24: 888–899.

Hesselman, L. (1983) 'The macroeconomic role of relative price variability in the USA and the UK', *Applied Economics* 15: 225–233.

Hercowitz, Z. (1981) 'Money and the dispersion of relative prices', *Journal of Political Economy* 89: 328–356.

Hercowitz, Z. (1982) 'Money and price dispersion in the United States', *Journal of Monetary Economics* 10: 25–37.

Hicks, J. R. (1940) 'The valuation of the social income', *Economica* 7: 105–124.

Hillier, B. and M. V. Ibrahimo (1993) 'Asymmetric information and models of credit rationing', *Bulletin of Economic Research* 45: 271–304.

Hirshleifer, J. (1971) 'The private and social value of information and the reward to inventive activity', *American Economic Review* 61: 561–574.

Holland, A. S. (1984) 'Does higher inflation lead to more uncertain inflation?', Federal Reserve Bank of St. Louis, *Review*, February, 15–26.

Holland, A. S. (1986) 'Wage indexation and the effect of inflation uncertainty on employment: An empirical analysis', *American Economic Review* 76: 235–243.

Horrigan, B. R. (1987) 'The CPI futures market: The inflation hedge that won't grow', Federal Reserve Bank of Philadelphia, *Business Review*, May–June, 3–14.

Horwitz, S. (1990) 'Competitive currencies, legal restrictions and the origins of the Fed: Some evidence from the panic of 1907', *Southern Economic Journal* 56: 639–649.

Horwitz, S. (1991) 'The political economy of inflation: Public and private choices', Paper presented to the Durell Foundation Conference, *American Money and Banking: Financial Fitness for the 1990s*, Scottsdale, AR.

Horwitz, S. (1992) *Monetary Evolution, Free Banking and Economic Order*, Boulder: Westview.

Horwitz, S. and G. A. Selgin (1987) 'Interstate banking: The reform that won't go away', Cato Institute, *Policy Analysis* 97. Washington, DC: Cato Institute.

Hoshi, T., A. Kashyap and D. Scharfstein (1990) 'Bank monitoring and investment: Evidence from the changing structure of Japanese corporate banking relationships', in R. G. Hubbard (ed.), *Asymmetric Information, Corporate Finance and Investment*, Chicago and London: Chicago University Press: 105–126.

Hoshi, T., A. Kashyap and D. Scharfstein (1991) 'Corporate structure, liquidity and investment: Evidence from Japanese industrial groups', *Quarterly Journal of Economics* 106: 33–60.

Houston, J. F. and S. Venkataraman (1994) 'Optimal maturity structure with multiple debt claims', *Journal of Financial and Quantitative Analysis* 29: 179–197.

Howitt, P. (1986) 'Indexation and the adjustment to inflation in Canada', in J. Sargent (ed.), *Postwar Macroeconomic Developments*, Toronto: University of Toronto Press: 175–224.

Howitt, P. (1990a) 'Zero inflation as a long-term target for monetary policy', in R. G. Lipsey (ed.), *Zero Inflation: The goal of price stability*, Toronto: C. D. Howe Institute: 67–108.

Howitt, P. (1990b) 'A comment', in R. C. York (ed.), *Taking Aim: The debate on zero inflation*, Toronto: C. D. Howe Institute: 104–108.

Howitt, P. W. (1992) 'Optimum quantity of money', in P. Newman, M. Milgate and J. Eatwell (eds), *The New Palgrave Dictionary of Money and Finance*, vol. 3, London: Macmillan: 81–83.

Hubbard, R. G. and A. Kashyap (1990) 'Internal net worth and the investment process: An application to US agriculture', National Bureau of Economic Research, *Working Paper* 3339.

Humphrey, D. B. (1984) *The US Payments System: Costs, pricing, competition and risk*, New York University Graduate School of Business, Salomon Brothers Center for the Study of Financial Institutions, *Monograph* 1984-1/2. New York: New York University.

Humphrey, D. B. (1986) 'Payments finality and risk of settlement failure', in A. Saunders and L. J. White (eds), *Technology and the Regulation of Financial Markets: Securities, futures and banking*, Lexington, MA: DC Heath: 97–120.

Humphrey, D. B. and A. N. Berger (1990) 'Market failure and resource use: Economic incentives to use different payment instruments', in D. B. Humphrey (ed.), *The US Payment System: Efficiency, risk and the role of the Federal Reserve: Proceedings of a symposium on the US payment system sponsored by the Federal Reserve Bank of Richmond*, Boston/Dordrecht/London: Kluwer Academic: 45–86.

Humphrey, T. M. (1982) 'The real bills doctrine', Federal Reserve Bank of Richmond, *Economic Review*, September–October, 3–13.

Humphrey, T. M. (1990) 'Fisherian and Wicksellian price-stabilization models in the history of economic thought', Federal Reserve Bank of Richmond, *Economic Review*, May–June, 3–12.

Hunter, W. G. and S. G. Timme (1986) 'Technical change, organizational form and the structure of bank production', *Journal of Money, Credit and Banking* 18: 152–166.

İmrohoroğlu, A. (1992) 'The welfare cost of inflation under imperfect insurance', *Journal of Economic Dynamics and Control* 16: 79–91.

Innes, R. (1993) 'Financial contracting under risk neutrality, limited liability and *ex ante* asymmetric information', *Economica* 60: 27–40.

Ippolito, R. A. (1992) 'Mutual funds', in P. Newman, M. Milgate and J. Eatwell (eds), *The New Palgrave Dictionary of Money and Finance*, vol. 2, London: Macmillan: 831–832.

Ireland, P. N. (1994) 'Money and growth: An alternative approach', *American Economic Review* 84: 47–65.

Iwai, K. (1988) 'The evolution of money: A search-theoretic foundation of monetary economics', University of Pennsylvania Center for Analytic Research in Economics and the Social Sciences, *Working Paper* 88-03.

Jacklin, C. J. (1987) 'Demand deposits, trading restrictions and risk sharing', in E. C. Prescott and N. Wallace (eds), *Contractual Arrangements for Intertemporal Trade*, Minneapolis, MN: University of Minnesota Press: 26–47.

Jacklin, C. J. (1988) 'Demand equity and deposit insurance', Graduate School of Business, Stanford University, mimeo.

Jacklin, C. J. and S. Bhattacharya (1988) 'Distinguishing panics and information-based bank runs: Welfare and policy implications', *Journal of Political Economy* 96: 568–592.

Jaffee, D. and E. Kleiman (1977) 'The welfare implications of uneven inflation', in E. Lundberg (ed.), *Inflation Theory and Anti-inflation Policy*, London: Macmillan: 285–307.

Jaffee, D. and T. Russell (1976) 'Imperfect information, uncertainty and credit rationing', *Quarterly Journal of Economics* 90: 651–666.

James, C. (1987) 'Some evidence on the uniqueness of bank loans', *Journal of Financial Economics* 19: 217–235.

James, C. (1988) 'The use of loan sales and standby letters of credit by commercial banks', *Journal of Monetary Economics* 22: 395–422.

James, C. and P. Wier (1988) 'Are bank loans different? Some evidence from the stock market', *Journal of Applied Corporate Finance* 1: 46–54.

James, C. and P. Wier (1990) 'Borrowing relationships, intermediation and the cost of issuing public securities', *Journal of Financial Economics* 28: 149–171.

Jansen, D. W. (1989) 'Does inflation uncertainty affect output growth? Further evidence', Federal Reserve Bank of St. Louis, *Review*, July–August, 43–54.

Japelli, T. (1990) 'Who is credit constrained in the US economy?', *Quarterly Journal of Economics* 105: 219–234.

Jarrett, J. P. and J. G. Selody (1982) 'The productivity-inflation nexus in Canada, 1963–1979', *Review of Economics and Statistics* 64: 361–367.

Jensen, M. C. (1968) 'The performance of mutual funds in the period 1945–1964', *Journal of Finance* 23: 389–416.

Jensen, M. C. (1986) 'Agency costs of free cash flow, corporate finance and takeovers', *American Economic Review* 76: 323–339.

Jensen, M. C. (1992) 'Market for corporate control', in P. Newman, M. Milgate and J. Eatwell (eds), *The New Palgrave Dictionary of Money and Finance*, vol. 2, London: Macmillan: 657–666.

Jensen, M. C. and W. H. Meckling (1976) 'Theory of the firm: Managerial behavior, agency costs and ownership structure', *Journal of Financial Economics* 3: 305–360.

Jensen, M. C. and R. S. Ruback (1983) 'The market for corporate control', *Journal of Financial Economics* 11: 5–50.

Jensen, M. C. and C. W. Smith, Jr. (1985) 'Stockholder, manager and creditor interests: Applications of agency theory', in E. I. Altman and M. G. Subrahmanyam (eds), *Recent Advances in Corporate Finance*, Homewood, IL: Richard D. Irwin: 93–128.

Jevons, W. S. ([1875] 1907) *Money and the Mechanism of Exchange*, 16th edn, London: Kegan Paul, Trench, Trubner and Co.

John, K. and A. Kalay (1985) 'Informational content of debt contracts', in E. I. Altman and M. G. Subrahmanyam (eds), *Recent Advances in Corporate Finance*, Homewood, IL: Richard D. Irwin: 133–161.

Johnson, H. G. (1967) 'Money in a neo-classical one-sector growth model', in H. G. Johnson, *Essays in Monetary Economics*, London: George Allen Unwin: 143–178.

Johnson, H. G. (1968) 'Problems of efficiency in monetary management', *Journal of Political Economy* 76: 971–990.

Johnson, H. G. (1970) 'Is there an optimal money supply?', *Journal of Finance* 25: 435–442.

Johnson, H. G. (1972) *Further Essays in Monetary Economics*, London: George Allen Unwin.

Jones, R. A. (1976) 'The origin and development of media of exchange', *Journal of Political Economy* 84: 757–775.

Jonung, L. (1989) 'The economics of private money: The experience of private notes in Sweden, 1831–1902', Stockholm School of Economics, mimeo.

Jorgenson, D. W. (1963) 'Capital theory and investment behavior', *American Economic Review* 53: 247–259.

Kafka, A. (1974) 'Indexing for inflation in Brazil', in H. Giersch, M. Friedman, W. Fellner, E. M. Bernstein and A. Kafka, *Essays on Inflation and Indexation*, Washington, DC: American Enterprise Institute for Public Policy Research: 87–98.

Kahn, J. A. (1990) 'Debt, asymmetric information and bankruptcy', Rochester Center for Economic Research, *Working Paper* 238.

Kanatas, G. (1987) 'Commercial paper, bank reserve requirements and the informational role of loan commitments', *Journal of Banking and Finance* 11: 425–448.

Kanatas, G. (1992) 'Collateral', in P. Newman, M. Milgate and J. Eatwell (eds), *The New Palgrave Dictionary of Money and Finance*, vol. 1, London: Macmillan: 381–383.

Kane, E. J. (1988) 'Fedbashing and the role of monetary arrangements in managing political stress', in T. D. Willett (ed.), *Political Business Cycles: The political economy of money, inflation and unemployment*, Durham, NC and London: Duke University Press: 479–489.

Kantor, L. G. (1986) 'Inflation uncertainty and real economic activity: An alternative approach', *Review of Economics and Statistics* 68: 493–500.

Karni, E. (1981) 'A note on Lucas's equilibrium model of the business cycle', *Journal of Political Economy* 88: 1231–1236.

Katsimbris, G. M. (1985) 'The relationship between the inflation rate, its variability and output growth variability: Disaggregated international evidence', *Journal of Money, Credit and Banking* 17: 179–188.

Katsimbris, G. M. and S. M. Miller (1982) 'The relation between the rate and variability of inflation: Further comments', *Kyklos* 35: 456–467.

Katz, M. L. and C. Shapiro (1986) 'Network externalities, competition and compatibility', *American Economic Review* 76: 424–440.

Kaufman, G. G. (1987) 'The truth about bank runs', Federal Reserve Bank of Chicago, *Staff Memorandum* SM-87-3.

Kaufman, G. G. (1988) 'Bank runs: causes, benefits and costs', *Cato Journal* 7: 559–587.

Kaufman, G. G. (1989) 'The savings and loan rescue of 1989: Causes and perspectives', Issues in Financial Regulation, *Working Paper* 89-23. Federal Reserve Bank of Chicago.

Kaufman, G. G. (1992) 'Capital in banking: Past, present and future', *Journal of Financial Services Research* 5: 385–402.

Kearl, J. R. (1978) 'Inflation and relative price distortions: The case of housing', *Review of Economics and Statistics* 60: 609–614.

Kearl, J. R. (1979) 'Inflation, mortgages and housing', *Journal of Political Economy* 87: 1115–1138.

Keeton, W. R. (1979) *Equilibrium Credit Rationing*, New York and London: Garland Publishing.

Kenen, P. B. (1969) 'The theory of optimum currency areas: An eclectic view', in R. A. Mundell and A. K. Swoboda (eds), *Monetary Problems of the International Economy*, Chicago: Chicago University Press: 41–60.

Keynes, J. M. ([1923] 1971) *A Tract on Monetary Reform*, London and Basingstoke: Macmillan.

Keynes, J. M. ([1930] 1971) *A Treatise on Money*, Two volumes. London and Basingstoke: Macmillan.

Keynes, J. M. ([1936] 1977) *The General Theory of Employment, Interest and Money*, London and Basingstoke: Macmillan.

Kimbrough, K. P. (1986) 'The optimum quantity of money rule in the theory of public finance', *Journal of Monetary Economics* 18: 277–284.

Kindleberger, C. P. (1983) 'Standards as public, collective and private goods', *Kyklos* 36: 377–396.

King, R. G. (1983) 'On the economics of private money', *Journal of Monetary Economics* 12: 127–158.

Kirzner, I. (1973) *Competition and Entrepreneurship*, Chicago: Chicago University Press.

Kiyotaki, N. and R. Wright (1989) 'On money as a medium of exchange', *Journal of Political Economy* 97: 927–954.

Kleiman, E. (1989) 'The costs of inflation', Hebrew University of Jerusalem Department of Economics, *Working Paper* 211.

Klein, B. (1975a) 'The impact of inflation on the term structure of corporate financial investments: 1900–1972', in W. L. Silber (ed.), *Financial Innovation*, Lexington, MA: Lexington: 125–149.

Klein, B. (1975b) 'Our new monetary standard: measurement and effects of price uncertainty, 1880–1973', *Economic Inquiry* 13: 461–484.

Klein, B. (1976) 'The social costs of the recent inflation: The mirage of steady "anticipated" inflation', *Carnegie–Rochester Conference Series on Public Policy* 3: 185–212.

Klein, B. (1978) 'The measurement of long- and short-term price uncertainty: A moving regression time series analysis', *Economic Inquiry* 16: 438–452.

Klein, B. and M. Melvin (1982) 'Competing international monies and international monetary arrangements', in M. B. Connolly (ed.), *The International Monetary System: Choices for the future*, New York: Praeger: 199–225.

Knapp, G. F. (1905) *Die Staatlich Theorie des Geldes*, Abridged and translated into English as *The State Theory of Money* (1924). London: Macmillan.

Korajczyk, R. A., D. Lucas and R. McDonald (1990) 'The effect of information releases on the pricing and timing of equity issues', in R. G. Hubbard (ed.), *Asymmetric Information, Corporate Finance and investment*, Chicago: Chicago University Press: 257–277.

Kormendi, R. C. and P. G. Meguire (1985) 'Macroeconomic determinants of growth: Cross-country evidence', *Journal of Monetary Economics* 16: 141–163.

Krasa, S. and A. P. Villamil (1990) 'Monitoring the monitor: An incentive structure for a financial intermediary', University of Illinois, Urbana-Champaign, mimeo.

Krasa, S. and A. P. Villamil (1992) 'A theory of optimal bank size', *Oxford Economic Papers* 44: 725–749.

Kydland, F. E. and E. C. Prescott (1977) 'Rules rather than discretion: The inconsistency of optimal plans', *Journal of Political Economy* 85: 47–491.

Lacker, J. M. (1989) 'Limited commitment and costly enforcement', Federal Reserve Bank of Richmond, *Working Paper* 90–2.

Lacker, J. M. (1990) 'Collateralized debt as the optimal contract', Federal Reserve Bank of Richmond, *Working Paper* 90-3.

Lacker, J. M. and J. A. Weinberg (1989) 'Optimal contracts under costly state falsification', *Journal of Political Economy* 97: 1345–1363.

Lacker, J. M., R. J. Levy and J. A. Weinberg (1990) 'Incentive compatible financial contracts, asset prices and the value of control', *Journal of Financial Intermediation* 1: 31–56.

Laidler, D. (1975) 'Thomas Tooke on monetary reform', in D. E. W. Laidler *Essays on Money and Inflation*, Chicago: Chicago University Press: 211–227.

Laidler, D. (1976) 'Concerning currency unions', University of Western Ontario Department of Economics, *Research Report* 7618.

Laidler, D. (1977) 'The welfare costs of inflation in neoclassical perspective – Some unsettled problems', in E. Lundberg (ed.), *Inflation Theory and Anti-inflation Policy*, London: Macmillan: 314–328.

Laidler, D. (1981) 'Adam Smith as a monetary economist', *Canadian Journal of Economics* 14: 185–200.

Laidler, D. (1984) 'Misconceptions about the real-bills doctrine: A comment on Sargent and Wallace', *Journal of Political Economy* 92: 149–155.

Laidler, D. (1985) *The Demand for Money: Theories, evidence and problems*, 3rd edn, New York: Harper and Row.

Laidler, D. (1990) *Taking Money Seriously*, Hemel Hempstead: Philip Allan.

Laidler, D. and M. Parkin (1975) 'Inflation: A survey', *Economic Journal* 85: 741–809.

Lane, F. C. and R. C. Mueller (1985) *Money and Banking in Medieval and Renaissance Venice*, vol. 1. Baltimore: Johns Hopkins University Press.

Larcker, D. (1983) 'The association between performance plan adoption and corporate capital investment', *Journal of Accounting and Economics* 5: 3–30.

Law, J. (1705) *Money and Trade Considered*, Edinburgh: Anderson.

Leach, J. (1983) 'Inflation as a commodity tax', *Canadian Journal of Economics* 16: 508–516.

Lee, C.-W. J. and C. R. Petruzzi (1986) 'The Gibson paradox and the monetary standard', *Review of Economics and Statistics* 189–196.

Leijonhufvud, A. (1981) *Information and Coordination: Essays in macroeconomic theory.* New York and Oxford: Oxford University Press.

Leijonhufvud, A. (1983) 'Constitutional constraints on the monetary powers of government', in J. A. Dorn and A. J. Schwartz (eds), *The Search for Stable Money: Essays on monetary reform*, Chicago: Chicago University Press: 129–143.

Leijonhufvud, A. (1988) 'Foreword', in T. D. Willett (ed.), *Political Business Cycles: The political economy of money, inflation and unemployment*, Durham and London: Duke University Press: xv–xxii.

Leland, H. E. and D. H. Pyle (1977) 'Informational asymmetries, financial structure and financial intermediation', *Journal of Finance* 32: 371–387.

Leser, C. V. (1983) 'Short run and long run relative price changes', *Journal of the Royal Statistical Society* 146: 172–181.

Levhari, D. and N. Liviatan (1977) 'Aspects of the theory of indexed bonds', in E. Lundberg (ed.), *Inflation Theory and Anti-inflation Policy*, London: Macmillan: 488–501.

Levhari, D. and D. Patinkin (1968) 'The role of money in a simple growth model', *American Economic Review* 58: 713–753.

Levi, M. D. and J. Makin (1980) 'Inflation uncertainty and the Phillips curve: Some empirical evidence', *American Economic Review* 70: 1022–1027.

Levine, R. and D. Renelt (1992) 'A sensitivity analysis of cross-country growth regressions', *American Economic Review* 82: 942–963.

Lewis, M. K. (1989) 'Market making and liquidity', University of Ulster, *Financial Services Seminar Series* 6.

Lewis, M. K. (1990) 'Liquidity', in J. Creedy (ed.), *Foundations of Economic Thought*, Oxford: Basil Blackwell: 290–330.

Lewis, M. K. (1992a) 'Modern banking in theory and practice', *Revue Economique* 43: 203–227.

Lewis, M. K. (1992b) 'Balance sheets of financial intermediaries', in P. Newman, M. Milgate and J. Eatwell (eds), *The New Palgrave Dictionary of Money and Finance*, vol. 1, London: Macmillan: 120–122.

Lewis, M. K. (1992c) 'Off-the-balance-sheet activities', in P. Newman, M. Milgate and J. Eatwell (eds), *The New Palgrave Dictionary of Money and Finance*, vol. 3, London: Macmillan: 67–72.

Lewis, M. K. and K. T. Davis (1987) *Domestic and International Banking*, Cambridge, MA: MIT Press.

Liebowitz, S. J. and S. E. Margolis (1994) 'Network externality: An uncommon tragedy', *Journal of Economic Perspectives* 8: 133–150.

Linn, S. and J. McConnell (1983) 'An empirical investigation of the impact of "antitakeover amendments" on common stock prices', *Journal of Financial Economics* 11: 361–399.

Lintner, J. (1956) 'Distribution of incomes of corporations among dividends, retained earnings and taxes', *American Economic Review* 46: 97–113.

Logue, D. E. and R. J. Sweeney (1981) 'Inflation and real growth: Some empirical results', *Journal of Money, Credit and Banking* 13: 497–501.

Logue, D. E. and T. D. Willett (1976) 'A note on the relation between the rate and variability of inflation', *Economica* 43: 151–158.

Lucas, R. E., Jr. (1972) 'Expectations and the neutrality of money', *Journal of Economic Theory* 4: 115–138.

Lucas, R. E., Jr. (1973) 'Some international evidence on output-inflation tradeoffs', *American Economic Review* 62: 326–334.

Lucas, R. E., Jr. (1976) 'Econometric policy evaluation: A critique', in K. Brunner and A. H. Meltzer (eds), *The Phillips Curve and Labor Markets, Carnegie–Rochester Conference Series on Public Policy* 1: Amsterdam: North Holland: 19–45.

Lucas, R. E., Jr. (1981) '"Discussion" of Stanley Fischer "Towards an understanding of the costs of inflation: II"', in K. Brunner and A. H. Meltzer (eds.) *The Costs and Consequences of Inflation. Carnegie–Rochester Conference Series on Public Policy* 15, Amsterdam: North Holland: 43–52.

Lucas, R. E., Jr. and N. Stokey (1983) 'Optimal fiscal and monetary policy in a world without capital', *Journal of Monetary Economics* 12: 55–93.

Lucas, R. F. (1989) 'The Bank of Canada and zero inflation: A new cross of gold?', *Canadian Public Policy* 15: 84–93.

Lummer, S. L. and J. J. McConnell (1989) 'Further evidence on the bank lending process and the capital-market response to bank loan agreements', *Journal of Financial Economics* 25: 99–122.

MacKie-Mason, J. K. (1990) 'Do firms care who provides their financing?', In R. G. Hubbard (ed.), *Asymmetric Information, Corporate Finance and Investment*, Chicago and London: Chicago University Press: 63–103.

Mains, N. E. (1977) 'Risk, the pricing of capital assets and the evaluation of investment portfolios', *Journal of Business* 50: 371–384.

Makin, J. H. (1982) 'Anticipated money, inflation uncertainty and real economic activity', *Review of Economics and Statistics* 65: 374–384.

Makinen, G. E. and G. T. Woodward (1986) 'Some anecdotal evidence relating to the legal restrictions theory of the demand for money', *Journal of Political Economy* 94: 260–265.

Malatesta, P. H. and R. A. Walkling (1988) 'Poison pill securities: Stockholder wealth, profitability and ownership structure', *Journal of Financial Economics* 20: 347–376.

Mankiw, N. G. (1986) 'The allocation of credit and financial collapse', *Quarterly Journal of Economics* 101: 455–470.

Marshall, A. ([1886] 1926) 'Answers from Professor Marshall to questions on the subject of currency and prices circulated by the [Royal] Commission [on the Depression of Trade and Industry]', Reprinted in A. Marshall, *Official Papers*, London: Macmillan and Co.: 1–16.

Marshall, A. ([1887a] 1926) 'Preliminary memorandum' [to the Royal Commission on the Values of Gold and Silver]. Reprinted in A. Marshall, *Official Papers*, London: Macmillan and Co.: 19-31.

Marshall, A. ([1887b] 1966) 'Remedies for fluctuations of general prices', Reprinted in A. C. Pigou (ed.), *Memorials of Alfred Marshall*, New York: Augustus M. Kelley: 188–211.

Mason, W. E. (1963) *Clarification of the Monetary Standard: The concept and its relation to monetary policies and objectives*, Pittsburgh?: Pensylvania State University Press.

Matatko, J. M. (1992) 'Investment trusts', in P. Newman, M. Milgate and J. Eatwell (eds), *The New Palgrave Dictionary of Money and Finance*, vol. 2, London: Macmillan: 525–527.

McCallum, B. T. (1985) 'Bank deregulation, accounting systems of exchange and the unit of account: A critical review', *Carnegie–Rochester Conference Series on Public Policy* 23: 13–46.

McCallum, B. T. (1989) *Monetary Economics: Theory and policy*. New York: Macmillan.

McCallum, B. T. (1990a) 'Inflation: Theory and evidence', in B. M. Friedman and F. H. Hahn (eds), *Handbook of Monetary Economics*, vol. 2, Amsterdam: North Holland: 963–1012.

McCallum, B. T. (1990b) 'Comments on "Empirical predictions of the new monetary economics: Perspectives on velocity"', *Journal of Policy Modelling* 12: 281–287.

McCallum, J. (1988) 'Les taux de chomage canadien et americain dans les années 1980: Un test de trois hypotheses', *L'Actualité Economique* 64: 498–508.

McCulloch, J. H. (1986a) 'Bank regulation and deposit insurance', *Journal of Business* 59: 79–85.

McCulloch, J. H. (1986b) 'Beyond the historical gold standard', in C. D. Campbell and W. R. Dougan (eds), *Alternative Monetary Regimes*, Baltimore: Johns Hopkins University Press: 73–81.

McCulloch, J. H. (1991) 'An error-correction mechanism for long-run price stability', *Journal of Money, Credit and Banking* 23: 619–624.

McCulloch, J. H. and M.-T. Yu (1989) 'Bank runs, deposit contracts and government deposit insurance', Ohio State University, mimeo.

McDermott, J. (1987) 'Adding exhaustibility to the traditional theory of the gold standard', *Journal of Macroeconomics* 9: 545–566.

McKinnon, R. I. (1963) 'Optimum currency areas', *American Economic Review* 53: 717–724.

Meade, J. E. (1957) 'The balance of payments problems of a free trade area', *Economic Journal* 67: 379–396.

Meisel, A. (1992) 'Free banking in Colombia', in K. Dowd (ed.), *The Experience of Free Banking*, London: Routledge: 93–102.

Meltzer, A. H. (1983) 'Monetary reform in an uncertain environment', *Cato Journal* 3: 93–112.

Meltzer, A. H. (1986) 'Some evidence on the comparative uncertainty experienced under different monetary regimes', in C. D. Campbell and W. R. Dougan (eds), *Alternative Monetary Regimes*, Baltimore and London: Johns Hopkins University Press: 122–153.

Melvin, M. (1988) 'Monetary confidence, privately produced monies and domestic and international monetary reform', in T. D. Willett (ed.), *Political Business Cycles: The political economy of money, inflation and unemployment*, Durham, NC and London: Duke University Press: 435–459.

Menger, K. (1892) 'On the origin of money', *Economic Journal* 2: 239–255.

Mengle, D. L. (1985) 'Daylight overdrafts and payments systems risks', Federal Reserve Bank of Richmond, *Economic Review*, May–June, 14–27.

Mengle, D. L. (1990) 'Legal and regulatory reform in electronic payments: An evaluation of payment finality rules', in D. B. Humphrey (ed.), *The US Payment System: Efficiency, risk and the role of the Federal Reserve: Proceedings of a symposium on the US payment system sponsored by the Federal Reserve Bank of Richmond*, Boston/Dordrecht/London: Kluwer Academic: 145–180.

Mengle, D. L. (1992) 'Behind the money market: Clearing and settling money market instruments', Federal Reserve Bank of Richmond, *Economic Review*, September–October, 3–11.

Meulen, H. (1934) *Free Banking: An outline of a policy of individualism*, London: Macmillan.

Miles, M. (1984) *Beyond Monetarism: Finding the road to stable money*, New York: Basic Books.

Mikkelson, W. H. and M. M. Partch (1986) 'Valuation effects of security offerings and the issuance process', *Journal of Financial Economics* 15: 31–60.

Miller, M. and K. Rock (1985) 'Dividend policy under asymmetric information', *Journal of Finance* 40: 1031–1052.

Miller, W. I. (1990) *Blood Taking and Peacemaking: Feud laws and society in Saga Iceland*, Chicago: Chicago University Press.

Miller, T. F. (1991) 'The political stalemate behind the crisis in banking', Paper presented to the Durell Foundation Conference *American Money and Banking: Financial Fitness for the 1990s?* Scottsdale, AR.

Mills, T. C. (1990) 'A note on the Gibson paradox during the gold standard', *Explorations in Economic History* 27: 277–286.

Mills, F. C. (1927) *The Behavior of Prices*, New York: National Bureau of Economic Research.

Mints, L. W. (1945) *A History of Banking Theory in Britain and the United States*, Chicago: University of Chicago Press.

Mishkin, F. S. (1990) 'Asymmetric information and financial crises: A historical perspective', National Bureau of Economic Research, *Working Paper* 3400.

Mitchell, D. W. (1981) 'Determinants of inflation uncertainty', *Eastern Economic Journal* 7: 111–117.

Mizon, G. E., J. C. Stafford and S. H. Thomas (1983) 'Relative price variability and inflation: Empirical evidence for the UK', University of Southampton, mimeo.

Modigliani, F. and M. Miller (1958) 'The cost of capital, corporation finance and the theory of investment', *American Economic Review* 48: 261–297.

Mookherjee, D. and I. Png (1989) 'Optimal auditing, insurance and redistribution', *Quarterly Journal of Economics* 104: 399–415.

Moore, R. R. (1993) 'Asymmetric information, repeated lending and capital structure', *Journal of Money, Credit and Banking* 25: 393–409.

Morgan, D. P. (1991) 'Imperfect information and financial constraints: New evidence using bank loan commitments', Federal Reserve Bank of Kansas City, mimeo.

Mullineaux, D. J. (1980) 'Unemployment, industrial production and inflation uncertainty in the United States', *Review of Economics and Statistics* 62: 163–169.

Mullineaux, D. J. (1987) 'Competitive monies and the Suffolk Bank system: A contractual perspective', *Southern Economic Journal* 54: 884–898.

Mundell, R. A. (1961) 'A theory of optimal currency areas', *American Economic Review* 51: 657–665.

Munn, C. W. (1981) *The Scottish Provincial Banking Companies, 1747–1864*, Edinburgh: John Donald.

Munn, C. W. (1985) 'Review' [of L. H. White *Free Banking in Britain*], *Business History* 27: 341–343.

Mussa, M. (1977) 'The welfare cost of inflation and the role of money as a unit of account', *Journal of Money, Credit and Banking* 9: 276–286.

Mussa, M. (1981) 'Sticky individual prices and the dynamics of the general price level', *Carnegie–Rochester Conference Series on Public Policy* 15: 261–296.

Myers, S. C. (1977) 'Determinants of corporate borrowing', *Journal of Finance* 5: 147–175.

Myers, S. C. (1984) 'The capital structure puzzle', *Journal of Finance* 39: 575–592.

Myers, S. C. and N. Majluf (1984) 'Corporate financing and investment decisions when firms have information that investors do not have', *Journal of Financial Economics* 13: 187–221.

Narayanan, M. P. (1992) 'Callable bonds', in P. Newman, M. Milgate and J. Eatwell (eds), *The New Palgrave Dictionary of Money and Finance*, vol. 1, London: Macmillan: 269–270.

Nataf, P. (1992) 'Free banking in France (1796–1803)', in K. Dowd (ed.), *The Experience of Free Banking*, London: Routledge: 123–136.

Nelson, R. W. (1985) 'Branching, scale economies and banking costs', *Journal of Banking and Finance* 9: 177–191.

Nelson, C. R. and C. I. Plosser (1981) 'Trends and random walks in macroeconomic time series: Some evidence and implications', *Journal of Monetary Economics* 10: 139–162.

Newcomb, S. (1879) 'The standard of value', *North American Review* 129: 223–237.

Niehans, J. (1978) *The Theory of Money*, Johns Hopkins University Press: Baltimore and London.

Nordhaus, W. D. (1973) 'The effects of inflation on the distribution of economic welfare', *Journal of Money, Credit and Banking* 5: 465–504.

Nordhaus, W. D. (1975) 'The political business cycle', *Review of Economic Studies* 42: 169–190.

Novin, F. (1991) 'The productivity-inflation nexus revisited: Canada, 1969–1988', Bank of Canada, *Working Paper* 91-1, February.

Nozick, R. (1974) *Anarchy, State and Utopia*, New York: Basic Books.

Nyborg, K. (1991) 'Signalling through convertible debt call policy and the mode of external financing', London Business School, mimeo.

O'Driscoll, G. P, Jr. (1985) 'Money in a deregulated financial system', Federal Reserve Bank of Dallas, *Economic Review*, May, 1–12.

O'Driscoll, G. P., Jr. (1988) 'Deposit insurance in theory and practice', in C. England and T. Huertas (eds), *The Financial Services Revolution: Policy directions for the future*, Washington, DC: Cato Institute and Boston: Kluwer Academic Press: 165–179.

Oh, S. (1989) 'A theory of a generally acceptable medium of exchange and barter', *Journal of Monetary Economics* 23: 101–119.

Okun, A. M. (1971) 'The mirage of steady inflation', *Brookings Papers on Economic Activity* 2: 485–498.

Okun, A. M. (1975) 'Inflation: Its mechanics and welfare costs', *Brookings Papers on Economic Activity* 2: 351–390.

Orphanides, A. and R. M. Solow (1990) 'Money, inflation and growth', in B. Friedman and F. H. Hahn (eds), *Handbook of Monetary Economics*, vol. 1, Amsterdam: North Holland: 223–261.

Osborne, D. K. (1985) 'What is money today?", Federal Reserve Bank of Dallas *Economic Review*, January, 1–15.

Osborne, D. K. and T. S. Zaher (1992) 'Reserve requirements, bank share prices and the uniqueness of bank loans', *Journal of Banking and Finance* 16: 799–812.

Pagan, A. R., A. D. Hall and P. K. Trivedi (1983) 'Assessing the variability of inflation', *Review of Economic Studies* 50: 586–596.

Paroush, J. (1986) 'Inflation, search costs and price dispersion', *Journal of Macroeconomics* 8: 329–336.

Park, S. (1991) 'Bank failure contagion in historical perspective', *Journal of Monetary Economics* 28: 271–286.

Parks, R. W. (1978) 'Inflation and relative price variability', *Journal of Political Economy* 86: 79–95.

Patinkin, D. (1961) 'Financial intermediaries and the logical structure of monetary theory', *American Economic Review* 51: 95–116.

Patinkin, D. (1965) *Money, Interest and Prices*, 2nd edn, New York: Harper and Row.

Patinkin, D. (1993) 'Irving Fisher and his compensated dollar plan', Federal Reserve Bank of Richmond *Economic Review*, Summer, 1–33.

Pearce, D. K. (1979) 'Comparing survey and rational measures of expected inflation: forecast performance and interest rate effects', *Journal of Money, Credit and Banking* 11: 447–456.

Peden, J. R. (1977) 'Property rights under Irish celtic law', *Journal of Libertarian Studies* 1: 81–95.

Peltzman, S. (1970) 'Capital investment in commercial banking and its relationship to portfolio regulation', *Journal of Political Economy* 78: 1–26.

Peltzman, S. (1984) 'Comment on "Bank market structure and competition: A survey"', *Journal of Money, Credit and Banking* 16: 650–656.

Pennacchi, G. G. (1988) 'Loan sales and the cost of bank capital', *Journal of Finance* 43: 375–396.

Pesando, J. (1983) *The Use of "Excess" Pension Fund Earnings to Provide Inflation Protection for Private Pensions*, Toronto: Ontario Economic Council.

Phelps, E. S. (1973) 'Inflation in the theory of public finance', *Swedish Journal of Economics* 75: 67–82.

Poitevin, M. (1989) 'Financial signalling and the "deep-pocket" argument', *Rand Journal of Economics* 20: 26–40.

Porter, R. C. (1961) 'A model of bank portfolio selection', *Yale Economic Essays* 1: 323–359.

Postlewaite, A. and X. Vives (1987) 'Bank runs as an equilibrium phenomenon', *Journal of Political Economy* 95: 485–491.

Pringle, J. J. (1974) 'The capital decision in commercial banks', *Journal of Finance* 29: 779–795.

Radford, R. A. (1945) 'The economic organisation of a P.O.W. camp', *Economica* 12: 189–201.

Ramakrishnan, R. T. S. and A. V. Thakor (1984) 'Information reliability and a theory of financial intermediation', *Review of Economic Studies* 51: 415–432.

Ravenscraft, D. and F. Scherer (1987) *Mergers, Sell-offs and Economic Efficiency.* Washington, DC: Brookings Institution.

Raviv, A. (1987) 'Alternative models of investment banking', in S. Bhattacharya and G. M. Constantinides (eds), *Financial Markets and Incomplete Information: Frontiers of modern financial theory*, Totowa, NJ: Rowman and Littlefield: 225–232.

Redish, A. (1990) 'The evolution of the gold standard in England', *Journal of Economic History* 50: 789–805.

Ringer, F. K. (1969) *The German Inflation of 1923*, New York and London: Oxford University Press.

Ritter, J. A. (1992) 'The transition from barter to fiat money', Federal Reserve Bank of St. Louis, mimeo.

Rockoff, H. (1975) *The Free Banking Era: A re-examination,.* New York: Arno.

Rolnick, A. J. and W. E. Weber (1982) 'Free banking, wildcat banking and shinplasters', Federal Reserve Bank of Minneapolis, *Quarterly Review*, Fall, 10–19.

Rolnick, A. J. and W. E. Weber (1983) 'New evidence on the free banking era', *American Economic Review* 73: 1080–1091.

Rolnick, A. J. and W. E. Weber (1984) 'The causes of free bank failures: A detailed examination', *Journal of Monetary Economics* 14: 267–291.

Rolnick, A. J. and W. E. Weber (1985) 'Banking instability and regulation in the US free banking era', Federal Reserve Bank of Minneapolis, *Quarterly Review*, Summer, 2–9.

Rolnick, A. J. and W. E. Weber (1986) 'Inherent instability in banking: The free banking experience', *Cato Journal* 5: 877–890.

Rooke, J. (1828) *Inquiry Into the Principles of National Wealth*, Edinburgh: A. Balfour.

Rose, D. (1988) 'The NAIRU in Canada: Concepts, determinants and estimates', Bank of Canada, *Technical Report* 50, Ottawa: Bank of Canada.

Ross, S. (1977) 'The determination of financial structure: The incentive signalling approach', *Bell Journal of Economics* 8: 23–40.

Rothbard, M. N. (1977) 'Robert Nozick and the immaculate conception of the state', *Journal of Libertarian Studies* 1: 45–57.

Rothbard, M. N. (1978) *For a New Liberty: The libertarian manifesto*, London and New York: Collier-Macmillan.

Rothschild, M. and J. E. Stiglitz (1976) 'Equilibrium in competitive insurance markets: An essay on the economics of imperfect information', *Quarterly Journal of Economics* 90: 629–649.

Rothwell, W. T. (1897) *Bimetallism Explained*, London: Chapman and Hall.

Roubini, N. and X. Sala-i-Martin (1991) 'The relation between trade regime, financial development and economic growth', Yale University, mimeo.

Rozeff, M. S. (1977) 'The association between firm risk and wealth transfers due to inflation', *Journal of Financial and Quantitative Analysis* 12: 151–163.

Rozeff, M. S. (1982) 'Growth, beta and agency costs as determinants of dividend payout ratios', *Journal of Financial Research* 2: 249–259.

Ruback, R. S. (1983) 'Assessing competition in the market for corporate acquisitions', *Journal of Financial Economics* 11: 141–153.

Ryngaert, M. (1988) 'The effect of poison pill securities on shareholder wealth', Journal of Financial Economics 20: 377–417.

Salsman, R. (1990) *Breaking the Banks: Central banking problems and free banking solutions*, Great Barrington, MA: American Institute for Economic Research.

Samuelson, P. A. (1968) 'What classical and neoclassical monetary theory really was', *Canadian Journal of Economics* 1: 1–15.

Samuelson, P. A. (1969) 'Nonoptimality of money holding under *laissez faire*', *Canadian Journal of Economics* 2: 303–308.

Santomero, A. M. (1984) 'Modelling the banking firm: A survey', *Journal of Money, Credit and Banking* 16: 576–602.

Sappington, D. (1983) 'Limited liability contracts between principal and agent', *Journal of Economic Theory* 29: 1–21.

Sargent, T. J. and N. Wallace (1982) 'The real-bills doctrine versus the quantity theory: A reconsideration', *Journal of Political Economy* 90: 1212–1236.

Sarnat, M. (1973) 'Purchasing power risk, portfolio analysis and the case for index-linked bonds', *Journal of Money, Credit and Banking* 5: 836–845.

Scarth, W. (1990) 'Fighting inflation: Are the costs of getting to zero too high?", in R. C. York (ed.), *Taking Aim: The debate on zero inflation*, Toronto: C. D. Howe Institute: 81–103.

Schleifer, A. and R. W. Vishny (1986) 'Large stockholders and corporate control', *Journal of Political Economy* 94: 461–488.

Schmidt, R. (1991) 'Is inflation risk associated with the rate of inflation – New evidence for cointegrated time series', University of Bonn Institut für Internationale Wirtschaftspolitik, mimeo.

Schnadt, N. and J. Whittaker (1990) 'Inflation-proof currency? The feasibility of variable commodity standards', University of Cape Town, mimeo.

Schnadt, N. and J. Whittaker (1993) 'Inflation-proof currency? The feasibility of variable commodity standards', *Journal of Money, Credit and Banking* 25: 214–221.

Schoenmaker, D. (1993) 'Externalities in payments systems: Issues for Europe', London School of Economics Financial Markets Group, *Special Paper* 55.

Schreft, S. L. and A. P. Villamil (1990) 'Liquidity constraints in commercial loan markets with imperfect information and imperfect competition', Federal Reserve Bank of Richmond and University of Illinois, mimeo.

Schuler, K. (1992a) 'Free banking in Canada', in K. Dowd (ed.), *The Experience of Free Banking*, London: Routledge: 79–92.

Schuler, K. (1992b) 'The world history of free banking: An overview', in K. Dowd (ed.), *The Experience of Free Banking*, London: Routledge: 7–47.

Schwartz, A. J. (1986) 'Alternative monetary regimes: The gold standard', in C. D. Campbell and W. R. Dougan (eds), *Alternative Monetary Regimes*, Baltimore: Johns Hopkins University Press: 44–72.

Sealey, C. W., Jr. (1987) 'Finance theory and financial intermediation', *Proceedings of a Conference on Bank Structure and Competition: Merging commercial and investment banking: Risks, benefits, challenges*, Chicago: Federal Reserve Bank of Chicago: 423–431.

Sechrest, L. J. (1993) *Free Banking: Theory, history and a laissez-faire model*, Westport, CT: Quorum Books.

Selgin, G. A. (1988a) *The Theory of Free Banking: Money supply under competitive note issue*, Totowa, NJ: Rowman and Littlefield.

Selgin, G. A. (1988b) 'The price level, productivity and macroeconomic order', University of Hong Kong, mimeo.

Selgin, G. A. (1989) 'The analytical framework of the real-bills doctrine', *Journal of Institutional and Theoretical Economics* 145: 489–507.

Selgin, G. A. (1990) 'Monetary Equilibrium and the Productivity Norm of Price-Level Policy', *Cato Journal* 10: 265–287.

Selgin, G. A. (1991) 'The "productivity norm" vs. zero inflation in the history of economic thought', University of Georgia, mimeo.

Selgin, G. A. (1992a) 'Bank lending "manias" in theory and history', *Journal of Financial Services Research* 6: 169–186.

Selgin, G. A. (1992b) 'Free banking in Foochow', in K. Dowd (ed.), *The Experience of Free Banking*, London: Routledge: 103–122.

Selgin, G. A. (1992c) 'On foot-loose prices and forecast-free monetary regimes', *Cato Journal* 12: 75–80.

Selgin, G. A. (1993) 'In defense of bank suspension', *Journal of Financial Services Research* 7: 347–364.

Selgin, G. A. (1994a) 'Free banking and monetary control', *Economic Journal* 104: 1449–1459.

Selgin, G. A. (1994b) 'On ensuring the acceptability of a new fiat money', *Journal of Money, Credit and Banking* 26: 809–826.

Selgin, G. A. (1995) 'The case for a "productivity norm": Comment on Dowd', *Journal of Macroeconomics* 17: 735–742.

Selgin, G. A. and L. H. White (1987) 'The evolution of a free banking system', *Economic Inquiry* 25: 439–457.

Selgin, G. A. and L. H. White (1988) 'Competitive monies and the Suffolk Bank system: Comment', *Southern Economic Journal* 55: 215–219.

Selody, J. G. (1990a) 'The goal of price stability: A review of the issues', Bank of Canada, *Technical Report* 54, Ottawa: Bank of Canada.

Selody, J. G. (1990b) 'The benefits and costs of price stability: An empirical assessment', Bank of Canada, mimeo.

Sharpe, S. A. (1989) 'Asymmetric information, bank lending and implicit contracts: A stylized model of customer relationships', Federal Reserve Board Finance and Economics *Discussion Series* 70.

Sheshinski, E. and Y. Weiss (1977) 'Inflation and the costs of price adjustment', *Review of Economic Studies* 44: 287–303.

Sheshinski, E. and Y. Weiss (1983) 'Optimum pricing policy under stochastic inflation', *Review of Economic Studies* 50: 513–529.

Shughart, W. F. (1988) 'A public choice perspective of the Banking Act of 1933', in C. England and T. Huertas (eds), *The Financial Services Revolution: Policy directions for the future*, Boston, MA: Kluwer: 87–105.

Sidrauski, M. (1967) 'Rational choice and patterns of growth in a monetary economy', *American Economic Review (Papers and Proceedings)* 57: 534–544.

Sims, C. A. (1972) 'Money, income and causality', *American Economic Review* 62: 540–552.

Singleton, J. C. (1984) 'Inflation and systematic wealth transfers in the capital markets', in M. B. Ballabon (ed.), *Economic Perspectives: An annual survey of economics,* vol. 3, New York: Harwood Academic: 57–67.

Sinkey, J. F., Jr. (1992) *Commercial Bank Financial Management*, 4th edn, New York: Macmillan.

Small, D. H. (1979) 'Unanticipated money growth and unemployment in the United States: Comment', *American Economic Review* 69: 996–1003.

Smith, A. ([1776] 1911) *An Inquiry into The Nature and Causes of the Wealth of Nations,* vol. 1. London: J. M. Dent and Sons; New York: E. P. Dutton and Co.

Smith, B. D. (1984) 'Private information, deposit-interest rates and the stability of the banking system', *Journal of Monetary Economics* 14: 293–317.

Smith, B. D. (1991) 'Bank panics, suspensions and geography: Some notes on the "contagion of fear" in banking', *Economic Inquiry* 39: 230–248.

Smith, C. W. (1977) 'Alternative methods for raising capital: rights issues versus underwritten offerings', *Journal of Financial Economics* 5: 273–307.

Smith, C. W. and J. B. Warner (1979) 'On financial contracting: An analysis of bond covenants', *Journal of Financial Economics* 7: 117–161.

Smith, V. C. (1936) *The Rationale of Central Banking*, London: P. S. King.

Smyth, D. J. (1994) 'Inflation and growth', *Journal of Macroeconomics* 16: 261–270.

Solomon, E. H. (1992) 'Electronic funds transfer', in P. Newman, M. Milgate and J. Eatwell (eds), *The New Palgrave Dictionary of Money and Finance*, vol. 1, London: Macmillan: 745–747.

Spier, K. E. (1992) 'Incomplete contracts and signalling', *Rand Journal of Economics* 23: 432–443.

Sprague, O. M. W. (1910) *History of Crises Under the National Banking System*, U.S. National Monetary Commission monograph. Washington, DC: Government Printing Office.

Sprenkle, C. M. (1985) 'On the precautionary demand for assets', *Journal of Banking and Finance* 9: 499–515.

Sprenkle, C. M. (1987) 'Liability and asset uncertainty for banks', *Journal of Banking and Finance* 11: 147–159.

Stein, J. C. (1992) 'Convertible bonds as backdoor equity financing', *Journal of Financial Economics* 32: 3–21.

Stevens, E. J. (1993) 'Price isn't everything', Federal Reserve Bank of Cleveland, *Economic Commentary*, April 1.

Stigler, G. (1961) 'The economics of information', *Journal of Political Economy* 69: 213–225.

Stigler, G. and J. K. Kindahl (1970) *The Behavior of Industrial Prices*, New York: Columbia University Press.

Stiglitz, J. E. and A. Weiss (1981) 'Credit rationing in markets with imperfect information', *American Economic Review* 71: 393–410.

Stockman, A. C. (1981) 'Anticipated inflation and the capital stock in a cash-in-advance economy', *Journal of Monetary Economics* 8: 387–393.

Stockman, A. C. (1990) 'Comments on "Should the unit of account be stabilized in terms of a commodity bundle?" by Tyler Cowen and Randy Kroszner', University of Rochester, mimeo.

Stockton, D. J. (1988) 'Relative price dispersion, aggregate price movement and the natural rate of unemployment', Economic Inquiry 26: 1–22.

Stulz, R. M. (1988) 'Managerial control of voting rights: Financing policies and the market for corporate control', *Journal of Financial Economics* 20: 25–54.

Summers, L. H. (1983) 'The nonadjustment of nominal interest rates: A study of the Fisher effect', in J. Tobin (ed.), *Macroeconomics, Prices and Quantities: Essays in memory of Arthur M. Okun*, Washington, DC: Brookings Institute: 201–241.

Sumner, S. (1989) 'Using futures instrument prices to target nominal income', *Bulletin of Economic Research* 41: 157–162.

Sumner, S. (1990) 'The forerunners of "new monetary economics" proposals ot stabilize the unit of account', *Journal of Money, Credit and Banking* 22: 109–118.

Sumner, S. (1991) '"The Development of Aggregate Economic Targetting', *Cato Journal* 10: 747–759.

Sumner, S. (1995) 'The impact of futures price targeting on the precision and credibility of monetary policy', *Journal of Money, Credit and Banking* 27: 89–106.

Tallman, E. (1988) 'Some unanswered questions about bank panics', Federal Reserve Bank of Atlanta, *Economic Review*, November–December, 2–21.

Tannehill, M. and L. Tannehill (1970) *The Market for Liberty*, Lansing, MI: published privately.

Tatom, J. A. (1976) 'The welfare cost of inflation', Federal Reserve Bank of St. Louis *Review*, November, 9–22.

Taussig, F. W. (1913) 'The plan for a compensated dollar', *Quarterly Journal of Economics* 27: 401–416.

Taylor, J. B. (1981) 'On the relation between the variability of inflation and the average inflation rate', *Carnegie–Rochester Conference Series on Public Policy* 15: 57–86.

Thakor, A. V., H. Hong and S. I. Greenbaum (1981) 'Bank loan commitments and interest rate volatility', *Journal of Banking and Finance* 5: 497–510.

Thompson, E. A. (1986) 'A perfect monetary system', Paper presented to the Liberty Fund/ Manhattan Institute Conference on Competitive Monetary Regimes. New York.

Thomson, J. B. (1993) 'The cost of buying time: Lessons from the thrift debacle', Federal Reserve Bank of Cleveland, *Economic Commentary*, January 1.

Thornton, H. ([1802] 1978) *An Enquiry Into the Nature and Effects of the Paper Credit of Great Britain*, Edited, with an introduction, by F. A. Hayek. Fairfield, NJ: Augustus M. Kelley.

Timberlake, R. H., Jr. (1984) 'The central banking role of clearinghouse associations', *Journal of Money, Credit and Banking* 16: 1–15.

Timberlake, R. H., Jr. (1986) 'Institutional evolution of Federal Reserve hegemony', *Cato Journal* 5: 743–763.

Timberlake, R. H., Jr. (1987) 'Private production of scrip-money in the isolated community', *Journal of Money, Credit and Banking* 19: 437–47.

Timberlake, R. H., Jr. (1991) *Gold, Greenbacks and the Constitution*, Berryville, VA: George Edward Durell Foundation.

Timberlake, R. H., Jr. (1993) *Monetary Policy in the United States: An intellectual and institutional history*, Chicago: Chicago University Press.

Tobin, J. (1963) 'Commercial banks as creators of "money"', in D. Carson (ed.), *Banking and Monetary Studies*, Homewood, IL: Richard D. Irwin: 408–4419.

Tobin, J. (1965) 'Money and economic growth', *Econometrica* 33: 671–84.

Tobin, J. and W. C. Brainard (1963) 'Financial intermediaries and the effectiveness of monetary controls', *American Economic Review* 53: 383–400.

Tolley, G. S. (1957) 'Providing for growth in the money supply', *Journal of Political Economy* 65: 465–485.

Tower, E. (1971) 'More on the welfare cost of inflationary finance', *Journal of Money, Credit and Banking* 3: 850–860.

Townsend, R. M. (1979) 'Optimal contracts and competitive markets with costly state verification', *Journal of Economic Theory* 21: 265–293.

Townsend, R. M. (1980) 'Models of money with spatially separated agents', in J. H. Kareken and N. Wallace (eds), *Models of Monetary Economiess*, Minneapolis: Federal Reserve Bank of Minneapolis: 265–303.

Townsend, R. M. (1982) 'Optimal multiperiod contracts and the gain from enduring relationships under private informaton', *Journal of Political Economy* 90: 1166–1186.

Triplett, J. E. (1983) 'Three studies of indexes and indexing', *Journal of Money, Credit and Banking* 15: 377–385.

Trivoli, G. (1979) *The Suffolk Bank: A study of a free-enterprise clearing system*, London: Adam Smith Institute.

Ullman-Margalit, E. (1978) 'Invisible-hand explanations', *Synthèse* 39: 263–291.

Usher, A. P. (1943) *The Early History of Deposit Banking in Mediterrranean Europe*, Cambridge, MA: Harvard University Press.

Vaubel, R. (1984) 'The government's money monopoly: Externalities or natural monopoly?", *Kyklos* 37: 27–58.

Vaubel, R. (1986) 'Currency competition versus governmental money monopolies', *Cato Journal* 5: 927–942.

Veitch, J. M. (1992) 'Loan commitments', in P. Newman, M. Milgate and J. Eatwell (eds), *The New Palgrave Dictionary of Money and Finance*, vol. 2, London: Macmillan: 605–606.

Villamil, A. P. (1990) 'Demand deposit contracts, suspension of convertibility and optimal financial intermediation', University of Illinois at Urbana-Champaign, mimeo.

Vining, D. R., Jr. and T. C. Elwertowski (1976) 'The relationship between relative prices and the general price level', *American Economic Review* 66: 699–708.

Wachter, M. L. and O. E. Williamson (1978) 'Obligational markets and the mechanics of inflation', *Bell Journal of Economics* 9: 549–571.

Waldo, D. G. (1985) 'Bank runs, the deposit-currency ratio and the interest rate', *Journal of Monetary Economics* 15: 269–277.

Wall, L. D. (1992) 'Interest rate swaps', in P. Newman, M. Milgate and J. Eatwell (eds), *The New Palgrave Dictionary of Money and Finance*, vol. 2, London: Macmillan: 445–446.

Wallace, N. (1983) 'A legal restrictions theory of the demand for "money" and the role of monetary policy', Federal Reserve Bank of Minneapolis, *Quarterly Review* 7: 1–7.

Wallace, N. (1989) 'Another attempt to explain an illiquid banking system: The Diamond and Dybvig model with sequential service taken seriously', Federal Reserve Bank of Minneapolis, *Quarterly Review* 12: 3–16.

Wallace, N. (1990) 'A banking model in which partial suspension is best', Federal Reserve Bank of Minneapolis, *Quarterly Review* 14: 11–23.

Walras, L. (1954) *Elements of Pure Economics*. (trans W. Jaffe), London: George Allen Unwin.

Warner, J. B. (1977) 'Bankruptcy costs: Some evidence', *Journal of Finance* 32: 337–347.

Wärneryd, K. (1989) 'Legal restrictions and the evolution of media of exchange', *Journal of Institutional and Theoretical Economics* 145: 613–626.

Wärneryd, K. (1990) 'Legal restrictions and monetary evolution', *Journal of Economic Behavior and Organization* 13: 117–124.

Watts, R. L. and J. L. Zimmerman (1983) 'Agency problems, auditing and the theory of the firm: Some evidence', *Journal of Law and Economics* 26: 613–633.

Webb, D. C. (1986) '"Comment" on "Competitive banking in a simple model" by Anderlini', in J. Edwards *et al.* (eds), *Recent Advances in Corporate Finance, Investment and Taxation*, Cambridge: Cambridge University Press: 177–181.

Weber, E. J. (1988) 'Currency competition in Switzerland, 1826–1850', *Kyklos* 41: 459–478.

Weber, E. J. (1992) 'Free banking in Switzerland after the liberal revolutions in the nineteeenth century', in K. Dowd (ed.), *The Experience of Free Banking*, London: Routledge: 187–205.

Weisbach, M. S. (1988) 'Outside directors and CEO turnover', *Journal of Financial Economics* 20: 431–460.

Wells, D. R. and L. S. Scruggs (1986) 'Historical insights into the deregulation of money and banking', *Cato Journal* 5: 899–910.

Wesslau, O. E. (1887) *Rational Banking Versus Banking Monopoly*, Edited by B. Cooke, London: Elliot Stock.

White, A. D. ([1959] 1980) *Fiat Money Inflation in France*, San Francisco: Cato Institute.

White, E. N. (1984) 'A reinterpretation of the banking crisis of 1930', *Journal of Economic History* 44: 119–138.

White, E. N. (1986) 'Before the Glass–Steagall Act: An analysis of the investment banking activities of national banks', *Explorations in Economic History* 23: 33–55.

White, E. N. (1991) 'Experiments with free banking during the French revolution', in F. Capie and G. E. Wood (eds), *Unregulated Banking: Chaos or order?*, London: Macmillan: 131–150.

White, L. H. (1984a) *Free Banking in Britain: Theory, Experience and Debate, 1800–1845*, Cambridge: Cambridge University Press.

White, L. H. (1984b) 'Competitive payments systems and the unit of account', *American Economic Review* 74: 699–712.

White, L. H. (1986) 'Regulatory sources of instability in banking', *Cato Journal* 5: 891–897.

White, L. H. (1987) 'Accounting for non-interest-bearing currency: A critique of the legal restrictions theory of money', *Journal of Money, Credit and Banking* 19: 448–456.

White, L. H. (1989) *Competition and Currency*. New York: New York University Press.

White, L. J. (1989) 'The reform of federal deposit insurance', *Journal of Economic Perspectives* 3: 11–29.

White, M. J. (1983) 'Bankruptcy costs and the new bankruptcy code', *Journal of Finance* 38: 477–487.

White, M. J. (1984) 'Bankruptcy liquidation and reorganization', in D. Logue (ed.), *Handbook of Modern Finance*, Boston: Warren, Gorham and Lamont: 1–49.

White, M. J. (1989) 'The corporate bankruptcy decision', *Journal of Economic Perspectives* 3: 129–151.

White, M. J. (1992) 'Costs of bankruptcy', in P. Newman, M. Milgate and J. Eatwell (eds), *The New Palgrave Dictionary of Money and Finance*, vol. London: Macmillan: 495–496.

Whited, T. M. (1992) 'Debt, liquidity constraints and corporate investment: Evidence from panel data', *Journal of Finance* 47: 1425–1460.

Wicker, E. (1982) 'A reconsideration of the causes of the banking panic of 1930', *Journal of Economic History* 42: 571–583.

Wicker, E. (1987) 'Can the money-of-account be divorced from medium of exchange? The verdict from the historical evidence', Indiana University, mimeo.

Wicker, E. (1988) 'How robust is par-value deposit banking?', Indiana University, mimeo.

Wicksell, K. ([1898] 1936) *Interest and Prices*, (trans R. F. Kahn), London: Macmillan.

Wicksell, K. (1907) 'The influence of the rate of interest on prices', *Economic Journal* 17: 213–220.

Wicksell, K. (1919) 'The Riksbank and the commercial banks: Proposal for the reform of the Swedish currency and credit system', *Ekomisk Tidskrift* 21: 177–188.

Willett, T. D. and K. Banaian (1988) 'Models of the political process and their implications for stagflation: A public choice perspective', in *Political Business Cycles: The political economy of money, inflation and unemployment*, Durham, NC and London: Duke University Press: 100–128.

Williams, A. (1892) 'A "fixed value of bullion" standard – A proposal for preventing general fluctuations of trade', *Economic Journal* 2: 280–289.

Williamson, S. D. (1986) 'Costly monitoring, financial intermediation and equilibrium credit rationing', *Journal of Monetary Economics* 18: 159–179.

Williamson, S. D. (1987) 'Costly monitoring, loan contracts and equilibrium credit rationing', *Quarterly Journal of Economics* 102: 135–145.

Williamson, S. D. (1988) 'Liquidity, banking and bank failures', *International Economic Review* 29: 25–43.

Williamson, S. D. (1992) 'Laissez-faire banking and circulating media of exchange', *Journal of Financial Intermediation* 2: 134–167.

Wilson, C. (1992) 'Markets with adverse selection', in P. Newman, M. Milgate and J. Eatwell (eds), *The New Palgrave Dictionary of Money and Finance*, vol. 2, London: Macmillan: 670–672.

Wilton, D. (1980) 'An analysis of Canadian wage contracts with cost-of-living allowance clauses', Economic Council of Canada, *Discussion Paper* 165, Ottawa: Economic Council of Canada.

Winton, A. (1993) 'Limitation of liability and the ownership structure of the firm', *Journal of Finance* 48: 487–512.

Winton, A. (1995) 'Costly state verification and multiple investors: The role of seniority', *Review of Financial Studies* 8: 91–123.

Woodford, M. (1990) 'The optimum quantity of money', in B. Friedman and F. H. Hahn (eds), *Handbook of Monetary Economics*, vol. 2, Amsterdam: North Holland: 1067–1152.

Wooldridge, W. C. (1970) *Uncle Sam, the Monopoly Man*, New Rochelle, NY: Arlington.

Woolsey, W. W. (1987) *The Black-Fama-Hall Payments System: An analysis and evaluation*, PhD dissertation, George Mason University.

Woolsey, W. W. (1989a) 'Indirect convertibility', The Citadel Department of Business Administration, mimeo.

Woolsey, W. W. (1989b) Letter to author. November 2, 1989.

Woolsey, W. W. (1992a) 'Index future convertibility and a cashless payments system', The Citadel Department of Business Administration, mimeo.

Woolsey, W. W. (1992b) 'Stabilizing the expected price level in a BFH payments system', The Citadel Department of Business Administration, mimeo.

Woolsey, W. W. (1992c) 'The search for macroeconomic stability: Comment on Sumner', *Cato Journal* 12: 475–492.

Worthington, P. R. (1992) 'Investment and market imperfections', Mimeo. Federal Reserve Bank of Chicago.

Yeager, L. B. (1983) 'Stable money and free-market currencies', *Cato Journal* 3: 305–326.

Yeager, L. B. (1985a) 'Deregulation and monetary reform', *American Economic Review (Papers and Proceedings)* 75: 103–107.

Yeager, L. B. (1985b) 'Separated functions in monetary reform', Auburn University, mimeo.

Yeager, L. B. (1987) 'The BFH system – Objections and extensions', Auburn University, mimeo.

Yeager, L. B. (1992) 'Toward forecast-free monetary institutions', *Cato Journal* 12: 53–73.

Yeager, L. B. and W. W. Woolsey (1991) 'Is there a paradox of indirect convertibility?', Paper presented to the Durell Foundation Conference *American Money and Banking: Financial Fitness for the 1990s?* Scottsdale, AR.

Yohe, W. P. and D. S. Karnowsky (1969) 'Interest rates and price-level changes, 1952–69', Federal Reserve Bank of St. Louis, *Review*, December, 18–38.

Zarnowitz, V. and L. A. Lambros (1987) 'Consensus and uncertainty in economic prediction', *Journal of Political Economy* 95: 591–621.

Zeckhauser, R. J. and J. Pound (1990) 'Are large shareholders effective monitors? An investigation of share ownership and corporate performance', in R. G. Hubbard (ed.), *Asymmetric Information, Corporate Finance and Investment*, Chicago and London: Chicago University Press: 149–180.

Zeldes, S. P. (1989) 'Consumption and liquidity constraints: An empirical investigation', *Journal of Political Economy* 97: 305–346.

Zender, J. (1991) 'Optimal financial instruments', *Journal of Finance* 46: 1645–1663.

Zilberfarb, B.-Z. (1992) 'Automated payments systems', in P. Newman, M. Milgate and J. Eatwell (eds), *The New Palgrave Dictionary of Money and Finance*, vol. 1, London: Macmillan: 96–98.

Author Index

Subject Index

566